# Beginning Access 2002 VBA

Robert Smith

Dave Sussman

Ian Blackburn

John Colby

Mark Horner

Martin Reid

Paul Turley

Helmut Watson

**wrox**

Programmer to Programmer

# Beginning Access 2002 VBA

Published by
**Wiley Publishing, Inc.**
10475 Crosspoint Boulevard
Indianapolis, IN 46256
www.wiley.com

Copyright © 2003 by Wiley Publishing, Inc., Indianapolis, Indiana

Published simultaneously in Canada

Library of Congress Card Number: 2003107092

ISBN: 0-7645-4402-0

Manufactured in the United States of America

10 9 8 7 6 5 4 3 2

1M/RX/QW/QT/IN

# Trademark Acknowledgments

Wrox has endeavored to correctly render trademarks for all the companies and products mentioned in this book with the appropriate use of capitals. However, Wrox is unable to guarantee the accuracy of this information.

# Credits

**Authors**
Robert Smith
Dave Sussman
Ian Blackburn
John Colby
Mark Horner
Martin Reid
Paul Turley
Helmut Watson

**Commissioning Editor**
Paul Jeffcoat

**Technical Editors**
Catherine Alexander
Ewan Buckingham
Robert Shaw
Michelle Everitt

**Managing Editor**
Laurent Lafon

**Project Manager**
Nicola Phillips

**Technical Reviewers**
Chris Crane
Cristof Falk
Susan Harkins
Humberto Lozano Ruiz
Fredrik Normen
Scott E. Robertson
David Schultz

**Production Coordinator**
Neil Lote

**Production Assistant**
Paul Grove

**Cover**
Natalie O'Donnell

**Proof Readers**
Dev Lunsford
Chris Smith

**Index**
Martin Brooks
Adrian Axinte

# About the Authors

## Robert Smith

Robert Smith has been developing solutions with Access for over 10 years, in fact, ever since its original launch in November 1992. He currently works for EH3 Consulting, a software consultancy with offices in Edinburgh and Bath, where most of his time is spent designing Access or SQL Server - based solutions for a variety of companies throughout the UK and Europe.

When not working, Rob takes a keen interest in the progress (or otherwise) of Crystal Palace Football Club, as well as indulging his other passion for collecting (and occasionally sampling) fine wines. In practice, the varying fortunes of the former normally mean that he spends a lot more time sampling than collecting.

## Dave Sussman

Dave Sussman has spent the majority of his professional life as a developer, using both Unix and Microsoft-based products. After writing his first two books while in full time employment, he realized that being an author sounded more glamorous than being a programmer. The reality is somewhat different. He now spends most of his time writing books for Wrox Press, speaking at conferences, and playing with most beta products that Microsoft ships.

## Ian Blackburn

Ian Blackburn is director of Blackburn IT Services Ltd (http://www.bbits.co.uk) – an IT firm based in Kent, UK, offering technical training, development, and consultancy. He has long experience in many areas including Microsoft Office development, ASP and ADO, SQL Server, Site Server, Visual InterDev, Visual Studio .NET, ASP.NET, and e-commerce. He is an MCSE and has been a MCP since 1993.

## John Colby

John Colby is an independent consultant who has specialized in Access development since 1994, designing databases for companies in the U.S., Canada, Mexico, and Ireland. John is past president and current board member of Database Advisors Inc., (www.databaseadvisors.com), a not-for-profit organization dedicated to providing fellow Access and Visual Basic developers with a place to discuss what we do, why we do it, what works, and what doesn't. Database Advisors Inc. also allows developers to showcase their talents by sharing databases, wizards, and various code packages.

John lives in Connecticut with his family. He enjoys music, travel, and all things computers, and dreams of getting back to Europe someday soon.

## Mark Horner

Mark Horner is Senior Architect and Development Consultant with Torville Software, which specializes in decision support and web-centric knowledge systems. He has worked in a variety of roles with Australian, UK, and US corporations including: ANZ Banking Group, Aspect Computing, British Aerospace, Citibank, Hewlett Packard, and Tenix Defence Systems.

Mark holds a bachelor of business degree from Swinburne University of Technology and an MBA from Monash University, Australia. He is a member of the Internet Society (www.isoc.org) and a Dilbert devotee (www.dilbert.com).

*I would like to thank the Wrox team for their determination "to make the books that make the difference" and the engineers at Redmond for more great development tools. Special thanks to Sarah Bowers for getting me into technical reviewing and to Beckie Stones for getting me into writing.*

## Martin Reid

Martin W. P. Reid is an Analyst at The Queen's University of Belfast. Martin has been working with Microsoft Access since version 1 and his main interest is working with Access Data Projects. He has contributed several articles to Smart Access, Inside SQL Server, and Inside Microsoft Access, and is a contributor to TechRepublic (www.techrepublic.com) and www.builder.com. He is also co-author of *SQL: Access to SQL Server*, published by Apress, and has been the technical editor on books involving technologies from VB.NET database programming to Oracle 9*i* PL/SQL and Macromedia Dreamweaver MX.

## Paul Turley

Paul Turley, his wife Sherri, and their four children live in the small community of Port Orchard, Washington, on the shores of the Puget Sound. He works for Netdesk, Corp in downtown Seattle as a Developer Instructor and Project Consultant. He began his IT career in 1988, installing and supporting medical billing systems and obtained his MCSD certification in 1996. Paul began using Access version 1.0, SQL Server 4.21, and Visual Basic 3.0. Since then, he has built custom database systems for several businesses including Hewlett-Packard, Nike, Microsoft, and Boise Cascade. He has worked with Microsoft Consulting Services on large scale, multi-tier solutions employing new Microsoft technologies. As an independent trainer/consultant, he traveled for Microsoft and various training providers to teach project design and management, application development, and database design.

Paul currently maintains www.scout-master.com, a web-based service that enables Boy Scout units around the world to maintain their membership and advancement records on-line using ASP.NET and SQL Server. He has published course materials and has been a contributing author on books and articles, including *Professional Access 2000 Programming* and *SQL Server Data Warehousing with Analysis Services* from Wrox Press.

## Helmut Watson

Helmut Watson started his IT career nearly twenty years ago writing games for the BBC micro. Soon after that he had to get a proper job so he moved into databases, initially using PC-Oracle v1.0. He quickly decided to change to DBMS that actually worked – Dbase, Clipper, Paradox, Informix, SQL Server, etc. After twenty years, there aren't many on the list left to try now.

Helmut specializes in database analysis and GUI design and runs a consultancy called "Nearly Everything" from his home in Essex, UK.

Known as Woof! to his friends (or anyone else who buys him a beer), he is a keen cyclist and a finalist in the 2000 British Marbles-on-Sand championships. Most people think he's a bit odd until they meet him – then they're sure!

# TABLE OF CONTENTS

# Table of Contents

## Table of Contents

## Chapter 4: Controlling the Program    145

## Chapter 5: Using Access Objects    175

## Chapter 6: Using DAO　　　　　　　　　　　　　　　　　　　　211

## Table of Contents

# Table of Contents

## Chapter 15: Libraries and Add-Ins      603

## Chapter 16: Automation      649

## Chapter 17: Multi-User      687

# Table of Contents

# INTRODUCTION

# Introduction

Microsoft's Access development community has grown to 600,000 members or thereabouts, and they form an important part of the several million developers that develop Microsoft Office solutions. Access plays key roles in the Microsoft Office suite by allowing us to rapidly develop applications that store, query, exchange, and report information.

Access 2002 is used typically in the following scenarios:

- Small-scale functional applications (Fixed Asset Register, for example)
- Knowledge Management systems
- Decision support applications
- Supporting client-server and Internet applications, perhaps as a front-end to SQL Server databases (via Access Data Projects)
- Exchanging data in popular data formats (for example, XML)

From this list, you can see that the types of programming opportunities available to you are broad and varied. As you gain experience, you may be developing the schema of a database, exporting data in XML, developing a suite of reports to be published on the Internet, or using Access to seamlessly front a large SQL Server database. This book will give you the skill set to begin all these types of jobs.

## The Structure of this Book

We had a quandary while planning this book because we were initially unsure as to which direction we should take. Since the first edition of this book, for Access 95, the functionality and versatility of Access has grown significantly, as has the underlying power of **Visual Basic for Applications** (**VBA**). So – should we stick with the older features of Access in this 2002 edition, or radically change the structure to implement new features?

We decided to keep in focus the fact that this is a VBA book, and the fundamentals of VBA itself haven't changed greatly. Consequently, in this fourth edition of the book, we have carefully selected the aspects of Access 2002 that are relevant to beginning VBA development, and merged them with a reworking of our core content that is based upon feedback from industry sources, reviewers, and readers.

In other words, we are not going to cover every new feature of Access 2002 in this book and, while our coverage of VBA techniques will be very comprehensive, we are not going to mention every single method. Our goal is to teach you VBA programming from scratch and, for that reason, we're not interested in including anything that would complicate this task unnecessarily.

The decision that caused us the most difficulty concerned which data access method we should use. Access 2002 comes with ADO, although DAO is still available for use. Should we switch to ADO, or stick with the older, simpler DAO technology? You might think that the obvious solution would be to use the newest, but this is not necessarily the case because of the different ways that Access 2002 can be used.

Access is used in two main ways:

❑ As a standalone database. This is the most common usage and programming Access 2002 with VBA in this scenario remains largely unchanged. The new data-access method, ADO, can be used here but DAO still gives better performance.

❑ As the front-end to a client-server database. Although this was possible in previous versions of Access, it's been taken a step further with Access 2002 to provide a better client-server environment. Only ADO works in this situation.

We'll examine the performance benefits of working with DAO in the standalone situation in later chapters but, for now, it's worth pointing out that, although DAO is a much older technology, its performance benefits and simplicity mean that it is still in very widespread use.

There are other good reasons for continuing to teach DAO in this book, though. DAO and the standalone scenario are *much* simpler to teach. The client-server scenario, where Access is, in effect, used as a front-end (or user interface) to a back-end database server (like SQL Server), introduces a range of architectural issues and the need to be able to use the back-end database effectively. This kind of material requires a steep learning curve and is a big enough topic for several books in itself!

In the 2000 edition, we stayed with DAO for the bulk of the development examples throughout the book, although we looked at ADO briefly and included an ADO appendix. In this 2002 edition, as a consequence of DAO aging further, we have decided that it is important to give a full introduction to the client-server scenario and ADO but, because DAO is quicker to learn and remains effective, we have retained our use of DAO through the majority of the book. This balanced coverage of the two data access techniques should prepare you effectively for Access development as it is in the real world today, and for any future decay in the use of DAO.

# How is Access Changing?

The key changes that Access 2002 brings to developers involve better integration with SQL Server, assisting Access's use in client-server situations, and enhanced XML support, which makes it easier to publish data to the Web and exchange it with other organizations. We'll look at these types of new functionality later in the book. However, it's worth remembering that, while we can use the powerful new leading-edge technologies, we can also choose to ignore them. Access continues to be widely employed as a humble repository of names and addresses on a standalone PC. This versatility is part of the reason for Access's success.

While Microsoft will probably wish to enhance Access's role in client-server architectures in the future, it will undoubtedly continue to protect its capabilities in the standalone situation, and it will be interesting to see how VBA fares alongside the new Microsoft .NET software development technologies and the Visual Basic .NET language in particular.

# Who is this Book For?

There are two types of user in particular that will benefit from this book:

❑ You have some experience of Access, but have not begun to learn VBA. You have spent a bit of time familiarizing yourself with the different Access objects – tables, forms, queries, reports – and may have used macros to achieve a little automation. You have not really programmed before, but are keen to learn how to tap the power that VBA offers.

❑ You have programmed a little with another language, perhaps Visual Basic or some of the scripting languages (such as VBScript or JScript), and need a primer on VBA and its use within Access. Even if you know a little VBA you'll find plenty in the book to keep you occupied.

# What Does this Book Cover?

Beginning Access 2002 VBA Programming covers everything that you need to gain the confidence to go away and experiment on your own. Programming is an art and cannot simply be taught – like anything worth doing in life, it's a question of "practice makes perfect". This book will provide the necessary information to get you up and running, and will show you enough interesting and practical examples to whet your appetite and ensure that your experiences of VBA don't end with the last page of the book.

After looking at application design, we will examine event-driven programming and what it really means in terms of programming Access. We'll then introduce you to the coding environment and basic principles such as variables, controls structures, data types, and procedures. We'll also look at objects and classes within Access, which will help you to get the best from your code.

Once we have some solid foundations to build on, we'll start to look at how to use VBA in a more practical sense, looking at how to create recordsets and other objects at run time, how to import and export data, and how to work with reports. We'll also look at some issues that you must bear in mind when programming any application, for example, errors – including what they are, how to find them, how to correct them, and, most importantly, how to prevent them.

In the latter part of the book, we'll take a look at some more advanced topics, such as working in a multi-user environment, using libraries and add-ins, and using automation with other applications. Finally, we'll look at applying the finishing touches to add that final polish to your application.

# What You Need for this Book

Apart from a bit of time and dedication to learn, you'll need access to a PC running Windows 2000 or Windows XP and a copy of Access 2002.

For one of the later chapters, you'll need Office XP and Internet Information Services (which comes with Windows 2000 Professional or Windows XP Professional).

# The Book's CD

As we work through this book, we will build up a sample database built around a fictitious wholesale supplier of ice cream.

The CD-ROM that accompanies this book contains the sample databases used in the book. The `CodeDatabases/Begin` folder contains the `IceCream.mdb` database you should start with, and develop as you work through the chapters. When you reach the end of the book, and implement all the functionality we cover, you should end up with the `IceCreamComplete.mdb` in the `CodeDatabases/Complete` folder.

The CD also contains some freeware (which we'll mention later in the book) and Microsoft Data Access Components v2.7 (including ADO 2.7). You can download this from www.microsoft.com, but Microsoft kindly gave us permission to include the install file on the CD so that you could avoid lengthy download times.

> *The use of the MDAC 2.7 software is governed by an end user license agreement contained in the software. This software was reproduced by Wrox Press under an arrangement with Microsoft Corporation. If your CD-ROM is faulty, please return it to Wrox Press, which will arrange for its replacement. **Please do not return it to Microsoft Corporation. Microsoft Corporation does not provide any product support for this software; please do not contact it for product support.***

*End users of the MDAC 2.7 software included shall not be considered "registered owners" of a Microsoft product and therefore shall not be eligible for promotions, automatic upgrades and regular notices or other benefits extended to "registered owners" of a Microsoft product.*

*All of the software on the CD-ROM provided with this book is provided as is, with no warranty of any kind expressed or implied, including but not limited to the warranties of merchantability and fitness for a particular purpose. Neither the manufacturer, the publisher, nor its dealers or distributors assumes any liability for any alleged or actual damages arising from the use of this software.*

Finally, the CD contains some appendices:

- ❑ Appendix A – Access Object Model
- ❑ Appendix B – Access Events
- ❑ Appendix C – ADO 2.7 Object Model
- ❑ Appendix D – Microsoft DAO 3.6 Object Library Reference
- ❑ Appendix E – ODBC and IIS

To help you navigate around the CD, start by opening the `menu.html` file.

# Exercise Solutions

Solutions to the end of chapter exercises can be found online at this web site:

http://p2p.wrox.com/exercises/

# Conventions

We use a number of different styles of text and layout in the book to help differentiate between the various styles of information. Here are examples of the styles we use along with explanations of what they mean:

**Try It Out**     **Conventions**

The *Try It Out* is an exercise you should work through, following the text in the book.

**1.** They usually consist of a set of steps.

**2.** Each step has a number.

**3.** Follow the steps through with your copy of the database.

## How It Works

After each *Try It Out*, the code you've typed in will be explained in detail.

*Background information will look like this.*

> **Not-to-be missed information looks like this.**

Bulleted information is shown like this:

- **Important words** have a special font.
- Words that appear on the screen (such as menu options) are in a similar font to the one used on the screen, for example the File menu.
- Keys that you press on the keyboard, like *Ctrl* and *Enter*, are in italics.
- All file names are in this style: `IceCream.mdb`.
- Any `code fragments` within normal text are highlighted in this `special font`.

Code shown for the first time, or other relevant code, is in the following format:

```
Dim intVariable As Integer

intVariable = 10
Debug.Print intVariable
```

...while less important code, or code that you have seen before, looks like this:

```
intVariable = 10
```

# Customer Support

We always value hearing from our readers, and we want to know what you think about this book: what you liked, what you didn't like, and what you think we can do better next time. You can send us your comments, either by returning the reply card in the back of the book, or by e-mail to feedback@wrox.com. Please be sure to mention the book's title in your message.

# Errata

We've made every effort to make sure that there are no errors in the text or in the code. However, no one is perfect and mistakes do occur. If you find an error in one of our books, like a spelling mistake or a faulty piece of code, we would be very grateful for feedback. By sending in errata you may save another reader hours of frustration and, of course, you will be helping us provide even higher quality information. Simply e-mail the information to support@wrox.com. Your information will be checked and, if correct, posted to the errata page for that title, or used in subsequent editions of the book.

To find errata on the Web, go to http://www.wrox.com/ and locate the title through our Find a Book search engine or our book list. Then click on the book's View errata link.

# E-mail Support

If you wish to directly query a problem in the book with an expert who knows the book in detail then e-mail support@wrox.com, with the title of the book and the last four numbers of the ISBN in the subject field of the e-mail. A typical e-mail should include the following things:

❑ The **title of the book, last four digits of the ISBN** (821X), and **page number** of the problem in the Subject field.

❑ Your **name, contact information**, and the **problem** in the body of the message.

We won't send you junk mail. We need the details to save your time and ours. When you send an e-mail message, it will go through the following chain of support:

❑ Customer Support – Your message is delivered to our customer support staff, who are the first people to read it. They have files on most frequently asked questions and will answer anything general about the book or the web site immediately.

❑ Editorial – Deeper queries are forwarded to the technical editor responsible for that book. They have experience with the programming language or particular product, and are able to answer detailed technical questions on the subject.

❑ The authors – Finally, in the unlikely event that the editor cannot answer your problem, they will forward the request to the author. We do try to protect the author from any distractions to their writing; however, we are quite happy to forward specific requests to them. All Wrox authors help with the support on their books. They will e-mail the editor with their response and, again, all readers should benefit.

The Wrox Support process can only offer support to issues that are directly pertinent to the content of the published title. Support for questions that fall outside the scope of normal book support is provided via the community lists of our http://p2p.wrox.com/ forum.

# p2p.wrox.com

For author and peer discussion, join the P2P mailing lists. Our unique system provides **programmer to programmer™** contact on mailing lists, forums, and newsgroups, all in addition to our one-to-one e-mail support system. If you post a query to P2P, you can be confident that it is being examined by the many Wrox authors and other industry experts who are present on our mailing lists. At p2p.wrox.com you will find a number of different lists that will help you, not only while you read this book, but also as you develop your own applications. Particularly appropriate to this book are the vba_access and access lists.

To subscribe to a mailing list just follow these steps:

1. Go to http://p2p.wrox.com/.

2. Choose the appropriate category from the left menu bar.

3. Click on the mailing list you wish to join.

4. Follow the instructions to subscribe and fill in your e-mail address and password.

5. Reply to the confirmation e-mail you receive.

6. Use the subscription manager to join more lists and set your e-mail preferences.

## Why this System Offers the Best Support

You can choose to join the mailing lists or you can receive them as a weekly digest. If you don't have the time, or facility, to receive the mailing list, then you can search our online archives. Junk and spam mails are deleted, and your own e-mail address is protected by the unique Lyris system. Queries about joining or leaving lists, and any other general queries about lists, should be sent to listsupport@p2p.wrox.com.

# CHAPTER 1

# Designing Applications

Access 2002 is mostly a very intuitive and easy to use application. From the early days of Access, usability has always been one of the primary development focuses behind Access. In fact it was this ease of use that was a major factor in the incredible speed with which Access came to be accepted as the definitive desktop database development tool.

But Access has always appealed to a wider audience than simply end users and inexperienced developers. Behind its ease of use, Access has always provided a very powerful database and application development tool – more recent releases of Access have extended this power even further with the introduction of features such as Access Database Projects (ADPs), Data Access Pages (DAPs) and the adoption of VBA (Visual Basic for Applications) version 6 as its programming language.

In this chapter, we introduce the application we will be developing throughout the course of this book. After that, we'll contrast the differences between macros and VBA, and highlight one of the limitations you will encounter when using macros.

But before any of this, let's begin by defining what an Access Application is, and take you through the design processes you ought to consider before you even begin coding.

# What Is an Access Application?

An Access application is just the same as any other kind of application, but one built using Access tools. It is a collection of interrelated objects working together to achieve a specific objective, usually business-orientated.

That didn't tell us that much, did it? Maybe we should have asked a different question:

### What makes an Access application different from any other kind of application?

The main difference is that Access is designed from the ground up to handle data, quickly, efficiently, and lots of it. Access applications therefore tend to be data intensive. Using Access to create such applications can be easier and faster and can produce better results than using anything else. Obviously today's applications also need to be able to present a modern and efficient graphical user interface and to allow for all sorts of additional functionality, like connections to other applications or to the Internet – Access provides for this as well, but this is not its primary goal. It is, for example, entirely possible to create an Access application that simulates shooting missiles at alien spacecraft as they move across a Martian landscape but this would certainly not be the best way to do it!

When you create a new database file (.mdb file) in Microsoft Access 2002, the first thing that you see is the database window. This is a container that will eventually hold a wide variety of different objects. Tables will be used to store data; queries will be designed to retrieve data in meaningful ways; forms, reports, and data access pages will all be used to display the results of those queries in ways that users can understand; and macros and VBA modules will provide the program logic which 'glues' the whole application together.

If you use Access 2002 to create a project (.adp file) instead, then the database window will also show additional server-side objects (such as database diagrams and stored procedures), which may also be included to make up the application.

All of these objects can play an important role in providing the functionality of the end product – whether it is hosted solely in an Access database or uses a client-server database project.

The aim of this book is to illustrate the important role played by VBA in orchestrating these objects, in binding them together through the use of logic to control workflow and to implement specific business rules, and in turning a collection of individual objects into a coherent and effective application. Yes, we want to teach you how to use VBA, but to do that without first telling you how to design an application would be irresponsible.

# The Development Process

There are many skills involved in the development and delivery of successful Microsoft Access 2002 applications. The database designers need to be able to understand the principles of relational database design, so that they can design the tables that will hold the data and the relationships between those tables. The application developers need to have a feel for the graphical user interface (GUI) design, so that the forms they design for users to interact with will be intuitive and easy to use. They will also need to understand both SQL (Structured Query Language) and VBA so that they can write queries and procedures that not only return the correct data or perform the required task, but also do so quickly and efficiently.

There are other less technical (but no less complex) skills to master. Analysts need to be able to understand the business requirements of the users for whom the application is being designed, and to translate these requirements into a design specification from which the developers can work. Technical documenters need to be able to articulate how the application works, to anticipate confusions that users might experience and to clearly express their thoughts in documentation that is both accessible and informative. Test engineers need to be rigorous in their approach, perhaps using formal methodologies to check for errors, and must not take anything for granted when evaluating the application. Last, but certainly not least, project managers need to know how to monitor progress and track resource usage to ensure that the application is delivered on time and within budget.

Sometimes, if the application being developed is large-scale or complex, then there will be many different people involved in the application development lifecycle. Some will be responsible purely for analysis or design, others will work solely on designing queries or developing forms, and yet others will be responsible for other tasks, such as migrating legacy data into the Access database or producing user documentation. But at other times, particularly if the application is less complex, or if resources (such as money or people) are scarcer, then it is not uncommon for many of these tasks to be undertaken by individuals. Indeed, in many situations, a single person can be responsible for the entire analysis and development process.

Irrespective of the number of people involved, or the development methodology employed, the development lifecycle for an Access application will typically involve the following steps:

Analysis ➔ Design ➔ Coding ➔ Testing ➔ Documentation ➔ Acceptance ➔ Review

In practice, however, these steps do not rigidly follow one after another. There can be significant overlaps and the project can iterate through some of these steps before progressing on to others. It is beyond the scope of this book to enter into a detailed discussion of different project lifecycle plans. However, it is undoubtedly true that the speed with which Access forms and reports can be produced makes Access an excellent tool for using in a more iterative lifecycle model. In such a situation, the lifecycle would look more like this:

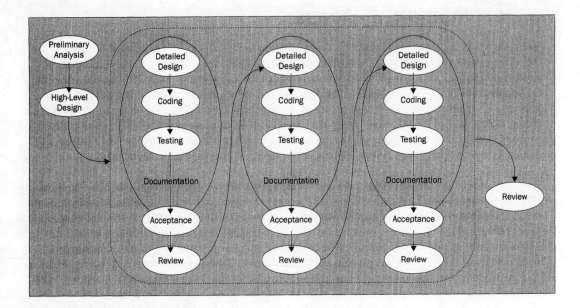

## The Analysis Phase

Irrespective of the type of project lifecycle mode, the first stage, and one of the most important to get right, is inevitably one of analysis. Without adequate analysis you will not be able to determine what the user wants from the application, the technical infrastructure within which the application will be implemented, and the constraints imposed by the data with which you will be working. Repairing the damage done by inadequate analysis, at a later date, can prove very costly or even kill a project completely.

### Requirements Analysis

The starting point for creating any successful Access application is to have a clear understanding of what the users of an application want out of it. You need to know this before you can even start to think about how to design any solution. The sorts of questions you will need to ask in this stage include, among others:

- ❑ What is the business process we are trying to automate?

- ❑ What benefit is the new application designed to achieve? How will we measure the benefit?

- ❑ Do we simply want to automate the existing process, or restructure the process and automate it?

- ❑ Will the application have to interoperate with other existing or planned systems or processes?

- ❑ What volume of data will the application be expected to handle?

- How many users will be using the system at the same time (concurrently)? How many in total?

- What is the anticipated mix of insert and update activity compared to query and reporting activity?

The problem is that the only people who can answer these questions are the customers who will use the finished application, and sometimes it can prove difficult to get answers out of them. It might be that the demands of their current business are so pressing that they have little time to answer questions about some future application. It might be that the sensitivities of internal office politics will make them unwilling to be too helpful in designing an application in which they feel they have too little ownership. Or it may be that they are trying to be helpful, but just don't know the answers to these questions, because it is something they have never thought about. Don't feel bashful about asking questions, however stupid some of them might sound. What might seem illogical and "obviously wrong" to an outsider might turn out to be a vital, but unspoken, business practice that simply must be implemented in order for the application to be acceptable. Once you think you understand a process it is often useful to run it past the client again for confirmation. Use these discussions to prompt further questioning to fill in any gaps. In any case, it is vital to try to approach this phase of the project with as few preconceptions as possible.

Requirements analysis is a skilled art and many organizations fail to appreciate the fact that good developers do not necessarily make good analysts. In fact, in many ways, developers make the worst analysts. By their very nature, good developers are constantly looking for detailed solutions to problems. Someone mentions a business requirement and you can almost hear the cogs whirring in their brains as their eyes glaze over and they start working out how they will produce a solution to that requirement; without stopping to ask what the value of satisfying that requirement is, or even if the requirement truly exists. That is not what you want from an analyst. You want an analyst to be able to take an objective look at the requirement expressed by the user, to check that they understand it correctly, to ask what the relevance of this requirement is to the business, to determine the metrics (ways of measuring) by which the successful implementation of the requirement can be judged and to express that requirement in a way that other parties involved in the project will understand.

A variety of tools and methods are available to assist the requirements analysis process. For example, JAD (Joint Application Development) is a technique that assists requirements definition by bringing all of the various parties who are interested in the development together in intense off-site meetings to focus on the business problem to be solved rather than worrying about specific technical issues.

Whether you use such techniques is up to you. What is important is that you value the requirements analysis process. This phase of a project is so important because it is the fundamental mechanism for defining both the scope of the project and the critical success factors that show when the project has achieved its requirements. It forms the basis for the contract between the users and the developers, and is the touchstone to be used when resolving conflict or confusion later on in the project lifecycle.

Ironically, the importance of sound requirements analysis is most clearly seen in its absence. When requirements are not properly defined or documented, one of two consequences almost inevitably follows. Either the requirements remain unmodified, with the result that the application fails to achieve its client's objectives; or the requirements are modified later in the development cycle. Late changes such as these can have a huge impact on project costs as their effects 'ripple' out and affect other areas such as documentation, design, coding, testing, personnel assignments, subcontractor requirements, and so on. Indeed, some studies indicate that such changes can be 50 to 200 times more expensive than they would have been if they had been made at the appropriate time!

## Prototyping

Prototypes, pre-development versions, proof of concepts, nailed-up versions – it doesn't matter what name you give them; they are all attempts to further refine the analysis phase of the project. Access used to be seen as being "only" a prototyping tool with the "real" development given over to something more "industrial strength". This is no longer the case, however (if indeed it ever really was). Access is perfectly up to the job of all but the most demanding projects. It still makes a marvellous tool for prototyping though.

A prototype is a scaled-down version of the final application, which can be achieved at low cost and within a short timescale. It may have certain functionality incomplete or missing entirely. It may even only implement a tiny part of the whole project. The whole point of the prototype is to test those areas of the design that are currently uncertain. This may include a number of different methods to achieve the desired functionality, or perhaps alternative GUI designs to see which is easiest to use, or maybe sample queries with test data to determine what kind of hardware platforms will be required to attain the desired performance.

One thing you should never see is a prototype as v1.0 of the application. This is invariably a recipe for disaster. The temptation is to take the prototype and keep developing it without first going through all the other formal processes described below. You should always see the prototype as part of the analysis phase of the project and not the end of it; it exists to ask questions and to get them answered. If certain parts of the prototype later make their way into the final application (the GUI design would be a good example) then all well and good, but ideally you should plan and cost the work separately.

## Technical Analysis

As well as determining the nature of the solution required by the users of the application, it is also necessary to determine the technical infrastructure that will support this solution. The types of questions posed are ones such as these:

- ❑ What operating system will the application run on?
- ❑ Will we need different versions of the application for different clients (for example, one for customers and one for managers)?
- ❑ What is the specification (that is, in terms of processor, memory, disk space) of the machines that the application will run on?

❑ What type of network will connect the computers? Will lack of available bandwidth prove a problem?

❑ What security policy will the application need to operate?

❑ What type of fault tolerance or recovery issues will need to be considered?

The purpose of the technical analysis should be to produce an application architecture and implementation framework within which the resultant application will nestle. Again, it may well turn out that developers are not the best people to undertake this type of analysis. Technical analysis requires a good understanding of networking, security, and technical issues and these skills may not be present in all of your developers.

## Data Analysis

By this stage, you should have a contract in place that defines what the application is meant to provide and you will probably have a good idea of the technical infrastructure within which the design will be implemented. The next stage is to analyze the data that you will be working with. Now, I must confess that I frequently find this task less than stimulating, but I know that it is imperative if I am to achieve a sound database design. As tedious as data analysis is, it sure beats the pants off rewriting an application because a fundamental misunderstanding of the underlying data only comes to light two weeks before the project is due to be delivered.

Now this is not a primer on data analysis. Although simple enough in theory, data analysis can be quite complex in practice and if you are new to the subject, you would do well to get some specialized training in this discipline.

One term you are likely to come across again and again is **normalization**. This is a formal technique for the elimination of dependencies in our data. This, in turn, realizes the twin benefits of reducing redundancy and minimizing opportunities for inconsistency being introduced into our data. Some of the principles of normalization are intuitive and you probably already follow them (like trying not to store a company's address twice in two different tables), but it can take a high degree of skill and substantial experience to know when and how to apply some of the more detailed rules, and gains can be elusive. Because of this we will not attempt to cover the subject here. In any case, for smaller projects, formal normalization is rarely useful.

> *If you are likely to be doing a lot of data analysis or are simply interested in the subject then one of the most authoritative discussions of the theory of normalization can be found in 'An Introduction to Database Systems' by CJ Date (Addison-Wesley, 1995, ISBN 0-201-54329-X). A less theoretical (and thus much more accessible) approach can be found in Database Design for Mere Mortals: A Hands-On Guide to Database Design by Michael J. Hernandez (Addison-Wesley, 1997, ISBN 0-201-69471-9) and Professional SQL Server 2000 Database Design by Louis Davidson (Wrox Press, 2001, 1-861004-76-1).*

The principles behind sound data analysis are straightforward enough:

❑ Identify all of the data entities you will be dealing with

❑ Establish the attributes of these entities

❑ Define the relationships between these entities

❑ Document, document, document...

As with the requirements analysis and the technical analysis, a variety of methods and tools can be employed to assist in the task of data analysis. Whichever you choose to employ, I would encourage you to bear the following two principles in mind.

First, when selecting a tool, it is paramount that you choose one that allows you to clearly document the results of the analysis in formats that everyone involved can understand. Remember that you may have to present your designs to a wide range of people from clients through developers and possibly up to management – they will all have different technical abilities and focus, so bear in mind that you will need to be able to easily vary the level of detail included. Your primary audience, however, is technical, so use diagrams to illustrate the relationships between your entities, by all means, but don't forget the fine detail (however boring it might be to gather!). Complex entity relationship diagrams may look very impressive and professional, but if you can't use your documentation to tell you whether Widget Part Codes are 8 or 9 characters long, then you are going to struggle.

Second, it is very seldom that I have come across data analysis that has suffered from being **too** detailed. Document everything – data types, field lengths, allowable values, calculated values – get it all down on paper and do so while it is fresh in your mind. If there is something you are not sure about, don't guess. Go back, check it out, and write it down. The temptation is always there to wrap up the data analysis early and get on with the fun part of the project (design and development). Resist the temptation. You'll thank yourself for it later on.

## Design and Coding

So then, now that the analysis is out of the way, it's time to get on with coding. Right? Wrong! As tempting as it might be to just plunge in and start coding straight away, you first need to spend some time deciding on an appropriate design for the application. One of the chief aims of the design process is to establish the blueprints from which the application can be built. A few of the issues that you will need to consider when designing the solution are:

❑ Data Storage / Location

❑ Import / Export Mechanisms

❑ Error Handling

❑ Portability Issues

❑   Performance Considerations

❑   Calculation Methods

But design is not just about establishing an immutable set of blueprints. Successful applications are normally those where the application designers have designed for change.

## Designing for Change

The concept of "Designing for Change" was first discussed by David Parnas in the early 1970s. It is a principle that recognizes the fact that, however good the analysis has been, there will frequently occur during the lifetime of a project a number of influences that will necessitate change to occur after the initial design has been completed. It might be a change in the legal or business environment in which the customers operate, a change in available technology, or simply a change in understanding on the part of either the customer or the developer. The purpose of designing for change is to ensure that these changes can be accommodated into the project with the minimum possible disruption or delay.

Three of the most important techniques involved in designing for change are described below:

### Identify Volatile Areas

Some issues are more liable to change than others during a development project. These include business rules, file formats, sequences in which items will be processed, and any number of other difficult design areas. The first step is to identify all such volatile areas and document them.

### Use Information Hiding

Once these issues have been listed, you can employ information hiding. The principle here is to wrap up, or encapsulate, these volatile issues in a module or procedure that hides, or partitions off, the complexity or volatility of the processes involved. These modules or procedures should have an interface that can remain the same, irrespective of any changes that may occur within the module or procedure as a result of any of the influences we identified earlier. If a change occurs, it should only affect that module or procedure. Other modules that interact with it should not need to be aware of the fact that anything has changed. This is often called "black box" coding, in that "stuff goes in" and "stuff comes out" but what happens in the box is hidden.

For example, you might be designing an application that is used for sending out pre-renewal reminder notices to customers prior to the expiry of their insurance policies. Perhaps a business rule states that pre-renewal notices are to be sent out 2 months before expiry. This is just the type of rule that could easily change and a good design will account for this. Accordingly, a procedure could be written which encapsulated that rule and which was invoked whenever various parts of the application needed to know when the reminder should be sent. Changes to the business rule would only need to be incorporated in a single procedure; the procedure would still be invoked in the same way and yet the effects of the change would be available throughout the application. We will look at this subject in more detail when we examine the use of classes in Access in Chapter 13.

### *Employ a Change Plan*

As well as information hiding, there are other techniques that can assist in reducing the impact of change, and these should be prescribed in a change plan. For example, the change plan might specify that:

❑ Named constants should be used wherever possible in place of hard-coded values.

❑ If the application is to be multi-lingual, then care must be taken to identify and separate out all the text to be used so that it can be easily localized (translated). This may mean allowing additional screen space to accommodate certain languages or considering the use of pictorial icons in place of text.

❑ Settings and configuration options should be stored in the Registry rather than hard-coded within the application itself.

❑ Generic and widely used processes should be identified and grouped together in modules, separate from code with specialized functionality only called by specific parts of an application.

One of the best ways to determine which elements to incorporate into a change plan is to perform post-implementation reviews just after a project has been delivered (or post-mortems if they don't get that far!). Identify what changed during the project lifecycle, what impact that change had, and how the impact of that change could have been lessened. Then put that knowledge into your next change plan and make sure you don't make the same mistake twice!

## Coding

Once your design is complete, you can start to code. That's the part of the process that we will be examining in most detail throughout the rest of this book. We will start by looking at the specifics of the VBA language and the structure of VBA procedures and modules. Then we will look at the Access object model and how this can be manipulated in code. After a short look at some more advanced programming techniques, we will look at how to handle errors that might occur in our application, how to make the best use of class modules, libraries and add-ins, and how to optimize the performance of our application. We will also look at some of the issues we need to be aware of if our application is being used in a multi-user environment and how we can bring some of the power of the Internet to our Access application. Finally, we will look at the finishing touches we can apply to round out our application and give it a more professional look and feel.

# Testing

There are a number of quality assurance practices that you can apply to your project, but by far the most basic is testing. This involves unit testing (or component testing) where the developer verifies that the code he or she has written works correctly; system testing where someone checks that the entire application works together as expected; and acceptance testing, where the users of the application check that the results the application produces are those they desire (or, at least, that they are those they asked for in the first place!).

The purpose of testing is to break code, to determine ways of making an application misbehave, to expose flaws in either the design or execution of the development process. For this reason, many developers dislike the testing phase (in the same way that many authors dislike the editing phase). If you have spent endless weeks working late to get a tough reporting module finished, if you have missed the ball game for the last four weeks in a row trying to get that import routine to work, if you couldn't make the Christmas party because you were wrestling with a suite of reports that you had to finish, then it is unlikely that you will approach the testing phase with anything other than fear and loathing.

The problem is that testing has a propensity for delivering bad news at the wrong time. The solution is to allow plenty of time for testing, to test early in the development cycle, and to build plenty of time for reworking code after the testing has completed. Being told that a routine you have written does not produce the right results is seldom welcome news to any developer, but it is a lot easier to bear if the developer is told this early on and knows that there is plenty of time to correct the offending code. *Test early and allow for rewrites!*

It also bears mentioning that a proper test plan is essential for both system and user acceptance testing, and the basis for this test plan should be the documentation that was produced during the requirements analysis stage. In particular, the test plan should define not just what is to be tested, but also what results the application should generate in response to that testing.

*One particularly effective technique that is growing more and more popular is the use of "Use Cases". These provide a method for describing the behavior of the application from a user's standpoint by identifying actions and reactions. For more information on how to produce Use Cases, you might want to have a look at Jake Sturm's VB6 UML Design and Development, ISBN 1-861002-51-3, from Wrox Press.*

## Documentation

Documentation is a bit like ironing. It's one of those things you have to do, but I have yet to meet anyone who enjoys doing it. It's one of those things that we all know we should do, but we all find boring. It's not surprising. I enjoy playing soccer, but I would soon get bored if I had to write a detailed game report every time I played, explaining what tactics we employed, why we employed them, when we scored, and so on. It's the same with documenting development projects. For most developers, the fun is in creating the solution and putting it into action. Writing it up is major-league boredom.

However, few people who play soccer are called upon to remember what color boots they were wearing at a match 2 years ago, what the coach said before the game started, and how many oranges were on the refreshments table at half-time. Programmers are frequently called upon to fix or update code many months after it was first written. Often they will be in the middle of an entirely different project, maybe even 2 or 3 projects down the line. It might not even be their code! It's at times like these that those little notes you made to yourself when you wrote the original code are worth their weight in gold. A few well chosen words can save days or weeks of making exactly the same mistakes you did the first time around.

Yes, I know it is important. I know that I am as likely to benefit from it as anyone else when I revisit my code later. I know that the users have paid for it! I know it makes the difference between a good application and a great application. That's why I do it and why I make sure that everyone working with me does it and does it well. But I am not going to pretend for a moment that I enjoy it!

In practice, the best approach to this time-consuming chore is a mixture of notes and in-line comments made as you write the code, followed by reports and descriptions when you're done. Then all you have to do is check everything through carefully and keep everything up to date every time anything gets changed at the last minute!

## Acceptance

Ah, the bliss! It's all over and the users love the application you have written for them. Great! If you have any sense, you will seize the moment and make sure that three things happen.

First, get the users to sign off the project. If you have drawn up a comprehensive requirements definition and have met all of the success factors identified by the users at the start of the project, this should be a formality. But it is no less an important step for all that.

Second, get the users to tell their colleagues about the new application they are using. Many users have very short memories, and it won't be long before the users forget just how bad the manual processes were that they had to rely on before you wrote this application for them and just what a difference this application makes. Get them to sing your praises while they are still hooked. That's when you will get the best recommendations, whether you are collecting them for your company's marketing brochure or for your own personnel review (and, hopefully, pay rise) in three months' time.

Finally, get the users to start thinking about the next release. Some features might have been axed because there wasn't time to implement them; others might have been identified too late to make it into this release; and others might have always been destined for future releases. Once you are convinced that the users love the product you have given them, remind them about what it doesn't do... yet!

## Review

The final stage is the post-implementation review. This is the point where you look back at the project and decide what worked and what didn't, what caused problems, and how those problems could have been avoided or their impact minimized. Did you hit all of your deadlines? Did all of the intended functionality make it into the final product? How are relations with the customer at the end of it all? What state are your developers in at the end of it all? Given the opportunity, would you do it all again?

The purpose of the post-implementation review is not just to give everyone a chance to whine and moan about what went wrong. Instead, the purpose is to identify the changes that need to be made to your project methodology and practices to make sure that the same problems don't happen again next time. At the same time, it is an opportunity to identify the successes and to make sure that the benefits of these can be reaped by future projects.

A final benefit of conducting post-implementation reviews is that it gives an appropriate opportunity for recognizing the efforts and contributions of everyone who worked on the project. Sincere praise in response to specific achievements is essential to the self-respect of individual developers and the continued morale of the team as a whole.

### *Further Reading*

OK, that's enough for now on the theory behind designing and delivering software projects. If you want to learn some more about this subject there is ample reading material available, but perhaps one of the most interesting books on this subject is *"Clouds to Code" (Wrox Press, 1998, ISBN 1-861000-95-2)* in which Jesse Liberty documents the design and delivery of a real project with no holds barred. But this is where we leave behind the theory. From now on, this book will be a hands-on guide with real code examples for you to try out yourself and as we go through the book, we will rapidly find that we are building up a fully functional Access application.

# The Ice Cream Shop Application

Once we have completed the design phase of our project, we should be in a position to answer the two following questions:

- ❑ What data items (or entities) and application objects will we need?

- ❑ How should these entities and objects fit together?

This book is not about how to design the data items and other application objects that make up the application. We are assuming that you know enough about tables, forms, reports, and queries from your previous exploration of Access. This book is about how you use VBA (Visual Basic for Applications) to control the way that these objects interoperate as part of a larger system. In one sense, VBA can be thought of as the 'glue' that holds the whole application together.

The best way to understand how VBA fits in is, of course, not through theory but through practice. In the rest of this chapter, we will run through the process of starting to create an application – the Ice Cream Shop database that accompanies this book. At a certain point we will hit a brick wall, when we try to automate our application and get it to display some intelligence. We'll then look at the two options available to us for solving the problem: VBA or macros. We will see why VBA is often the best and sometimes the only satisfactory choice.

You may find that this section covers a lot of familiar territory. However, if you do take the time to read it, it will acquaint you with the structure of the Ice Cream Shop database so that, when the crunch comes, and we have to use VBA, we will have a familiar database structure to work with.

# *Designing the Ice Cream Shop Database*

As its name suggests, the Ice Cream Shop database is an application that has been designed to track stock and sales for an ice cream wholesaler called Dave and Rob's Ice Cream Shop. The requirements analysis we conducted indicated to us that the primary purpose of the database is to store information about the following things:

- ❏ Stock carried by the Ice Cream Shop
- ❏ Orders placed by companies
- ❏ Customer and supplier details

Our analysis has also indicated that ease of data entry and maintenance is a key requirement for the application, and that the forms used by the staff at the shop must be intuitive and simple to use. The fact that there will a fair amount of data to handle is enough for us to decide to use Access to build the application with (which is just as well or we wouldn't have an example to write about).

We have also conducted the appropriate technical analysis, which indicates that Access 2002 is an appropriate application development tool for the delivery of this database solution (otherwise this would be a very short book!).

Our data analysis has indicated that there are five primary objects or **entities**. We decided on these particular entities by dividing up the data requirements into self-contained "lumps". For a complex application there may be several different possible entity models (or ways of arranging your data) and at the end of the day the choice of which model to use will come down to your judgement, your experience and the type of requirements to be met. In this case the basic model is fairly obvious:

- ❏ Suppliers
- ❏ Customer Companies
- ❏ Ice Creams
- ❏ Ingredients
- ❏ Sales

The four key processes that indicate the relationships between the entities are as follows:

- ❏ Ice Creams are sold to Customer Companies
- ❏ Each Ice Cream is composed of one or more Ingredients
- ❏ Each Ingredient can be used in one or more Ice Creams
- ❏ Ingredients are purchased from Suppliers

A more detailed analysis has revealed the attributes of the five entities that we need to record and our preliminary **entity relationship diagram** (ERD, or more simply, database design) looks like this:

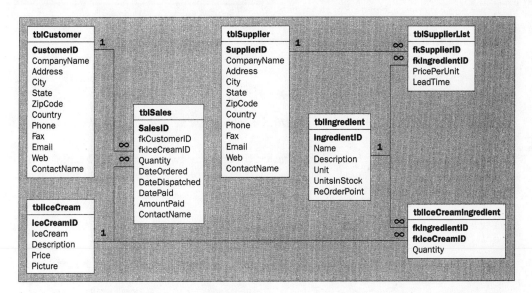

As you can see from the database diagram above, five tables have been created to represent the five basic entities identified in the data analysis:

| | | |
|---|---|---|
| tblSupplier | *represents* | the Suppliers entity |
| tblCustomer | *represents* | the Customers entity |
| tblIceCream | *represents* | the Ice Creams entity |
| tblIngredient | *represents* | the Ingredients entity |
| tblSales | *represents* | the Sales entity |

One-to-many relationships between the entities have been denoted by creating straightforward one-to-many relationships between the tables:

```
tblCustomer        (1)          ➜      (n)        tblSales
```

*A sale can only involve one customer, but a customer can have more than one sale*

```
tblIceCream        (1)          ➜      (n)        tblSales
```

*Only one type of ice cream can be sold in a particular sale, but an ice cream can be sold more than once*

Many-to-many relationships have been handled by creating two intermediate tables (tblIceCreamIngredient and tblSupplierList) and placing one-to-many relationships on either side of the intermediate table:

```
tblIce      (1)  ➜  (n)  tblIceCream     (n)  ⬅  (1)   tblIngredient
Cream                    Ingredient
```

*An ice cream is composed of many ingredients and the same Ingredient can be used in many ice creams*

```
tbl         (1)  ➜  (n)  tblSupplier     (n)  ⬅  (1)   tblIngredient
Supplier                 List
```

*A supplier can provide many ingredients and the same ingredient could be provided by many suppliers*

> *This use of intermediate tables is the standard way in which we join two tables together when the two tables have a many-to-many relationship. It is part of a process called normalization, which is a series of steps you go through to make sure your database is designed correctly. This process is really beyond the scope of this book, but there are plenty of books specializing in it. One such book is (as we've mentioned earlier) 'Database Design for Mere Mortals', Michael J. Hernandez, Addison-Wesley, ISBN 0-201-69471-9.*

## Typical Dilemmas Regarding Data Storage

A few features of this database structure are worthy of note. Firstly, note the duplication of the ContactName attribute in the tblSupplier, tblCustomer, and tblSales tables. This is deliberate and caters for the fact that although there is one primary contact for each supplier and for each customer, the Ice Cream Shop also wants to be able to assign separate contacts to individual sales.

Secondly, note the fact that the `tblSupplier` and `tblCustomer` tables have identical structures. Whenever we see this in a database structure it should alert us to the fact that what we have represented as two discrete entities might instead be represented as a single entity. So what is it that differentiates a supplier from a customer? Obviously, we buy from suppliers and customers buy from us. But is that sufficient reason for treating them as separate entities? After all, what happens if a supplier is also a customer? If this was to occur, and we were maintaining separate `tblSupplier` and `tblCustomer` tables, then changes to, say, the address of the company involved would necessitate a change to both the `tblSupplier` and `tblCustomer` tables.

A better alternative might be to combine the two tables into a generic `tblCompany` table:

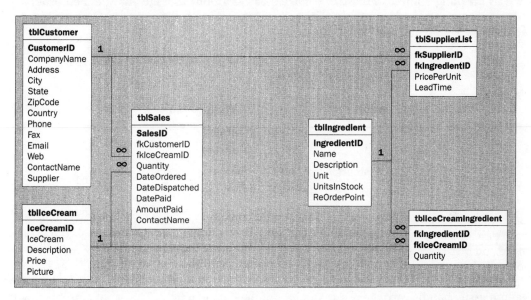

This is actually the database design that has been employed in the Ice Cream Shop database that accompanies this book. The `tblCompany` table now holds details of both suppliers and customers. In order to distinguish between those companies that appear in the `tblCompany` table (because they are either customers or suppliers) we have added a new `Supplier` field to the table. This field has a Yes/No data type and we will use to indicate whether the company should appear in supplier lists.

This is not the only way that we could have chosen to implement the physical design of the database. There is often no one correct database design. A fully normalized design might please the relational database theorists, but they are not the ones who will have to maintain the database or account for its performance in a production environment. Database design, as with most aspects of system design and development, is all about achieving the best compromise. There is nothing inherently wrong with denormalizing a database and it can be an excellent tool for increasing query performance. However, before you decide to denormalize a database, you should ensure that it doesn't introduce any significant data anomalies and that either:

- ❑ It will allow you to achieve a measurable improvement in performance, with a minimal increase in administrative overhead, or

- ❑ It will allow you to achieve a measurable reduction in administrative overhead, with a minimal degradation of performance

Another aspect of the `tblCompany` table that required careful consideration was the question of how to hold address information. Look at the structure of the table. The address information has been broken down into five fields (`Address`, `City`, `State`, `ZipCode`, and `Country`). Why do you think this has been done, instead of holding the address in a single field? The answer is that by breaking it into five fields, we make it easier for our users to analyze their orders by city, state, zip code and country individually. This would be difficult, if not impossible, if the address were stored in a single field.

*Note, however, that only one field is used for the first part of the address (the lines that precede the city, state, zip code and country).*

| | |
|---:|:---|
| **Address:** | 37 Walnut Grove |
| **City:** | Nutbush |
| **State:** | Tennessee |
| **Postcode/Zip Code:** | 38053 |
| **Country:** | USA |

Even though this first part of the address might contain more than one line (especially if the address contains a building name) we can store it in a single field, because Access allows us to store and display multi-line values in one field. We store these in one field because they logically belong together and you shouldn't need to split them up at all. Sometimes you will see databases with tables that store this part of the address in multiple fields, because the database cannot easily handle carriage returns as part of the data in a field. That's not a problem with Access though.

The other advantage with storing the first part of the address in a single field is that it makes it a lot easier to amend the address. Just imagine if you had stored the above address with a separate field for every line of the address and then had to change it to:

| | |
|---:|:---|
| **Address:** | **Unit 17** |
| | 37 Walnut Grove |
| **City:** | Nutbush |
| **State:** | Tennessee |
| **Postcode/Zip Code:** | 38053 |
| **Country:** | USA |

## Choosing a Storage Engine

Another choice which developers of Access 2002 applications will now need to make is which database engine they will use to store the application's data in. Traditionally, Microsoft Access has always used JET as its native database engine. Additionally, however, Access developers are offered the choice of using a second desktop database engine, the Microsoft SQL Server 2000 Desktop Engine (henceforth MSDE).

To keep this chapter concise and to the point, we have placed the discussion of which storage engine to use in Chapter 20. It is also worth reiterating at this point that the purpose of this book is to teach how to use VBA in Access and for that reason all of the data access examples will be against JET databases.

# Entering and Viewing Data

So far, we've considered the need for careful analysis and table design. But that's only the start. Now we have to consider how the users of our system are going to enter information into the tables. Of course, they could type information straight into the tables in datasheet mode, but that would be inelegant and inefficient, and would make it difficult to check data entry properly. There may also be security issues involved as it is unlikely that we will want all the users to be able to access sensitive data and this is impossible to achieve if the users have access to the "raw" data tables. We therefore need to put an acceptable face on our application and shield the users from the complexity of the table structure.

## Designing a Form

The simplest way to create a quick-and-easy form is to use one of the Form Wizards. Using a wizard to produce a form will give you all the fields you require from one or more tables. This is great, but sometimes you'll need to add extra functionality to the form, in which case you'll have to make any additional modifications yourself. We're going to use a Form Wizard to create one of the key forms in the application – the form for maintaining company information.

**Try It Out** — **Creating a Form Using the AutoForm Wizard**

As we explained in the Introduction, your starting point for the *Try It Out* sections in this book is the `IceCream.mdb` database, found on the CD-ROM. We have also included on the CD partially completed databases that reflect each chapter's development, in case you lose your own copy, or want to jump in at a later chapter. The databases are numbered such that they correspond to the state at the end of a chapter – in other words, IceCream03 is the database you'd get when you'd worked through to the end of Chapter 3. We think it's better if you work through all of the *Try It Out*s, though, so you can really get a feel for how everything works and fits together.

OK. Let's get started!

**1.** Load up the database file `IceCream.mdb`. In the **Database** window, select the **Tables** tab and then the `tblCompany` table:

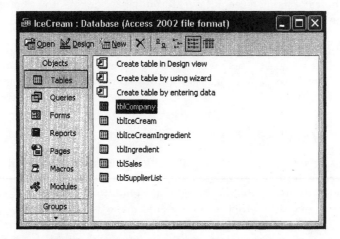

**2.** Select **AutoForm** from the **Insert** menu, or click the down arrow next to the **New Object** button on the toolbar and select **AutoForm** from the drop-down menu:

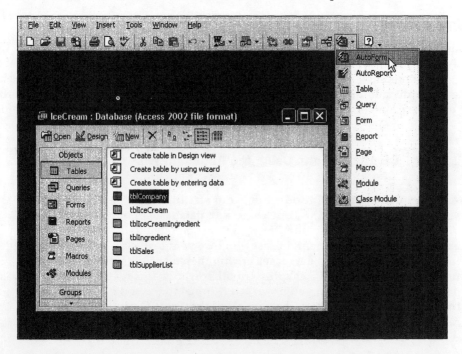

**3.** Access will now generate a form with all the fields from the tblCompany table and display the first record:

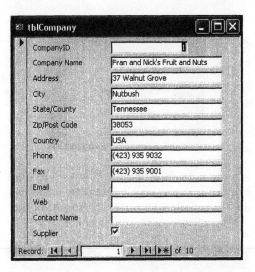

This is OK, but it's not perfect. There are several things that we can improve:

❏ The form caption is tblCompany, which isn't very instructive to the user.

❏ We will probably want to hide the CompanyID field, as it's of little relevance to the user.

❏ Some of the fields are the wrong shape. For example, we will want to make the Address textbox taller, to accommodate larger addresses.

❏ The navigation buttons at the bottom of the form are a bit small and fiddly – this is a key form and must be as easy to use as possible.

So let's change the form so that it looks a little more professional.

**Try It Out** **Changing a Form's Appearance in Design View**

**1.** Save the form you've just created by choosing Save from the File menu or by hitting *Ctrl + S*. A dialog box will appear allowing you to type in a name for the form. Call it frmCompany:

**2.** Now switch to **Design** view for the newly saved form by selecting **Design View** from the **View** menu or by clicking the **Design View** button:

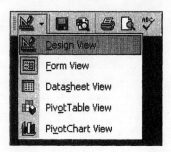

**3.** We can now attempt to make the changes that we highlighted earlier. To change the form's caption, you bring up the form's property sheet by double-clicking the Form Selector (the small gray box in the upper left corner of the form where the rulers meet), or by clicking the **Properties** button on the toolbar:

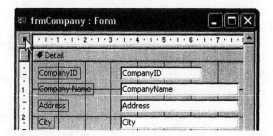

**4.** When the **Properties** window appears, make sure that the **Format** tab is selected, and then change the text of the **Caption** property to **Company Details**:

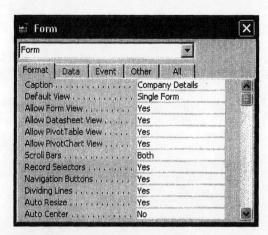

**5.** Next we must delete the CompanyID textbox and its label. To do this, we must select the textbox on the form by clicking it once, and then hitting the *Delete* key. The CompanyID textbox and its label will be deleted:

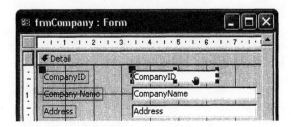

**6.** Next we'll change the size of the Address textbox. To do this, first select all of the controls on the form below the Address textbox. You can do this by dragging a rectangle around them with the primary mouse button held down or by clicking them in turn with the *Shift* key held down. Once the controls have been selected, place the mouse over one of the selected controls. The mouse pointer will turn into a small hand, indicating that the controls can be moved:

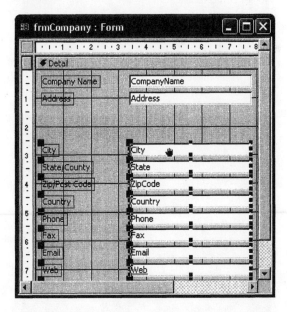

**7.** Hold down the primary mouse button and drag the controls down the form to leave some space for the Address text box, which we are going to resize.

*You may have noticed that the wizard initially generated the form with just enough room for the controls. Don't worry about it, the form will automatically extend when you move the controls down.*

*There is an alternative method for moving controls around on a form once they are selected: Use the arrow keys on your keyboard whilst holding down the Ctrl key. This method is slower, but can be more precise.*

**8.** Once you have created some space, resize the **Address** textbox. To do this, we select the **Address** textbox by clicking it and then click the resizing handle (it looks like a black square) at the bottom center of the text box. Dragging the resizing handle down will give us a taller shape for the textbox:

*You can also use a similar method to move, by using the arrow keys plus the Shift key, to more precisely resize all the controls selected.*

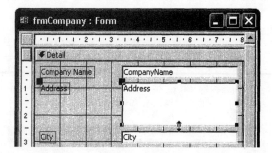

**9.** Finally, change the form back to Form View to see the changes you've made. You can do this by selecting Form View from the View menu or by clicking the button that has replaced the Design View button:

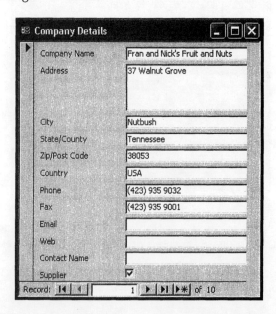

We've now made the first three changes we decided on, and our form certainly looks a little more professional. But what about the other change? We still need to put more manageable navigation buttons on the screen. This is where things get a little more advanced!

## Creating Navigation Buttons

To make the form easier to use, we can place some command buttons on the screen to replace the present navigation buttons. We can then use macros to move through the records behind the form. A macro is simply a stored collection of instructions that correspond to the actions that a user might carry out. So, in this case, our macro would contain the instructions to move to the next, previous, first or last records.

Of course, this book is about VBA, not macros. However, using them here will help show you their limitations.

---

**Try It Out**     **Adding Simple Navigation Buttons to a Form**

**1.** Switch back to **Design View**. We're going to use headers and footers, so go to the **View** menu and select the **Form Header/Footer** option. A header section and footer section will then appear on the form. We don't have to add the buttons to the footer of the form. We could add them onto the Detail section of the form instead. However, putting them on the footer keeps them in one place and we don't have to worry about them getting in the way if we decide to change around the other controls in the Detail section:

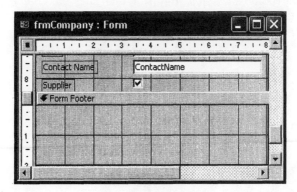

**2.** Next, we must remove the navigation buttons that Access supplies by default. So, click the **Form Selector** to bring up the form's property sheet, and on the property sheet's **Format** tab, change the value of the **Navigation Buttons** property from **Yes** to **No**. You can do this by double-clicking the property value or by clicking on the arrow and selecting **No** from the drop-down list that appears:

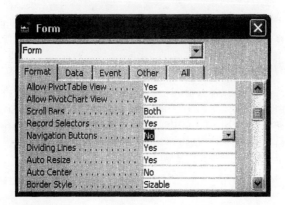

**3.** Once you have done this, you can also set the following form properties:

| Scroll Bars | Neither |
| --- | --- |
| Record Selectors | No |
| Dividing Lines | No |

**4.** Now you can add the first of your own navigation buttons. We'll start by creating a **Next Record** button.

**5.** Check that the Toolbox is visible. If it isn't, then click the Toolbox button on the toolbar:

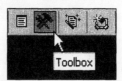

**6.** Then, make sure the **Control Wizards** button isn't depressed (that's the one in the toolbox with the magic wand on it), and select the **Command Button** tool from the toolbox. This will allow us to place a command button on the form:

**7.** Draw the button a suitable size on the footer:

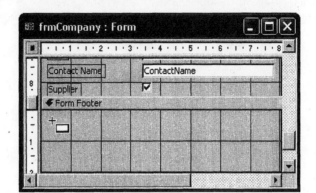

**8.** Now go to the property sheet and change the **Name** property of the button (found under the **Other** tab) to **cmdNext** and its **Caption** property (found under the **Format** tab) to **Next**.

*Note that when you name controls on a form it is a good idea to use a prefix that matches their type (like* cmd *for a command button). This makes the type obvious when you come to use the control in your VBA code, which makes your programs more readable and can help to reduce errors. Unfortunately there is no common standard for prefixes. Every company I've ever seen seems to use different ones (for example* tb, txb, txtbx, textbox, *for text boxes) and Microsoft have never published consistent guidelines. The best advice I can give is to find out what standards your company uses or, if none, use your own (sensible) prefixes and then be ready to change them at a later date!*

**9.** Now we must instruct the button to display the next record whenever it is clicked. To do this, you right-click on the button and select **Build Event...** from the pop-up menu which appears:

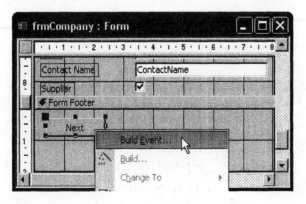

**10.** This will, in turn, bring up the Choose Builder dialog. For the moment, we want to use a macro, so select Macro Builder and hit the OK button:

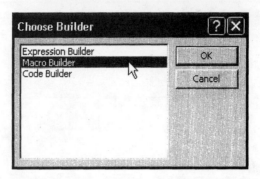

**11.** We've said that we want a macro behind the button, so Access now helps us to build it. It displays the macro design window and prompts us for the name that we want to give the macro. We will call it macNextButton, so you should type in macNextButton and then press OK.

**12.** Now we get to specify the macro commands that will be carried out when we hit the command button. We want the button to make the form go to the next record. To get it to do this, you must click the down arrow in the Action column and select GoToRecord from the drop-down list that appears:

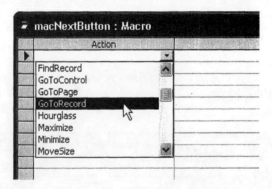

**13.** We then need to specify which record we want the command button to move us to. Click in the Record box in the lower pane of the screen, click the down arrow and select which record you want to go to from the drop-down list. We want to go to the next record, so make sure Next is selected. In fact, Next is the default selection in the drop-down list:

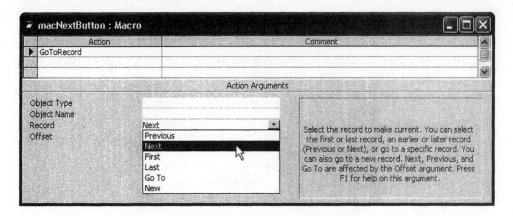

**14.** Now close the macro window and choose **Yes** when prompted to save the macro you have just created. Then change the frmCompany form to **Form** view and save the changes you made to it. When you open the form in form view, there should be a navigation button on it that allows you to move forward through the records in the form.

*If you look at the button's properties, you will see that the name of the macro is listed in the **On Click** property on the **Event** tab. This is how Access knows to run the macro when the button is clicked. The macro name was inserted automatically into the event property because you right-clicked the button to select **Build Event...** and the* Click *event is the default event for buttons. If you had built the macro yourself, you could still make Access use it whenever you click the **cmdNext** button, but you would have to insert the macro's name manually into the* On Click *event property before it would work. We'll look at this whole area in a lot more detail in the next chapter.*

**15.** Finally, complete the form by adding navigation buttons to enable you to move to the previous, first, last, and new records. You should be able to work out how to do this simply enough by referring to the steps described above.

## The Finished Product

So there we have it! Your own handcrafted navigation buttons! You can customize these further if you wish – you may want to change the caption on the **Next** button to add a 'greater than' sign (>). You may even want to add a tooltip by modifying the **ControlTipText** property of each button.

You can also provide a hotkey for each of the buttons. This allows the user to activate the button from the keyboard by pressing *Alt* and a particular letter. To set this up, you simply type an ampersand (&) in the button's **Caption** property, before the letter that you want to activate the button. So, for example, if you typed **&Next** the user could select the button by pressing *Alt-N*. The hot key (in this case *N*) will appear underlined on the button.

Once you have added the other buttons, your form should look something like the one shown overleaf:

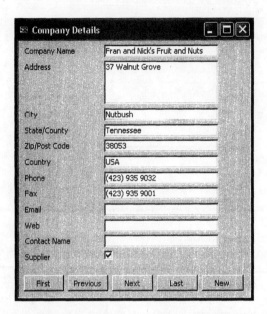

The form looks better, but it's still not perfect. If you haven't already done so, try clicking the **First** button to move to the first record. Now try clicking the **Previous** button to move to the previous record. Obviously, there's no record previous to the first record, so an error occurs and an error message box appears:

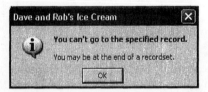

This is quickly followed by another error message which just gives you some additional information to try to help you debug (fix) the problem:

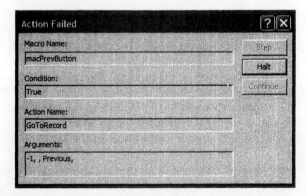

In this case of course, we know exactly what caused the problem: the user, right? Wrong. Ask the user: sloppy programming caused the problem!

*Rule #1 of programming – the user is always right because they pay the bills.*

While we cannot guard against absolutely every single incorrect action the user may take, we really ought to try to do something against a common possibility like this. One way to solve the problem would be to make the buttons intelligent so that they only allowed you to click them if they represented a valid choice? In other words, if you were already at the first record, the Previous button should appear grayed out or **disabled**.

Sure, you may say, but how? There doesn't appear to be any way to determine where you are in the table when you're using macros. So how is it done? You have just come across one of the shortcomings of macros. Macros are good at automating simple tasks, but they're less useful when the task (or the logic behind the task) becomes more complex. The only way to make these buttons intelligent is to use VBA, and we'll show you how to do this in the next chapter.

# Macros Or VBA?

Obviously, there are some simple tasks that can be performed happily by macros, but the example above should have highlighted one of their limitations. We could create navigation using macros, but we could not disable or enable them according to where we were in the records behind the form. That may not be a problem for some people, but if you want a slick interface that will win over your end-users, you'll probably want to enable and disable buttons. Our users will be sitting in front of this screen a lot, so we want to get it right.

## *Why You Should Use VBA*

The advantages that VBA has over macros can be summarized as follows:

**VBA enables you to provide complex functionality.**
You'll remember that when we tried to move back to the previous record from the first record we encountered an error and Access displayed an error message. What if we wanted to display our own error message instead? This type of intelligence isn't possible with macros.

**You can trap (intercept) and handle errors using VBA.**
Handling errors is impossible with macros but simple enough with VBA. Also, in some circumstances, you *have* to handle errors yourself. If you don't, your application could easily crash! We look in detail at error handling in Chapter 12.

**VBA is faster to execute than macros.**
VBA code is executed faster than macros. Although you may not notice the difference in a one-line macro, the difference in speed becomes more noticeable the longer and more complex the macro you are creating. Since speed is normally a critical factor in impressing end-users, we have another notch in favor of VBA.

**Using VBA makes your database easier to maintain.**

Macros are completely separate from the objects that call them. Although we created the navigation button macro from within the form, the macro is actually stored as a separate object in the database window. Click the Macros tab and you'll see it's there. In contrast, you can save VBA code with the form itself. This means that if you want to move the form into another database, the code automatically goes with it. With macros, you would have to find out for yourself which macros you needed to take as well.

**Using VBA allows you to interact with other applications.**

With VBA you are able to make full use of Automation. This facility allows you to access the functionality of applications like Excel and Word from within your Access application. It also allows you to control Access programmatically from applications like Excel and Word. More on this in Chapter 15.

**Using VBA gives you more programmatic control.**

Macros are good at performing set tasks where there's little need for flexibility. They can't pass variables from one macro to another in the form of parameters, are unable to ask for and receive input from the user, and they have extremely limited methods for controlling the sequence in which actions are performed.

**VBA is easier to read.**

Because you can only view one set of Action arguments at a time in the lower pane of the macro window, it is difficult to see the details of a macro. You have to select each action one after the other and look at its arguments in turn. In contrast, VBA is very easy to read with its color-coded text and Full Module View.

**VBA is common to all Microsoft applications (well, almost!)**

Finally, VBA is the language on which all Microsoft applications are now standardizing. VBA code written in Access is easily portable to Excel, Word, and any other applications that use VBA (we shall be showing you more about this in Chapter 15). In contrast, macros are highly specific to their native application.

# When to Use Macros

By this stage, you may be wondering why you should ever bother to use macros if VBA has so much in its favor! Well, there are still a couple of things that you can't do in VBA that you need macros for, and we'll look at these below. They are:

❑ Trapping certain keystrokes throughout the application

❑ Carrying out a series of actions whenever a database is opened (this is done via the Autoexec macro)

But, apart from these, you'll find that with VBA you can do all that you could with macros and lots more besides.

*In early versions of Access, you also had to use macros if you wanted to create custom menu bars or attach custom functionality to buttons on toolbars. However, from Access 97 onwards, both of these tasks are now achieved from the **Customize...** dialog box available from **Toolbars** on the **View** menu.*

Before we move on to the next chapter and completely discard macros in favor of VBA, let's just take a look at the two things mentioned above where we still need macros.

## Trapping Keystrokes Throughout an Application

Something you may want to do to make your application more user-friendly is to assign frequently used actions to certain keystrokes. For example, you may want your application to print the current record when your users hit *Ctrl+P*.

We have already seen that on a specific form you can implement a hotkey by using an ampersand (&) in the caption for a control. That's what we did with the navigation button on the **Company Details** form. However, if you want to implement a global keyboard shortcut – one that is available throughout your application – you can do so by creating a special macro.

First create a new macro (click the down arrow next to the **New Object** button on the toolbar and select **Macro** from the drop-down menu). You will need to save the macro with the name **Autokeys**, as this is the name of the macro in which Access looks for keyboard shortcuts. To display the **Macro Name** column, click on the **Macro Names** button on the toolbar. This button toggles the column between visible and invisible. You can also do this by selecting **Macro Names** from the View menu:

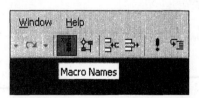

Then you specify the keystroke that you wish to instigate the required action in the **Macro Name** column, and the action itself in the **Action** column. For example, the following macro will cause the currently selected records to be printed whenever *Ctrl+P* is pressed:

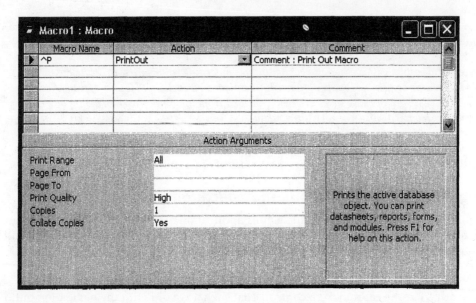

The lower pane of the macro window lists the arguments that you can pass to the PrintOut action to define exactly how it should operate. For example, we've specified **Selection** as the **Print Range** argument. This causes Access to only print out those records that were selected when the key combination *Ctrl+P* was pressed. If we had only wanted to print out the first two pages of the currently selected object, we could have chosen **Pages** as the **Print Range** argument and then typed 1 as the **Page From** argument and 2 as the **Page To** argument.

*The caret sign (^) is used to indicate that the Ctrl key is held down at the same time as the P key. For more information on these key codes, search Microsoft Access Help using the phrase "Autokeys Key Combinations".*

## Carrying Out Actions when a Database is Opened – the Autoexec Macro

When you open up an existing database, the first thing that Access does is to set any options that have been specified in the **Tools/Startup...** dialog. After this, it checks to see if a macro called **Autoexec** is present. If it is, then Access executes it immediately. This handy feature allows you to carry out actions such as writing a record to a log file to indicate that your application has started up.

*Users of versions of Access 2.x and earlier should note that many of the conventional uses of the **Autoexec** macro have now been replaced by the **Startup...** option on the **Tools** menu. If you're converting an application from a version 2.x or earlier, you may want to remove the functionality from the **Autoexec** macro and use the **Startup...** dialog instead.*

If you want to perform an action whenever the database is opened, but want to get the benefits of using VBA rather than macros, then you should write a procedure in VBA and call the procedure from the Autoexec macro. You can do this by using the RunCode action in your Autoexec macro:

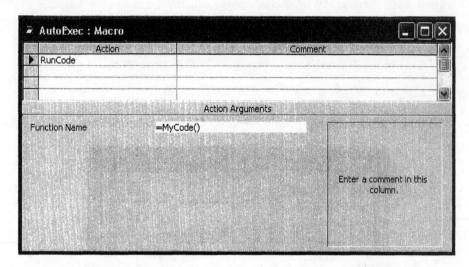

In this situation, when the database opens, the Autoexec macro is executed and this causes the MyCode() procedure – written in VBA – to be executed.

> **Be aware, however, that a user can prevent the Tools/Startup... options or the Autoexec macro from running by holding down the *Shift* key when the database is being opened.**

You can prevent a user from bypassing the Tools/Startup... options and the Autoexec macro by setting the database's AllowBypassKey property to False. However, the AllowBypassKey property isn't available normally, and so can't be set in the usual way. We'll look at how to set this property from VBA later on.

## Moving to VBA

Macros have their purposes then, but while undoubtedly useful for some things, they don't offer the power of VBA. We've just demonstrated in a few pages how and where you should apply macros. We'll now use the rest of the book describing how and where you can use VBA.

Just before we do that, however, there is one last useful trick that macros can give us: Access will allow us to convert macros into VBA code, and it can even go one step further by adding useful error trapping code if we ask it to. This can be a very useful technique for those new to VBA.

**Converting a Macro to VBA**

> **Your first sight of the Visual Basic Editor can be a bit daunting. Don't panic! We'll lead you through all the details as we continue through the book.**

**1.** Load up the database file `IceCream.mdb`. In the Database window, select the Macros tab and then the macNextButton macro that we created earlier.

**2.** Select File and then Save As... from the main menu.

**3.** When the Save As dialog appears select As Module and click OK:

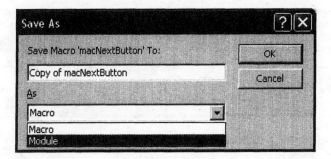

**4.** Another dialog appears. Just accept the default settings of Add error handling and Include macro comments and press the Convert button:

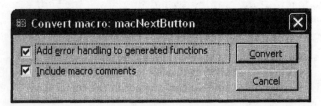

**5.** Access will now open the Visual Basic editor and finish the conversion. When the conversion is complete, click OK.

**6.** Double-click on the new module that Access has created for us in the project viewer pane:

**7.** The Project Explorer will open the module for us, and we can view the code it created:

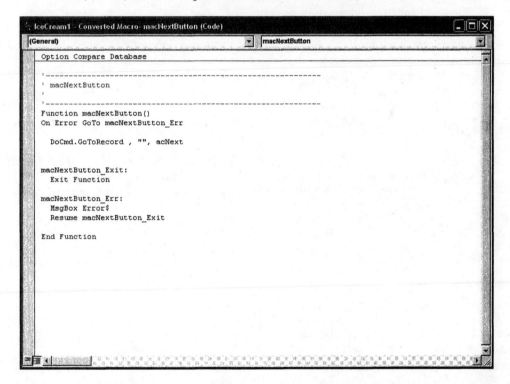

**8.** You might be able to recognize that the line that does all the work is the one that starts DoCmd.GoToRecord. Most of the rest is (necessary) padding and error handling code.

*This technique is a useful learning tool and can help you to convert any existing macros you may have into working code that you can use 'as is' or simply copy into your own modules as you become more proficient with VBA.*

# Summary

In this chapter, we've worked our way through the process of creating part of an Access application with one aim in mind – to deliberately hit a brick wall. That brick wall is the implementation of the intelligent navigation buttons. We just can't implement them properly using macros. Instead, we need VBA...

So, in brief, we have covered:

❑ How to go about designing an application

❑ An introduction to the application that forms the basis of this book – `IceCream.mdb`

❑ Creating the main form for the application and adding custom navigation buttons

❑ Why macros aren't sufficient for our needs

❑ When to use VBA and when to use macros

In the next chapter, we'll look at how you can polish up the Company Details form using VBA. If this chapter has been a success, you'll hunger for the power to solve the problems we've come up against – so let's get on with it.

# Exercise

**1.** The Autokeys macro is used to associate macro actions with keyboard shortcuts. Try using the Autokeys macro to display the property window whenever you hit *F4*. When does this shortcut not work? What happens if you try to associate this action with *Alt+F4* and why?

# CHAPTER 2

# Introduction to Event-Driven Programming

This chapter introduces a key concept in VBA programming. Indeed, the concept of event-driven programming is one that is central to all Windows programming, whether it is in low-level languages such as Visual C++ or higher-level languages such as Visual Basic for Applications (VBA) or Visual Basic Scripting Edition (VBScript). In essence, when we say that Access is an event-driven application, what we mean is that nothing happens in Access unless it is in response to some event that Access has detected.

In itself, that should not be a very difficult concept to grasp. After all, most of us are event-driven in the way that we behave. The phone rings, so we answer it. It gets dark, so we switch the lights on. We feel hungry, so we buy some food. That's event-driven behavior at its simplest.

These examples all have something in common, which characterizes the way that event-driven programming works:

❑ **An event occurs**
The events that occurred in the three examples above are the phone ringing, it getting dark, and us feeling hungry. Events are sometimes triggered by external forces (such as a visitor ringing the doorbell), and sometimes they are triggered by an internal change of state (we start to feel hungry).

❑ **The event is detected by the system**
We are only concerned about events that can be detected. For example, if a phone three blocks away rings we are not bothered, either because we cannot hear it or because we know that it is someone else's responsibility to handle the phone call. It is like that in Windows programming. Windows applications can only respond to events if they can detect them, and they will only handle events that they know are their responsibility to handle.

❑ **The system responds to the event**
The response can take the forms of various explicit actions, such as turning on the light or buying a burger. Alternatively, the system can respond to the event in a less dramatic fashion, by incrementing a counter which keeps track of how many times the event has occurred. In fact, the system can acknowledge the event and choose to do nothing. The important thing to note is that once the system has carried out its predefined response to the event, the event is said to have been handled and the system can go back to its dormant state, waiting for the next event to occur.

Now that's fine as far as we are concerned, but how does that help us with Windows programming in general and Access VBA programming in particular? What are the events that arise in Windows and in Access? And what actions do Windows and Access come up with in response to those actions?

## *Examples of Events*

Here is an item that should be familiar to all of us. It is the Windows Desktop.

Whenever we start one of the Windows family of operating systems we will see something similar to this. So what do we do next? Well, that depends on what we want to achieve. Let us suggest that we want to delete the documents in our Recycle Bin. So we right-click the icon representing the Recycle Bin and choose Empty Recycle Bin – a seemingly simple enough event. Only it is not quite as simple as all that. When we look more closely we will see that there are a number of events and responses underlying this seemingly simple action:

- **Move the mouse pointer**
  This event is detected by Windows, which responds by repainting the mouse pointer at the new location on the screen. In fact, this event occurs repeatedly and Windows responds repeatedly until the mouse comes to rest over the Recycle Bin.

- **Right-click the mouse button over the Recycle Bin**
  This event is also detected by Windows and the response is two-fold. First, the Recycle Bin icon is shaded to indicate that it has been selected. Second, a popup menu specific to the Recycle Bin is displayed at the location of the mouse pointer.

- **Move the mouse to the Empty Recycle Bin menu item**
  Notice how Windows again detects the mouse moving and responds by repainting the mouse pointer. This time, however, because the mouse is over a menu, the menu is repainted to highlight the menu items over which the mouse passes.

- **Click the Empty Recycle Bin menu item**
  The popup menu item detects that the Empty Recycle Bin menu item has been selected, and in response displays a dialog box asking whether we really want to delete the items in the Recycle Bin. At the same time, it hides the popup menu.

- **Move the mouse to the dialog box**
  Again, Windows detects the mouse movement and repaints the cursor.

- **Click the Yes button**
  The message box determines that we have clicked the mouse button over the Yes button and responds by causing the Recycle Bin to delete all items within it. In addition, the Recycle Bin icon is changed to an image of an empty trashcan.

Notice that in every case, the same three steps occur:

- **An event occurs**

- **The event is detected by the system**

- **The system responds to the event**

# *How Windows Handles Events*

So far, we have looked at what events are and we have seen an example of a typical series of events and responses. But, before we go any further, let's have a look in a little more detail at what was happening when we emptied the Recycle Bin. Just who or what was detecting the events? And what is it that determines which action is carried out in response to the event?

Whenever Windows detects that an event has occurred – the mouse may have been moved or a mouse button clicked – Windows generates a message and directs it to the specific window to which the event relates. So, when the user clicks the mouse over the Yes button on the Confirm File Delete dialog box, Windows generates a message and directs it to the Yes button. Windows can direct messages to windows or controls either by sending them directly or by placing the message in a message queue and marking it with the handle (identifier) of the window or control the message is destined for.

The type of message generated will be different for every type of event that Windows detects. For example, when Windows detects that the mouse has been moved, it generates one type of message. And when it detects that the user has clicked a mouse button, it generates a different message. All of these messages, irrespective of their type, are automatically generated by Windows and directed to the window to which the event relates. It is then up to the window that receives the message to decide how to handle the event indicated by the message it received.

When the window receives the message it can carry out some particular action in response to the message – such as displaying a dialog box. Alternatively, the window can decide that it does not need to take any specific action. In this case it can elect for the default action for that event to be carried out – the default action is what Windows does if we haven't told it to do anything different. In fact, most windows will only process a few messages specifically and will pass the rest of the messages back for the system to handle with the default action.

So how does this help us? Well, a few more things should have become apparent:

- ❑ The Windows operating system automatically detects when events occur
- ❑ The operating system automatically notifies windows or controls as events arise which relate to them
- ❑ If the window decides it does not want to do anything special, it can simply pass the message back to allow the default response to occur

The implication of all this is that as programmers, we can limit ourselves to writing code that handles specific events in a specific manner. We don't need to bother with the hassle of detecting events – Windows does that for us. And we don't need to write code to handle events where we want our windows or controls to react in the default manner.

We can see this if we take a look back at the form we created in the previous chapter.

**Try It Out**    **Examining Event Properties**

**1.** Open the `IceCream.mdb` database and, if necessary, press *F11* to display the database window:

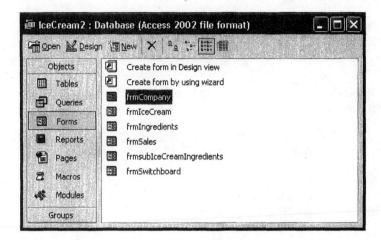

**2.** Now open the `frmCompany` form in design view by right-clicking it and selecting Design View:

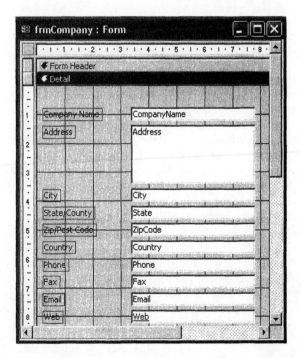

**3.** Select the `cmdFirst` button (First) at the bottom of the form and display the Properties window. You can do this by choosing **Properties** from the **View** menu, by right-clicking the command button and choosing **Properties**, or by selecting the command button and depressing the **Properties** toolbar button:

**4.** Select the **Event** tab on the **Properties** sheet. This will display all of the events that can occur for the selected command button. There are quite a few, aren't there!

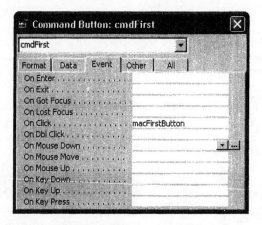

Twelve different events that we can handle for a single command button! As it happens there is only one event that we are concerned with. We want to carry out a specific action when the user **clicks** the button. We don't care what happens when the mouse moves over the button; we don't care what happens when the user presses a key when the button is selected; all we care about is what happens when the button is clicked. That is why we have specified a macro (`macFirstButton`) to be run when the `Click` event occurs. If we had wanted an action to occur whenever the user moved the mouse pointer across the button, we would have specified a macro to be run when the `MouseMove` event occurs and so on.

Two important characteristics of event handling in Access that we examined a little earlier – characteristics that are major contributing factors in making Access such an excellent tool for rapid design and prototyping – are worth repeating here. The first is that the programmer does not need to determine when a particular event happens. We don't have to work out when the user clicks one of our buttons or when the user moves the mouse pointer over it. Windows automatically detects the event and the operating system notifies Access, which in turn causes the specific event to be raised, so executing the code or macro that the programmer has specified in the property sheet for that particular event.

The second noteworthy characteristic of this method of event handling is that the programmer need only supply macros or code for those events that the programmer wants to be handled in a 'non-default' manner. For example, clicking on a button causes the appearance of the button to change to reflect the fact that it has been depressed, whether or not we supply our own event handling macro or code. We don't need to worry about that because it is a type of default behavior common to all buttons. So for the `cmdFirst` button, all we need to worry about is the code or macro that is required to move the form to the first record.

## Some Definitions

We have introduced a few new terms in this chapter and it is probably worthwhile clarifying just what they mean. They are terms that we will be using throughout the rest of the book, so it is as well to make sure that we all know what we are talking about!

An **event handler** is any VBA code (or macro) that the programmer constructs to be executed when a specific event occurs for a specific object. In the example above, we specified that the `macFirstButton` macro should be the event handler for the `Click` event of the `cmdFirst` button.

An **event property** is the mechanism that Access provides to allow us to attach an event handler to a specific event for a specific object. These event properties are exposed on the **Event** tab of an object's property sheet (kind of logical, huh!). In the example above, we can see that our command button has 12 event properties. That means that there are 12 different events that we can choose to handle through VBA code or macros. It is worth noting that the same event handler can, in fact, be assigned to many different event properties on many different objects.

The same types of object will always have the same number and type of event properties. So, every command button that you place on a form in Access will have the same 12 event properties that are listed in our example above. Event properties often start with the word **On** and their names reflect the event they allow the programmer to handle. So, the **On Click** event property is where we specify the VBA code or macro that we will use to handle the `Click` event. The **On Mouse Move** property is used to handle the `MouseMove` event, and so on.

So, to recap terminology, in our earlier example we can see that the `cmdFirst` button has a `Click` event. We can write a macro or piece of VBA code to act as an event handler for that event. And we specify that the macro or VBA code is the event handler for the `Click` event, by entering its name in the **On Click** event property for the button.

## So Many Events...

Reading through the previous paragraphs, you might well have thought "Whaaaat? 12 events for a measly little button!" VBA gurus call this a rich programmatic interface. Most other folk call it downright scary... It can be daunting when you start programming and are faced with a vast number of events to choose between. Sometimes it is obvious which to use. We want our form to move to the first record when the user clicks the button, so we use the `Click` event. But it is not always that straightforward. For example, report sections have an **On Retreat** event property. What's that all about? And what is the **On No Data** event property of a report used for?

Well, you don't have to worry. In the first place, there are excellent reference materials available in the shape of Access Help. And secondly, you'll find that there are a few core events that you will use time and time again, and you will soon become familiar with what these are. For example, let's look at command buttons again. Although there are 12 possible events, you will soon discover that for (at least) 99% of the time, you will only ever need to handle the `Click` event. Why? Because that's what people are used to. Sure, you could write an elegant and highly inventive handler that makes use of one or more of the other events. But bear in mind that users, like horses, scare easily. They are not used to things happening when they move their mouse over buttons. They are used to things happening when they click buttons. Buttons are to be clicked – no more, no less. Please don't misinterpret this as either an attack on the intelligence of users or an attempt to limit the creativity of developers. It is just that people are used to interacting with the Windows interface in a certain manner. They expect buttons just to sit there and wait to be clicked; they don't expect strange things to happen when you move the mouse over them. A user's expectation of how your application will behave is a very powerful force. Use it to your advantage, make your application conform to the standards of Windows interface behavior and you will find that the task of getting users to feel comfortable with your application will be ten times easier than if you attempt to surprise them with cool new methods of interaction.

*That is (more than) enough on interface design considerations. If you want to know more about this subject, an excellent reference is About Face by Alan Cooper (IDG, ISBN: 1-568843-22-4). Alternatively, you could consult the Windows Interface Guidelines for Software Design, which is available online on the Microsoft Developer Network (MSDN) web site.*

## Default Events

One of the helpful things about the way that Access exposes events to programmers is that each object has a **default** event. The default event is the event that Microsoft believes programmers are most likely to want to use when handling events for that type of object. For example, the default event for command buttons is the `Click` event. That is obviously because the event we are most likely to want to handle when using command buttons is the `Click` event. By way of contrast, for a textbox the default event is the `BeforeUpdate` event. This is because Microsoft believes that, as programmers, we are more likely to want to write a piece of VBA code or macro to handle the `BeforeUpdate` event than any other event that occurs with textboxes.

In fact, we have come across default events before. In the previous chapter, when we wanted to attach a macro to the `cmdNext` button, we did so by right-clicking the button in design view and selecting **Build Event...** from the popup menu.

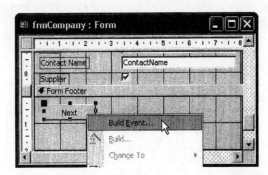

This brought up the **Choose Builder** dialog that allowed us to select the technique we wanted to use to write the logic that would handle the button's behavior. We selected **Macro Builder**, built a macro and when we closed the macro window, Access entered the name of the macro into the **On Click** event property:

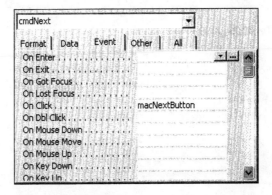

Right-clicking an object and selecting **Build Event...** will always create an event handler for the object's default event. If, instead, we want to create an event handler for a non-default event, we have to do it through the object's property window. For example, if we wanted to create a macro to handle the `MouseMove` event of the `cmdFirstButton` command button, we could type the name of a saved macro directly into the property sheet for the button's **On Mouse Move** event:

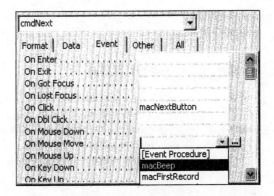

Alternatively, we could click in the event box and then click the builder button (the one with the ellipsis or three dots) to the right of the **On Mouse Move** event in the buttons **Property** window. This would allow us to invoke the Macro Builder to build a macro to handle the `MouseMove` event:

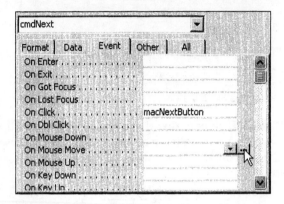

## One Action, Many Events...

Something else to bear in mind when deciding which event to handle is the fact that what seems like a single action may actually result in a number of different events being triggered. For example, let's consider what happens when a user has changed the text in a textbox (`txtFirst`) and then hits the *Tab* key to move to a new textbox (`txtSecond`). The single action of hitting the *Tab* key will trigger the following events in order:

Which event you decide to handle depends very much on just what you want to do. For example, the `BeforeUpdate` event occurs after the text in the text box has been changed on screen but before the value is actually saved. As such it is an excellent candidate for holding validation rules that can check the validity of what has been entered in the control before the value actually gets saved.

> *For a fuller listing of the order in which events happen as a result of common actions, type "Find out when events occur" in the Answer Wizard of the Access online help.*

## Handling Events in Access with VBA

So far then, we have looked at what events are and how we can use macros to perform certain tasks as those events occur. The example we have used is the `frmCompany` form that we created in the previous chapter. That form has five buttons on it, whose purpose is to allow the user to navigate through all of the records in the underlying table. Each of the buttons has a macro attached to its **On Click** property that determines which record the form will move to when the button is clicked:

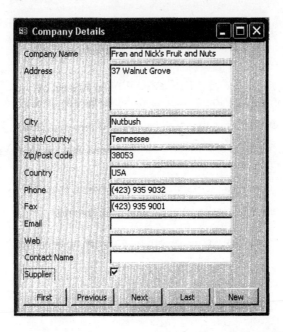

You should also recall that this solution is not perfect. If we click the **First** button (`cmdFirst`) to move to the first record in the form and then click the **Previous** button (`cmdPrevious`), a dialog box tells us that an error has occurred, because Access tried to move to the record before the first record (and obviously there isn't one):

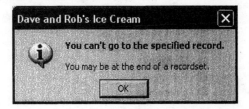

What we decided we needed was some intelligent navigation buttons – buttons which knew what record the form was on and therefore buttons which could enable and disable themselves depending on whether the actions they represented were valid at that point in time. That degree of intelligence simply isn't possible with macros. Macros are great for automating very simple tasks, but they just don't have the flexibility to allow us to use them for anything too sophisticated.

The alternative to using macros is to write your event handlers in VBA. In fact, you will find that in almost all professional Access applications VBA is used for event handlers. Some of the reasons for this were mentioned in the previous chapter but, to recap, the most important are as follows:

- ❑ VBA allows you to add more complex logic to your event handlers

- ❑ VBA allows you to execute a more varied selection of actions than are available through macros

- ❑ VBA allows you to extend the functionality of Access by making use of other components or applications, such as Excel or Word, through automation

- ❑ VBA code executes faster than the equivalent macro actions

- ❑ VBA code is portable between any applications that support VBA, whereas macros are proprietary to Access

- ❑ VBA allows you to trap errors and handle them gracefully

- ❑ VBA code is easier to read and print out than macros

Put simply, VBA gives you more control. So, let's waste no more time and rewrite our event handlers in VBA code.

**Try It Out      Writing VBA Event Handlers**

**1.** If you haven't done so already, open the `IceCream.mdb` database and, if necessary, hit *F11* to display the database window:

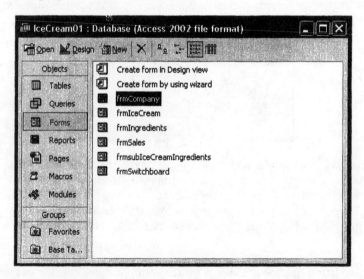

**2.** Now open the `frmCompany` form in design view by right-clicking it and selecting Design View:

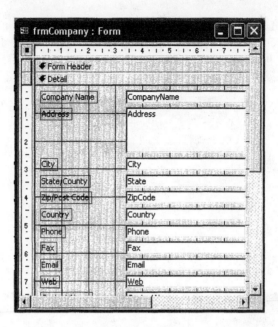

**3.** Select the `cmdFirst` button at the base of the form and display the **Properties** window. You can do this by choosing **Properties** from the **View** menu, by right-clicking the command button and choosing **Properties,** or by selecting the command button and depressing the **Properties** toolbar button.

**4.** Select the **Event** tab on the **Properties** sheet. Notice that the event handler for the `Click` event is the `macFirstButton` macro:

**5.** Select the **On Click** event property and delete the text `macFirstButton`. Note that by doing this we are not deleting the actual macro. We are simply instructing Access that the macro is no longer to be used as the handler for the `Click` event of this button.

**6.** Click the Builder button (the one with the ellipsis or three dots) to the right of the **On Click** event property. This will display a dialog box asking us how we want to build our event handler. We want to use VBA code rather than macros, so select **Code Builder** and hit the **OK** button:

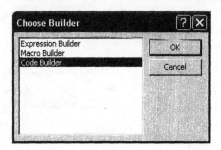

**7.** Clicking **OK** opens up the VBA integrated development environment (IDE). A new window should appear looking something like this:

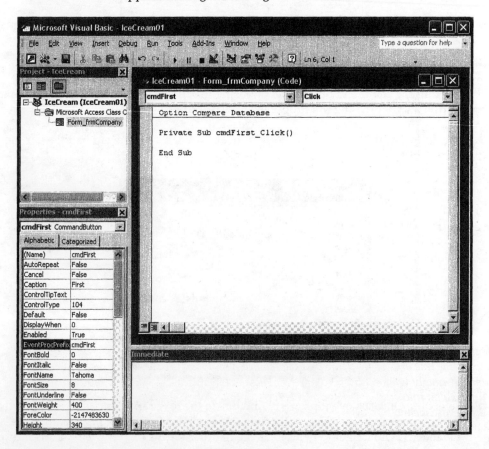

The first line `Option Compare Database` determines the method for comparing text strings. The default is fine for us so just ignore it for now.

The last two lines of code shown in the window in the above form is the VBA event handler for the `Click` event of the `cmdFirst` button. These are automatically entered by VBA when you decide to use the `Click` event of `cmdFirst`. The event procedure (that's another term for an event handler written in VBA) starts with the line:

```
Private Sub cmdFirst_Click()
```

and ends with the line:

```
End Sub
```

Everything that goes between these two lines will be executed whenever the `cmdFirst` button is clicked. At the moment there is nothing there, so nothing beyond the default action (the button appears to be pressed down) will happen when the button is clicked.

**8.** Type the following line of code in the event procedure, making sure that you type it exactly as it appears below, including the two commas:

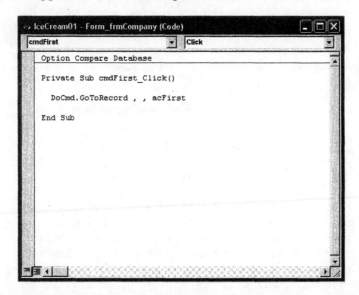

*Don't worry if some strange popups (looking a bit like tooltips) appear while you are typing the line of code. They are designed to help you to write code more efficiently but you can simply ignore them if you prefer. These two features – **Auto List Members** and **Auto Quick Info** – are discussed a little later in this chapter. Microsoft calls this Intellisense technology and you will soon find it is an indispensable tool which aids in Rapid Application Development.*

**9.** Now switch back to Access by hitting *Alt + F11*. The words [Event Procedure] should now appear against the **On Click** property of the `cmdFirst` button. This indicates that the `Click` event for this button is now being handled by VBA code:

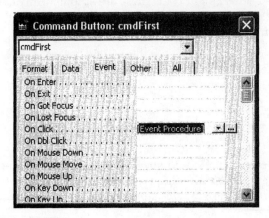

**10.** Close the **Properties** window, switch to **Form View** and move to the second record by hitting the **Next** button. Then click the **First** button. If you've done everything correctly, you will be able to use the button to navigate back to the first record on the form. Congratulations! You have written your first VBA procedure!

## How It Works

OK, so let's have a look in more detail at the code you typed in:

```
DoCmd.GoToRecord , , acFirst
```

It's really quite simple. We'll look at each part in turn.

The `DoCmd` at the start of the line indicates that we want Access to carry out an **action**. In other words, we want Access to do something that we could have performed using either the keyboard (or mouse) or a macro. The action that we want to carry out is the `GoToRecord` action. This is what would happen if we selected **Go To** from the **Edit** menu when the form's open in **Form View**. You may remember from the last chapter that this is also the name of the action we selected in the macro that was originally behind this button.

Once we've specified the action, we need to tell Access which record we want to go to. This is the purpose of the constant `acFirst` – the record we want is the first record. We'll be looking at constants in detail in the next chapter. For now you should simply be aware that the constant is a useful named placeholder for a value that is set somewhere else in the program or internally within VBA.

The two commas before acFirst indicate that there are additional optional arguments we could have supplied to make our code more specific. In this case, we could have specified the type of object we want to move within (in our case a form) and the name of the object, frmCompany. So, we could have written the code like this:

```
DoCmd.GoToRecord acForm, "frmCompany", acFirst
```

If we omit these two arguments, Access will assume that we mean the current object. This is fine in our case, so we can leave the optional arguments out. However, we still have to insert a comma to indicate where arguments have been omitted. So that's how we end up with the line of code:

```
DoCmd.GoToRecord , , acFirst
```

*If arguments are still a mystery to you, don't worry, as we will be covering them in more depth in the next chapter.*

## What are Actions and Methods?

At this stage you might be getting a little confused over just what the difference is between actions and methods. After all, there is a GoToRecord action (which we used in the original macro) and a GoToRecord method (which we used in VBA) and they both do the same thing. What's the difference?

**Actions** are the building blocks of **macros**. Many of them correspond to tasks carried out by the user by selecting items from a menu. Others allow you to perform different tasks that a user can't, such as displaying a message box or making the computer beep. The main thing to remember, however is that actions occur in macros.

**Methods**, however, occur in **VBA**. A method is used to instruct an object to behave in a certain way and we'll look at the idea of objects and methods in more detail in Chapter 5. Because you cannot use actions outside of macros, you use methods to achieve the same ends in VBA. There are two objects whose methods you use to perform almost all of the macro actions in VBA. These are the Application object and the DoCmd object.

So, if we want to write a VBA statement that performs the same function as the Quit action in a macro, we would use the Quit method of the Application object:

```
Application.Quit
```

In fact, the Application object is the default object, and refers to Access itself, so we can omit it and simply type this as our line of code:

```
Quit
```

*Defaults are a useful way to abbreviate your code and to speed up the writing process. Only use defaults where you are sure of their meaning, however. Assuming the wrong default will lead to errors that may prove very difficult to track down – if in doubt use the fully qualified version.*

Almost all of the macro actions, however, correspond to methods of the DoCmd object. So if we want to write a line of VBA that does the same as the Beep macro action, we would write this:

```
DoCmd.Beep
```

*To find out the VBA equivalent of a macro action, simply look up the action in the Access help. If there is an equivalent VBA method, it will be described on the help page for the action.*

## Why is the Code in Different Colors?

One of the nice things about VBA is colored code. This is not just a pretty device. The different colors are used to distinguish the different components of code and can make your code easier to read. You can set these colors yourself on the **Editor Format** tab of the **Options...** dialog on the **Tools** menu in the VBA IDE:

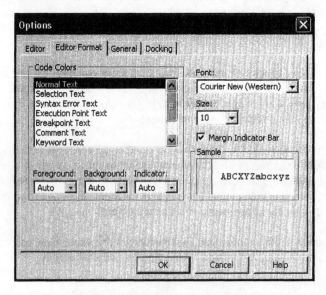

The colors really can make it easier for you to read and understand the code. For example, you can alter the color of the line of code that is due to be executed next. This makes it easier to see what is happening when you step through your code one line at a time. Or you can choose to have all your comments in gray so that they don't appear too intrusive.

*Stepping through the code by running it line by line is useful for debugging the code. This is covered later in the book, in Chapter 12.*

You can also use different colors to distinguish between the different types of word you use in your code. **Keywords** – reserved words, such as DoCmd, which always have a special meaning to Access – can be in one color, and **identifiers** – such as the names of forms you have created or messages you want to display – can be in another color. This can make it easier to understand what your code (or someone else's code!) is doing.

## *What were all those Popup Thingies?*

Good question! Before you have finished typing even half a word you may find VBA trying to butt in and finish the job for you. It all looks a bit disconcerting at first but, once you get used to the way it works, it can make your code both easier to write and less prone to errors. The proper terms for these popups are Auto List Members and Auto Quick Info. We'll look at them now in more detail. As we go through this over the next few pages, it would be worth your while to keep the VBA IDE open, and just have a play around to become accustomed to how these pop-ups operate.

> *The Auto List Members and Auto Quick Info features can be turned on and off via* **Tools/Options.../Editor** *on the menu of the VBA IDE. Make sure that these options are checked if you want to observe the behavior described below.*

The Auto List Members feature of the VBA IDE suggests a list of all the valid words that can come next in your VBA code. (More specifically, it lists the relevant methods, properties, events, members or constants. We'll be looking at what these terms mean in the next few chapters.) You can see this at work if you type the phrase DoCmd. in VBA. As soon as you have done so, VBA suggests a list of possible methods that could come next:

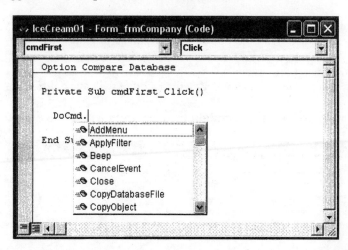

All of the words in the popup list box are valid methods that can follow the DoCmd object. We saw earlier how the DoCmd object allows us to carry out the same actions we can perform in macros. Well, once we have decided that we want to use the DoCmd object, the popup lists all of those actions for you.

You can either select an item from the list by double-clicking it or by hitting the *Tab* key, or the spacebar. Or if you want you can carry on typing your code. If you do carry on typing your code, VBA will highlight the word that matches most closely what you are typing.

The other popup you may have seen is displayed by the **Auto Quick Info** feature. This one helps you to remember the syntax of difficult-to-remember commands. You'll see it whenever you type the name of a recognized function or sub procedure in VBA. So, in our example above, once you had typed `DoCmd.GotoRecord`, VBA displayed the **Auto Quick Info** popup to help you with the rest of the command:

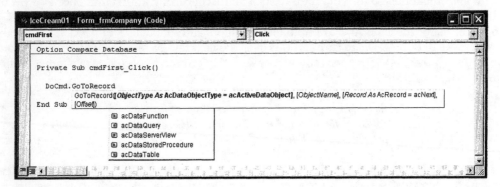

The popup window acts as a memory aid, to remind you what arguments you need to type in after `DoCmd.GoToRecord`. The next argument you need to type in is always highlighted in bold, and any optional arguments are displayed inside square brackets.

In the example above, the next argument we should type in is the `ObjectType` argument. There is even an **Auto List Members** popup behind the **Auto Quick Info** popup to list the possible values you can type in for the `ObjectType` argument! Since the `ObjectType` argument is shown in square brackets, we can ignore it, as it is an optional argument. However, we still need to type a comma to acknowledge the fact that we have omitted the optional argument.

Typing the comma causes VBA to highlight the next argument in the **Auto Quick Info** popup:

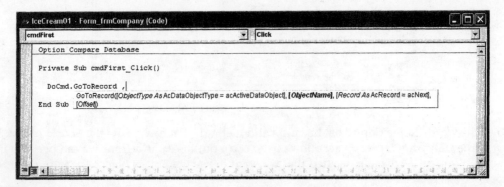

Again the argument is optional, so we can ignore it and simply type a comma in its place. The highlight then moves to the third argument:

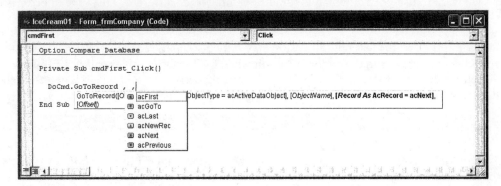

Even though the Record argument is optional, we want to use it, as this is the one that tells VBA which record we want to move to. And what's cool is that VBA displays an Auto List Members popup that lists the possible values we can supply for this argument. We can click acFirst and VBA inserts that argument in our line of code. The last argument, Offset, is also optional, so we can ignore it and just hit the *Enter* key to complete our line of code.

Auto List Members and Auto Quick Info aren't just gimmicks. They really help you to get your VBA code right the first time without needing to spend time looking through the Help, or other manuals. As such they are a great aid to productivity.

## What if I Still Get it Wrong?

None of us are perfect! Even with Auto List Members and Auto Quick Info looking over our shoulder and telling us what to write we still make mistakes. Another way in which VBA makes the job of writing code a bit easier is that it will inform you if you have made a mistake in a line of code. For example, you might have mistyped the line of code as:

```
Do Cmd GoToRecord , , acFirst
```

Then, when you tried to move off the line, VBA would have highlighted the line of code (and the word Cmd) and displayed this dialog box:

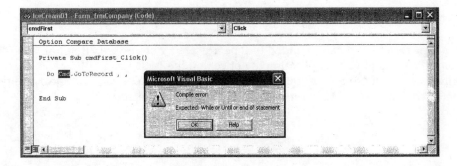

This indicates that the word Do must always be followed by the words While or Until (we'll cover this in Chapter 4), or se it must appear on its own. Of course, we don't want the word Do – we want to use DoCmd, which is something altogether different. This type of error is called a **syntax error**.

However, if the error is less obvious, VBA may only be able to recognize the fact that it's an error when you try to run the code (when you click the button). This is called a **run-time error** and will result in a rather unfriendly dialog box being presented to the user when they click the button. For example, if you had missed out a comma and typed:

```
DoCmd.GoToRecord , acFirst
```

VBA wouldn't have generated a syntax error when you moved off the line but, when the cmdFirst button was clicked at run time it would have interpreted acFirst as the second argument (rather than the third) and would have displayed the following dialog box:

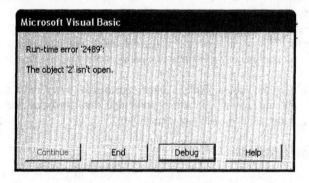

*Here, the constant acFirst has the value 2 within VBA, a value that the missing optional parameter should not have. Later in the book we shall be looking at how to prevent these run-time errors and how to handle them more gracefully.*

The third type of error that you can create when writing code occurs when the code that you type in is syntactically correct, but does not produce the desired effect. In this situation, the program appears to function normally, but in fact doesn't perform as you intended. For example, you may have accidentally typed:

```
DoCmd.GoToRecord , , acLast
```

This is a **logic error** – you had intended to type acFirst not acLast. It might take some time for you or the users of your application to notice that the cmdFirst button was moving the current record pointer to the last rather than the first record. You may also hear this type of error referred to as a **semantic error** because it changes the meaning of the code.

## Compiling Code

You've seen how VBA checks for the more obvious errors as you type. However, there is another method that can be used to prevent errors. This is the process known as **compiling**, and is used to trap the less obvious errors that might crop up in your code. When your code is compiled, routine checks are performed – such as checking that variables have been declared (if Option Explicit has been set) and that procedures you call are named in your application. Compiling involves assembling the code in preparation for execution, but doesn't actually execute the code. Compiling can't catch all errors, but it will pick up general consistency problems in your code. If compiling doesn't produce any errors, then control is returned to you. You don't need to worry about this now, as we look at the issue of compiling code in more detail in Chapter 19, and variables and Option Explicit are covered in more detail in the next chapter.

## Other Events

So where are we now? We have looked at what events are, and how fundamental they are to the operation of Windows and Access. We have also looked at how we can use macros and VBA to write event handlers. But so far we have only mentioned one or two events. We'll take a quick look at some of the more common events that can be handled within Access, what triggers them and how they can be useful to us. We've included a comprehensive list of the events that Access handles on the CD that accompanies this book. It should give you an idea of just how much you can achieve in Access through the careful use of event handlers.

| Event Property | Belongs to... | Occurs... | Used for... |
|---|---|---|---|
| On Change | Controls on a form | after the contents of a control change (say, by typing a character). | triggering the update of related controls on the form. |
| On Click | Forms, Controls and sections on a form | when the user clicks the mouse button over a form or control; when the user takes some action which has the same effect as clicking (like pressing the spacebar to check a checkbox). | just about anything – this is one of the most used of all events, and is about the only event used with command buttons. |
| On Close | Forms, Reports | after a form or report has been closed and removed from the screen. | triggering the opening of the next form, and for "cleaning up" or checking entries on the current form. |

*Table continued on following page*

| Event Property | Belongs to... | Occurs... | Used for... |
| --- | --- | --- | --- |
| On Current | Forms | when the form is opened or requeried; after the focus moves to a different record, but before the new record is displayed. | implementing intelligent navigation buttons (see example below) or "startup" code. |
| On Dbl Click | Forms; Controls and sections on a form | when the user depresses and releases the left mouse button twice over the same object. | selecting an item in a list and carrying out the actions of the OK button in one go. |
| On Delete | Forms | when the user attempts to delete a record. | preventing the user from deleting records. |
| On Dirty | Forms | after the user has updated any data in the current record but before the record has been saved. | determining whether you need to ask the user if any changes should be saved. |
| On Error | Forms; Reports | when a run-time database engine error occurs (but not a VBA error). We look at this in more detail in Chapter 13. | intercepting errors and displaying your own custom error messages. |
| On Mouse Move | Forms; Controls and sections on a form | when the mouse pointer moves over objects. | displaying X and Y coordinates of the mouse pointer. |
| On Mouse Up | Forms; Controls and sections on a form | when the user releases a mouse button. | detecting whether the user has a mouse button depressed when clicking an object. |

*The final column of the table is only intended to give an indication of the type of action that you can perform in the event handler. It isn't meant to be an exhaustive or comprehensive list of the uses of each event handler. If you feel a burning desire to use the On Delete event to start a video clip playing then you can if you really want to!*

You will notice that the table lists event properties rather than events. Remember, an event property is a property that appears in the property sheet and allows you to handle a specific event. Therefore, the event handler for the `Click` event of a command button is exposed via the button's On Click event property.

# The VBA IDE

Now that we have written our first procedure, it is probably as good a time as any to take a look at the VBA integrated development environment (IDE). The VBA IDE is the place where you will type all of your VBA code, and if you have not seen it before it can appear quite daunting.

> *You will sometimes see the VBA IDE referred to simply as the VBE or Visual Basic Editor. Don't be confused; they are just two different names for the same thing.*

If you have used Access before, one of the first things that you may have noticed is that the VBA IDE is now in a separate window from Access itself. So, even though the code we are writing relates to Access objects, we enter the code in the VBA IDE window rather than within Access itself. Actually, the VBA IDE is now common to all of the VBA-enabled applications that make up Microsoft Office XP as well as to Visual Basic itself. So, whichever Office XP application you are in, if it supports VBA you will be able to use the VBA IDE to write VBA code.

> *In previous versions of Access, the code editor was integrated within Access itself. It might seem a little counter-intuitive to abstract the code development environment into a separate window, rather than retaining it within the application itself. However, the benefits – in terms of ease of learning and portability of code – of sharing a common, **integrated** development environment between all of the Office XP applications is, in the author's opinion, well worth the effort of occasionally having to Alt+Tab (or Alt+F11) between windows.*

OK, so let's have a look in a little more detail at the VBA IDE.

# Components of the VBA IDE

When we wrote our first event procedure in VBA earlier in this chapter, we concentrated on just one window, the code window. In fact, the VBA IDE is comprised of 7 different windows, each of which can be hidden or displayed according to the user's preferences. The screenshot below shows what the VBA IDE looks like with all seven windows displayed:

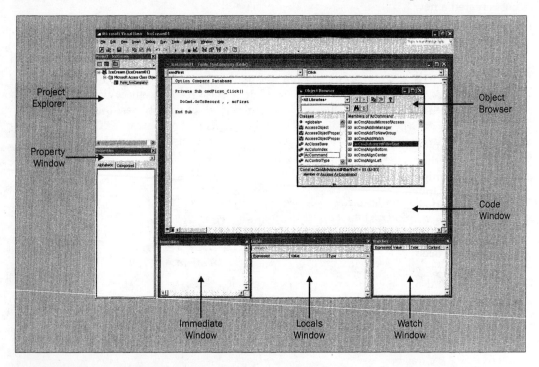

*Remember, if the VBA IDE isn't displayed, press Alt+F11, or select **Code** from the **View** menu when you're in Design view. Note also that when you call it up, it may not show all seven windows automatically.*

We will look at how all of these windows can be used throughout this book, but before we go much further, it probably makes sense to familiarize ourselves with two of them in particular, the **Project Explorer** and the **Code Window**.

## *Project Explorer*

All code within VBA must be stored within a **project**. As far as we are concerned, all of the code that we use within an Access database is stored within a single project. By default the name of the VBA project that holds our code is given the same name as the Access database to which the code relates. So, when we created our first event procedure in the IceCream.mdb database, Access created a new VBA project and called it IceCream.

> Be careful not to confuse a VBA project with an Access project. A *VBA project* is the mechanism used by VBA to store all of the code that is associated with a specific database. By contrast, an *Access Data Project* (or **.adp** file) is a special type of lightweight database front-end to facilitate client-server development against databases such as SQL Server or Oracle.

Within a VBA project, code is arranged within a series of **modules**. These are simply a method of grouping together related chunks of code. If it makes it any easier, think of a filing cabinet at the office – you might use the top drawer for product detail files, the second for customer files and the third for invoices and sales details. The drawers of a filing cabinet allow you to store similar files together, but in a way that keeps them separate from each other. In the same way, a module allows you to store related chunks of code together. The Project Explorer window allows us to navigate our project and locate individual modules and individual chunks of code (we call them **procedures**, and will explain more about them in the next chapter) within those modules. The three types of module that are displayed in the Project Explorer window are class modules, form and report modules, and standard modules.

*If the Project Explorer window is not immediately visible in the VBA IDE, it might be hidden. To make it visible, just hit* Ctrl+R.

### Form and Report Modules

Every form and report can have a built-in module, called a **class module**, associated with it that contains all the code for that form or report. This code includes both event procedures – such as the cmdFirst_Click() event we wrote earlier – and other general procedures. The class module is tightly bound to the form or report object – so if you copy a form or report into another database and the form or report has a class module, the class module is automatically copied as well.

*Note that new forms and reports do not automatically have a module associated with them. Instead, the module is only created if you decide to use VBA code in your form. This helps to reduce the size of the project and improves performance generally.*

### Standalone Class Modules

Class modules can also exist without an associated form or report. When created without an associated form or report, they are used to create custom objects. We will look at this use of class modules in more detail in Chapter 13.

### Standard Modules

Standard modules always exist outside of forms or reports as objects in their own right, and are used for grouping together procedures that aren't associated with any one form or report in particular. These procedures can then be used by any form or report in the database. For example, you may have a standard module that contains specific functions that your company uses. These may carry out complex calculations such as wind loading in a construction company, or they may format and check the text of a site-visit report in line with your company's safety policy. These can also be included in code libraries. We discuss these in Chapter 15.

### Working with Modules

The three types of module (class modules associated with Access forms or reports, standalone class modules and standard modules) are all displayed hierarchically in the **Project Explorer** window in the VBA IDE. In the example below, we can see how VBA groups together:

❑ Class modules associated with forms or reports (referred to as **Microsoft Access Class Objects**)

❑ Standard modules (referred to just as **Modules**)

❑ Standalone class modules (referred to as **Class Modules**)

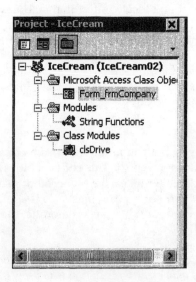

In this example, Form_frmCompany is the class module associated with the frmCompany form, String Functions is a standard module, and clsDrive is a standalone class module.

> *The last two modules – String Functions and clsDrive – will not appear in IceCream.mdb, the database accompanying this book, but are shown here for illustrative purposes only.*

To open a module from within the VBA IDE, simply select the module in the Project Explorer window, and then either double-click it or right-click it and select View Code from the popup menu. Alternatively, you could hit the View Code button on the toolbar.

If we were to select the Modules tab in the Database window in Access, we would see the standalone class module and the standard module displayed like this:

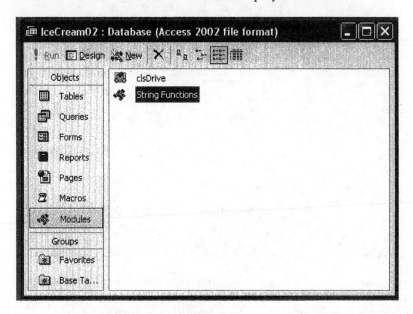

You can open one of these modules in number of ways. For example, you can select it and hit the Code button on the toolbar, or you can simply double-click it. Other ways of opening the module include right-clicking it and selecting Design View or selecting it and choosing Code from the View menu.

Note that the class module associated with the frmCompany form is not displayed in the Database window. To open that class module from within Access, you should select the form in the Database window or open it in design view and then either hit the Code button or choose Code from the View menu.

> *If you want to toggle between the Access window and the Visual Basic IDE, you can just hit Alt+F11.*

## *Code Window*

When we open up a module, whether it's a class module associated with a form or report, a standalone class module or a standard modules, the **Code Window** is displayed. As its name suggests, the code window is where we type our VBA code:

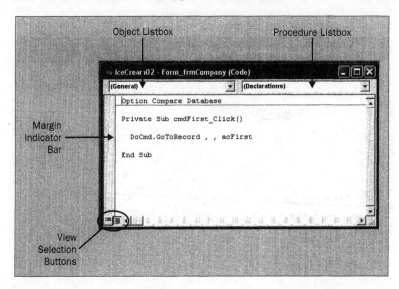

Each separate code window contains all of the code within a module, so opening a new module will open a new code window. You can view the code in a module one procedure at a time or you can decide that the procedures should be shown continuously. To toggle between full module view and single procedure view, simply click the appropriate **View Selection** button in the lower left corner of the code window.

*You can determine whether the code window will default to full module view or single procedure view by checking or unchecking the **Default to Full Module View** checkbox on the **Editor** tab of the dialog displayed when you select **Options...** from the **Tools** menu.*

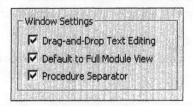

*If you do decide to use Full Module View, you can use the **Procedure Separator** checkbox to determine whether or not procedure separators (thin gray lines) should be displayed in the code window to demarcate where one procedure ends and another starts.*

At the top of the code window you will notice two drop-down lists, referred to as the **object listbox** and the **procedure listbox**. The object listbox is used to select the object whose code you want to look at. For standard modules, the only option listed is (General) as standard modules do not contain objects, only procedures. For class modules associated with forms or reports (also called form or report modules), the object listbox will also contain in alphabetical order a list of all of the objects (such as command buttons) contained on the form or report.

The procedure listbox details the events associated with the specific object selected in the object listbox. For example, if we opened the form module for our frmCompany form and selected the cmdFirst button in the object listbox, the procedure listbox would display all of the event procedures that we could write for that object. If we have actually chosen to handle one of these events by entering code in the event handler, the name of the event will appear in bold in the procedure listbox:

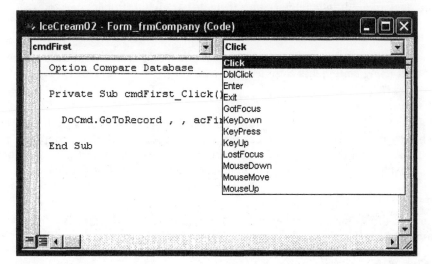

It is also possible to display code from two different procedures, or parts of procedures, from the same module in the same window. To do this select Window | Split from the main menu:

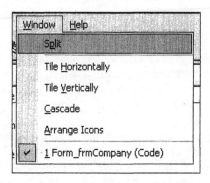

The code window then splits in two. Initially these views show exactly the same thing but you can scroll them individually or use the object and procedure listboxes to jump to the desired procedure. It is also possible to move the split up or down by clicking and dragging the split bar in the middle.

Using split windows can be very useful for cutting and pasting between procedures or perhaps viewing variable declarations alongside the code where they are used (see below).

## The (General) Object

The (General) object isn't really an object at all, but it's where everything goes that relates to the module as a whole. So, in a form or report module, you could put procedures here that aren't necessarily event procedures tied to a particular object, but are procedures that are general to the form. In standard modules, all procedures go in this section. This is also the place where you declare module-level variables (**Private**) or global (**Public**) variables.

### Options

You also set Options in the (General) section of a module. Every module has certain options that can be set using statements commencing with the Option keyword.

### Option Explicit

This is the most widely used of the options. If it's set, it means that all variables have to be declared before being used. You will see why this is a good idea in later chapters. You can turn on Option Explicit by default in new modules by selecting **Options** from the **Tools** menu (in the VBA IDE) and checking **Require Variable Declaration** on the **Editor** page.

### Option Base

This statement allows you to set the default lower limit for arrays. This is normally 0. Arrays are explained later on in the book, so you don't need to worry about this at the moment.

### Option Compare

This is one statement that you will frequently see. It determines how VBA compares strings (text values). Normally, this is set to Database, but it can be Binary or Text instead.

When Option Compare Binary is set, VBA will use the internal binary representation of characters when comparing them in that module. This means that it will regard lower and upper case versions of the same letter as different. It also means that when VBA sorts values it will place all upper-case letters before all lower-case letters, so whereas a word beginning with a upper-case Z is placed after one starting with an uppercase Y, a word beginning with a lower-case a is placed after both of these.

Option Compare Database, which is the default setting, causes VBA to use the Access database's sort order when comparing strings in that module. The sort order of the database is determined by what the setting of the **New Database Sort Order** option on the **General** tab of the **Tools/Options...** dialog (in Access) was when the database was created.

If the value in the New Database Sort Order drop-down box is General, then the database will be created with a sort order defined by the system locale. We can change the system locale by using the Regional Settings utility in the Control Panel. As well as defining the sort order, the system locale also affects other features such as the way that dates are formatted or how currency values are displayed. Alternatively, if we want to use a sort order different from that specified by the system locale, we can select a different sort order in the New Database Sort Order drop-down box.

Changes we make to the New Database Sort Order drop-down box are only reflected in new databases that are created after we change the setting. Note, however, that when we tell Access to compact a database, it physically creates a new database into which it compacts the old. This means that the new database that is created will have the new sort order. In fact, this is the recommended way of changing the sort order of a database. Option Compare Text uses the system locale to determine the sort order, but is always case insensitive.

> *Make sure you have good reasons for changing the default sort order as this affects every table in the database.*

### Option Private

This makes the whole module private, so that none of the code within it can be accessed from another module. This saves you having to use the Private keyword on each procedure. Again, we'll explain these concepts in more detail in later chapters, so don't worry too much about them for now.

> *You will not normally need to modify any of these Option settings in day-to-day use. The only one to keep an eye on is Option Explicit. We'll look at the reasons for that in Chapter 4.*

### Declarations

As well as setting options, the (General) section can also be used to declare external functions, variables, and constants that apply to the whole module. We'll look at this subject in more detail in the next chapter.

# Adding Intelligent Navigation Buttons to the Company Contacts Form

So how does all this help us? If you remember, our original mission in this chapter was to produce intelligent navigation buttons. That is to say, we need to create navigation buttons that disable themselves when they are unavailable. How can we do this? Well, first of all we'll show you the answer, and then we'll explain how it works.

**Creating an 'Intelligent' Navigation Button**

**1.** Open the `frmCompany` form in Design view.

**2.** Make sure that the form's properties are visible by double-clicking on the form selector at the top left, where the rulers meet:

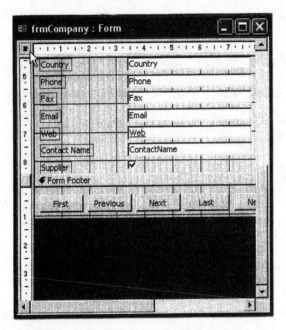

**3.** Open the form's `Current` event procedure by clicking on the builder button to the right of the **On Current** property and selecting **Code Builder**:

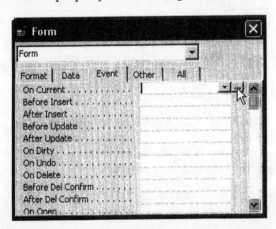

**4.** Add the following code to the form's `Current` event procedure:

```
Private Sub Form_Current()

    'If the form is on a new record, we should disable the Next button.

    'To do this we have to shift the focus first. If there is
    'a value in CompanyID, we must enable the button.

    If Me.NewRecord = True Then
        cmdPrevious.SetFocus
        cmdNext.Enabled = False
    Else
        cmdNext.Enabled = True
    End If

End Sub
```

**5.** Switch back to Access by hitting *Alt+F11*. Close the `frmCompany` form and save it when you are prompted. When you open the form again, what do you know! You've got an 'intelligent' **Next** button! When you get to the end of the records (by hitting the **New** button, for example), the **Next** button becomes disabled. However, clicking the **Previous** button enables the **Next** button again:

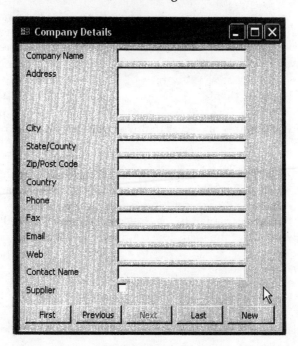

Well, it looks simple enough, but bear in mind that we are only dealing with one button here – and in fact it's the easiest one to handle! The first thing to note is that we have used the **On Current** event property. We need to enable or disable the button as soon as the form is opened, and then whenever the user moves from one record to another. Looking through the list of events, there is only one that fits the bill, and that is the **On Current** event. This event occurs whenever a form is opened and then when moving between records on that form – the very times that we need to check whether the button should be enabled or disabled.

After deciding which event handler to use, we must determine what rules we will use for enabling and disabling the **Next** button. Well, we want the **Next** button disabled only when the user cannot move any further forward through the records. That means that the **Next** button should be disabled when the user is in a new (blank) record.

> **Bear in mind that Access provides a new blank record at the end of every updateable table or form. For now, we will allow the user to move to this record so that they can enter details of a new company. We will modify this behavior a little in Chapter 7 to cater for situations where the user cannot add new records.**

If we are on a new record, the **Next** button should be disabled. If not a new record, the button should be enabled. We can determine whether or not the form is currently on a new record by inspecting the value of the form's `NewRecord` property. This property returns `True` if the form is on a new record and `False` otherwise:

```
If Me.NewRecord = True Then
```

The `Me` keyword simply indicates to Access that we want to use the current object (which is our `frmCompany` form).

However, it's not quite that easy – we can't just disable the **Next** button directly because it has the focus – it has just been clicked. Access does not allow us to disable an item that has the focus, and if we try to do so we'll get a run-time error. So first we must move the focus somewhere else, and where better than to the **Previous** button. This is likely to be the one you want to use next anyway. To set the focus to a control, we just call its `SetFocus` method:

```
If Me.NewRecord = True Then
    cmdPrevious.SetFocus
    cmdNext.Enabled = False
```

You'll notice that to enable or disable a control, we just set its `Enabled` property to `True` or `False`.

As it stands, the button will be disabled when we find ourselves in a new record (or if there are no records in the form when it opens) but it will also remain grayed out when we scroll back to an existing record. We must re-enable it each time the current record is *not* a new one...

```
Else
    cmdNext.Enabled = True
End If
```

*This code uses the* `If...Then...Else` *construct which may be new to you. This is pretty intuitive, but in case you aren't familiar with branching statements, they are explained in more detail in Chapter 4.*

# Adding to the User Interface

We have added intelligent buttons to provide visual clues to help the user navigate through the data as painlessly as possible. The user interface is not all about forms and buttons though. What happens if the user accidentally presses the *Ctrl* and *Z* keys? This has the same effect as selecting Edit | Undo Current Field/Record from the menu. If the user has modified several fields in the record then all this work could be lost in a split second. If the form was large and complex then this data may have taken an hour or more to compile and input – the user is not going to be happy even though, strictly speaking, it was "their fault". As a programmer you have a professional responsibility to try to make your applications as "foolproof" as possible.

We will add a confirmation dialogue to give the user a second chance if they inadvertently trigger an undo operation. Follow the steps below and then go through the explanation that follows.

**Try It Out**    **Foolproofing**

**1.**   As before, open the `frmCompany` form in Design view (making sure that the form's properties are visible). Then open the form's Undo event procedure by clicking on the builder button to the right of the On Undo property and selecting Code Builder:

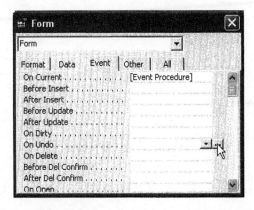

**2.** Add the following code to the form's Undo event procedure:

```
Private Sub Form_Undo(Cancel as Integer)

Dim intResult As Integer

    'ask the user what to do
    intResult = MsgBox("Are you sure you want to discard all changes " _
                    & "you have made to this record?", vbYesNo)

    If intResult = vbYes Then
        'user confirmed so go ahead and allow undo to continue
        Cancel = False
    Else
        'user changed their mind - cancel the undo
        Cancel = True
    End If

End Sub
```

**3.** Switch back to Access by hitting *Alt+F11*. Close the `frmCompany` form and save it when prompted. Open the form again and make a few changes to a record. Now press *Ctrl+Z* (or select Undo from the menu).

*Note: you may have to activate undo more than once as the first Undo will simply undo typing changes you have made to that field only. This time, instead of simply throwing away the changes, we now get asked to confirm our actions.*

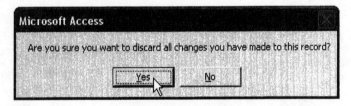

**4.** If we select Yes then the undo action continues as normal. Select No and it is cancelled.

### How It Works

Lets go through the code in detail:

```
Dim intResult As Integer
```

First be we declare an integer variable ready to hold the results of our dialog:

```
'ask the user what to do
intResult = MsgBox("Are you sure you want to discard all changes " _
                   & "you have made to this record?", vbYesNo)
```

Then we go ahead and display the dialog. MsgBox is a standard Access function and saves us the chore of creating our own forms to do the same thing. The vbYesNo constant tells MsgBox to display two buttons for the user to press, one **Yes** and one **No**. After MsgBox returns (completes its task) the user's answer is placed into intResult.

*You will see more of MsgBox in future chapters but if you want to check out some of its other possibilities feel free to look it up in Microsoft Visual Basic Help.*

```
If intResult = vbYes Then
    'user confirmed so go ahead and allow undo to continue
    Cancel = False
Else
    'user changed their mind - cancel the undo
    Cancel = True
End If
```

Finally we set Cancel accordingly. You may have noticed that Cancel appeared in the procedure's declaration line as a parameter. Don't worry too much about this at the moment. It is enough to know that this is simply a mechanism for us to return a result back to Access. All we need to do is set Cancel correctly and Access takes care of the rest.

That's it! Obviously it is not possible to guard against every eventuality, nor is it always desirable. For example, if undo is legitimately required frequently in the course of normal data entry then it will quickly become tiresome for the user to have to confirm their actions each and every time. You will always have to balance inconvenience to some users against the risk of letting them mess up.

# Summary

So, there we are. In this chapter we have had our first taste of VBA code. The chapter should also have given you some idea of how an application is built. As a developer, you build your forms and reports and then write code that causes the objects you have created to respond to events in a particular way. In an event-driven environment like Access, you can let the users decide the order in which your code modules are executed.

We have spent some time looking at the different events that can occur in Access and how these can be put to use. You have seen, for example, how the **On Current** event can be used to solve one of the tasks we set ourselves at the start of the chapter – enabling and disabling navigation buttons depending on our position in the recordset. We shall complete this feature for all the buttons in later chapters, once we have a few more programming concepts under our belt.

We have also spent some time looking at the VBA IDE, and by now you should feel comfortable with:

❑ What events are

❑ How to make an Access object respond to an event

❑ The VBA IDE

❑ What modules are and how they are used to store code

❑ How to use the **On Current** event to make a navigation button intelligent

Finally we saw how to improve the user's interface experience by using the **On Undo** event automatically guarding against their possible mistakes.

In the next couple of chapters, we will be looking at the nuts and bolts of VBA so that you will be able to write your own event handlers more easily. Ponder on the following points before moving on to the next chapter.

# Exercises

**1.** One of the most important things to remember when working with events in VBA is the order in which events occur. For example, when you save a record on a form, several events occur, one after another. By looking at the list of events on the property sheet, try to work out the order in which they happen.

**2.** Take some time to read through the list of events and their uses. You will find that some events are more useful than others – in other words, you will find yourself writing custom event handlers for some events more often than for other events. Look at the list and try to think about which events you would most commonly handle with custom event handlers.

**3.** We saw how to use the On Undo event to help guard against user error. Hopefully, you should already be thinking of other ways to foolproof the application even if you are not sure how to actually code them. What would happen if the user closed the form halfway through adding a new record? Code a new dialog to ask the user to confirm that they really wish to exit the form.

*Hint: you can use the* `Form Unload` *event to detect when the user has attempted to exit the form.*

# CHAPTER 3

# Creating Code

Well, we really should start looking deeper at some code. The next two chapters are going to lay the foundations of programming and using VBA. So far, we've looked at the programming environment, and seen how event-driven programming works, so now it's time to start putting this into practice.

In this chapter we will be dealing with what code is, and how you can build up code in small segments to make programming easier. In particular we shall look at:

- ❏ What procedures are and how you use them
- ❏ How to pass information into procedures
- ❏ What variables are and how they store data
- ❏ The different types of data you can store
- ❏ How to make decisions in your code

This is the heart of the VBA language, and will lay the foundations for all programming you do later.

## Procedures

You use procedures in life every day, even if you don't think about it. From making breakfast to requesting that brand new PC you've always wanted, there's a procedure to follow. A specific set of actions you take to get it done. The whole idea of a procedure is to break down a task into smaller, more manageable tasks. Let's look at making some chocolate ice cream. What are the tasks you would need to perform?

1. Beat egg yolks lightly

2. Beat in sugar

**3.** Heat the cream/milk on the stove

**4.** Beat in cocoa powder

**5.** Heat cream/milk/cocoa mix until steaming

**6.** Stir into egg/sugar mix

**7.** Add vanilla extract

**8.** Cool

**9.** Freeze in ice cream maker

This is the procedure we would follow to make basic chocolate ice cream.

Now we have defined this set of instructions, we don't need to write them out again. We can just refer to the recipe by its name. So what's this got to do with programming? Well, in programming you can do the same sort of thing. You can group together a set of instructions under a single name, and then use this name when you want to run those instructions. This is a good thing for several reasons:

❑ It allows us to break complex problems into smaller, more discrete tasks. This can often make the problem easier to solve.

❑ It makes your code smaller, because you only need the instructions entered once.

❑ It makes your code easier to maintain, because if there is an error in the instructions, you only need to correct it in one place.

❑ It makes it easy to use the instructions in other applications.

❑ You can change the inner workings of your procedure without worrying about others who use it. As long as it has the same result, no one will know the difference.

You may not think this is a big issue, but as your programs start to get more complex you'll find that dealing with procedures is much easier than having a single large chunk of code. The last point in the list is one you'll see mentioned again later in the book, as it means you can change the internal workings of a procedure, perhaps to improve performance, without changing the end result of the procedure. Think about our 'making ice cream' example. If you make ice cream by hand, you don't use Step 9 above. There may be two or three steps here instead, describing how long you should place the ice cream in the freezer for, and how often you should stir it. But if you buy an ice cream making machine, you could replace these steps with Step 9, and the end result would be the same.

# Modules

One term that you've already seen is **modules**. From the pictures in the previous chapter you saw that the Visual Basic IDE can have many modules. But what exactly are they? A module is really just a place to store procedures.

We generally group procedures into logical units. So, if we created a set of string handling procedures, we could put them all together in a single module, and call the module String Handling. As you go through the book you'll see this in practice. Each chapter has its own code module where the code for the chapter goes. This makes it easy to find.

# Subroutines and Functions

In VBA programming terms there are two types of procedures: **subroutines** and **functions**. They really only have one difference, which is that a function returns a value to you. Let's say you ask someone to make some ice cream for you. They wander off to the kitchen and make the ice cream, and then come back, but they don't tell you anything about how the process went or whether it's ready or not. That's a subroutine. On the other hand, if they come back and bring you a dish of chocolate ice cream, then that's a function.

Let's make this a bit clearer by turning the steps involved in making ice cream into a subroutine, and then into a function. The first thing we have to do is give the procedure a name – MakeIceCream. It is in this format because procedure names can't have spaces in them. We then use a special keyword called Sub to tell Access that we are starting a new subroutine. We put our steps after that, followed by more keywords to tell Access that we've reached the end of the subroutine. Note that the following two examples are just for teaching purposes and won't actually run. Soon, we'll translate some of these English phrases into VBA code that Access can understand. Here's how it looks:

```
Sub MakeIceCream()
   Beat egg yolks lightly
   Beat in sugar
   Heat the cream/milk on the stove
   Beat in cocoa powder
   Heat cream/milk/cocoa mix until steaming
   Stir into egg/sugar mix
   Add vanilla extract
   Cool
   Freeze in ice cream maker
End Sub
```

Now, anywhere in our program, we can just say MakeIceCream, and this subroutine is run. Access starts at the first line in the subroutine, and runs each line in turn until it gets to the end. You can see how much easier this is than typing in all of the lines again. So, the actual details of the procedure are just typed once, and to run it you don't type the details again, just the procedure name.

For a function, we need the procedure to tell us something – perhaps whether vanilla extract was added or not. The way it is used is slightly different:

```
Function MakeIceCream()
   Beat egg yolks lightly
   Beat in sugar
   Heat the cream/milk on the stove
   Beat in cocoa powder.
   Heat cream/milk/cocoa mix until steaming
   Stir into egg/sugar mix
   Add vanilla extract (if there is any)
   Cool
   Freeze in ice cream maker.

   If vanilla extract added Then
     MakeIceCream = "Vanilla"
   Else
     MakeIceCream = "No Vanilla"
   End If
End Function
```

Notice that instead of Sub we use Function. At the end of the function we determine whether or not vanilla extract was added, and we set the function name to a value to indicate this.

When calling a function from within our code we can now see what happened – its return value tells us what kind of ice cream was made. For example:

```
If MakeIceCream = "Vanilla" Then
   Chocolate vanilla ice cream was made
Else
   Plain chocolate ice cream was made
End If
```

Don't worry too much if you don't understand some of the things here. The important thing is to remember that we are making little blocks of code, and then we'll use these blocks to build bigger blocks and programs.

# Naming Conventions

Naming conventions are one of the most important concepts in programming and yet are rarely taught. It's easy to ignore the importance of a systematic approach to naming variables, procedures, and so on – but once you start programming in earnest, you'll realize that not only does a set of conventions make thinking up new names easier, but it is a tremendous help when it comes to understanding the code you have written. For example, if you follow a set of conventions, you will be able to tell at a glance a variable's type and where it was declared (that is, whether it is local or public). This will save you having to look for the variable declaration to find this out – a process which can be especially tedious if you have several modules and public variables.

Naming conventions are, of course, a matter of personal taste and you should use whichever set of standards you prefer. An important consideration is to use standards that will help others maintain your code in the future. There are no hard and fast rules (the ones shown here are fairly standard, although other people may use slightly different prefixes that the ones we've shown). All we can do is list our favorite set of conventions and let you make your own mind up.

## Keep Names Meaningful

The first rule is to make variable names meaningful. They should describe what they hold. If you have a variable that holds someone's age, then call it `Age`. A birth date should be stored as `DateOfBirth`, or `date_of_birth`. We prefer the first method without the underscores, since we think it looks neater, but you can choose any style. The important point is to be consistent. If you have a system, then stick to it.

## Mixed Case Naming

There are some generally accepted rules about procedure naming that are worth mentioning here. Long ago it was necessary to use vary short and cryptic names due to the system limitations at the time. Early operating systems didn't differentiate between upper and lower case characters. These days, disk space and memory is not so much of a premium commodity and lengthy names don't significantly affect performance. Since you can't have spaces in a procedure name, you take the name for your procedure (usually a short phrase), cram all of the words together, and capitalize the first letter of each word. This is known as PascalCase. For example, if we're creating a function to return a list of ingredients, we might call it `GetIngredientsList()`.

## Prefix All Variables and Constants With Their Type

If you use a prefix, you can easily see what type the variable is. For example, if `Age` was stored as an integer, then you should use `int` as the prefix, giving `intAge`. The prefix is lower case to separate it from the variable name. This form of naming is known as Hungarian notation, and we will be using throughout the book. The most commonly used prefixes are listed below:

| Variable Type | Prefixes | Variable Type | Prefixes |
|---|---|---|---|
| Integer | `int` | Variant | `var` |
| Long | `lng` | Date | `dat` |
| | | | `dte` |
| Single | `sng` | Boolean | `bln` |
| Double | `dbl` | Byte | `byt` |
| Currency | `ccy` | Object | `obj` |
| | `cur` | | |
| String | `str` | Hyperlink | `hyp` |

It's also a good idea to add a double prefix for the variant type. Use `var` to denote that a variant is in use, but add another prefix to denote the type of data the variant will store. For example, if the age was to be stored in this way, you could use `intvarAge`.

### Prefix Global Variables with their Scope

Yet another prefix. Will it never stop? This is the last one and, in some ways, the most useful since it can be a great time saver. Use a prefix to denote the scope, that is, whether it is a local, module or public variable. You can leave the prefix for local variables blank, since most will be local, but use `m_` for module level, `g_` for public (global) variables, and `s` for static variables in procedures. Thus if `Age` was a public variant holding an integer value, it would become `g_intvarAge`.

OK, so in this case the prefixes are now larger than the variable name, but on the other hand you can see everything about this variable from its name. What could be clearer?

## Naming Conventions for Controls

In the same way that you use conventions for variables, you should also consider using them for controls on forms and reports, especially if you are going to refer to these controls in your code.

| Control | Prefix | Control | Prefix |
|---------|--------|---------|--------|
| Chart (graph) | cht | Option button | opt |
| Check box | chk | Option group | grp |
| Combo box | cbo | Page break | brk |
| Command button | cmd | Rectangle | rec |
| Frame | fra | Subform/report | sub |
| Label | lbl | Textbox | txt |
| Line | lin | Toggle button | tgl |
| Listbox | lst | Hyperlink | hyp |

The principle is exactly the same as for variables and, again, will make your code easier to read:

```
Function GetName () As String

   Dim strName As String

   strName = txtFirstName & " " & txtLastName
   GetName = strName

End Function
```

It immediately becomes obvious that the first and last names are stored on the form in textboxes.

Now that the use of ActiveX controls is becoming widespread, you may find you wish to use controls that do not fit into the above list. In this case just use a prefix that you find suitable. For example, we will be looking at the Calendar control later on, and for this you could use `cal`.

## Naming Conventions for Objects

The same principle should be applied to objects, both in code and in the database window. So when you save your tables, queries, forms, and so on, follow the same principle:

| Object | Prefix | Object | Prefix |
|--------|--------|--------|--------|
| Table | tbl | Group | grp |
| Query | qry | Container | con |
| Form | frm | Document | doc |
| Report | rpt | Index | idx |
| Macro | mac | Field | fld |
| Module | mod | Property | pty |
| User | usr | Page | pag |

You may not have come across many of these objects yet, but you will meet a few more as the book progresses.

## Naming Conventions for Constants

For constants you follow a similar style to variables, although some people prefer to have their constants all in capitals. We recommend using a c at the front of the name, to indicate a constant, and then the prefix for the type, making sure that you always specify the type of the constant. For example:

```
Const clngSpeedOfLight As Long = 299792458
Const cstrCleverPerson As String = "Albert Einstein"
```

or a slightly shorter form:

```
Const clSpeedOfLight As Long = 299792458
Const csCleverPerson As String = "Albert Einstein"
```

## *Naming Conventions Summary*

All of this may seem rather cumbersome and a waste of effort, but as your programs become larger, you will find it essential to be able to identify different variables/controls/objects. If you start using conventions as you learn the language, it will soon become second nature and, after a while, you won't even have to think about it!

One of the greatest advantages of naming conventions is in maintenance. You will inevitably spend a proportion of time maintaining code, and not necessarily your own code. If a standard set of conventions has been used, it makes your job so much easier. You will automatically know where global variables are stored, what type variables are, and what their scope is, and the chance of introducing errors is automatically reduced. If you follow this procedure, then it benefits others who have to maintain your code. No one likes maintenance, we all want to write cool new apps, so the quicker and more efficient you can make the process the better.

> **The really important thing to remember is consistency. Whichever style you choose, you should be consistent with its use. Don't think that just because you are writing a small program or a single procedure that naming conventions have no place. If you are going to use a style, then use it everywhere.**

# Procedure Declaration

The act of telling Access what a procedure is called is known as the **declaration**. When you declare a procedure you must follow some special rules. For a subroutine, the syntax (just like sentence structure in English) is like this:

```
Sub SubroutineName (Arguments)
```

For a function it's like this:

```
Function FunctionName (Arguments) As Type
```

There are two new things you haven't seen here, the arguments and the type, but we'll be covering those in the next section. For the name there are some special rules that apply:

- ❏ It must start with a letter.
- ❏ After the first letter, it can contain letters, numbers, or the underscore character (_).
- ❏ It cannot be more than 255 characters long.
- ❏ It shouldn't be the same name as an existing VBA keyword.

Apart from that, you can name procedures as you like, although it's always best to keep the names meaningful and descriptive of the task they perform. For example, calling our ice cream making routine `CalculatePayRise` would be perfectly legal, but it doesn't make any sense because that's not what the procedure does.

## Function Types

For the function syntax shown above you saw `As Type` added to the end of the declaration. This allows us to tell Access what sort of value the function is going to return (for example, a number, a date, and so on), and allows Access to perform checking on the values. This can stop errors later on in the code.

For our ice cream making function we return a character string, either `Vanilla` or `No Vanilla`, so our type would have been `String`. So our function should really be declared like this:

```
Function MakeIceCream() As String
```

You can actually leave the function type out and you won't get an error, but it's best to explicitly state the type. Leaving the type out means you get a generic catch-all type, which may not be what you really want. One of the reasons why we have these special types is so that VBA can try to understand what we are trying to do.

The value being sent back by the function is called the **return value**, and always involves using the function name. Its format is:

```
FunctionName = ReturnValue
```

In the example above this was:

```
MakeIceCream = "Vanilla"
```

**Try It Out**　　　**The MakeIceCream Function**

Since we've talked about functions, let's create a simple ice cream making function to see how they work.

1. Open your working database (`IceCream03.mdb`), press *F11* to view the main Access window, and select **Modules** from the database window.

2. From the Insert menu, select **Module** to insert a new VBA module. If you can't see the **Module** option, just click the double chevron at the bottom of the menu to see all of the menu options. (This is one of those Office XP 'intelligent features' that hides options you don't use so often).

**3.** In the new module, type the following code below any text that appears in the window:

```
Option Compare Database
Option Explicit

Function MakeIceCream() As String
   Debug.Print "Making ice cream"
   Debug.Print "Adding Vanilla"
   MakeIceCream = "Vanilla"
End Function
```

**4.** From the View menu, select **Immediate Window** (or hit *Ctrl-G*).

*The Immediate window is where we print values to with* Debug.Print *and what we use to test procedures. We'll be looking at it in depth in Chapter 12, when we look at error handling and debugging.*

**5.** In the Immediate window type the following, followed by the *Enter* key:

```
? MakeIceCream
```

You'll see the function being run, and its result:

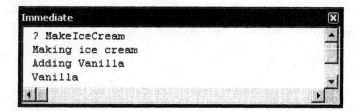

### How It Works

You've seen how a function is declared, but what about the code we put in it? The statement Debug.Print just prints things out to the Immediate window. It's often used for debugging and tracing functions. In the last line we set the return value to Vanilla.

In the Immediate window we used a question mark before the function name. The question mark is a shortcut for the word *Print* and tells VBA to print out the return value. You can try typing in just the function name without the question mark. The function will still run, but the return value isn't printed.

---

**Try It Out    Calling Functions from Functions**

Let's add another procedure to call the first one.

1. In the module window, move the cursor to below the `End Function` line, and type the following:

```
Sub Hungry()
   MakeIceCream
End Sub
```

2. Back in the Immediate window, type the following:

```
Hungry
```

Notice that the return value isn't printed out this time.

3. Now try typing this:

```
? Hungry
```

We get an error. But don't worry, we meant for this to happen. You can press **OK** to clear the error box. Remember that in the Immediate window the question mark prints out the return value of a function. Well `Hungry` isn't a function, but a subroutine, so it doesn't have a return value. So, how do we see the return value?

4. Switch back to the code window and place a `Debug.Print` statement in front of the function call:

```
Sub Hungry()
   Debug.Print MakeIceCream
End Sub
```

Now try the Immediate window procedure again, without the question mark. This time the return value is printed, because `MakeIceCream` returned its return value to the procedure that called it. Confused? Have a look at this diagram:

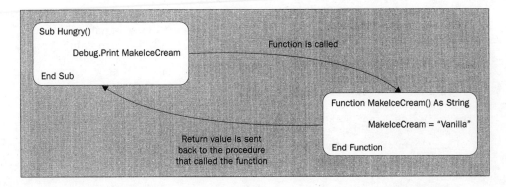

This means that the calling procedure has the return value, and it has to do something with it. In this case it prints it to the Immediate window, but it could also store it for later use.

# Parameters or Arguments

The one limit to our procedure now is that there is no way for us to pass any information into it – no way to tell it anything. In some situations that's fine, all we might want to say is MakeIceCream. But what if we want to make some ice cream that's not chocolate based? You could have another procedure, MakePlainIceCream, that just skips this step, but then you have two pieces of very similar code. Wouldn't it be better if we could have just one procedure that we can tell whether or not cocoa powder is to be added? This is where **arguments** (often called **parameters**) come in.

The argument is our way of passing a value into the procedure. Let's look at an example:

```
Function MakeIceCream (CocoaToBeAdded As Boolean) As String
```

Here we have added the argument within the parentheses of the function. The syntax of an argument is:

```
Name As Type
```

The *Name* follows the same rules as a procedure name, and is the variable that will hold the value of the argument. The As *Type* part is the same as in the function – it tells Access what type of data is to be held in the variable. We'll be looking at variables and data types later on.

Within the procedure you can use this variable to make choices. For example, our function could now look like this:

```
Function MakeIceCream (CocoaToBeAdded As Boolean) As String
    Beat egg yolks lightly
    Beat in sugar
    Heat the cream/milk on the stove

    If CocoaToBeAdded = True Then
      Beat in cocoa powder
    End If

    Heat cream/milk/cocoa mix until steaming
    Stir into egg/sugar mix
    Add vanilla extract (if there is any)
    Cool
    Freeze in ice cream maker

    If vanilla extract added Then
      MakeIceCream = "Vanilla"
    Else
```

```
      MakeIceCream = "No Vanilla"
   End If
End Function
```

If we wanted to make chocolate ice cream we could then call this function with the following line:

```
MakeIceCream (True)
```

To make plain ice cream, we'd use this:

```
MakeIceCream (False)
```

Remember, don't worry about the values. We'll explain those in a minute. The term we use is to **pass in** a value. So, in the latter example, we are **passing in** a value of `False`.

You aren't limited to just one argument – there can be as many as you need. You separate multiple arguments with a comma. For example:

```
Function MakeIceCream (CocoaToBeAdded As Boolean, _
                VanillaToBeAdded As Boolean) As String
```

*The underscore character, when it's the last character on a line and preceded by a space, tells Access that the statement isn't finished, and it continues onto the next line. This allows you to split long lines into easily readable chunks.*

To call this you would use this type of command:

```
MakeIceCream (True, False)
```

Here we are passing in two values. The first is `True`, and would be passed into the first argument, `CocoaToBeAdded`. The second is `False`, and would be passed into the second argument, `VanillaToBeAdded`.

---

**Try It Out**   **Arguments**

Let's add some arguments to our existing function.

**1.** Modify the `MakeIceCream` function so it looks like this:

```
Function MakeIceCream (VanillaToBeAdded As Boolean) As String

   Debug.Print "Making ice cream"
```

```
      If VanillaToBeAdded = True Then
         MakeIceCream = "Vanilla"
      Else
         MakeIceCream = "No Vanilla"
      End If
   End Function
```

**2.** Switch to the Immediate window and type the following:

```
? MakeIceCream (True)
```

Notice the return value.

**3.** Now type this:

```
? MakeIceCream (False)
```

See how the return value has changed?

This shows that arguments allow you to build procedures that can change their behavior depending upon how they are called.

## Optional Arguments

If you have a procedure that accepts two arguments, then you have to pass in both arguments every time. We would get an error if we tried to call the procedure without both arguments. It would be nice if we could make the procedure clever, so that it could go ahead and make chocolate vanilla ice cream by default. Fortunately we can make our arguments **optional**, allowing us to test whether they have been supplied or not. This is achieved by putting Optional in front of the arguments:

```
Function MakeIceCream (Optional CocoaToBeAdded As Boolean, _
                   Optional VanillaToBeAdded As Boolean) As String
```

However, this leads to a problem. Since we've now said that these arguments don't have to be supplied, how do we know if they have been supplied or not? If we created a function like the one above, then if we didn't supply the arguments, they would have a default value of False. The program would have no way of telling the difference between the situation where the arguments were supplied with values of False, and that where the arguments were left out. The same problem occurs if our optional arguments are of other data types, although the default values differ depending upon the type – strings are empty, and numbers are 0.

To get around this problem, you can declare your optional arguments to be of a special type – Variant. This doesn't affect the data they can hold because a Variant can hold different types of data. So what we have to do is this:

```
Function MakeIceCream (Optional CocoaToBeAdded As Variant, _
                 Optional VanillaToBeAdded As Variant) As String
```

Now within the code we need to check whether those arguments have been supplied, since they are optional. For this we use the IsMissing() function. This is a built-in function, supplied by Access, which returns a value of True if the argument is missing, and False if it is present. So if we wanted to make our default ice cream have chocolate and vanilla, we could modify our code to look like this:

```
Function MakeIceCream (Optional CocoaToBeAdded As Variant, _
                 Optional VanillaToBeAdded As Variant) As String

    If IsMissing(CocoaToBeAdded) Then
      CocoaToBeAdded = True
    Else
      CocoaToBeAdded = False
    End If

    If IsMissing(VanillaToBeAdded) Then
      VanillaToBeAdded = True
    Else
      VanillaToBeAdded = False
    End If

    rest of code goes here
End Function
```

This shows that we test both of the arguments, and if they are missing we simply set their values to True. You can now call this procedure in a few ways:

| | |
|---|---|
| MakeIceCream (True, False) | This is the original syntax, using both arguments. |
| MakeIceCream | This doesn't supply any arguments. In both cases the IsMissing() test sets the value of CocoaToBeAdded and VanillaToBeAdded to True. |
| MakeIceCream (True) | This only supplies one argument; this is the first one (CocoaToBeAdded). The IsMissing() test for the first argument fails, but the second sets the value of VanillaToBeAdded to True. |

*Table continued on following page*

```
MakeIceCream (, False)
```

This only supplies one argument, but the supplied comma indicates that the first argument is skipped. Here `CocoaToBeAdded` would be missing, and therefore gets set to `True`, but `VanillaToBeAdded` wouldn't be. If you are skipping arguments, you must supply the comma.

*As we'll see later on, a new `Variant` variable has a default value of `Empty`, which is why we can use the `IsMissing()` function to check it.*

One important point to note is that optional arguments must be the last arguments in the argument list. In our example, both of the arguments are optional, so that's all right. We could also make the first argument required and the second optional – that would be fine too. What we can't do is make the first optional and the second required.

## Default Values

Another way to get around the problem of missing optional arguments is to use default values. This allows us to tell VBA what the default value of the variable should be if the user does not supply a value. For example:

```
Function MakeIceCream (Optional CocoaToBeAdded As Boolean = True, _
                       Optional VanillaToBeAdded As Boolean = True) _
                       As String
```

Here, after the variable type, we put the equals sign followed by the default value. Now if the argument is not supplied, it will automatically supply the value `True`. The thing to remember with this method is that if you omit an argument that has a default value, VBA fills in the default. This means that `IsMissing()` would never work correctly, because all it sees is a correctly supplied variable. The fact that VBA supplied the value, rather than the user, is immaterial.

If you are using optional arguments, and you need to supply default values, then use the method shown above, rather than using `IsMissing()`. However, if you need to check whether the argument has been supplied (and not filled in by VBA), then you will need to use `IsMissing()` and not supply default arguments.

# Named Arguments

So far you've seen a simple procedure with two arguments, but what happens if you have a procedure with lots of arguments? For example, imagine our `MakeIceCream` procedure had an argument for every ingredient type, to indicate how much of that ingredient to use. When using this procedure it would get confusing as to which argument is which. To avoid this confusion you can name the arguments as you use them. For example, imagine our procedure was declared like this:

```
Function MakeIceCream (EggYolks As Integer, Sugar As Integer, _
                       Cream As Integer, Milk As Integer, _
                       Cocoa As Integer, Vanilla As Integer, _
                       Optional CocoaToBeAdded As Boolean = True, _
                       Optional VanillaToBeAdded As Boolean = True) _
                       As String
```

If you came across a line of code that called this function you might be confused as to which of the arguments represented which ingredient:

```
MakeIceCream (3, 25, 1, 1, 2, 2, True, False)
```

Confusing? To get around this you can use the name of the argument as it is used:

```
MakeIceCream (EggYolks:=3, Sugar:=25, _
              Cream:=1, Milk:=1, _
              Cocoa:=2, Vanilla:=2, _
              CocoaToBeAdded:=True, VanillaToBeAdded:=False)
```

Note the colon just before the equals sign. You can now easily see which argument is which. Since you are explicitly naming the arguments, you can also put them in any order.

Now imagine how useful this is if you have a procedure with lots of optional arguments. Remember how we said that to skip an argument you must supply the comma? Well, with named arguments you don't have to, because if you name them VBA knows which argument you are supplying. So, if all of our arguments to `MakeIceCream` were optional, we could call it like this:

```
MakeIceCream (CocoaToBeAdded:=True)
```

All of the other arguments are simply taken to be missing, or use their defaults if they have them. Note that even though you are using named arguments, you still have to follow the rules as to whether the arguments are optional or not. Using named arguments just means that you can explicitly name the argument, and put it in any order, but if it's a required argument you still have to supply a value for it.

# Built-In Functions

So far you've seen what procedures are and how they can be used. VBA has a whole host of functions built in to make things easy for you. You've already seen an example of one – IsMissing().

We're not going to give a full list of functions in the book because there are far too many of them, and anyway the Access documentation has a good list. You can find it under the Microsoft Visual Basic Help Contents, under Visual Basic Language Reference: Functions.

You'll see some of these in use as we explain variables in the next section, and plenty of examples throughout the rest of the book.

# Variables

A **variable** is a temporary holding place for data while your application is running. When your application stops running, the variable is destroyed. Variables reside in memory, which is much faster than being written to the hard disk.

You've actually already seen variables in action, because arguments are variables. These are used to store the details of what information is to be passed into a procedure. Within the procedure itself we can have other variables, to store other information.

Let's look at a simple example. Looking back to our ice cream making procedure from earlier, and how we set the return value of the function, we used IsMissing() to determine if the argument was missing or not, and then used this to make a decision.

```
If IsMissing(VanillaToBeAdded) Then
   VanillaToBeAdded = True
Else
   VanillaToBeAdded = False
End If
```

Now what happens if we need to make this decision twice in the same procedure? We could do this:

```
If IsMissing(VanillaToBeAdded) Then

' some more code here

If IsMissing(VanillaToBeAdded) Then
```

This is a little wasteful because we are calling the same function twice with the same argument, so the result will be the same. What we can do is use a variable to store the result of the function, and then test the variable:

```
blnMissing = IsMissing (VanillaToBeAdded)
If blnMissing Then
   VanillaToBeAdded = True
Else
   VanillaToBeAdded = False
End If
```

Now if we need to see if the argument is missing more than once, we don't have the overhead of running the function every time. Remember how we said that using procedures allows us to call a set of instructions just by a single name? That saves us having to type out all of those lines again. Well, assigning a variable to the result of a function saves VBA from having to call the function more than once. In this case `IsMissing()` is not a very complex function, and therefore runs very quickly, but if we were calling a long and complex function, then calling it more than once would be a little wasteful.

*Don't worry too much about the `If` statement, as we'll be covering that in the next chapter.*

You can see that to set the value of a variable, we use the equals sign. The general rule is:

```
Variable = Value
```

In the above example we set our variable to hold the return value from a function, but you can set variables directly. For example:

```
blnMissing = True
strName = "Janine Lloyd"
intAge = 27
ccyPrice = 24.95
```

## Declaring Variables

You've seen a few examples of variables but may not realize exactly what they are, or why we need them. The reason is that VBA is very ordered, and it can't put things just anywhere. If VBA is storing something, it needs a place to store it, and that place has to be suitable. Declaring a variable tells VBA to put aside some memory to store the variable in, and specifying the variable type tells VBA what sort of data will be stored. That way it knows how much memory to put aside, as different variable types take different amounts of memory.

We have variable types to store different types of information. Strings, for example, need to be stored in a different way from numbers, and the variable type tells VBA how to handle that variable as well as how to store it.

To declare a variable we use the `Dim` statement:

```
Dim VariableName As VariableType
```

`VariableName` is the name of the variable, and follows the same conventions as procedure names. We also frequently prefix the variable name with the type of data it is going to hold. For example, in the above example we used the variable `blnMissing`, using `bln` as the prefix to indicate a `Boolean` value (which can be either `True` or `False`). Keep in mind that wherever you see a variable used, the prefix indicates its data type.

`VariableType` indicates the type of data that this variable will hold, for example string, number, date, boolean, and so on. We'll also look at data types in more detail later on.

For our boolean variable we would have used the following declaration:

```
Dim blnMissing As Boolean
```

Variable names are not case-sensitive, and VBA will convert variables to the case they were declared in. There is no specific place where variables must be declared, but by convention they are generally put at the top of procedures. This makes them all easy to find.

There are many different data types all designed to hold specific kinds of data.

## Manipulating Variables

Remember back to your math classes? Remember how you used to have all this stuff about x, y and z, and if x is 3, then z should be half of y...? And you used to write things like this:

$$x = y^2 + z^2$$

This is manipulating variables, and you can do it just the same in VBA. You can use any of the standard math operators just like you did back then:

```
intX = intY * intY + intZ * intZ
```

Addition, subtraction, it all works the same way, with all of the numeric data types.

When dealing with strings, though, you can't do some of this. But one thing you can (and will) do is join (another term is **concatenate**) strings together. For this you use the `&` sign, as follows:

```
Dim FirstName As String
Dim LastName As String
Dim FullName As String

FirstName = "Janine"
LastName = "Lloyd"

FullName = FirstName & LastName
```

This gives you:

JanineLloyd

But this doesn't look too good, since the first name and last name are right next to each other, which is probably not quite what you wanted. What would be better was if we could add a space in the middle of the two names. You might think that you'd need to create a new variable and assign it a string that just contains a space, but you can actually concatenate strings without them being in a variable:

```
FullName = FirstName & " " & LastName
```

This just adds a space in between the two strings. You're also not limited to just using strings in the middle of expressions, as the following lines show:

```
FullName = "Janine " & LastName
FullName = FirstName & " Lloyd"
```

So don't think that once you've stored a value in a variable it's untouchable. You can continue to manipulate it as much as you wish.

## Variable Types

The following table shows the standard variable types and how they are used:

| Type | Used For |
|------|----------|
| Boolean | True or False values only |
| Byte | Single values between 0 and 255 |
| Currency | Numbers with 4 decimal places, ranging from –922,337,203,685,477.5808 to 922,337,203,685,477.5807 |
| Date | Store dates in the range 1 January 100 to 31 December 9999, and times from 0:00:00 to 23:59:59 |
| Double | Floating point numbers in the range $-1.79769313486231*10^{308}$ to $-4.94065645841247*10^{-324}$ for negative numbers and $4.94065645841247*10^{-324}$ to $1.79769313486232*10^{308}$ for positive numbers |
| Hyperlink | Text that identifies a hyperlink address |
| Integer | Whole numbers in the range –32,768 to 32,767 |

*Table continued on following page*

| Type | Used For |
|------|----------|
| Long | Whole numbers in the range –2,147,483,648 to 2,147,483,647 |
| Object | Any type of Object |
| Single | Floating point numbers in the range $-3.402823*10^{38}$ to $-1.401298*10^{-45}$ for negative numbers and $1.401298*10^{-45}$ to $3.402823*10^{38}$ for positive numbers |
| String | Character data with up to 2 billion ($2^{31}$) characters for a variable length string, or 64,000 ($2^{16}$) for fixed length strings |
| Variant | Different types of data (we'll go into detail later) |

You can also define your own complex types of data; this will be covered later in the book, when we look at advanced programming topics.

> **It is extremely important to declare your variables as the correct type, otherwise unpredictable results can occur, both during the writing and running of your code.**

## Boolean

Booleans are used to stored values that can only be one of two values – True or False. They allow us to store values that can be used to make decisions with.

When numbers are converted to Boolean, 0 becomes False and any other number becomes True. When converting from Boolean to a number, False becomes 0 and True becomes -1.

## Byte

The Byte data type is probably one of the least used. Not because it's not useful, but because the type of data it holds is less used than other types of data. A Byte can hold a single value between 0 and 255. By itself this isn't great, but in a large, multidimensional array it can be used to hold binary data, such as the bitmap for an image. Don't worry. This is not something you are typically going to do in an Access application.

You can assign a value to a Byte like so:

```
bytChar = 243
```

## Currency

The `Currency` type is specifically designed for dealing with numerical currency information, such as prices. It is often more accurate than `Single` or `Double` values because it doesn't suffer from rounding errors. This is due to the way the data is stored internally by VBA. A currency value can be assigned like this:

```
ccyPrice = 19.99
```

## Double and Single

`Double` and `Single` values are for floating point numbers (rather than a fixed number of decimal positions) which aren't currency based. They have a greater range than `Currency` but can suffer from rounding problems if a particularly large number of decimal places is used. The reason we have both `Single` and `Double` is that they take up different amounts of memory – `Single` being the smaller. Therefore, if you know your number will not exceed the range of a `Single`, use a `Single` because it will take up less memory. However, you should always consider the largest possible value that the variable could store, because assigning a value that is outside the range of a variable will cause an error.

`Singles` or `Doubles` can be assigned like so:

```
sngNumber = 123.456
dblNumber = 789.012
```

## Integer and Long

`Integer` and `Long` are used for dealing with whole numbers. Like `Single` and `Double` they take up different amounts of memory, and `Integer` is the smaller. This of course means that the `Integer` has a smaller range, so remember not to assign a very large number to it, otherwise an error will be generated.

`Integers` and `Longs` can be assigned like this:

```
intNumber = 123
lngLongNumber = 123456
```

## String

`Strings` are used to hold any form of character data, such as names, descriptions, and so on. When assigning `Strings` you must use double quotes, like this:

```
strName = "Janine Lloyd"
strDescription = "Jan's favorite ice cream is Strawberry Cheesecake"
```

## *Object*

The `Object` type is used to hold objects for which we don't know the exact object type. Usually we know what type of object we are dealing with (`Recordset`, `Form`, a `Word Document`, and so on), but there are times when the type of object is decided after the code has been written, (such as when the program is running, or if the user decides upon the object type). You'll see examples of this later in the book.

You use a `Set` statement to assign a value to an object:

```
Set objWordDocument = Word.ActiveDocument
```

## *Hyperlink*

A `Hyperlink` allows us to store details about Internet hyperlinks, such as web addresses. The `Hyperlink` variable contains several pieces of information, and we discuss this more in Chapter 19, *Optimizing Your Application* when we look at developing features for the Internet.

## *Variant*

Since a `Variant` can hold different types of data, in fact any type shown in the previous table, we'll examine it in more detail. If you read any of the documentation you might see that the `Variant` is the default variable type, which means that if you leave off the As Type clause from a `Dim` statement, you'll get a `Variant`. For example, both statements below declare the variable as a `Variant`:

```
Dim varAnyThing
Dim varAnyThing As Variant
```

However, it's a good idea to explicitly declare variants, as it makes your code easier to maintain if you can easily see what your variables are.

Since a `Variant` can hold any type of data, you can do things like this:

```
Dim varAnyThing As Variant

varAnyThing = 31
varAnyThing = "Any old thing"
```

This first assigns the variable an integer value of 31, and then a string. VBA doesn't care what type of data it is.

So far this isn't any advantage over an `Integer` or a `String`, but what about the following:

```
Dim varAnyThing As Variant

varAnyThing = 31
varAnyThing = varAnyThing & " is half of 62"
```

This firstly stores an integer in the `Variant`. We then append a string onto the end of the number, which doesn't really make any sense. But, since a `Variant` can hold different types of data, VBA realizes what is happening and treats the first number as though it was a string. The result of this is that we end up with a string containing:

```
31 is half of 62
```

Let's look at a converse example:

```
Dim varAnyThing As Variant

varAnyThing = "31"
varAnyThing = varAnyThing + 10
```

This time we start with a string (note the quotation marks), and add a number onto it. VBA recognizes that the string contains a number and converts it into a number, and adds 10, giving us a result of 41.

Where this can get confusing is under these circumstances:

```
Dim varAnyThing As Variant

varAnyThing = "31"
varAnyThing = varAnyThing + "10"
```

Does this convert both strings to numbers? Well, no, it doesn't. You've seen the plus sign being used for addition, but it can also be used to concatenate strings together, so the answer you get here is a string containing 3110. Remember that a number inside a string is treated as a string. This behavior is by design. If you need to treat a value as a number, either use conversion functions or declare the variable as a specific numeric type. It is inadvisable to use a `Variant` to combine data in this way.

This illustrates an important point: VBA will convert variants into the appropriate type when they are used in expressions.

If you use the + operator on variants, remember the following:

❑ If both values are strings, but contain numbers, they are treated as strings, and joined together.

❏   If both values are numbers, then they are treated as numbers.

❏   If one of the values is a number and the other a string, VBA attempts to convert the string into a number. If successful, the two values are added together. If unsuccessful, an error occurs.

This latter case can be demonstrated with the following code:

```
Dim varAnyThing As Variant

varAnyThing = 31
varAnyThing = varAnyThing + "thirty four"
```

This gives a **Type Mismatch** error, indicating that we are trying to do addition with incompatible types.

### Determining the Type of a Variant

You've seen that `Variants` can hold different types of data, but what do you do if you need to find out the exact type of data held in a variant? VBA provides a function called `VarType()` for this purpose, which returns a value to indicate the exact data type. The table below shows these values:

| Value | Variant type |
|-------|--------------|
| 0 | Empty (unitialized) |
| 1 | Null (no valid data) |
| 2 | Integer |
| 3 | Long Integer |
| 4 | Single |
| 5 | Double |
| 6 | Currency |
| 7 | Date |
| 8 | String |
| 9 | Object |
| 10 | Error value |
| 11 | Boolean |

| Value | Variant type |
|-------|-------------|
| 12 | Variant (only used with arrays of variants) |
| 13 | Data access object |
| 14 | Decimal value |
| 17 | Byte |
| 36 | User Defined Type |
| 8192 | Array |

There are a few things here that you haven't seen yet. The `Empty` and `Null` values are described a little later in this chapter. The `Decimal` value doesn't exist as a type on its own, and can only exist as sub-type of a variant. We won't be covering it here. The `User Defined Type` will be covered later in the book.

---

**Try It Out**     **Examining a Variant**

**1.** Open up `IceCream03.mdb`, and select **Modules**.

**2.** Add a new module by selecting **New** from the toolbar; when saving the module call it Chapter 3 Code:

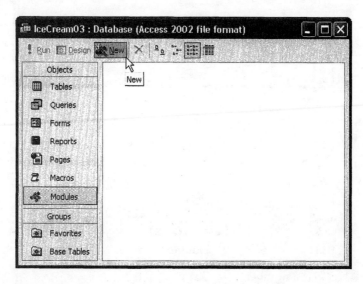

**3.** In the Visual Basic Editor, create a new subroutine called `VariantExample`:

**119**

**4.** Add the following code:

```
Sub VariantExample()
  Dim varAnyThing As Variant

  varAnyThing = 12.345
  Debug.Print VarType(varAnyThing)

  varAnyThing = 12.345
  varAnyThing = varAnyThing & " is a number"
  Debug.Print VarType(varAnyThing)

  varAnyThing = 12.345
  varAnyThing = varAnyThing + "10"
  Debug.Print VarType(varAnyThing)

  varAnyThing = 12345
  Debug.Print VarType(varAnyThing)

  varAnyThing = 123456
  Debug.Print VarType(varAnyThing)
End Sub
```

**5.** Switch to the Immediate window (remember *Ctrl-G* is a shortcut for this) and type `VariantExample`, followed by the *Enter* key.

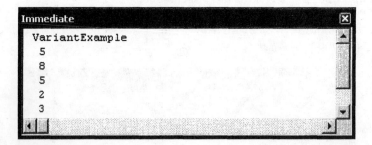

## How It Works

You can see that five values have been printed out, and that two are the same. Let's see what value `VarType` was looking at:

| Value | Is a... | So VarType returns |
| --- | --- | --- |
| 12.345 | Double | 5 |
| 12.345 is a number | String | 8 |

| Value | Is a... | So VarType returns |
|---|---|---|
| 12.345 + "10" | Double | 5 |
| 12345 | Integer | 2 |
| 123456 | Long | 3 |

Notice that the two numbers with decimal points are assigned to a Double. This is because VBA plays it safe and picks the largest numeric type, rather than a Single. Also notice that when dealing with 123456 a Long is automatically picked, as VBA realizes that this is too big a number to fit into an Integer.

### The Empty Value

When numeric variables are declared they have an initial value of 0, and strings are initially a zero length string (that is, ""). But when a variant data type is first declared it is **empty**, because VBA doesn't know what type of data it is going to hold, so an initial value cannot be assigned. The empty value is special in that it is not the same as 0, "", or the **null** value, which we'll look at a little later.

A variant has the empty value before it is assigned. When used in expressions, a variant that is empty is treated as 0 or "", depending upon the expression. For example:

```
Dim varAnyThing As Variant

varAnyThing = varAnyThing + 1.23
```

This leaves varAnyThing as 1.23, since it was initially treated as 0.

Assigning any value to a variant overwrites the empty value. You can use the IsEmpty() function to determine whether a variant has been assigned or not.

```
If IsEmpty(varAnyThing) Then
```

### The Null Value

The null value is another value special to the variant. In fact, a variant is the only data type that can hold this value – if you assign null to any other type of value an error will occur. You can use the IsNull() function to test for the null value:

```
If IsNull(varAnyThing) Then
```

The null value behaves differently from the empty value, as it is said to **propagate** through expressions. That means that if you use a null value in an expression, the whole expression will become null. For example:

```
Dim varAnyThing As Variant

varAnyThing = Null
varAnyThing = varAnyThing + 1.23
```

Unlike the empty value, this doesn't result in 1.23, but Null.

## Try It Out — How Null Propagates

1.  Insert a new procedure called VariantStringTest into your existing module – it doesn't matter if it is a subroutine or a function.

2.  Add the following code:

```
Dim varFirstName As Variant
Dim varLastName As Variant
Dim varFullName As Variant

varFirstName = "Janine"
varLastName = Null

varFullName = varFirstName & varLastName

Debug.Print varFullName
```

3.  Run the procedure by typing VariantStringTest into the Immediate window. Notice that only the first name is printed.

4.  Now change the & into a + and run the procedure again.

When you use &, and one of the expressions is null, it is treated as a zero-length string. So initially we only see the first name. If both parts of the name had been null an empty string would have been returned. Using the + operator, however, a null value is returned. This is because nulls propagate through expressions when the + operator is used, meaning that if any part of the expression is null, then the whole expression is null.

This shows one very important point:

> **Do not use the + operator to concatenate strings.**

### When to Use Variants

There are some good reasons for using variants:

- ❏ They make coding very easy, since you don't have to worry about data types.

- ❏ They are the only data type that can hold a null value. Databases often use null values to show that data hasn't been assigned, so you often have to use a Variant if you are unsure about the source of the data.

- ❏ They have to be used when dealing with Optional arguments to procedures if you want to use the IsMissing() function.

But, remember that there are also some very good reasons for not using them:

- ❏ Variants slow your application because every time a variant is accessed, VBA must determine the type of data that is being stored.

- ❏ They can encourage bad programming. Assigning the correct data type to a variable allows VBA to automatically prevent certain errors from occurring.

In general you should always use the explicit data types, rather than variants.

## Date

The Date type is one that requires a little explanation, since it can often be confusing when using it in VBA. The first thing to remember is that when assigning a date variable to a specific date you need to enclose the date within # signs, to tell VBA that the value is a date (and not a numerical division):

```
datToday = #12/31/02#
```

You can type in dates in almost every recognizable format, and VBA will convert them into an internal value that it uses to for all dates and times. This is partly to stop errors in code, but also to get around the year 2000 problem. Years from 00 to 29 are treated as 2000 to 2029, and 30 to 99 are treated as 1930 to 1999. When a date is displayed, Access uses a format based on the current Windows Regional settings. This enables users in different regions to view such values in a format appropriate for their country.

Date arithmetic is something that is quite common. We often want to find out the differences between two dates, or how many days ahead a certain date is. The great thing about dates is that you can use + and – just as you can with normal numbers. For example:

```
Dim datToday As Date
Dim datNextWeek As Date
Dim datLastWeek As Date
Dim datePaymentDate As Date

datToday = Date()
datNextWeek = datToday + 7
datLastWeek = datToday - 7
datPaymentDate = datToday + 30
```

Date() is a function that returns the current date. You can then just add or subtract days from a date variable and VBA works it all out for you, including the running over of months and years if necessary. If you want to work with values other than days, such as weeks or months, then there are some other functions you can use:

❑   DateAdd() allows us to add dates together.

❑   DateDiff() allows us to work out the difference between two dates.

❑   DatePart() allows us to extract a specific part of a date.

Let's have a look and see how these can be used, and then we'll explain more about them.

**Try It Out      Dates**

1.   Create a new procedure called DateTest in the module you're using for this chapter.

2.   Add the following code:

```
Sub DateTest()
    Dim datDec As Date
    Dim datMay As Date
```

```
    datMay = #5/1/2002#
    datDec = #12/1/2002#

    Debug.Print DatePart("m", datDec)

    Debug.Print DateDiff("m", datMay, datDec)

    Debug.Print "August is " & DateAdd("m", 3, datMay)
End Sub
```

**3.** Now switch to the Immediate window, and type in `DateTest` followed by the *Enter* key to run the procedure.

Let's take this line by line, and look at each of these new functions in turn.

With the first statement we used `DatePart` to find out a specific part of the date:

```
    Debug.Print DatePart("m", datDec)
```

`DatePart` takes four arguments, two of which are optional. (We'll look at the optional arguments when we discuss the `Format` function):

```
    DatePart(Interval, Date [, FirstDayOfWeek [, FirstWeekOfYear]])
```

`Interval` identifies which part of the date to return. We used "m" which stands for month and it returned 12, for December. We could have used "yyyy" for the year, "d" for the day, or one of the others. We won't go into the other intervals here, but you can always look them up in the help file if you want.

With the second statement we used `DateDiff` to find the difference between dates:

```
    Debug.Print DateDiff("m", datMay, datDec)
```

`DateDiff` takes five arguments, of which the latter two are again optional:

```
DateDiff(Interval, Date1, Date2 [, FirstDayOfWeek] [, FirstWeekOfYear])
```

The interval has the same settings as for `DatePart`, and we used "m" to return the difference in months. `Date1` and `Date2` are the two dates we want to find the difference between. In our case we wanted to find the number of months' difference between May and December.

For the third line we used `DateAdd` to add a number to a date:

```
Debug.Print "August is " & DateAdd("m", 3, datMay)
```

`DateAdd` takes three arguments

```
DateAdd(Interval, Number, Date)
```

`Interval` has the same settings as before. `Number` is the number of `Intervals` to be added to `Date`. We added 3 months to May, to get a date in August. You can use negative numbers to subtract numbers from a date. The date printed appears in the format as set in the Regional Settings in the Control Panel.

## Times

The `Date` type also stores times, either on their own, or as part of a date. VBA will accept a date and/or time in a variety of formats. Time values are separated by colons and date parts are separated by forward slashes, hyphens, spaces, and commas. You can assign a time to a date variable like so:

```
Dim datTime As Date

datTime = #3:20:15#
```

which sets it to twenty past three and fifteen seconds in the morning. As you type this in it will be converted by VBA to:

```
datTime = #3:20:15 AM#
```

If you type in a 24-hour date (for example, 15:35) it is converted to 12-hour format and PM is added. Again this is only the internal storage, and not how times are shown on forms.

To assign both a date and a time you use this format:

```
datTime = #6/30/2002 3:20:15#
```

### Other Useful Date and Time Fuctions

There are a few useful date and time functions that you haven't seen already:

- ❏   `Time()` returns the current time

- ❏   `Date()` returns the current date

- ❏   `Now()` returns the current date and time

You can use these quite effectively in your code to work out the difference between the current date and a user-supplied date, or for calculating a date a number of days in advance. For example, let's assume you are printing an invoice and want to give the payee 60 days; you could use this formula:

```
Dim datPayBy as Date

datPayBy = Date() + 60

Debug.Print "Payment is due by " & datPayBy
```

**Try It Out**     **Using DatePart in a Query**

You can see that although these date functions are quite simple, they give you quite a lot of power. For example, imagine you have sales data and you need to find out how many sales have taken place on a month-by-month basis. You can do a summary query quite easily, but how do you group by month? Well, using the `DatePart()` function you could do this easily. Return to the Access Database Window and do the following:

**1.** Create a new query based upon the sales data from `tblSales`. You can do this from the main database window by selecting the **Queries**, and then double-clicking on **Create query in Design view**. When the **Show Table** dialog appears select `tblSales`, click **Add**, and then click **Close**.

**2.** Add the **DateOrdered** and **Quantity** fields to the query. You can do this by just double-clicking on these.

**3.** In the **DateOrdered** field, change the field so that it looks like this:

```
SalesMonth: DatePart ("m", [DateOrdered])
```

**4.** Click on the **View | Total** menu so that the **Total** row appears in the Design view.

**5.** In the `DateOrdered` column add some sorting, click in the **Sort** field and choose **Ascending**. Also make sure the **Show** checkbox is still selected, so that the field appears in the query.

6. In the Quantity column make this a summary query, by changing the Total field from Group By to Sum. Sum is one of several aggregate functions that return a single value for a group of records; aggregate functions allow us to evaluate a set of records. The query should now look like this:

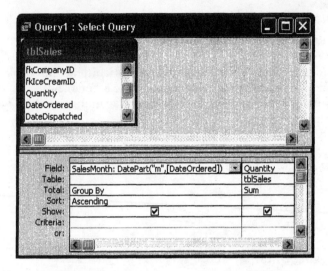

7. Now run the query:

So, not only can you use functions in code, you can use them in queries too. If you want to keep this query, don't forget to save it.

## Formatting Variables

You've seen from the examples above that when used within VBA, dates and times are stored using a standard format, but when they are printed out they use the local settings of the Windows user. This happens for numbers too. But what happens if you want to print out dates in a different format, or specify a format for a number? The solution to this is to use the formatting functions supplied with VBA.

## *Formatting Numbers*

To format numbers you can use one of the formatting functions:

❑   `FormatCurrency()` to format a number into a currency style.

❑   `FormatNumber()` to format a number into a normal number style.

❑   `FormatPercent()` to format a number into a percent style.

All of these functions have several arguments, most of which are optional. They allow us to change the number of digits after the decimal point, whether or not to include a leading 0 for fractions, whether or not to use parentheses for negative numbers, and whether or not a grouping separator is used. Look at the help file in the VBA IDE for the exact details of these arguments.

You can see the difference between these functions easily. Consider this code:

```
Dim dblNumber As Double

dblNumber = 1234.567

Debug.Print dblNumber
Debug.Print FormatCurrency(dblNumber)
Debug.Print FormatNumber(dblNumber)
Debug.Print FormatPercent(dblNumber)
```

This code gives the following output:

```
1234.567
$1,234.57
1,234.57
123,456.70%
```

You can see some interesting things here:

❑   All functions use the system's Regional Options to determine the grouping of numbers and the number of decimal places.

❑   `FormatCurrency()` adds the local currency sign to the front of the number.

❑   `FormatNumber()` adds no special formatting apart from grouping and rounding.

❑   `FormatPercent()` multiplies the number by 100 and adds a percent sign to the end of the number. (Although this looks odd, it makes sense – 0.5 is 50%).

### Formatting Dates

To format dates you can use the `FormatDateTime` function, which takes two arguments. This first is the date to be formatted, and the second (optionally) is the format. Have a look at the code below:

```
Dim datDateTime As Date

datDateTime = #11/30/2002 10:54:17#

Debug.Print datDateTime
Debug.Print FormatDateTime(datDateTime, vbGeneralDate)
Debug.Print FormatDateTime(datDateTime, vbLongDate)
Debug.Print FormatDateTime(datDateTime, vbLongTime)
Debug.Print FormatDateTime(datDateTime, vbShortDate)
Debug.Print FormatDateTime(datDateTime, vbShortTime)
```

The values used for the second argument are constants, predefined by VBA. We'll be looking at constants later in the chapter.

This code gives the following output:

```
11/30/2002 10:54:17 AM
11/30/2002 10:54:17 AM
Saturday, November 30, 2002
10:54:17 AM
11/30/9
10:54
```

This shows that the general format is used by default when printing dates.

### Custom Formats

The functions described above for formatting numbers and dates are all very well, but what if you want to specify the format yourself. For this you can use the `Format` function, which has the following syntax:

```
Format (Expression [, Format [, FirstDayOfWeek [, FirstWeekOfYear]]])
```

As you can see three of the arguments are optional. Let's look at them in turn.

- ❏ `Expression` is the item of data to be formatted.
- ❏ `Format` is the format we want the data to appear in. There are some predefined formats that allow quick formatting, but you can specify your own format too.

❑    `FirstDayOfWeek` allows us to specify which is the first day of the week. By default this is Sunday, but you could set this to Monday if you prefer to start your week on a Monday, as some countries do. This is quite important when converting dates into week numbers, as the day the week starts on could affect which week a date appears in. There are intrinsic constants for all days of the week – see the help file for a list.

❑    `FirstWeekOfYear` allows us to specify which week is defined as the first of the year. By default this is the week in which January 1$^{st}$ occurs, but it could be the first week with at least four full days, or the first full week. This is important when dealing with week numbers, especially as it allows you to set the starting week of a fiscal year.

We are only going to concern ourselves with the first two arguments. In fact, we're really going to look at the second argument – the format.

For dates you have a number of options for the format. You may either specify a named format string to the `Format` function or an intrinsic constant to the `FormatDateTime` function. Intrinsic constants will be explained in greater detail later on.

❑    `Short Date`, which is the same as `FormatDateTime` with `vbShortDate`

❑    `Short Time`, which is the same as `FormatDateTime` with `vbShortTime`

❑    `Long Date`, which is the same as `FormatDateTime` with `vbLongDate`

❑    `Long Time`, which is the same as `FormatDateTime` with `vbLongTime`

❑    A custom format

For the custom format you can use, among others, a combination of:

❑    d or dd for the day number

❑    ddd for the shortened day name, for example Mon

❑    dddd for the full day name

❑    m or mm for the month number

❑    mmm for the shortened month name, for example Mar

❑    mmmm for the full month name

❑    yy for the two-digit year

❑    yyyy for the four-digit year

❑    h or hh for the hour

❑    m or mm for the minute

❑    s or ss for the seconds

❑    AMPM for an AM/PM indicator

❑    Any other text, which is printed out verbatim.

For example, with `datDateTime` set to 11/30/1998 10:54:17 AM:

| Format | Results in |
|---|---|
| Format(datDateTime, "Short Date") | 11/30/02 |
| Format(datDateTime, "Long Date") | Saturday, November 30, 2002 |
| Format(datDateTime, "dd mmm yy") | 30 Nov 2002 |
| Format(datDateTime, "yyyy-mm-dd") | 2002-11-30 |
| Format(datDateTime, "mm dddd hh:mm") | 11 Saturday 10:54 |
| Format(datDateTime, "yymmddhhnnss") | 021130105400 |

You can see that although m and mm appear to be shared between months and minutes, their use is often worked out depending upon the context. To be more explicit, n may be used to specify minutes.

Formatting numbers follows similar lines, where you can use:

❑ Currency (giving the same as FormatCurrency)

❑ Percent (giving the same as FormatPercent)

❑ A custom format

For a custom format you can use a combination of:

❑ 0 to display a digit or a zero. This allows you to pad the string with zeros.

❑ # to display a digit. Nothing is displayed if no number is present.

❑ . for a decimal placeholder. You always use a decimal point here and not the placeholder specified in the regional settings.

❑ % for a percentage placeholder. Like FormatPercent the number is multiplied by 100.

❑ , for a thousands separator. You always use a comma here and not the separator in the regional settings.

For example, with dblNumber set to 12345.678:

| Format | Results in |
|---|---|
| Format(dblNumber "0.00") | 12345.68 |
| Format(dblNumber "000000.00") | 012345.68 |
| Format(dblNumber "#####0") | 123456 |

| Format | Results in |
|---|---|
| Format(dblNumber "###,##0.00") | 12,345.68 |
| Format(dblNumber "Currency") | $12,345.68 |

You can see that you can put any number of these placeholders in the format string to achieve exactly what you want. The latter example depends upon the regional settings in Windows and will display currency values for the current locale.

# Constants

Constants are static names for constant data. They are declared while you are writing your code, and can be used anywhere in the code, but they cannot be changed programmatically – that's why they are called constants. They are a great way to improve the readability and maintainability of your code because, like variables, they have a name, and you can therefore use the name instead of the actual value in your code.

You add constants to your code using the Const statement. For example:

```
Const clSpeedOfLight = 299792458
```

Once defined you can use the name in your code instead of the value. So what's the use of this? Well firstly it makes your code more readable. Seeing 299792458 in your, or someone else's, code might not be very meaningful (unless you're a rocket scientist), but seeing clSpeedOfLight instantly gives you more information. Another great reason is that should you want to change the value of a constant, you only have to change it once, where it is defined, and not everywhere in the code.

You can use constants anywhere in code, even in other constant definitions:

```
Const csMinute = 60
Const csHour = csMinute * 60
Const csDay = 24 * csHour
```

Constants also allow you to declare a type, which can improve the error checking that VBA can do:

```
Const clSpeedOfLight As Long = 299792458
Const csCleverPerson As String = "Albert Einstein"
```

Notice that there are also some naming standards applied to these constants – this is the cs and cl you see at the start of the constant name.

# Intrinsic Constants

Intrinsic constants are ones that are automatically defined by Access or VBA. You can find a full list of these in the Access help file, under the **Visual Basic Language Reference** section.

For example, earlier in the chapter we used the `VarType()` function to determine the type of a variant. If you wanted to test a variant to see whether it contained a string you could do this:

```
If VarType(varAnyThing) = 8 Then
```

However, this has the immediate disadvantage in that you must know what the value 8 means. Luckily there is a set of intrinsic constants just for this purpose. Let's have another look at the table:

| Value | Variant type | Constant |
|-------|--------------|----------|
| 0 | Empty (uninitialized) | vbEmpty |
| 1 | Null (no valid data) | vbNull |
| 2 | Integer | vbInteger |
| 3 | Long Integer | vbLong |
| 4 | Single | vbSingle |
| 5 | Double | vbDouble |
| 6 | Currency | vbCurrency |
| 7 | Date | vbDate |
| 8 | String | vbString |
| 9 | Object | vbObject |
| 10 | Error value | vbError |
| 11 | Boolean | vbBoolean |
| 12 | Variant (only used with arrays of variants) | vbVariant |
| 13 | Data access object | vbDataObject |
| 14 | Decimal value | vbDecimal |
| 17 | Byte | vbByte |
| 36 | User Defined Type | vbUserDefinedType |
| 8192 | Array | vbArray |

Now our code becomes much more readable:

```
If VarType(varAnyThing) = vbString Then
```

You'll see plenty of uses of intrinsic and user-defined constants as we go through the book.

# Variable Scope and Lifetime

Whether or not you can use a variable within a particular procedure depends on where and how the variable was declared, that is, the **scope** of a variable. Scope is the term given to the visibility of a variable, in other words, where it can be seen from. A variable that is created within a procedure can only be seen, and therefore can only be changed, from within that procedure. Its scope is **local** to the procedure. However, a variable can also be declared outside a procedure in the (General) (Declarations) section. In this case, it can be seen by all procedures in that module (and sometimes other modules as well). Thus, its scope is either **private** (to the procedures only in the local module) or **public** (to procedures in all modules).

The **lifetime** of a variable is defined as how long the variable can be seen for; in other words, how long it will contain the value assigned to it. Normally, local variables 'live' for as long as their procedure has the control – so when the procedure ends the variable ceases to exist. The next time the procedure is called, the local variables are recreated.

If you want local variables to exist even when the procedure exits, you can use the Static keyword. Making a variable **static** ensures that its contents are not lost. You can also declare a procedure as Static, which makes all of the local variables within the procedure Static. However, static variables still have the same scope as non-static variables. They cannot be seen outside of their procedure, even though their lifetime is longer than the procedure.

A Public variable exists as long as the database is open and retains its contents throughout the life of the program.

> With VBA, you can apply scope to the procedures themselves by using the Public and Private keywords. A Private procedure can only be called from within the module in which it is declared, whereas a Public procedure can be seen from everywhere.

A procedure has to be Public for it to be called from the Immediate window. A Private procedure is only visible to other procedures in the same module. So if you are creating Private procedures and you need to test them from the Immediate window, you will have to change them to Public to test them. Don't forget to change them back though, once you've finished testing.

Let's look at these concepts in more detail.

## *Local Variables*

You have already seen local variables in the VariantExample procedure and others that you created earlier. Remember that the variables are local to the procedure, no matter where the procedure can be seen from. So local variables in a Public procedure have the same scope as local variables in a Private procedure – it is just the procedure that can be seen from outside, not the variables. This means that you can have different procedures with local variables that have the same name.

Let's have a look at some simple examples that illustrate this.

**Try It Out**     **Local Variables**

**1.** Create a new subroutine and call it Procedure1. Make sure it's a Public procedure. Enter the following lines:

```
Public Sub Procedure1()
   Dim intVariable1 As Integer
   Dim intVariable2 As Integer

   intVariable1 = 1
   intVariable2 = 2

   Debug.Print intVariable1
   Debug.Print intVariable2
End Sub
```

**2.** Now create another subroutine, a Private one this time, called Procedure2, with these lines:

```
Private Sub Procedure2()
   Dim intVariable1 As Integer

   intVariable1 = 100

   Debug.Print intVariable1
End Sub
```

**3.** Now you need a third subroutine (another Private one) called TestLocal, that calls the first two:

```
Public Sub TestLocal()
   Procedure1
   Procedure2
   Procedure1
End Sub
```

**4.** Now open the Immediate window and run the `TestLocal` subroutine:

As you can see, the variables in `Procedure1` are only seen in that procedure. Likewise with the variable in `Procedure2`. With local variables, you can have the same variable name in different procedures without them affecting each other.

**5.** Now try accessing `intVariable2` from within `Procedure2` by adding the following line before the `End Sub`:

```
Debug.Print intVariable2
```

Before running the example again, think about what you expect to happen.

Now try typing `TestLocal` in the Immediate window again. Were you surprised at receiving the error? Whether yes or no, the reason is simple. `Procedure1` declared `intVariable2` as local. Therefore, no other procedure can see the variable. Don't forget to remove this last line, otherwise it will cause error messages later.

**Try It Out    Local Scope**

Now let's look at another example to explain local scope.

**1.** Stop the module running by selecting the **Reset** button on the toolbar (the one that's a filled in square). Then create another `Public` subroutine, `TestLocal1`, and add the following lines:

```
Public Sub TestLocal1()
   Dim intVariable1 As Integer

   intVariable1 = intVariable1 + 1
   Debug.Print intVariable1
End Sub
```

Here, you are adding 1 to the variable even though it has not been used before. This is allowed, since an integer is set to 0 when first declared. This should give you a clue as to what happens when you run the program.

2. Now type TestLocal1 in the Immediate window. Now type TestLocal1 again. You should see:

You can see that intVariable1 is reset each time the procedure is called.

*Local variables only exist while a procedure has the control. When the procedure ends, local variables 'die'. When the procedure is called again, local variables are reset.*

## Static Variables

To allow a variable to retain its value over multiple calls, you must declare it as Static. This means that the variable is only initialized once – the first time the procedure is called. To declare a variable in this manner, you replace the Dim with Static:

```
Static intVariable1 As Integer
```

**Try It Out — Static Variables**

1. Create another subroutine called StaticScope. Add the same code as before, but this time change the variable declaration line from Dim to Static:

```
Public Sub StaticScope()
   Static intVariable1 As Integer

   intVariable1 = intVariable1 + 1
   Debug.Print intVariable1
End Sub
```

2. Run the subroutine several times from the Immediate window.

So, just by changing one word, you have dramatically altered the way the program works. You'll find this a useful feature; for example, you can use static variables to create a function that keeps a running total each time a new value is passed in, or one that keeps track of the number of times it has been called. This could be used, for instance, as a user name and password system for securing a system. You could limit the user to three tries before shutting the system down.

If you want all variables in a procedure to be static, just put `Static` before the procedure declaration:

```
Static Sub AllVariablesAreStatic ()
```

All variables within that procedure will now be `Static` irrespective of whether they are declared with `Static` or `Dim`.

# Global Variables

If you need other procedures to see your variables, you can use a global variable, defined in the (Declarations) section of a module. These are known as **module-level** variables. There are two types of global variables:

- ❑ Those that can be seen by every procedure in the module but can not be seen outside of the module. These are module-level **private** variables. You declare these using the `Private` keyword.

- ❑ Those that can be seen everywhere in the program, even outside of the module. These are called **public** variables. You declare these using the `Public` keyword.

## Private Variables

We will create an example here to clarify the principle of a module-level private variable.

## Try It Out — Module Variables

We'll create two subroutines called TestProc1 and TestProc2 within the same module that you've been using throughout this chapter.

**1.** Move to the (Declarations) section of the module window and enter the following line under the Option statements:

```
Private intModuleVariable As Integer
```

**2.** Now add the code to the new subroutine, TestProc1, as follows:

```
Public Sub TestProc1

    intModuleVariable = intModuleVariable + 1

End Sub
```

**3.** Now add the code to the new subroutine TestProc2, as follows:

```
Public Sub TestProc2

    Debug.Print intModuleVariable

End Sub
```

**4.** Try calling the two procedures from the Immediate window to see what happens:

Here you can see that although neither procedure declared intModuleVariable, they can both access it. However, procedures in other modules or forms will not be able to access it.

*A module- or form-level variable has the scope of the module or form. If, for example, you declare a variable in the (Declarations) section of a form, all procedures in that form will have access to it. When the form is unloaded, the variable and its contents will die and will be reset when the form is next loaded.*

**5.** Now add a third new procedure `TestProc3`, as follows:

```
Public Sub TestProc3
   Dim intModuleVariable As Integer
   intModuleVariable = 100
   Debug.Print intModuleVariable
End Sub
```

This declares `intModuleVariable` as a local variable when you already have it as a module-level variable.

**6.** Run through the procedure again to see what happens:

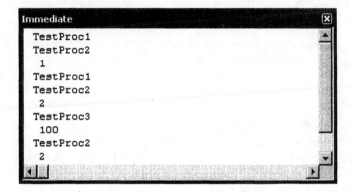

The call to `TestProc3` does not change its own (separate) variable `intModuleVariable`, but also does not affect the public `intModuleVariable` variable. Only its own copy is in scope within the procedure.

So, not only can you have procedures with local variables of the same name, but you can also have local variables with the same names as public ones. In this case, the procedure with the local variable will always use its own variable, rather than the global one. You can probably see that it is not a very good idea to create local and public variables with the same name, as it can lead to confusion when looking at the code later. It is much better practice to use different names for your variables.

## Public Variables

A public variable is one that can be accessed from all modules and forms. They can only be created in modules, not within the (`Declarations`) section of a form. To declare a public variable, replace the `Private` keyword with `Public`:

```
Public intModuleVariable As Integer
```

This variable is now accessible to all modules and forms and has a lifetime until the database is closed.

You cannot declare `Public` variables within a procedure.

### Public vs. Private

There are some general principles that you should bear in mind when deciding on the scope and lifetime of your variables:

❏ Unless you are writing a general routine, make procedures private. This is especially true if you are developing in teams or writing add-ins, as then there is no danger of your procedure clashing with another of the same name. However, you should never really have more than one procedure with the same name. The names of procedures should actually be decided at the design time, specifically to avoid this sort of confusion.

❏ Wherever possible, you should avoid manipulating variables that are declared outside a procedure. Instead, pass the value of the variable into the procedure using an argument. Inside the procedure, you can perform the calculations required and return the new value to the code that calls it. This not only protects you from errors that are difficult to find, but also makes your procedures far more generic and reusable.

❏ Use public variables sparingly and with care. You will generally find that only a small number of public variables are used in most programs. It is sometimes much easier to use a public variable than to have the same variable declared in several procedures and passed as a parameter. However, do not always take the easy route. Think about how a variable is going to be used and try to plan ahead.

# Summary

This chapter has covered an awful lot of ground, but it's really important stuff. The techniques we've looked at are the building blocks of programming. Every program is made up from procedures, and these all use variables, other procedures, built-in functions, and so on. Having a good understanding of this will make it easier to understand other code that you see, as well as making your own code better.

In this chapter, we looked at:

❏ What procedures and functions are. They are small sections of code that perform a task. Sometimes that task may be small, and other times it may be quite large, but the chunk of code is usually a logical unit, with a defined purpose. Making ice cream and making frozen yogurt are two separate tasks, although their procedures might be similar.

❏ Naming conventions, to show the importance of consistency. As you see more and more code, this can ease your understanding, as well as making it quicker to maintain.

❑ What variables are, and how they can be used. Variables are where we store temporary information during a procedure. They allow us to store and manipulate different types of data.

❑ The scope (where the variable can be seen from) and lifetime (how long the variable keeps its value) of variables. It's important to always think about how great a scope you want for each variable, and how their lifetime will affect the code you're writing.

Now that you've got a good understanding of these techniques, let's move on to look at how we can make decisions in our code, and use looping to help us with repetitive tasks.

# CHAPTER 4

# Controlling the Program

Most of the procedures that you have seen so far have been fairly simple – they start at the first line, finish at the last, and execute the lines in between one after the other. However, there are times when you want to run only one section of code, or perhaps run a section of code more than once, depending on certain conditions. To do this, you have to introduce **control structures** into your code. These are what we'll look at in this chapter.

We'll cover:

- ❑ How to make decisions in a program
- ❑ How to perform repetitive tasks
- ❑ How to store variables in an array
- ❑ The difference between static and dynamic arrays

## Programming Structures

There are three main structures that are used in programming. Firstly, **sequential**, where we need to do things one after the other, or in a certain order. We saw some of that in the previous chapter, and you'll see plenty more as we go through the book. Next comes **selection**, where we often need to make a choice based upon some piece of information, so we either do one thing or another. Lastly comes looping, or **repetition**, where we do the same thing over and over again.

# Expressions

With VBA, you can check something and perform different operations depending on the results of the check. This check is usually called a **condition** or an **expression**. An expression always has a Boolean result – that is, it's either `True` or `False`. The easy way to think about expressions is to just think about everyday decisions, like 'Do I want to open a large tub of ice cream?' That's probably going to be `True` (it is for me, anyway). You are not limited to just one statement – how about 'Do I want to stop work and open a large tub of ice cream?' Here, we've got two statements.

When dealing with multiple statements you generally join them together, either by an `And` or by an `Or`. In the above example we used `And`, which means that both statements have to be True for the whole expression to be `True`. If you want to stop work but don't feel like ice cream at the moment, then the expression is `False`. If we had used `Or`, then only one of the statements needed to have been `True` for the whole expression to be `True`. 'Do I want to stop work `Or` do I want to open a large tub of ice cream?'

When joining statements together in expressions, the rule is quite simple:

❑ If you use `Or` to join the statements, then only one statement has to be `True` for the expression to be `True`.

❑ If you use `And` to join the statements, then all statements have to be `True` for the expression to be `True`.

You can also mix the two types of statements. 'Do I want to stop work and open a large tub of ice cream, or do I want a cup of coffee?'

You'll see plenty of expressions as we go through this chapter, and we'll be revisiting them again in a little while, once we've looked at how we make decisions.

# Decision Structures

We know that everyday life has many decisions, and VBA code often has plenty of them too. We use decision structures to make those decisions; these structures are the VBA statements that mean we can perform one task or another.

## If...Then...

We've already come across this statement back when we were creating an intelligent navigation button. We'll now take a look at the structure of the statement and then run through a couple of examples. You use `If...Then` when you want to execute a piece of code only when a certain statement is true. It has two formats; the single line format is as follows:

```
If expression Then statement
```

The multi-line format runs like this:

```
If expression Then
   statement1
   statement2
End If
```

Both of the above perform the same operation. (The second example, however, allows more than one line as the statement). For example:

```
If strName = "" Then Exit Function
```

is the same as:

```
If strName = "" Then
   Exit Function
End If
```

Here, you test whether the argument strName is an empty string (denoted by the two double quotes together), and if so, exit the function directly.

The expression can also contain other functions:

```
Sub Test()

   Dim strNumber As String

   strNumber = "1234"

   If IsNumeric(strNumber) Then
      Debug.Print strNumber & " is a number"
   End If

   strNumber = "one two three four"

   If IsNumeric(strNumber) Then
      Debug.Print strNumber & " is a number"
   End If

End Sub
```

The function IsNumeric returns a value of True if the string passed in is a number. The above code would print out the following:

    1234 is a number

There would be nothing printed for the second example If statement because the string passed in does not contain a number.

## *If...Then...Else...*

You can use the `If...Then...Else...` statement to decide which of two actions to perform. Let's revisit our number test, adding in a few lines:

```
Sub Test()

   Dim strNumber As String

   strNumber = "1234"

   If IsNumeric(strNumber) Then
      Debug.Print strNumber & " is a number"
   Else
      Debug.Print strNumber & " is not a number"
   End If

   strNumber = "one two three four"

   If IsNumeric(strNumber) Then
      Debug.Print strNumber & " is a number"
   Else
      Debug.Print strNumber & " is not a number"
   End If

End Sub
```

Here we test the string to see if it contains a number. If it does, we run the code as before. If the string is not a number, then we run some other code. This would produce:

**1234 is a number**
**one two three four is not a number**

You can include variables and numerical and relational operators in your expressions too:

```
Dim intAbc As Integer
Dim intDef As Integer
Dim strName As String

intAbc = 1
intDef = 2
strName = "Janine"

If intAbc = 1 Then Debug.Print "Abc is 1"
If intAbc = intDef Then Debug.Print "Two variables the same"
If intAbc > intDef Then Debug.Print "Abc is greater than Def"
If intAbc + 1 = intDef Then Debug.Print "Adding 1 to Abc gives Def"
if strName = "Janine" Then Debug.Print "Hello Jan"
```

*Note that you can use any normal arithmetic operators within an If statement, such as +, -, \*, /, or the relational operators <, >, = in conjunction with variables and values, to determine whether or not a condition is true.*

# ElseIf...

The `ElseIf` statement is used for joining a set of `If` conditions together. This is quite common when you need to check the results of several different conditions:

```
If intAbc = 1 Then
   Debug.Print "Abc is 1"
ElseIf intAbc = intDef Then
   Debug.Print "Two variables the same"
Else
   Debug.Print "Abc is not 1 and it is not the same as Def"
End If
```

If the first condition is true, then only the code between the `Then` statement and the `ElseIf` is executed and no more conditions are tested. If the first condition isn't true, the second is tried. If that isn't true, the `Else` statement is executed.

# Logical Operators with the If statement

You can also make more complex queries with this statement by using logical operators. The three most common logical operators are `And`, `Or` and `Not`. You can use these to test a combination of expressions together to get a true or false answer. The answer is calculated via a set of truth tables which are applied for each operator:

| AND | Expression 1 | Expression 2 | Result |
|-----|--------------|--------------|--------|
| | TRUE | TRUE | TRUE |
| | TRUE | FALSE | FALSE |
| | FALSE | TRUE | FALSE |
| | FALSE | FALSE | FALSE |

| OR | Expression 1 | Expression 2 | Result |
|----|--------------|--------------|--------|
| | TRUE | TRUE | TRUE |
| | TRUE | FALSE | TRUE |
| | FALSE | TRUE | TRUE |
| | FALSE | FALSE | FALSE |

| NOT | Expression | Result |
|-----|------------|--------|
| | TRUE | FALSE |
| | FALSE | TRUE |

**149**

It's as easy, though, to use common sense to deduce what the answer should be. Think of it in terms of the English language; for example, if you break the speed limit OR you rob a bank, it's true that you've broken the law. Let's look at the earlier example to make the criteria slightly more complex.

```
Dim intAbc As Integer
Dim intDef As Integer
Dim strName As String

intAbc = 1
intDef = 2
strName = "Janine"

If intAbc = 1 And intDef = 2 Then Debug.Print "Abc is 1 and Def is 2"
If intAbc = 1 Or intDef = 2 Then Debug.Print "Either Abc is 1 or Def is 2"
```

# Select Case

There's no limit to the number of `ElseIf` statements that you can have:

```
If datOrderDate >= #7/1/02# Then
...
ElseIf datOrderDate >= #6/1/02# And datOrderDate <= #6/30/02# Then
...
ElseIf datOrderDate < #6/1/02# Then
...
Else
...
End If
```

*Remember that the # sign around the dates just tells VBA that this is a date value, otherwise VBA would take 6/1/02 as 6 divided by 1 divided by 2.*

You can see that the code is starting to look messy. There's a much better way – using the `Select Case` statement:

```
Select Case datOrderDate
Case Is >= #7/1/02#
   MsgBox "Your order was placed during or after July, 2002"
Case #6/1/02# To #6/30/02#
   MsgBox "Thank you for your June, 2002 order."
   ...
Case Else
   ...
End Select
```

This is much clearer to read. If datOrderDate is equal to or after the 1st of July then the section of code under the first Case statement would be executed. The second Case statement checks for datOrderDate being from June 1st to June 30th, and any code within the Case Else will be run if datOrderDate is any other date. Adding a Case Else statement is not compulsory, but it's always a good idea to include one, just in case the variable you are testing has an unexpected value. Even if you don't think you need a Case Else, it's best to put one in anyway, and put an error message there. That way, if some unexpected value appears you'll know about it, and be able to act accordingly.

You can also test for more than one value with Case:

```
Select Case intMainCount
Case 1, 2, 3
...
Case 4 To 6
...
Case Else
...
End Select
```

This shows two different ways of testing the condition. If intMainCount is 1, 2, or 3, the first section is executed. If it's between 4 and 6 inclusive, the second section is executed, and so on. You can achieve the same result using the Is keyword and an expression:

```
Select Case intMainCount
Case Is < 4
...
Case Is < 7
...
Case Else
...
End Select
```

Here, if intMainCount is less than 4, the first section is executed, and so on.

*Note that, as soon as a true expression is found in a Select Case statement, no more expressions are checked. An expression must fail one test to get to the next. This means that if you have an expression that matches two Case statements, only the first will be executed.*

Select Case isn't limited to numeric tests – you can also use strings:

```
Select Case strSalutation
Case "Mrs", "Miss", "Ms"
...
Case "Mr"
...
```

```
   Case Else
   ...
   End Select
```

You can also use the To form with strings:

```
   Case "Alfred" To "Bertrand"
```

This would be executed if the condition matched any string within the range specified. Don't be put off by the fact the string has a range – strings are checked in alphabetical order, so Alfred comes before Bertrand. They can be tested alphabetically, so a value such as Basil would be accepted in such a condition, while Roy would be excluded.

As you can see, not only is the Select Case statement very flexible, but it can also greatly increase the clarity of your code. Let's give this a go:

## Try It Out — Select Case

1. Create a new module, or if you are using the complete database go into the **Chapter 04 Code** module.

2. Create a new procedure called Seat, to find out where we are sitting on a plane. Add the following code:

```
Public Sub Seat(ByVal strSeatNumber As String)

   Dim intRow As Integer
   Dim strSeat As String

   intRow = CInt(Left(strSeatNumber, 2))
   strSeat = Right(strSeatNumber, 1)

   Select Case intRow
   Case 1
     Debug.Print "At the front eh? Must be the pilot"
   Case 2 To 5
     Debug.Print "First Class - a lottery winner"
   Case 6 To 10
     Debug.Print "Business Class - on a business trip"
   Case 11 To 54
     Debug.Print "Cattle Class - squeeze up now"
   Case Else
     Debug.Print "No seat - must be on the tail!"
   End Select

   Select Case strSeat
   Case "a" To "c"
```

```
      Debug.Print "To the left of the plane"
   Case "d" To "g"
      Debug.Print "In the middle"
   Case "h" To "j"
      Debug.Print "To the right of the plane"
   Case Else
      Debug.Print "In the aisle"
   End Select

End Sub
```

**3.** Switch to the Immediate window and try it out with a few seat numbers. These should have a two-digit row and a single character seat.

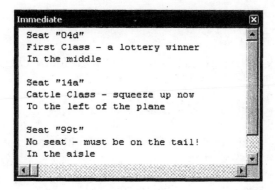

Firstly we have two variables, to store the row number and the seat letter.

```
Dim intRow As Integer
Dim strSeat As String
```

Before we can decide where you are sitting, we need to work out the row number. We use Left for this, which extracts the leftmost characters from a string. Here, we are extracting the two characters at the left of the strings, as these will be the row number. We assign this to the integer variable, allowing VBA to automatically convert the string containing numbers into an integer number.

```
intRow = Left(strSeatNumber, 2)
```

We then use Right for a similar purpose, this time to extract the very rightmost character from the string. This will be the seat number.

```
strSeat = Right(strSeatNumber, 1)
```

Now we can go ahead with our `Select` statement, first checking the row number. The first case will only happen if the row number is 1:

```
Select Case intRow
Case 1
   Debug.Print "At the front eh? Must be the pilot"
```

If the row is between 2 and 5 inclusive then the second case is run:

```
Case 2 To 5
   Debug.Print "First Class - a lottery winner"
```

For seats including 6 to 10 we have the third case:

```
Case 6 To 10
   Debug.Print "Business Class - on a business trip"
```

For the seats at the back of the plane, 11 through to 54, the fourth case is run:

```
Case 11 To 54
   Debug.Print "Cattle Class - squeeze up now"
```

If your row number is anything else then I hope you brought a coat, as it's quite windy on the tail!

```
Case Else
   Debug.Print "No seat - must be on the tail!"
End Select
```

Once the row number is decided, you can find out which side of the plane you are on. Seats a to c are on the left, d to g are in the middle, and h to j are on the right.

```
Select Case strSeat
Case "a" To "c"
   Debug.Print "To the left of the plane"
Case "d" To "g"
   Debug.Print "In the middle"
Case "h" To "j"
   Debug.Print "To the right of the plane"
Case Else
   Debug.Print "In the aisle"
End Select
```

You can easily see how much clearer this is than if we had used `If` statements.

# IIf

There are certain places (such as in queries, but more on that later) where you need to be able to return one of two values, but you can't use the If statement. In these cases, you can use the **immediate if**, or IIf:

```
strName = "Janine"

strWhoAreYou = IIf (strName = "Janine", "Hi Jan", "Who are you?")
```

The IIf statement takes three arguments:

- ❑ The condition to test for
- ❑ The value to return if the condition was True
- ❑ The value to return if the condition was False

So, the statement below is exactly the same as the If statement above:

```
If strName = "Janine" Then
  strWhoAreYou = "Hi Jan"
Else
  strWhoAreYou = "Who are you?"
End If
```

Some people prefer using the IIf since it looks slightly neater, as it's all on one line, but it can be a cause of confusion, especially for new programmers. There is also a major drawback you have to be aware of. When using the IIf statement, all three arguments are evaluated by VBA. "So what?" you may ask. Consider the following examples, where we divide one number by another:

```
Public Function Divide (ByVal intNumber1 As Integer, ByVal intNumber2 As
Integer) As Double

  If intNumber2 = 0 Then
    Divide = 0
  Else
    Divide = intNumber1 / intNumber2
  End If

End Function
```

```
Public Function Divide (ByVal intNumber1 As Integer, ByVal intNumber2 As
Integer) As Double

  Divide = IIf (intNumber2 = 0, 0, intNumber1 / intNumber2)

End Function
```

The two functions look as though they should work the same, but this isn't the case. If intNumber2 is 0, the second version will give a Divide by Zero error because intNumber1 / intNumber2 is always evaluated. You must bear this in mind when you use IIf.

Because IIf evaluates all the arguments, it's slower to use than the normal If statement. Admittedly, you'll probably never notice this, but if you were to use IIf in a large loop, that small delay would gradually build up. You might not think that a small delay is a problem, but you can be sure that your users will think otherwise!

The real use for IIf is in queries and on forms and reports. You'll see examples of this later in the book.

## *Operator Precedence*

When combining conditions and expressions, it's very important that you understand operator precedence. This defines the order in which parts of an expression are evaluated and is similar to the lessons that you learnt in mathematics when you were at school. The rules are recapped below and may, at first, seem complex, but do persevere. There are some examples later to make everything clear.

When operators from more than one category are combined in an expression, arithmetic operators are evaluated first, comparison operators next, and logical operators last. The order of operator evaluation is shown below, from top downwards:

| Arithmetic | Arithmetic Symbol |
|---|---|
| Exponentiation | ^ |
| Negation | - |
| Multiplication and Division | * / |
| Integer division | \ |
| Modulo arithmetic | Mod |
| Addition and Subtraction | + - |
| String concatenation | & |

Some miscellaneous points are:

❑ All comparison operators, such as =, <, and Like, have equal precedence, the same level as addition and subtraction. This means that they are evaluated from left to right as they appear in expressions.

❑   Arithmetic operators with the same precedence are also evaluated from left to right.

❑   Operations within parentheses (brackets, like this) are always performed before those outside. This means that you can force the order in which evaluation takes place by using parentheses. However, normal precedence is maintained within the parentheses.

If that all sounds rather complex, don't worry. Here are some examples to help you.

You have four numbers: A, B, C, and D, and you want to multiply the sum of A and B by the sum of C and D:

```
A = 1
B = 2
C = 3
D = 4

E = A + B * C + D
```

This doesn't produce 21, but 11, as multiplication has a higher precedence than addition. What happens is that B and C are multiplied, then A and D are added. To correct this, use:

```
E = (A + B) * (C + D)
```

This forces the additions to be performed first. In the example below, the parentheses have no effect (although, to some, they make the intention clearer):

```
E = A * B + C * D
```

```
E = (A * B) + (C * D)
```

With expressions in If statements, you have to follow a similar set of rules for using And and Or. You can liken And to * and Or to + in the previous examples, since And has a higher order of precedence. For example, consider the following, where A, B, C, and D are all integers, all with the value of 1:

```
If A = 1 Or B = 1 And C = 1 Or D = 1 Then
```

This expression will be True if any of these conditions are True:

❑   A is equal to 1

❑   B is equal to 1 and C is equal to 1

❑   D is equal to 1

However, consider the expression if we add parentheses:

```
If (A = 1 Or B = 1) And (C = 1 Or D = 1) Then
```

This expression will be True only if these conditions are True:

❑   Either A is equal to 1 or B is equal to 1

❑   Either C is equal to 1 or D is equal to 1

This is a fairly simplistic example, but you can clearly see the differences between the two sets of expressions. Most of the time, you will find that your expressions are more advanced, but it's important to know what happens when things get more complicated.

*If you are at all unsure of the order of precedence of an expression, use parentheses to force your meaning. If the order was correct anyway, then you won't have lost anything, plus you will have made your code clearer.*

# Repetition

We've now considered how to deal with conditions but, sometimes, you need to go through a portion of code several times to arrive at a certain condition. Performing repetitive tasks that would otherwise drive the user crazy is one of the best programming tricks on offer. You don't want to know if your computer has to check a database with 10,000 entries, adding an extra 1 to every international phone number each time the codes are changed; you only want to know when it's finished.

## Loops

VBA provides the For...Next and Do...Loop statements for this purpose. A loop is a piece of code that is executed repeatedly while or until a certain condition is met. We'll have a look at both these structures.

### For...Next

The For...Next loop is useful when you know how many times you want to execute the statements within the loop:

```
For intLoop = 1 To 10
...
Next
```

This starts the intLoop at 1 and then executes the code between the For and Next statements. When the Next is reached, VBA moves you back to the For statement and adds 1 to intLoop. This continues until intLoop is greater than 10.

The basic syntax is shown below:

```
For counter = start To end [Step increment]
...
Next [counter]
```

where the terms are defined as:

| Argument | Description |
| --- | --- |
| counter | The variable you assign to the loop |
| start | The number with which you wish to start the loop |
| end | The number with which to stop the loop |
| increment | The number you add to start each time round the loop (this is optional, and defaults to 1 if you omit the Step section) |

The argument increment can be either positive or negative, allowing loops to count both up and down. (If you leave out the Step and increment part of a For...Next loop, Access will assume that you just want to increment the value by one each time). For example, to get just the odd numbers you could do this:

```
For intLoop = 1 To 10 Step 2
```

Here, instead of adding 1 to intLoop every time the loop is run, VBA adds 2.

The counter after the Next statement is also optional and is usually left out. This isn't a bad thing but, if you have loops within loops, you may find that using the complete format is clearer, since you can easily see to which loop a Next statement refers. For example, imagine three loops within each other:

```
For intX = 1 To 10
  For intY = 1 To 10
    For intZ = 1 To 10
      ...
    Next intZ
  Next intY
Next intX
```

Here you can see exactly which Next statement belongs to which For statement. If you indent the code as a disciplined programmer (as shown above), even in nested loops it is easy to see which Next statement belongs to which For statement. Ultimately it boils down to personal preference, but do follow a partcular style consistently.

## Do...Loop

The For...Next loop is ideal if you know how many times the loop is to be executed. There are occasions, however, when you want to perform loops until a certain condition is met. For those cases, you should use Do...Loop:

```
intSpeed = 0
intAcceleration = 5
Do Until intSpeed > 55
    intSpeed = intSpeed + intAcceleration
Loop
```

This executes until the variable intSpeed is greater than 55. If the variable is already greater than 55, the loop isn't entered and the code isn't executed. There is a second form of this loop, however, which allows you to test the condition at the end of the loop instead of at the beginning:

```
Do
    intSpeed = intSpeed + intAcceleration
Loop Until intSpeed > 55
```

This is basically the same as the previous example, but the code in the loop is always executed at least once. Even if intSpeed is greater than 55 when the loop is first started, the code in the loop is still executed once. This may cause errors if intSpeed is being used in other expressions.

You can also replace the Until with While, which allows loops to be performed *while* a condition is True, rather than *until* it is True. For example:

```
Do
    intSpeed = intSpeed + intAcceleration
Loop While intSpeed < 55
```

This performs the same task as the Until version, but the condition is reversed, because now we want to continue the loop While the expression is True, not Until it is True. Which version you use is up to you, and may depend upon the expression and how easy it is to read.

> You should always be careful about the conditions, because you can generate endless loops. This occurs when the loop test never becomes True (for Do...Until loops) or never stops being True (for Do...While loops). If you suspect that this is happening you can press *Ctrl-Break* to halt your code.

# Nested Control Structures

We have only looked at single control structures so far, but VBA does allow you to **nest** them (putting one structure inside another). Here is a trivial function that executes a loop ten times and uses the Mod function (which divides two numbers and returns the remainder) to determine whether the loop counter intLoop is odd or even:

```
Sub OddEven()

    Dim intLoop As Integer
    Dim intMainCount As Integer
    Dim strOutFinal As String

    intMainCount = 10

    For intLoop = 1 To intMainCount
        If (intLoop Mod 2 = 0) Then
            strOutFinal = "Even"
        Else
            strOutFinal = "Odd"
        End If
        Debug.Print intLoop, strOutFinal
    Next

End Sub
```

Here, the If structure is nested inside the For...Next loop. The code for both structures is indented to make it clear where they start and end. There's no limit to the amount of nesting that can be performed, but if you nest too many loops you'll find that your code becomes almost impossible to read (unless you've got a very wide monitor). If you need more than three or four levels of nesting, you should consider restructuring your code – perhaps by creating a new procedure, or maybe just by adjusting your tab width.

# Exiting a Control Structure

The loops that we have looked at so far have all started and stopped at set places. Suppose, though, that because of some action that took place in a loop, you need to exit it straight away, without reaching the condition that normally terminates it. In this case, you can use the Exit *structure* statement. For example:

```
For intLoop = -1 To 10
    If (intLoop = 6) Then
        Exit For
    End If
    Debug.Print intLoop
Next
```

If the condition on the `If` line is true, (that is, if `intLoop` equals 6), the `Exit For` statement immediately exits from the loop, rather than waiting until `intLoop` is larger than 10.

You can also use the `Exit Sub` or `Exit Function` statement to immediately exit a procedure:

```
If strInName = "" Then Exit Function
```

This will directly exit the function if `strInName` is an empty string.

You'll now have a good idea of the power and versatility that a loop can offer. However, loops can also serve another very useful purpose which we will look at now. They can be used to populate **arrays**.

# Arrays

Your first question is probably, "What is an array?" Earlier, we said that variables are just temporary storage. If you think of a variable as a can of cola, then you can think of an array as a six-pack of cola. They are collections of variables, all with the same name and the same data type. Elements in an array are identified by their index – a number indicating their position in the array.

Arrays are used for collecting together a number of similar variables. Variables themselves are useful for holding specific information about a certain object, property, or value. For example, if you want to store a number suggested by the user, you can create a variable to hold that value and then assign the value to the variable. These are the two lines of code that you might use to do that:

```
Dim intNum As Integer
intNum = InputBox("Please enter guess number 1", "Guess!")
```

The first line of code declares the variable as an integer. That is to say that the variable `intNum` will be able to hold any whole number between -32,768 and +32,767.

The second line of code assigns to the variable a number that has to be entered by the user. If you wanted the user to enter two numbers and you wanted to store the two values concurrently, you could create two variables as shown in the code below:

```
'Declare variables
Dim iNum As Integer
Dim iNum2 As Integer

'Assign values to variables
iNum = InputBox("Please enter guess number 1", "Guess!")
iNum2 = InputBox("Please enter guess number 2", "Guess!")
```

What if you want the user to be able to make five guesses... or twenty... or more? The answer is that your code could become very lengthy and repetitive. Given that the potential number of bugs in any program usually increases in proportion to the number of lines of code, you probably won't want to use the method shown above. What you need is a method for storing a collection of related variables together. That's just what an array provides.

The following are examples of items of data that you may want to collect in an array:

- ❑ The values of ten guesses made by the user

- ❑ Each individual letter making up a single string

- ❑ The enabled property of a number of different command buttons on a form

- ❑ The values of all the controls on a specific form

To show this at work, let's rewrite the code above to allow the user to make 10 initial guesses:

**Try It Out — Declaring and Populating an Array**

**1.** Open `IceCream.mdb` if it's not open already, and select the Modules tab from the database window. Open your module for the chapter and enter the following code:

```
Public Sub ArrayExample()

    Dim i As Integer
    Dim intNum(1 To 10) As Integer

    For i = 1 To 10
        intNum(i) = InputBox("Please enter guess " & i, "Guess!")
    Next i

    For i = 1 To 10
        Debug.Print "Guess number " & i & " = " & intNum(i)
    Next i

End Sub
```

**2.** Run the `ArrayExample` procedure by typing `ArrayExample` in the Immediate window and hitting the *Enter* key. You'll be prompted to enter ten integers. Once you have entered the last of the ten integers, all ten will be displayed.

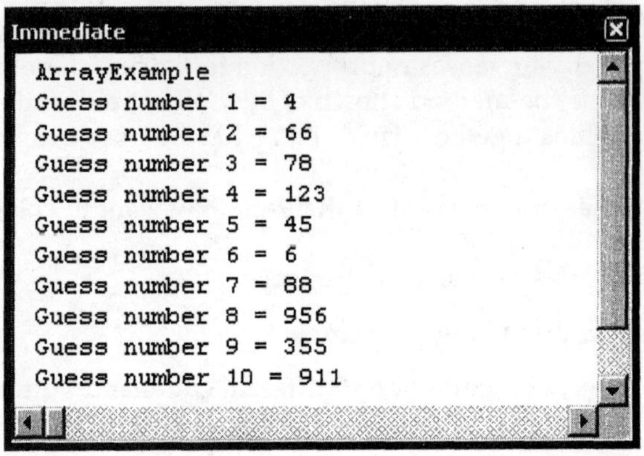

```
Immediate                                        [X]
ArrayExample
Guess number 1 = 4
Guess number 2 = 66
Guess number 3 = 78
Guess number 4 = 123
Guess number 5 = 45
Guess number 6 = 6
Guess number 7 = 88
Guess number 8 = 956
Guess number 9 = 355
Guess number 10 = 911
```

## How It Works

Declaring an array is easy. We simply place parentheses indicating the array's dimensions after its name. So whereas this:

```
Dim intNum As Integer
```

declares an `Integer` type variable called `intNum`, this:

```
Dim intNum (1 To 10) As Integer
```

declares an array of ten `Integer` type variables called `intNum`. This tells VBA that `intNum` is to hold ten separate values, each of which will be a whole number between -32,768 and 32,767.

Note that an array need not hold `Integer` type variables. An array can hold any of the following data types:

- ❑ Integer
- ❑ Long
- ❑ Single
- ❑ Double
- ❑ Variant
- ❑ Currency
- ❑ String
- ❑ Boolean
- ❑ Byte
- ❑ Date

❑   Hyperlink

❑   Object

❑   User Defined Types

However, all elements of the array must be of the same data type. In other words, one array will not be able to store both strings and integers (although it could store `Variant` type variables with differing subtypes).

```
For i = 1 To 10
  intNum(i) = InputBox("Please enter guess" & i, "Guess!")
Next i
```

Now all that's needed is to populate the ten elements of the array with guesses from the user. Individual elements of the array are identified by their index (the number which appears in parentheses after the variable's name) so we create a simple `For...Next` loop and use the loop counter – in this case, the variable `i` – to refer to the elements of the array.

The ten elements of the `intNum` array are referred to as `intNum(1)`, `intNum(2)`, `intNum(3)`, ...`intNum(10)`.

```
intNum(i) = InputBox("Please enter guess " & i, "Guess!")
```

To make this rather tedious task easier on the user, we have also used the loop counter, `i`, to indicate to the user how many guesses they have had:

```
For i = 1 To 10
  Debug.Print "Guess number " & i & " = " & intNum(i)
Next i
```

Having stored the results of all the guesses in an array, we then loop through the elements of the array to display the results in the debug window.

Note that if we wanted to allow the user to make twenty guesses instead of ten, we need only alter three lines of code. In fact, we could reduce this to one line by replacing the value 10 in the code above with the constant `ciNumberOfGuesses`. The procedure would then look like this:

```
Sub ArrayExampleWithConstant()

  Const ciNumberOfGuesses = 10
  Dim i As Integer
  Dim intNum(1 To ciNumberOfGuesses) As Integer

  For i = 1 To ciNumberOfGuesses
    intNum(i) = InputBox("Please enter guess " & i, "Guess!")
  Next i
```

```
    For i = 1 To ciNumberOfGuesses
        Debug.Print "Guess number " & i & " = " & intNum(i)
    Next i

End Sub
```

To change the number of guesses that the user is allowed, we now need only to change the value of `ciNumberOfGuesses`.

# Static Arrays

The examples above all made use of **static arrays**. That is to say, the number of elements in the array was fixed when the array was first declared. When you declare an array in this manner, the number of elements can't be changed.

> Don't confuse static arrays with static variables. A static variable is one which has been declared with the `Static` statement and preserves its values between calls. A static array is one whose dimensions are fixed when it is declared.

Static (that is, fixed-dimension) arrays can be declared with any of the following statements `Dim`, `Static`, `Private`, or `Public`.

For example, typing the following in the `Declarations` section of a form's code module would declare an array with a fixed number of elements which would be visible to all procedures in that form:

```
Option Compare Database
Option Explicit

Private intNum(1 To 10) As Integer
```

Whereas the following, if typed in the `Declarations` section of a standard code module, would declare an array with a fixed number of elements which was visible to all procedures throughout all code modules, forms, and reports.

```
Option Compare Database
Option Explicit

Public intNum(1 To 10) As Integer
```

After you have created a static array, the elements of the array are initialized. All that means is that VBA gives these elements default values. The values with which they are initialized depend on the data type of the elements.

| Data type | Initialization value |
|-----------|---------------------|
| Any numeric | 0 |
| String (variable length) | Zero-length string (" ") |
| String (fixed length) | A fixed-length string of `Chr$(0)` characters |
| Variant | `Empty` |

## *Upper and Lower Bounds*

The bounds of an array are its lowest and highest indexes. The lower bound of an array can be set to any integer value (but we usually set it to 0). Had we wanted to, we could have typed:

```
Dim intNum(23 to 32) As Integer
```

This would also have given us an array which could hold a maximum of ten integers, but whose index would run from 23 to 32. To populate this array, we could use the following For...Next loop:

```
For i = 23 To 32
  intNum(i) = ...
Next i
```

Alternatively, if we had wished, we could have omitted the lower bound and typed instead:

```
Dim intNum(10) As Integer
```

However, you should note that, if you do not explicitly specify a lower bound, Access will use 0 as the lower bound. In other words, the line of code above is evaluated as:

```
Dim intNum(0 to 10) As Integer
```

This means that the array intNum() will be able to hold eleven values.

If you want Access to use 1 instead of 0 as the default lower bound for arrays, you should include the following line of code in the Declarations section of the code module:

```
Option Base 1
```

Just so you know, you can no longer change the option base to anything other than 0 in the newer VB.NET. For this reason, it's probably not good practice in VBA.

## Dynamic Arrays

You may not know at the outset how many elements are required in your array. In this case, you should declare a **dynamic** array. You do this by placing **empty** parentheses after the array name you can still use the `Dim`, `Static`, `Private`, or `Public` keywords. The `ReDim` statement is then used later in the procedure to dynamically set the lower and upper bounds of the array.

For example, we could modify our original procedure to allow the user to specify how many guesses they want:

**Try It Out**    **Dynamic Arrays**

**1.** Create a new procedure called `DynamicArrayExample` with the following code:

```
Sub DynamicArrayExample()

  Dim i As Integer
  Dim intGuessCount As Integer
  Dim intNum() As Integer

  intGuessCount = InputBox("How many guesses do you want?")

  ReDim intNum(1 To intGuessCount)

  For i = 1 To intGuessCount
    intNum(i) = InputBox("Please enter guess " & i, _
      "Guess!")
  Next i

  For i = 1 To intGuessCount
    Debug.Print "Guess number " & i & " = " & intNum(i)
  Next i

End Sub
```

**2.** Switch to the Immediate window and run the procedure.

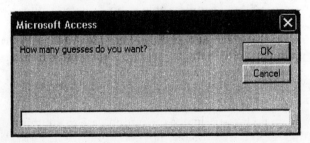

First, you're asked how many guesses you want.

**3.** Enter the number of tries you are going to have and press the OK button.

**4.** For each new dialog enter any integer (within reason!).

**5.** When you're finished you'll see the results in the Immediate window:

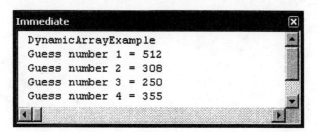

```
Immediate                                    ×
DynamicArrayExample
Guess number 1 = 512
Guess number 2 = 308
Guess number 3 = 250
Guess number 4 = 355
```

### How It Works

You've seen some of the code before, so we'll just look at the new stuff here. The first thing to notice is that in the Dim statement we don't specify how many elements the array will contain:

```
Dim intNum() As Integer
```

The next thing to do is ask the user how many guesses they want – this will determine the number of array elements:

```
intGuessCount = InputBox("How many guesses do you want?")
```

Now we have the number of elements we can use ReDim to specify the size of the array:

```
ReDim intNum(1 To intGuessCount)
```

And finally, we use the number of guesses as the maximum in the loop.

```
For i = 1 To intGuessCount
```

This technique saves having to declare a large array just because you aren't sure how many elements it's going to have. In fact you can take this one step further, and increase or decrease the size of the array as you go along, and here, you only use as much memory as you need.

**Very Dynamic Arrays**

**1.** Create another procedure called `VeryDynamicArray`, like so:

```
Public Sub VeryDynamicArray()

    Dim i As Integer
    Dim intGuess As Integer
    Dim intNum() As Integer

    ReDim intNum(0)
    i = 1

    Do
        intGuess = InputBox("Please enter guess " & i & _
            vbCr & "Use -1 to exit", "Guess!")
        If intGuess <> -1 Then
            ReDim Preserve intNum(i)
            intNum(i) = intGuess
            i = i + 1
        End If
    Loop Until intGuess = -1

    For i = 1 To UBound(intNum)
        Debug.Print "Guess number " & i & " = " & intNum(i)
    Next i

End Sub
```

**2.** Switch to the Immediate window and run this code by typing in `VeryDynamicArray` followed by the *Enter* key.

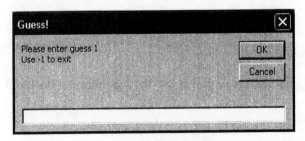

Notice that you haven't been asked how many guesses you want. You can just type in as many guesses as you like, and when you are finished you should enter –1.

**3.** Now switch back to the Immediate window to see the results:

```
Immediate                                    [x]
VeryDynamicArray
Guess number 1 = 980
Guess number 2 = 526
Guess number 3 = 399
```

## How It Works

This is quite different from the previous two examples, so we'll look at this in more detail.

The first thing is defining the variables:

```
Dim i As Integer
Dim intGuess   As Integer
Dim intNum()   As Integer
```

Then we ReDim the array to make sure it's got at least one element in it and set the initial count number. We'll need these later.

```
ReDim intNum(0)
i = 1
```

Now we can start our loop. Notice that we are using a Do loop, so we can decide at run time when to end the loop.

```
Do
```

Now we are inside the loop so we ask for our guess. We've used a constant, vbCr (carriage return), to force the string to be split onto two lines. This just makes it easier for the user to read.

```
intGuess = InputBox("Please enter guess " & i & _
    vbCr & "Use -1 to exit", "Guess!")
```

Now we check to see if the user has entered –1, as we only want to add the number to the array if they haven't:

```
If intGuess <> -1 Then
```

If they have entered a number other than –1, we do three things. First, we increase the size of the array. Notice the use of Preserve to make sure that any existing array elements are kept (we'll look at this a little later). Then we assign the new array element to the user guess, and then we increase the count number, before ending the If statement.

**171**

```
      ReDim Preserve intNum(i)
      intNum(i) = intGuess
      i = i + 1
   End If
```

Now we come to the end of the loop, and we only stop the loop if the user has entered −1.

```
Loop Until intGuess = -1
```

Now we need to print out the guesses. To find out how many times we should loop, we use UBound to find out the upper bound of the array.

```
For i = 1 To UBound(intNum)
   Debug.Print "Guess number " & i & " = " & intNum(i)
Next i
```

So, you can see that arrays are quite flexible, and you don't need to know in advance how many elements are required.

## Redimensioning Existing Arrays

The ReDim statement can also be used to change the size of a dynamic array that already has a known number of elements set by a previous ReDim statement. For example, if you have an array of ten elements, declared with the following code:

```
Dim iNum() As Integer
...
ReDim iNum(1 To 10)
```

You can reduce the number of elements in the array later in the procedure to four, with the single line of code:

```
ReDim iNum(1 To 4)
```

You might want to do this if you had a large array but now only need a small one. Reducing the size of the array will save memory.

Normally, when you change the size of an array, you lose *all* the values that were in that array – it is reinitialized. However, you can avoid this by using the Preserve keyword. The following line of code would have the same effect as the previous one, except that the values stored in iNum(1), iNum(2), iNum(3), and iNum(4) would remain unchanged.

```
ReDim Preserve iNum(1 To 4)
```

### The Dangers of ReDim

There's one important point to notice when using ReDim, which can be shown with a couple of lines of code:

```
Dim intNum() As Integer

ReDim intNun(10)
```

Notice that the variable in the second statement is different from that in the first. This can happen quite easily as a typing mistake. So what happens here? Usually when you use a variable that hasn't been declared, VBA gives you an error – but not with ReDim. This is because the ReDim command acts like a declaration if you don't use Option Explicit. In the above example this leads to two arrays, which can cause errors in your code. This actually happened to us while we were creating one of the above examples.

If you are getting errors telling you that an index is out of bounds, but you are sure you have dimensioned it correctly, then check your spelling – you might have given the wrong name to the variable in your ReDim statement. Using Option Explicit in all of your code modules will eliminate this problem.

# Summary

In this chapter we've covered the important aspects of building code into useful sequences of statements, decision structures, and loops. In the previous chapter we showed variables and their use – here we've looked at putting those variables into practice, and used them to help us control procedures.

In particular we've looked at:

❑ Using the If and Select statements to make decisions. These allow us to make our code change its behavior according to user input.

❑ Using loops to avoid unnecessarily repeating statements of code, and allowing actions to continue until user input decides otherwise.

❑ Using arrays to store several pieces of information of the same type. This allows the program to be flexible in allowing any number of user defined inputs.

Now that we've spent a while building these fundamentals it's time to start delving into Access, and the objects it controls.

# CHAPTER 5

# Using Access Objects

While using Access, you might get the impression that it's one big application. In reality, it consists of many smaller pieces, all working in harmony. These pieces are generally described as **objects**. For example, you have **tables** for storing data, **queries** that allow you to get at the data, in a specific way, and **forms** to allow the data to be displayed in a user-friendly way. These objects can also contain other objects – forms, for example, contain controls, such as text boxes and command buttons. Access allows you to program against these objects.

In this chapter, we are going to look at the different Access objects and how they provide a framework that you can use to build robust applications.

In particular we are going to look at:

- ❑ What objects are
- ❑ How they are used within Access 2002
- ❑ What collections are, and the different types available in Access
- ❑ How to use properties and methods

## Object Oriented Programming

There is much talk these days about **object-oriented programming (OOP)**, and many debates over what the term actually means. Generally, OOP perceives objects (which we will look at shortly) to be programmable representations of entities. The objects demonstrate the behavior and characteristics of the entity as methods, properties and events. By using objects to represent entities, we can more easily describe a complex system than by using traditional programming methodologies.

VBA itself is not a full OOP language because it lacks key features. However, VBA has many object-oriented aspects to aid the programmer, some of which we will be considering in this chapter. There are several reasons why object-oriented aspects have been added to many languages, not just the VBA programming language. The main problems are that traditional **procedural** languages make it hard to reuse code efficiently in other applications and, as applications become larger and more complex, maintaining and modifying procedural code becomes very tricky.

Of course, what puts many people off OOP in the first place is the obscure and esoteric terminology in which it is often described. So let's start by defining our terms.

# Objects

In the real world we use the word **object** to describe a whole number of things. A car, a computer, a house – they are all objects. An object can also be a collection of other objects: for example, a car is made up of a chassis, wheels, a transmission system and many other components which are objects in their own right.

The key thing about all these objects is that they **encapsulate** or contain everything they need to know in order to do what they do, and we don't need to know this information in order to be able to use them. In other words, when the ignition key is turned, the battery, distributor and spark plugs each know what they have to do to start the car; when the brake pedal is depressed, the braking mechanism knows what it has to do to slow the car down – it doesn't have to confer with the battery, for example. We, meanwhile, are not aware of this happening. It is the same when we use an object; its essential characteristics are what matter to us, not how it works underneath, which gives us a lot less to think about.

Likewise, in Access, a form is an object. It knows everything it needs to know in order to do what it does. When you hit the Close button, the form closes itself. When you hit the Minimize button, the form reduces itself to a minimized state. Here we see **encapsulation** or self-containment at work.

Encapsulation is one of the pillars of OOP along with **inheritance**, **polymorphism**, and **abstraction**. We'll look at each of these terms shortly, but first, we need to look more at what constitutes an object.

## Properties

All objects have **properties**. These are simply its characteristics or attributes. Just as a car has a size, weight, and color, objects have their own properties. For example, forms have a `Caption` property, a `Filter` property, a `DefaultView` property, and so on. `QueryDefs` have properties, too, for example, an `SQL` property and an `Updateable` property. You can alter the value of an object's properties, either on the property sheet in design view, or with VBA code.

## Methods

**Methods** are behavioral actions of an object. Our `car` object might have a `LightsOn` method for turning on the headlights and a `LightsOff` method for turning them off. In Access, objects have methods for performing actions. For example, among the `Database` object's methods is the `OpenRecordset` method for creating a new recordset (refer to Chapter 6 for a discussion of these methods).

## Events

**Events** are notifiable actions or occurrences that can be raised by an object. In our car analogy, a `car` object may have a `NeedToRefuel` event that is raised when the fuel level property falls to a given level or value.

## The Interface

We've said that an object encapsulates all of its inner workings so that the outside world doesn't need to worry about them. An object achieves this encapsulation with its **interface**. The interface of an object is comprised of the object's methods, properties, and events (or, being more precise, those methods, properties, and events that the object makes public; it can keep some private and hidden from other objects). The interface is essentially the view of the object provided to the outside world, and all communication to the object is achieved through the methods, properties and events that make up its interface.

## Classes

The interface – that is, the properties, methods, and events – of an object are fairly straight-forward. The next OO concept we need to introduce is slightly more unintuitive, but it's vitally important.

A **class** is a template, or blueprint, for an object. If we stick with our car analogy, then the class could be equated to the technical drawings for the car. At the blueprint stage, we don't actually have a car, just the template, and to create the car we must build it. This gives us an **instance** of a car, and if we build more cars from the same template, we have multiple instances.

The same holds true for objects. To create the object we **instantiate** the class, which creates an object based on the class template – just like building a car from the blueprints. An object's interface is defined by the blueprints contained within the class from which it is instantiated. Also, we can create or instantiate multiple instances of the same object from a single class, just as we could produce many identical cars from the same blueprints. This means we can have several objects of the same type, all instantiated (created) from the same class template. It's important to note that although these objects are instances of the same class, they are not the same object – they each exist in their own right.

Generally, if you need multiple instances of an object you have a **collection**. If you've got lots of money you might have a collection of cars, all stored in a nice air-conditioned building. A collection of objects is similar – it's a way of grouping related objects together, and letting you work on them in a similar fashion.

Classes are examined in more detail in Chapter 13.

Now we understand the concepts of objects, their interfaces (properties, methods, and events), and that you instantiate an object from a class, let's look at the other pillars of OOP – **inheritance**, **polymorphism**, and **abstraction**.

## *Inheritance*

**Inheritance** provides the ability for a object to take on the functionality of another object, without having to replicate any code. It has two forms: class inheritance and interface inheritance.

❑ **Class inheritance** is where one class inherits the code of another class. Fully object-oriented languages have class inheritance; VBA doesn't and this is one of the reasons why it is not considered a full object-oriented programming language.

❑ **Interface inheritance** is where a class inherits only the interface to the class, and then will provide all the functionality to support the interface. In other words, one class inherits a list of properties, methods, and events from another class, but not the actual code within that class which defines how each of the properties, methods, and events actually works. That code must be supplied separately. VBA offers interface inheritance.

**Polymorphism** refers to having many (poly) implementations of the same thing – we can have one method which can operate on different objects in different ways, but yet achieve the same overall goal. For example, we may have one employee object (`CarSalesperson`) with a `phoneCustomer` method which is implemented differently from the `phoneCustomer` method of another employee object (`AccountsClerk`) – the `CarSalesperson` may use a mobile phone to phone a customer, while the `AccountsClerk` may use a landline phone to phone a customer. The same named method, `phoneCustomer`, does the same thing – phone a customer – but they do it in different ways for the two different objects.

**Abstraction** in an OOP context is a way of describing the essential characteristics of an object that distinguish it from all other objects. This provides us with a hypothetical model of the object, rather than a real object. This provides us with an abstract class that can not be instantiated itself, and hence it can only be used to derived other classes from it (VBA doesn't support class abstraction). **Abstraction** may also be used in a generic context (real versus abstract), so you need to be alert to the context in which the term is used.

## *The Advantages of Object-Orientation*

This all seems very complicated, but there are several related reasons why this class and object approach is extremely powerful:

❑   It simplifies complexity by allowing us to define a large and complex system by using smaller sets of interrelated objects.

❑   Designing an application using objects usually means that we are modeling real-life objects, such as orders or products. This allows our program design to naturally map the real world (or domain), enabling us to work more intuitively.

❑   It gives us a vocabulary by which we can more effectively discuss a system or application with co-workers. It is much easier to discuss functionality in terms of a method of an object than in general terms of one of the hundreds of functions which reside in a general code module.

❑   Classes have their own self-contained properties, methods, and events (**encapsulation**), so they are generally self-sufficient. This makes your code more ordered and easier to maintain, as most things to do with that class are stored within the class template. We can, however, have a class that is composed of other classes, which delegates functionality to these contained classes, which themselves encapsulate functionality.

❑   Encapsulation means that code reuse is easy, since you can just copy the class templates and the changes will automatically be reflected in any classes which inherit from the base class you've altered. This is useful when sharing code with others, or when reusing code from old projects, and, over time, reduces development times and costs.

# Object Models

When an application consists of many smaller objects, as Access does, then we use the term **Object Model** to show those objects and identify the relationship between them. This is generally shown in a diagrammatic form, and you'll see occurrences of these diagrams later in the book, for the data access object models.

The Access 2002 Object Model is quite large, so we won't be showing it here. However, showing you a bit of the model and how the diagram looks can help to understand how some of the Access objects fit together:

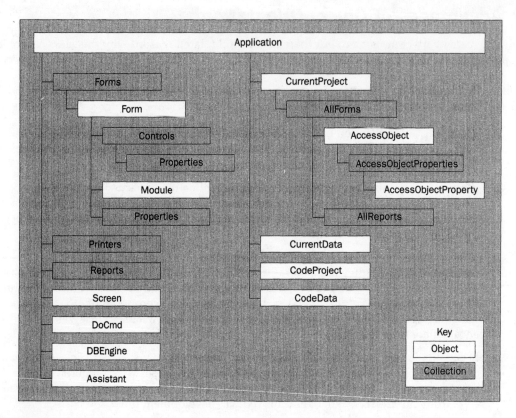

At the top we have the Application, which is the main Access application. This contains several smaller objects and numerous collections of objects, such as the Forms collection, which contains instances of Form objects. Each of these Form objects contains other objects. There are also some objects, such as the DoCmd object, which don't have any collections belonging to them.

Remember that this is just a portion of the object model – if you want to look at the full model, then you can find it in the Access Help File, assuming that you have chosen a complete install, and therefore have the full Help Files installed. In the **Contents** tab, it's under: **Programming in Visual Basic | Microsoft Access Visual Basic Reference | Microsoft Access Object Model**. As this is a help file it allows you to drill down into the objects for a more detailed look. Otherwise we provide a cut-down version of the object model in Appendix D.

## Using Object Models in VBA

Using object models in VBA is quite intuitive, because you can just use a period to separate the various objects and collections. For example, to get to the Forms collection you would do something like this:

```
Application.Forms
```

As the `Application` object is the main object, it can generally be omitted when referencing sub-objects. For instance, the example above could simply be written as:

```
Forms
```

To reference an individual item in an object you must either know its name, or its position in the collection. For example, if you have a form called `frmSwitchboard`, then you could do this:

```
Forms("frmSwitchboard")
```

Here we are using the name ("`frmSwitchboard`") to find the object in the `Forms` collection. This is a bit like the way we used a variable to index into a loop, in the previous chapter, and you can use that methodology too:

```
Forms(0)
```

This would give you the first object in the collection – it's the first object because collections start at 0.

To get further into the hierarchy of the model you just add the next item, separated by a period. For example:

```
Forms("frmSwitchboard").Controls(0)
```

This would get the first control on the form `frmSwitchboard`.

A practical benefit of using indexes rather than names is that we can loosely couple our code; that is, if the name of the form or the quantity of forms changed, then we do not need to adjust our code. However, we may need to if we had hard-coded (or tightly-coupled) the name ("`frmSwitchboard`") into our code. Don't worry too much about this now, because you'll be seeing lots of examples using objects and collections as we go through this chapter.

# Access 2002 Objects

There are several sets of objects that you might come across in Access, and they can be categorized quite simply:

- ❑ General Access Objects
- ❑ Data Access Objects
- ❑ ActiveX Data Objects

In this chapter we're only going to concern ourselves with the first of these – the General Access Objects. The Data Access Objects will be covered in the next chapter, and ActiveX Data Objects are discussed in the appendices.

But before we do, we will look briefly at the new features added to the AccessObject model in the latest version of Access.

# New Objects in Access 2002

These tables show what is new, so that you can see the technical trends or direction that Microsoft are applying to Access.

Access 2002 has only modestly added to the list of objects, all of which allow the programmer greater flexibility when dealing with Access – the new objects are listed below:

| Access Object | Refers to | Used in Chapter |
| --- | --- | --- |
| AllFunctions | A collection that holds an AccessObject object for each function in CurrentCode or CurrentData object | Not Applicable |
| LanguageSettings | An object that holds the details of the language settings | Not Applicable |
| Printers (Printer) | A Printer collection that holds a Printer object for each available printer on the system | Chapter 10 |

*Items marked* Not Applicable *are beyond the scope of this book, and are therefore not covered.*

In summary the new features of immediate interest to us include (please see the Help for full listing of new features):

## New Objects

| Object | Particulars |
| --- | --- |
| AllFunctions collection | Provides the ability to refer to a function object in the CurrentData or CurrentCode collections – in a similar vein to the AllTables, AllQueries, and AllViews collections. |
| Printers collection & Printer object | Enables us to programmatically control the printers of the system. |

## New Object Properties & Methods

| Object(s) | Method/Property | Particulars |
|---|---|---|
| AccessObject | DateCreated property | Returns date & time when object design was created (read-only) |
| | DateModified property | Returns date & time when object design was last modified (read-only) |
| Application | BrokenReference property | Indicates if the current database has broken references to type libraries or databases |
| | FileDialog property | Returns a file dialog box |
| | Printer property | Sets or returns an object that represents an available system printer |
| | Printers property | Returns a collection that represents available printers |
| | Versions property | Returns version number of current copy of Microsoft Access (read-only) |
| | ConvertAccessProject method | Converts the version of a Microsoft Access file using the constant acFileFormat: acFileFormat can be Access XP, 2000, 97, 95 & 2 |
| | ExportXML method | Exports in XML file format: data, schema & presentation details |
| | ImportXML method | Imports from XML file: data, schema & presentation details |
| CodeData | AllFunctions property | Returns a collection that represents the functions (user-defined) in a SQL Server database |
| CurrentData | AllFunctions property | Returns a collection that represents the functions (user-defined) in a SQL Server database |
| CurrentProject | FileFormat property | Returns the Microsoft Access version or file format of a given project (read-only) |
| | RemovePersonal Information property | Returns or sets a boolean that indicates if personal (user) information is stored in the active data access page or current project |

| Object(s) | Method/Property | Particulars |
|---|---|---|
| Form (there are approximately 48 new properties & methods: for brevity a selection is shown – see Help for a complete list) | DataChanged property | Returns or sets an event procedure, user-defined function or macro that is called on the DataChange event |
| | OnConnect property | Returns or sets an event procedure, user-defined function or macro that is called on the OnConnect event |
| | OnDisconnect property | Returns or sets an event procedure, user-defined function or macro that is called on the OnDisconnect event |
| | OnUndo property | Returns or sets an event procedure, user-defined function or macro that is called on the Undo event |
| ListBox & ComboBox | AddItem method | Adds an item to the list of items in either a listbox or combo box control |
| | RemoveItem method | Removes an item from the list of items in either a listbox or combo box control |

# The AccessObject Object

This shows the complete AccessObject object that we can program against; in one way or another almost all code is programmed against one of these object containers.

The AccessObject object refers to one of the following:

- ❑ AllForms
- ❑ AllReports
- ❑ AllMacros
- ❑ AllModules
- ❑ AllTables
- ❑ AllDataAccessPages
- ❑ AllQueries
- ❑ AllViews

❑ AllStoredProcedures

❑ AllFunctions

❑ AllDatabaseDiagrams

You can probably guess what these are. AllForms, for example, refers to all of the forms in a database or project. This allows us to easily get access to all of the objects stored. In previous versions of Access, you would have had to use the Data Access Objects, and the Containers and Documents collections. This method is much easier. Let's have a look at a quick example:

**Try It Out**     **Viewing the Access Objects**

1.  Open IceCream.mdb and select Modules. If you are using the complete database open Chapter 05 – Module and Module2 modules.

2.  Insert a new module, and add the following procedure:

```
Public Sub ShowObjects()

    Dim objAO As AccessObject
    Dim objCP As Object

    Set objCP = Application.CurrentProject

    For Each objAO In objCP.AllForms
        Debug.Print objAO.Name
    Next

End Sub
```

3.  Switch to the Immediate window and run the procedure:

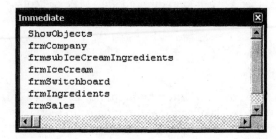

4.  Now change AllForms to AllReports and run the procedure again:

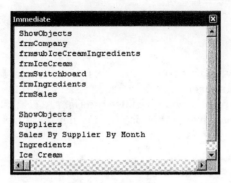

This code is quite simple, but there are a few things that need explaining. Let's start with the variable declarations.

```
Dim objAO As AccessObject
Dim objCP As Object
```

The first declares a variable to hold an Access object – this will be one of the All objects shown earlier. The second variable will hold the current project – this is the current database. We have to use a generic object type here, because, oddly enough, there isn't a specific type for an Access project.

Next we set this object to point to the current project. This will allow us access to all of the objects in the current database:

```
Set objCP = Application.CurrentProject
```

Once the current project is set, we can loop through the AllForms collection, printing out the name:

```
For Each objAO In objCP.AllForms
  Debug.Print objAO.Name
Next
```

You'll be familiar with loops by now, but you might not have seen this particular version. The For Each statement is used with collections, allowing us to loop through the collection. The way this works is that you declare a variable that matches the type of the elements in the collection – in this case it's AccessObject, because we are looping through the AllForms collection. The general rule is:

```
Dim objObject As ObjectType

For Each objObject In Collection.Objects
```

This has the effect of running the loop for each object in the collection, and each time around, the loop variable (`objObject`, or `objAO` in the example above) is set to point to the individual collection member.

If this sounds confusing, just have a look at the diagram below:

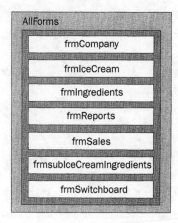

Each time around the loop `objAO` points to the next form. If you think of a collection as similar to an array then you'll get the general idea (that is, each form is an item in the array or collection).

## Dynamic Listboxes

So what we have is an easy way to find out what objects are within our database. Why is this useful? Given the way applications change, it's a good idea to build in some form of future proofing, to allow you to perform less maintenance as the application inevitably changes. Refer to the earlier section *Using Object Models in VBA* where we discussed the benefits of not having to hard-code form names: note that the same principle applies here. We loop through the `Reports` collection with no maintenance required to our code and we automatically get the changes that have been made to the report names or additions/deletions of reports that currently reside in the `Reports` collection.

Consider you have a form listing all of your reports. You've built this using a single form and hard-coded the hyperlinks, one hyperlink for each form. Something similar to this:

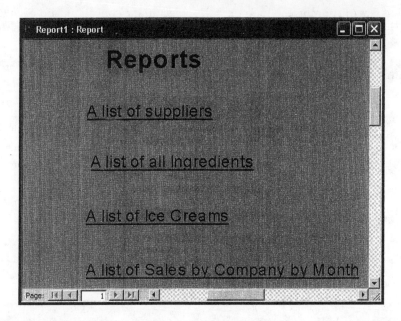

But what happens if you need to add another report? Or even two? You have to edit the form, squash things up so it fits on, and so on. Wouldn't it be simpler to provide a dynamic list of reports? Maybe something like this:

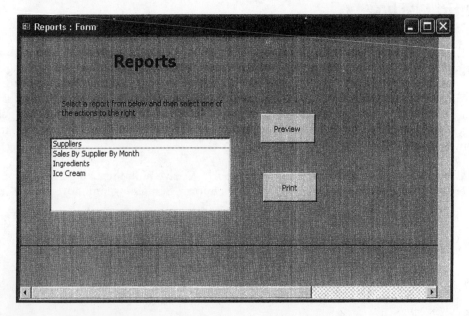

Now when you add a new report to the database it will automatically be added to the list box. Let's have a look and see how we can do this:

**Using the AccessObject**

**1.** Create a new form and add a listbox onto it, calling the listbox `lstReports` (note that the name of the listbox starts with lowercase letter `l` and not the number one).

**2.** Press the **Code** button on the toolbar to create a code module, and add the following code to the `Load` event for the Form:

```
Private Sub Form_Load()

  Dim objAO As AccessObject
  Dim objCP As Object
  Dim strValues As String

  Set objCP = Application.CurrentProject

  For Each objAO In objCP.AllReports
   strValues = strValues & objAO.Name & ";"
  Next objAO

  lstReports.RowSourceType = "Value List"
  lstReports.RowSource = strValues

End Sub
```

**3.** Switch the form into **Form** mode to see the results:

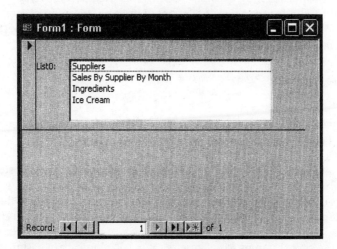

**4.** Switch the form back into design view; right-click outside the form and select **Properties**. Set the **Record Selectors** and **Navigation Buttons** properties to **No**.

**5.** Save the form as `frmReports`.

**How It Works**

This method of filling a listbox is really simple, and relies on you supplying a list of values for a listbox, just by separating the values by a semi-colon. So let's look at how this is done.

Firstly we have the variables, the first two of which you've seen before. This will be used to help us loop through the Report objects. The last variable, strValues, is a string that we will use to build up a list of report names.

```
Dim objAO As AccessObject
Dim objCP As Object
Dim strValues As String
```

Next we set a variable to point to the current project.

```
Set objCP = Application.CurrentProject
```

Then, we loop through the AllReports collection, adding the name of each report to a string. Notice how we add a semi-colon after the name of each report, as this is our list separator.

```
For Each objAO In objCP.AllReports
  strValues = strValues & objAO.Name & ";"
Next objAO
```

Finally we set the properties for the listbox. The first is the RowSourceType property, which when set to Value List means that what's shown in the listbox comes from a list of values. The second line actually sets those values, by setting the RowSource property to the contents of the string containing the report names.

```
lstReports.RowSourceType = "Value List"
lstReports.RowSource = strValues
```

That's it – a really simple way to use VBA to fill a listbox. However, this isn't the only way to fill a listbox using code; we can use the AddItem method of the listbox.

As we saw in the above example, to get all the names of the reports into the listbox (lstReports), we moved through the AllReports collection and progressively built a string (strValues) to hold all the names of the reports. We then assigned the strValues string to the row source property of lstReports, which then listed the names of the reports on separate rows.

Rather than add the report names to a string (strValues) and then assign the string to a property of the listbox (lstReports), we can added them directly from the AllReports collection to the listbox and remove the need to use a string to build the list of names.

So let's modify the above example and see how the AddItem method works.

**Using the AddItem method of the Listbox control**

**1.** Reopen the form code module and make the following changes to the Load event of
the form:

```
Private Sub Form_Load()

   Dim objAO As AccessObject
   Dim objCP As Object
   Dim strValues As String

   Set objCP = Application.CurrentProject
   lstReports.RowSourceType = "Value List"

   For Each objAO In objCP.AllReports
   'strValues = strValues & objAO.Name & ";"
    Me.lstReports.AddItem (objAO.Name)
   Next objAO


   'lstReports.RowSource = strValues

End Sub
```

**2.** Switch the form into **Form** view to see the results:

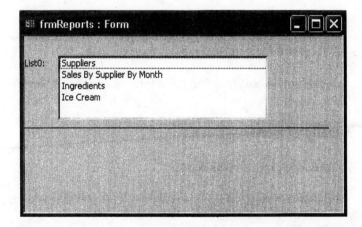

**3.** You can save the form with the changes or reverse the changes that we made to
demonstrate the AddItem method (we have elected not to save the changes).

We moved the line of code that sets the `RowSourceType` property to `Value List`, to precede the `AddItem` method; we do this to set the `RowSourceType` to `Value List` before we add the items.

```
lstReports.RowSourceType = "Value List"
```

We then commented out the lines of code that build the string `strValues` and assign that value to the row source – we don't need to use them in this example. (Commenting out code is a cool way to effect changes and it helps you if you need to restore the changes at a later date).

```
'strValues = strValues & objAO.Name & ";"

'lstReports.RowSource = strValues
```

Next we insert the line of code that will call the `AddItem` method of the listbox to add the names of the reports to the listbox. Note the object referencing: `Me` (the `Me` property is discussed shortly) refers to the form, `lstReports` is the name of the listbox that is contained by the form, `AddItem` is a method of the listbox and we pass to this method the name of the report. Because we have this code nested inside a `For Each...Next` loop we move through the `AllReports` collection progressively adding items (report names) to the list until each one has been added.

```
Me.lstReports.AddItem (objAO.Name)
```

As the above example shows, using the `AddItem` method of the listbox is quite intuitive. Both of the above examples underscore the value of thinking in terms of objects and their properties and methods when you want to perform a task or a set of tasks.

Now that we have a working listbox, let's add those buttons so we can view or print the reports.

## Try It Out     Adding the Print buttons

1. Switch the form back into Design mode.

2. Add two command buttons. If you have the wizards enabled you can just cancel out of the screen it shows – we want to code these ourselves.

3. Name the buttons `cmdPreview` and `cmdPrint`, and set their captions accordingly.

4. Add a label at the top of the report, for a title, and change the label for the listbox. Your form should now look something like this:

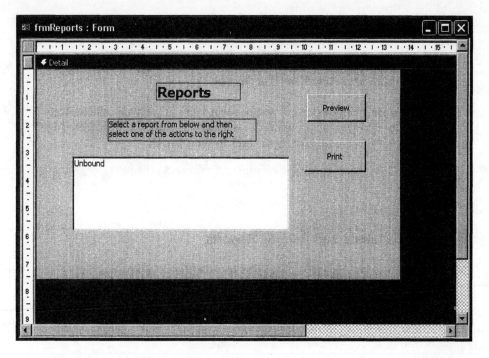

**5.** From the View menu, select **Code**, to create a code module for the form. This will switch us to the Visual Basic Editor (VBE).

**6.** Add the following subroutine:

```
Private Sub ProcessReport(intAction As Integer)

    If Not IsNull(lstReports) Then
      DoCmd.OpenReport lstReports, intAction
    End If

End Sub
```

**7.** Select cmdPreview from the object combo box (that's the one at the top left of the code window), and then select Click from the event combo box (the one on the right).

**8.** Enter the following line of code:

```
ProcessReport acViewPreview
```

**9.** Select cmdPrint from the object combo box, and Click from the event combo box.

**10.** Add the following line of code:

```
ProcessReport acNormal
```

**11.** Save the module and switch back to Access.

**12.** Switch the form from design view into form view and try out the buttons. Selecting Preview will open (in preview mode) whichever report is highlighted in the listbox, and selecting Print will print it straight to the printer.

With just a few lines of code you have a couple of command buttons to preview and print any report.

---

**How it Works**    **Previewing and Printing Reports**

The ProcessReport procedure first checks to see whether a report has been selected in the listbox. The listbox value will be Null if no report has been selected. So, if a report has been selected, we call the OpenReport method of the DoCmd object, passing in the report name (this name comes straight from the listbox – if you refer to a listbox in code, the value you get is whatever is selected). The second argument to OpenReport is the action – what we want to do. This is passed into ProcessReport as an argument.

```
If Not IsNull(lstReports) Then
  DoCmd.OpenReport lstReports, intAction
End If
```

Each of the command buttons calls ProcessReport passing in a different constant (predefined by Access). We either want to preview the report (acViewPreview) or we want to open the report normally (acNormal).

```
ProcessReport acViewPreview
ProcessReport acNormal
```

That's all there is to it.

## Changing the Switchboard

Since we've just looked at opening reports, let's have a quick diversion into the switchboard, just to point out a couple of facts. If you've tried to use the switchboard to open other forms you'll notice that only two of the buttons are working – those for the Ice Cream Details and the Ingredients. You might also have noticed the method used to open these forms – using hyperlink addresses. Now we'll be covering these in more detail later in the book, but basically they give you a simple way to jump from form to form without any code.

We have a minor issue with using hyperlinks:

❑ The Web toolbar may appear when we click the switchboard's Ice Cream Details or Ingredients buttons, which tends to be a bit confusing: after all, we're not dealing with a web page in this circumstance.

A thing to do under these circumstances is to remove the hyperlinks and use VBA to open the forms.

## Try It Out — Opening Forms

**1.** Open the switchboard in **Design** view.

**2.** Select the **Ice Cream Details** button, and delete the contents of the Hyperlink SubAddress property.

**3.** Now move to the **On Click** event and add an event procedure. You can do this by pressing the builder button to the right of the property (and selecting **Code Builder** from the next dialog if you don't default to always using event procedures).

**4.** Add the following code:

```
DoCmd.OpenForm "frmIceCream"
```

**5.** Now do the same (repeat Steps 2-4) for the **Ingredients** button, this time using frmIngredients as the form name.

**6.** Now do the same (repeat Steps 2-4: however, the **Hyperlink Sub Address** should be empty) for the **Suppliers Lists** button, with frmCompany as the form name.

**7.** Do the same (repeat Steps 2-4: however, the **Hyperlink Sub Address** should be empty) for the **Reports** button, using frmReports as the form name.

**8.** Switch back to Access, and view the respective forms in form view to see the results. Notice that the forms open after clicking the respective button, but that the Web toolbar doesn't appear (if you don't get this result check to see that you haven't got **Web** selected in the main menu: **View | Toolbars | Web**). There's still a problem with the **Suppliers** button, though, because it shows all the companies, and not just suppliers.

**9.** Switch back to the VBE and modify the code in the **Suppliers Lists** event procedure (cmdSuppliers_Click) so that it looks like this:

```
DoCmd.OpenForm "frmCompany", , , "Supplier = True"
```

**10.** Now switch back to Access and try again. Notice that only suppliers are shown.

We are utilizing the `Where` argument of the `OpenForm` command, which allows us to specify a SQL `WHERE` clause as part of the open. This means that instead of `frmCompany` showing all the records, it will only show records where the `Supplier` field is set to `True`.

# Forms and Reports

Two collections that we haven't discussed might seem a bit confusing. Remember how we said that `AllForms` and `AllReports` give us a list of forms and reports. Well, what about the `Forms` and `Reports` collections? What do they contain?

The `Forms` and `Reports` collections store details about the **open** forms and reports. So these are the ones that the user currently has open. This allows you to perform actions on the forms that the user currently has open, rather than the forms that are not being used. This is an important point, because you can use the `Forms` collection to change an open form, but any changes you make are not saved when the form is closed. The changes only exist while the form is open. If, however, the form is open in design view and you make changes, then these changes will be saved when you close the form, as long as you don't abandon the changes.

Let's just see this in action:

**Try It Out — The Forms Collection**

1. Close any open forms.

2. Create a new module, open the **Immediate** window, and type:

```
?forms(0).Name
```

3. Press *Enter* and you should see the following error message:

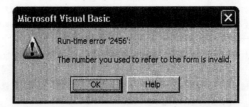

This is because there are no forms open, so the `Forms` collection is empty. The `Forms` collection, like an array, starts at 0, so trying to look at this entry when there are no forms in the collection causes an error.

**4.** Now open a form, perhaps `frmCompany`, and try this line again:

The `Forms` collection is very useful when you need to perform tasks on open forms. For example, you may want to change the color scheme or current font. This is really simple because each form has another collection, `Controls`. This contains an entry for each control on a form. So you could easily build a control that changes the current font for all controls, just by looping through this collection.

**Try It Out — Forms and Controls**

**1.** Create a new subroutine called `FormFonts`, like so:

```
Sub FormFonts (strFont As String)

   Dim frmCurrent As Form
   Dim ctlControl As Control

   For Each frmCurrent In Forms
    For each ctlControl In frmCurrent.Controls
       ctlControl.FontName = strFont
    Next
   Next

End Sub
```

**2.** Make sure that only the form `frmCompany` is open.

**3.** Run the new procedure from the **Immediate** window, passing in **Rockwell** as the font name, like so:

FormFonts "Rockwell"

*If you don't have this font, substitute the name of one you do, preferably one that is obviously different. Why not try Wingdings (if you don't mind not being able to read it)?*

**4.** Press *Return* to run the procedure, and you should see another error message:

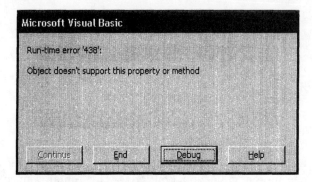

Now don't panic; this is expected. What we're doing is changing the font name for all of the controls. But what you may not realize is that not all controls have a font.

**5.** Switch back to Access and you'll see this:

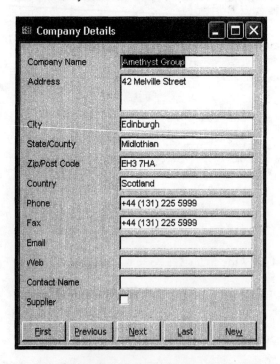

Notice that all of the text boxes have had their font changed, but we seemed to have stalled at the **Supplier**. That's because this is a check box field and it doesn't have a font, therefore it has no `FontName` property. Its associated label does, but the field itself doesn't. So we get the error. Notice that the command buttons haven't been changed either – they do have a `FontName` property, but since the **Supplier** field is before them in the collection they haven't been reached yet.

## Control Types

So how do we get around this problem? How do we check for controls that don't have an associated font? Well, there are two ways to tackle this:

The first way is to check each control in the loop to see if it is one of the controls that has a font. We use code similar to this:

```
For Each frmCurrent In Forms
 For Each ctlControl In frmCurrent.Controls
   If ctlControl.Type <> acCheckBox Then
    ctlControl.Font = strFont
   End If
 Next
Next
```

This uses the `ControlType` property of each control to see if the control is a checkbox (`acCheckBox` is an intrinsic constant), and only changes the font if it isn't a checkbox. But again we run into a problem here, because there are several control types that don't have fonts: images, lines, etc. Should we check each one? Yes, we could, but this would make our code hard to read and maintain.

The second way is to use the error handling of VBA and Access. We're going to discuss error handling in detail later on in the book, but you've already seen we've got an error – Run-time error '438'. This is a fixed error number telling us the property is not supported. So what it's really saying is that the property we are trying to use doesn't exist. Now wouldn't it be nice if we could just say 'OK, I know it doesn't exist, so just skip trying to set the font for this control, and move onto the next control'? Well, with error handling we can.

## The Err Object

Whenever a VBA error is generated, a special object is used to hold the error details – this is the `Err` object. We'll look at this in more detail later in the book, but for the moment all you have to know is that one of the properties of the `Err` object is the `Number` property – this is the error number that we were shown in the error dialog.

Using error handling allows us to tell VBA that when a given error occurs, it shouldn't just display an error message, but should run a special bit of code, which we can supply.

**Try It Out**     **Objects, Controls and Errors**

**1.** If you are in Access, switch back to the VBE.

**2.** Now change the code for the `FormFonts` procedure, so that it looks like this:

```
Sub FormFonts (strFont As String)

  On Error GoTo FormFonts_Err

  Dim frmCurrent As Form
  Dim ctlControl As Control

  For Each frmCurrent In Forms
   For Each ctlControl In frmCurrent.Controls
     ctlControl.FontName = strFont
   Next
  Next

FormFonts_Exit:
  Exit Sub

FormFonts_Err:
  If Err.Number = 438 Then
   Resume Next
  Else
   MsgBox Err.Description
   Resume FormFonts_Exit
  End If

End Sub
```

**3.** Switch back to Access, and close and reopen the form. This makes sure that the font is reset to its default – remember our changes aren't saved.

**4.** Switch back to the VBE and run the procedure again.

**5.** Now if you switch back to Access you'll see that all of the text has changed to our new font.

## How It Works

As we've said, we won't go into detail about the error handling, as this is covered fully in the debugging chapter. But let's briefly look at the collections a little more:

Every form has a collection of controls. This comprises everything on the form, and since it is held in a collection we can use the For Each statement to iterate through it. This sets the variable ctlControl to point to successive controls, and then tries to set the FontName property of this control. If the control doesn't support this property, then an error is generated. However, we are using On Error to trap errors, so our special bit of code is run. This is the bit of code after FormFonts_Err. In this section of code we check to see if the error number is 438 – remember this error number identifies that the FontName property doesn't exist. In this case we don't care, so we just tell the program to Resume at the Next statement. If the error number is anything other than 438, then the error message is displayed, and the function exits.

Don't worry too much about this error handling code, as we will cover it in detail later. The thing to remember is that we now have a procedure that works on all open forms, irrespective of the controls they have on them.

Another important thing to remember is that changes you make to an open form are not saved when you close the form. Later in the book we'll see ways of making permanent changes to forms and reports by opening the form in design mode and making changes there.

# Referring to Objects

So far, you have only used an index into the collection to reference the required item, but there are other ways to find the object you require. The first way we'll look at is probably the most common. It allows you to refer to an object explicitly as a member of a collection. For example, to set an object variable to the form frmCompany you can use:

```
Dim frmP As Form
Set frmP = Forms!frmCompany
```

You use the exclamation mark to separate the collection from the object. If the object has spaces in its name, you have to enclose it within square brackets. For example, if the form were called Company Details, then you would do this:

```
Set frmP = Forms![Company Details]
```

The second method is similar to using an index, but instead of a number you use the name of the object or a string variable:

```
Set frmP = Forms("frmCompany")
```

Or, using a string containing the name:

```
strFormName = "frmCompany"
Set frmP = Forms(strFormName)
```

Of course, you can use a number to refer to an object in a collection just like you would with an array:

```
Set frmP = Forms(3)
```

This would set frmP to point to the fourth form in the collection (collection numbers start at 0). So, you can access a form either from its name or its position in the Forms collection. If you use For Each to cycle through the collection, you use the numeric position in the collection. Using the name allows you to access single objects directly.

# Special Objects

There are some properties and objects in Access that we haven't covered yet, but which are quite useful. When changing the font earlier we used the Forms collection to look at all open forms, but what if we wanted this procedure to only work for the active form? Or what if we want to write a procedure where a form object is passed into it? Let's look at these special objects and properties, and see what they do:

| Object | Property | Refers to... |
|---|---|---|
| Screen | ActiveControl | The control that has the focus. |
| Screen | ActiveDataAccess Page | The data access page that has the focus. |
| Screen | ActiveForm | The form that has the focus, or contains the control with the focus. |
| Screen | ActiveReport | The report that has the focus, or contains the control with the focus. |
| Screen | PreviousControl | The control that had the focus immediately before the control with the current focus. |
| Form or Report | Me | The current form or report. This is actually a keyword and not a property. |
| Form or Report | Module | The form or report module. |
| Form or Report | RecordsetClone | A copy of the recordset that underlies a form or report. You'll see more of this in the next few chapters. |
| Subform, form, or the actual control | Form | For a subform control, this is the subform. For a form, it is the form itself. You'll see this in action later in the book. |
| Subreport, report, or the actual control | Report | For a subreport control, this is the subreport. For a report, it is the report itself. |
| Control | Parent | The form or report that contains the control. |
| Control | Section | The section of a form or a report upon which a control lies. |

Some of these you might not use, but there are some, such as ActiveForm, Me, and RecordsetClone, that you'll use quite often.

### Try It Out — The ActiveForm Property

**1.** Open the company form, `frmCompany`.

**2.** Switch to the VBE and show the **Immediate** window.

**3.** Type the following:

?Screen.ActiveForm.Name

**4.** Switch back to Access and open the Switchboard form (`frmSwitchboard`), keeping the company form open too.

**5.** Switch back to the VBE and try it again.

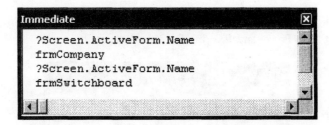

So you can see that the `ActiveForm` object changes, depending upon which form is the currently active one. This would be quite useful if you needed to write a procedure to act upon the current active form. For example, in the `FormFonts` procedure we created earlier, we used the `Forms` collection to loop through all open forms, but if we only wanted to act upon the current active form we could do this:

```
Dim frmCurrent As Form
Dim ctlControl As Control

For Each ctlControl In Screen.ActiveForm.Controls
  ctlControl.FontName = strFont
Next
```

## *The Me Keyword*

You'll find the Me keyword extremely useful because it refers to the object currently being executed. So, if you use Me in a form module, it refers to the form, and if you use it in a report module, it refers to the report. This allows you to write code that isn't dependent upon the form name, and that could be copied to another form module: another example of the benefit of loosely coupled code. For example, taking another look at the code to change the font of controls – it loops through the open forms. But what if we wanted to use this code in a single form – perhaps in response to a user request to change the font? One way would be to use the Forms collection, for example:

```
For Each ctlControl In Forms("frmCompany").Controls
```

One reason why this is bad is that you can't just copy the code – it would need changing if you pasted this into another form. Another reason is that it's wasteful – Access already knows what the active form is – Me:

```
Dim frmCurrent As Form
Dim ctlControl As Control

For Each ctlControl In Me.Controls
  ctlControl.FontName = strFont
Next
```

Now you might think that you could use ActiveForm, but Me and ActiveForm don't always refer to the same thing. For example, consider this diagram below:

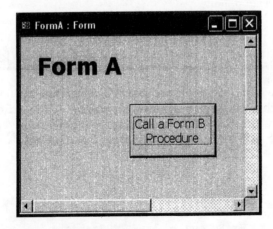

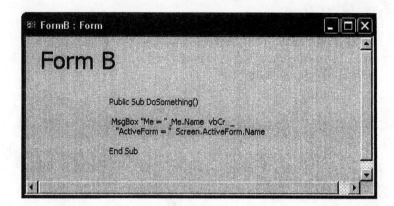

We have **Form A**, which is the active form (note: the highlighted toolbar). The button calls a public procedure in **Form B**, which displays the name of the form for Me and for the ActiveForm. Here's the result:

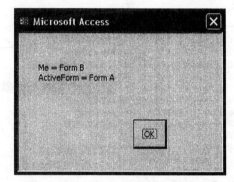

So this shows that even though DoSomething is executing in a different form, Me still points to the current form (that is the form under which the code is running), whereas ActiveForm is the form with the current focus.

# The Object Browser

The Object Browser is part of the VBE, and it allows you to look up definitions of objects, methods, properties, and constants. You can easily call up the object browser by pressing *F2* (when you're in the VBE); it looks like this:

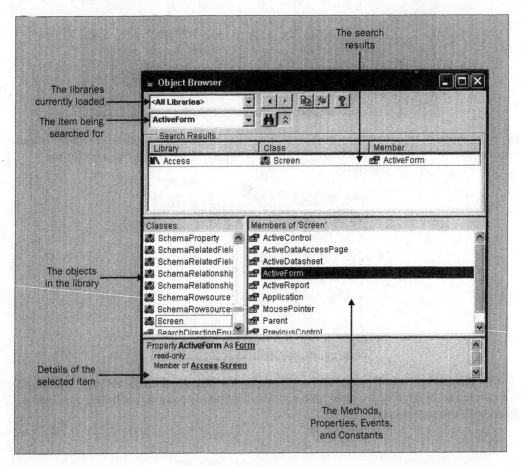

There's a lot of information available in the object browser. The first combo box allows you to select a specific library:

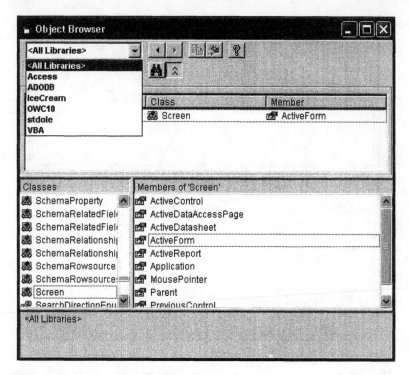

In this example, there are 6 libraries loaded:

- ❑ **Access** contains the objects for Access itself

- ❑ **ADODB** contains the ActiveX Data Objects

- ❑ **IceCream** contains the current database, so that includes forms, reports, and so on

- ❑ **OWC10** contains the standard Microsoft Office XP objects

- ❑ **stdole** contains some standard object features, which you'll never have to refer to

- ❑ **VBA** contains the objects for Visual Basic for Applications

In Chapter 16 you'll see how to add more objects to this list.

The search window and results pane allows you to search for specific items. In the above diagram, I searched for **ActiveForm**, and it only occurs once – in the Access library, belonging to the Screen object. This is extremely useful if you know the name of something (such as a method or property) but can't remember which object it belongs to.

In the above diagram you can see that we were looking at **<All Libraries>**, so every object is shown, in alphabetical order. To look at the objects within the current database, you can just change to the **IceCream** entry:

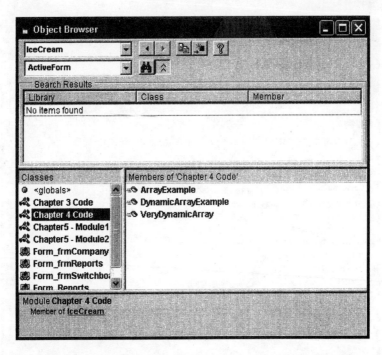

This shows a list of all of the objects in the IceCream database. The **Chapter 4 Code** module is selected, and the **Members** pane shows all of the items in that module. Notice that no reports appear here – this is because the reports in the database don't have any code behind them. Only objects with code appear in the object browser.

The object browser is very useful: you really can learn a lot from just browsing around in it. You'll be amazed at how many objects, properties, and methods there are, and you're bound to find plenty that you didn't know existed.

# Summary

In this chapter we've started to look into the object world, looking at the objects that Access has built in. This has concentrated on some of the main ones, such as forms, controls, and so on, but you will be seeing more throughout the rest of the book.

An important thing to remember from this chapter is collections. If there is more than one of a given type of object then it may be contained in a collection, with the collection name usually being the plural of the object. So to hold the form objects we have a Forms collection. Looping through these collections is easy with the For Each statement, so you can easily examine every item. To avoid hard-coding our code, we loosely couple it by making use of the index of an item in a collection – this cuts down on maintenance and supports code reuse in other Access applications: we also saw how the Me property helps us to loosely couple our code.

Once you have an object you can refer to its methods and properties, such as the `FontName` property for controls. So, from within your code, you have access to almost everything that you have access to when in design mode. This is a very powerful feature, and you'll see much more of it later. But for now, it's time you learned about data access.

# Exercises

**1.** Early on in the chapter in *Try It Out – Viewing the Access Objects*, we looked at viewing forms and reports using the `AllForms` and `AllReports` objects, go to that section and alter the code to look at the other `AccessObject` objects (`AllTables`, `AllFunctions` and `AllQueries` and so on). You should receive a **Run-time error 438 – Object doesn't support this property or method** when you try `AllFunctions` – because this property is supported in the Access Data Project and not normal Access projects, such as this one (we discuss Access Data Projects in Chapter 21).

**2.** An object may have properties and methods – what is the difference between a property and a method? Provide an example of a form property and a method.

# CHAPTER 6

# Using DAO

Having read this far, you should now be familiar with some of the basics of VBA programming. We have looked at the nature of event-driven programming; we have written our first code in VBA and investigated some of the programming constructs we can use to add more complex logic to our application; and we have taken a look at the object model of the Access application.

That's all fine – and we need to make sure that we understand the basics before we move onto some of the more advanced concepts – but so far the ground that we have covered has been fairly generic. That is to say that the concepts we have looked at so far have dealt more with the basics of VBA programming as opposed to the specifics of database programming. That's all about to change now, as we get to grips with using VBA to manipulate tables, queries, and data that we keep in our databases.

## DAO vs ADO

Anyone who has had dealings in the computer industry will know that use of the TLA (Three Letter Acronym) is rife. You will not be surprised to know that things are no different in the database world. Indeed, Microsoft have elevated the use of the TLA to new heights in recent years by not only repeatedly changing the TLAs that they use to describe their methods of database access, but by trying to devise as many TLAs as they can while using the fewest number of letters.

**Try It Out** — **Invent a Data Access Method (DAM)**

1. Take a photocopy of this page.

2. Cut out the following counters (Remember, scissors can be dangerous, so if you are not sure, ask an adult to do this for you):

3. Put all of the counters into an empty mug.

4. With your eyes closed, pull out three or four of the counters and lay them on the desk in front of you. Hey presto! You have your own Data Access Method. But we're not finished yet!

5. Wait for about a year until everybody has got use to using the new DAM you have invented. Now put all the counters back in the mug, pull out three or four more, and proclaim the resultant letters as your new (and even better!) Data Access Method.

They have been trying this for years in Redmond and in recent years we have had Microsoft espouse the following TLAs in their attempts to make database access as simple to understand as possible...

❑ DAO (Data Access Objects)

❑ RDO (Remote Data Objects)

❑ RDS (Remote Data Services)

❑ ADO (Active Data Objects, later ActiveX Data Objects)

So, before we plunge into looking at how we can use DAO from VBA, let's take a moment or two to look at what it is and how it has been developed.

> *For the latest information on Microsoft's data access strategy, check out the Universal Data Access section of Microsoft's web site at http://www.microsoft.com/data.*

# A Brief History of DAO

The initial release of Microsoft Access in November 1992 was popular enough, but one of its few failings was the relatively limited programmatic access that it allowed to the database objects within it. The database engine it used was JET 1.0, and it was possible to access tables and queries in JET from code (which at the time was Access Basic, not VBA) by using an interface known as Data Access Objects (DAO). But the number of operations that could be performed against JET objects through DAO 1.0 was very restrictive.

An interim release of Access in the following summer introduced JET 1.1 and DAO 1.1 which gave programmers the ability to perform more advanced operations against tables and queries, although again the feature set offered by DAO 1.1 still left significant room for improvement. The situation was not helped by the fact that the interim release of DAO was only available through Visual Basic 3 and not natively from within Access 1.1.

A little over a year later in the late spring of 1994, Microsoft released Access 2.0. Again, a new version of the database engine – JET 2.0 – accompanied the release along with a revised programmatic interface. DAO 2.0 was a significant improvement over its predecessors and exposed the objects within JET 2.0 as a complete hierarchical collection of objects with their own methods and properties with support for data definition (creating tables and queries) and security management as well as data manipulation.

A service pack released six months later introduced JET 2.5, but the next significant step forward came with Access 95, which provided the first full 32-bit implementation of JET. This not only offered significant performance improvements over its 16-bit predecessor, but also added support for replication.

With Access 97 came JET 3.5 and DAO 3.5. As the version numbering indicates, the changes from the previous version were fairly modest, with perhaps the most significant enhancement being the addition of **ODBCDirect**, a technology that allowed programmers to use the DAO interface to access data on remote enterprise servers (such as SQL Server or Sybase) efficiently.

JET 4.0, the version of the database engine that ships with Access 2002 shows a number of improvements over previous versions. This latest incarnation of JET supports Unicode and uses a SQL syntax which is not only ANSI compliant, but is also entirely compatible with SQL Server 7.0, making the task of upsizing a database from Access to SQL Server easier than ever. JET 4.0 also introduces row-level locking, improved replication functionality, and the ability to programmatically determine which users are currently accessing the database. As you would expect, the programmatic interface to JET 4.0 – DAO 3.6 – exposes all of this new functionality to the developer.

# The Future of DAO

Before we discuss the specifics of DAO, let's cut to the chase and talk about why this is an important topic. The choice of using DAO and ADO is a dilemma that, depending on your current and future needs, may not be an easy choice. DAO is still the easiest and most efficient method to access data from an Access database. However, DAO has limited capabilities. On the other hand, ADO is more flexible and works well with a client/server database like SQL Server. So, do you keep things simple by using the DAO object model – and accept the limitations of JET – or use the newer ADO objects and write additional code in lieu of many built-in features? The following will help you understand the strengths and weaknesses of this dated object model.

DAO has always been an excellent interface for working with native Access data, but companies keep data in a wide variety of databases other than Access. For example, a great number of companies keep their data in large client-server databases such as Microsoft SQL Server, Sybase, or Oracle. What if you want to join data in SQL Server with data that resides in an Access database?

One approach – which has proved highly effective – is to attach the SQL Server tables to an Access database. The data remains in the SQL Server database but, to all intents and purposes, the attached tables appear just like Access tables and can be accessed programmatically using DAO in the same way that native Access tables can. The 'glue' that is used to attach tables from these client-server databases is a technology called ODBC or Open Database Connectivity. A vendor-independent technology, it was devised in the early 1990s as a method of connecting any client application to any relational database.

Although admirable for its simplicity, this approach had its limitations. For example, by accessing SQL Server tables as if they were Access tables, the developer was often prevented from taking advantage of SQL Server-specific functionality. The primary reason for this was that in order for an Access developer to programmatically fetch data from the base SQL Server table, the developer would have to use DAO, which would in turn call JET, which would in turn determine that the table wasn't actually an Access table but was a remote ODBC table and so (take a deep breath…) would in turn call ODBC, which would in turn load the appropriate database driver, which would in turn fetch the data from the base table in SQL Server (whew!). Although much of this chain of delegation was transparent to the developer, there was an impact – both in terms of response time and memory overhead – resulting from the number of DLLs that needed to be loaded for even simple operations against an ODBC database.

To get around this problem, Access 97 introduced ODBCDirect. This was a development of the RDO (Remote Data Objects) technology that had been in use in Visual Basic for a while. The advantage of ODBCDirect was that it used DAO to call ODBC, completely bypassing JET. Not only could this improve query response times against ODBC databases, but because JET was completely bypassed it meant that developers had more control over low-level connection and query configuration options.

The diagram below illustrates where each of the components we have described so far fits into the big picture as far as accessing data from Access or VBA is concerned.

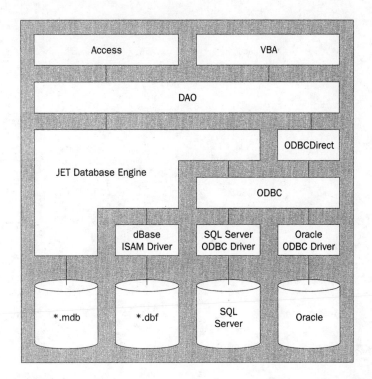

ODBCDirect was a big improvement, but there was still another problem. You see, ODBC was designed to work against relational databases like SQL Server and Oracle. At a pinch it could be made to work against non-relational tabular sets of data such as Microsoft Excel spreadsheets. But there was still an awful lot of data that ODBC wouldn't work with, simply because the data was not relational. For example, many companies have electronic mail systems such as Microsoft Exchange. Such a system holds a vast amount of information, both in the content of the messages and in the details of the senders themselves. If only we could get to this data…

## OLEDB and ADO

Enter **OLEDB**, stage left… OLEDB is a newer technology, developed by Microsoft, which provides access to both relational and non-relational data. So OLEDB can be used to extract data from Access databases and from SQL Server databases. But it can also be used to extract information from non-relational sources such as Microsoft Exchange, Microsoft Index Server, Active Directory Services in Windows 2000 and .NET Server, and decision support systems such as OLAP servers. It is the universality of the data that can be accessed through OLEDB – the underlying framework has been christened Universal Data Access (UDA) by Microsoft – that makes this technology so compelling. The diagram below shows the OLEDB architecture.

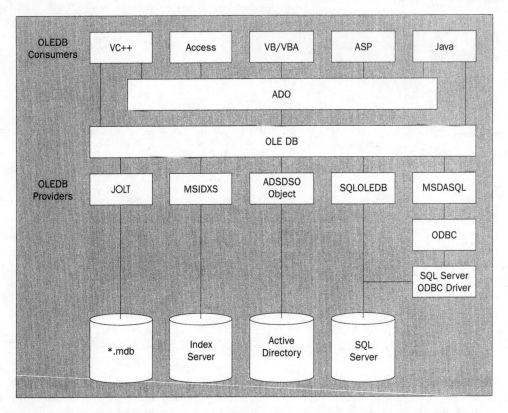

As you can see from this diagram, OLEDB is able to communicate with these disparate data sources through drivers which are known as "Data Providers". A number of native providers have been written– the provider for Access 2000 and 2002 is the Jet OLEDB 4.0 provider and the native provider for SQL Server is SQLOLEDB. It's possible to connect to ODBC databases for which there is no native provider by using the MSDASQL provider. This provider allows access via existing ODBC drivers.

So that is how OLEDB communicates with the different data sources. What is really cool, however, is how client applications communicate with OLEDB. OLEDB has a single programmatic interface called ADO (ActiveX Data Objects) and this is what client applications use irrespective of the type of provider. So you use the same syntax whether you are connecting to tables in SQL Server, tables in Access, or data that is in an Exchange Server or in Index Server. That's a real big plus. So, where does that leave DAO?

Microsoft has made it clear that DAO has a limited shelf-life. There will be no further development to DAO and Microsoft assert that the presence of DAO in Access 2002 is primarily intended to ease the migration path for developers whose Access 97 applications contain a large DAO codebase. That is the reason why – despite substantial changes between JET 3.x and JET 4.0 – the changes between DAO 3.5 (Access 97) and DAO 3.6 (Access 2000 and 2002) are minimal.

However, it is not as simple as that (it never is!). You see, DAO really is very, very good for working with data in Access. And ADO? Well, like any newcomer it's got quite a lot to learn. The incarnation of ADO included with Access 2002 and, more specifically, the native provider for JET (Jet OLEDB 4.0) just don't offer the same functionality. True, there are some things you can do with ADO that you can't do with DAO (such as viewing who is currently logged in to the database) but for a lot of the bread-and-butter tasks, DAO still has the edge. For example, if an Access form is based on an ADO recordset (the data in the form comes from Access tables via ADO rather than DAO) then the records are not updateable. Now that's quite a significant limitation. So, is it back to DAO then? The advice we would offer is this:

❑   If you will be working primarily with data in Access tables and you are unlikely to upsize your application to a client-server database such as SQL Server, then stick with DAO.

❑   If you will be using Access as a front end to a client-server database, then use ADO instead (and create an Access project).

❑   If you are working primarily with data in Access but think that you might upsize the application to a client-server database like SQL Server, then it's your call. Using ADO from the start will make the migration to a client-server database much easier but, such are the limitations of the current version of the JET 4.0 OLEDB provider, you will probably be counting down the days until you can upsize the database and use ADO in an environment which shows it off in its best light.

The decision over whether to base this book around DAO or ADO is one that has vexed the authors considerably. The problem is that for working with Access data – which is the primary focus of this book – DAO is still both faster and more feature-rich. For the moment, it is a question of choosing the trusty old linebacker over the promising new draft pick.

> If you want to know more about ADO, you will be glad to know that we will be using it (albeit briefly) in Chapter 13 (Classes). In addition, there are two appendices at the back of this book with information about ADO. The first (Appendix B) goes into more detail about choosing between ADO and DAO. The second (Appendix C) details the ADO object model.

## ADO.NET and the Future of Data Access

Before we jump into this topic, let's make sure you understand that Access 2002 and .NET have nothing to do with each other and that you need not concern yourself with any of this in the current version of Access. It will certainly be important as you work with future versions of Access.

The fate of DAO (and ADO for that matter) is a little uncertain. The one thing that is very certain is that things will be changing in Access – significantly – in the near future. In February of 2002, Microsoft officially released Visual Studio .NET and the .NET Framework after nearly three years of intensive development and testing. This technology is changing the face of enterprise application development. The new data access method, ADO.NET, is built into the .NET Framework, which is a collection of some 64,000 object classes that replace practically everything software developers have used in the past. The interesting thing is that, aside from some similarly named objects, ADO.NET has little in common with ADO. In fact, it's not even an acronym for anything! Apparently the marketing folks at Microsoft figured that they had positive name recognition with ADO and wanted to leverage that as they moved forward. The main advantage of ADO.NET is that it allows data to be moved around over the Internet which was challenging or impossible using DAO, RDO, or ADO.

My crystal ball is a little cloudy but we will probably see more emphasis placed on using Access as a front end for SQL Server databases rather than for JET and then ADO will eventually be replaced by ADO.NET. I think that DAO will continue to be the right tool to use with native Access (JET) databases as long as this type of Access database is available (which should be a long while). Support for ADO.NET and the .NET Framework should be part of the next version of Microsoft Office where they will begin to move us from VBA to Visual Studio for Applications (VSA) which will look and feel more like Visual Studio.NET. For the present time, DAO is your best choice for programming an Access database in Access 2000 and Access 2002.

# The DAO Hierarchy

So, DAO here we come... If we are to use DAO effectively, then we must start with an understanding of the DAO hierarchy. We saw in the previous chapter how we can interact programmatically with the Access application via the Access object model. This contained a number of objects, grouped together into collections, all arranged in a hierarchical manner.

For example, the Forms collection contains a number of Form objects representing every form that is currently open.

Each of these Form objects has a Controls collection that contains a Control object for every control appearing on that form.

Each Control object has a Properties collection that contains a Property object for every property of that control.

> **Make sure that you appreciate the difference between the Access object model and the DAO object model. The Access object model is what we use to interact programmatically with the Access user interface (forms and reports). The DAO hierarchy is what we use to programmatically interact with JET databases.**

The good news is that the DAO hierarchy is arranged in the same similar manner to the Access object model, with collections of objects, each of which has its own methods and properties. However, before we look at the DAO hierarchy, we need to make sure that we have a reference to DAO in our database.

Forms and reports in Access 2002 still use DAO rather than ADO to fetch the data that they display. Originally it was intended that they should use ADO, but Microsoft changed tack during the development cycle when it was clear that the limitations of ADO/JOLT would mean the loss of a great deal of functionality to which Access developers had grown accustomed.

However, despite the fact that DAO is the mechanism used for retrieving data in forms and reports, the default database access method from Visual Basic is now ADO. What do we mean by that? Well, if you open the `IceCream.mdb` database, switch to the VBA IDE by hitting *Alt+F11* and then look at the references that are set by default (by choosing **References**... from the **Tools** menu) you should see this, if you scroll down:

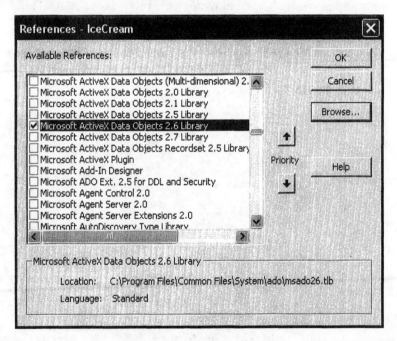

As you can see from the **References** dialog box, there are quite a number of libraries that we can reference from within VBA. We will look at libraries in more detail in Chapters 13 and 15, but for the moment you can think of them as collections of pre-built objects and functions that we can use in our code. Even though there might be many such libraries installed on our computer, it is unlikely that we will want to use them all in every database. So we can use the **References** dialog box to select those libraries that we want to be available from VBA within each database. To make a library available from within VBA, we simply check the checkbox beside it. Unchecking the checkbox makes the library unavailable, which means that we will get an error if we try to refer to any of the objects or functions in that library.

The `IceCream.mdb` database has references to the four libraries that are available by default in new Access 2002 databases:

- ❏ Visual Basic for Applications
- ❏ Microsoft Access 10.0 Object Library
- ❏ OLE Automation
- ❏ Microsoft ActiveX Data Objects 2.6 Library (ADO)

Now we are not going to be using ADO in this chapter, but will be using DAO. So we need to remove the reference to ADO and add a reference to DAO. We do that by unchecking **Microsoft ActiveX Data Objects 2.6 Library** and checking **Microsoft DAO 3.6 Object Library**. Once we have done that and clicked **OK**, we will be able to use DAO 3.6 from within our code.

> **Strictly speaking, we don't need to remove the reference to ADO. However, some of the objects in the ADO hierarchy have the same names as objects in the DAO hierarchy and retaining the reference to ADO could lead to confusion when writing code that uses the DAO version of those objects.**

So let's have a look at the DAO 3.6 hierarchy:

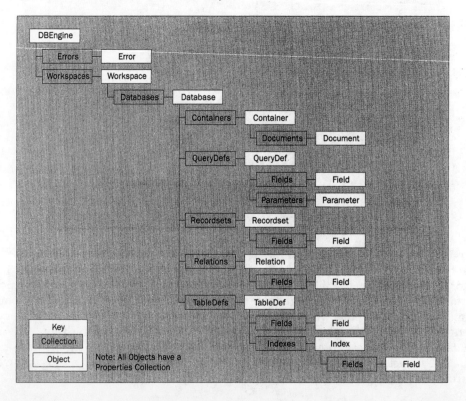

*Two collections (Users and Groups) have been omitted from this diagram for the sake of simplicity. Don't worry; we'll be looking at these in a lot more detail when we deal with security in Chapter 15.*

Hopefully, after reading the previous chapter, you should be familiar with the concept of object hierarchies. But probably the best way to learn how the DAO hierarchy works is to walk through the object model by using the Immediate window. And that's what we will do. So, pour yourself a nice strong cup of coffee, make sure you are sitting comfortably, open the Immediate window and get ready for a whistle-stop tour of the DAO hierarchy, starting from the top.

## The DBEngine Object

In the Access object hierarchy, the topmost object was the Application object, representing the Access application. Well, as you can see from the diagram above, the topmost object in the DAO hierarchy is the DBEngine object. This represents the DAO interface into the JET engine – the database engine which Access uses for all of its native database management – and ODBCDirect, which is used for accessing remote ODBC databases. So what can we do with the DBEngine object? Well, we can start by determining what version of DAO we are using. To do this, type the following in the Immediate window and hit *Enter*:

```
? DBEngine.Version
```

The result 3.6 should be displayed, indicating that we are using version 3.6 of DAO.

The DBEngine object contains two collections, the Errors collection and the Workspaces collection. The Errors collection is populated with Error objects every time a database-related error occurs, and we will look at this in more detail in Chapter 12 when we get to grips with error handling.

*To be honest, there isn't that much else that you can do with the DBEngine object per se. In fact, you will probably find that most of the time you won't use the DBEngine object for anything other than as a way of getting to the Errors or Workspaces collections.*

## The Workspace Object

The other collection is the Workspaces collection, which we can think of as representing a single session or instance of a user interacting with the database engine.

For example, to find out the name of the currently logged-on user of Access, we could execute the following code in the Immediate window:

```
? DBEngine.Workspaces(0).UserName
```

If you are using an unsecured system database, and have not logged into Access, the name of the default user will be displayed:

```
admin
```

But if you have manually logged into Access, the user name you logged in with will be displayed instead. Notice that to get to this property we used the syntax `DBEngine.Workspaces(0)`. This expression returns the first (and most of the time only) `Workspace` object in the `Workspaces` collection. This represents the currently logged on interactive session that you have with the database engine.

> *Earlier in this chapter we mentioned that Access 97 (or, more accurately, version 3.5 of DAO) saw the introduction of ODBCDirect, a technology that enables Access developers programmatic access to remote ODBC databases such as SQL Server or Oracle. In order to give developers tight control over the security and session management features of these databases, there is a special type of `Workspace` object that should be used when working with ODBCDirect. However, we don't need to worry about that because in this book we won't be dealing with ODBCDirect.*

The `Workspace` object used by JET contains a `Users` collection and a `Groups` collection that contain details of all users and groups defined in the current system database.

It also contains a `Databases` collection that holds a `Database` object representing every database that the current user for that `Workspace` object has open.

> *The `Workspace` object will be dealt with more fully in Chapter 17, when we consider multi-user and security issues.*

## The Database Object

Normally, we will only have one database open at a time, so there will only be one `Database` object in the `Databases` collection for the current workspace. You can see this for yourself by typing this in the **Immediate** window and hitting *Enter*:

```
? DBEngine.Workspaces(0).Databases.Count
```

which should return 1. To inspect this `Database` further, we could refer to it by its position in the `Databases` collection like this:

```
DBEngine.Workspaces(0).Databases(0)
```

So, to find the name of the currently open database we could type this in the **Immediate** window:

```
? DBEngine.Workspaces(0).Databases(0).Name
```

Alternatively, because the `Workspaces` collection is the default collection of the `DBEngine` object and the `Databases` collection is the default collection of the `Workspace` object, we could omit the collection names and use a shorthand notation like this:

```
? DBEngine(0)(0).Name
```

Or we could use this more friendly shortcut:

```
? CurrentDB.Name()
```

*Although practically synonymous, the `CurrentDB()` function and `DBEngine(0)(0)` are subtly different. `CurrentDB()` creates a new instance of the current database and returns a reference to it, whereas `DBEngine(0)(0)` returns a reference to the current instance of the open database. For subtle reasons, which we will not go into here, you should use `CurrentDB()` rather than `DBEngine(0)(0)` wherever possible. If you want to know more, take a look at Microsoft Knowledge Base article Q131881 http://support.microsoft.com/support/kb/articles/q131/8/81.asp).*

To inspect the properties of the currently open database, we simply examine the properties of the object returned by `CurrentDB()`. For example:

```
? CurrentDB.Name
```

will return the file name and location of the currently open database, and

```
? CurrentDB.Version
```

will return the version of JET with which the current database was created. So, if we are in a database which was created with Access 2000 or Access 2002, the value of `CurrentDB.Version` would be 4.0, because Access 2002 uses JET 4.0. However, if we were to use Access 2002 to open (not convert) a database created in Access 97, the value of `CurrentDB.Version` would be 3.0 instead, indicating that the database was created by JET 3.0.

So, what collections does the `Database` object contain? Well, if we look at the diagram, we can see that there are five of them.

| This collection... | ...contains these objects |
| --- | --- |
| Containers | One `Container` object for every collection of `Documents` |
| QueryDefs | One `QueryDef` object for every saved query that exists within the database |

*Table continued on following page*

| This collection... | ...contains these objects |
|---|---|
| Recordsets | One Recordset object for every recordset that is currently open in the database |
| Relations | One Relation object for every relationship defined between tables in the database |
| TableDefs | One TableDef object for every table (including system tables, but excluding linked tables) which exists within the database |

We'll take a brief take look at the TableDefs and QueryDefs collections, just to make sure that we understand what they represent. Then we will focus on one collection in particular – the Recordsets collection – in a fair amount of detail. We shall not look at the Relations collection, as it is used so infrequently, and we shall leave our examination of the Containers collection to Chapter 17 when we discuss multi-user security.

## The TableDefs Collection

First of all, let us use the TableDefs collection to determine the number of tables in our database. Going back to the Immediate window in the IceCream.mdb database, if we type the following and hit the *Enter* key:

```
? CurrentDB.TableDefs.Count
```

we should see that the current database has 11 tables in it. "Hold on!", you might say, as you switch to the Database window, "There are only six tables there!"

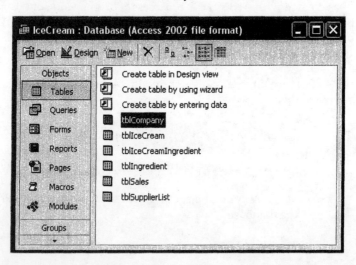

There certainly are six visible user-created tables, but the `TableDefs` collection also includes any hidden tables and system tables. If we view these, by checking the **Hidden Objects** and **System Objects** checkboxes on the **View** tab of the **Options…** dialog, we will see that there are indeed 11 tables in the database:

## The QueryDefs Collection

If we examine the `QueryDefs` collection, then we would expect to see that the number of objects in the collection is equal to the number of queries in the database. So let's try it:

```
? CurrentDB.QueryDefs.Count
```

Now this is even more perplexing. If you evaluate this line of code in the **Immediate** window in `IceCream.mdb`, you will find that there are a great number of them! But if you go to the Query pane of the Database window, you will see that there are no saved queries. So where did these `QueryDef` objects come from?

The answer is that there are occasions when queries are stored in an Access database even though they may not be visible in the Database window. For example, if you create a form which contains a combo box, and then use a SQL statement as the **Row Source** to populate that combo box, Access will compile the SQL and save the resulting query internally as a `QueryDef`. So the `QueryDefs` collection contains not just the queries that you explicitly created as queries and saved, but also any internal queries that exist within forms and reports.

# The Recordsets Collection

The third collection contained within the Database object is the Recordsets collection. Recordsets are fundamental to data access through VBA and are something that you will really need to get to grips with. But don't worry; it's really not that tough! Now even if you don't know what a recordset is, you will almost certainly have used one already. Put simply, a Recordset is just what its name suggests – a set of records. When you open a table in Datasheet view, you are looking at a set of records. When you open a form, it will normally have a set of records behind it that supply the data for the form. Relational databases are all about sets of records (as opposed to flat-file databases which tend to deal with records on an individual basis) and you will find that the Recordset object will probably become the single most used of all of the Data Access Objects that you will come across in VBA. So, we will spend some time now looking in detail at the different types of Recordset and how we can use them in code.

**Try It Out — Recordsets**

1. Open up IceCream.mdb, create a new standard module and call it **Chapter 6 Code**. In the new module, add a subprocedure called OpeningARecordset.

2. Add the following code to the subprocedure:

```
Public Sub OpeningARecordset()

Dim db As Database
Dim rec As Recordset
Dim intRecords As Integer

Set db = CurrentDb()
Set rec = db.OpenRecordset("tblIceCream")

intRecords = rec.RecordCount
MsgBox "There are " & intRecords & " records in the tblIceCream table"
rec.Close

End Sub
```

3. Now run the procedure. Remember, there are four ways to do this: you can hit *F5*, select **Run Sub/User Form** from the **Run** menu, hit the **Run Sub/User Form** button on the toolbar or type OpeningARecordset in the **Immediate** window and hit the *Return* key. You will get a message box telling you how many records there are in the table tblIceCream:

*If you get a Compile Error when trying to run this code, go to **References...** in the
**Tools** menu of the VBE, and make sure **Microsoft DAO 3.6 Object Library** is checked,
and not **Microsoft ActiveX Data Objects 2.1 Library**. Note that depending on what
software or Office service packs you may have installed on your computer, there may be
newer versions of ADO libraries listed. Make sure that none of them are checked.*

You can check that this is correct by opening the table in Datasheet view and having a look.

| | IceCreamID | IceCream | Description | Price | Picture |
|---|---|---|---|---|---|
| | 1 | Walnut Wonder | Wondering how many walnut pieces can be packed into an ice cream. In which | £0.00 | |
| | 3 | Strawberry Surprise | Lazy summer days by the river. Stawberries and cream, captured into a | £0.00 | Bitmap Image |
| | 4 | Admirable Apricot | Sharp and refreshing. One for those hot summer days. | | |
| | 5 | Blushing Blueberry Berg | A tangy taste of fresh Blueberries, buried deep beneath rich vanilla ice cream. | | |
| | 6 | Chocs Away | Rich, dashing and full of sauce. The very best dark chocolate ice cream, for those | | |
| | 7 | Barely Cinnamon | One for the animal in you. This cool cinnamon flavored ice will sooth the bear | | |
| | 8 | Chocolate Chip | Pieces of rich dark chocolate buried within luscious vanilla ice cream | | |
| | 9 | Chocolate Chip Cookie Dough | For those who can't make up their mind whether to have some cookies or an ice | | |
| | 10 | Strawberry Cheesecake | Fancy a large slice of cheesecake, but don't want to sit in a hot diner. Cool down | | |
| | 11 | Fudge Brownie | Horribly sweet and rich. The perfect brownie, now in ice cream form. | | |
| | 12 | Crunchy Coconut | Smooth ice cream and real coconut flesh give a rich and crunchy eastern feel. | | |
| | 13 | Apple Pie | For those who prefer Mom's apple pie, we've captured the very best in fresh | | |
| * | (AutoNumber) | | | | |

Record: ◄◄ ◄ [ 1 ] ► ►► ►* of 12

You should be getting a feel for the VBA code by now, so we won't explain every line that we write. Instead, we'll concentrate on the new or interesting parts.

In this example, we fill a variable with the data from the table `tblIceCream`,

```
Set rec = db.OpenRecordset("tblIceCream")
```

and then use the `MsgBox` function to display the count of the records in the `Recordset`:

```
intRecords = rec.RecordCount
MsgBox "There are " & intRecords & " records in the tblIceCream table"
```

Notice also that we close the `Recordset` at the end of the procedure:

```
rec.Close
```

Once a `Recordset` has been closed, you can't do anything else with it. This allows VBA to free any resources associated with the `Recordset` and is particularly necessary in a multi-user environment or when you are dealing with linked tables. (These are tables that are stored in other currently open Access or non-Access databases, but which are linked and so can be manipulated as such if they were in the current Access database).

As we mentioned above, a `Recordset` is just that – a set of records. While a `Recordset` is open in your code (after it has been filled with records with the `OpenRecordset` method and before it is closed with the `Close` method), you can do what you like with the records in that `Recordset` – edit them, delete them, or even add new records.

## Different Types of Recordset

In VBA there are five different types of `Recordset` object that you can use. Which one you use depends on a combination of factors, such as:

❑ How many tables the underlying data comes from

❑ Whether you want to update the records or just view them

❑ Whether the tables are in Access or some other type of database

❑ How many records there are in the recordset

We'll look in detail at when to use each of the five types of `Recordset` a little later, but first let's have a look at what they are. The five types of `Recordset` object are:

❑ `Table` – type Recordset objects

❑   Dynaset – type Recordset objects (normally just called dynasets)

❑   Snapshot – type Recordset objects (or just snapshots)

❑   Forward-only – type Recordset objects

❑   Dynamic – type Recordset objects

Dynamic Recordset objects aren't actually part of JET and are instead part of ODBCDirect technology. They are used for accessing data in remote ODBC databases, rather than data in Access databases, so we need not concern ourselves with them here. Instead, we will concentrate on the four JET recordsets: table-type, dynaset-type, snapshot-type and forward-only-type recordsets.

We'll look at the differences between these four types in just a moment.

You open all four different types of Recordset object in the same way – using the OpenRecordset method against a Database object. Have another look at the portion of code that we used just now:

```
Dim db As Database
Dim rec As Recordset

Set db = CurrentDb()
Set rec = db.OpenRecordset("tblIceCream")
```

First we create a Database object that corresponds to the database we are currently in. Then we create a Recordset object within the current database and fill it with records from the table tblIceCream.

By default, this statement creates a table-type Recordset object because it is based on a single table. If we had wanted to be more explicit, we could have used the intrinsic constant, dbOpenTable, as a parameter to the OpenRecordset method just to make sure that the Recordset object would be a table-type Recordset object:

```
Set rec = db.OpenRecordset("tblIceCream", dbOpenTable)
```

If we had wanted a dynaset-type Recordset object instead, we would have used the dbOpenDynaset constant instead:

```
Set rec = db.OpenRecordset("tblIceCream ", dbOpenDynaset)
```

And, not surprisingly, if we had wanted a snapshot-type Recordset object or a forward-only-type Recordset object, we would have created them like this:

```
Set rec = db.OpenRecordset("tblIceCream ", dbOpenSnapshot)
```

```
Set rec = db.OpenRecordset("tblIceCream", dbOpenForwardOnly)
```

We can see from the above statements, then, that there are three things we need to think about when we are creating a `Recordset` object:

❑   Which database are the records in?

❑   Whereabouts in that database are those records?

❑   What type of `Recordset` object do we want?

There are, in fact, further optional levels of control we can apply when we open `Recordset` objects, but we'll look at those a little later in Chapter 17 when we consider multi-user issues.

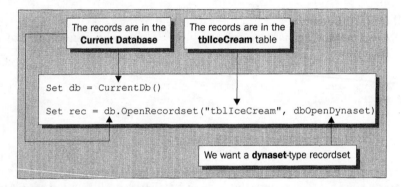

*Access allows you to create a `Recordset` object in a single line of code, without having to create a `Database` object. So you could say:*

```
Set rec = CurrentDB.OpenRecordset("tblIceCream",
dbOpenDynaset)
```

*However, the method we have used throughout this chapter, using an intermediate `Database` object, is usually preferable, and is more efficient if you need to refer to the same database somewhere else in your procedure.*

Now we know how to create `Recordset` objects, which type should we use? Let's look at the different types in turn, and see which situations they are best suited to.

### Table-type Recordset Objects

This is the default type for any `Recordset` objects where the records come from a single local or attached Access tables. In other words, if we try to create a `Recordset` object to retrieve records from a single Access table and we do not specify the type of `Recordset` object we want to open, Access will create a table-type `Recordset` object:

```
Set rec = db.OpenRecordset("tblIceCream")
```

Table-type `Recordset` objects are updateable (which means that we can make changes to the records in the `Recordset` and the changes will be reflected in the underlying table) objects. Another great advantage of using a table-type `Recordset` object is that you can use indexes on the table to speed up the process of searching for specific records. By contrast, you cannot use indexes against the other `Recordset` objects. In fact, we look at using indexes to locate records in a table-type `Recordset` later on in this chapter.

### Dynaset-type Recordset Objects

A dynaset-type `Recordset` object can be based on either a local or attached table, or it can be based on the result of a query. There are two key features of dynaset-type `Recordset` objects:

❑ You can edit a dynaset and the results will be reflected in the underlying tables.

❑ While a dynaset is open, Access will update the records in your dynaset to reflect the changes that other people are making in the underlying tables.

To understand better the way that dynasets operate, it is probably helpful to see how they are created. Whenever a dynaset-type `Recordset` object is created, Access starts to build a copy of the **key values** from the result. That is, it copies the field or group of fields that uniquely identifies each of the records in the result. The copy that it creates is, sensibly enough, called a keyset, because it is the set of key values. Then, whenever you want to view the records in the `Recordset` object, Access fetches the latest version of the non-key fields from the database based on the key values it has stored. Because of this behavior, you might sometimes see dynasets referred to as keyset-driven cursors. We will look at some of the implications of this behavior a little later.

*Note that the keyset is not fully complete until the last record (key value) in the table has been accessed.*

You should use dynaset-type `Recordset` objects if:

❑ You will need to update the records in the `Recordset` object.

❑ You want to see updates other users are making to those records.

❑ The `Recordset` object is very large.

❑ The `Recordset` object contains OLE objects such as bitmaps or Word documents.

### Snapshot-type Recordset Objects

In contrast, snapshot-type `Recordset` objects are not updateable and do not reflect the changes that other users make to the records. In fact, just as the name suggests, you are taking a 'snapshot' of the data at a certain point in time. Whereas Access creates a copy of just the key values to create a dynaset, it takes a copy of the entire set of results to form a snapshot.

One of the advantages of snapshots is that with modestly sized `Recordset` objects, snapshots are generally faster to create than dynasets. This is because the entire structure sits in memory without references back to the data source. You would use a snapshot-type `Recordset` object in a situation where you don't wish to update the data and when the recordset won't contain too many records – let's say no more than about 500 records.

> *The terms dynaset and snapshot were introduced in early versions of Access, but Microsoft suggests that they should both be referred to just as recordsets. Throughout this chapter, if we mention dynasets and snapshots, we will be referring to dynaset-type* `Recordset` *objects and snapshot-type* `Recordset` *objects respectively.*

### Forward-Only-type Recordset Objects

Conceptually, forward-only-type `Recordset` objects are very similar to snapshots. They are read-only, do not reflect other users' changes, and are created by taking a copy of the entire qualifying set of results. Where they differ from snapshots is that they only allow you to move through them in one direction. In other words, with a forward-only recordset, you can read the records from it one after the other, but you can't then move back to previous records. Forward-only recordsets are sometimes referred to as firehose cursors.

What makes forward-only recordsets so attractive is the fact that they are very fast for moderately sized sets of results. So, if you are concerned about performance, if you can put up with the limited functionality then forward-only recordsets are a good choice.

## Building Recordsets Dynamically

We have already seen how `Recordset` objects can be created with the `OpenRecordset` method. The examples that we have looked at so far have all involved creating `Recordset` objects directly from tables. However, you can also create a `Recordset` object from a saved query or from a SQL `SELECT` statement. To do this, you simply substitute the query's name or the SQL `SELECT` statement for the table name. For example, if you had a query called `qryTotalOrders` in your database, you could create a dynaset-type `Recordset` object that contained the records from the query like this:

```
Set db = CurrentDb
Set rec = db.OpenRecordset("qryTotalOrders", dbOpenDynaset)
```

or by entering a SQL `SELECT` statement directly:

```
Set db = CurrentDb
Set rec = db.OpenRecordset("SELECT * FROM Order", dbOpenDynaset)
```

Using saved queries (as in the first of these two examples) will typically give slightly better performance, as the query will already be compiled and so JET will not have to go through the process of compiling the query before it is run. However, the second technique affords more flexibility and is often the only way out if you want to build up a query's definition dynamically in code (for example, in response to a user's selections on a form). There is an extended example of just this technique in the next chapter.

### Default Types

If you do not specify the type of Recordset object that you want to open, Access will choose what is normally the best-performing type of Recordset object available:

❑ If the Recordset object is based on a single named table in the current database, Access will return a **table-type** Recordset object.

❑ If the Recordset object is based on a query or a SQL SELECT statement (or if it's from a table in a non-Access database), and if the underlying query or table can be updated, Access will return a **dynaset-type** Recordset object.

❑ In all other situations, Access will return a **snapshot-type** Recordset object.

However, there may be situations where you want to return a recordset of a different type than the one Access would normally return. For example, dynaset-type recordsets are generally quicker to open than snapshots, if the recordset will contain more than a few hundred records. So in a situation where Access would otherwise have created the recordset as a snapshot, you might want to explicitly create a dynaset instead.

## Requerying Data in Recordsets

If you want to make sure that the data in your Recordset is up-to-date, you can refresh it by executing the Requery method of the Recordset object:

```
rec.Requery
```

This re-executes the query that the Recordset object is based on, thus ensuring that the data is up to date. You can only do this, however, if the Recordset object supports requerying. In order to determine whether this is so, you should inspect the Recordset object's Restartable property. If the Recordset object's Restartable property is True, you can use the Requery method. You could test for this as follows:

```
If rec.Restartable = True Then rec.Requery
```

However, if the Recordset object's Restartable property is False, attempting to requery the recordset will generate an error. Table-type recordsets always have a Restartable property of False and so can never be requeried.

# Working with Recordsets

So far, we have only really looked at how to create `Recordset` objects and ensure that the data in them is up to date. But, of course, what we normally want to do is to look at the data itself.

To refer to individual fields within a `Recordset` object, you can use a variety of different methods. We'll create a subprocedure that opens a dynaset-type `Recordset` object based on the `tblIceCream` table.

**Try It Out**     **Looking at Values in a Recordset**

**1.** In `IceCream.mdb`, in the same module you created earlier in this chapter, insert a procedure called `OpenIceCreamRecordset`:

```
Sub OpenIceCreamRecordset()

    Dim db As Database
    Dim rec As Recordset

    Set db = CurrentDb()
    Set rec = db.OpenRecordset("tblIceCream")

    rec.Close

End Sub
```

**2.** Now place a **Stop** command after the `OpenRecordset` command. This has the effect of suspending execution of the code (see Chapter 12 for more on this):

```
Set rec = db.OpenRecordset("tblIceCream")

Stop

rec.Close
```

**3.** Run the procedure, either by hitting *F5*, by selecting **Run Sub/User Form** from the **Run** menu, hitting the **Run Sub/User Form** button on the toolbar, or typing the name of the procedure in the **Immediate** window and hitting the *Enter* key. When the line containing the `Stop` command is reached, execution of the code should pause and the line should be highlighted. We can now use the **Immediate** window to inspect the records in the recordset.

**4.** Make sure the **Immediate** window and **Locals** window are both visible. The **Locals** window should look like this. (If you have named your module differently, you will see a reference to the name you have given the module, rather than to **Chapter 6 Code**).

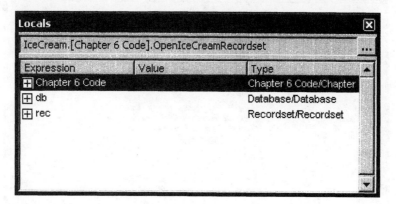

**5.** Now type the following in the **Immediate** window:

```
? rec(0), rec(1), rec(2)
```

**6.** Hit the *Enter* key and the value of the first three fields for the first record in the tblIceCream table should be displayed:

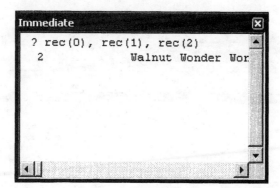

**7.** Now go to the **Locals** window and find the variable called rec. If you click on the plus sign to the left of the variable's name, the tree will expand to display the properties of the rec variable. There are quite a few of them!

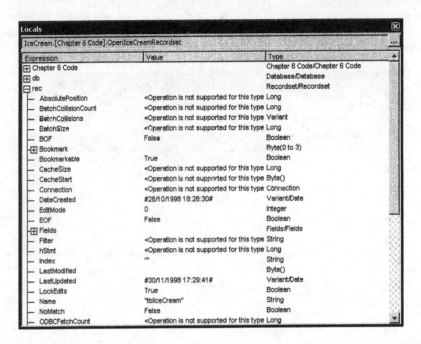

**8.** If you expand the entry for the Fields collection by clicking the plus button to its left, you will see it has five items (because there are five fields in the Recordset represented by the variable rec):

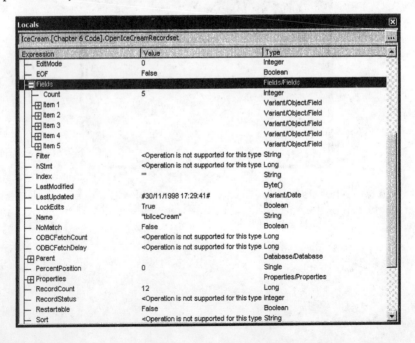

**9.** Expand Item 2, again by clicking the plus button to its left. You should see the properties of that particular Field object:

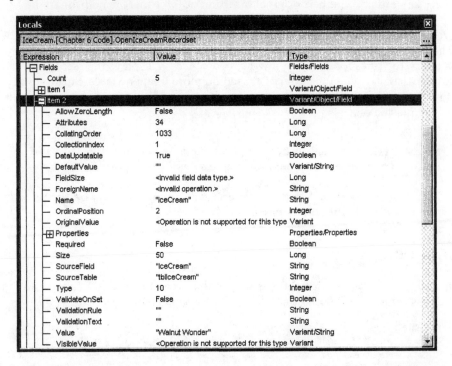

| Locals | | | ⊠ |
|---|---|---|---|
| IceCream.[Chapter 6 Code].OpenIceCreamRecordset | | | ... |
| Expression | Value | Type | ▲ |
| ⊟ Fields | | Fields/Fields | |
| — Count | 5 | Integer | |
| ⊞ Item 1 | | Variant/Object/Field | |
| ⊟ Item 2 | | Variant/Object/Field | |
| — AllowZeroLength | False | Boolean | |
| — Attributes | 34 | Long | |
| — CollatingOrder | 1033 | Long | |
| — CollectionIndex | 1 | Integer | |
| — DataUpdatable | True | Boolean | |
| — DefaultValue | "" | Variant/String | |
| — FieldSize | <Invalid field data type.> | Long | |
| — ForeignName | <Invalid operation.> | String | |
| — Name | "IceCream" | String | |
| — OrdinalPosition | 2 | Integer | |
| — OriginalValue | <Operation is not supported for this type | Variant | |
| ⊞ Properties | | Properties/Properties | |
| — Required | False | Boolean | |
| — Size | 50 | Long | |
| — SourceField | "IceCream" | String | |
| — SourceTable | "tblIceCream" | String | |
| — Type | 10 | Integer | |
| — ValidateOnSet | False | Boolean | |
| — ValidationRule | "" | String | |
| — ValidationText | "" | String | |
| — Value | "Walnut Wonder" | Variant/String | |
| — VisibleValue | <Operation is not supported for this type | Variant | ▼ |

**10.** Note the values of the CollectionIndex, Name, Size, and Value properties. From this you should be able to determine that the index of this field in the Fields collection of the Recordset is 1 (remember, these collections are zero-based); the name of the field is IceCream; the maximum length of values in this field is 50 characters; and the value of this field in the current record is Walnut Wonder.

**11.** Finally, return to the code window and hit either *F5* or the **Run Sub/User Form** button on the toolbar. This allows the procedure to run from where it is (at the Stop statement) to the end of the procedure and close the Recordset object.

### How It Works

Whenever you create a Recordset object, the first row of the recordset becomes the current record. As we created a table-type Recordset object, the records are ordered according to the primary key (IceCreamID) and so the current row is the record containing data for the ice cream called Walnut Wonder. We can then examine the value of any of the fields in this record. In this example, we inspected the values of the first three fields of that record, the IceCreamID, IceCream, and Description fields respectively.

At this point, you should note that the order of records in a query may not always be what you expect. If a query is based on a single table and you have not chosen to sort the records in some other way when you designed the query, then records in the query will normally be displayed in primary key order, or in their original insertion order if there is no primary key.

However, if your query contains a criterion for a field that is not the primary key, the records will usually be displayed in insertion order (that is, the order in which they were entered in the table). In fact, the rules for deciding in what order Access displays the records are even more complex, particularly when the query is based on more than one table. Suffice to say that you cannot rely on the records in a query being sorted in any particular order unless you have explicitly requested one.

> If you want the records in a query to be sorted, you should specify a sort criterion (or an **ORDER BY** clause) when you design the query.
>
> If you have not specified any sort criteria, you should not rely on the records in the result set being in any particular order.

## Examining Field Values

To look at the values of individual fields within the current record, we can use any number of conventions that we could with other objects within collections. They are as follows:

| General Syntax | Example |
| --- | --- |
| RecordsetName!FieldName | rec!IceCreamID |
| RecordsetName("FieldName") | rec("IceCreamID") |
| RecordsetName(FieldIndex) | rec(0) |
| RecordsetName.Fields(FieldIndex) | Rec.Fields(0) |

*When using the RecordsetName(FieldIndex) syntax to refer to fields in a Recordset object, you should remember that Access will always give the first field an index of 0 rather than 1, irrespective of any Option Base setting you may have stated. So, rec(2) refers to the third field in the Recordset object, rec, not the second.*

## Moving Through Recordsets

So far, however, things have been rather static. We are able to open a Recordset object and inspect all the values in the current record, but what if we want to move around the recordset? Suppose we wanted to move to the next record down and look at the values in that? Well, it's simple enough. If, after our Stop statement, we had applied the MoveNext method to the Recordset object in the last example by typing this into the Immediate window:

```
rec.MoveNext
```

and then checked the value of the `IceCream` field, we would have found that it was
`Strawberry Surprise`:

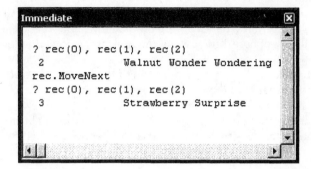

Moving around a recordset is really very simple. The methods that you can use are:

| Method | Description |
|---|---|
| MoveNext | Makes the next record the current record |
| MovePrevious | Makes the previous record the current record |
| MoveFirst | Makes the first record the current record |
| MoveLast | Makes the last record the current record |
| Move *n* | Makes the record *n* records away from the current record (rec.Move 3 or rec.Move -2) |

This is all very well, but we are still faced with the problem that we encountered back in the
first couple of chapters with our "unintelligent" navigation buttons. If we wanted to print the
value of the `IceCream` field for every record in our recordset, we could keep on using the
`MoveNext` method and then print the value of `IceCream`, but at some point we'll hit the last
record. Access will let us try another `MoveNext`, but when we try to print the value of
`IceCream`, we'll get a warning message telling us that there is no current record:

In Chapter 2, we had the same problem. We added logic to the buttons on the `frmCompany` form to enable us to move to the first, next, last, or previous records or to the blank record at the end of the recordset that is used for inserting a new record, but there was nothing to stop us trying to move beyond this, in which case we also got an error message.

To make the form more user friendly, we decided to disable certain buttons, depending on where we were in the recordset. In Chapter 3, we started to implement this feature and wrote code to disable the Next button when we were on the new blank record at the end of the table. Well, it's taken a while to get here, but now we can look at the code that looks after *all* the buttons.

We're in a position to deal with the problem for all of the buttons, because we have a set of methods at our disposal that allow us to test where we are in a recordset and actually move to the last record or first record in one straightforward action. Once we've executed these methods, we can then take appropriate action to disable the correct buttons. Before we move on to the actual code, however, let's make sure that we understand exactly when we want the navigation buttons to be enabled or disabled.

| Position | First | Previous | Next | Last | New |
|---|---|---|---|---|---|
| First Record | Disabled | Disabled | Enabled | Enabled | Enabled |
| Intermediate Records | Enabled | Enabled | Enabled | Enabled | Enabled |
| Last Record | Enabled | Enabled | Disabled | Disabled | Enabled |
| New (Blank) Record | Enabled | Enabled | Disabled | Enabled | Enabled |

Looking at the table above, we can see that when we are on the first record of the form we want the Previous button to be disabled, while the rest of the buttons will be enabled. On the last record of the form we want the Next button to be disabled. On a blank, new record we would want to have both the Previous and Next buttons disabled.

We also need to consider what will happen if the form does not allow new records to be added. By disabling the Next button on the last record, we prevent the user from using the Next button to try to move from the last record into the blank, new record. So we are covered in that situation. However, we will also need to make sure that the New button is disabled if the form does not allow new records to be added.

Finally, we will need to make sure that all of the buttons except for the New button are disabled if there are no records at all in the form (or rather in the underlying recordset).

Now that we have sorted out the rules of engagement, we can go into battle…

**1.** If you haven't already done so, open up the `IceCream.mdb` database and switch to the VBA IDE by hitting *Alt + F11*.

**2.** Double-click the `Form_frmCompany` class module and locate the `Current` event. This should contain the code we wrote in Chapter 3.

**3.** Locate the `Private Sub Form_Current()` subprocedure, and replace it with the code given below:

```
Private Sub Form_Current()

Dim recClone As Recordset

'Make a clone of the recordset underlying the form so
'we can move around that without affecting the form's
'recordset

Set recClone = Me.RecordsetClone()

'If we are in a new record, disable the <Next> button
'and enable the rest of the buttons
If Me.NewRecord Then
  cmdFirst.Enabled = True
  cmdPrevious.Enabled = True
  cmdNext.Enabled = False
  cmdLast.Enabled = True
  cmdNew.Enabled = True
  Exit Sub
End If

'If we reach here, we know we are not in a new record
'so we can enable the <New> button if the form allows
'new records to be added
cmdNew.Enabled = Me.AllowAdditions

'But we need to check if there are no records. If so,
'we disable all buttons except for the <New> button
If recClone.RecordCount = 0 Then
  cmdFirst.Enabled = False
  cmdNext.Enabled = False
  cmdPrevious.Enabled = False
  cmdLast.Enabled = False
Else

  'If there are records, we know that the <First> and
  '<Last> buttons will always be enabled, irrespective
  'of where we are in the recordset
```

```
      cmdFirst.Enabled = True
      cmdLast.Enabled = True

      'Synchronize the current pointer in the two recordsets
      recClone.Bookmark = Me.Bookmark

      'Next, we must see if we are on the first record
      'If so, we should disable the <Previous> button
      recClone.MovePrevious
      cmdPrevious.Enabled = Not (recClone.BOF)
      recClone.MoveNext

      'And then check whether we are on the last record
      'If so, we should disable the <Next> button
      recClone.MoveNext
      cmdNext.Enabled = Not (recClone.EOF)
      recClone.MovePrevious
   End If

   'And finally close the cloned recordset
   recClone.Close

End Sub
```

**4.** Now check that the code compiles by selecting **Compile IceCream** from the **Debug** menu.

**5.** Save the changes to the module and switch back to Access by hitting *Alt + F11*.

**6.** Close the frmCompany form (which should be in **Design View**) and open it up in **Form** view. Try moving through the records – you'll see that you now have intelligent navigation buttons:

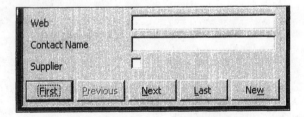

## How It Works

The code is not complicated but there are a few new things, so let's have a look at it in detail.

```
Set recClone = Me.RecordsetClone()
```

The first thing we did was to create a duplicate copy of the form's `Recordset` object, using `RecordsetClone()`. This is an alternative to using the `OpenRecordset` method to create a `Recordset` object. Using the `RecordsetClone()` method against the form to create a **separate** copy of the recordset means that we can navigate or manipulate a form's records independently of the form itself. This is desirable, as we are going to want to move around the recordset behind the scenes and don't want our maneuvers to be reflected in the form itself. Instead, we are able to use a separate, cloned, read-only `Recordset` object that acts just as if it had been created using the `OpenRecordset` method.

```
If Me.NewRecord Then
```

The first condition that we check for is whether or not we are in a new record. The simplest way to do this is to check the `NewRecord` property of the form. If we are in a new record, we disable the **Next** and **New** buttons and then use the `Exit Sub` to exit the procedure without executing any more code.

```
cmdNew.Enabled = Me.AllowAdditions
```

We then need to work out whether the form allows new records to be added. Again we can determine this by inspecting a property of the form – in this case, the `AllowAdditions` property. If this returns `True` we want to enable the **New** button; if it returns `False` we want to disable the **New** button. In other words, the `Enabled` property of the **New** button should be set to the same as the `AllowAdditions` property of the form.

```
If recClone.RecordCount = 0 Then
```

The next step is to check whether there are any records behind the form. It is often easy to forget to make this check but, if we try to move around a `Recordset` object with no records, Access will generate an error and cause our code to break. The easiest way to determine whether there are any records is to inspect the cloned `Recordset` object's `RecordCount` property. This will tell us the number of records in the recordset. If it is equal to zero, there are no records in the recordset and the only button that should be enabled is the **New** button.

> *It's worth mentioning here that the `RecordCount` property of some types of `Recordset` object is not always immediately available. You might need to move to the last record in the recordset to update it. However, here the form is based on a single table and so the form's recordset is a table-type `Recordset` object that doesn't suffer from this problem. You'll see more of this in a moment.*

So, by now we have determined that we are not in a new record and that there is more than one record in the recordset. We can therefore enable the **First** and **Last** buttons. Once we have done that, we need to work out where in the recordset we are – at the top, the bottom, or somewhere in the middle?

Before we can do this, we need to make sure that the current record in our cloned Recordset object is the same as the current record in the form. Whenever you create a Recordset object, the first record in that Recordset object becomes the current record. However, our procedure is called from the form's Current event (not only when the form is opened, but also whenever the user moves to a different record). When a clone is created, it doesn't have a current record. So, we need some sort of mechanism to set the current record in the cloned Recordset object to match that on the form. We can do this with a Bookmark (we'll discuss these later in the chapter):

```
recClone.Bookmark = Me.Bookmark
```

A Bookmark is simply way of identifying each individual row in a recordset. This is what Access uses in place of record numbers. A Bookmark consists of a Byte array. We shall be looking at them in a little more detail later on in this chapter when we discuss how we can find specific records in a recordset. For the moment, however, all we are concerned with is ensuring that the cloned Recordset object and the form are in sync. By assigning to the Bookmark property of the cloned Recordset object the same value as the Bookmark property of the form, we ensure that the clone has the same current record as the one the user can see displayed on the form.

So now it is time to work out where the current record is in the recordset. If the current record is the first record, we must disable the Previous button. If the current record is the last record, we must disable the Next button. To determine whether the current record is at an extremity of the recordset, we use the BOF and EOF properties. BOF stands for **Beginning Of** File and EOF stands for **End Of** File.

The BOF property of a Recordset object is True if the current record pointer is placed immediately before the first record, and the EOF property is True if the current record pointer is placed immediately after the last record. Consequently, if we attempt to move to the record previous to the current one and we find that the recordset's BOF property is True, we know that the current record is the first record in the recordset:

```
recClone.MovePrevious
cmdPrevious.Enabled = Not (recClone.BOF)
recClone.MoveNext
```

If this code seems a little hard to fathom at first, just remember that the BOF and EOF properties return a True or False value. If recClone.BOF returns True, we're at the beginning of a recordset and we need to disable the cmdPrevious button by setting its Enabled property to False. We use the NOT operator to simply reverse the Boolean value returned by the recClone.BOF expression. If False is returned, however, it means we're not at the beginning of a recordset, so we want the cmdPrevious button to be enabled by having a True value placed in its Enabled property.

If we had wanted to, we could also have expressed this with the following less succinct If...Then structure.

```
recClone.MovePrevious
If recClone.BOF = True Then
   cmdPrevious.Enabled = False
Else
   cmdPrevious.Enabled = True
End If
recClone.MoveNext
```

Similarly, if we attempt to move to the record after the current record and we find that the EOF property of the cloned Recordset object is True, we know that the current record is the last record in the recordset.

```
recClone.MoveNext
cmdNext.Enabled = Not (recClone.EOF)
recClone.MovePrevious
```

And that's about it. We just close the cloned recordset and the code is complete.

# Counting Records in a Recordset

In the last example, we used the RecordCount property of a Recordset object to determine how many records it contained. The behavior of the RecordCount property is, in fact, a little more complex than we let on, and depends on the type of recordset in question.

### Table-Type Recordsets

When you open a table-type recordset, Access knows the number of records in the table, and so the RecordCount property of the recordset is instantly set to that number.

### Dynasets and Snapshots

In order to increase the performance of your code when creating dynaset-type Recordset objects and snapshot-type Recordset objects, Access doesn't fully populate the recordset until navigating to the end of the table or query. Therefore, Access does not always immediately know the number of records in these types of Recordset object. In order to force Access to calculate the number of records in a dynaset-type Recordset object or in a snapshot-type Recordset object, you have to use the MoveLast method of the Recordset object.

```
Set rec = db.OpenRecordset("qryTotalOrders", dbOpenDynaset)
rec.MoveLast
Debug.Print rec.RecordCount
```

This forces Access to fetch all the rows in the recordset before continuing, and so enables it to determine the precise number of rows in the recordset.

> *If you only want to know whether there are any records in the recordset, as opposed to finding out how many, you do not need to use a MoveLast method. When you use the OpenRecordset method and the recordset is not empty, Access waits until the first record has been returned before executing the next line of code. In other words, if the RecordCount property of a recordset is equal to zero, there are definitely no more rows to be returned.*

If you add or delete records in a dynaset-type `Recordset` object, the `RecordCount` property of the object increases or decreases accordingly. However, if other users add or delete records in the underlying tables, these changes are not reflected until the `Recordset` object is requeried (using the `Requery` method). Again, you will need to use the `MoveLast` method after the `Recordset` object has been requeried, to ensure that the `RecordCount` property is accurate.

## AbsolutePosition and PercentPosition

The record counting behavior has implications for two other recordset properties. The `AbsolutePosition` property returns the position of the current record in the recordset relative to 0. When using the `AbsolutePosition` property, bear these factors in mind:

- ❑ If there is no current record, the `AbsolutePosition` property returns –1.

- ❑ It is by no means certain that records will always appear in the same order every time a recordset is opened unless a sort criterion (ORDER BY clause) has been specified.

- ❑ Remember that the `AbsolutePosition` of a record will change as records are inserted or deleted. For this reason, do not be tempted to use the `AbsolutePosition` property instead of a bookmark.

The `PercentPosition` property indicates the absolute position of the current record as a percentage of the total number of records that is returned by the `RecordCount` property. With regard to accuracy of the values returned, the same considerations apply to the `PercentPosition` property as to the `RecordCount` property. In order to ensure that the `PercentPosition` property returns an accurate figure, you should use the `MoveLast` method after opening or requerying `Recordset` objects, and before inspecting the `PercentPosition` property.

> *The AbsolutePosition and PercentPosition properties only apply to dynasets and snapshots. Trying to use them against table-type Recordset objects will result in a run-time error.*

The following procedure can be used to display the record count and the absolute and percent positions returned by Access in the Ice Cream database.

```
Sub ShowPositions()

Dim db As Database
Dim rec As Recordset

Set db = CurrentDb()
Set rec = db.OpenRecordset("tblIceCream", dbOpenDynaset)

Debug.Print "Records", "Absolute", "Percent"

Do While Not rec.EOF
   Debug.Print rec.RecordCount, rec.AbsolutePosition, rec.PercentPosition
   rec.MoveNext
Loop

rec.Close

End Sub
```

If you run this procedure in the Ice Cream database, you will see that it creates a dynaset-type `Recordset` object based on the `tblIceCream` table and then loops through it, one record at a time. For each record, it displays the `RecordCount`, `AbsolutePosition`, and `PercentPosition` properties of the recordset. The output it would print into the **Immediate** window would look like this:

| Immediate | | |
| --- | --- | --- |
| ShowPositions | | |
| Records | Absolute | Percent |
| 1 | 0 | 0 |
| 12 | 1 | 8.333333 |
| 12 | 2 | 16.66667 |
| 12 | 3 | 25 |
| 12 | 4 | 33.33333 |
| 12 | 5 | 41.66667 |
| 12 | 6 | 50 |
| 12 | 7 | 58.33333 |
| 12 | 8 | 66.66666 |
| 12 | 9 | 75 |
| 12 | 10 | 83.33334 |
| 12 | 11 | 91.66666 |

There are three things in particular that are worth noting in this procedure:

❑ Firstly, you can see that the `RecordCount` property returns the wrong value the first time around.

❑ Secondly, the `AbsolutePosition` property is zero-based and so returns 0 for the first record, 1 for the second record, and so on.

❑ And finally, take a good look at the `Do While...Loop` structure seen here. This technique is commonly used in procedures that need to loop through every record in a recordset.

# Looking for Specific Records

So far, we have only concerned ourselves with moving through a `Recordset` object using the various `Move` methods. But there may be occasions when you know exactly which record you wish to find. In that situation, you will find that the `Seek` and `Find` methods are more suited to your task.

## Finding Records in Table-Type Recordsets

The quickest way to find a record in a table-type `Recordset` object is to use the `Seek` method.

One of the important processes involved in designing a database is to determine how the tables within the database are to be indexed. If you search on an indexed field, Access is able to find records much more quickly. Also, Access can perform operations, such as joins and sorts, much faster if the fields which are being joined or sorted are indexed. Bear in mind, however, that one downside of indexes is that they add an overhead to the length of time it takes Access to update records (as the index needs to be updated in addition to the data) so they should only be used where they will provide a measurable improvement in performance.

As a programmer, you can take advantage of the extra speed provided by indexes if you use the `Seek` method. This allows you to perform a fast search on an indexed field. Using `Seek` is a two-step process:

❑ First select the indexed field that you wish to search on

❑ Then specify the criteria for finding the record

As an example, we'll search the `tblSales` table for sales that cost a certain amount.

---

**Try It Out**    **Using the Seek Method**

**1.** Open the `tblSales` table in design view and select the `AmountPaid` field.

**2.** If there is not one already, add a non-unique index to the field by changing its Indexed property to Yes (Duplicates OK).

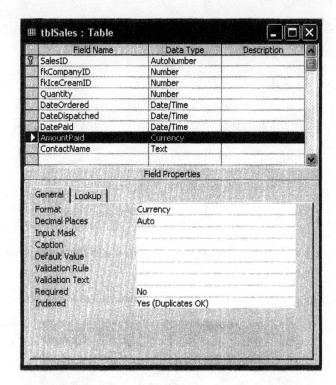

3. Now switch to **Datasheet** view, save the table design (if prompted), and sort the records by **AmountPaid**. This should be fast as the **AmountPaid** field is now indexed and, in any case, there are not too many records in the table.

4. Look for orders that cost the same amount, for instance, orders with a **SalesID** of 120 and 357 both cost $210.00. Make a note of the **SalesID**, **DatePaid** and **AmountPaid** values. We shall be using these in a moment.

5. Close down the table, saving your changes as you do so.

6. Now create a new procedure in the **Chapter 6** module you created earlier in the chapter and type in the following code:

```
Sub SeekByPrice(curPrice As Currency)

    Dim db As Database
    Dim rec As Recordset
    Dim strSQL As String
    Dim strMsg As String

    strSQL = "tblSales"
```

```
    Set db = CurrentDb()
    Set rec = db.OpenRecordset(strSQL)

    rec.Index = "AmountPaid"
    rec.Seek "=", curPrice

    strMsg = "Order No. " & rec("SalesID") & " placed on " & _
      FormatDateTime(rec("DateOrdered"), vbLongDate) & _
      " cost " & FormatCurrency(rec("AmountPaid"))

    MsgBox strMsg

    rec.Close

End Sub
```

**7.** Run the code by typing SeekByPrice 210 in the **Immediate** window and hitting the *Enter* key.

**8.** A message box appears telling you the first order it has found with the price of $210.00.

## How It Works

This example makes use of the Index property and Seek method to locate the required record in the table.

```
Set rec = db.OpenRecordset(strSQL)
```

The first thing we do is to create a table-type Recordset object. Note that we did not need to explicitly request that the Recordset object should be a table-type Recordset object as it is based on a single local Access table; table-type is the default type for Recordset objects created from local Access tables.

```
rec.Index = "AmountPaid"
```

The next step is to specify the index that we want to use when seeking the required record. When setting the `Index` property of the `Recordset` object, you should use the name of the index as it appears in the **Indexes** window of the table in Design view (you can view this by pressing the **Indexes** button on the toolbar). If you try to set the `Index` property of a `Recordset` object to an index that does not exist, Access will generate a run-time error.

```
rec.Seek "=", curPrice
```

Once we have chosen an index, we are ready to look for the record we require. We do this using the `Seek` method. When using `Seek`, we need to specify two arguments. The first indicates the type of comparison we want to carry out and the second indicates the value we want to compare against the index.

In our example, we want to find records for which the value of the indexed field is equal to `210`, so the type of comparison is an equality comparison and the value we are comparing against the index is `210`. The following list shows the type of comparisons that can be carried out using the `Seek` method:

| Comparison argument | Has this effect... |
| --- | --- |
| `"="` | Finds the first record whose indexed field is equal to the value specified |
| `">"` | Finds the first record whose indexed field is greater than the value specified |
| `">="` | Finds the first record whose indexed field is greater than or equal to the value specified |
| `"<"` | Finds the first record whose indexed field is less than the value specified |
| `"<="` | Finds the first record whose indexed field is less than or equal to the value specified |

Note that the comparison argument is enclosed in quotes. If you prefer, you can specify a string variable – or a variant variable of type `vbString` – in place of the string literal. In other words, we could have written our code like this:

```
strComparison = "="
rec.Seek strComparison, curPrice
```

However, the important thing to remember is that the comparison argument must be a valid string expression.

```
strMsg = "Order No. " & rec("SalesID") & " placed on " & _
    FormatDateTime(rec("DateOrdered"), vbLongDate) & _
    " cost " & FormatCurrency(rec("AmountPaid"))
```

Once the Seek method has found a record matching the criterion we set, we display the result in a dialog box.

*Remember that there was more than one record that matched our criterion; the Seek method returns the first match it finds.*

The above example assumes that Seek is going to be successful in finding a matching record. What happens, though, if this isn't the case?

**1.** Run the SeekByPrice procedure again, but this time pass it as an argument a value which you know will have no matching records, such as 3.64. The result of this is that the code breaks and Access displays a dialog box telling you that there is no current record.

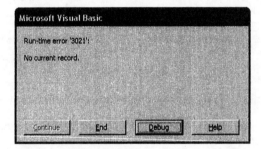

In order to work out how to solve this problem, we must first determine which line of our code caused the error to happen.

**2.** Hit the Debug button. Access displays the code window with the offending line of code highlighted:

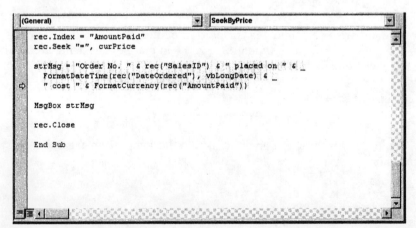

```
(General)                                    SeekByPrice

    rec.Index = "AmountPaid"
    rec.Seek "=", curPrice

    strMsg = "Order No. " & rec("SalesID") & " placed on " & _
      FormatDateTime(rec("DateOrdered"), vbLongDate) & _
⇨     " cost " & FormatCurrency(rec("AmountPaid"))

    MsgBox strMsg

    rec.Close

    End Sub
```

As you can see, the line that caused the error to occur was the one in which we attempted to display the dialog box informing the user of the matching record. The code did not break simply because there was no record which matched. In fact, it broke because when the Seek method fails to find a matching record, it doesn't know which record to make the current record and leaves the current record in an indeterminate state. So, when you subsequently try to perform an operation that requires the current record to be known, Access does not know which record is the current record, and displays an error message.

What we need, therefore, is some mechanism that allows us to determine whether or not the Seek method found a record, so that we only attempt to display the result if we know it was successful.

**3.** Stop the code from executing, by either hitting the **Reset** button or selecting **Reset** from the **Run** menu.

**4.** Modify the SeekByPrice procedure so that it now looks like this:

```
. . .
If rec.NoMatch = True Then
   strMsg = "No orders cost " & FormatCurrency(curPrice)
Else
   strMsg = "Order No. " & rec("SalesID") & " placed on " & _
         FormatDateTime(rec("DateOrdered"), vbLongDate) & _
         " cost " & FormatCurrency(rec("AmountPaid"))
End If
. . .
```

*The NoMatch property of a Recordset object is set to True when the Seek method (or any of the Find methods discussed below) fails to locate a record.*

**5.** Now run the procedure from the **Immediate** window, and pass 3.64 again. This time, you get a message box telling you what has happened:

This is a much more friendly way of doing things!

*As we've explained, one problem of failed Seek or Find (see below) operations is that if no matching record is found, the current record is left in an indeterminate state. We will look at how to deal with this situation a little later in this chapter when we look at the Bookmark property.*

## Finding Records in Dynasets and Snapshots

Using the Seek method is a very quick way of finding records, but it has a couple of notable limitations:

❑   It can only be used on indexed columns, which means that…

❑   It can only be used against table-type recordsets

If we want to find records in dynaset- or snapshot-type Recordset objects, or in non-indexed fields of table-type Recordset objects, we must use one of the Find methods. There are four of these and their uses are described below:

| This method... | Works like this... |
| --- | --- |
| FindFirst | Starts at the beginning of the recordset and searches downwards until it finds a record which matches the selected criteria and makes that record the current record. |
| FindLast | Starts at the end of the recordset and searches upwards until it finds a record which matches the selected criteria and makes that record the current record. |
| FindNext | Starts at the current record and searches downwards until it finds a record which matches the selected criteria and makes that record the current record. |
| FindPrevious | Starts at the current record and searches upwards until it finds a record which matches the selected criteria and makes that record the current record. |

As with the Seek method, if any of the Find methods fail to find a record matching the specified criterion, the current record is left in an indeterminate state. This means that if you then try to perform any operation that requires the current record to be known, Access will generate a run-time error.

The syntax of the Find methods is somewhat different from that of the Seek method, as we need to specify the field we are searching on, as well as the value we are looking for. For example, if we had opened a snapshot-type Recordset object based on the tblSales table and wanted to use the FindFirst method to find the first with a DateOrdered after 10th July 2002, we would write this:

```
rec.FindFirst "DateOrdered > #07/10/2002#"
```

*The argument we supply for a Find method is just the WHERE clause of a SQL statement, but without the WHERE in front.*

It's quite intuitive really – the only thing you need to remember is that the criteria must be enclosed in quotes.

As with the `Seek` method, we could use a string variable to specify the criteria:

```
strCriterion = "DateOrdered > #07/10/2002#"
rec.FindFirst strCriterion
```

**Try It Out**       **Using the Find Methods**

Let's try rewriting the last example using the `FindFirst` and `FindNext` methods.

**1.** Insert a new procedure and add the following code:

```
Sub FindByPrice(curPrice As Currency)

Dim db As Database
Dim rec As Recordset
Dim strSQL As String
Dim strMatches As String
Dim intCounter As Integer

strSQL = "tblSales"

Set db = CurrentDb()
Set rec = db.OpenRecordset(strSQL, dbOpenSnapshot)

rec.FindFirst "AmountPaid = " & curPrice
Do While rec.NoMatch = False
  intCounter = intCounter + 1
  strMatches = (strMatches & vbCrLf) & rec("SalesID")
  rec.FindNext "AmountPaid = " & curPrice
Loop

Select Case intCounter
  Case 0
  MsgBox "No orders cost " & FormatCurrency(curPrice)
  Case 1
  MsgBox "The following order cost " & _
    FormatCurrency(curPrice) & " : " & _
    vbCrLf & strMatches
  Case Else
   MsgBox "The following " & intCounter & " orders cost " & _
    FormatCurrency(curPrice) & " : " & _
    vbCrLf & strMatches
End Select
```

```
rec.Close

End Sub
```

**2.** Open the **Immediate** window and run the procedure, using the price 3.64. There are no matching records and the following dialog box is displayed:

**3.** Now run it again, but this time pass 77 as the argument, for which there is one match.

**4.** Finally, run the procedure again and pass a price for which there are several matches, like 210.

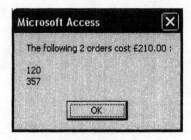

<hr/>

**How It Works**

The main difference in this portion of code is the method we use to find the matching records:

```
rec.FindFirst "AmountPaid = " & curPrice
```

We start by looking for the first record with a price matching the one entered:

```
Do While rec.NoMatch = False
  intCounter = intCounter + 1
  strMatches = strMatches & Chr$(10) & rec("SalesID")
  rec.FindNext "AmountPaid = " & curPrice
Loop
```

If there is no order with this price, rec.NoMatch is True and so the subsequent Do...Loop structure is not entered. However, if a matching order is found, rec.NoMatch is False and we enter the loop.

Once inside the loop, three things happen. First we increment a counter to indicate how many matches have been made; then we build up a string using the linefeed character Chr$(10) (which causes a new line to be created) and the SalesID of the matching record; and finally we have a look to see if there is another record which matches our criterion.

If there is, we return to the start of the loop and, as rec.NoMatch is False, we run through the whole process again.

When there are no more matches found, rec.NoMatch is True and the loop terminates. Then, all that is left is to display the results in a message box.

```
Select Case intCounter
  Case 0
  MsgBox "No orders cost " & FormatCurrency(curPrice)
  Case 1
  MsgBox "The following order cost " & _
    FormatCurrency(curPrice) & " : " & _
    Chr$(10) & strMatches
  Case Else
  MsgBox "The following " & intCounter & " orders cost " & _
    FormatCurrency(curPrice) & " : " & _
    Chr$(10) & strMatches
End Select
```

intCounter contains a count of the number of times we went through the loop, and, therefore, how many matches were found.

## Notes on Formatting Dates and Currency Amounts in VBA

Among the most frequent types of data that you will search for in Recordset objects are dates and monetary amounts. For example, you may want to find orders placed on a certain day or worth a certain amount. If you do so, you need to be aware of how VBA handles date and currency formats, especially if you are working through this book somewhere other than in the United States.

VBA will format date and currency outputs according to the settings you make in the **Regional Settings** section of the **Control Panel**. No problem there.

**257**

You may, for example, have your computer set up to display dates in the British format (so that the 31st of October, 2002 is displayed as 31/10/02). This isn't a problem for VBA when formatting date or currency **output** – if VBA encounters a date of 31-Oct-02 and your Short Date Style is set to dd/mm/yy, VBA will display the date as 31/10/02. Just what you want.

However, VBA operates slightly differently when requesting date **input**. The locale of VBA is always **English (United States)** irrespective of the way that you have configured the **Regional Settings** in your **Control Panel**. As a result, if you enter a date in either a SQL statement or as in VBA, it will be interpreted as if it were in the format mm/dd/yy, that is, in US format.

To ensure that all of the dates you enter will be interpreted correctly, it is best to explicitly convert all dates to US format before using them in SQL statements or in VBA. To convert a date to US format, you would replace a statement like this:

```
rec.FindFirst "OrderDate = " & dtOrder
```

with one like this:

```
rec.FindFirst "OrderDate = #" & Format(dtOrder, "mm/dd/yy") & "#"
```

When entering currency values, similar considerations apply. VBA expects currency values in 9.99 format – even if the currency separator defined in **Control Panel** is something other than a period.

> **The problem of non-US date and currency formats only exists when you are dealing with dates and monetary amounts in VBA. In forms and in the query designer, you can enter dates and currency amounts in your own local format, and Access will convert them for you.**

## When to Use Find and Seek

So far, we have looked at how to use the Seek and Find methods to locate records in a recordset. However, in all of the examples, our task could have been completed more quickly by opening a Recordset object based on an SQL string which defined our search criteria. Don't worry if you don't know much about Structured Query Language, the SQL in this example is very simple and we will be looking at SQL in more detail in the next chapter few chapters.

```
strSQL = "SELECT * FROM tblSales WHERE AmountPaid = " & curPrice
```

It simply assigns to the string strSQL an SQL statement which selects every field (using the * symbol) for each record of the tblSales table where the AmountPaid is equal to the price held in the variable curPrice. So, if we add this to our code, the FindByPrice() procedure could be rewritten like this:

```
Sub FindByPrice2(curPrice As Currency)

Dim db As Database
Dim rec As Recordset
Dim strSQL As String
Dim strMatches As String
Dim intCounter As Integer

strSQL = "SELECT * FROM tblSales WHERE AmountPaid = " & curPrice

Set db = CurrentDb()
Set rec = db.OpenRecordset(strSQL, dbOpenSnapshot)

Do Until rec.EOF
  strMatches = strMatches & Chr$(10) & rec!SalesID
  rec.MoveNext
Loop

intCounter = rec.RecordCount

Select Case intCounter
  Case 0
  MsgBox "No orders cost " & FormatCurrency(curPrice)
  Case 1
  MsgBox "The following order cost " & _
    FormatCurrency(curPrice) & " : " & _
    Chr$(10) & strMatches
  Case Else
  MsgBox "The following " & intCounter & " orders cost " & _
    FormatCurrency(curPrice) & " : " & _
    Chr$(10) & strMatches
End Select
rec.Close

End Sub
```

The difference in speed between executing FindByPrice() and FindByPrice2() could be particularly noticeable if you run the procedures against attached tables in a remote ODBC server such as SQL Server over a Local Area Network or particularly over a Wide Area Network.

The reason for this difference in speed is that, in the first example, we are opening a Recordset object that contains the entire contents of the tblSales table. All of these records would have to be read from disk on the remote computer, sent across the network and then read into cache locally – although, if it was a dynaset-type Recordset object, only the keys from each row are cached. Then we would have to search through all of the records for the few that meet our criteria.

In the second example, however, we are opening a Recordset object that contains only as many rows as there are matching records. This will be much more efficient and will result in considerably less network traffic, as only two or three rows will need to be retrieved.

**259**

Although the difference in speed might go unnoticed for relatively small tables, for other larger tables with many thousands of records the difference could be very great indeed.

For this reason, it is wiser to restrict the use of the Find methods to local tables, and to use SQL WHERE clauses in queries against attached tables in ODBC databases. If performance against local tables is still a problem, check whether the field you are searching on is (or can be) indexed, and use the Seek method instead.

# Bookmarks

Earlier in the chapter, we used the Bookmark property to synchronize the current records in two Recordset objects that were clones of each other. The Bookmark property of a recordset is stored internally by Access as an array of bytes which uniquely identifies the current record. When you reference the Bookmark property in VBA code, however, you should always assign it to a String or Variant variable:

```
Dim strBookmark As String
strBookmark = rec.Bookmark
```

or:

```
Dim varBookmark As Variant
varBookmark = rec.Bookmark
```

> *Note that you can only use the Bookmark property to synchronize current records in Recordset objects that are clones of each other. If the Recordset objects have been created separately – even if they are based on the same query or SQL – the bookmarks of individual records may not match.*

You can also use bookmarks to help you to return to records that you have already visited. This is done by storing the Bookmark property of the recordset in a variable when you are on a specific record, and then setting the Bookmark property of the recordset to that value when you want to return to that record. This is especially useful when used in conjunction with Seek or Find operations. Remember, if you are using Find or Seek and a matching record cannot be found, the current record will be left in an indeterminate state. So it makes sense to store the Bookmark property of the recordset before the operation and then reassigning this value to the Bookmark property of the recordset if the Find or Seek operation fails.

Our code would then look like this:

```
Dim strBookmark As String
strBookmark = rec.Bookmark

rec.FindFirst "DateOrdered > #07/10/2002#"
```

```
If rec.NoMatch = True Then
   strMsg = "No orders cost " & FormatCurrency(curPrice)
   rec.Bookmark = strBookmark
Else
   strMsg = "Order No. " & rec("SalesID") & " placed on " & _
       FormatDateTime(rec("DateOrdered"), vbLongDate) & _
       " cost " & FormatCurrency(rec("AmountPaid"))
End If
```

## Comparing Bookmarks

Sometimes, you may wish to compare two Bookmark properties. For example, you may want to check whether the current record is one that you visited earlier and whose Bookmark you had saved.

Although you can store a Bookmark as a String variable, you need to remember that a Bookmark is stored internally as an array of Bytes. For this reason, you should use **binary comparison** when comparing two bookmarks with each other.

If the Option Compare Database statement is present in a module, which it is by default, comparisons will be made according to the sort order determined by the locale of the database. In other words, when you compare two strings together in Access, the default for US English is for the comparison to be case-insensitive. You can prove this by opening the Immediate window and evaluating the following expression:

```
?"aaa" = "AAA"
```

When you hit the *Enter* key, the result should be True, which means that string comparisons are not case-sensitive.

In contrast, when **binary comparison** is enabled, comparisons are made according to the internal binary representation of the characters, which is case-sensitive. Because lower case characters (for example "a") are represented differently internally than upper case characters ("A"), a binary comparison of "aaa" and "AAA" should return False.

When you compare Bookmark properties, you want to make sure that the comparison is case-sensitive, otherwise you may find that the comparison returns True when the Bookmarks are not completely identical. The safest way to do this is to compare string variables with the StrComp function, which returns 0 if the two variables that are being compared are identical. This has an argument that allows you to choose what type of comparison you wish to perform:

❑    If the comparison argument is set to vbBinaryCompare (0), it forces binary comparison of the two variables.

❑    If it is set to vbTextCompare (1), it forces textual comparison.

❑ And if it is set to `vbDatabaseCompare` (2), or is omitted, the comparison is performed based on the sort order that was in place when the database was created.

```
intResult=StrComp(strBkMk1, strBkMk2, 1vbTextCompare) 'Textual comparison

intResult=StrComp(strBkMk1, strBkMk2, 0vbBinaryCompare) 'Binary comparison
```

*Recordset objects based on native Access tables should all support bookmarks. However, Recordset objects based on linked tables from some databases, such as Paradox tables with no primary key, may not support bookmarks. Before you attempt to use bookmarks, you can test whether the Recordset object supports them by inspecting its Bookmarkable property. This will be True if the Recordset object supports bookmarks.*

## Editing Records in Recordsets

You now know how to find particular records within a `Recordset` object, but what if you want to edit them once you've found them? There are five main methods that can be used for manipulating data in recordsets. These are listed here:

| This method... | Has this effect... |
| --- | --- |
| Edit | Copies the current record to the copy buffer to allow editing. |
| AddNew | Creates a new record in the copy buffer with default values (if any). |
| Update | Saves any changes made to the record in the copy buffer. |
| CancelUpdate | Empties the copy buffer without saving any changes. |
| Delete | Deletes the current record. |

From the table above you should be able to see that changes to records are made in the copy buffer rather than in the recordset itself. What this means in practice is that adding or amending a record is a three-part process:

❑ Copy the current record into the copy buffer with the `Edit` method, or place a new record in the copy buffer with the `AddNew` method

❑ Make any required changes to the fields in that record

❑ Save the changes from the copy buffer to disk with the `Update` method

*Note that if you try to make changes to a record without first copying it to the copy buffer (without using the Edit method), Access will generate a run-time error. And if you move to a new record without saving the changes to the current record in the copy buffer (using the Update method) – or by canceling the change, those changes will be lost.*

If you want to empty the copy buffer without moving to a new record, you can use the `CancelUpdate` method on the `Recordset`. This will undo any changes you may have made to the record in the copy buffer, but does not change the current record.

If you want to know whether any records have been copied into the copy buffer and not saved, you can inspect the `EditMode` property of the recordset. This can hold any of three values represented by the constants in the table below.

| This constant... | Has this value... | And means this... |
| --- | --- | --- |
| `dbEditNone` | 0 | There is no record in the copy buffer. |
| `dbEditInProgress` | 1 | The current record is in the copy buffer (the `Edit` method has been invoked). |
| `dbEditAdd` | 2 | The record in the copy buffer is a new record that hasn't been saved (the `AddNew` method has been invoked). |

If you use the `Delete` method the deletion is immediate; you do not have to follow it with an `Update` method to make the deletion permanent. However, although the record is deleted, it is still regarded as the current record. You need to make a different record the current record before you perform any more operations that require a valid current record. Once you have moved away from a deleted record, you cannot make it current again.

*We shall be looking at how Access locks records when editing and updating `Recordset` objects when we consider multi-user aspects of Access in Chapter 17.*

**Try It Out — Editing Records in VBA**

**1.** Open the `tblCompany` table and have a look at the place names in the `Country` field. They are currently in mixed case. Note the following illustration that shows these values before they are updated.

**2.** Close the table and then, in the code module you created earlier in this chapter, add the `Capitalize` procedure:

```
Function Capitalize(strTable As String, strFld As String)

Dim db As Database
Dim rec As Recordset

Set db = CurrentDB()
Set rec = db.OpenRecordset(strTable)

'Loop through all records until we go beyond the last record
Do While Not rec.EOF

  'Copy the current record to the copy buffer
  rec.Edit

  'Make changes to the record in the copy buffer
  rec(strFld) = UCase$(rec(strFld))

  'Save the contents of the copy buffer to disk
  rec.Update
```

```
'Make the next record the current record
rec.MoveNext


Loop

Capitalize = True

End Function
```

**3.** Now make sure that the **Immediate** window is visible and type the following line of code.

```
? Capitalize ("tblCompany", "Country")
```

**4.** When you hit the *Enter* key, if the Capitalize function executes correctly, it will convert all the names of the places in the Country field of the tblCompany table to upper case and then return True to indicate success.

**5.** Open the tblCompany table again and have a look at the names of the places in the Country field. They should now be in upper case.

*Note that this example is simply an illustration of the sequence of events required when editing a record. In practice, using an **action query** would be considerably more efficient than stepping through all the records.*

### When a Recordset Can't be Updated

We started the chapter by pointing out the differences between the various types of recordset. One of the most obvious differences between snapshot-type `Recordset` objects and dynaset-type `Recordset` objects is that snapshots are static images of the data and are never editable. So, if you try to use the `Edit`, `AddNew`, or `Delete` methods against a snapshot-type `Recordset` object, Access will generate a run-time error. However, there are also several occasions when a dynaset-type `Recordset` cannot be edited, such as:

❑   When it is based on a crosstab query.

❑   When it is based on a union query.

❑   When you have not been granted permission to update the records in the table on which the recordset is based.

In order to be sure that your `Recordset` object can be edited, you can inspect its `Updatable` property. This will be `True` if the recordset can be updated, and `False` otherwise.

```
If rec.Updatable = True Then
  rec.Edit
  . . .
  . . .
  . . .
  rec.Update
End If
```

# Summary

In this chapter, we have looked at one of the key features that differentiates VBA from macros – the ability to work with sets of records at the record level. With macros, you can only see the big picture – you can deal with sets of records as a whole but there is no mechanism for manipulating individual records. With VBA, however, you can go down to the record level and then work on individual fields within each record. You will find that creating and manipulating `Recordset` objects is one of the most frequent and useful operations that you will perform if you choose to use DAO in VBA. If you can master the use of the `Recordset` object you have won most of the battle.

This chapter has covered:

- ❑ What the Data Access Object hierarchy is and how it has developed.

- ❑ What ActiveX Data Objects (ADO) is all about.

- ❑ The chief components of DAO.

- ❑ When to use the different types of `Recordset` objects – particularly tables, dynasets, and snapshots.

- ❑ How to examine data in a `Recordset` using VBA.

- ❑ Creating intelligent navigation buttons using the `Move` methods.

- ❑ How to use `Find` and `Seek` to locate particular records.

- ❑ The `Bookmark` property and what it is used for.

- ❑ How to edit records in a `Recordset`.

However, that is just the beginning. In the next chapter we will look at some of the more advanced capabilities of the JET 4.0 engine and how we can access them through DAO.

# Exercises

**1.** Earlier in this chapter we looked at the `AbsolutePosition` property of the recordset. See if you can use this to create a record indicator on the **Company** form (`frmCompany`). What are the limitations of this record indicator?

**2.** We mentioned earlier on that the `Relations` collection contains a `Relation` object for every relation defined between tables in a database. See whether you can write a procedure to document these relations in the **Immediate** window like this:

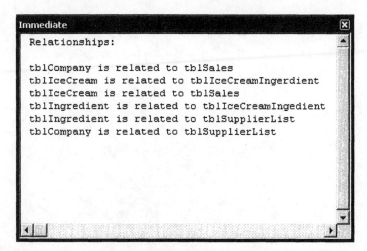

```
Immediate                                        ☒
 Relationships:

 tblCompany is related to tblSales
 tblIceCream is related to tblIceCreamIngerdient
 tblIceCream is related to tblSales
 tblIngredient is related to tblIceCreamIngedient
 tblIngredient is related to tblSupplierList
 tblCompany is related to tblSupplierList
```

# CHAPTER 7

# Data Management Techniques

In the previous chapter, we looked at how recordsets are created and how we can move through records within a recordset one at a time, giving us a much finer degree of control than we have with macros. In this chapter, we will look at some of the other DAO objects – in particular the `QueryDef` object – and how, as developers, we are able to manipulate them to our best advantage.

Here, we will be concentrating on methods of creating queries at run time. This is a particularly useful technique which can allow users a great deal of freedom over the types of query they want to produce, without the developer having to relinquish too much control. The main topics that we will consider are:

❑    Creating queries at run time

❑    Displaying records selected at run time

❑    Modifying the form's record source

❑    Using Structured Query Language (SQL)

❑    Creating a table of matching records

## The Challenge – Flexibility vs. Manageability

We have already seen how we can navigate around and modify the data in recordsets. The main theme running throughout this chapter, however, is the dynamic creation and modification of actual database objects such as queries at run time. In other words, we will see how it is possible to programmatically modify the structure of the underlying database objects while they are in use in a production environment.

You may wonder why anyone would want to create or modify a query at run time. Why not just create the query correctly at design time? Well, it's true that you should try to create as many of your queries at design time as possible – this has definite performance benefits, as we will see later, and allows complete control over the actions of the user. However, sometimes you just don't have enough information at design time to allow you to build all the queries that will be necessary for your application to run. Having to drop everything and create new queries for your users every time they think up yet another minor variation would quickly become a chore. Or perhaps the user needs to run so many different queries that their pre-definition is simply too uneconomical.

In the example we will be using, we have to enable the users to design queries while the application is running. In the Ice Cream database, frmCriteria is a simple form, which allows users to select sales based on a set of criteria that they specify themselves.

We'll start off by examining what our users want the application to be able to do. This is often more formally known as **user requirements analysis**. Once we have done that, we can work out how we are going to implement this functionality.

# The Requirement – Ad Hoc Query Functionality

If you remember, one of the tables within the Ice Cream database is the tblSales table. This contains details of all of the sales (orders) that have been made for the ice creams that our shop produces. As well as detailing who ordered the ice cream, it also stores payment and delivery details. To remind you, here is the structure of the tblSales table.

| Column | Data Type |
| --- | --- |
| SalesID | AutoNumber |
| fkCompanyID | Long Integer |
| fkIceCreamID | Long Integer |
| Quantity | Integer |
| DateOrdered | Date/Time |
| DateDispatched | Date/Time |
| DatePaid | Date/Time |
| AmountPaid | Currency |
| ContactName | Text |

And here is a diagram of the relationships between the various tables:

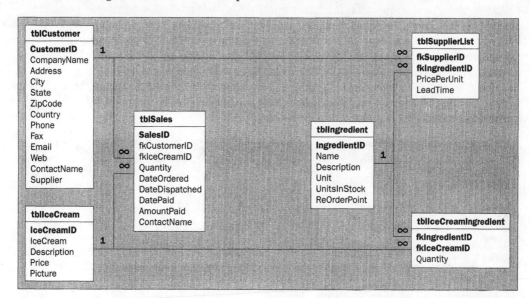

As you can see, relationships between the `tblSales`, `tblCompany`, `tblIceCream`, `tblIngredients`, and `tblIceCreamIngredient` tables allow us to determine which companies ordered which ice creams and what ingredients were in those ice creams.

Now one of the requirements of our application is that it should allow users to look up previous sales that meet certain conditions or criteria. The criteria identified by the users are as follows:

- All sales made to a certain company
- All sales of a particular ice cream
- All sales of ice creams containing a particular ingredient
- All sales of ice creams ordered between certain dates
- All sales which it took longer than a certain period of time to fulfill
- All sales for which it took the customer longer than a certain period of time to pay

In itself, this might seem fairly daunting, but our users are even more demanding and want to be able to combine any or all of these criteria into a single query. For example, they might want to find out: *Which orders for ice creams were made by Jane's Diner in November 2002 where it took more than 7 days for us to fulfill the order?*

When they run the query, the users want to know how many orders match the criteria that they have specified. They should then be presented with the opportunity of viewing those results in detail and printing a report containing the matching results.

Now this is not an uncommon type of request. In most database applications there is some type of requirement for flexible querying functionality. One of the characteristics of relational databases is that they divide up complex pieces of information into a number of smaller, related elements. There is more about this characteristic, more formally known as **normalization**, in the next chapter. The consequence of this division is that it allows us to view our data and analyze our data across multiple dimensions. For example, by division our data into separate tables for sales, ice creams, companies, and ingredients, we have made it a fairly simple task to allow a query to be created which finds the answer to the question posed above. In fact the query required to provide the answer is shown below:

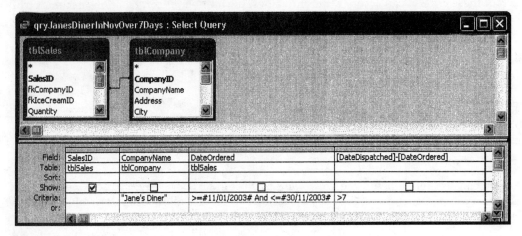

Alternatively, if we wanted to write the query in SQL, we would express it like this:

```
SELECT tblSales.SalesID
FROM tblCompany
   INNER JOIN tblSales
   ON tblCompany.CompanyID = tblSales.fkCompanyID
WHERE (((tblCompany.CompanyName)="Jane's Diner")
   AND ((tblSales.DateOrdered)>=#11/01/2002# And
(tblSales.DateOrdered)<=#11/30/2002#)
   AND (([DateDispatched]-[DateOrdered])>7));
```

*Structured Query Language, or SQL, is the language that databases use for manipulating data. Later on in this chapter, we'll look at the basics of how SQL works. If you want to learn more about SQL, why not look at Beginning SQL Programming, from Wrox Press (ISBN 1-861001-80-0)?*

Now writing that one query might not seem too complex in itself. But that is just one example of one of the queries that could have been requested. If you cast your mind back to the list of criteria that the users of the application want to search on, we can see that there are 6 of them, any of which can be combined to form a more complex query. Those of you with a mathematical inclination (and a knowledge of Pascal's triangle) will realize that this means that there are $2^6 = 64$ different ways in which these criteria can be combined (That's 1 combination involving no criteria, 6 combinations involving 1 criterion, 15 involving 2 criteria, 20 involving 3, 15 involving 4, 10 involving 5 and 1 combination involving all 6 criteria). Pascal's triangle or no Pascal's triangle, that is still a lot of combinations. In fact, when you add to this the fact that each of these criteria can accept different values, the number of combinations becomes truly daunting. So what are we to do?

> Our first reaction – and quite a tempting one – is simply to tell our users not to be so demanding. This may annoy our users, so we will assume that we cannot offer this response and that this is the functionality we have to deliver! In any case this is a perfectly reasonable request and exactly the kind of thing you will come across frequently out there in the real world.

## Why Not Use Parameterized Queries?

One solution might be to devise a parameterized query to solve this problem. To see how this would work, let us assume that we are working with just three possible criteria: `Quantity`, `AmountPaid`, and `DatePaid`. If we were to allow our users to select records based on these criteria, they could combine them in $2^3 = 8$ ways.

Now we could cater for all of these combinations with the following query:

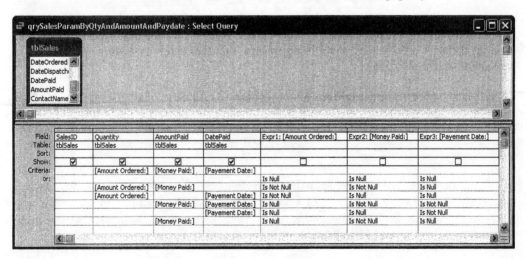

The user will be prompted for values for the three different criteria and the query will return the correct values irrespective of which of the criteria the user chooses to fill in. But it is not the most intuitive of queries, especially if you see how the query looks in SQL.

```
SELECT tblSales.SalesID, tblSales.Quantity, tblSales.AmountPaid,
tblSales.DatePaid
FROM tblSales
WHERE (((tblSales.Quantity)=[Amount Ordered:])
  AND ((tblSales.AmountPaid)=[Money Paid:])
  AND ((tblSales.DatePaid)=[Payement Date:]))
  OR ((([Amount Ordered:]) Is Null) AND (([Money Paid:]) Is Null)
  AND (([Payement Date:]) Is Null))
  OR (((tblSales.Quantity)=[Amount Ordered:])
  AND ((tblSales.AmountPaid)=[Money Paid:])
  AND (([Amount Ordered:]) Is Not Null)
  AND (([Money Paid:]) Is Not Null) AND (([Payement Date:]) Is Null))
  OR (((tblSales.Quantity)=[Amount Ordered:])
  AND ((tblSales.DatePaid)=[Payement Date:])
  AND (([Amount Ordered:]) Is Not Null) AND (([Money Paid:]) Is Null)
  AND (([Payement Date:]) Is Null))
  OR (((tblSales.AmountPaid)=[Money Paid:])
  AND ((tblSales.DatePaid)=[Payement Date:])
  AND (([Amount Ordered:]) Is Null)
  AND (([Money Paid:]) Is Not Null) AND (([Payement Date:]) Is Not Null))
  OR (((tblSales.DatePaid)=[Payement Date:])
  AND (([Amount Ordered:]) Is Null)
  AND (([Money Paid:]) Is Null) AND (([Payement Date:]) Is Not Null))
  OR (((tblSales.AmountPaid)=[Money Paid:])
  AND (([Amount Ordered:]) Is Null)
  AND (([Money Paid:]) Is Not Null) AND (([Payement Date:]) Is Null));
```

Now if you scale that up to 6 criteria, then you will find that the query needs 64 criteria rows, with various combinations of Is Null and Is Not Null – and the SQL doesn't even bear thinking about! We think that you will appreciate that this is not a prudent way of implementing the solution.

An alternative (and equally nightmarish) approach would be to create 64 queries and run whichever one corresponded to the particular combination of criteria selected by the user. Trust us, we wouldn't wish the implementation and administration of that solution on anyone. Even minor changes to the database might force us to modify each and every query (without introducing any errors, of course!).

The problem with the first approach, using the parameterized query, is that a very complex query is always run whenever the user asks a question, however simple the question is. Even if the user just wants to find the sales made on 1st November, the parameterized query approach will always require a beast of a query to be run.

The problem with the second approach is that you have to write and administer 64 separate queries, only one of which is ever used at any one time, irrespective of the questions the user asks. Both of these solutions, then, are very inefficient. What we really want is to have a single query, and for that query to be only as complex as the question posed by the user demands. And to do that we need to modify the query on the fly, in response to the user's selection of criteria. That's what we are going to do in this chapter; we will learn how to programmatically build and use a SQL query string.

*By the way, the ability to view the SQL generated by the Query Designer grid in Access is very useful, particularly when dealing with complex joins between tables. Even experienced VBA database developers sometimes use it to design a query. Then they switch to SQL view and copy the SQL it has generated into their VBA code. To do this simply select View menu and then SQL View.*

*And it works just as well the other way. If you are using VBA to build a SQL string, then you can always copy and paste the SQL string into the Query Designer's SQL window. Then you can switch to design view and/or run the query so that you can check that the SQL string really does produce the results you intended.*

## Building a Query by Form Interface

Our first challenge is working out how we are going to present the user with an intuitive way of selecting one of the 64 different combinations of criteria that are available. One of the best approaches to this problem is to use what is often referred to as a query by form (QBF) interface.

A QBF interface is, at its simplest, just a form containing textboxes or combo boxes for each of the criteria that the user can specify. In our case, there are 6 criteria so the form would look something like this:

As you can see, the user clicks the checkbox to indicate that a particular criterion is to be used. The process of clicking this checkbox enables the text boxes or combo boxes in which the values for the criterion are then entered. The screenshot above illustrates how the form could be used to ask the question we highlighted earlier: *Which orders for ice creams were made by Jane's Diner in November 2002 where it took more than 7 days for us to fulfill the order?*

In fact, the way the form has been designed, it actually allows substantially more than 64 queries to be produced as the user can specify either a lower or upper limit (or both) for the Order Date and can also select sales with a Payment Delay or Dispatch Delay either more than or less than a certain number of days. And yet this form uses only one query to answer all of those combinations of criteria, and it only takes a few dozen lines of code to make the whole thing work. We'll spend the rest of this chapter implementing this QBF functionality in the Ice Cream database. Once you have seen how it works in this situation you should be able to adapt the ideas that we will be covering to pretty much any situation that calls for QBF functionality. Here's what we are trying to do:

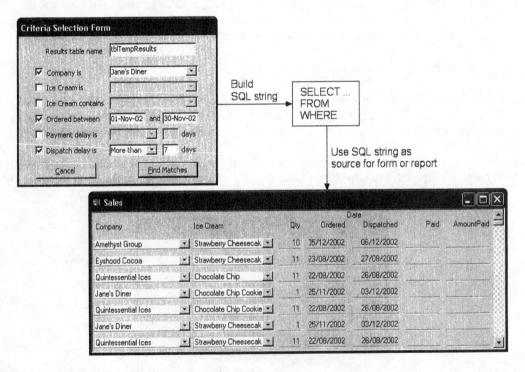

We are going to create the Criteria Form, which will allow us to select our criteria. This will build a SQL query, and this query will be used as the basis for a form or a report.

Before we start to modify any queries we first need to create the QBF form that is shown above. If you want to, you could try your hand at building it yourself, but to make life easier for you, there is a shell criteria form provided in the `IceCream07.mdb` database.

**Try It Out**    **Importing the Criteria Form**

**1.** Open the `IceCream.mdb` database you have been building as you have been working through the book (or open the `IceCream07.mdb` database from the CD).

**2.** If the Database window is not displayed, make it visible by hitting *F11*.

**3.** From the File menu, select Get External Data and then Import.

**4.** A dialog box will then appear and you will be asked to select the database from which you want to import objects. Select the `IceCream07.mdb` database and hit the *Enter* key.

**5.** You will then be asked which objects you wish to import. Click the Forms tab and select `frmCriteria`.

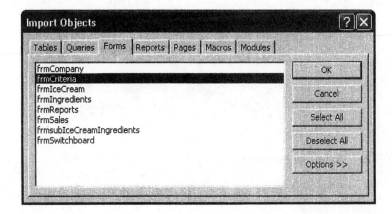

**6.** Press the OK button and the `frmCriteria` form will be imported into the current database.

Now that we have a copy of the `frmCriteria` form in our database, we can take a look at what happens when the user selects values in it.

**Try It Out**    **Using the Criteria Form**

**1.** Open the version of the `IceCream.mdb` database you have been using or building.

**2.** Open the `frmCriteria` form.

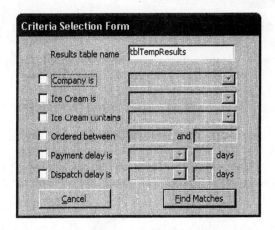

**3.** Check and uncheck the checkboxes on the left hand side of the form. Note how the associated text boxes and combo boxes are enabled and disabled as you check and uncheck the checkboxes.

**4.** Check the **Company is**, **Ordered between**, and **Dispatch delay is** checkboxes and enter the following values into the textboxes on the form.

| Field | Value |
|---|---|
| Company is | Jane's Diner |
| Ordered between | 01-Nov-02 and 30-Nov-02 |
| Dispatch delay is | More than 7 days |

**5.** Now hit *Ctrl+G* to open the VBA IDE and display the Immediate window.

**6.** In the Immediate window, we are going to look at the values held by some of the various combo boxes and text boxes on the form. To find the values they hold, evaluate the following expressions in the Immediate window. To do this, type each of the lines in turn into the Immediate window and hit the *Enter* key after each.

```
?forms("frmCriteria")("chkCompanyID")
?forms("frmCriteria")("cboCompanyID")
?forms("frmCriteria")("chkDateOrdered")
?forms("frmCriteria")("txtDateFrom")
?forms("frmCriteria")("txtDateTo")
?forms("frmCriteria")("cboDispatchDelay")
?forms("frmCriteria")("txtDispatchDelay")
```

You should see the following values returned:

```
Immediate                                                    ⊠
?forms("frmCriteria")("chkCompanyID")
-1
?forms("frmCriteria")("cboCompanyID")
10
?forms("frmCriteria")("chkDateOrdered")
-1
?forms("frmCriteria")("txtDateFrom")
01/11/2002
?forms("frmCriteria")("txtDateTo")
30/11/2002
?forms("frmCriteria")("cboDispatchDelay")
>
?forms("frmCriteria")("txtDispatchDelay")
7
```

So, although we have still quite a way to go, at least we have a good starting point. We have a form that we can use to gather all of the criteria required to run the various queries that our application needs to be able to cope with. But before we look at how to build the query, let's have a brief look at some of the other functionality in the frmCriteria form.

Firstly, if you want to know how the textboxes and combo boxes are enabled and disabled, just take a peek at the code behind the form (open the form in Design view and then click the Code button or choose **Code** from the **View** menu). Each of the checkboxes has an event procedure handling its Click event. For checkboxes, the Click event is not only fired when the user clicks the checkbox with the mouse; it is also fired when the user carries out any action which has the same effect as clicking the checkbox with the mouse, such as pressing the space bar while the checkbox is selected.

```
Private Sub chkCompanyID_Click()

   cboCompanyID.Enabled = chkCompanyID

End Sub
```

So what the piece of code above does is to interrogate the value of chkCompanyID. If the checkbox has just been checked, its value will be True (-1); otherwise it will be False. All we then need to do is to assign this value to the Enabled property of any combo boxes or textboxes associated with the checkbox.

*The Value property is the default property of a checkbox object, so evaluating chkCompanyID is equivalent to evaluating chkCompanyID.Value.*

Secondly, have a look at the values that the textboxes and combo boxes contain. Some of them are obvious, but others bear further investigation. For example, the top three combo boxes return numbers rather than the values that are selected. We do this on purpose as shall become clear. The combo boxes are populated by a query with two columns. One of these columns is the one that is displayed on the form; other is hidden (by having its Width set to 0) and contains the CompanyID for the value being displayed. For example, the cboCompanyID combo box has been populated with the results of this query, which is stored in the Row Source property of the combo box:

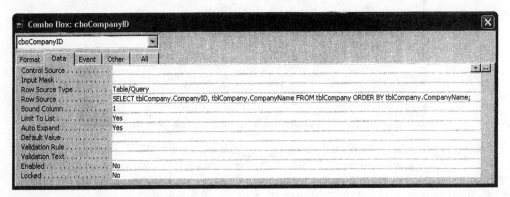

So, when Jane's Diner is selected in the combo box, the bound column contains the value 10, which is what is returned when we interrogate the value of cboCompanyID. Now that's all very interesting, but why bother? To answer that, let us have another look at the SQL that we used earlier in this chapter to evaluate this query:

```
SELECT tblSales.SalesID
FROM tblCompany
  INNER JOIN tblSales
  ON tblCompany.CompanyID = tblSales.fkCompanyID
WHERE (((tblCompany.CompanyName) = "Jane's Diner")
  AND ((tblSales.DateOrdered) >= #11/01/02#)
  AND ((tblSales.DateOrdered) <= #11/30/02#)
  AND ((tblSales.[DateDispatched] - tblSales.[DateOrdered]) > 7));
```

You see, the company name is the only part of this query which needs to be retrieved from a table other than the tblSales table. The tblSales table contains the CompanyID, not the CompanyName for the company that bought the ice cream. So, if we wanted to, we could re-write this query like this:

```
SELECT tblSales.SalesID
FROM tblSales
WHERE tblSales.fkCompanyID=10
  AND tblSales.DateOrdered>=#11/1/02#
  AND tblSales.DateOrdered<=#11/30/02#
  AND [DateDispatched]-[DateOrdered]>7
```

Now rewriting the query in this fashion has two advantages. Firstly, the query should run faster, because there is no need to create a join to a second table. (Indeed if the tables have a lot of data and we have specified a lot of joins then the performance gain may be substantial.) More importantly for us though, the query is much simpler to construct. Remember, we are going to need to be able to create a variety of different queries, depending on what the user selects. The more we can avoid joins, the easier that task will be for us.

The final thing to notice about this form is what happens when we hit the **Find Matches** button. Have a look at the code in the event handler for the `Click` event of the `cmdFind` button and you will see this:

```
Private Sub cmdFind_Click()

    Call EntriesValid

End Sub
```

So, when the `Click` event is fired, this code runs the `EntriesValid` procedure. As its name suggests, the `EntriesValid` procedure checks that each of the selections made by the user is valid. So if a user has, for example, checked the "**Company is**" checkbox, but has not selected a company, the `EntriesValid` function will display an error message warning the user of this inconsistency.

So, we have a convenient way of collecting input from the user, but how do we go about reflecting the user's selections in the query we will run? In order to do that, we need to know how to manipulate queries. Once we have done that, we will come back and implement that functionality in the `frmCriteria` form.

# Creating and Modifying DAO QueryDefs

You will probably remember from the previous chapter that a `QueryDef` is the name given to a query object variable in VBA. Just as we can create a `String`-type variable to hold a piece of text, so we can create a `QueryDef` object to hold a query definition. Note that a `QueryDef` object holds the **definition** of a query, not the results. Query results, as we saw in the previous chapter, are held in `Recordset` objects. If you want, you can think of the `QueryDef` as being like a query in design view and a `Recordset` as representing a query in datasheet view.

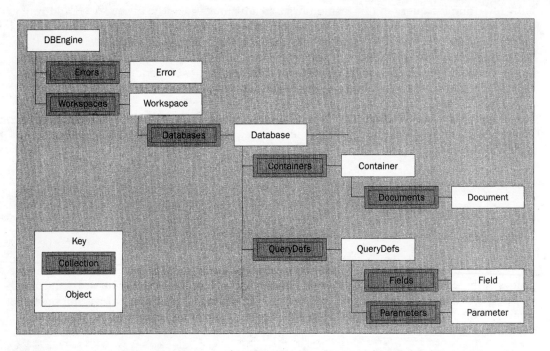

As you can see from the diagram above which shows a section of the DAO hierarchy, the QueryDefs collection belongs to the Database object. This is fairly logical really – after all, a database can have multiple queries in it, but a query can only exist in one database.

**Try It Out** — **Creating and Modifying a QueryDef**

1. Create a new standard code module and call it Chapter 7 Code.

2. Type in the procedure as it appears below.

```
Function MakeQueryDef(ByVal strSQL As String) As Boolean

    Dim qdf As QueryDef
    Dim boolResultCode As Boolean

    If strSQL = "" Then
        boolResultCode = False              'no query string to use!
    Else
        On Error Resume Next                'get ready to handle any errors
```

```
     'Create the new query object
     Set qdf = CurrentDb.CreateQueryDef("qryExample")
     If Err.Number <> 0 Then
        boolResultCode = False        'failed for some reason so cannot continue
     Else
        qdf.SQL = strSQL              'succeeded so load the query object with
                                      'the query string

        qdf.Close                     'finished with the query object so close it
        RefreshDatabaseWindow             'update the Query window
        boolResultCode = True             'report a success
     End If
     On Error GoTo 0                  'reset error handler
   End If

   MakeQueryDef = boolResultCode      'report what happened

End Function
```

To run the procedure, open the Immediate window. Type in the following and hit *Enter*:

```
?MakeQueryDef("SELECT * FROM tblCompany WHERE CompanyID = 10")
```

**3.** The word `True` should appear in the Immediate window, indicating that the function completed successfully.

*If you try to execute this procedure for a second time it will return `False` indicating that it has failed. This is because there is already a query called `qryExample` in the database. We will look at how to handle this situation later on in the chapter. You can check this by commenting out the `On Error Resume Next` line in the code then running the procedure again. This time the error will not be trapped and instead you will see the Access error message "Object 'qryExample' already exists."*

> **You don't have to worry if you don't quite understand the error handling techniques used in this chapter. We will be revisiting this code in more detail in Chapter 12 when we look at error handling. For the moment, you only need to understand that the use of `On Error` allows us to handle run-time errors gracefully without confusing messages popping up in front of the user.**

**4.** Press *Alt+F11* to view the Database window and change to the **Queries** tab. You should see a query there called `qryExample`.

**5.** Open `qryExample` in design view. The design of the query should match the criteria that you passed as an argument to the `MakeQueryDef` function.

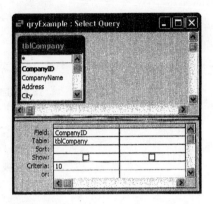

**6.** Now go back to the VBA IDE and type the following procedure in the code window for the `Chapter 7 Code` module:

```
Function ChangeQueryDef(ByVal strQuery As String, ByVal strSQL As String) As
Boolean

    Dim qdf As QueryDef
    Dim boolResultCode As Boolean

    If (strQuery = "") Or (strSQL = "") Then
        boolResultCode = False              'no query name or query string to use!
    Else
        On Error Resume Next                'get ready to handle any errors

        'modify the query object with the name given
        Set qdf = CurrentDb.QueryDefs(strQuery)
        If Err.Number <> 0 Then
            boolResultCode = False          'failed for some reason so cannot continue
        Else
            qdf.SQL = strSQL                'succeeded so load the query object with
                                            'the query string

            qdf.Close                       'finished with the query object so close it
            RefreshDatabaseWindow           'update the Query window
            boolResultCode = True           'Report a success
        End If
        On Error GoTo 0                     'reset error handler
    End If

    ChangeQueryDef = boolResultCode         'report what happened

End Function
```

**7.** Run the procedure by typing the following in the Immediate window and hitting *Enter*:

```
?ChangeQueryDef("qryExample", "SELECT * FROM tblCompany ORDER BY
CompanyName")
```

**8.** The word `True` should appear in the Immediate window, indicating that the function completed successfully.

**9.** Press *Alt+F11* to view the Database window and change to the Queries tab. Open `qryExample` in design view. The design of the query should now have changed to match the new SQL you passed to the `ChangeQueryDef` function.

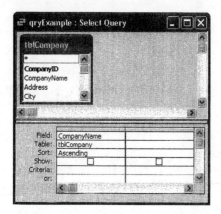

**How It Works**

Creating a `QueryDef` is very simple.

```
Dim qdf As QueryDef

Set qdf = CurrentDb.CreateQueryDef("qryExample")
```

First, we create an empty `QueryDef` object. The `CreateQueryDef` method both creates a `QueryDef` object and assigns it the name that it will have when it is saved. If you don't intend to save it and will only use it in the current procedure, you can give it an empty string (`" "`) as its name and it won't be saved. However, we do want to save our `QueryDef` so we can use it again later and so we'll call it `qryExample`.

> If you try to create a **QueryDef** object with a name that is the same as a saved query that already exists in the database, Access will generate a run-time error. In our example we have decided to trap errors and return a false value (which we would then have to deal with appropriately) rather than let Access fill the screen with its error message and kill the application. Notice that we also handle the possibility of sending the function an empty SQL string, which would not actually cause an error but it would obviously make no sense to create a query which didn't do anything.

```
qdf.SQL = strSQL
```

Next, we assign the SQL property of the QueryDef object. If you aren't too sure about how to write SQL, you can always try designing the query normally in the Query Designer and then switching the query to SQL view to see the SQL created. You can then copy the SQL to the clipboard and paste it into your procedure from there.

Finally, we close the QueryDef, with the following line:

```
qdf.Close
```

The act of closing the QueryDef saves it to the database. Then we refresh the database window to show the changes:

```
RefreshDatabaseWindow
```

The RefreshDatabaseWindow method causes any changes to database objects such as forms, reports, and queries to be immediately reflected in the database window.

Modifying the QueryDef is just as simple as creating it. First you use a variable to reference the QueryDef called qryExample in the current database.

```
Dim qdf As QueryDef

Set qdf = CurrentDb.QueryDefs(strQuery)
```

And then you modify its SQL property, save it, and refresh the database window like we did in the previous function.

## Working with SQL

A QueryDef object has over a dozen different properties, but you will find that there is one property in particular that you will use more than any other; the SQL property. As we saw above, the SQL property is used to set the SQL statement that will be run when the QueryDef object is executed.

If the frmCriteria form is to be used to allow users to frame their queries in a manner of their own choosing, we will then need to convert the entries that the user makes on the form into an SQL statement and use that SQL statement to select the records that should be displayed.

SQL SELECT statements generally consist of three clauses:

```
SELECT fields
FROM source table AS alias name
WHERE criteria
```

The SELECT clause indicates the columns or fields that will be displayed in the result set of the query.

The FROM clause indicates the base table or tables from which the results are drawn. The AS keyword is optional but if used gives the alias name to the table or tables specified. For example SELECT tblSales AS s means that you can use s instead of the longer tblSales throughout the rest of the query. Using aliases can save a lot of typing and if used carefully can make queries much easier to read and, therefore, to maintain. It is also possible to abbreviate this clause by omitting the AS keyword but retaining the alias name, for example: SELECT tblSales s

The WHERE clause indicates the criteria for determining which rows or records will be represented in the result set of the query.

Put another way, if you think of the table as a kind of spreadsheet, the SELECT clause is a form of vertical partitioning, and the WHERE clause a method of horizontal partitioning:

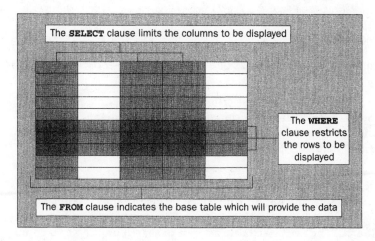

The **SELECT** clause limits the columns to be displayed

The **WHERE** clause restricts the rows to be displayed

The **FROM** clause indicates the base table which will provide the data

So let's see how this works when we apply it to the frmCriteria form in the Ice Cream database.

Well, we know which fields we want displayed. We know that the user is to be shown details of each sale and so we will have to display all of the fields from the `tblSales` table. That will be fixed and won't change, irrespective of the criteria we select on `frmCriteria`. In other words, the `SELECT` clause will not change and will always be:

```
SELECT tblSales.*
```

which selects all of the fields from the `tblSales` table.

Things get slightly more complicated with the `FROM` clause. Most of the time we will only need to use the `tblSales` table. This is because most of the criteria on the `frmCriteria` form represent columns in the `tblSales` table. In fact, if we look at the following table, we can see which columns are represented by which criteria on the `frmCriteria` form.

| This criterion... | ...relates to this field |
|---|---|
| Company is | `tblSales.fkCompanyID` |
| Ice Cream is | `tblSales.fkIceCreamID` |
| Ice Cream contains | `tblIceCreamIngredient.fkIngredientID` |
| Ordered between | `tblSales.DateOrdered` |
| Payment delay is | `tblSales.DatePaid - tblSales.DateOrdered` |
| Dispatch delay | `tblSales.DateDispatched - tblSales.DateOrdered` |

As you can see, however, one of these criteria is dependent on a field in a separate table. If we want to view sales of ice creams that contain specific ingredients, then we need to join the `tblSales` table with the `tblIceCreamIngredient` table and then search for records with an `fkIngredientID` matching the one selected on the criteria form.

> Remember, although the combo box on `frmCriteria` displays the ingredient's name, the bound column contains the ingredient's `fkIngredientID`. Without this `fkIngredientID`, we would have needed to join the `tblIngredient` table as well to search on the `Name` column. This would have been slower to run as well as more complicated to implement.

So, we can see that most of the time our `FROM` clause will look like this:

```
FROM tblSales
```

The only variation is when the user chooses to restrict by ingredient, when the FROM clause will look like this:

```
FROM tblSales INNER JOIN tblIceCreamIngredient
  ON tblSales.fkIceCreamID = tblIceCreamIngredient.fkIceCreamID
```

This FROM clause implements the join between the two tables. The two tables to be joined are tblSales and tblIceCreamIgredients:

```
FROM tblSales INNER JOIN tblIceCreamIngredient
```

And the fields participating on either side of the join are both called fkIceCreamID:

```
ON tblSales.fkIceCreamID = tblIceCreamIngredient.fkIceCreamID
```

Now for the WHERE clause, this one is certainly going to change. What we are interested in is building up a SQL statement which will restrict the rows selected to those which meet our criteria and as we know, it is the WHERE clause which restricts the rows that are returned. Each of the criteria selected by the user will add at least one extra element to the WHERE clause. So, in the specific example we have been looking at so far, the following WHERE clause would be generated.

```
WHERE tblCompany.CompanyID=10
  AND tblSales.DateOrdered>=#11/01/02#
  AND tblSales.DateOrdered<=#11/30/02#
  AND [DateDispatched]-[DateOrdered]>7
```

Anyway, enough of the theory; let's get on with writing a procedure which converts our criteria into a SQL string.

**Try It Out**     **Building a SQL String**

1. Open your version of the IceCream.mdb database and open the code module for the frmCriteria form.

2. Now create a new function called BuildSQLString and add the following code to it:

```
Function BuildSQLString(ByRef strSQL As String) As Boolean

    Dim strSELECT As String
    Dim strFROM As String
    Dim strWHERE As String

    strSELECT = _
        "SELECT s.*.* "                 'set the columns to return results from
                                        '(all columns in this case)
```

```
'set an alias "s" for tblSales and "i" for tblIceCreamIngredient
strFROM = "FROM tblSales AS s "
If chkIngredientID Then
    strFROM = strFROM & " INNER JOIN tblIceCreamIngredient i " & _
        "ON s.fkIceCreamID = i.fkIceCreamID "

    'check for 2nd or more WHERE term
    If strWHERE <> """" Then strWHERE - strWHERE & " AND "
    strWHERE = "i.fkIngredientID = " & cboIngredientID
End If


If chkCompanyID Then
    'check for 2nd or more WHERE term
    If strWHERE <> "" Then strWHERE = strWHERE & " AND "
        strWHERE = strWHERE & "s.fkCompanyID = " & cboCompanyID
End If


If chkIceCreamID Then
    'check for 2nd or more WHERE term
    If strWHERE <> "" Then strWHERE = strWHERE & " AND "
    strWHERE = strWHERE & "s.fkIceCreamID = " & cboIceCreamID
End If


If chkDateOrdered Then
    If Not IsNull(txtDateFrom) Then
        'Check for 2nd or more WHERE term
        If strWHERE <> "" Then strWHERE = strWHERE & " AND "
        strWHERE = strWHERE & "s.DateOrdered >= " & _
            "#" & Format$(txtDateFrom, "mm/dd/yy") & "#"
    End If
    If Not IsNull(txtDateTo) Then

        'Check for 2nd or more WHERE term
        If strWHERE <> "" Then strWHERE = strWHERE & " AND "
        strWHERE = strWHERE & "s.DateOrdered <= " & _
            "#" & Format$(txtDateTo, "mm/dd/yy") & "#"
    End If
End If


If chkPaymentDelay Then
    'check for 2nd or more WHERE term
    If strWHERE <> "" Then strWHERE = strWHERE & " AND "
    strWHERE = strWHERE & "(s.DatePaid - s.DateOrdered) " & _
        cboPaymentDelay & txtPaymentDelay
End If


If chkDispatchDelay Then
    'check for 2nd or more WHERE term
    If strWHERE <> "" Then strWHERE = strWHERE & " AND "
    strWHERE = strWHERE & "(s.DateDispatched - s.DateOrdered) " & _
        cboDispatchDelay & txtDispatchDelay
End If
```

```
        strSQL = strSELECT & strFROM
        If strWHERE <> "" Then strSQL = strSQL & "WHERE " & strWHERE

        BuildSQLString = True

End Function
```

**3.** Next, amend the event handler for the `Click` event of the `cmdFind` button so that it looks like this:

```
Private Sub cmdFind_Click()

    Dim strSQL As String
    Dim strTableName As String

    If Not EntriesValid(strTableName) Then Exit Sub

    If Not BuildSQLString(strSQL) Then
      MsgBox "There was a problem building the SQL string"
      Exit Sub
    End If

    MsgBox strSQL

    CurrentDb.QueryDefs("qryExample").SQL = strSQL

End Sub
```

**4.** Now save the changes you have made to the `Form_frmCriteria` module and switch back to Access by hitting *Alt+F11*.

**5.** Open the `frmCriteria` form and enter the following criteria.

| Field | Value |
| --- | --- |
| Company is | Jane's Diner |
| Ordered between | 01-Nov-02 and 30-Nov-02 |
| Dispatch delay is | More than 7 days |

**6.** When you hit the **Find Matches** button, a message box will appear displaying the SQL string that has been constructed.

**Microsoft Access**

SELECT s.SalesID FROM tblSales AS s WHERE s.fkCompanyID = 10 AND s.DateOrdered >= #11/01/02# AND s.DateOrdered <= #11/30/02# AND (s.DateDispatched - s.DateOrdered) >7

[ OK ]

**7.** Hit the **OK** button and then open the `qryExample` query in design view. It should reflect the criteria that you entered.

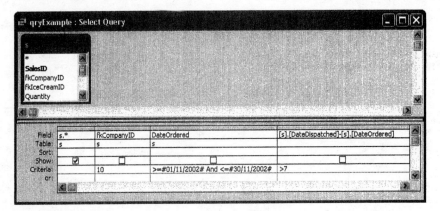

**8.** When you run the query it displays the records that meet your criteria.

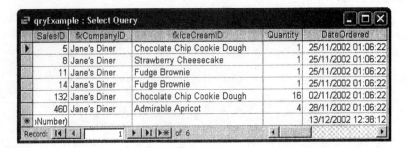

### How It Works

The principle behind this procedure is simple enough, although it may look a bit daunting at first! The general idea is that a variable of type `String`, `strSQL`, is passed into the procedure by reference. We do this rather than passing the variable by value as we would normally do so that the function can modify it. Note that we can't simply return the string using the function's return value as we are already using this to indicate success or failure of the operation. The procedure eventually puts into that variable a SQL statement that reflects the choices entered by the user on `frmCriteria`.

In fact, there is nothing in this exercise that we have not already covered in this chapter. The first step was to create a procedure that generates an SQL string from the criteria that were selected. The heart of this procedure is three variables that correspond to the three parts of the SQL string.

```
Dim strSELECT As String
Dim strFROM As String
Dim strWHERE As String
```

As we said earlier, the SELECT clause is invariant, so we can populate that immediately.

```
strSELECT = "SELECT s.* "
```

The next step is to complete the FROM clause. Again, we looked at this earlier and decided that it should contain just the tblSales table unless the user chose to restrict by ingredient, in which case the tblIceCreamIngredient table should be joined to it. We also alias tblsales to s and tblIceCreamIngredient to i. This simply helps to make the rest of the string shorter and easier to read.

```
    strFROM = "tblSales AS s "
    If chkIngredientID Then
      strFROM = strFROM & " INNER JOIN tblIceCreamIngredient i " & _
        "ON s.fkIceCreamID = i.fkIceCreamID "
      If strWHERE <> """" Then strWHERE = strWHERE & " AND "
      strWHERE = " AND i.fkIngredientID = " & cboIngredientID
End If
```

*You can use the "+" (addition) operator instead of the "&" (concatenation) operator to build strings with instead but the "&" operator is able to perform automatic type casting and so is preferable. For example, if you had a string called strTestString and an integer called intTestInt then the equivalent of "strTestString & intTestInt" is "strTestString + Str(intTestInt)" – if you don't explicitly cast the integer variable by using the Str() function then you get a "Type Mismatch" error.*

Next we construct the WHERE clause. To build the WHERE clause, we look at each of the textboxes in frmCriteria in turn. If the user has checked the checkbox for a criterion and has entered something in the relevant textbox, we add that criterion to the WHERE clause, after first checking to see if we need to add an and or not as whenever we add a new section to the end of the WHERE clause we must also add an AND in front of it to link the sections together.

Remember that the variable that is being populated with the SQL string is the one that was passed into the function at the start.

```
Function BuildSQLString(strSQL As String) As Boolean

    ...
```

```
    strSQL = strSELECT & strFROM
    If strWHERE <> "" Then strSQL = strSQL & "WHERE " & strWHERE

    BuildSQLString = True

End Function
```

*This variable was passed in by reference which means that we can amend the contents of the variable and those changes will persist when the function exits.*

All that is left in this procedure is to return `True` to indicate that the procedure completed successfully. Strictly speaking this is unnecessary as we don't actually perform any validation checks on the string we build. We could have just used a subroutine rather than a function, that is, we don't strictly need to return a value here and so we don't need to use a function. However, it is standard practice to use a function that returns a Boolean value to indicate success or failure, and if at a later date we decide to modify the function to include checking code then we will not need to change any code that calls the function.

Having built the function, we then need to make sure that it is invoked when the user presses the **Find Matches** button on the criteria form. So we modify the `cmdFind_Click` procedure by declaring a variable to hold the SQL string and then passing it into the `BuildSQLString` procedure.

```
    Dim strSQL As String
    Dim strTableName As String

    If Not EntriesValid(strTableName) Then Exit Sub

    If Not BuildSQLString(strSQL) Then
        MsgBox "There was a problem building the SQL string"
        Exit Sub
    End If
```

Note how we check the return value of the `BuildSQLString` procedure and display an error message if it's `False`. If it is `True`, however, we display the string in a message box and then modify the `qryExample` query to contain the SQL string that we built:

```
    MsgBox strSQL

    CurrentDb.QueryDefs("qryExample").SQL = strSQL
```

That is fine as far as it goes and we are well on the way to achieving the functionality that we originally stated. If you remember, we stated earlier that when they run the query, the users want to know how many sales match the criteria that they have specified and should then be presented with the opportunity of viewing:

❑    the matching results in detail on screen

❑    a report containing the matching results

Well, so far we have a way of determining the criteria that the user wants to use to restrict the sales records that he or she wants to view, and we have a method of programmatically modifying a query in Access to express the user's choice. So, where do we go from here?

# Two Approaches to Displaying Results

It should be clear that the requirements expressed above would require a separate form and report to be written to satisfy them. We will need a form to display the matching results in detail, and if the user wants to print off the results, then we will also need a report showing the matching sales. Now we already have a form displaying details of sales (frmSales), and we will use this to display the results that match our criteria.

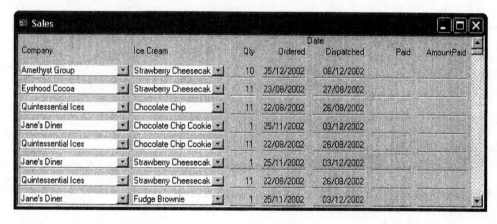

What we want to do now is to create a report that will display those results as well, so we can print them out. That is what we'll do now.

---

**Try It Out**        **Saving a Form as a Report**

**1.**  Open the IceCream07.mdb database and display the Database window if it is not already visible, by pressing *F11*.

**2.**  Select the sales details form (frmSales) and right-click it. From the resultant popup menu, select **Save As...**

**3.**  In the dialog that then appears, specify that you want to save the form as a report called rptSales.

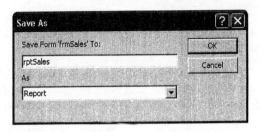

**4.** Now switch to the database window and open the report you have just created. It looks OK, but it could sure do with some tidying up.

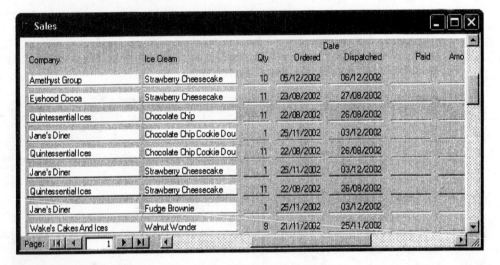

**5.** Switch to design view and make the following changes to the report. (You might also need to resize some of the controls to make sure that they all fit within the width of one page).

| Object | Property | Setting |
|---|---|---|
| Report Header | Back Color | 12632256 (Gray) |
| Detail | Back Color | 16777215 (White) |
| fkCompanyID, fkIceCreamID, Quantity, DateOrdered, DateDispatched, DatePaid, AmountPaid | Special Effect | Flat |
| | Border Style | Transparent |

**6.** Now switch back to report view. The report should now look like this:

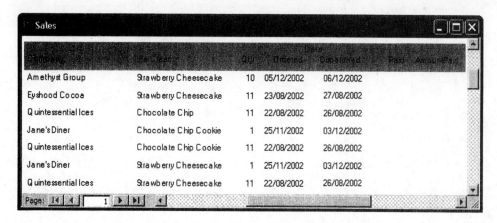

7. Close the report, saving the changes when prompted to do so.

Now we have a form (frmSales) and a report (rptSales) both based on the tblSales table. So, how do we go about ensuring that the form and the report display only the records that match the criteria selected by the user? In fact, there are two common methods that we can use to restrict the records displayed to those the user has selected. The first involves modifying the underlying QueryDef and the second involves creating a table of matching records. We will look at each of those in turn in some detail now.

## Modifying the QueryDef

Perhaps the most intuitive way of restricting the records on a form or report is to modify the QueryDef object to which the form is bound. That is, after all, what we have been looking at so far. Why not simply bind the form and the report to the qryExample query that we modified above? That way, whenever the user hits the **Find Matches** button and the qryExample query is redesigned, the population of the form and report will be automatically be redefined to match the selected criteria.

This is a frequently used method and has the advantage of being fairly straightforward. In order to modify one form and one report, we simply modify one QueryDef object.

**Try It Out** — **Modifying the QueryDef**

1. Open the rptSales report in design view and change its RecordSource property to be qryExample. Then close the report, saving changes when prompted to do so.

2. Now open the frmSales form in design view and change its RecordSource property to be qryExample as well. Instead of closing the form, place a command button in the footer of the form calling it cmdPrint and setting its Caption property to Print.

**297**

**3.** Open the property window and select the print button's On Click event property. Select [Event Procedure] from the drop-down list and then hit the Builder button to the right of the property to create a VBA event handler for the Click event.

**4.** Add the following code to the cmdPrint_Click event.

```
Private Sub cmdPrint_Click()
  DoCmd.OpenReport "rptSales", acViewPreview
End Sub
```

**5.** Now switch back to Access and add another button to the frmSales form and call it cmdClose. Add the following code to the event handler for the button's Click event and then close frmSales, saving changes when prompted to do so.

```
Private Sub cmdClose_Click()
  DoCmd.Close acForm, Me.Name
End Sub
```

**6.** Next, switch back to the VBA IDE and open the code module for the form frmCriteria. Modify the code in the cmdFind_Click event procedure by adding a command to open the frmSales form and remove the MsgBox strSQL command as we no longer need to see this. The procedure should now look like this.

```
Private Sub cmdFind_Click()

  Dim strSQL As String
  Dim strTableName As String

  If Not EntriesValid (strTableName) Then Exit Sub

  If Not BuildSQLString(strSQL) Then
    MsgBox "There was a problem building the SQL string"
    Exit Sub
  End If

  CurrentDb.QueryDefs("qryExample").SQL = strSQL

  DoCmd.OpenForm "frmSales", acNormal

End Sub
```

**7.** Save the changes to this module and, after switching back to Access, save the changes to frmCriteria.

**8.** Finally, run frmCriteria by clicking on the Form View button in the toolbar, and enter the following criteria.

| Field | Value |
|---|---|
| Company is | Jane's Diner |
| Ordered between | 01-Nov-02 and 30-Nov-02 |
| Dispatch delay is | More than 7 days |

**9.** When you hit the Find Matches button, the sales details form is displayed containing only the records that match the criteria you specified. When you hit the Print button, the report containing those records is previewed on screen ready for printing to paper if we are happy with it.

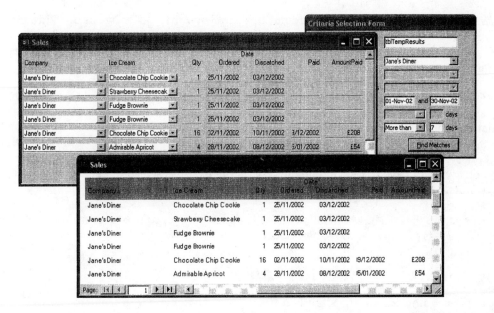

Now that really is something! We are well on our way to implementing the functionality that we set out to achieve at the start of this chapter. In fact the only thing that we haven't put in place is a message informing the user of the number of qualifying records. Don't worry about that, though; we'll look at that a little later. For the moment, let's consider in a little more detail the solution we have implemented.

To recap, then, the steps involved in producing this solution are as follows:

❑ The user selects various criteria

❑ The application modifies the query upon which frmSales and rptSales is based

❑ frmSales (and optionally rptSales) are then opened

In this particular situation this works fine. However, this method does have a drawback. It will only work if the form and the report can both use exactly the same query as their record source. What if we had wanted the report to contain two grouping levels such that the report was grouped first by company name and then by ice cream name? Not too difficult, you might think, until you try to implement it.

You see, if you have a look at the query on which the report is based, you will discover that it does not contain either the company name or the ice cream name. Just like the `frmSales` and `frmCriteria` forms, the `rptSales` report contains only the ID of the ice cream and the company. And, like the form, the report uses combo boxes to display the details of the ice cream and company. The combo box is populated by a query that displays the name of the ice cream or company, but stores its ID. What that means is that, as it stands, we could group on `fkIceCreamID` or `fkCompanyID` but not on the ice cream's name or the company's name, as they are not contained in the query.

Now in this situation we could get around this problem fairly easily by simply adding the ice cream name and company name into `qryExample` (although this would mean that the query now involves two join operations). In practice, however, once you have allowed your users to isolate the sales they are interested in, they might want to carry out a large number of operations on these results. They might want to use them in a mail merge; they might want to count how many of them there are; they might want to display the results in reports which have very different record sources, but use the same criteria to select from among those records. What we would like is to be able to run a complicated query once to determine the records we want to deal with and then achieve some kind of permanence or persistence to the results of that query. We might want to base all sorts of queries on the results that are returned to us, but we don't want to have to re-evaluate the criteria the user has selected. Let's do that once, save the results, and then we are free to do whatever we want with the results.

So the method that we have looked at so far – modifying `qryExample` every time we change our criteria – is good as far as it goes. But is there a better way?

## Using a Matching Records Table

We are now going to look at a slightly different way of tackling this problem and then we will look at some of the pros and cons of this new way of restricting records in a form and a report based on criteria selected by the user.

What we are going to do is to dynamically build a query – as before – but this time we are going to use it to generate a small table of matching key values rather than a table of matching rows. This table of key values (the values of `SalesID` for every record which matches the selected criteria) will be called `tblResults` and can be used in any query to restrict the results of that query to records that match the user's criteria.

It will probably become clearer once we have tried it out.

**Building a Matching Records Table**

**1.** Open the IceCream07.mdb database (if it's not already open).

**2.** Now open Form_frmCriteria, the code module behind the frmCriteria form, and modify the cmdFind_Click procedure so that it now reads like this:

```
Private Sub cmdFind_Click()

   Dim strSQL As String
   Dim lngRecordsAffected As Long
   Dim strTableName As String

   If Not EntriesValid(strTableName) Then Exit Sub

   If Not BuildSQLString(strSQL) Then
     MsgBox "There was a problem building the SQL string"
     Exit Sub
   End If

   If Not BuildResultsTable(strSQL, "tblResults", lngRecordsAffected) Then
     MsgBox "There was a problem building the results table"
     Exit Sub
   End If

   DoCmd.OpenForm "frmSales", acNormal

End Sub
```

**3.** Next, open the BuildSQLString function and change it so that it only returns the SalesID column.

```
Function BuildSQLString(ByRef strSQL As String) As Boolean

   Dim strSELECT As String
   Dim strFROM As String
   Dim strWHERE As String

   strSELECT = "SELECT s.SalesID " 'set the column to return results from

   strFROM = "FROM tblSales s " 'set an alias "s" for tblSales and "i" for
tblIceCreamIngredient

   . . .
```

**4.** Now create a new function in Form_frmCriteria called BuildResultsTable. The function should look like this:

```
Function BuildResultsTable(ByRef strSQL As String, _
                          ByVal strTableName As String, _
                          ByRef lngRecordsAffected As Long) As Boolean

    Dim db As Database
    Dim qdfAction As QueryDef
    Dim boolResultCode As Boolean

    boolResultCode = True 'so far so good!
    Set db = CurrentDb

    On Error Resume Next
    db.TableDefs.Delete strTableName 'delete the existing table
    If Err.Number <> 0 Then
       'failed for some reason - probably because it doesn't exist
       'not a problem - continue
    End If
    On Error GoTo 0

    'modify the SQL string
    strSQL = Replace(strSQL, " FROM ", " INTO " & strTableName & " FROM ")

    If boolResultCode Then 'check everything is still OK to continue
      On Error Resume Next
      Set qdfAction = db.CreateQueryDef("", strSQL) 'create the new query
      If Err.Number <> 0 Then
        boolResultCode = False 'failed for some reason - cannot continue
      End If
      On Error GoTo 0
    End If

    If boolResultCode Then 'check everything is still OK to continue
      On Error Resume Next
      qdfAction.Execute dbFailOnError 'execute the new query
      If Err.Number <> 0 Then
        boolResultCode = False 'failed for some reason - cannot continue
      Else
        'suceeded so get the results
        lngRecordsAffected = qdfAction.RecordsAffected
        qdfAction.Close 'close the query
      End If
      On Error GoTo 0
    End If

    BuildResultsTable = boolResultCode 'report what happened

End Function
```

**5.** Save the changes to this module and switch back to Access by hitting *Alt+F11*.

**6.** Now open the criteria form `frmCriteria` in form view and hit the **Find Matches** button without entering any criteria.

**7.** The `frmSales` form should now appear. Close it down and switch to the **Tables** tab of the database window. There should now be a table called `tblResults`.

**8.** Next, create a new query with the following definition and save it as `qryResults`:

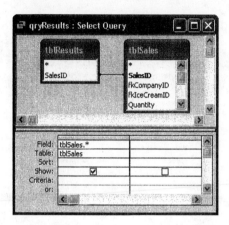

**9.** Now open the `frmSales` and `rptSales` forms and change their `RecordSource` property to be the name of the new query, `qryResults`. Close these objects, saving changes when prompted to do so.

**10.** Finally open the criteria form `frmCriteria` in form view and enter the following criteria:

| Field | Value |
| --- | --- |
| Company is | Jane's Diner |
| Ordered between | 01-Nov-02 and 30-Nov-02 |
| Dispatch delay is | More than 7 days |

**11.** When you hit the **Find Matches** button, the `frmSales` form should be displayed showing the results that match the criteria you have entered. When you hit the **Print** button the `rptSales` report should appear with the same results displayed.

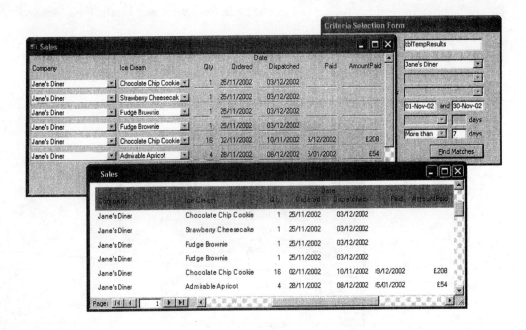

## How It Works

There's quite a bit going on here, and it may seem that the end result is no different from what we had before. But bear with us, and you will see just what the benefits are of using this method of implementing the criteria functionality. To better understand what is happening, let's take a look at the query `qryResults` that now sits behind `frmSales` and `rptSales`.

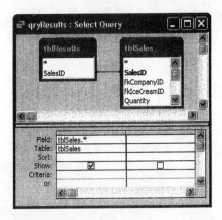

```
SELECT tblSales.*
FROM tblResults INNER JOIN tblSales ON tblResults.SalesID = tblSales.SalesID
```

This query joins the list of all sales with a list of the key values (`SalesID`) of those sales that meet the criteria we have specified. In order to implement this, we need to build a table containing those key values. Now obtaining the key values themselves is not too tricky – we simply modify the `BuildSQLString` procedure so that instead of returning all rows from `tblSales`:

```
strSELECT = "s.* "
```

it simply returns the key values:

```
strSELECT = "s.SalesID "
```

Now what we need to do is to somehow get those key values into a permanent table. The simplest way to do that is to change our **select** query into a **make-table** query.

Select queries always use this general syntax:

```
SELECT select-list
FROM table-list
WHERE criteria-list
```

Whereas make-table queries use this syntax:

```
SELECT select-list
INTO new-table
FROM table-list
WHERE criteria-list
```

So to turn our select query into a make-table query, we simply have to insert `INTO` and the name of the table we want to create between the `SELECT` and `FROM` clauses in our query. We can do that by using the `Replace` function, which replaces a number of characters in a string with other characters:

```
strSQL = Replace(strSQL, " FROM ", " INTO " & strTableName & " FROM ")
```

In this case we are replacing

```
" FROM "
```

with

```
" INTO " & strTableName & " FROM "
```

This has the effect of inserting the required `INTO` clause into our query string (`strSQL`). For more information on the `Replace` function consult the help file.

Then we take this SQL string and create a temporary query with `strSQL` as its `SQL` property.

```
Set qdfAction = db.CreateQueryDef("", strSQL)
```

Until now, we have only been dealing with saved queries that are visible in the database window. However, if we create a `QueryDef` object and give it an empty string as its name, VBA knows that we only want a temporary query. As soon as we close the `QueryDef` object later in this procedure, the query will be deleted.

```
qdfAction.Execute dbFailOnError
```

Having created the query, and checking for any errors, we now execute it by calling the `Execute` method of the `QueryDef` object. Notice that we use the optional `dbFailOnError` argument with the `Execute` method. If we had not specified the `dbFailOnError` argument and our query could not be executed for some reason, VBA would have ignored the error and executed the next line of code without warning us. By specifying the `dbFailOnError` argument, we are instructing VBA to alert us if the query could not be run and we can then report this back to the procedure that called this function.

When we run the query, a new table is created and is called whatever we set the value of the argument `strTableName` to. In our example we set the value of this argument to `tblResults` so that is the name of the new table we created.

```
lngRecordsAffected = qdfAction.RecordsAffected
```

After running the query, we can then inspect the `QueryDef` object's `RecordsAffected` property. As its name suggests, this lets us know how many records were affected by the query. In this case it tells us how many records met the criteria we specified and were therefore inserted into the new `tblResults` table by our make-table query. If you remember, one of the demands made by our users was the ability to see how many records met the criteria they specified. The `RecordsAffected` property gives us just that ability.

```
qdfAction.Close
```

Finally, we close the `QueryDef` object. Because this was only a temporary query, the `QueryDef` is not saved as a query in the database window. Strictly speaking we don't really have to close the query as it will be destroyed automatically after the function returns its result. It is always good practice to explicitly use close, however, as this frees up resources more quickly and guarantees that it really does get closed.

Of course, one potential problem is that the next time we run the `BuildResultsTable`, there will already be a table called `tblResults`. If we did not pre-empt this situation, then VBA would generate a run-time error telling us that the table already existed. To get around this problem we delete the table before running the query:

```
On Error Resume Next
db.TableDefs.Delete strTableName 'delete the existing table
If Err.Number <> 0 Then
   'failed for some reason - probably because it doesn't exist
   'not a problem - continue
End If
On Error GoTo 0
```

The first line (On Error Resume Next) instructs VBA that we will deal with any errors that may occur when we try to delete the table. If an error occurs then Err.Number will be set to the error number and the error handling code between the If...EndIf is run, if not then it will remain 0 and execution will continue with the line after the EndIf. In fact we don't actually do anything if an error occurs as it's probably just because it's the first time we ran this function. In that case there will be no tblResults table to delete. At some point in the future we could easily add some more sophisticated error handling code to check that this really was the case and that we have not encountered a more serious error. For now we'll just leave the comment there to remind us what's going on.

The last line (On Error GoTo 0) instructs VBA not to ignore errors in any subsequent lines of code, that is, this is the end of our error checking code.

> You don't have to worry if you don't quite understand the error handling in this section of the code. We will be revisiting this code in more detail in Chapter 12 when we look at error handling. For the moment, you only need to understand that these lines of code delete the tblResults table if it already exists and doesn't crash horribly if it doesn't.

It might also be worth mentioning that rather than exit the function immediately when we detect an error we instead continue. A series of If...Then...End Ifs make sure that code further down the function is only executed if everything is still OK. This is an alternative method to using Exit Subs that allows us more control over what code is executed and what is not. We could, for example, add some code to retry some of the operations if they fail or perhaps some code near the bottom to inform the user what errors we have encountered and offering helpful suggestions on how to cure the problems. As is usual with any form of programming, there are a number of different ways to achieve the end result. Unfortunately, there are often no fixed rules on the best choice to make – you must rely on experience.

Now as you can see from the example above, the end result of rewriting this part of our application is that it yields exactly the same results as our previous attempt where we embedded the user's criteria directly within the query itself. So why bother? There are a couple of reasons for implementing this method of building a table of matching records as opposed to merely modifying a query to include the new criteria inline.

The first benefit of the 'matching-keys' method is that we only have to run the complicated query that evaluates which sales meet the user's criteria once, irrespective of the number of times that we want to use those results. By contrast, in the 'modify-query' method we used earlier, that complicated WHERE clause that was used to restrict the sales to those that met the user's criteria was run when both the frmSales form and the rptSales report were opened.

Now there is obviously going to be an overhead involved in creating the initial table of matching keys, and it is really the way that your application works that will determine whether this overhead is one that is worth bearing. In our example there is little difference between the overall time taken to open the form and report using either method. However, in many situations the user will want to select a number of records and then perform a large number of different operations against those records. If there were, for example, 2 forms and 10 reports that needed to be run against these records, we would see the following overheads:

| Modify-Query Method | Matching-Keys Method |
| --- | --- |
| Build SQL string | Build SQL string |
| Modify query | Create make-table query |
| Run complex select query x 12 | Run complex make-table query x 1 |
| | Run simple select query x 12 |

Obviously, the more complex the initial query, the greater the benefits of the 'matching-keys' method will be. The initial query might be slow because it contains complex criteria or because the client PC has a modest processor or little RAM. Because the 'matching-keys' method will only need to run the more complex query once, it will tend to give better performance than the 'modify-query' method which will have to run it whenever a form or report based on those results is to be opened.

Another benefit of the 'matching-keys' method comes from the fact that the results of the query are persisted (saved). This means that a user can exit the database and reopen it and the results of the last criteria search will still be there. We will look at the implications of this in more detail in Chapter 11 when we look at what we can do with custom properties.

A final and significant benefit of the 'matching keys' method is the flexibility that this method affords us. Using this technique, we no longer have to base a report and form on the same query. And once we have the key-set saved, we can use this in any subsequent queries without having to deal with the added complexity of redefining the selection of records in those queries.

## *Other Considerations*

There are two normal methods of deploying Access database solutions in a networked (multi-user) environment:

❑ The first, most basic, solution employs a single database stored on a shared network drive. This one database contains all of the data as well as the other Access objects (for example forms, queries, reports, and modules) that comprise the application. This solution makes installation very easy.

❑ The second, and generally preferable, solution uses two or more databases. One is located on a shared network drive, and contains the base data in Access tables. The other database(s) are located individually on each user's PC, and contains the other Access objects (for example forms, queries, reports, and modules) that comprise the application. This local database contains links to the base data in the shared network database and the data appears, to all intents and purposes, to reside locally even though it is located elsewhere. This solution may give significant performance benefits as less data has to be passed over the network.

You should employ the second of these two architectures if you want to use either the 'modify-query' or 'matching-keys' method. That is because you want to ensure that the objects that the user is modifying (either `tblResults` or `qryExample`) are objects that belong solely to that user. If `tblResults` or `qryExample` existed in a central database that everyone shared, then one user's modifications would affect the result set that everyone else used.

It is also for this same reason that we don't just add an extra column to our main data tables to keep track of which rows have been selected and which haven't – again changes made by one user running a query would be seen by all users.

It is possible to employ the first solution successfully but only if all queries and results tables are additionally identified as belonging to each particular user. We could, for example, add the user's name to the beginning of each table name to achieve this. Generally speaking, though, it is usually easier to employ the second, local table, solution.

*For information on how to obtain user names please see Chapter 17: Multi-User.*

Something else to be aware of is the fact that constantly deleting and creating tables can lead to a condition that goes by the name of 'database bloat'. What that means is that Access allocates storage space when new objects are created, but does not always reclaim that space when the object is deleted. The result is that frequent deletion and creation of tables will cause the database size to grow steadily, so causing a decrease in performance.

The good news is that this condition is easily cured. Either manually compact the database at frequent intervals or use the new Compact on Close option on the General tab of the Tools | Options… dialog, which causes the database to be automatically compacted whenever it is closed.

> 'Compact on Close' only causes the database to be compacted if it calculates that doing so will reduce the size of the database by 256 Kb or more.

# Summary

In this chapter, we have spent a good deal of time looking at the different methods that we can use to manipulate QueryDef objects at run time. The first part of the chapter was concerned with how to generate criteria to restrict the display of the records we needed. We used the user's input to create a SQL string using the BuildSQLString procedure.

Once we had created the SQL string, we had two choices for displaying the records we wanted to display:

❑ Base the frmSales and rptSales objects on a saved query and modify the query before we opened the form and report

❑ Create a table of matching records and use this in the record source for the sales form and report

You should have realized by this stage that the key to the whole thing is the Data Access Object hierarchy. If you have a sound knowledge of how this fits together, you should have little problem putting into practice any of the techniques we have used in this chapter.

Knowledge of SQL is also very important. It's a big subject, and we've only really scratched the surface. Hopefully, you've seen how useful it can be. It's definitely something that you should consider learning if you intend to use run-time queries at all.

If you work at these two areas, you will find that you become more and more inventive with the things you attempt and the results you achieve.

# Exercises

**1.** In this chapter, we used the BuildResultsTable procedure to build up the tblResults table from a given SQL string. We built the table by running a make-table query. See if you can rewrite the BuildResultsTable procedure to build the table using the Data Access Object hierarchy instead. Once the table has been built using DAO, the procedure should populate it with an append query, for example:

```
INSERT INTO tblResults SELECT SalesID FROM …
```

**2.** Modify `frmCriteria` to allow the user to enter a name for the results table. Then modify `cmdFind_click` to use the name given to save the results table under (after first checking that a valid name has been entered, of course). This is a useful feature to add to the application. The user can then create any number of different queries and view the stored results from each at any time.

**3.** Next (if you are feeling really brave) see if you can modify the `BuildResultsTable` so that it looks like this:

```
Function BuildResultsTable(ByRef strSQL As String, _
                    ByVal strTableName As String, _
                    ByRef lngRecordsAffected As Long, _
                    Optional blnIndexed As Boolean = False, _
                    Optional strMethod As String = "Query") as Boolean
```

| This argument... | Does this... |
|---|---|
| `strSQL` | Supplies the SQL statement that was built up from the selections made on the criteria selection form. |
| `strTableName` | Supplies the name for the table to be created. |
| `lngRecordsAffected` | Is used to return a long integer signifying the number of records placed into the new table. |
| `blnIndexed` | Is a Boolean value (default `False`) used to indicate whether the new table should be indexed on the `SalesID` field. If this argument is not supplied, the field will not be indexed. |
| `strMethod` | Is used to specify what method will be used to build the new table. If this argument is "`Query`" or is not supplied, the table will be created using a make-table query. The alternative, used when `strMethod` is "`DAO`", is to use DAO, which you should have completed in the previous exercise. |

**4.** Finally, see if you can modify the application so that it informs the user how many records met the criteria and asks whether the `frmSales` form should be displayed. Use this for the `cmdFind_Click` procedure on the criteria form and then put the required functionality into the `DisplayResults` procedure.

```
Private Sub cmdFind_Click()

  Dim strSQL As String
  Dim lngRecordsAffected As Long
```

```
    If Not EntriesValid Then Exit Sub

    If Not BuildSQLString(strSQL) Then
      MsgBox "There was a problem building the SQL string"
      Exit Sub
    End If

    If Not BuildResultsTable(strSQL, "tblResults", lngRecordsAffected,
strMethod:="DAO", _
      blnIndexed:=True) Then
      MsgBox "There was a problem building the results table"
      Exit Sub
    End If

    If Not DisplayResults(lngRecordsAffected) Then
      MsgBox "There was a problem displaying the results"
      Exit Sub
    End If

End Sub
```

# CHAPTER 8

# Working with Tables

In the previous chapter, we looked at how to handle queries and `QueryDef` objects. In this chapter we will look at ways to work with tables and how to change their structures programmatically as using the IDE GUI. In particular, we will be looking at the DAO object `TableDef`. We will also look at some other ways to build and modify tables such as using XML and sub-datasheets.

Modifying tables at run time can be a very useful tool. It potentially allows tables to be altered as and when the user's requirements change, without having to wait for a database administrator to make the changes for them manually. It can be used to create and destroy tables on-the-fly, perhaps in order to store temporary data. It also allows you to write code that can then be shipped to the client and run on their data in situ – very useful for maintenance updates.

The main topics that we will cover in this chapter are:

❑    Create a table complete with a number of fields and indices using the DAO hierarchy.

❑    Adding a new field to an existing table.

❑    Creating a table by importing an XML schema.

❑    Sub-datasheets – what they are and how to use them.

## Working with Tables

In the previous chapter we created a table by building a make-table query. We'll now see how to build a table using the Data Access Object hierarchy. One of the advantages of using DAO to create the table is that it gives us more control over the way the table is constructed. When you use a make-table query to create a table, Access determines the data types for the fields in the tables. In addition, tables created from make-table queries don't have any indexes created initially. In contrast, however, if we create a table using DAO, we can specify the data types of the fields in the table and add whatever indexes we want.

Using tables this way also enables us to change their existing structure at runtime, perhaps allowing the user to specify a number of additional columns to be added.

> The judicious use of indexes can have a dramatic impact on the performance of queries. You can think of an index as a list of shortcuts to the data that are sorted independently of the data rows they refer to and so can be searched extremely quickly. It is also possible to have multiple indices for a table, each sorted in a different way ready for different types of queries. Conversely, inappropriate use of indexes can hugely increase data storage requirements as all those shortcuts have to be stored somewhere!

However, in order to do this, we must first understand exactly how tables are constructed. Aside from the data that is held in them, tables have two major constituents: Fields and Indexes.

❑ A Field is a column of data with a specified data type and length. Fields may expose certain properties. For example, a Field has a DefaultValue property that, not surprisingly, indicates the default value that Access places there if the user doesn't supply one. Another property is the Required property that is False if a Field allows Null values and True if Null values aren't allowed.

❑ An Index is an object that holds information about the ordering and uniqueness of records in a field. Just as is it is faster to look up a page in a large book if it has an index at the back, so it is faster for Access to retrieve records from a large table if the table is indexed. As well as containing Fields an Index object also has Properties. For example, the Unique property of an Index object indicates whether all values in the Field to which that Index applies should be unique.

We'll now take this opportunity to introduce the TableDef object. A TableDef object is an object that holds a complete table definition. Just as we saw with a QueryDef object, a TableDef object holds the definition of a table and not the actual data. If you want, you can think of the TableDef as being like a table in design view.

| Access | VBA Equivalent |
| --- | --- |
| Table (Design View) | TableDef object |
| Table (Datasheet View) | Table-type Recordset object |
| Query (Design View) | QueryDef object |
| Query (Datasheet View) | Dynaset-type, Snapshot-type, or Forward-only-type Recordset object |

The lower portion of the following diagram indicates how TableDef objects, Field objects, and Index objects fit into the overall Data Access Object hierarchy.

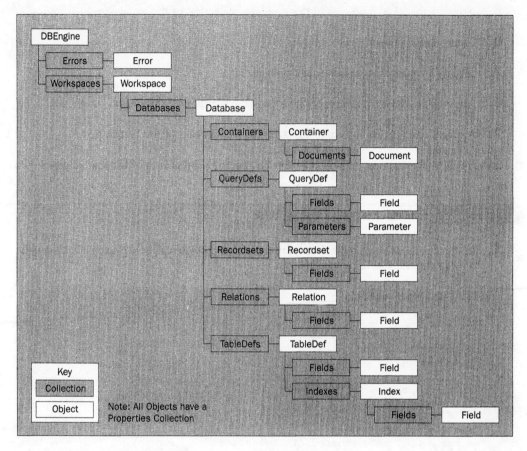

Once you understand the diagram above, creating tables in VBA is a relatively simple process. If you aren't sure you understand how objects and collections work, you should re-read Chapter 5 and Chapter 6 where they are described in detail. These are the fundamental building blocks of the Data Access Object hierarchy and you need to make sure that you are familiar with how they work.

## The Ten Steps

To create an empty table using VBA, you will always carry out the following steps:

1. Create a `TableDef` object.

2. Set any properties for the `TableDef`.

3. Create one or more `Field` objects.

4. Set any properties for the `Field` objects.

**5.** Append the `Field` objects to the `Fields` collection of the `TableDef`.

**6.** Create one or more `Index` objects.

**7.** Set any properties for the `Index` objects.

**8.** Append any `Field` objects to the `Fields` collection of the Index.

**9.** Append the `Index` objects to the `Indexes` collection of the `TableDef`.

**10.** Append the `TableDef` object to the `TableDef`'s collection of the `Database`.

### Try It Out — Creating a Table Using VBA

**1.** In the `IceCream.mdb` database, create a new module called `Chapter 8 Code` and type in the following procedure:

```
Public Sub MakeATable()

    Dim db As Database
    Dim tbl As TableDef
    Dim fld As Field
    Dim idx As Index

    'Start by opening the database
    Set db = CurrentDb()

    'Create a TableDef object
    Set tbl = db.CreateTableDef("tblCountries")

    'Create a field; set its properties; add it to the TableDef
    Set fld = tbl.CreateField("CountryID", dbLong)

    fld.OrdinalPosition = 1
    fld.Attributes = dbAutoIncrField

    tbl.Fields.Append fld

    'Create another; set its properties; add it to the TableDef
    Set fld = tbl.CreateField("CountryName", dbText)

    Fld.OrdinalPosition = 2
    fld.Size = 50
    fld.Required = True
    fld.AllowZeroLength = False

    tbl.Fields.Append fld
```

```
'Create an index and set its properties
Set idx = tbl.CreateIndex("PrimaryKey")

idx.Primary = True
idx.Required = True
idx.Unique = True

'Add a field to the index
Set fld = idx.CreateField("CountryID")
idx.Fields.Append fld

'Add the index to the TableDef
tbl.Indexes.Append idx

'Finally add table to the database
db.TableDefs.Append tbl

'And refresh the database window
RefreshDatabaseWindow

'Indicate creation was successful
MsgBox "The " & tbl.Name & " table was successfully created"

End Sub
```

**2.** Now run the procedure, either by hitting *F5* or the Go/Continue button on the toolbar.
You should see a message box informing you that the table has been successfully
created. You will get an error message if this table already exists, so you might want to
make sure the table doesn't exist before running this function:

**3.** Hit the OK button and then hit *Alt+F11* to switch to Access. If you go to the database
window, the table that you have just created should be visible there. Open it in Design
View and have a look at the two fields that you have created. Note the properties in
the lower half of the window:

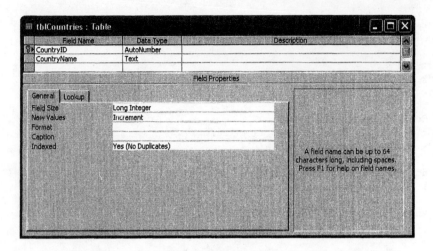

4. Now look at the indexes, either by clicking the **Indexes** button or by selecting **Indexes** from the **View** menu. Does everything look as you expected?

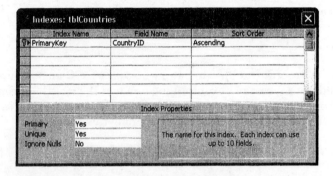

## How It Works

Although the code may look a little tortuous, it's actually very easy to follow if you bear in mind the Data Access Object hierarchy and follow the steps listed above.

After opening the database, the first thing we must do is create a new `TableDef` object:

```
Set tbl = db.CreateTableDef("tblCountries")
```

Creating any Data Access Object is a simple task. All you need to do is use the `Create<Object>` method on the Data Access Object which is the next highest in the hierarchy. The `TableDefs` collection belongs to a `Database` object so, to create a `TableDef`, you use the `CreateTableDef` method on the `Database` object.

As with `QueryDefs`, when we create a `TableDef` object, we give it a name by which we can refer to it later and which will appear in the database window when it is saved.

We don't want to set any other properties for the `TableDef` (the next step in the process), and so we move on and create a `Field` object:

```
Set fld = tbl.CreateField("CountryID", dbLong)
```

`Fields` are a collection within the `TableDef` object, so we use the `CreateField` method on the `TableDef` object that will contain the `Field`, and give it a name by which we can refer to it later. We also need to specify the type of data that this `Field` will hold. We want the field to be an AutoNumber field, and as AutoNumber fields are long integers, we specify `dbLong` as the data type.

Next, we must set properties for the `Field`:

```
fld.OrdinalPosition = 1
fld.Attributes = dbAutoIncrField
```

The `OrdinalPosition` property indicates where a `Field` appears in a table. The leftmost `Field` in a table has an `OrdinalPosition` property of 1, the next has an `OrdinalPosition` property of 2, and so on. The `OrdinalPosition` property of the rightmost `Field` is equal to the number of `Fields` in the `TableDef`.

The `Attributes` property is used to specify how an object behaves. By setting the `Attributes` property of our `Field` to `dbAutoIncrField`, we are indicating that the field should behave like an AutoNumber field and increase by one every time a new record is added.

Now we must add the `Field` to the `Fields` collection of the `TableDef` using the `Append` method:

```
tbl.Fields.Append fld
```

We then repeat the process to create another `Field` and append it to our `TableDef` object.

Once all the `Field` objects have been added, we create an `Index` for the table and call it `PrimaryKey`:

```
Set idx = tbl.CreateIndex("PrimaryKey")
```

We then set its properties:

```
idx.Primary = True
idx.Required = True
idx.Unique = True
```

The `Primary` property indicates whether an `Index` is the primary key for the `TableDef` to which it is to be added. The `Required` property determines whether the `Index` can accept `Null` values – if it is `True`, `Null`s will not be accepted. The `Unique` property determines whether duplicate values are allowed within the `Index`. We have set this to `True`, so duplicate values will not be allowed.

*The proper use of indexes can make a dramatic difference to the performance of applications, particularly where large amounts of data are involved. As this is primarily a book about VBA we don't have space to cover indexes in detail here. If you are still baffled by indexes, their properties, and their uses then I suggest you read more about them in Beginning SQL Programming, from Wrox Press (ISBN 1-861001-80-0).*

The next stage is to specify the `Field` that will be indexed:

```
Set fld = idx.CreateField("CountryID")
idx.Fields.Append fld
```

Here, we use the familiar `Create<Object>` syntax to create a `Field` object within the `Index` object. By setting the name of the `Field` object to `CountryID`, we are indicating that the `Field` called `CountryID`, which we created earlier in the procedure, is the one to be indexed. Next, we add the `Index` to the `TableDef`:

```
tbl.Indexes.Append idx
```

Finally, we add the `TableDef` to the database:

```
db.TableDefs.Append tbl
```

Note that if a table of the same name already exists then this line will raise an error – the existing table will not be replaced. You cannot use the `Append` method to modify an existing table either. The method for this is explained below.

That's all there is to it!

If you cast your mind back to the `BuildResultsTable` function in the previous chapter, you may remember that we created the `tblResults` table using a make-table query. It is left to you as an exercise at the end of this chapter to rewrite the procedure to allow the table to be created using the DAO hierarchy, but if you want to see how this is done, you can have a look at the `BuildResultsTable` function in the **Chapter 07 Code** module of the database.

You need to be aware of the fact that the table might already exist in the database, in which case this statement will cause a run-time error to be generated. You should make sure you delete the table before running this code.

## *Modifying the Table*

Modifying tables is even easier than creating them in the first place. Here we will add an extra field, `CountryCode`, to the `tblCountries` table that we created before. To do this we will need to carry out the following steps:

**1.** Retrieve the `TableDef` object for this table

**2.** Create a new `Field` objects

**3.** Set the properties for the `Field` object

**4.** Append the `Field` object to the `Fields` collection of the `TableDef`

**Try It Out** — **Adding an Extra Field using DAO**

**1.** In the `IceCream.mdb` database, open the `Chapter 8 Code` module that you created earlier and enter the following subprocedure:

```
Sub ModifyATable()

    Dim db As Database
    Dim tbl As TableDef
    Dim fld As Field

    'Start by opening the database
    Set db = CurrentDb()

    'Retrieve the tabledef object
    Set tbl = db.TableDefs("tblCountries")

    'Create a field; set its properties; add it to the tabledef
    Set fld = tbl.CreateField("CountryCode", dbText)

    fld.Size = 5
    fld.Required = True
    fld.AllowZeroLength = False

    tbl.Fields.Append fld

    'Indicate creation was successful
    MsgBox "The " & tbl.Name & " table was successfully modified"

End Sub
```

**2.** Now run the procedure, either by hitting *F5* or the **Go/Continue** button on the toolbar. You should see a message box informing you that the table has been successfully modified. You will get an error message if this table does not already exist, so you might want to make sure the table does exist before running this function:

**3.** Hit the **OK** button and then hit *Alt+F11* to switch to Access. If you go to the database window, the table that you have just modified should still be visible there. Open it in **Design View** and have a look at the new field that you have created. Again note the properties in the lower half of the window:

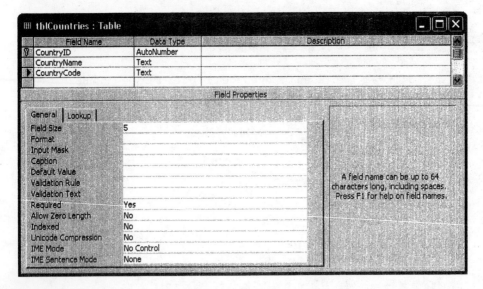

After opening the database, the first thing we must do is to retrieve the `TableDef` object for `tblCountries`:

```
Set tbl = db.TableDefs("tblCountries")
```

As before, the `TableDefs` collection belongs to the `Database` object, so to retrieve a `TableDef`, you use the `TableDefs` method on the `Database` object.

We don't want to modify any properties for the `TableDef` (if we did then the code for this would come here), and so we move on and create a new `Field` object using the same method we used earlier:

```
Set fld = tbl.CreateField("CountryCode", dbText)
```

Next, we must set properties for the new `Field`:

```
fld.Size = 5
fld.Required = True
fld.AllowZeroLength = False
```

We have not bothered to specify the `OrdinalPosition` property so the field will simply be added onto the end of the current list of fields.

Now we must add the `Field` to the `Fields` collection of the `TableDef` using the `Append` method:

```
tbl.Fields.Append fld
```

We are now done!

Adding indexes, modifying field properties, and so on, all require a similar method to the one above. We won't cover them in detail here but by referring to this example and the create table example given before, together with the DAO hierarchy, you should have no problems.

## Creating a Table Using an XML Schema

By importing an XML schema (`.xsd` file), perhaps downloaded from a web site, you can create new tables. If you are not familiar with XML then you should know that XML files are an excellent way to transfer table structures because they contain simple ASCII text which makes them easy to receive by e-mail or download through a firewall.

> *The subject of XML and schemas is complex and wide-ranging. It will certainly have a major impact on data interchange over the next few years. To read more about XML we suggest Beginning XML 2nd Edition, from Wrox Press (ISBN 1-861005-59-8).*

Here's the XML schema for the `Countries` table we created above:

```
<?xml version="1.0" encoding="UTF-8"?>
<xsd:schema xmlns:xsd="http://www.w3.org/2000/10/XMLSchema"
xmlns:od="urn:schemas-microsoft-com:officedata">
<xsd:element name="dataroot">
<xsd:complexType>
<xsd:choice maxOccurs="unbounded">
<xsd:element ref="tblCountries"/>
</xsd:choice>
</xsd:complexType>
</xsd:element>
```

```
<xsd:element name="tblCountries">
<xsd:annotation>
<xsd:appinfo>
<od:index index-name="PrimaryKey" index-key="CountryID " primary="yes"
unique="yes" clustered="no"/>
</xsd:appinfo>
</xsd:annotation>
<xsd:complexType>
<xsd:sequence>
<xsd:element name="CountryID" od:jetType="autonumber" od:sqlSType="int"
od:autoUnique="yes" od:nonNullable="yes">
<xsd:simpleType>
<xsd:restriction base="xsd:integer"/>
</xsd:simpleType>
</xsd:element>
<xsd:element name="CountryName" minOccurs="0" od:jetType="text"
od:sqlSType="nvarchar">
<xsd:simpleType>
<xsd:restriction base="xsd:string">
<xsd:maxLength value="50"/>
</xsd:restriction>
</xsd:simpleType>
</xsd:element>
<xsd:element name="CountryCode" minOccurs="0" od:jetType="text"
od:sqlSType="nvarchar">
<xsd:simpleType>
<xsd:restriction base="xsd:string">
<xsd:maxLength value="5"/>
</xsd:restriction>
</xsd:simpleType>
</xsd:element>
</xsd:sequence>
</xsd:complexType>
</xsd:element>
</xsd:schema>
```

The first thing to say about this is "DON'T PANIC!" You really don't need to know anything about XML in order to use it to create tables.

To import this database just follow these simple steps:

1. From the main menu select File | Get External Data | Import:

2. In the Import dialog that appears make sure that you have selected Files of Type XML Documents. Then select the schema to be imported, tblCountries in this case:

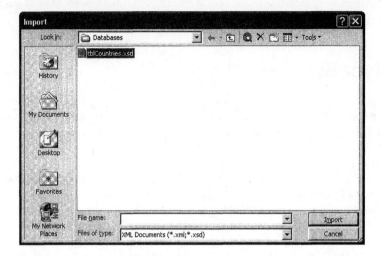

**3.** In the next dialog, if you press the Options>> button you can choose whether you want to import an empty table (structure only) or include the data (if there is any). You can also add just the data to an existing table. We will choose to import the structure only as we know that there is no data in this file anyway:

**4.** Hit the OK button. After a few moments the import completes.

**5.** If you now look at the database window again you will see that the table has been added. You might also notice that because we already had a table called tblCountries Access has thoughtfully renamed the imported table tblCountries1 rather than overwriting the original:

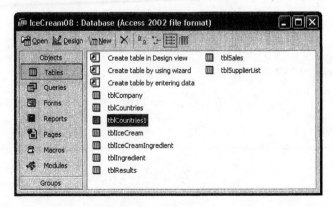

That's all there is to it. Exporting tables, or even entire databases, to XML is just as easy so we won't cover it here.

# Sub Datasheets

**Sub Datasheets** are a way to provide lookup and edit functionality with tables engaged in a one-to-many or one-to-one relationship. In the table on the 'one' side of the relationship we place the sub datasheets that enables us can lookup and edit the rows in the table on the 'many' side of the relationship.

Sub datasheets may be used in tables, queries, form datasheets, or in sub-forms. Microsoft Access automatically creates a sub datasheet on the "one" side of the relationship, provided that the sub datasheet Name property of the table is set to [Auto] – which is the default. So if everything went smoothly up to this point, all the setting up of sub datasheets has been already been done for us when the tables were originally created. So we are going to remove all setting up that Access has automatically done, and redo it manually and learn what it all means for ourselves. Once we have an understanding gained from setting up sub datasheets manually, then we will write a generic VBA subprocedure to automate the process on any table in the current database.

Lets get some background first: below we have a screenshot of our table relationships – focus on two relationships: 1. tblIceCream table and tblIceCreamIngredient and 2. tblIngredient and tblSupplierList. Note that they are both one to many relationships.

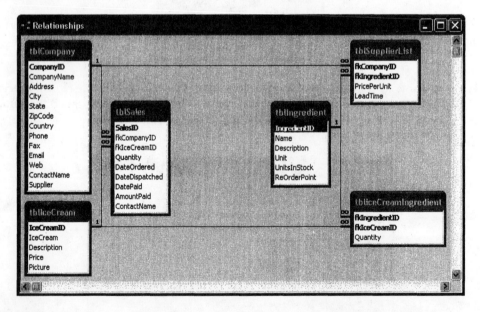

We are going to set up two sub datasheets:

❑ In the tblIceCream (One) and tblIceCreamIngredient (Many) One-to-Many relationship

❑ In the tblIngredient (One) and tblSupplierList (Many) One-to-Many relationship

The sub datasheet is placed in the Subdatasheet Name property of the table on the One side of the relationship.

The reason why these sub datasheets are useful is because: In the first example, when a user opens tblIceCream they can view the ingredients that are used in a selected ice cream. So in this case we may have a situation where they want to add an ingredient to a selected ice cream, so by looking up Walnut wonder ice cream in tblIceCream they can use the sub datasheet (tblIceCreamIngredients) and see all the ingredients that are currently used for that ice cream and so add a new valid ingredient, Apple for example.

In the second example, when a user opens up tblIngredient they can view the suppliers that supply the selected ingredient and they can edit the list of Suppliers that supply that selected ingredient – which is a very intuitive way of working. For example, they may need to order more apples, and so looking up Apples in the tblIngredient they use the sub datasheet (tblSupplierList) to see which company supplies apples – 'Fran and Nick's Fruit and Nuts'.

In the *Try It Out* we will do this manually so that we get a feel for what we are doing, and then once we feel comfortable with that, then we will use VBA code. It is good practice to slowly work through a manual process – in "slow motion" – until you get a feel for what the code will have to do and the sequence in which it will carry out its role, and then start coding. What we are trying to build up is a mental picture or visualization to take with us to the code editor – coding is less frustrating once you have that all important mental picture of the way things work.

Now let's manually create two sub datasheets and reinforce what we have just discussed.

**Try It Out      Creating Sub Datasheets (Manually)**

Before we begin to create the sub datasheets we need to remove the sub datasheets that were automatically added by Access. We do the following in the tblIceCream and tblIngredient tables:

**1.** Open tblIceCream in datasheet view and remove the sub datasheet by selecting the following from the menu: Format | Subdatasheet | Remove, save the table and close it – do the same to tblIngredient.

**2.** To create a sub datasheet open up tblIceCream in datasheet view and select from the menu Insert | Subdatasheet... An Insert Subdatasheet dialog should appear – select tblIceCreamIngredient from the listbox and make the respective selections from the drop-down boxes as shown below, and then click OK and save the table.

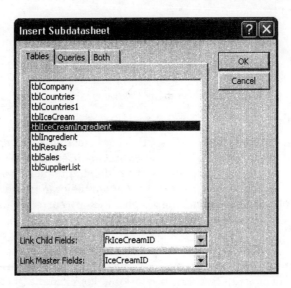

**3.** Now repeat the process with **tblIngredient** by opening it in datasheet view and selecting **Insert | Subdatasheet…** – select **tblSupplierList** in the listbox and ensure the following selections are in the drop-down boxes, then click **OK**, and save the table.

**4.** We have now created both sub datasheets, and so let see what effect this has had on the properties of the table. If you select **tblIceCream** in design view and select the table properties you should have the same as below:

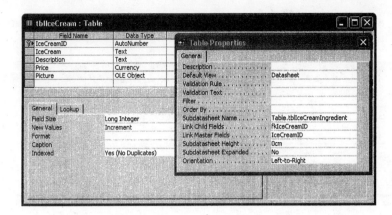

**5.** If you now select tblIngredient in design view and select the table properties you should have the same as below:

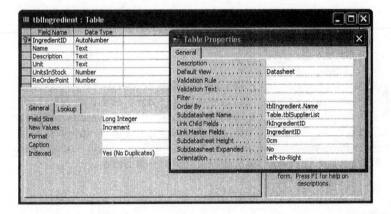

**6.** Let's now take a look at the effect of the sub datasheets: open up tblIceCream in datasheet view and click on the top left + and you should see the contents of tblIceCreamIngredient in the sub datasheet, as shown below:

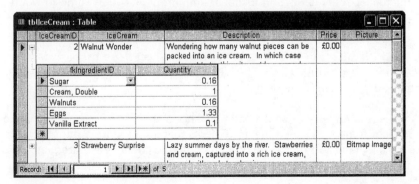

**7.** Now open up tblIceIngredient in datasheet view and click on the top left + and you should see the contents of tblSuppliesList in the sub datasheet, as shown below:

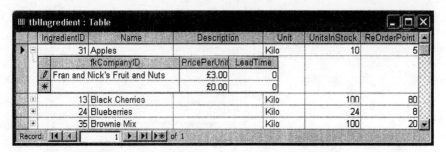

**8.** Now we are going to make some changes to the data. Make tblIceCream the active table (it should be in datasheet view). Click on the + alongside Walnut Wonder ice cream and it should be the same as the screenshot in Step 6 above. To this product we want to add another ingredient – an Apple – so if you click in the grid below Vanilla Extract, a drop-down box should list the ingredient choices that are available from the tblIceCreamIngredient table. Select **Apples** and enter **1** in the **Quantity** column, then click **Save**.

**9.** Now make tblIngredient the active table (it should be in **Datasheet** view). Click on the cross alongside **Apples** – it should be the same as the screen shot in Step 7 above. To this ingredient we want to add another supplier – Amethyst Group – so if you click in the grid below **Fran and Nick's Fruit and Nuts**, a drop down should list the company choices that are available in the tblSupplierList table – select **Amethyst Group** and enter **2.95** in the **PricePerUnit** column, then click **Save**.

## How It Works

In the introduction we said that we were going to set up two sub datasheets:

❑   In the tblIceCream (One) and tblIceCreamIngredient (Many) One-to-Many relationship

❑   In the tblIngredient (One) and tblSupplierList (Many) One-to-Many relationship

We did this and we can see in tblIceCream the subdatasheet Name property is Table.tblIceCreamIngredient. The **Link Child Fields** and **Link Master Fields** properties were automatically filled in from the dialog

We said that the reasons why these two sub datasheets are of value are: In the first example when we opened tblIceCream we viewed the ingredients that are used in Walnut Wonder ice cream, so we can use the sub datasheet (tblIceCreamIngredients) to add a new ingredient, Apple.

In the second example when we opened up `tblIngredient` we viewed the suppliers that supply the Apple ingredient: so we use the sub datasheet (**tblSupplierList**) to add a new Apple supplier: **Amethyst Group**.

From having worked through the exercise manually we are now well placed to understand the process and replicate it using VBA code. In our code we will write a generic subprocedure that will accept as parameters all that we need to set up a sub datasheet on any suitable table combination: to be suitable the tables need to be in a one-to-one or one-to-many relationship. In our code we target the properties of the table on the 'one' side of the relationship.

Let's open up our chapter code module (**Chapter 8 Code**) and start coding.

## Try It Out — Creating Sub Datasheets (Code)

**1.** Enter the following code:

```
Sub SubDataSheet(ByVal strSDN As String, ByVal strLCF As String, _
                 ByVal strLMF As String, ByVal strTbl As String)

   Dim db As Database
   Dim tbl As TableDef

   'Open the database
   Set db = CurrentDb()

   'Open the table
   Set tbl = db.TableDefs(strTbl)

   'before: comment out the following With block when finished debugging
   With tbl

      Debug.Print .Properties("SubdatasheetName")
      Debug.Print .Properties("Linkchildfields")
      Debug.Print .Properties("Linkmasterfields")

   End With

   'Set the property values - this will override the current values
   'saving us from having to remove them beforehand.
   With tbl

      .Properties("SubdatasheetName") = strSDN
      .Properties("Linkchildfields") = strLCF
      .Properties("Linkmasterfields") = strLMF

   End With

   'after: comment out the following With block when finished debugging
   With tbl
```

```
         Debug.Print .Properties("SubdatasheetName")
         Debug.Print .Properties("Linkchildfields")
         Debug.Print .Properties("Linkmasterfields")

     End With

End Sub
```

**2.** Now test the code by opening up the Immediate window and entering the following, then pressing *Enter*.

SubDataSheet "Table.tblIceCreamIngredient", "fkIceCreamID", "IceCreamID", "tblIceCream"

**3.** You should see the following:

```
Immediate                                                                    ☒
SubDataSheet "Table.tblIceCreamIngredient", "fkIceCreamID", "IceCreamID", "tblIceCream"
Table.tblIceCreamIngredient
fkIceCreamID
IceCreamID
Table.tblIceCreamIngredient
fkIceCreamID
IceCreamID
```

### How It Works

We create a generic subprocedure passing (ByVal) the necessary string values:

```
Sub SubDataSheet(ByVal strSDN As String, ByVal strLCF As String, ByVal strLMF
As String, ByVal strTbl As String)
```

Then we drill down the Access object model until we hold the table that we want to address in the variable tbl.

```
Dim db As Database
  Dim tbl As TableDef

  'Open the database
  Set db = CurrentDb()

  'Open the table
  Set tbl = db.TableDefs(strTbl)
```

After which we print out the current property settings before we change them:

```
'before: comment out the following With when finished debugging
With tbl

    Debug.Print .Properties("SubdatasheetName")
    Debug.Print .Properties("Linkchildfields")
    Debug.Print .Properties("Linkmasterfields")

End With
```

Having done that we then get down to the business of assigning the property values passed in as parameters:

```
'Set the property values - this will override the current values
'saving us from having to remove them beforehand.
With tbl

    .Properties("SubdatasheetName") = strSDN
    .Properties("Linkchildfields") = strLCF
    .Properties("Linkmasterfields") = strLMF

End With
```

And just to check everything is OK we print the updated property value to the Immediate window and then close the subprocedure:

```
'after: comment out the following With when finished debugging
With tbl

    Debug.Print .Properties("SubdatasheetName")
    Debug.Print .Properties("Linkchildfields")
    Debug.Print .Properties("Linkmasterfields")

End With

End Sub
```

# Summary

In this chapter, we covered some of the methods we can use to manipulate TableDef objects at run time from within our own VBA code.

While it is true that not every Access application will require these techniques (in many cases creating tables by manually entering fields and indexes will be sufficient), working through this chapter will improve your knowledge of how Access stores information and how to improve your program's use of it.

Perhaps more than any other chapter you should have noticed that knowledge of the Data Access Object hierarchy is the key to everything. A little time studying the DAO Object Library Reference (which we have reproduced for you in Appendix B) will really help.

We also went through the useful technique of creating tables from XML schemas. You may know that Microsoft has placed XML right at the core of their corporate strategy so I'm sure that you will be hearing a great deal more about XML over the next few years.

Finally we had a look at the topics of relationships and sub datasheets and had a go and creating them both manually and programmatically.

# Exercises

1. You can use the Immediate window to inspect the properties of data access objects. What line would you have to type in the lower pane of the immediate window to determine how many fields there are in the tblCountries table?

2. See if you can use the Immediate window to determine how many properties each of the fields in the tblCountries table has. Why do some have more properties than others?

3. Modify the MakeATable sub to automatically allow for the possibility that a version of tblCountries might already exist by deleting the old table before adding the new one instead of having to do this manually. HINT: you can use a For Each...Next loop to scan through the collection of Tabledefs for a matching name and the Delete method of the collection to remove it if it does exist.

# CHAPTER 9

# External Data

The main reason for owning a database is obviously to store data. So far, you've seen a lot about manipulating data within Access using VBA. But in business, you'll often have data in a variety of formats: text files, spreadsheets, and so on. When you're designing new business applications in Access you might need a way to get this data into and out of Access, so that you can incorporate it into your application.

Access has a very good wizard for importing data, but you might want data imports to be something that users can run, and you probably don't want them to have the (potentially dangerous) freedom of running the wizard. So what we're going to cover in this chapter is how to bypass that wizard (however nice it might be), and move data in and out of Access with code. That way it's you who are in control of the import and export process, and not the user.

In particular we shall be looking at:

- ❑ Importing and exporting data to other applications

- ❑ Importing and exporting data to text files, both in a fixed format, and a CSV (Comma Separated Values) format

- ❑ Importing and exporting data to XML and using XML to generate Web Reports

- ❑ Sending data via electronic mail

- ❑ Using data that is stored in other databases

# Other Applications

As mentioned briefly in Chapter 1, the world today is full of data, and not all of it is stored in databases. Daily we have to deal with text files, spreadsheets, mail systems, and so on, and it never seems to stop. We as programmers would like it if our bosses (and every one else's too, come to think of it) just junked all those old machines and applications, and brought us heaving and groaning into the 21st century. However nice an idea that is, it seems unlikely to happen, especially considering that by the time you've upgraded the whole office, the first machine you bought is now out of date.

So we're stuck with our own old applications, and other people's, too. These applications may hold their data in a different format. This isn't a bad thing, as Access has built-in support for the most common data formats.

## Databases

You've already seen that there are different versions of Access, and there are many more databases around than you'd realize. Transferring between these other databases and Access is pretty straightforward, because we can do it with one simple command – the `TransferDatabase` method of the `DoCmd` object:

```
DoCmd.TransferDatabase [TransferType], DatabaseType, DatabaseName,
    [ObjectType], Source, Destination, [StructureOnly], [StoreLogin]
```

This is quite simple to use. For example, to export our ice cream details to a database called **Prices**, we could use this:

```
DoCmd.TransferDatabase acExport, "Microsoft Access", _
    "C:\IceCream\Prices.mdb", acTable, "tblIceCream", "tblIceCream"
```

This says the following:

- ❑ The `TransferType` is `acExport`, so we are exporting something. There is one of three values (intrinsic constants) that can be used here, the other two being `acImport` to import some data, and `acLink` to create a link to some data. Linking means that Access stays connected to the data source, so that it is always up to date. Of course, linking also means that the original data source needs to be available whenever you use the transferred data in Access.

- ❑ The `DatabaseType` is "Microsoft Access", because we are transferring to another Access database.

- ❑ The `DatabaseName` is "C:\IceCream\Prices.mdb", which is the database where the data is being transferred to.

- ❑ The `ObjectType` is `acTable`, to indicate we are exporting a table.

❑ The Source is "tblIceCream", which is the name of the table in our current database.

❑ The Destination is "tblIceCream", which is the name the table will take when it's in the new database. If this table already exists it will be overwritten.

When you use this method you need to make sure that both the directory and the target database exist, otherwise an error will be generated. One way to deal with this would be to use error handling – we'll be discussing this in chapter 11.

Importing some data would be just as simple:

```
DoCmd.TransferDatabase acImport, "Microsoft Access", _
  "C:\IceCream\Prices.mdb", acTable, "tblIceCream", "tblIceCream"
```

Here the difference is the TransferType argument, which in this case is acImport. This tells Access that we are going to import data. Notice that nothing else has changed. The DatabaseName stays the same, but since we are now importing, it becomes the source of the data, and the current database becomes the destination. That's an important point, because it shows that the DatabaseName argument changes its role depending on which way the data is going.

Since there are several options for these arguments, let's have a look at them in detail:

| Argument | Description |
| --- | --- |
| TransferType | The action to be performed. It must be one of: <br><br> acImport, to import data <br><br> acExport, to export data <br><br> acLink, to link data <br><br> If you leave this blank, the default of acImport is used. |
| DatabaseType | The type of database that you wish to transfer from or to. It must be one of: <br><br> Microsoft Access Jet 2.x <br><br> Jet 3.x dBase III <br><br> dBase IV dBase 5 <br><br> Paradox 3.x Paradox 4.x <br><br> Paradox 5.x Paradox 7.x <br><br> ODBC Databases |

*Table continued on following page*

| Argument | Description |
| --- | --- |
| DatabaseName | The full name of the database to import from or export to. This must include the path, and if exporting, this must already exist. If the DatabaseType is "ODBC Databases" then this parameter is the ODBC Data Source Name, and not the database path. |
| ObjectType | The type of object to be exported. it must be one of:<br><br>acDataAccessPage<br><br>acDefault<br><br>acDiagram<br><br>acForm<br><br>acFunction<br><br>acMacro<br><br>acModule<br><br>acQuery<br><br>acReport<br><br>acServerView<br><br>acStoredProcedure<br><br>acTable<br><br>If you leave this blank, the default of acTable is used. |
| Source | The name of the object that is supplying the data. |
| Destination | The name of the object once it is transferred. |
| StructureOnly | You should set this to True to indicate that only the structure of the object should be transferred, and set it to False (which is the default) to transfer the structure and the data. This allows you to just copy table details without copying the data. |
| StoreLogin | You should set this to True if you are connecting to an ODBC database and wish the user details to be saved with the connection. That way if you connect to the same source, you won't have to enter the user details again. Setting this to False (which is the default) ensures that each time you connect to an ODBC database you have to supply the user details. |

**Exporting to a Database**

1.  Select New... from the File menu.

2.  In the New Task pane, select Blank Database. Name the new database `Sales` and place it in the same directory as your other databases from the book (on the download CD, we've placed this file inside a `Chapter08Files` subfolder to keep things tidy):

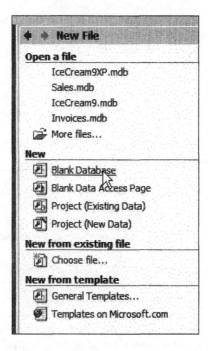

3.  Now close this database and switch back to `IceCream.mdb`.

4.  Create a new form, not based on a table or query, and put a command button on it. Call this button `cmdSales` and give it a suitable caption:

**5.** In the Click event for this button place the following code (remember you can create this event procedure by clicking the right mouse button and selecting the Build Event option from the menu that appears):

```
Application.DoCmd.TransferDatabase acExport, "Microsoft Access", _
   "C:\BegAccessVBA2002\Sales.mdb", acTable, "tblSales", "IceCreamSales"
MsgBox "Sales data exported"
```

Note that this assumes C:\BegAccessVBA2002 is your database directory. If your databases are elsewhere then change this directory name. Note also that you do not need to include the Application object prefix for DoCmd, since it is implicit. We have included here for clarity, but DoCmd would also work just fine by itself, and the rest of the examples in this chapter will use DoCmd by itself.

**6.** Switch back to Access, run the form, and press the button to export the data.

**7.** When the message box pops up, you can close this database. Don't forget to save your changes – save the form as frmImportExport.

Open up the Sales database (Sales.mdb) and have a look at the new table that you've just created.

Notice that the fkCompanyID and fkIceCreamID now only show numbers whereas before (in the IceCream.mdb) they showed the names of the company and "IceCream"

This is because the fields fkCompanyID and fkIceCreamID are **lookup fields**, and get their values from other tables – the company table and the ice cream table to be precise. Since we've not transferred these tables Access can no longer look up the text values, and so displays the underlying foreign key values instead, which in this case happen to be numbers. You can also see that Access still displays the fields as combo boxes but with nothing in the drop-down list. Again this is because it has nothing to look up. If you are happy with the numbers but want to remove the combo boxes then you can open the table in Design view, and remove the Row Source property of each field (on the Lookup tab), or choose TextBox from the Display Control property.

If you would really like to display the text in the fields, instead of just the numbers you should export the missing tables (Company and IceCream) using the TransferDatabase method you have just tried.

## Spreadsheets

Transferring to spreadsheets is probably more common than transferring to databases. Access is really good at reporting, but most people who need to analyze figures are more familiar with spreadsheets. Things like Pivot Tables and Charting are very powerful and useful in Excel, and although you can use them in Access, most people are more familiar with the Excel environment. You probably won't be surprised to learn that there's a `TransferSpreadsheet` command:

```
DoCmd.TransferSpreadsheet [TransferType], [SpreadsheetType],
    TableName, FileName, [HasFieldNames], [Range]
```

You can probably piece together how it works, but let's have a look at the arguments:

| Argument | Description |
| --- | --- |
| TransferType | The action to be performed. It must be one of: |
| | acImport, to import data |
| | acExport, to export data |
| | acLink, to link data |
| | If you leave this blank, the default of acImport is used. |

*Table continued on following page*

| Argument | Description |
| --- | --- |
| SpreadsheetType | The type of spreadsheet you wish to transfer to, or import from. It must be one of:<br><br>acSpreadsheetTypeExcel3   acSpreadsheetTypeExcel4<br><br>acSpreadsheetTypeExcel5   acSpreadsheetTypeExcel7<br><br>acSpreadsheetTypeExcel8   acSpreadsheetTypeExcel9<br><br>acSpreadsheetTypeLotusWK1 acSpreadsheetTypeLotusWK3<br><br>acSpreadsheetTypeLotusWK4 acSpreadsheetTypeLotusWJ2<br><br>If you leave this blank, the default is acSpreadsheetTypeExcel8. **You may have expected to see an** acSpreadsheetType10 **or** acSpreadsheetTypeXP **here, but they are not available or needed, since Excel XP can happily open on files created in** acSpreadsheetType9**, so we can use that instead.** |
| TableName | The table name that the data should be imported into, or linked into; or a table name or query that is the source of the data to export from or link from. |
| FileName | The full name of the spreadsheet, including the path. If this file does not exist before you use the TransferSpreadsheet command, it will be created automatically. However if it *does* already exist, then it will be overwritten without warning. |
| HasFieldNames | When importing or linking, you can set this to True if the source of the data has field names as the first row. The default of False is taken if you leave this argument empty, which assumes that the first row contains data. |
| Range | A valid range of cells, or the name of a range, in the spreadsheet. You cannot supply a range when exporting. The syntax must be valid for the spreadsheet type you are importing. |
| useOA | This is a strange one – though listed in the documentation, there is no mention of what it does, and setting it to true/false (or anything else since it is a variant), appears to have no effect! Further research seems to suggest that it really does nothing of use for us, and can be safely ignored. |

*If you are exporting to an existing workbook, then the data is created in the next available worksheet.*

**Exporting to a Spreadsheet**

**1.** Back in `IceCream.mdb`, open up `frmImportExport` in design mode.

**2.** Add another button, call it `cmdSalesSheet`, and give it a caption of **Sales Spreadsheet**.

**3.** Create a new query, adding the `tblCompany`, `tblSales`, and `tblIceCream` tables. You need to add all of the fields from the sales table to the query (except for `fkCompanyID` and `fkIceCreamID`, as these are just the ID numbers, and not the names). Instead of these two fields add `CompanyName` from `tblCompany` and `IceCream` from `tblIceCream`. Your query should look like this:

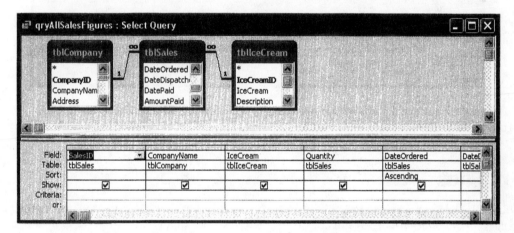

This just links the three tables together, and outputs their names. You should also add a sort on the `DateOrdered` field. Save the query as `qryAllSalesFigures`.

**4.** Now in the code `cmdSalesSheet` command button, enter the following code:

```
DoCmd.TransferSpreadsheet acExport, acSpreadsheetTypeExcel9, _
   "qryAllSalesFigures", "C:\BegAccessVBA2002\Sales.xls"
MsgBox "Sales data exported"
```

**5.** Switch back to Access. Click the button, and a spreadsheet should be created at the specified location. You'll have to open in to see it though:

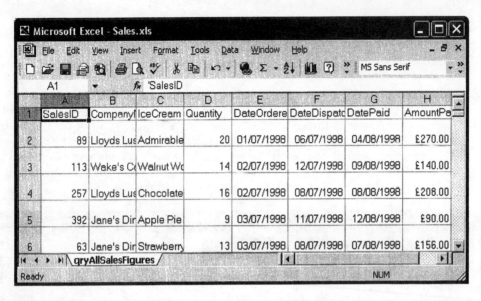

Later in the book we'll show you other ways of transferring data to Excel, using OLE Automation. Now, though, we're going to look at importing and exporting simple text files.

# Text Files

Importing and exporting to text files is quite common, because this is really the one method that nearly all systems support. There are two types of text files that you might have to deal with:

❑   **Fixed width** – where the columns of data are aligned to a specific width. With this format you have to know in advance how wide each column is.

❑   **Comma separated values (CSV)** – (also known as **delimited** text files), where the columns are not aligned, but placed **next to** each other. Each column is separated from the next by a special character. Traditionally this separator character is a comma, but if you're using something else you'll need to tell Access what it is.

> You may have heard of something called XML (Extensible Markup Language). This is also a text-based format for exchanging data and one that is fast replacing CSV and fixed-width files as the best way to move data between different systems. We will look at Exporting XML and the **ExportXML** method after this section, and then later in the book, during the Internet chapter, we'll look at XML in a bit more depth.

To export to fixed-width or CSV files, you use the `TransferText` command:

```
DoCmd.TransferText [TransferType], [SpecificationName],
    TableName, FileName, [HasFieldNames],
    [HTMLTableName], [CodePage]
```

The arguments are fairly obvious, but let's look at them anyway:

| Argument | Desciption |
| --- | --- |
| TransferType | The type of transfer to be performed. This must be one of:<br><br>acExportDelim  acExportFixed<br><br>acExportHTML   acExportMerge<br><br>acImportDelim  acImportFixed<br><br>acImportHTML   acLinkDelim<br><br>acLinkFixed    acLinkHTML<br><br>If you leave this blank, the default of acImportDelim is used.<br><br>Only acImportDelim, acImportFixed, acExportDelim, acExportFixed, or acExportMerge transfer types are supported in a Microsoft Access project (.adp). |
| SpecificationName | The name of the specification. This is required for fixed-width transfers, but isn't always necessary for CSV files. If you are using a CSV file and leave this out then the default values are used. We'll look at specifications next. |
| TableName | The table or query name to be exported, or the table name to import or link. |
| FileName | The full name, including the path, of the file to export to or import or link from. If this file does not exist before you use the TransferText command, it will be created automatically. However if it *does* already exist, then it will be overwritten without warning. |
| HasFieldNames | When importing or linking, you can set this to True if the source of the data has field names as the first row. The default of False is taken if you leave this argument empty, which assumes that the first row contains data. |

*Table continued on following page*

| Argument | Desciption |
|---|---|
| HTMLTableName | The name of the table or list in the HTML document that you wish to import or link from. This is determined by the `<caption>` tag, or by the `<title>` tag. This argument is ignored unless `acImportHTML` or `acLinkHTML` are being used. |
| CodePage | A number that indicates the character set of the text file. A quick way to determine the number you need for this parameter, is to create a new macro, select the Transfer Text Action, then use the drop-down list for the `CodePage` property – it will show the number and a text description. It is just the number that you need. |

## Specifications

When dealing with fixed-width files, or with CSV files with a separator other than a comma, you need to create a specification to tell Access how the text file is structured. This could have all been set by arguments in the `TransferText` method, but then it would have many more arguments and would be far harder to read. To make things easier, you can create a specification including all of these details. In early versions of Access this had its own menu item, but now it's buried within the import/export area, in a very unfriendly manner. Here's how to do it:

**Try It Out       Creating Specifications**

1. Make sure you are in the Tables view of the database window, and select `tblCompany`.

2. From the File menu select Export....

3. On the Export dialog, select Text Files in the Save as type combo box at the bottom of the screen:

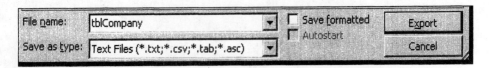

*Don't worry about the file name, since you're not actually going to export anything, (although if the name in here already exists you will be asked if you want to overwrite it).*

4. Click the Save button. This will start the Export Text wizard. Don't run through any of the wizard.

**5.** Click the **Advanced** button. This will show the specification box:

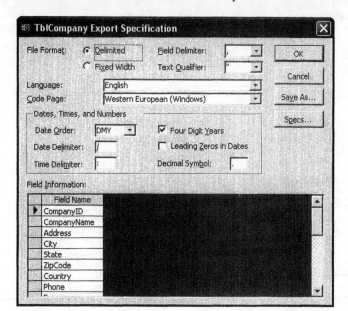

**6.** The above picture shows the view for CSV files. The two important items here are the **Field Delimiter** and **Text Qualifier**.

By way of explanation, look at this example text file:

```
1,"Fran and Nick's Fruit and Nuts","37 Walnut Grove
Nutbush","Tennessee","38053","USA","(423) 935 9032","(423) 935 9001",,,,1
2,"Candy's Cones","26 Wafer Street
Redwood City","California","94056","USA","(650) 456 3298","(650) 456
3201",,,,1
```

The **Field Delimiter** is what the fields will be separated by (it's usually a comma, as it is here). The **Text Qualifier** is what is placed around text fields, and is usually double quotation marks. Anything within these marks is treated as a single field. This means that a field can contain the field delimiter character without causing confusion. For example, if one of our address fields contained a comma, enclosing the field in quotes would mean that the comma in the field wasn't treated as the end of the field.

**7.** Save this specification by clicking the **Save As...** button. Give it a name of `CompanyDelimited`.

**8.** Now change from a delimited file format to a fixed-width format, by selecting the appropriate radio button for the **File Format** at the top of the screen. Notice that the **Field Information** section has changed to show the start and width of each column:

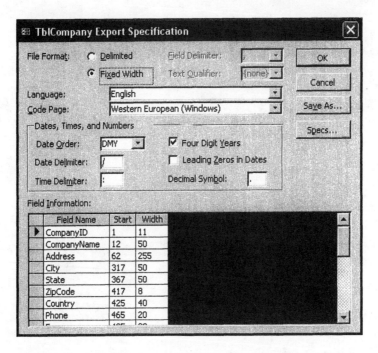

9. Click the **Save As...** button once more, and save this as `CompanyFixed`, in the `BegAccessVBA2002` directory that you've previously used.

10. Press the **OK** button to return to the **Export Text** wizard, and then click on **Cancel** to close it. This returns you to the database window.

So those are the two types of specification. Let's have a look and see what sort of results we get when importing and exporting data with them.

---

**Try It Out**     **Export to a Fixed-Width File**

1. Open up `frmImportExport` in design view.

2. Add another button, calling it `cmdExportFixed`, and give it a caption of **Export Company Fixed**.

3. In the `Click` event of the button, add the following code:

```
DoCmd.TransferText acExportFixed, "CompanyFixed", "tblCompany", _
  "C:\BegAccessVBA2002\CompanyFixed.txt", True
MsgBox "Company details exported"
```

**4.** Flip back to Access, switch the form into Form view, and click the Export Company Fixed button.

**5.** When the export has finished, take a look at the file it's created:

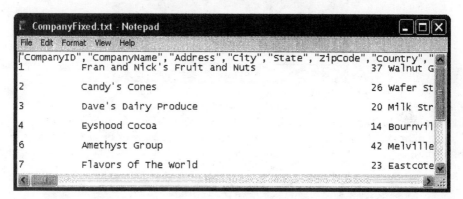

Notice that the first column, CompanyID, is 11 characters wide, as laid out in the specification. Also note that the second column contains no quotes around it, even though it's a text field. That's because we've specified the length of the field, so there's no need to contain text fields in quotes.

You'll also notice something very odd here. Our line of code set the HasFieldNames argument to True, and you can see that the first line it has generated does indeed contain the field names. But (and this is the weird part), the fixed width format isn't used for these field names. We can only assume that the rationale behind this is that the field names themselves don't really fit as part of the specification, and so are output in the CSV default format.

**Try It Out**　　　**Importing from a Fixed Width File**

**1.** In Access, create a new button on our import and export form. Call this one cmdImportFixed, and caption it Import Company Fixed.

**2.** Add the following code to the Click event:

```
DoCmd.TransferText acImportFixed, "CompanyFixed", "tblCompanyFixed", _
    "C:\BegAccessVBA2002\CompanyFixed.txt", True
MsgBox "Company details imported"
```

**3.** Flip back to Access, switch the form into Form mode and press the new import button. This will import the file you've just exported into a new table.

If you look at the list of tables you'll see two new ones – tblCompanyFixed and CompanyFixed_ImportErrors. The first is the new table you imported, and the second is automatically created by Access because there were some import errors. If you open the errors table, you'll see what the problem is:

Yeah, right. That's really useful. What this means is that Access has tried to add some data from the text file into the CompanyID field, but it was not the correct format. But hold on. Hasn't Access just exported this data – how can it be wrong? The answer lies in the record for Flavors Of The World:

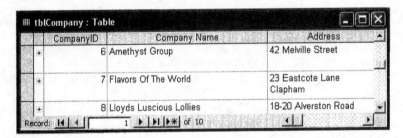

Notice that the address field appears on two lines – it has a carriage return character in it. This isn't a problem in Access, but think about how the text file handles this – the carriage return indicates a new line. With fixed-width text files, the import routine assumes that each new line is a new record. So when it imports this text file you get an error, as it is expecting a number (the CompanyID) at the beginning of the line, not part of the address. That's why we've got a Type Conversion Failure – Access is trying to convert a string into a number. If you open the newly imported table, tblCompanyFixed, you'll see what Access has done:

| CompanyID | CompanyName | Address | City | State | ZipCode | Country | P |
|---|---|---|---|---|---|---|---|
| | | S | | +4 | 76 2232 | | |
| 1 | Fran and Nick's | 37 Walnut Grov | Nutbush | Tennessee | 38053 | USA | (423) ! |
| 2 | Candy's Cones | 26 Wafer Street | Redwood City | California | 94056 | USA | (650) |
| 3 | Dave's Dairy Pr | 20 Milk Street | Boston | Massachusetts | 02119 | USA | (617) ! |
| 4 | Eyshood Cocoa | 14 Bournville St | Birmingham | Alabama | 35210 | USA | (205) : |
| 6 | Amethyst Grou | 42 Melville Stre | Edinburgh | Midlothian | EH3 7HA | SCOTLAND | +44 (1 |
| 7 | Flavors Of The ' | 23 Eastcote La | | | | | |
| 8 | Lloyds Lusciou: | 18-20 Alverston | | | | Godalmir | |
| 10 | Jane's Diner | 1827 East 1st A | Denver | CO | 80206 | USA | 303 3: |
| 11 | Wake's Cakes . | 72 High Street | Birmingham | | B27 2AA | UK | +44 1: |

Notice that there is a record at the top without a CompanyID field – this is the extra record caused by the carriage return in the address field. The record for **Flavors Of The World** has incorrect information for its address fields, as does the record for **Lloyds Luscious Lollies**. That's because the record count is now incorrect and Access has difficulty catching up.

This is pretty disastrous, as it might mean a lot of data becomes corrupted. The way to solve this problem is to use delimited files with a text qualifier, as these import and export correctly. That's because the text qualifier marks the start and the end of a text field, so the carriage return is taken to be part of the field because it is within the quotes.

**Try It Out** — **Export to a Comma-Separated File**

1. Add another button to your form. Call it cmdExportSeparated and caption it **Export Company Separated**.

2. Add the following code to the Click event for this button:

```
DoCmd.TransferText acExportDelim, "CompanyDelimited", "tblCompany", _
   "C:\BegAccessVBA2002\CompanyDelimited.txt", True
MsgBox "Company details exported"
```

3. Back in Access, click this button.

4. When done, have a look at the file it's produced:

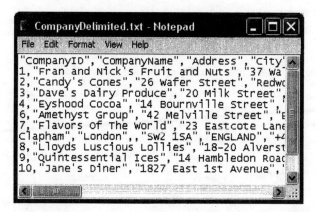

As you can see, now everything is in the same format as the header line. The comma is used to delimit the fields, and quotes are used around all text fields.

## Try It Out — Importing from a Comma-Separated File

**1.** OK, add the last in our little line of buttons. This time call it `cmdImportDelimited` and caption it Import Company Delimited.

**2.** Add the following code to the `Click` event:

```
DoCmd.TransferText acImportDelim, "CompanyDelimited", "tblCompanyDelimited", _
  "C:\BegAccessVBA2002\CompanyDelimited.txt", True
MsgBox "Company details imported"
```

**3.** Now, back in Access, click this button.

**4.** When it's done, have a look at the database window:

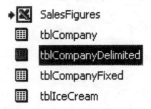

You now have a new table, containing exactly the same details as the company table. Although we used the standard layout with a comma, just changing the specification can let us easily use other characters. (In fact, because we used the default values, we could have quite easily omitted the specification).

### A Couple of Gotchas to be aware of when Importing from Text files

If the table that you import into does not already exist, then it will be created automatically. This is fine. However if you run the import again, when the table does exist, the data will be appended to the existing data, and you will get duplicate records. This would not usually be what you or you users want, so make sure that once they have performed the import, they are protected from immediately doing it again by mistake (by disabling the import button, perhaps, or showing a different form).

But wait, you say, I have a primary key in the table, so duplicate records will not be accepted! Which brings me on to my next point: the text files cannot contain any detailed information about the structure of your tables – so information such as primary keys, the size of a text field, or indexes are lost during the export/import you performed above. Take a look at the text sizes for the `CompanyName` field for example in both the `tblCompany` and the `tblCompanyDelimited` tables by opening them up in design view. You will see that the original table had a text size of 50, whereas the imported table has 255 – Access had to take a guess during the import and 255 is the best it could do. Probably of more concern though is the `CompanyID` field, this was an `AutoNumber`, but now it is just a plain old Long Integer, and it has lost its status as a primary key. This could of course have ramifications for the rest of system.

# XML

XML (eXtensible Markup Language) is a hot new buzzword that seems to be on everyone's lips at the moment. Ask some people any question you like, and they'll tell you XML is the answer! But what is it? And why are people so interested in it?

Actually it's a very simple idea, and simple ideas that are good tend to go a long way. XML is just way to describe data in a text-based format, and in a standard way. I like to think of an XML file as a super-powered CSV file. We saw that CSV files were a nice way to transfer data in and out of a database (or any system as a matter of fact), but that they lost crucial information during the process, such as the details of the data types or indexes. XML gives us the mechanism to keep all that data, and any other data safe and sound. But it doesn't lose the ability to be used in pretty much any system, and there in lies its strength. It has all the convenience of CSV files, because anything can use it, and it adds a strong way to describe the data in as much detail as we want.

We'll be exploring XML in more detail in Chapter 18, but for this section, we are going to see how easy it is to export our data to an XML format.

To export data to XML we use the `ExportXML` method:

```
Application.ExportXML (ObjectType, DataSource, DataTarget, SchemaTarget, ,
PresentationTarget, ImageTarget, Encoding, OtherFlags)
```

| Argument | Desciption |
|---|---|
| ObjectType | The type of transfer to be performed. This must be one of:<br><br>acExportDataAccessPage<br><br>acExportForm<br><br>acExportFunction<br><br>acExportQuery<br><br>acExportReport<br><br>acExportServerView<br><br>acExportStoredProcedure<br><br>acExportTable |
| DataSource | The name of the Access object you want to export. If left blank it will use the currently open object of the type specified in the ObjectType argument. |
| DataTarget | The file name and path for the exported data. If you skip this, then data is not exported, which may be desirable if you just want to export to one of the other targets. |
| SchemaTarget | This is file name and path for the exported schema information. Schema information describes the structure of the data, such as the data types used, or if a particular field is the primary key. If this argument is omitted, schema information is embedded in the data document rather than as a separate file. |
| Presentation Target | The file name and path for the exported presentation information. If this argument is omitted, presentation information is not exported. This file will contain XSL that is used to "transform" the XML to HTML, and as such would usually have an .xsl extension. |

| Argument | Desciption |
|---|---|
| Encoding | The text encoding to use for the exported XML. Can be one of:<br><br>acEUCJ<br><br>acUCS2<br><br>acUCS4<br><br>acUTF16<br><br>acUTF8<br><br>If not specified acUTF8 will be used (8-bit Unicode) and will be fine for more cases. |
| OtherFlags | The OtherFlags argument allows you to specify among other things if the web page that performs the actual transformation should be HTM or ASP. It does this through a bit mask with the following values:<br><br>1  Related tables – Means that the export includes the "many" tables for the object specified by DataSource.<br><br>2  Relational properties – If you export related tables, this will also creates relational schema properties.<br><br>4  Run from server – Means the export pages will be created as ASP pages (Active Server pahges); otherwise, default is HTML. Only applies when exporting reports.<br><br>8  Special properties – Creates extended property schema properties.<br><br>To use a bit mask for this argument, just add the values up. So if you want related tables, relational properties, and ASP you would add 1+2+4 giving you 7 as the value to set. We'll take a more detailed look at bitmasks later in the book. |

If you want to import XML data into the database then you can use the ImportXML method:

```
Application.ImportXML (Datasource, ImportOptions)
```

| Argument | Desciption |
|----------|------------|
| DataSource | This is a string specifying the name and path of the XML file to import. Note that the file name of the XML file does NOT have to relate to the name of the table you are importing, rather it is the XML tags inside the file that determine the table that the data will be imported to. This is important when considering the next parameter (ImportOptions). |
| ImportOptions | One of the following instrinsic constants :<br><br>acAppendData – this option means that if the table to be imported already exists then the imported data will be appended to it. If the table does not exist then the import will fail and Access will create an ImportErrors table detailing the failure.<br><br>acStructureAndData – Access will create the table and import the data into it. If a table with the same name as the table to be imported already exists then Access will create a new table and append a number to the end of the name (for example Company1). For Access to be able to import the structure then there must be an embedded or linked schema file (XSD) for the XML file. We will see an example of this below.<br><br>acStructureOnly – Access will create the table structure only but will not import the data into it. If a table with the same name as the table to be imported already exists then Access will create a new table and append a number to the end of the name (for example Company1) For Access to be able to import the structure then there must be an embedded or linked schema file (XSD) for the XML file. We will see an example of this below. |

## Try It Out — Exporting a Table to XML

1. Open up frmImportExport in design view.

2. Add another button, calling it cmdExportXML, and give it a caption of Export Company XML.

In the Click event of the button, add the following code:

```
Application.ExportXML acExportTable, "tblCompany",
"c:\BegAccessVBA2002\Company.xml", _
  "c:\BegAccessVBA2002\company.xsd", "c:\BegAccessVBA2002\company.xsl"
MsgBox "Company details exported to XML"
```

**3.** Flip back to Access, switch the form into Form view, and click the Export Company XML button.

**4.** When the export has finished, take a look at the files it's created:

**5.** Company.xml – this contains the XML data. Open it up in Internet Explorer or Notepad and you will see how the data is represented. This is not meant for human consumption, rather it is just a storage for the data.

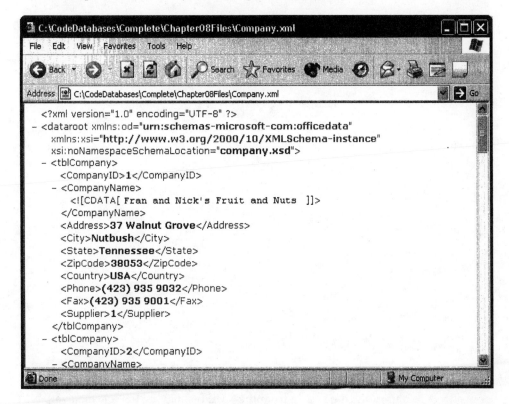

Company.xsl – this is the XSL code that was executed by Access to produce the HTML file. XSL stands for eXtensible Style Language and is a way of 'transforming' XML into something more human-friendly.

```
<?xml version="1.0"?>
<xsl:stylesheet xmlns:xsl="http://www.w3.org/TR/WD-xsl"
language="vbscript">
<xsl:template match="/">
<HTML>
<HEAD>
<META HTTP-EQUIV="Content-Type" CONTENT="text/html;charset=UTF-8" />
<TITLE>
tblCompany
</TITLE>
<STYLE TYPE="text/css">
</STYLE>
</HEAD>
<BODY link="#0000ff" vlink="#800080">
<TABLE BORDER="1" BGCOLOR="#ffffff" CELLSPACING="0" CELLPADDING="0"><TBODY>

<xsl:for-each select="/dataroot/tblCompany">
<xsl:eval>AppendNodeIndex(me)</xsl:eval>
</xsl:for-each>
<xsl:for-each select="/dataroot/tblCompany">
<xsl:eval>CacheCurrentNode(me)</xsl:eval>
<xsl:if expr="OnFirstNode">
<TR><TH style="width: 2.38cm">
CompanyID
</TH>
<TH style="width: 6.269cm">
Company Name
</TH>
<TH style="width: 4.312cm">
Address
</TH>
<TH style="width: 2.38cm">
City
</TH>
<TH style="width: 2.38cm">
State/County
</TH>
<TH style="width: 2.38cm">
Zip/Post Code
</TH>
<TH style="width: 2.38cm">
Country
</TH>
<TH style="width: 3.121cm">
Phone
</TH>
<TH style="width: 3.227cm">
```

Company.xsd – this is the schema for the data – it describes the structure of the data. If we were to import the data again from the XML file, having the schema available too means that we won't lose important information such as which field is the primary key. Open it up in notepad to see the description of the structure of the Company table:

```
<?xml version="1.0" encoding="UTF-8"?>
<xsd:schema xmlns:xsd="http://www.w3.org/2000/10/XMLSchema"
xmlns:od="urn:schemas-microsoft-com:officedata">
<xsd:element name="dataroot">
<xsd:complexType>
<xsd:choice maxOccurs="unbounded">
<xsd:element ref="tblCompany"/>
</xsd:choice>
</xsd:complexType>
</xsd:element>
<xsd:element name="tblCompany">
<xsd:annotation>
<xsd:appinfo>
<od:index index-name="PrimaryKey" index-key="CompanyID " primary="yes" unique="yes"
clustered="no"/>
<od:index index-name="PostCode" index-key="ZipCode " primary="no" unique="no"
clustered="no"/>
<od:index index-name="SupplierID" index-key="CompanyID " primary="no" unique="no"
clustered="no"/>
</xsd:appinfo>
</xsd:annotation>
<xsd:complexType>
<xsd:sequence>
<xsd:element name="CompanyID" od:jetType="autonumber" od:sqlSType="int"
od:autoUnique="yes" od:nonNullable="yes">
<xsd:simpleType>
<xsd:restriction base="xsd:integer"/>
</xsd:simpleType>
</xsd:element>
<xsd:element name="CompanyName" minOccurs="0" od:jetType="text" od:sqlSType="nvarchar">
<xsd:simpleType>
<xsd:restriction base="xsd:string">
<xsd:maxLength value="50"/>
</xsd:restriction>
</xsd:simpleType>
</xsd:element>
<xsd:element name="Address" minOccurs="0" od:jetType="text" od:sqlSType="nvarchar">
<xsd:simpleType>
<xsd:restriction base="xsd:string">
<xsd:maxLength value="255"/>
</xsd:restriction>
</xsd:simpleType>
```

Company.htm – here is a HTML representation of our table – not that pretty perhaps, but in the next step we'll export a report with much nicer formatting:

---

**Try It Out**  **Exporting a Report using XML to get a HTML Web Report**

**1.** Open up `frmImportExport` in design view.

**2.** Add another button, calling it `cmdExportXMLReport`, and give it a caption of Export Suppliers XML Report.

**3.** In the `Click` event of the button, add the following code:

```
Application.ExportXML acExportReport, "Suppliers",
"c:\BegAccessVBA2002\Suppliers.xml", _
    "c:\BegAccessVBA2002\Suppliers.xsd", "c:\BegAccessVBA2002\suppliers.xsl"
MsgBox "Suppliers report exported to XML"
```

**4.** Flip back to Access, switch the form into Form view, and click the Export Company XML button.

**5.** When the export has finished, take a look at the `suppliers.htm` file it's created: it is a pretty good representation of our Access report that we can now publish on the Web. One thing to bear in mind is that even if your original report spanned multiple pages, it will now be displayed on a single HTML page.

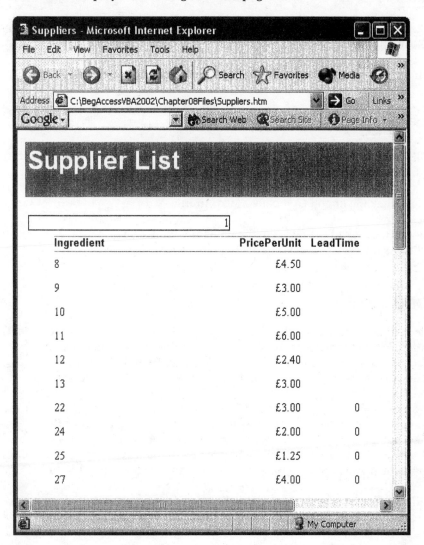

---

**Try It Out**    **Importing XML Data**

**1.** Open up `frmImportExport` in design view.

**2.** Add another button, calling it `cmdImportXML`, and give it a caption of Import Company XML.

**3.** In the `Click` event of the button, add the following code:

```
Application.ImportXML "c:\BegAccessVBA2002\Company.xml", acStructureAndData
  MsgBox "Company Details Imported from XML file"
```

**4.** Flip back to Access, switch the form into Form view, and click the Export Company XML button, so that we have some XML data to import.

**5.** Now click the Import Company XML button.

If you now take a look at the tables in the database window, you will see that you have a new table, **Company1**, which contains the data you have just imported.

# Electronic Mail

Electronic mail is ubiquitous nowadays. Everyone has an e-mail account. OK, that's a slight exaggeration. My Mom doesn't have e-mail yet. Or even a computer, actually. My brother builds electrical things. I program them. And Mom looks on in that way that only parents can, saying 'Yes dear, very nice. Pour me another whiskey, would you please?'

Not only has e-mail brought the world closer, it has opened up lines of communication. No longer do you have to print off a twenty-page report and fax it to your office in Outer Elbonia, only to find out they've run out of fax paper. You can simply pick names from an electronic address book, and with a single click your report is on its way. Having data quicker means decisions can be made in a more timely fashion. Let's face it: it's just less effort all around.

The e-mail facilities in Access are not specific to any e-mail software. I'll show you samples with Microsoft Outlook, because that's what I use, but other packages should work just as well.

To send e-mail you use the `SendObject` method:

```
DoCmd.SendObject [ObjectType], [ObjectName], [OutputFormat],
  [To], [CC], [BCC], [Subject],
  [MessageText], [EditMessage], [TemplateFile]
```

You can probably guess what some of these arguments are, but let's look at them in more detail:

| Argument | Description |
|---|---|
| ObjectType | The type of object you wish to send. It must be one of:<br><br>acSendDataAccessPage    acSendForm<br><br>acSendModule          acSendNoObject<br><br>acSendQuery           acSendReport<br><br>acSendTable<br><br>If this argument is omitted, acSendNoObject is used, which just sends mail, without attaching any objects. |
| ObjectName | The name of the object you wish to send. |
| OutputFormat | The format the object is to be sent in. It must be one of:<br><br>acFormatDAP   acFormatHTML<br><br>acFormatRTF   acFormatText<br><br>acFormatXLS<br><br>You will be prompted for a format if you leave this argument blank. |
| To | The recipient name, or list of recipient names, to whom the mail should be sent. You will be prompted for names if you leave this argument blank. To include multiple recipients, you just separate their names by a semi-colon. This name should be a valid address book entry, or the actual email address. |
| CC | The recipient name, or list of recipient names, to whom the mail should be CC'd. |
| BCC | The recipient name, or list of recipient names, to whom the mail should be BCC'd. |
| Subject | The text that comprises the subject line of the message. |
| MessageText | The text that comprises the main body of the message. |
| EditMessage | Set this to True, which is the default, to open your mail application and allow editing of the message before it's sent. Set this to False to send the message straight away. |
| TemplateFile | The full name (including the path), of an HTML template file, to be used when sending HTML files. |

Let's see this in action.

It's important to note that the following code will only work if you have an e-mail program installed on your computer. You don't actually have to have it connected to anything, as long as it is installed and set up to send mail. While writing this, I installed Outlook 2002 and set up a profile, even though I didn't have e-mail on the test machine. Just follow the installation instructions for installing Outlook, and then follow the wizard to set up a service provider. It doesn't matter what you put into the wizard fields, because you're not actually going to be sending mail anyway.

## Try It Out — Sending Mail

1. Open the import and export form in design view and add another button. Name this `cmdEmailPriceList`, and caption it Email Price List.

2. Add the following code to the `Click` event:

```
DoCmd.SendObject acSendTable, "tblIceCream", acFormatXLS, _
    "Janine Lloyd", "Karen Wake; Jane Donnelly", _
    "IceCreamLovers", "Latest Prices", _
    "Hot off the press - our latest price list."
```

*If you want to really send mail, you should change the names here to some of your own contacts.*

3. Back in Access, switch to Form view and press the e-mail button. Since we left out the `EditMessage` argument, the default is to show the message before sending:

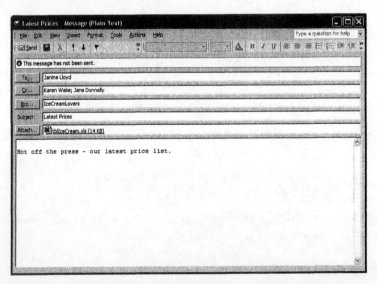

Notice how the names in the three address fields match those in our code? Also notice that because we specified `acFormatXLS` the table has been turned into an Excel spreadsheet before being attached to the mail message. If we had set the `EditMessage` argument to `False` the message would have been delivered without any user interaction. It's a simple as that. You'll be seeing other ways to send mail in a later chapter.

NOTE: It's important to realize that your application could actually send mail without the user being aware of it. You may consider this a security risk. Depending on the version of Outlook the user may see the following dialog:

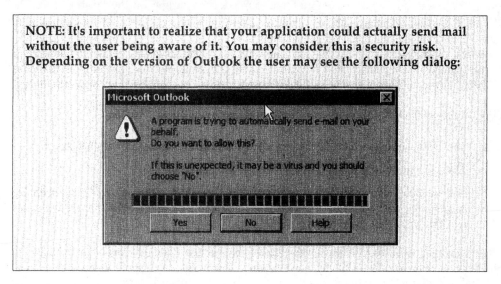

# Using External Data

So far in this chapter we've looked at how to get data into and out of Access, but we haven't addressed the point that imported data isn't live. In other words, when you import a set of data you'll be unaware of any subsequent changes that are made. In order to get access to live data, you have to **link** objects into Access as tables. They look like tables, they act like tables... heck, they even smell like tables. But in fact, they are really just a pointer back to the original data.

This technique allows you to link into Access a variety of other objects. This is pretty important, because it allows you to use data that might not be yours to control. Other departments, for example, might not want you to control the data, even if they do let you access it.

## The Database Splitter

One quite useful advantage of this linking is the ability to split your database into two without damaging it. There's actually an add-in supplied called the **Database Splitter**. We're not going to run through this here, but it is worth mentioning why it's a good idea.

Let's take a typical business scenario. You've just developed a database for use in your department. You've spent months developing it, and have finally rolled it out. It's stored on your central server, so there's only one copy, and everyone has been using it – the data has started to accumulate quite rapidly. It's been a few weeks, and then your boss comes to you and says 'I want you to add this feature. By tomorrow.' Great. Now you've got to stop everyone from using the database, because you have to make the changes on the master, since it's the one with all of the data. They all complain, and you're now under pressure. Not a good way to work.

But, what if you've got two databases? One with all of the tables, and one with everything else – forms, queries, reports, and so on, with the actual data tables just linked from the other database. You can quite happily make changes to the forms database without affecting the data.

In fact, when redeveloping your front end, you can have three databases:

❑　The Data database. This is the one whose structure almost never changes.

❑　The Live forms database. This is the one the users use.

❑　A Test database, which is a copy of the Live database. You can make your changes to forms, etc., without affecting the users. You can test against the live data if necessary, just by linking in the tables.

In this situation, once you've made the changes to the test database, you can just copy it onto the server, overwriting the Live forms database. The tables are linked, so no data is lost. The users will only have a few moments delay while you perform the copy, and then they have the new changes.

This sort of scenario is used quite often. Many companies start using Access as their main development tool, and then grow beyond its capabilities. So they move their data into a bigger database, such as SQL Server, but leave the front end, the forms, in Access, and link the tables from SQL Server. This way the only cost, both in terms of time and resources, is the movement of the data, not the redevelopment of the whole application. This is one of the reasons why Access now has the ability to work with MSDE and SQL Server in a much more integrated way.

## Linked Tables

Since we've talked about linked tables, it's about time to give them a try. Let's use the `Sales.xls` spreadsheet we created earlier. If you've deleted it, you can simply recreate it from the import and export form.

**Try It Out**　　**Linking a Spreadsheet**

**1.**　Open `frmImportExport` in design view and add another button. Call it `cmdLink` and give it a caption of Link Spreadsheet.

**2.**　In the `Click` event, add the following code:

```
DoCmd.TransferSpreadsheet acLink, acSpreadsheetTypeExcel9, _
  "SalesFigures", "C:\BegAccessVBA2002\Sales.XLS", True
MsgBox "Spreadsheet linked"
```

**3.** Go back to the form and, in **Form** mode, click the **New** button.

**4.** Then, have a look at the database window:

Notice the new table, the icon to indicate its source, and the arrow, to indicate it's a linked table. There are a few things you can't do (such as deleting data), but otherwise this behaves exactly like a normal table. If you change data, you are actually changing the spreadsheet. There's only one copy, and you've just got a link to it.

> *You can delete the link anytime you want, and it doesn't delete the original spreadsheet. All it does is delete the link. It's a bit like shortcuts in Windows – if you delete the shortcut, you don't delete the file it points to.*

This technique is quite useful as it allows you to have a copy of the data on a central server, but it allows users to have a copy of the front-end database on their local machines. This would mean that it's quicker to open the database because it's stored locally. In fact, one often-used technique is to store some tables locally as well. These would be tables that change very rarely, or not at all. So the only data stored centrally is the data that changes frequently.

## *Differences between Linked and Local Tables*

Linked tables have several advantages over local ones:

❑ You can store the data in its most appropriate location. For example, if the data is supplied by the finance department, and they are happier working in Excel than in Access, you can let them work in Excel. Linking the spreadsheet into Access lets you use the data as if it was an Access table.

❑ Linking tables allows you to access data you don't own, but need to use. This is especially true as companies start using data more for decision making.

❑ They allow you to separate your data from your user interface, allowing easier maintenance.

There are, however, certain drawbacks of linked tables:

❑ Linked tables aren't part of your database, so the records have to be retrieved from another file. This could lead to speed problems if the source of the data is on another machine on the network.

❑ Linked tables must be opened as dynaset or snapshot-type recordsets, and they therefore don't support the Seek method.

❑ You must be careful when joining tables from different places, such as one local table and one remote table, as the field type may not be completely compatible. JET 4 has reduced the possibility of incompatibilities, but you should just be aware that this could be a problem.

❑ You should be careful when joining large remote tables to small local tables. If both tables are local Access can optimize the join, but if the large table is linked, all of the data must be brought across the link before the join can take place. This can lead to speed problems.

Don't let the above put you off linking tables, or even trying the database splitter with its back end/front end approach. This is the first step towards client/server systems, and can bring some big benefits.

# Summary

In this chapter we've concerned ourselves purely with data from outside of the current database – what it is, where it is, and how to use it. We've looked at how we can use data from other sources, as well as supplying data to other sources. This is quite a common request, and you've seen that the programming required for this is fairly simple.

In particular we've looked at:

- ❏ How to import and export text files, spreadsheets, and database objects
- ❏ How to export to XML, and to generate web reports using this technique
- ❏ How to send electronic mail, incorporating data from Access
- ❏ How to use other data sources, whilst keeping the original source of the data

Now that we've got all of this data into Access, it's about time to see how reports can make it easier for us to view it.

# Exercises

**1.** Use the Database Splitter to create a back-end and front-end database. Are there any changes you need to make to the front end to make sure that it still works correctly?

**2.** If you are connected to a mail system, create a form to allow users to fill in Bug Reports and Enhancements Requests, and use the SendObject method to let the user send them to you.

**3.** Create a form that lets users select any report then export it to HTML format for inclusion in their web site.

# CHAPTER 10

# Reports

The reporting facility is one of the best features of Access, and even though this is a VBA book, there are certain areas of reports that need covering. Reports, just like forms, can have code underneath them, and there are several events that you can use: for example we can code an **Open** event to raise a message box reminding a user that the report is best run overnight because it takes hours to run. You generally don't need much code on reports, but what little you do use can turn an ordinary report into a great report.

In particular we will be looking at:

- ❑ How to use expressions on reports
- ❑ Adding totals and summaries
- ❑ Events, and which ones to use

## Starting Off

As we work through this chapter, we're going to need a report to work on, so we're going to create a report that summarizes the sales data. We're not going to create this with the Report Wizard, because the wizard automatically does some of the things we want to do manually. That's not to say that you should never use the wizard, but if you work through some of the steps you'll understand what it does.

**Creating the Query**

**1.** This report is going to be based on a query, so create a new query, and add `tblCompany` and `tblSales` to it:

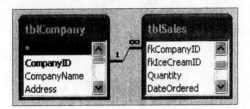

**2.** Click on the Totals button on the toolbar – that's the one that looks like this:

**3.** Select `CompanyName` from `tblCompany` and add it to the query by double-clicking it. Now place the cursor in the empty **Field** box in the next column to the `CompanyName` and type the following:

```
MonthName: Format([DateOrdered], "mmmm")
```

**4.** Next, add `Quantity` from `tblSales` to the query, as the third field. Then place the cursor in the fourth empty **Field** box and type the following:

```
MonthNumber: DatePart("m", [DateOrdered])
```

**5.** Now check and alter the `Total` and `Sort` values. Your query needs to be setup like the following:

| Field | Total | Sort |
| --- | --- | --- |
| CompanyName | Group By | Ascending |
| MonthName | Group By | |
| Quantity | Sum | |
| MonthNumber | Group By | Ascending |

The `MonthName` and `Quantity` fields should have empty `Sort` boxes.

**6.** Your query should now look like this:

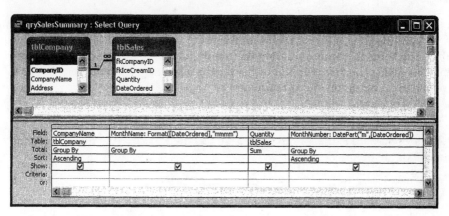

**7.** Save the query as `qrySalesSummary`.

**8.** Run the query – you should have something that looks like this:

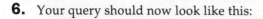

Before we explain our query in the *How It Works* section we should understand what the design grid is actually doing for us behind the scenes. The design grid is giving us a user-friendly way to develop a **SQL query**. While we drag and drop fields to the grid, behind the scenes the design grid is building a SQL query; it is that query that will run against the database when we call it. To see code of the SQL query either click the designer tool and select **SQL View** or select **View | SQL View** from the menu and you should see the SQL query code that has been developed, as the following illustrates:

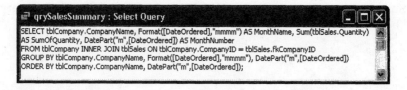

## How It Works

Let's just look at those bits of code we typed in, so you'll understand what's happening. In this report we want the company, the month of the order, and the total of the orders for that month, ordered by the company name and then the month. Ordering by the company name is not a problem since we can just sort on it, but the date is a bit of a problem. We want to show the full month name, but sort on the month number.

- ❑ So, the first field is the company name and we sort by that.

- ❑ The second field is the month name. We use the Format function to give us the full name of the month:

```
MonthName: Format([DateOrdered], "mmmm")
```

- ❑ The third field is Quantity, which will be the sum of sales for that month.

- ❑ The fourth field is the month number. Remember from an earlier chapter, where we looked at DatePart – using a format of "m" allows us to just get the month number of the order:

```
MonthNumber: DatePart("m", [DateOrdered])
```

Why do we need this? Well, what we want to show is the sum of the sales for each month, and we'd like the months to be shown in chronological order. However, the month name is a string, and if we sort on the name we don't end up with the correct order, because strings are sorted in alphabetical order. That means that February would come before January, which is not what we want. So we use another field, which is the number of the month, and we sort on that. This gives us the correct ordering.

So we end up with a correctly formatted query. OK, on to the report.

## Try It Out          Creating the Report

1. Now we need to create a new report based on the above query. Don't use the Report Wizard, as we want to create this manually. Select **Reports**, and then click the **New** button.

2. On the **New Report** dialog, select **Design View** from the list at the top, and select qrySalesSummary from the drop-down list at the bottom. This is the query the report will be based upon.

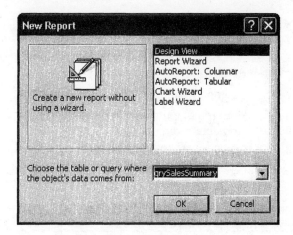

**3.** Press the OK button to create a blank report.

**4.** Click the Sorting and Grouping button. That's the one that looks like this:

**5.** Add CompanyName to the Field/Expression list, and set both the Group Header and Group Footer to Yes.

**6.** Add MonthNumber to the Field/Expression list. Now close the Sorting and Grouping window:

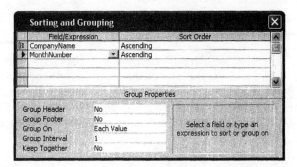

**7.** Now add the fields to the report. To see the fields, select Field List from the View menu. You can just drag the fields from the list and drop them in the appropriate place on the report.

- ❏ You need to drag and drop the CompanyName into the **CompanyName Header**, and MonthName and SumOfQuantity into the **Detail** section.
- ❏ Add a Label in the **CompanyName Header** above the **SumOfQuantity** field with its **Caption** property as Qty.
- ❏ You can leave the **CompanyName Footer** and **Page Footer** blank for now.
- ❏ You might also like to remove the labels for the fields you've just added, so that the report doesn't look cluttered.
- ❏ You can also add a label in the **Page Header** to act as the report heading and change the background colour to accent the header – the report should now look like this:

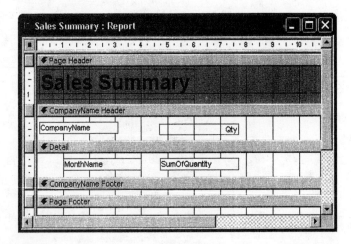

Save the report as Sales Summary. There's no need to close it, as we'll be using it straight away. There is a voluntary naming convention that recommends that the name of a report is prefixed by 'rpt' and comprises one word, that is, rptSalesSummary. It is a convention that also applies to other Access objects: we have followed it in naming our query (qrySalesSummary).

While this convention is widely followed there are developers and users that prefer to have the name of the report to be the same as the title of the report as it appears on the actual report; as we have done here: "Sales Summary". Both methods are valid, but when you develop reports for different users you may need to be able to use both styles. So, in this example we show you how to use the voluntary naming convention when we name the query and the alternative when we name the report.

OK, that's the report set up. Let's look at what code we can now use on it.

# Page Numbers

The report wizard automatically puts page numbers onto reports, or you can put them in yourself in design mode (you can simply add them from the Insert menu), but let's add them manually so you can see what these other methods actually do.

**Page Numbers**

1. In the page footer add a new textbox. Place it at the right of the page.

2. Bring up the Properties for the new textbox, select the **Data** tab and add the following code into the `Control Source` property:

```
= "Page " & [Page] & " of " & [Pages]
```

3. Delete the label for this textbox, as we won't need it.

4. Switch the report to **Preview** mode and have a look at the bottom of the page.

This is really simple. You know that we use the and symbol (`&`) to join strings together in expressions. Well, `Page` and `Pages` are predefined fields within any report, and identify the current page number and the total number of pages. We enclose them in square brackets to tell Access that these are fields and not strings.

# IIf

We mentioned `IIf` earlier in the book (Chapter 4), and warned you of its dangers (all of the arguments are run), but there are some times when it can be really useful. For example, suppose we want to print our report out double sided, and would like the page numbers to appear at the outer edge on both odd and even numbered pages. This means that for some pages it must be on the left, and for the others it must be on the right. Note that as an alternative, we could write our own function to do this: we probably would if we wanted more flexibility than the `IIf` function offers.

## Try It Out — The IIf Function

1. Switch the form back into design mode.

2. Move the page number field to the very left of the page, and set the text to be left aligned using the Align Left button on the toolbar.

3. Modify the Control Source property of the page number field, so it now looks like this:

```
=IIf([Page] Mod 2 = 0, "Page " & [Page] & " of " & [Pages], "")
```

4. Add another textbox, this time at the right of the page and set the text to be right aligned using the Align Right button on the toolbar. You can delete the label again.

5. Add the following code to this textbox's Control Source property:

```
=IIf([Page] Mod 2 = 1, "Page " & [Page]  & " of " & [Pages], "")
```

6. Now switch to preview mode to see what effect the changes have had. Step forward a few pages to see what happens for odd and even pages.

Notice that for the first page, and all odd numbered pages, the page numbers are on the right of the page. For all even numbers they are on the left.

## How It Works

Let's look again at the arguments for the IIf function:

```
IIf (Expression, TruePart, FalsePart)
```

The arguments are:

- ❑   Expression, which is the expression to test
- ❑   TruePart, which is the value to return if Expression is True
- ❑   FalsePart, which is the value to return if Expression is False

So, for the page numbers on the left we have this:

```
=IIf([Page] Mod 2 = 0, "Page " & [Page]  & " of " & [Pages], "")
```

That means the `Expression` we are testing is:

```
[Page] Mod 2 = 0
```

This uses `Mod` to return the integer remainder of dividing the page number by two. This will be 0 if the page number is even, so the expression will only be `True` on even pages.

If the `Expression` is `True`, then the `TruePart` of the `IIf` function:

```
"Page " & [Page]  & " of " & [Pages]
```

is returned.

If `Expression` is `False`, then the `FalsePart` of the `IIf` function is returned, which is empty.

So this whole field will only show up on even numbered pages, which produces the page count we are looking for.

The page number field for page numbers on the right is pretty similar. The only difference is in the expression to test:

```
[Page] Mod 2 = 1
```

Here we check to see whether the page number is odd or not. If it is, then the same `TruePart` is returned.

This shows that with just one simple function you've made your report look much better than it did before.

Still confused about `Mod`? We need to use it because we don't have a programmatic concept of what is an odd or even page, and so we use the `Mod` operator to help us out. We know that if we set the `Mod` operator to 2, that all page numbers (numerator) will be divided by 2 (denominator). It just so happens that whenever a page number is divided by two that if there is a remainder the page number is odd and whenever there is no remainder the page number is even.

So by using `Mod` 2 in this instance we can determine an odd from an even page number.

> *You can find more about the `Mod` operator by keying "Mod" into the help index when in the V-E (remember online help is context sensitive).*

# Dates

In Access 2002, Microsoft has introduced two new date properties: `DateModified` and `DateCreated` (we previewed them in Chapter 5 – *Using Access Objects*). Now we are going to add these two dates and a `DatePrinted` field (based on the `Now()` function) to the Sales Summary report.

While we are adding these dates to our report, it is a convenient time to reflect on how we can use the `AllReports` collection and `Report` object (actually it was a variable of type `AccessObject`, that we used to represent a "**Report Object**") that we previewed earlier (Chapter 5). Previously we looped through the `AllReports` collection extracting the `Name` property of each report in the collection. We then used this property to add to a list of report names in a listbox. Now we will explore how we can use these two new properties, `DataModified` and `DateCreated`, of a report.

Placing a `DatePrinted` value on a report is as simple as setting the control source of a text box to the `Now` function, however, the `DateModified` and `DateCreated` dates pose a challenge: they are properties of a **Report Object** (`AccessObject`) that resides in the `AllReports` collection. The approach that we will take is to develop a custom function (`ReportHistory`) that will return all the dates and property values in a string and set it as the control source of a textbox.

Note: we use a function and not a subroutine because a function returns a value and a subroutine doesn't.

The `ReportHistory` function will be passed one string parameter – the name of the report – and it will return a string that will include the three dates that we want (`DatePrinted`, `DateModified`, and `DateCreated`), the printer's port, and device names from the `Printers` collection. We will then create a textbox (`txtReportHistory`) on the report and set its control source to the `ReportHistory` function.

In a real-world situation, `ReportHistory` function would be useful on many reports, so to enable us to re use the function we will write it generically, that is, there will be no hard-coding of names (this is referred to as 'loose coupling').

The information returned by `ReportHistory` will be useful for users of reports, because it will tell them when the report was run, the port and device it was run on, and the date when the report (not the data) was last modified and first created.

---

**Try It Out** — **Writing the ReportHistory Function**

**1.** In Modules: Create a new module.

**2.** Enter the following code and save the module as Chapter 9 Code.

```
Function ReportHistory(ByVal sRpt As String) As String

    Dim acObj As AccessObject
    Dim sRptIn As String
    Dim sDatePrinted As String
    Dim sDateModified As String
    Dim sDateCreated As String
    Dim sPort As String
    Dim sDevice As String
    Dim sBuild As String

    sRptIn = sRpt
    sPort = "Port name: " & Application.Printers(0).Port
    sDevice = "Device name: " & Application.Printers(0).DeviceName
    sBuild = ""

    For Each acObj In CurrentProject.AllReports
      With acObj
        If acObj.Name = sRptIn Then
          sDatePrinted = "Date printed: " & Now()
          sDateModified = "Date modified: " &.DateModified
          sDateCreated = "Date created: " & .DateCreated
          Exit For
        End If

      End With
    Next acObj

    sBuild = sDatePrinted & ", " & sPort &", " & sDevice & ", " _
          & sDateCreated & ", " & sDateModified & "."

    ReportHistory = sBuild

End Function
```

## How It Works

We create a function header that takes one String argument (the report name) and returns a String:

```
Function ReportHistory(sRpt As String) As String
```

Then we declare an AccessObject – the AllReports collection contains AccessObjects that represent reports. Next we declare seven String variables to hold respective strings:

```
Dim sRptIn As String
Dim sDatePrinted As String
Dim sDateModified As String
```

**385**

```
Dim sDateCreated As String
Dim sPort As String
Dim sDevice As String
Dim sBuild As String
```

Next we assign values to four `String` variables: `sRptIn` is assigned the value passed in by the parameter (`sRpt`); `sPort` and `sDevice` are assigned the respective property of the `Printer` object. We prefix each of these strings with a descriptor (for example, `Port name:`) and then access the respective property by using its qualified name: for example, the `Port` property is addressed through the `Application` object (the Access application), which has a collection of `Printers`, and the first `Printer` object in the collection has an **index value** of 0, and this printer has a `Port` property (in this case we have only one printer). Finally we assign "" to `sBuild` to assure ourselves that it holds no value:

```
sRptIn = sRpt
sPort = "Port name: " & Application.Printers(0).Port
sDevice = "Device name: " & Application.Printers(0).DeviceName
sBuild = ""
```

Having done that, we commence a `For Each...Next` block and with each `AccessObject` in the `AllReports` collection we progress through the collection:

```
For Each acObj In CurrentProject.AllReports
    With acObj
```

We progress through the collection until the `If` statement is `True`. We use an `If` statement to see if the `AccessObject` represents the report that we are looking for (`Sales Summary` which is the value held in `sRptIn`). If the `AccessObject` does match the string value in `sRptIn`, then we have located our report in the `AllReports` collection and we can assign respective string variables to hold the `Now` function and the two properties of the `AccessObject` (`DateModified` and `DateCreated`). The `Exit For` is used to exit the `For Each` loop as we have the report we want: after that we close with `End If` and `End With`:

```
If acObj.Name = sRptIn Then
    sDatePrinted = "Date printed: " & Now()
    sDateModified = "Date modified: " & .DateModified
    sDateCreated = "Date created: " & .DateCreated
    Exit For
End If

End With
```

If, on the other hand, the `AccessObject` doesn't match the string value in `sRptIn` it moves onto the `Next AccessObject` in the `AllReports` collection. (We could add some error code in an `Else` statement to handle the situation where the parameter passed was invalid – but we won't for brevity.)

```
Next acObj
```

Finally we build our `sBuild` string and assign it to the functions return, and then end the function:

```
sBuild = sDatePrinted &", " & sPort & ", " & sDevice & ", " _
    & sDateCreated & ", " &sDateModified & "."

ReportHistory = sBuild

End Function
```

# Testing the ReportHistory Function in the Immediate Window

We don't know for sure if our code has error-free syntax or is logical until we test it, and the best place for that is in the Immediate Window.

**Testing the ReportHistory Function in the Immediate Window**

**1.** From the code module window, open the Immediate Window (View | Immediate Window)

**2.** Enter the following line of code into the Immediate Window:

```
?ReportHistory("Sales Summary")
```

The Immediate window should look similar to the following:

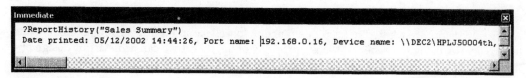

```
Immediate
?ReportHistory("Sales Summary")
Date printed: 05/12/2002 14:44:26, Port name: 192.168.0.16, Device name: \\DEC2\HPLJ50004th,
```

Now we have our function written and tested so we can add it to the Sales Summary report – so open up the report in design mode, if it is not already open, and let's finish building our report.

**Adding Dates to the Sales Summary report**

**1.** In the Page Footer section, add a textbox from the toolbox, change the name of the textbox to `txtReportHistory`, change the label for the textbox to read `Report History`, and then add the following as the control source in `txtReportHistory`:

```
=ReportHistory([Name])
```

**2.** The Page Footer should now look like this:

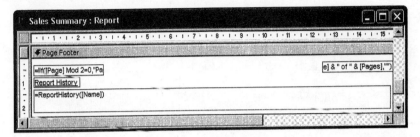

**3.** Switch to preview mode and you should see the following:

## How It Works

We set the control source of `txtReportHistory` to the string value returned by `ReportHistory` function. The function needs to be passed a string parameter that represents the name of the report. We do this by passing the `[Name]` property of the report to the `ReportHistory` function.

As we said before we wanted to keep this function loosely coupled (that is, not tied to any one report) and by using the generic `[Name]` property of the report we can achieve our design objective.

# Summarizing

One thing this report lacks is totals. Since we are showing sales figures on a month-by-month basis, we really ought to show totals for each company.

## Try It Out — Adding Totals

**1.** Switch the report back to Design view.

**2.** Add a new textbox into the CompanyName Footer. Call it `txtCompanyTotal`.

**3.** Change the label of the new text box to **Total**:

**4.** Put the following in the **Control Source** for the new field:

```
=Sum([SumOfQuantity])
```

**5.** Switch to **Preview** mode:

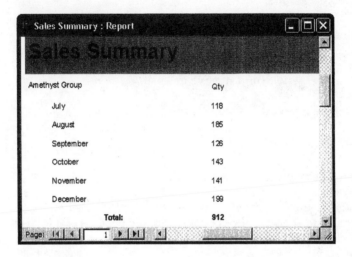

You've seen the use of functions in fields, and Sum is just another function. When sum is used on a group footer, the argument you give it is the name of the field in the **Detail Section**. In our case this is SumOfQuantity – that's the field from the underlying query. All Sum does is sum up the values for the field in the **Detail Section**. It's as simple as that.

# Expressions

You've already seen expressions in use in this chapter. Remember that an expression is just something that returns a value, and in the following Try It Out we will be using an expression to return the value to the control source property of a textbox that is placed on the report itself. The following are all examples of expressions:

- ❏ ccyTotal = ccyPrice * ccyQuantity
- ❏ strName = strFirstName & " " & strLastName
- ❏ strMonth = Format(datOrderDate, "mmmm")

So far you've seen expressions that use the page number, date, and the Sum function. With the latter, this was placed in the section footer, and produced a total of records in the preceding detail section. You can also do this the other way around, by putting a field in the detail that references the total. For example, let's assume we'd like to see what percentage of a company's total sales occur in each month.

**Expressions**

1.  Switch the form into design view.

2.  Place a new textbox on the form, in the **Detail** section. Place it to the right of the SumOfQuantity field, and remove its label.

3.  Put the following in the **Control Source** property:

```
= [SumOfQuantity]/[txtCompanyTotal]
```

4.  Change the **Format** property to Percent.

5.  Add a label to the **CompanyName Header** section changing its Caption property to %. If you wish add separator lines to break up the headers and totals from the data. Now preview the form:

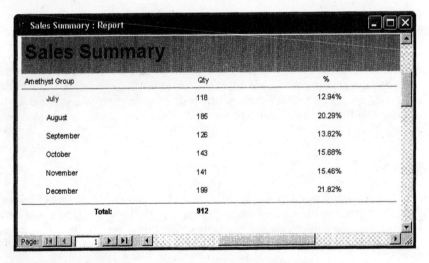

This just uses the total field we created earlier. So not only can you create new fields with expressions in them, but you can use those new fields in other expressions, too.

# Events

The examples above simply illustrate using expressions and functions on your reports, but it's not really a large amount of VBA. What you might not realize is that reports also respond to events, just like forms. So opening and closing a report generates events, and you can add code to the events just as you would with a form. Just as forms have form modules behind them, reports have report modules. There's no real difference to the way the code is created or used. The only difference is the number of objects and events that are available in reports.

You can easily see which events are available by looking at the Events tab in the Properties window for the report:

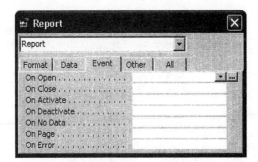

As you can see, the report has seven events. The page header and footer sections have two events, as shown below:

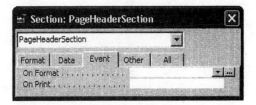

Group sections and the detail section have three events:

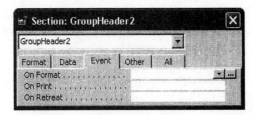

Let's look at all of these in a little more detail. We won't be building examples for most of these, but we will look at some code snippets for most events – we're covering them in case you want to use them.

# Open

The Open event is generated when a report is opened, before any printing takes place. There are several uses for this:

- ❑ On a report that takes a particularly long time to run, you could inform the user that they might have to wait a while, and offer them the option of not running it.

- ❑ In reports with sensitive information, you could ask for a password before letting anyone run the report.

- ❑ You could open a form to allow filtering of the report data. You'll see an example of this later.

The Open event has one argument, Cancel, which is something you can set. It allows you to cancel the opening of the report from within code, and thus the report isn't previewed or printed. For example:

```
Private Sub Report_Open (Cancel As Integer)

    Dim blnResultintResult As Integer
    Dim strWarningAs String

    strWarning = "This report may take some time." & _
      " I suggest you make a coffee, or perhaps do a little shopping!" &_
      " Or press Cancel to abort the operation."
    intResult = MsgBox (strWarning, vbOKCancel, "Warning")
    If intResult = vbCancel Then
      Cancel = True
    End If

End Sub
```

If you set the Cancel argument to True, then the report isn't opened.

# Activate

The Activate event is generated when a report has been opened and becomes the active window. It will therefore occur after the Open event, and any time the report becomes the main window. You could use this to display a custom menu bar or toolbar:

```
Private Sub Report_Activate()

    DoCmd.ShowToolbar "AllOrders", acToolbarYes

End Sub
```

## Deactivate

The Deactivate event is generated when a report stops being the active window, but before another Access window becomes active. This is an important point – it is not generated when another application becomes the active window, only when another Access window does. It can be used to reverse the actions of the Activate event. For example:

```
Private Sub Report_Deactivate()

   DoCmd.ShowToolbar "AllOrders", acToolbarNo

End Sub
```

## Close

The Close event is generated when a report is closed and removed from the screen, and will occur after the Deactivate event. You could perhaps use this (or indeed the Open event) to log usage of reports, possibly for auditing purposes. Or if you've opened a filter form (which we'll be seeing shortly) during the Open event, you could close it here:

```
Private Sub Report_Close()

   DoCmd.Close acForm, "frmReportFilter", acSaveNo

End Sub
```

## Error

The Error event is generated when an error occurs within the report. This includes database errors, but not VBA run-time errors. There are two arguments passed into this event:

❑ DataErr, which is the error number

❑ Response, which is an output parameter used to determine how the error is reported

Response can take one of two values:

❑ acDataErrContinue, which tells Access that the error should be ignored. This would be useful if you just want to log the error, and then continue silently without the user being aware of any problems.

❑ acDataErrDisplay, which tells Access to handle the error, so it shows the standard error details. This is the default value.

If you want to perform your own error logging, then some code like this would work:

```
Private Sub Report_Error(DataErr As Integer, Response As Integer)

    Response = acDataErrContinue
    LogError Me, DataErr

End Sub
```

This sets the response to indicate that Access should do nothing to handle the error, and then it calls a function called `LogError` (not included) to log the details.

# Format

The `Format` event is generated when Access knows what data it is going to put in a section, but before the data is formatted for previewing or printing. In previous versions of Access this tended to be used to display hidden fields. For example, at Rob and Dave's we try to flag up these items:

- ❑   Those orders that were dispatched 6 or more days after the order date.

- ❑   Unpaid orders that are 35 or more days old.

There are two ways to highlight these orders:

**Try It Out**        **Formatting with the Format Event**

1.  Open up the **Sales By Supplier By Month** report in design mode.

2.  Add a new label to the detail section. Call it `lblOverdue` and give it a `Caption` of **Payment Overdue**, and set the text alignment to 'center'. Place it over the **Date Paid** and **Amount** fields. It will only be visible for those orders where these fields are empty, so it will look OK.

3.  Select the `DateDispatched` field and change the background style from **Transparent** to **Normal**.

4.  Select the **Detail** bar and view the properties.

5.  Click the builder button for the **On Format** event and choose code builder.

6.  In the event procedure, add this code:

```
If IsNull(DatePaid) And (Date - DateOrdered) > 34 Then
   lblOverdue.Visible = True
Else
```

```
   lblOverdue.Visible = False
End If

If (DateDispatched - DateOrdered) > 5 Then
  DateDispatched.BackColor = vbRed
Else
  DateDispatched.BackColor = vbWhite
End If
```

**7.** Back in Access, switch the report into Preview mode:

| rptSales | | | | | | |
|---|---|---|---|---|---|---|

**Amethyst Group**

**July 2002**

| Ordered | Sent | Ice Cream | Qty | Paid | AmountPaid |
|---|---|---|---|---|---|
| 05/07/2002 | 07/07/2002 | Strawberry Cheesecake | 4 | 05/08/2002 | $60 |
| 06/07/2002 | 10/07/2002 | Admirable Apricot | 20 | Payment Overdue | |
| 06/07/2002 | 10/07/2002 | Strawberry Cheesecake | 6 | Payment Overdue | |
| 08/07/2002 | | Fudge Brownie | 6 | 17/08/2002 | $60 |
| 11/07/2002 | 14/07/2002 | Barely Cinnamon | 15 | 15/08/2002 | $180 |
| 13/07/2002 | 17/07/2002 | Chocolate Chip | 12 | 19/08/2002 | $132 |
| 16/07/2002 | | Fudge Brownie | 20 | 26/08/2002 | $200 |
| 19/07/2002 | 20/07/2002 | Fudge Brownie | 2 | 20/08/2002 | $20 |

Page: 1

Here you can see that the overdue warning only appears when the order is unpaid, and it is 35 days old; also, the dispatched date is highlighted if we took more than 5 days to dispatch the order. It shows up gray on the printed page, but it's red on the screen.

## How It Works

This code was added to the Format event for the Detail section, so it gets run for every row that appears in the Detail section. Within this code, we can refer to fields and set their properties just as we would on a form. So, in the first piece of code, we check to see if the DatePaid is Null, meaning a payment hasn't been received. We also see if the difference between the current date (remember Date returns the current date) and the order date is greater than 34. If both of these are true, then we make the Overdue label Visible. If not true, then the label is hidden.

```
If IsNull(DatePaid) And (Date - DateOrdered) > 34 Then
  lblOverdue.Visible = True
Else
```

```
    lblOverdue.Visible = False
  End If
```

In the second piece of code, we work out the difference between the order date and dispatch date (shown as **Sent** on the report). If this difference is greater than 5 days, we make the background of the dispatch date red (and set it to white if the order was dispatched on time).

```
  If (DateDispatched - DateOrdered) > 5 Then
    DateDispatched.BackColor = vbRed
  Else
    DateDispatched.BackColor = vbWhite
  End If
```

One thing to note about this is that the report preview will open slower than it did without this code. That's simply because it runs this code for every line.

## Conditional Formatting

**Conditional Formatting** is a feature that allows you to apply formatting to a field depending upon certain conditions – so be careful that the conditions are what you really want them to be. Sounds very similar to what we've just done in code, doesn't it? However there are certain limitations and it's not as flexible as the Format event. For example, you can't apply conditional formatting to a label, and you can only set the formatting of an object, not its visibility. However, white text on a white background is pretty hard to see, so you can get the same results.

Let's add some conditional formatting to the report to see how this works in comparison to the code method.

### Try It Out — Conditional Formatting

1. Switch the report back into design view.

2. Add a new textbox to the Detail section, and remove its associated label. Place this field to the very left of the Detail section, just to show it's different from our other overdue label. The name of the field isn't important; we've called it txtOverduePayment.

3. Set the Control Source property of the textbox to:

   ```
   ="Payment Overdue"
   ```

4. Set the Font/Fore Color to White.

**5.** With the textbox selected, from the Format menu pick Conditional Formatting...

**6.** Set up the condition so that it looks like this:

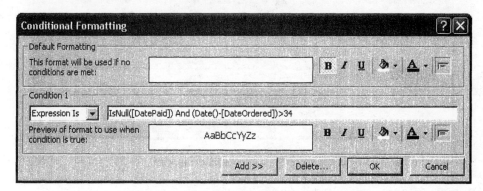

The important thing here is that the Font/Fore Color on this should be Black. So this field defaults to white text, and when the condition is true it becomes black. This emulates the visible/hidden idea we used earlier.

**7.** Press OK to close this dialog and switch the report into Preview mode:

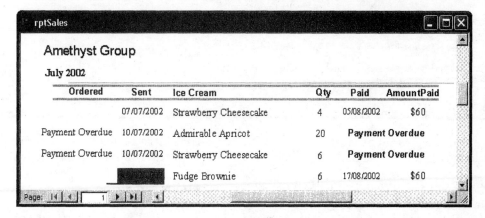

Notice how the new overdue field follows the same rules as the old one. But notice how the Date Ordered field is being overwritten. That's because this new field is not transparent, but even if it were, the white text would still overwrite the field below it. This means you must make sure that this field (payment overdue) is behind all other fields. You can do this from the Format menu, by selecting Send To Back.

**8.** Select the DateOrdered field. We'll add the dispatched date formatting to this field just so you can see the difference between this method and the code method.

**9.** From the Format menu pick Conditional Formatting...

**10.** Set up the condition so that it looks like this:

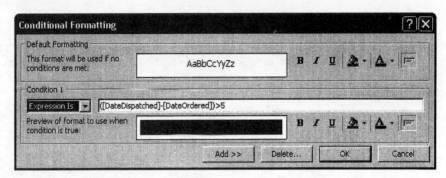

Here the back color is set to red if the condition is met.

**11.** Press OK to close this dialog and switch the form into Preview mode:

| rptSales | | | | | | |
| --- | --- | --- | --- | --- | --- | --- |

**Amethyst Group**

**July 2002**

| | Ordered | Sent | Ice Cream | Qty | Paid | AmountPaid |
| --- | --- | --- | --- | --- | --- | --- |
| | 05/07/2002 | 07/07/2002 | Strawberry Cheesecake | 4 | 05/08/2002 | $60 |
| Payment Overdue | 06/07/2002 | 10/07/2002 | Admirable Apricot | 20 | **Payment Overdue** | |
| Payment Overdue | 06/07/2002 | 10/07/2002 | Strawberry Cheesecake | 6 | **Payment Overdue** | |
| | | | Fudge Brownie | 6 | 17/08/2002 | $60 |

Page: 1

Of course, if we used this label instead of (and in the same place as) the VBA-formatted one, it would appear to behave similarly, as there wouldn't be any text for it to be masked by.

So there you have it. Two completely different ways to perform custom formatting on objects. Which is the best? It's really up to you. Use whichever method you feel more familiar with. The code method gives you more flexibility since you've got full control over the objects; the conditional formatting method is probably simpler, but here you've only got control of the formatting.

You might like to remove this new field and just stick with the coding method.

## Cancel and FormatCount

When you were editing code for the format event you might have wondered about the arguments. The first, `Cancel`, you've seen before and works in the same way as the argument to the `Open` event. If you set this argument to `True` in the event procedure, then the section is not formatted. To be honest, I would never use this option.

FormatCount is a complex issue, and again one we've never used. But there might be conditions under which you need to use it. To understand this you must understand how formatting of report sections works. When Access formats a section it checks certain properties of the section, such as Force New Page, New Row or Col, or Keep Together. This last one is pretty important because if it is True, then the whole section should be kept together on a single page. This means that Access has to calculate how big the section will be, and then see if that fits on the remainder of the current page. So, how does it know how big the section is going to be? Simple, it formats the section. If it doesn't fit on the remainder of the page, a new page is started, and the section is formatted again. So FormatCount identifies how many times the formatting has been run.

This means that the code you put into the Format event could be run several times. Now if all you are doing is setting some formatting properties this doesn't matter too much, but this might be important if you are keeping totals from within code. For example, you might have declared a report-level variable, intTotalOrdersNDOT, and then be adding up some custom totals – perhaps keeping track of the number of orders that weren't delivered within the allocated time. If the format event were run twice, you'd end up counting some items twice. So you could do something like this:

```
If FormatCount = 1 Then
   If (DateDispatched - DateOrdered) > 5 Then
      intTotalOrdersNDOT = intTotalOrdersNDOT + 1
   End If
End If
```

This ensures that the totals are only calculated once.

## Print

The Print event is generated after the section has been formatted, but before it is printed. You could use this to perform tasks that won't affect the layout of the report. In the above examples for the Format event, we set properties on some fields, but these were contained within the section, and didn't cause the section to shrink or expand, so they could easily have been coded in the Print event.

The thing to watch out for in the Print event is that it is only executed for sections that are printed. So if you open a report in preview mode and then flip to the last page, the Print event is only generated for sections on the first and last pages. That means you should never use the Print event for calculating totals, since the calculations might not get run for the middle pages.

Like the Format event, the Print event has Cancel and PrintCount arguments, which behave in a similar fashion.

## Retreat

The Retreat event is run in conjunction with the Format event. Remember how we said that formatting could occur several times? If a section doesn't fit on a page once it's been formatted, Access Retreats back through the section, and then formats the section on a new page. The Retreat event is triggered between the two formats, and allows you to undo anything, such as totals, that you might have performed while formatting.

## NoData

The NoData event, as its name implies, is generated when there is no data on the report. This could happen perhaps if the report was generated according to some user defined selections, and indicates that there is no data in the underlying query. You could use this to display a custom error message rather than just displaying a blank report. For example:

```
Private Sub Report_NoData(Cancel As Integer)

   MsgBox ("No records matched your selection. Please try again.")
   Cancel = True

End Sub
```

The Cancel argument here behaves exactly like it does in the Open event, so setting it to True cancels the opening of the report. Setting it to False will open the report, but no records will be displayed.

The NoData event occurs after the Open event and before the Activate event.

## Page

The Page event is triggered after a page is formatted, but before it is printed. You could use this to add graphics to a report as a whole, rather than just a section. For example, the following code draws a border around the whole report:

```
Me.Line(0,0) - (Me.ScaleWidth, Me.ScaleHeight),,B
```

This type of graphic is far more difficult to achieve by drawing it on the report in design view.

## When to Use the Different Events

As the Format, Print, and Retreat events are not used very often, deciding when to use which type of event can often be the hardest part of report design. Here are a few guidelines to help you:

## Format

You should use this when your procedure could affect the layout of the page, for example, for making controls invisible. Access will actually lay out (format) the section after your procedure has run.

You could also use this in conjunction with a hidden section. If you need to perform some totaling for a section which is not visible, you can't use the Print event procedure, since this will never be generated. In this case, you have to use the Format event procedure.

## Print

This should be used when your procedure does not modify the layout of the report, or when the procedure depends upon the page the records are printed on. It only affects sections that print, so if you only print the last page of a report, the Print event is not generated for the other pages. This is particularly important if you are using the event to calculate running totals.

## Retreat

This is best used in conjunction with the Format event. For example, if you have a Format event procedure that is calculating totals, you may wish to undo some of them if you are backing up (Retreating) over previously formatted sections.

## The FormatCount and PrintCount Properties

You should use these to ensure that actions within the format and print event procedures are only executed once. These properties increment each time a record is formatted or printed, including occasions where a record does not fit on a page.

You will probably calculate most of your totals by using the Sum command in the footer sections of the report, but the Format and Print event procedures provide a flexible way of adding totals which are not based on a grouping. However, do bear in mind the problems you can experience if you don't remember to check these.

# Filters

Reports are all very well, but their details are fixed at design time. What you really need to be able to do is allow users a little degree of customization, and this is where filtering comes in. A report has two properties to help with this:

❑   Filter, which holds the details of the filter, usually a SQL statement
❑   FilterOn, which indicates whether the filter is on or off

Generally there are a couple of ways of visibly interacting with a report to filter data: we can set a criteria parameter in the underlying query or we can develop a filter form. If we want a 'quick 'n' dirty' solution then we may opt – while in query design mode – to place a parameter in the criteria section of the appropriate field of the query grid (for example, place ["Enter Company Name"] in the criteria of the CompanyName field in qrySalesSummary) and when we try to preview the report, Access will automatically show an input box asking for a parameter, and by entering a valid company name we get a filtered report. However, if we want a professional result and one that offers better management of user input (for example, a list of valid input choices in a combo box) then we would opt for the filter form – this is the option that we will illustrate now.

What we are going to do next is create a form that gets shown when the report is opened. This will allow us to pick an Order Date, and whether to only show records that match, or are greater than or less than this date. A couple of buttons on the form will apply and clear the filter.

We'll use the same report we've been using throughout this chapter, so you might like to remove the duplicate formatting we did earlier. We took off the ones we added later, using conditional formatting, and kept the code versions. This is quite a long *Try It Out*, but it's fairly easy. A note of caution: some developers have experienced inefficiencies in using filters, so see the chapter on Data Management Techniques where we discuss alternatives.

**Try It Out**    **Adding a Filter Form**

**1.** Switch the Sales By Suppiler By Month form back into design view and add a new textbox to the Report Header section, like so:

**2.** Name the textbox txtFilter, and the label lblFilter and change the caption in lblFilter to 'Filtered:'. Set the Visible property for this textbox and its label to No.

**3.** Switch to the VBE, and in the NoData event for the report add the following code:

```
MsgBox "There were no records for your selection."
Cancel = True
```

**4.** In the Open event for the report add the following code:

```
DoCmd.OpenForm "frmReportFilter"
```

**5.** In the `Close` event for the report add the following code:

```
DoCmd.Close acForm, "frmReportFilter", acSaveNo
```

**6.** Now switch back to Access and close the report, making sure you save your changes. Create a new form and lay it out like this:

**7.** Name the combo box `cboOperator`, and set the **Row Source Type** property to **Value List**. In the **Row Source** property, type the following:

```
=;>;<;>=;<=
```

These are the operators which the user will use to search for dates.

**8.** Name the text box `txtValue`, and set the **Format** property to be **Short Date**. Now set the **Input Mask** property to the following:

```
99/99/00;0;_
```

**9.** Name the **Apply** button `cmdApply`, and the **Clear** button `cmdClear`.

**10.** Press the code button on the toolbar to create a code module for the form. This will switch you to the VBE. Now add the following variable declaration just after the `Option Explicit` statement:

```
Dim m_rptSales As Report
```

**11.** We're now going to code the various events for the filter form. Add the following line of code in the `Form_Load` event:

```
Set m_rptSales = Reports("Sales By Supplier By Month")
```

Now, in the `cmdClear_Click` event, add the following code:

```
txtValue = ""
With m_rptSales
  .Filter = ""
  .FilterOn = False
  txtFilter.Visible = False
  lblFilter.Visible = False
End With
```

Finally, in the cmdApply_Click event, add the following code:

```
Dim strWhere As String

strWhere = "[DateOrdered] " & _
  cboOperator & _
  " #" & txtValue & "#"

With m_rptSales
  .Filter = strWhere
  .FilterOn = True
  .txtFilter.Visible = True
  .txtFilter = strWhere
  .lblFilter.Visible = True
End With
```

**12.** Save all of your changes, and close the new form. Now open the report (**Sales By Supplier By Month**) in Preview mode. Notice that the form is displayed too – it may be hidden by the report, so you might have to move it around on the screen (or find it via the menu: Window | Sales Report Filter).

**13.** Select the = sign from the operator combo box and add 07/20/02 to the textbox. Now press the Apply button.

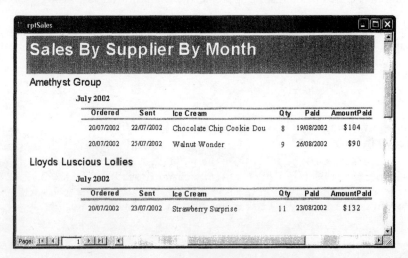

Notice how only those orders with an order date of 7/20/02 are shown.

**14.** Press the Clear button, and all of the records are restored.

Let's start with the code in the report first.

In the NoData event we just want to inform the user that their selection didn't produce any records. We set Cancel to True to cancel the opening of the report.

```
MsgBox "There were no records for your selection." & _
    vbCr & "Please try again."
Cancel = True
```

When the report is opened, the Open event is generated, and here we just make sure the filter form is opened at the same time.

```
DoCmd.OpenForm "frmReportFilter"
```

When the report is closed, the Close event is generated. There's no point keeping the filter form open once the report is closed, so we close the form.

```
DoCmd.Close acForm, "frmReportFilter", acSaveNo
```

That's all the code in the report. Now on to the filter form.

First, the variable declaration. Since we are going to be referring to an active report several times, we declare a form-level variable to hold a reference to the report. The variable has form-level scope because we placed it in the General Declarations section of the form code module.

```
Dim m_rptSales As Report
```

When the form (frmReportsFilter) is opened, we want to set this variable to point to the currently active report, so we have some code in the Open event for the form. We know what the report is called, so we use the report name to index into the Reports collection. Remember the Reports collection holds a list of all reports and can access the ActiveReport property. Once the variable is set we'll be able to use the variable to reference the currently active report, rather than using the collection. This is not only easier to read, but faster too (notice that we use the Set keyword because the report (Sales By Supplier By Month) is an object).

```
Set m_rptSales = Reports("Sales By Supplier By Month")
```

When the form is closing, the Close event is triggered, so we just set the variable to Nothing to clear the memory associated with it.

```
Set m_rptSales = Nothing
```

Now we need to look at what happens when we click the **Apply** button. The first thing we do is declare a string variable to hold the filter. This is a standard SQL WHERE clause, but without the WHERE.

```
Dim strWhere As String
```

To build this filter, we need the field we are filtering on, which is DateOrdered, followed by the operator, followed by the date. Notice that # signs have been put around txtValue, to tell VBA that the string is in fact a date:

```
strWhere = "[DateOrdered] " & _
    cboOperator & _
    " #" & txtValue & "#"
```

This gives us something like this:

```
[DateOrdered] = #7/20/02#
```

Now we have a filter statement, we need to set it on the report. We use the With construct here to save a bit of typing (it's more efficient, too).

```
With m_rptSales
```

We set the Filter property of the report to the filter statement we've constructed and then set the FilterOn property to True, indicating that a filter is in action.

```
    .Filter = strWhere
    .FilterOn = True
```

Since it's always a bad idea to show a filtered report without indicating that not all records are present, we set the textbox and label to indicate what the filter is. Otherwise, you'd give the user the impression that all records were shown, and this could have implications if the report is used to satisfy customer queries, or contains financial information.

```
    .txtFilter.Visible = True
    .txtFilter = strWhere
    .lblFilter.Visible = True
End With
```

To clear the filter we do almost the opposite. We clear the `Filter` property and set `FilterOn` to `False` to indicate that there is no filter in action.

```
txtValue = ""

With m_rptSales
   .Filter = ""
   .FilterOn = False
```

Since there is no filter in place anymore, we set the indicators to be hidden. So an unfiltered report has nothing extra on it, but a filtered one does.

```
   txtFilter.Visible = False
   lblFilter.Visible = False
End With
```

That's all there is to it. The steps are really quite simple:

- ❏ In the Report's `Open` event, you open your filter form.

- ❏ On the filter form, you construct the filter.

- ❏ To apply the filter, you set the `Filter` property to point to the filter string, and set the `FilterOn` property to `True`.

- ❏ To clear the filter, you can just turn the `FilterOn` property to `False`, set the `Filter` property to a blank string, or, as I did, do both.

Using this technique, you can construct filter forms quite easily. To construct a generic filter form that could be used to apply to any filter is a little more difficult, since you have to find out the fields on the report, what type of data they hold, and so on. It's something you might want to think about, but it's a little bit too involved to cover here.

# Summary

In this chapter we've looked at how you use code in reports. This varies from just using functions in fields to using events and larger sections of code in the code module behind the report. Even at its very simplest, you can see that adding code to reports can make a difference.

The important things to consider are:

- ❏ You can use expressions as the `ControlSource` of a field, just by placing an = sign in front of the expression.

- ❏ You can use the `Format` event to allow you to change the layout of reports, such as making fields visible, or changing the formatting of a field.

- ❏ You can use the `Open` and `Close` events to trigger other actions, such as loading a form.

You probably won't use much code in your reports, just limiting it to the samples shown here. Now that you've seen code behind both forms and reports, it's time to look at a little advanced programming.

# Exercises

**1.** How could you modify the filter form so that instead of being fixed to the date ordered, you can pick any of the fields on the form?

**2.** What report event occurs last: `Deactivate` or `Close` event?

**3.** To loop through the `AllReports` collection what data type would you use to represent a report?

Answer to 3: You would use the `AccessObject` type.

# CHAPTER 11

# Advanced Programming Techniques

At this stage of the book, we have covered most of the fundamentals of programming with VBA, including the use of objects in the Access object model and in the Data Access Object hierarchy. We will now take a look at some of the more sophisticated features of VBA. As such, this chapter is a mixed bag of ideas and techniques that have been either too complex to tackle until now, or that have required knowledge of other features before you could learn about them. We will also discuss in more detail a few items that we've already mentioned in some of the earlier chapters. In effect, we are going to be looking at four separate subject areas under the broad umbrella of advanced programming.

First, we'll take another look at arrays, because there is a lot that we haven't considered yet, such as how VBA distinguishes arrays from variables. Then we'll have a look at some of the more interesting ways that we can pass arguments between VBA procedures. After that, we will be investigating how we can extend the functionality of VBA by using code from Dynamic Link Libraries (DLLs). Finally, we'll look at how we can extend Data Access Objects by adding our own properties to them.

So, the main topics of discussion in this chapter are:

- ❏ Getting more out of arrays
- ❏ Passing parameters by reference and by value
- ❏ Using DLLs
- ❏ Creating custom properties for Data Access Objects

# Arrays

We first encountered arrays in Chapter 4 where we looked at what an array is, and the difference between static and dynamic arrays. You will remember that an array is simply a sequential set of data elements, all with the same name and data type, referenced by an index. We declare an array by placing parentheses after the variable name. If we know how many elements we want the array to contain, we can specify this when we create the array, the number indicates the upper bound of the array:

```
Dim intArray(2) As Integer      'Declares an array of 3 integers
```

In the example above, the bounds (0 To 2) indicate that the array will have three elements, `intArray(0)`, `intArray(1)`, and `intArray(2)`.

> Remember, in VBA all arrays are indexed from 0 upwards by default. If you want to override this behavior and make the first element of your array have an index of 1, you would put an **Option Base 1** statement in the **Declarations** section of the module.
>
> ```
> Option Compare Database
> Option Explicit
> Option Base 1
> ```

We can declare what is known as a **dynamic array** by omitting the bounds. We should do this if we do not know how many elements the array will contain, or if the array will need to be resized later:

```
Dim intArray() As Integer      'Declares a dynamic array of integers
```

Before using a dynamic array, but after declaring it, we always need to tell VBA how many elements the array should contain by using a `ReDim` command:

```
ReDim intArray(2)              'Resizes the array to hold 3 elements
```

## Multi-dimensional Arrays

So far, all the arrays that we have been using have been one-dimensional. However, we might wish to store data that relates to a position on a grid, map, or mathematical settings like matrices. Arrays can have two, three or up to 60 dimensions and can store information in this way. For instance, we could store the SalesID and CompanyID of a number of sales in a 2 x 3 array like this:

| SalesID | CompanyID |
|---------|-----------|
| 1       | 6         |
| 2       | 4         |
| 4       | 9         |

To declare a multi-dimensional array, like the one above, simply specify the bounds of each dimension separated by commas: note that we specify the columns and then the rows. For example, to specify an array of 2 (columns) x 3 (rows), for instance, 6 elements whose dimensions start at 1, use the following syntax:

```
Dim intNum(1 To 2, 1 To 3) As Integer
```

Alternatively, for an array of the same size, but whose dimensions start at 0, you could use:

```
Dim intNum(1, 2) As Integer
```

This would have the same effect as using this code:

```
Dim intNum(0 To 1, 0 To 2) As Integer
```

From another perspective, if we wanted to specify an array of 6 elements that had 3 columns and 2 rows (and not 2 columns and 3 rows as above), then we write the above styled declaration as:

```
Dim intNum(0 To 2, 0 To 1) As Integer
```

## Dynamic Multi-dimensional Arrays

As with normal one-dimensional arrays, there is the option to make the arrays dynamic (that is, resizeable), according to our needs. To declare a dynamic, multi-dimensional array, we would use the following syntax:

```
Dim intNum() As Integer

Redim intNum(1 To 2, 1 To 3)
```

Or, alternatively, for a dynamic array whose dimensions start at 0, we could use:

```
Dim intNum() As Integer

Redim intNum(1, 2)
```

## Referencing Elements in a Multi-dimensional Array

To reference elements in a multi-dimensional array, we simply specify the appropriate number of indexes to the array. The following code displays the results of raising the numbers 2 and 3 to the 3rd, 4th, and 5th power in turn. In other words, it displays the values of $2^3$, $2^4$, $2^5$, $3^3$, $3^4$, and $3^5$. We do this by using the exponent operator (^):

```
Sub MultiDimArray()

   Dim i As Integer
   Dim j As Integer
   Dim intNum() As Integer                    'Create a dynamic array

   ReDim intNum(2 To 3, 3 To 5)               'Resize the array

   For i = 2 To 3                             'Populate the array
     For j = 3 To 5
        intNum(i, j) = i ^ j
     Next j
   Next i

   For i = 2 To 3                             'Print the contents...
     For j = 3 To 5                           '...of the array
        Debug.Print i & "^" & j & "=" & intNum(i, j)
     Next j
   Next i

End Sub
```

This procedure produces the following results:

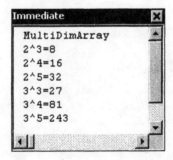

As you can see, the procedure has two parts: the calculation and then printing the results. Each part has two loops, one nested inside the other. The inside loop is executed three times (For j = 3 to 5) for each value of i in the outer loop, which is executed twice (For i = 2 to 3).

The number of elements in a multi-dimensional array (that is, the number of separate values that it can hold) is calculated by multiplying together the number of elements in each dimension of the array. For example, the array in the procedure above would be able to hold 2 x 3 = 6 values.

Similarly, the following declaration:

```
Dim intNum() As Integer

ReDim intNum(9, 19, 29)
```

would produce an array of 10 x 20 x 30 = 6000 elements (assuming there is no `Option Base 1` statement in the module).

## Memory Considerations

We mentioned in Chapter 3 that it's important to select the right data type for your variables. This helps to avoid errors, but it's also important because the different data types take up different amounts of memory. For example, a long integer takes up more memory than an integer.

Arrays require twenty bytes of memory, plus four bytes for each array dimension, plus the number of bytes occupied by the data itself. The memory occupied by the data can be calculated by multiplying the number of data elements by the size of each element.

Therefore, to calculate the memory that the integer array `intNum(9, 19, 29)` would take up, we multiply the number of elements in the array by the size of each of the elements:

```
10 x 20 x 30 = 6,000 elements
6000 x 2 bytes for an integer = 12,000 bytes
```

Then add the overhead, which is always equal to 20 bytes + 4 bytes per dimension:

```
20 bytes + (3 x 4 bytes) = 32 bytes
```

This gives a total of 12,032 bytes.

If we compare this to the amount of memory that the array would have taken up if it had been declared as a `Variant`, you'll see just why it is important to choose your data type carefully.

```
Dim varName As Variant

ReDim varName(9, 19, 29)
```

`Variant` type variables containing strings require (22 + the string length) bytes of memory per element. So, the memory requirements would have been:

```
10 x 20 x 30 = 6,000 elements
6000 x 22 bytes (minimum) for a Variant = 132,000 bytes
```

Add the overhead:

```
20 bytes + (3 x 4 bytes) = 32 bytes
```

This gives a total of at least 132,032 bytes – around 128K.

It is clear that the more dimensions you have in your array, the number of elements in each dimension, and the larger the data type, the easier it is to consume vast amounts of memory. Computer memory is a precious resource and like money you never seem to have enough of it, hence choose the data type of the right size depending on the application at hand.

In theory, the maximum number of dimensions that you can declare in an array is 60, as we noted earlier. In practice, though, you will probably find it very hard to keep track of what is happening in arrays of more than three, or perhaps four, dimensions.

## Erasing Arrays

When an array's lifetime expires, the memory that the array variable was taking up is automatically reclaimed by VBA. So, if you declare an array at the procedure level, then when the array is destroyed at the end of the procedure, VBA reclaims any memory that it was taking up.

However, you might want to explicitly free up the memory that an array was taking up without actually destroying the variable itself. For example, you might be using a module-level array variable (for instance, a variable declared in the Declaration section of a standard code module). Because standard code modules are always loaded into memory in Access, the array variable will only be destroyed when Access is closed down.

If, in the meantime, you want to "empty" the array and free up the memory that its contents were taking up, then you can use the Erase statement. If you use the Erase statement on a *dynamic* array, that's just what happens – we free up memory:

```
Erase intNum        'Empties contents of intNum array and reclaims its memory
```

However, this only works with dynamic arrays. Using the Erase statement on a *static* array will reinitialize the array, but will not reclaim the memory that it takes up. So, if you only need to use an array for part of the time – especially if it has a long lifetime – you should consider declaring it as a dynamic array.

> *When we say that an array is reinitialized, we mean that its elements are restored to their initial values. For numeric variables, the initial value is 0, for strings the initial value is an empty string ("") and for variants the initial value is the special Empty value.*

As we can see, the Erase statement has different effects on different types of arrays, and it even has different effects on different types of static arrays as the following table illustrates:

| Array Type | Using Erase on static array elements |
|---|---|
| Static numeric | Each element is set to zero |
| Static string (variable length) | Each element is set to zero length (that is "") string |
| Static string (fixed length) | Each element is set to zero |
| Static variant | Each element is set to Empty |
| Boolean | Each element is set to False |
| UDT (User Defined Types) | Each element is set to its default |
| Objects | Each element is set to Nothing |

# Parameter Arrays

VBA also allows you to pass parameter arrays to functions and sub procedures. A parameter array, as its name suggests, is an array of parameters: it is an Optional array of Variant type elements. In other words, a parameter array allows you to pass a variable number of arguments to a procedure. It can be useful if, at design-time, you don't know how many arguments you will want to pass to a procedure. Have a look at the following code:

```
Function Avge(ParamArray aValues() As Variant) As Double

    Dim varValue As Variant
    Dim dblTotal As Double

    For Each varValue In aValues
        dblTotal = dblTotal + varValue
    Next

    Avge = dblTotal / (UBound(aValues) + 1)

End Function
```

This function returns the average value of a series of numbers. If you add this procedure to a code module and use the **Immediate** window to determine the average of a series of numbers, you should see something like this when you hit the *Enter* key:

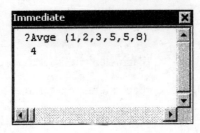

In the above example, aValues() is a parameter array. To declare an argument as a parameter array, you just prefix it with the keyword ParamArray. There are a few important things to remember when declaring parameter arrays:

- A ParamArray argument may only appear as the last argument passed to a Sub or Function.

- ParamArray arguments are of type Variant.

- ParamArray arguments may not be passed as Optional, ByVal, or ByRef (as we said before a ParamArray is itself an Optional Variant Array).

- A ParamArray may not appear with an Optional argument in the same list of arguments; however, it may be preceded, in an argument list, by other arguments that are passed ByRef and ByVal.

In the Avge function, we loop through each of the elements in the aValues() array and add it to a running total, dblTotal.

```
For Each varValue In aValues
   dblTotal = dblTotal + varValue
Next
```

We then divide the total by the number of elements in the array.

```
Avge = dblTotal / (UBound(aValues) + 1)
```

We've used the UBound() function which, if you remember from Chapter 4, returns the value of the highest index in the array. Note that, here, we calculate the number of elements as UBound(aValues) + 1. This is because parameter arrays always start at element 0 – *even if* you have specified Option Base 1 in the Declarations section of the module containing the procedure.

> That last sentence is important – if it didn't sink in just now, read it again. This is guaranteed to catch you out one day!

# The Array Function

If we have a series of values that we want to insert into an array, we can do so with the Array function. Look at the following subprocedure:

```
Sub MonthNames()

    Dim varMonth As Variant

    varMonth = Array("Jan", "Feb", "Mar", "Apr")

    Debug.Print varMonth(1)
    Debug.Print varMonth(2)

End Sub
```

If you were to execute this procedure, the values Feb and Mar would be displayed in the Immediate window.

The Array function accepts a comma-delimited list of values which it then returns as a one-dimensional array. Two things in particular are worth remembering when you use the Array function. Firstly – and somewhat counter-intuitively given the way parameter arrays work – the index of the first element in the returned variant array is determined by the current Option Base statement if there is one. In the example above, the code module had no Option Base statement, so the index of the first element of the array was 0. Hence, varMonth(1) contains Feb, the second element of the array. The second thing to remember is that the array returned by the Array function must be stored in a variable of type Variant.

Although conceptually different, in practice there is no difference between an array of Variant variables and a Variant variable containing an array.

# The GetRows() Method

Another way to use a `Variant` array is to use the `GetRows()` method of the `Recordset` object (refer to Chapter 6 if you want to freshen up on recordsets). This is used to copy a number of rows from a `Recordset` object into an array. The technique is very useful in a multi-user environment because it allows the `Recordset` object to be closed, minimizing potential locking conflicts, but still giving you access to the values in the records. In addition, it can be faster to perform repeated operations on the values stored in the array than continually re-reading the records from the `Recordset` object. That is because the array does not have the overhead of the sophisticated cursor functionality which Access provides via `Recordset` objects. Note, however, that because you will be working with a copy of the records, rather than the records themselves, any changes made to the values in the array will not be reflected in the recordset from which you copied them. So in practical terms, using this methodology is appropriate for tasks that are read-only, for example, analyzing last month's sales.

We'll now demonstrate with an example where we'll create an array which takes data from the first two rows of the `Sales` table.

**Try It Out      The GetRows() Method**

**1.** Create a new code module in `IceCream.mdb` and call it **Chapter 11 Code**. Then type in the following code:

```
Sub TestGetRows()

    Dim varValues As Variant
    Dim recSales As Recordset
    Dim intRowCount As Integer
    Dim intFieldCount As Integer
    Dim i As Integer
    Dim j As Integer

    Set recSales = CurrentDb().OpenRecordset("tblSales")
    varValues = recSales.GetRows(2)
    recSales.Close

    intFieldCount = UBound(varValues, 1)
    intRowCount = UBound(varValues, 2)

    For j = 0 To intRowCount
      For i = 0 To intFieldCount
        Debug.Print "Row " & j & ", Field " & i & ": ";
        Debug.Print varValues(i, j)
      Next i
    Next j

End Sub
```

**2.** Open the **Immediate** window and run `TestGetRows`. When you hit *Enter*, you should get a list of the contents of each field in each of the first two rows of the table `tblSales`.

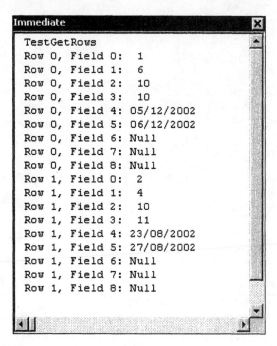

```
Immediate                                    ✕
TestGetRows
Row 0, Field 0:  1
Row 0, Field 1:  6
Row 0, Field 2:  10
Row 0, Field 3:  10
Row 0, Field 4: 05/12/2002
Row 0, Field 5: 06/12/2002
Row 0, Field 6: Null
Row 0, Field 7: Null
Row 0, Field 8: Null
Row 1, Field 0:  2
Row 1, Field 1:  4
Row 1, Field 2:  10
Row 1, Field 3:  11
Row 1, Field 4: 23/08/2002
Row 1, Field 5: 27/08/2002
Row 1, Field 6: Null
Row 1, Field 7: Null
Row 1, Field 8: Null
```

### How It Works

The `GetRows()` method takes as an argument the number of rows that we want to copy into the array:

```
varValues = recSales.GetRows(2)
```

Here, we copy the first two rows. The rows that are copied are relative to the current record. As the recordset has just been opened, the current record is the first row in the recordset, so the first two rows will be copied. If the number of rows requested is greater than the number of rows between the current record and the last record in the recordset, `GetRows()` will return all the available rows.

After the `GetRows()` method has been applied, the current row will be the one after those that have been copied. This is useful because it allows us to copy one block of records (say the first 50) into our array and process them. Then, when we have finished with them, we can read the next block.

Note that – as with the `Array` function – the rows are copied into a `Variant` variable, rather than into an array declared with the usual syntax.

```
Dim varValues As Variant
.
.
.
varValues = recSales.GetRows(2)
```

The array created by the `GetRows()` method is always two-dimensional. The first element corresponds to the field index, the second to the row index. To inspect the index of the last field returned, inspect the value of the highest index in the first dimension of the array:

```
intFieldCount = UBound(varValues, 1)
```

*When using `UBound()` with a multi-dimensional array, you should specify which dimension you want to find the highest index. Specify it as a number following the array name.*

To find the index of the last row returned, inspect the value of the highest index in the second dimension of the array returned:

```
intRowCount = UBound(varValues, 2)
```

*Note that the array returned by `GetRows()` is zero-based. This means that the number of fields is `intFieldCount+1` and the number of rows is `intRowCount+1`.*

Once we have determined the number of elements in each dimension of the array, we loop through each dimension, printing the results.

```
For j = 0 To intRowCount
  For i = 0 To intFieldCount
    Debug.Print "Row " & j & ", Field " & i & ": ";
    Debug.Print varValues(i, j)
  Next i
Next j
```

Using a semicolon as a separator in the **Immediate** window causes the two expressions to be printed next to each other without a carriage return. So placing a semicolon at the end of the first `Debug.Print` line means that there will be no carriage return before the next line is printed. In other words, in the **Immediate** window, the output of the two code lines will be printed together on one line.

You can also use a comma to separate expressions in the **Immediate** window. This causes the two expressions to be printed next to each other, but separated by a tab (which sometimes makes the results easier to read).

# Detecting Arrays

We have just seen two different uses of `Variant` variables to hold arrays. Of course, one of the problems with using `Variant` variables to hold arrays is that it isn't obvious whether the variable contains an array or just contains a single value. For example, in the `TestGetRows` procedure above, the variable `varValues` only contained an array after the `GetRows()` method was used.

There are actually three different ways you can determine whether a variable contains a single value or an array. These involve using one of the following functions:

- ❑  `IsArray()`
- ❑  `VarType()`
- ❑  `TypeName()`

## The IsArray() Function

This function returns `True` if the variable passed to it is an array, and `False` if it is not. Have a look at the following procedure:

```
Sub ArrayTest()

    Dim intNum1 As Integer
    Dim intNum(1 To 10) As Integer

    Debug.Print "intnum1: " & IsArray(intNum1)
    Debug.Print "intnum: " & IsArray(intNum)

End Sub
```

You can run this procedure by typing the above code into a module and then either hitting *F5*, or typing `ArrayTest` in the **Immediate** window and hitting *Enter*. Either way, you should see the words `False` and `True` appear in the **Immediate** window:

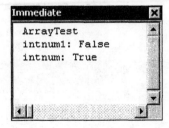

This is because `IsArray(intNum1)` is `False` and `IsArray(intNum)` is `True`. In other words, `intNum1` is not an array, whereas `intNum` is.

## *The VarType() Function*

Another method for determining whether or not a variable is an array is to use the `VarType()` function. We looked at this in Chapter 3 (See *Try It Out – Examining a Variant*) when we used it to determine the type of value being held within a variable of type `Variant`. In fact, we can also use this function to determine whether the variable holds an array. Have a look at this procedure:

```
Sub ArrayTest2()

    Dim intNum1 As Integer
    Dim intNum(1 To 10) As Integer

    Debug.Print "intnum1: " & VarType(intNum1)
    Debug.Print "intnum: " & VarType(intNum)

End Sub
```

If you run `ArrayTest2` by typing the above code into a code module and hitting *F5*, you should see the values **2** and **8194** in the **Immediate** window:

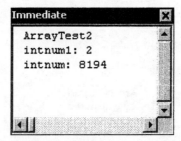

Now, you are probably asking yourself "What on earth does `8194` mean?" Well, if you cast your mind back to our discussion of the `VarType()` function in Chapter 3: `Sub VariantExample()` in *Try It Out – Examining a Variant*, you will remember that the subroutine prints out a number, via `Debug.Print`, indicating the type of data that the variable contains. The table below shows the values for each data type as well as the intrinsic constant that represents those numbers. For example, `2` or `vbInteger` indicates that the underlying data type of the variable is an integer.

| Constant | Value | Variable type |
|----------|-------|---------------|
| vbEmpty | 0 | Empty (uninitialized) |
| vbNull | 1 | Null |
| vbInteger | 2 | Integer |

| Constant | Value | Variable type |
| --- | --- | --- |
| vbLong | 3 | Long Integer |
| vbSingle | 4 | Single |
| vbDouble | 5 | Double |
| vbCurrency | 6 | Currency |
| vbDate | 7 | Date |
| vbString | 8 | String |
| vbObject | 9 | Object |
| vbError | 10 | Error value |
| vbBoolean | 11 | Boolean |
| vbVariant | 12 | Variant |
| vbDataObject | 13 | Data access object |
| vbDecimal | 14 | Decimal value |
| vbByte | 17 | Byte |
| vbUserDefinedType | 36 | UDT (User Defined Type) |
| vbArray | 8192 | Array |

As you can see from the table, arrays are denoted by the value 8192 (vbArray). In fact, vbArray is never returned on its own. If the variable passed to VarType() is an array, then the number that the VarType() function returns is a combination of vbArray and the underlying data type. So, in our example, both variables are of integer type (vbInteger, or 2), and the second one is an array (vbArray, or 8192) of integers, giving a total of vbArray + vbInteger = 8194.

Because the number 8192 can be represented by the intrinsic constant vbArray, we can modify the procedure to make the results a little more readable:

```
Sub ArrayTest3()

    Dim intNum1 As Integer
    Dim intNum(1 To 10) As Integer
```

```
    Debug.Print "Array: " & (VarType(intNum1) > vbArray),
    Debug.Print "Type: " & (VarType(intNum1) And Not vbArray)
    Debug.Print "Array: " & (VarType(intNum) > vbArray),
    Debug.Print "Type: " & (VarType(intNum) And Not vbArray)

End Sub
```

If you run this procedure, you should get the results shown below:

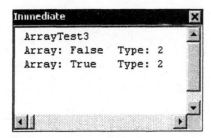

The code looks a little more complex, but isn't that hard to follow. The first thing to remember is that putting parentheses around an expression in VBA forces the expression to be evaluated first. So the parentheses around `(VarType(intNum) > vbArray)` force that expression to be evaluated first. The result of this expression is `True` because `VarType(intNum)` (which equals 8194) is indeed greater than `vbArray` (8192).

The next step is to determine the data type of each variable. We do that with this expression:

```
(VarType(intNum) And Not vbArray)
```

The parentheses again cause the expression to be evaluated. But what exactly is being evaluated? To understand the logical expression `And Not` we need to start thinking in binary again. If you remember, in Chapter 3 we looked at how an integer variable could be used as a set of flags. Well, that's how the `vbArray` constant is used.

To see how this works, let's look at what `VarType(intNum)` and `vbArray` look like in binary. We know from the previous procedure, `ArrayTest2()`, that the value of `VarType(intNum)` is 8194 and that `vbArray` is 8192. In binary those are 1000000000010 and 1000000000000 respectively.

| | | Array bit | | | | | | |
|---|---|---|---|---|---|---|---|---|
| | 16384 | 8192 | 4096 | 2048 | 1024 | 512 | 256 | 128 |
| Data type | 0 | 0 | 0 | 0 | 0 | 0 | 0 | 0 |
| Array flag | 0 | 1 | 0 | 0 | 0 | 0 | 0 | 0 |
| Total | 0 | 1 | 0 | 0 | 0 | 0 | 0 | 0 |

| | | Datatype bits | | | | | | |
|---|---|---|---|---|---|---|---|---|
| 64 | 32 | 16 | 8 | 4 | 2 | 1 | Total | |
| 0 | 0 | 0 | 0 | 0 | 1 | 0 | 2 | |
| 0 | 0 | 0 | 0 | 0 | 0 | 0 | 8192 | |
| 0 | 0 | 0 | 0 | 0 | 1 | 0 | 8194 | |

The rightmost five binary digits are used to indicate the data type of the variable. The binary digit 2nd from the left on the top set, whose value is 8192, is used to flag whether the variable is an array or not. If it is an array, this flag is set to 1, increasing the value of the VarType by 8192.

*Don't worry about the other 10 bits. They are reserved for use in future versions of VBA and don't hold any meaningful information for us.*

What we want to do is to determine the value of the digits without the influence of the 14th digit, that is, the vbArray digit. To do this we use the logical operator And against Not vbArray. Not vbArray is the reverse of vbArray. In other words, the 0s become 1s and the 1s become 0s. The result of an And operation is that bit flags in the result are set to 1 only if the bit was 1 in both the numbers being compared. So using an And with Not vbArray has the result of leaving 15 of the bits in the result the same as they were in the original number, while ensuring that the 14th bit is set to 0.

As you can see, the result of this is 2, which is what we were expecting, indicating that the underlying data type is an integer.

## The TypeName() Function

The TypeName() function does much the same as the VarType() function, except that it returns its result in plainer terms.

For example, the following procedure:

```
Sub ArrayTest4()

    Dim intNum1 As Integer
    Dim intNum(1 To 10) As Integer

    Debug.Print "intnum1: " & TypeName(intNum1)
    Debug.Print "intnum: " & TypeName(intNum)

End Sub
```

will give these results:

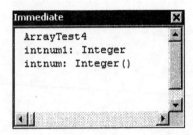

As you can see, the return value of the `TypeName()` function is a lot easier to understand. It returns the type of the variable in plainer terms, `Integer`, and adds a pair of empty parentheses if the variable is an array, `Integer()`. However, if you need to detect programmatically whether a variable contains an array, you will find it easier to use either the `IsArray()` function or the `VarType()` function (which has the advantage over `IsArray()` in that it also returns the underlying data type.)

This concludes our look at arrays. Hopefully, splitting the discussion over two separate chapters hasn't confused you. This was necessary as we needed to discuss the fundamentals of what static and dynamic arrays were early in the book before we could move on to more unusual topics such as multi-dimensional arrays and using the `GetRows()` method to create an array. The next topic is unrelated to arrays, but is a continuation of another concept learned earlier in the book: passing arguments.

# Arguments

Normally, when an argument is passed to a function, it is passed by **reference**. In other words, the procedure receiving the argument is passed a reference, or pointer, which indicates where in memory the variable is stored. It *doesn't* receive the actual **value** of the variable.

Passing variables by reference has two effects. The advantage is that it's faster – Access doesn't need to make a copy of the value in another location ready for the procedure to read. However, because the procedure has access to the original variable (it knows where it is stored in memory), it can change the value of this variable. When the procedure ends, the code that called the procedure will see and work with the new value.

This is useful if you *want* the procedure to change the value, but it can create unexpected results if the value is changed when you have not planned it.

In VBA the default is to pass arguments by reference (`ByRef`), however, where applicable, we suggest that you consider passing arguments by value (`ByVal`). It is good programming practice, if the value is not to be changed to pass it by value. Then you know when debugging that it was not changed in that function. Generally developers new to programming seem to experience problems when passing by reference (such as unintentionally changing values of variables). Another reason why we favor passing arguments by value, where appropriate, is that it is the default in the new VB.NET language, and traditionally many Access VBA developers advance to develop VB applications (or now VB.NET applications). Of course, there may be times when you pass by reference, for example, passing an object by reference. We will see as we work through this chapter where we should pass `ByRef` and `ByVal`.

## Passing Arguments By Value

Our favored choice is to pass arguments by value. As we have said, this is where VBA just makes a copy of the data and passes that copy to the procedure. In this way, if the value of the copy is changed, the original value remains the same.

Let's compare the two methods by using each of them to calculate the cube root of 8.

---

**Try It Out** — **Passing Arguments By Reference and By Value**

**1.** Open the **Chapter 11 Code** module and create the `CubeRoot()` subprocedure by typing in the following code:

```
Sub CubeRoot(dblNumber As Double)

   dblNumber = dblNumber ^ (1 / 3)

End Sub
```

**2.** Now create a procedure which will call the `CubeRoot()` procedure:

```
Sub CubeRootWrapper()

   Dim dblVariable As Double
   dblVariable = 8

   Debug.Print "Before: " & dblVariable
   CubeRoot dblVariable
   Debug.Print "After: " & dblVariable

End Sub
```

**3.** Run the `CubeRootWrapper()` procedure either by hitting *F5* or by entering its name in the Immediate window and hitting *Enter*. You should then see the following in the Immediate window:

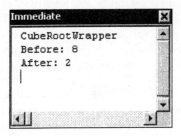

**4.** Now modify the `CubeRoot()` subprocedure by inserting the keyword `ByVal` before the argument, like this:

```
Sub CubeRoot(ByVal dblNumber As Double)

    dblNumber = dblNumber ^ (1 / 3)

End Sub
```

**5.** Run the `CubeRootWrapper()` procedure again. The output should now look like this:

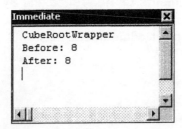

## How It Works

The `CubeRoot()` subprocedure simply calculates the cube root of a number (no surprises there). The main procedure then prints the number twice – once before the subprocedure is run and once after.

By default, VBA passes variables by reference. Therefore, the first time we run the `CubeRootWrapper()` procedure, we pass the variable `dblVariable` to the `CubeRoot()` procedure by reference. In other words, the `CubeRootWrapper()` procedure passes a pointer to the place where `dblVariable` is stored in memory.

```
CubeRoot dblVariable
```

The `CubeRoot()` procedure labels what it finds at this location as `dblNumber` and then modifies the contents of that memory location.

```
dblNumber = dblNumber ^ (1 / 3)
```

Consequently, when the `CubeRootWrapper` inspects what is at that location, it finds that its contents have changed.

```
Debug.Print "After: " & dblVariable
```

We then change the code in `CubeRoot()`. Placing the `ByVal` keyword before the argument means that it will be passed by value instead of by reference – the actual value of the variable will be passed, as opposed to just a pointer to its memory address.

```
Sub CubeRoot(ByVal dblNumber As Double)
```

This time, the `CubeRoot()` procedure has no idea where the original variable `dblVariable` in the calling procedure is located in memory – all it has got is its value. The variables `dblNumber` and `dblVariable` are now quite distinct from each other. It quite happily changes the value of `dblNumber`, but `dblVariable` is not modified.

Passing arguments by reference is quicker than passing by value, as we noted earlier, but you should consider passing arguments by value, especially in the following circumstances:

❑ When you do not want the contents of a variable to change, but you need to pass it to a procedure that someone else has written and you don't know how it works. After all, you've no idea what the procedure you are calling might do to your variable!

❑ When passing variables to procedures in DLLs.

If you have no idea what that last point means, don't worry. That's what we are going to look at now – how to extend the functionality of VBA through using DLLs.

# Dynamic Link Libraries (DLLs)

Even if you have not done any VBA or C coding before, you may well have come across DLLs. Just have a look in the **System** or **System32** subdirectories of the **Windows** directory on your computer and you will find tens, if not hundreds or even thousands of them. But what exactly are DLLs?

Well, clearly they are files. In fact, they are code files, similar to the modules that you get in Access. DLL stands for **dynamic link library** and if we look at what the name means, we begin to understand a little better how they work. They are called **libraries** because they contain a number of procedures (functions or subprocedures) that can be read and used. Similar to a real library where people can access the library, this form of library is a collection of procedures.

Other programs can access (or **link** to) the library to use a procedure whenever they want. This means that the other programs don't need to contain their own copy of the procedure, saving the programmer's expense and the user's disk space.

The **dynamic** part of the name comes from the fact that the DLL itself isn't loaded into memory until an application needs it. It's the same as saying that a book is only borrowed from a real library when someone wants to read it. There is no real limit on the number of applications that can link to a DLL at the same time. Windows keeps track of when the DLL needs to be loaded into memory, and when applications have finished with the DLL it can be unloaded from memory.

Some DLLs contain functions with fairly limited appeal. Others, such as `Kernel32.dll`, `User32.dll`, and `Gdi32.dll`, are used by every Windows application to provide their basic operations. `User32.dll` provides the code that Windows provides for all aspects of interaction with the user interface; `Gdi32.dll` provides the code that is used for graphics rendering and interaction with other types of display device, such as printers; and `Kernel32.dll` provides a host of routines for low-level system activities, such as memory management and file input and output.

As a Windows application, our VBA code can also use the functions in these DLLs to achieve things that aren't otherwise supported in Access. There are literally hundreds of functions in these three DLLs, so we have plenty of scope! Of course, we can make use of functions in other DLLs as well and, if none provide the function we need, we can even build our own DLL if we have tools like Visual Basic or Visual C++. They really do provide a useful way of extending the functionality of VBA without too much hard work. It is also possible to purchase new DLLs.

So let's move on and see how we use DLLs in VBA.

## Declaring a DLL in Code

Before we can use a procedure in a DLL, we must tell VBA where it is – both the name of the DLL itself, and which procedure (function or subprocedure) in that DLL we want to use. In our book and library analogy this is like telling a borrower (VBA), where the library (DLL) is located, and what book (Procedure) to borrow (Declare). VBA can then dynamically link to that routine, as required, while the application is running. VBA doesn't automatically check that the procedure exists, either when you compile or start the application. If it can't be accessed, you will only find this out when an error message appears as you make the call to the function at run time.

One very useful DLL function we can use is `timeGetTime` which can be found in `Winmm.dll`. This function returns the number of milliseconds that have elapsed since Windows started. It is useful because we can execute this function twice, once before and once after executing a portion of code and, by subtracting one from another, we can determine how long the code took to execute. This is a typical example of using a procedure in a DLL to enhance standard Access or VBA functionality – the `Timer` function in Access is only accurate to a whole second. Another function, `GetTickCount()` in `Kernel32.dll` can also be used to return the number of milliseconds that have elapsed since Windows started, but the accuracy of `GetTickCount()` varies between different operating systems and processors.

*The process of calling a procedure in a DLL is also referred to as 'making an API call'. API stands for **application programming interface** – the published set of procedures that a particular application or operating system provides for the programmer to use.*

In order to declare the `timeGetTime()` function, we place the following statement in the `Declarations` section of a module:

```
Declare Function timeGetTime Lib "WINMM" () As Long
```

This indicates that the function is called `timeGetTime()` and that it returns a `Long` type value. It is in the `WINMM` library (`Winmm.dll`) and it takes no parameters, hence the empty brackets towards the end of the function declaration.

> **Make sure that you type the function declaration exactly as it appears above. The names of functions and subprocedures in DLLs in 32-bit versions of Windows (for instance, Windows NT, 2000, and XP) are case-sensitive. If you do not capitalize the name of the function or subprocedure correctly Access will generate an error message and the code will not execute correctly.**

Once a function has been declared in this manner, all we have to do is execute it. If you type the above declaration in a module, and then enter the following in the **Immediate** window:

```
?timeGetTime()
```

The number of milliseconds since Windows was started will be returned. We will return to this function later on when we look at optimizing VBA in Chapter 17.

Did you know that there is also an API call (that is, DLL procedure) that can tell you whether or not the user has swapped the left and right mouse buttons around? To declare it, we place the following statement in the `Declarations` section of a module:

```
Declare Function GetSystemMetrics Lib "user32" (ByVal nIndex As Long) As Long
```

The function is called `GetSystemMetrics()` and is in the `User32.dll` library. We haven't specified a path in front of the library name, so the following directories are searched in turn to find the DLL.

- ❑ The current directory
- ❑ The Windows system directory
- ❑ The Windows directory
- ❑ The directories listed in the `PATH` environment variable

*If you want to use a DLL that resides anywhere else but these four locations, you need to qualify it with a full path.*

The GetSystemMetrics() function takes an argument nIndex of type Long and returns a Long. The function actually returns information about the layout of the user interface (for example, the height of window title bars, the width of scroll bars) as well as other juicy tidbits, such as whether the user has swapped the left and right mouse buttons (via the Control Panel). The argument nIndex is used to specify a constant indicating the type of information we want. In our case, we want to know whether the mouse buttons have been swapped. So we need to declare the following constant and pass it as an argument to the function:

```
Public Const SM_SWAPBUTTON = 23
```

In fact, you can try it out for yourself!

## Try It Out        Using a Function in a DLL

1. Open the **Chapter 11 Code** module.

2. In the Declarations section, type the following function declaration:

```
Declare Function GetSystemMetrics Lib "user32" (ByVal nIndex As Long) As Long
```

3. Now declare the following constant, again in the Declarations section:

```
Public Const SM_SWAPBUTTON = 23
```

4. Create the ShowHands() procedure by typing the following code into the module:

```
Sub ShowHands()

  If GetSystemMetrics(SM_SWAPBUTTON) = False Then
    MsgBox "Your mouse is right-handed!"
  Else
    MsgBox "Your mouse is left-handed!"
  End If

End Sub
```

5. Run the ShowHands() procedure and a dialog box should appear which indicates whether your mouse is configured for right- or left-handed use.

**6.** Now swap the left and right mouse buttons by altering the button configuration. You can do this by opening the **Control Panel**, selecting **Mouse**, and changing the **Button configuration** option on the **Buttons** tab of the dialog box that appears.

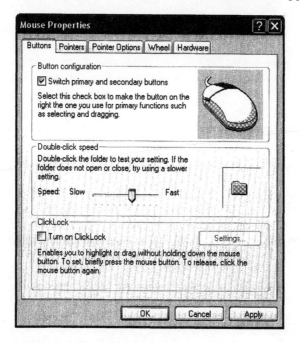

**7.** Hit the **OK** button to close the **Mouse Properties** dialog box and go back to the module that you have just created. You will probably notice at this stage that the mouse buttons have been swapped around.

**8.** Run the ShowHands() procedure again. This time, the message box that appears should indicate that the mouse buttons have been swapped. Click the **OK** button to close the message box:

9.  If you're still sitting there wondering why you can't seem to click the OK button, remember that you have swapped the mouse buttons round and you should be clicking the *other* button!

10. Finish up by changing the mouse buttons back to their original settings. (And then get even more annoyed on the way because you keep bringing up context-sensitive menus when you just want to click things!).

### How It Works

As we explained just before the example, the GetSystemMetrics function returns information about the screen layout. The actual information that is returned depends on the argument we pass to the function. We passed it the SM_SWAPBUTTON constant. But how did we know that was the constant to use? And how did we know that this was the declaration for the constant?

```
Public Const SM_SWAPBUTTON = 23
```

Come to think of it, how did we even know about the GetSystemMetrics function?

Well, in the real world, the most popular libraries have good indexes, and it's the same in the programming world. For OLE libraries and Access library databases, such an index is provided by the Object Browser. However, for DLLs, we rely on the vendor's documentation for information about the functions within the DLL – what arguments they take, what values they return and so on.

Because User32.dll is such a vital and frequently used component of Windows, it is very well documented. The authoritative source of such information is the *Microsoft Platform SDK* (where SDK stands for Software Development Kit). This information is also available online from http://msdn.microsoft.com/. You may find it easier to find the information by searching the Microsoft Developer Network or Microsoft TechNet CDs if you have a subscription. Alternatively, if you only want the function declaration and any constant or type declarations, you can use the Win32 API Viewer, which comes with Microsoft Office 2000 Developer Edition.

If you do look up the documentation, you will see that when GetSystemMetrics is called with the SM_SWAPBUTTON constant, it returns a non-zero value if the buttons have been swapped and False (that is, zero) if they have not. It's as simple as that!

## Enums

One cool feature of VBA is the ability to create enumerated constants or **Enums**. An Enum is simply a list of constants that you can use to represent allowable integer values that can be passed to certain procedures. In the previous example, we noted that 23 was an allowable value to pass as the nIndex argument to GetSystemMetrics and we declared a constant SM_SWAPBUTTON to represent this value. Let's see how we can make things even easier for the programmer by creating an Enum.

**Try It Out** — **Creating an Enum**

**1.** Open the Chapter 11 Code module.

**2.** In the Declarations section, delete the following line:

```
Public Const SM_SWAPBUTTON = 23
```

**3.** Now add the following lines to the Declarations section:

```
Public Enum SystemMetrics
    SM_MOUSEPRESENT = 19
    SM_SWAPBUTTON = 23
    SM_MOUSEWHEELPRESENT = 75
End Enum
```

**4.** Next, modify the GetSystemMetrics declaration so that it looks like this:

```
Declare Function GetSystemMetrics Lib "user32" (ByVal nIndex As
SystemMetrics) As Long
```

**5.** Now, go to the Immediate window and type in the following line:

```
?GetSystemMetrics(
```

Note how, as you get to the part of the line where you should enter the argument to the GetSystemMetrics function, the **Auto List Members** feature of VBA presents you with a list of the three valid selections (There are three of them; one is hidden behind the tooltip!).

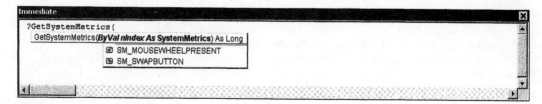

**6.** Select `SM_SWAPBUTTON`, close the parentheses and hit *Enter*. The result displayed should indicate whether you have configured your computer for left-handed use.

This example should be fairly self-explanatory. First, we provide the definition of the `SystemMetrics` Enum:

```
Public Enum SystemMetrics
   SM_MOUSEPRESENT = 19
   SM_SWAPBUTTON = 23
   SM_MOUSEWHEELPRESENT = 75
End Enum
```

As well as the value indicating whether the mouse buttons are swapped, we have also supplied another two values which, when passed to the `GetSystemMetrics` function, indicate whether a mouse is present or whether a mouse wheel is present. These both return a non-zero value to indicate the presence of the relevant item and zero to indicate its absence.

Once we have specified the constituents of the Enum, we can use it as a way of limiting the values that can be supplied as an argument to certain functions.

```
Declare Function GetSystemMetrics Lib "user32" (ByVal nIndex As
SystemMetrics) _ As Long
```

The great thing about using an Enum is that when we are writing our code, we are prompted with the acceptable values for a particular argument. It is one thing having the constant `SM_SWAPBUTTON` in place of the difficult to remember value 23. But by creating an Enum and binding it to the argument nIndex, we can ensure that the programmer is prompted with that – and any other acceptable values – when using that function in code.

> Note that you will only be prompted with the contents of the Enum if you the **Auto List Members** option on the **Editor** tab of the **Tools/Options…** dialog is checked in the VBA IDE.

## Aliases

Once you have declared the function within the DLL you want to use, you can call it by name from within VBA, as if it were a native VBA function. However, there may be occasions when you want to change the name of the DLL function. For example, VBA has a `SetFocus` method that applies to forms and controls. Now there is also a `SetFocus` API call (that is, there is a `SetFocus` function in the `User32.dll` library). If you were to declare it in the normal manner, it might cause confusion:

```
Declare Function SetFocus Lib "user32" (ByVal hwnd As Long) As Long
```

Now you would have both a `SetFocus` method and a `SetFocus` API call. To make things clearer, you could create an `Alias` for the API call. In other words, you could rename it. So, for example, you can declare the `SetFocus` API call, but rename it as `Win32SetFocus`:

```
Declare Function Win32SetFocus Lib "user32" Alias "SetFocus" _
    (ByVal hwnd As Long) As Long
```

The `Alias` keyword is also useful if the name of the DLL function isn't legal in VBA or Visual Basic (or is too long to keep typing!). The API functions `_lopen`, `_lread`, and `_lwrite` can't be declared directly because of the use of an underscore at the beginning of a function name is illegal in VBA. However, they can be declared if they are aliased to a legal name such as `LOpen`.

*You do not have to use aliases for your functions, but it is often a good idea, if only to avoid confusion and prevent the inconvenience of encountering name conflicts between the API library and VBA. For example, you might want to give functions aliases which begin with the prefix api_, such as api_SetFocus. This makes it easier for people reading your code to see when you are using native Access or VBA functions and when you are calling functions in other DLLs and this, in turn, can make the code easier to debug.*

## Using the ByVal Keyword

We saw earlier that, by default, VBA passes arguments to a procedure by reference. In other words, Access passes a pointer to the memory address of the variable that is being passed, rather than the actual value of the variable. However, many functions in DLLs expect to receive the value of the variable, rather than a pointer to its memory address. If this is the case, you need to pass the argument by value by placing the `ByVal` keyword in front of the argument when you declare the function:

```
Declare Function GetSystemMetrics Lib "user32" (ByVal nIndex As Long) As Long
```

## Passing Strings

The functions in most DLLs expect any strings which are passed to them to be **null-terminated** strings. A null-terminated string uses a null character (ASCII value 0) to indicate the end of the string. VBA, however, doesn't use null-terminated strings. Therefore, if you pass a string from VBA to a function in a DLL, you will need to convert it. This can also be done with the `ByVal` keyword.

When the `ByVal` keyword is used with a string argument, VBA converts the string variable into a null-terminated string and passes to the DLL function a pointer to the memory address of the null-terminated string (that is, it passes the null-terminated string **by reference**). Yes, this is the opposite of what we said earlier about using the `ByVal` keyword – but it only applies with VBA and VB strings.

Because the string is passed to the DLL function by reference, the DLL can modify it. This presents a problem. If the DLL attempts to modify the value of a null-terminated string and the new value is longer than the original one, the function doesn't increase the length of the string. Instead, it simply carries on writing the remainder of the string into the memory location adjacent to that of the null-terminated string. This is not good! In fact, if it happens, your application will probably crash.

To prevent this, you should make sure that the string you pass to the function is large enough to accept any value that the function may place in it. You do this by passing a **fixed length** string of a suitably large size:

```
Dim strFilename As String * 255
```

*You should consult the documentation for the DLL function to determine the maximum size, but 255 characters is usually sufficient.*

## Passing Arrays to a DLL

To pass an array of numeric values to a procedure in a DLL, you simply pass the first element of the array. You can do this because all the elements of a numeric array are laid out sequentially in contiguous memory space. After you have passed the first element of the array, the function is then able to retrieve the remaining elements by itself. However, you *can't* pass string arrays this way – attempting to do so may cause your application to crash!

## Type Conversion

Because most DLLs are written in C or C++, the data types used by the arguments to the procedures within the DLL aren't identical to the data types used by VBA. However, it's not difficult to map the C data types to the Visual Basic data types if you consult the following table:

| C Data type | Description | VBA Equivalent |
|---|---|---|
| BOOL | Boolean | ByVal b As Boolean |
| DWORD, LONG | Long Integer | ByVal l As Long |
| HWND | Handle | ByVal l As Long |
| INT, UINT, WORD | Integer | ByVal l As Long |
| LPDWORD | Pointer to a long integer | l As Long |
| LPINT, LPUINT | Pointer to an integer | l As Long |
| LPSTR | Pointer to a string | ByVal s As String |

| C Data type | Description | VBA Equivalent |
|---|---|---|
| LPRECT (for example) | Pointer to a type | See below |
| NULL | Null | See below |
| VOID | Void | Use a subprocedure |

## User-defined Data Types

Often, procedures in DLLs use **structures** as their arguments. A structure is the C-language equivalent of a user-defined type in VBA, that is, a type that you have defined yourself. If a procedure expects a structure, we can pass it a user-defined type so long as we pass it **by reference**.

*User-defined types allow you to place several different data types together in one type, allowing you to group together related variables. For example, in an Accounting system you might wish to create a type for a Customer which includes the name, account number, credit limit, and so on.*

One of the more frequently used structures in DLL functions is the RECT structure. This is a representation of a rectangular area and is composed of four elements representing the left, top, bottom, and right coordinates of the rectangle.

The RECT structure can be represented by the following user-defined type in VBA:

```
Type RECT
   Left As Long
   Top As Long
   Right As Long
   Bottom As Long
End Type
```

It's typically used to represent a rectangular area on the screen. You can see from the diagram below that the coordinates for the four elements are measured from the top left corner of the screen:

| | 32768 | 16384 | Array bit 8192 | 4096 | 2048 | 1024 | 512 |
|---|---|---|---|---|---|---|---|
| VarType (intNum1) | 0 | 0 | 1 | 0 | 0 | 0 | 0 |
| Not vbArray | 1 | 1 | 0 | 1 | 1 | 1 | 1 |
| Result | 0 | 0 | 0 | 0 | 0 | 0 | 0 |

| 256 | 128 | 64 | 32 | 16 | Datatype bits 8 | 4 | 2 | 1 |
|---|---|---|---|---|---|---|---|---|
| 0 | 0 | 0 | 0 | 0 | 0 | 0 | 1 | 0 |
| 1 | 1 | 1 | 1 | 1 | 1 | 1 | 1 | 1 |
| 0 | 0 | 0 | 0 | 0 | 0 | 0 | 1 | 0 |

An example of a DLL procedure which uses this structure is the `ClipCursor` function. When this is passed a `RECT` structure, it confines the mouse pointer to a rectangular area on the screen defined by the coordinates of the structure.

```
Type RECT
    Left As Long
    Top As Long
    Right As Long
    Bottom As Long
End Type

Declare Function ClipCursor Lib "user32" (lpRect As RECT) As Long

Sub Foo()

    Dim rectClipArea As RECT
    Dim lngRetVal As Long

    With rectClipArea
        .Top = 200
        .Left = 100
        .Bottom = 420
        .Right = 280
    End With
```

```
    lngRetVal = ClipCursor(rectClipArea)

End Sub
```

## Null Pointers

Sometimes a procedure in a DLL expects to be passed a **null pointer**. If you have confined the mouse pointer with the `ClipCursor` function, you can free it by passing a null pointer to the `ClipCursor` function. In VBA, the equivalent to a null pointer is just the value zero, usually written as:

```
ByVal 0&
```

The `&` is a type declaration character which indicates that the pointer is a long (that is, 32-bit pointer). Note that the null pointer *must* be passed by value. If the `ByVal` had been omitted, we would have found ourselves passing a pointer to `0&` rather than a null pointer.

It is also possible to use the friendlier VBA module constants `vbNull` or `vbNullChar` instead of the `ByVal 0&` syntax.

However, we told VBA in our function declaration that the argument is of type `RECT`, so it will generate its own error if we try and pass anything else – like a null pointer – to the function. The answer is to declare the argument with a type of `Any`:

```
Declare Function ClipCursor Lib "user32" (lpRect As Any) As Long
```

This turns off VBA's type checking and allows any data type to be passed to the function. So the call to free the mouse pointer would look like this:

```
    lngRetVal = ClipCursor(ByVal 0&)
```

## The Dangers of Using DLLs

Bear in mind when you use DLL functions that, as soon as execution passes into the DLL, you lose all the cozy protection that VBA offers. Although Windows API functions themselves, and all good third-party DLLs, are designed to trap their own errors and exit gracefully, they will not always do this if you supply the wrong parameter types or values.

Each time your code calls *any* procedure – either another VBA routine or a DLL – the data type of each argument is checked against those declared in the procedure. If you try to pass a wrong data type to any function or subroutine you get a **Type Mismatch** error. When you declare a DLL procedure in VBA, you can take advantage of the built-in type checking that occurs. That way, if you pass a wrong data type, you'll get a friendly VBA error message rather than a system crash.

You could, of course, declare all the arguments as type Any, and VBA would allow you to pass any data type you wanted. Almost without exception, your next step would then be *Ctrl-Alt-Del* because the format of the arguments doesn't match those required by the DLL. It's not that the DLL has caused the error directly, but simply that it can't make head nor tail of what you've sent it!

So, to minimize errors, you should always place as tight a definition on your DLL data types as possible when you declare them. Of course, there are times that you can declare a function in two different ways. In this situation, one step you can take to make your declarations safer is to use an Alias to rename one or more of them:

```
Declare Function ClipCursorOn Lib "user32" Alias "ClipCursor" _
                                      (lpRect As RECT) As Long


Declare Function ClipCursorOff Lib "user32" Alias "ClipCursor" _
                                      (lpRect As Any) As Long
```

Both can coexist in your code together, and you can call the correct forms of the function as you need them.

> **When you use DLL or API functions you should *always* save your work regularly and back up any databases before you modify them. If you are using Windows 2000 or XP, you should also ensure that no other applications (outside Access) have unsaved data in case you freeze Windows completely.**

Well, that's three of our topics down and one to go. This final topic, like the one we have just covered, is also concerned with extending the functionality of Access. It's all about extending Data Access Objects by adding user-defined or custom properties.

# Custom DAO Properties

As you know, a property is an attribute of an object. For example, all forms have a Caption property, which defines the text appearing in its title bar. This property can be read and written to, both at design and at run time. Reading the property allows its value to be stored in a variable. Writing to the property allows it to be changed.

Other properties are read-only. For example, the DBEngine object has a Version property which indicates the version number of the DAO interface. This can be inspected, but not changed.

With other properties, whether you can read or write to them depends on whether the object is in Design view, or whether it is being run. For example, the AutoResize property of a form can be read or written to at design time, but is read-only at run time.

A great deal of the time that you spend writing VBA will be spent modifying the in-built properties of Data Access Objects and other objects. But, even with all the versatility provided by these in-built properties, there are times when you would like that little bit more control. This is when you can take advantage of the custom properties which Access exposes.

The simplest way to create a custom property for a Data Access Object is to use the CreateProperty method. We are going to add a custom property to the tblResults table which we created in Chapter 7 and we are going to use the property to store the criteria which were used in the creation of the table.

## Try It Out — Creating Custom DAO Properties

1. Open your IceCream.mdb database (if it's not open already) and open the code module behind the form frmCriteria. To do this, open the form in **Design** view, and then select **Code** from the **View** menu.

2. Now find the BuildResultsTable function. This function builds a table of SalesIDs based on the selection made by the user on the form.

3. Add the following declaration to the list of variable declarations at the top of the BuildResultsTable function.

```
Dim tdf As TableDef
Dim prpCriteria As Property
Dim intWHEREPos As Integer
```

4. Now insert the following lines of code near the end of the function:

```
qdfAction.Close
```

```
'Now add a custom property to the table to hold the criteria
db.TableDefs.Refresh
Set tdf = db.TableDefs(sTableName)
Set prpCriteria = tdf.CreateProperty("Criteria")
prpCriteria.Type = dbText
iWHEREPos = InStr(sSQL, " WHERE ")
If iWHEREPos = 0 Then
    prpCriteria.Value = "All Records"
Else
    prpCriteria.Value = Mid$(sSQL, iWHEREPos + 7)
End If

tdf.Properties.Append prpCriteria

BuildResultsTable = True
```

**5.** Now compile the code and close the form, saving the changes you have made.

**6.** Open the `frmCriteria` form and specify that you are looking for sales that meet the following criteria:

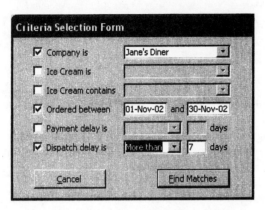

**7.** When a message box appears, asking you whether you want to see the results, hit the No button.

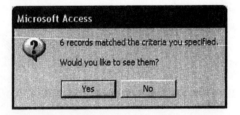

**8.** Now close the Criteria Selection form and switch to the Immediate window by hitting *Ctrl+G*. Then evaluate the following statement:

```
?currentdb.TableDefs("tblResults").Properties("Criteria")
```

**9.** The criteria you specified on the Criteria Selection form should now be displayed in the Immediate window (although you will probably notice that the Immediate window doesn't wrap the text for you):

```
Immediate
?currentdb.TableDefs("tblResults").Properties("Criteria")
s.fkCompanyID = 10 AND s.DateOrdered >= #11/01/02# AND s.DateOrdered <= #11/30/02# AND (s.DateDispat
```

We created a new property called `Criteria` for the new table, and used it to store the criteria which was used to generate the table. Let's look at how we did it in a bit more detail.

First, we declare a variable having the data type `Property`.

```
Dim prpCriteria As Property
```

Next, we create a reference to the table we have just created.

```
Set tdf = db.TableDefs(sTableName)
```

Then we create a new property for that object. When we create the property, we need to give it a name. We have called it `Criteria`.

```
Set prpCriteria = tdf.CreateProperty("Criteria")
```

The next step is to specify the type of value that the property can hold. We want the new `Criteria` property to hold a textual value, so we specify the intrinsic constant `dbText` as the property's type.

```
prpCriteria.Type = dbText
```

Then, we assign a value to the property. If the SQL string contains no `WHERE` clause (because no criteria were entered), we set the value of the property to `"All Records"`; otherwise we set it to the `WHERE` clause of the SQL string that was passed in.

```
intWHEREPos = InStr(sSQL, " WHERE ")
If intWHEREPos = 0 Then
  prpCriteria.Value = "All Records"
Else
  prpCriteria.Value = Mid$(sSQL, intWHEREPos + 7)
End If
```

Finally, we need to make the property **persistent**. In other words, we need to save it to disk, so it is preserved even when the application is closed. We do this by appending it to the `Properties` collection of the `TableDef` object for the table to which it belongs:

```
tdf.Properties.Append prpCriteria
```

The property can be inspected and set in the same way as any of the in-built properties, either in a procedure or in the **Immediate** window. So you can display the current value of the table's `Criteria` property by typing the following in the **Immediate** window:

```
?currentdb.TableDefs("tblResults").Properties("Criteria")
```

In the case where no criteria have been specified, "All Records" will be returned.

## Database Properties

Of course, tables aren't the only Data Access Objects which can have custom properties. Some of the most useful applications of custom properties concern the Database object. To start with, let's have a look at how many properties a Database object has by default.

**Try It Out** — **Custom Database properties**

1. Create a new Access database and call it DBProperties.mdb.

2. Create a new standard code module (accept the default module name when you save it) in the new database and then, in the **References** dialog (on the **Tools** menu in the VBE), make sure that there is a reference to **Microsoft DAO 3.6 Object Library**. You will need to remove the reference to the Microsoft ActiveX Data Objects 2.1 or 2.5 Library, or else this code will not work.

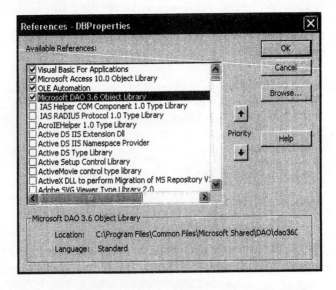

3. In the standard code module you have created, type in the following procedure:

```
Sub EnumDBProperties()

    Dim pty As Property
    Dim strTemp As String
```

```
   On Error Resume Next

   For Each pty In CurrentDb.Properties
     strTemp = pty.Name & ": "
     strTemp = strTemp & pty.Value
     Debug.Print strTemp
   Next

End Sub
```

**4.** Run the procedure. In the Immediate window, you should see a list of 14 properties, 10 of which have values displayed. Some of the values (such as the value of the Name property) might be different from the ones shown here, but you should still see 14 properties.

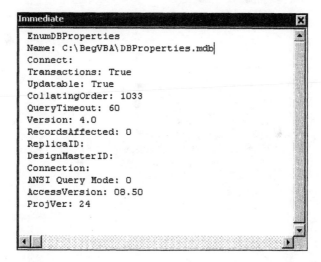

**5.** Now switch to the Database Window and open up the Startup… dialog from the Tools menu. Give your application a name of My New Database and hit the OK button.

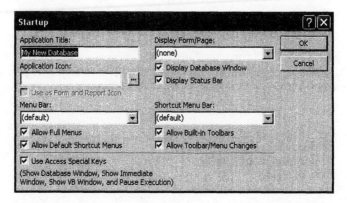

**6.** Now go back to the Immediate window and delete everything in it. Then run the
EnumDBProperties procedure again. Things should look quite a bit different (we've
highlighted the new properties that appear this time around).

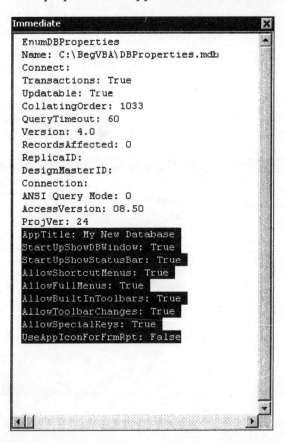

```
Immediate                                          ☒
EnumDBProperties
Name: C:\BegVBA\DBProperties.mdb
Connect:
Transactions: True
Updatable: True
CollatingOrder: 1033
QueryTimeout: 60
Version: 4.0
RecordsAffected: 0
ReplicaID:
DesignMasterID:
Connection:
ANSI Query Mode: 0
AccessVersion: 08.50
ProjVer: 24
AppTitle: My New Database
StartUpShowDBWindow: True
StartUpShowStatusBar: True
AllowShortcutMenus: True
AllowFullMenus: True
AllowBuiltInToolbars: True
AllowToolbarChanges: True
AllowSpecialKeys: True
UseAppIconForFrmRpt: False
```

## How It Works

The EnumDBProperties procedure displays the properties of the current database. In fact,
what we are doing here is looping through the Properties collection of the current
Database object, and for every Property object in that collection, we are displaying its Name
and Value.

```
For Each pty In CurrentDb.Properties
  strTemp = pty.Name & ": "
  strTemp = strTemp & pty.Value
  Debug.Print strTemp
Next
```

You may have wondered why we put in the error handling line.

```
On Error Resume Next
```

The reason for this is that, whereas all `Property` objects have a `Name` property, not all have a `Value` property. Of the 13 standard properties of the `Database` object, one of them – the `Connection` property – does not have a `Value`. If we try to print the `Value` of a `Property` which doesn't have one, VBA would normally generate a run-time error. By inserting the statement `On Error Resume Next` we are telling VBA to ignore any statements that cause errors and simply resume execution on the next line.

But once we make a change in the **Startup**… dialog from the **Tools** menu, we suddenly find that there are nine new properties. Where did these come from? The answer is that these are **application-defined properties**. In other words, they are not standard properties that exist in every new database, but are added by Access as needed.

You should also be aware that not all database properties can be accessed using the `db.propertyname` notation. So although we can do this in the **Immediate** window:

```
?Currentdb.Version
4.0
```

We can't do this:

```
?Currentdb.AppTitle
```

In order to determine the value of these non-standard properties, we have to get in through the `Properties` collection of the `Database` object. So to find the value of the `AppTitle` property, we would do this:

```
?Currentdb.Properties("AppTitle").Value
My New Database
```

This also means that we need to exercise a little care when setting the value of these properties. We need to check that the property exists before we set its value, and if it doesn't exist, we need to create it using the DAO hierarchy as we did earlier. So, if we wanted to programmatically prevent the user from bypassing the `Autoexec` macro or **Startup**… dialog options, we would set the `AllowBypassKey` property of the database to `False` like this:

```
Sub KeepEmOut()

    Dim db As Database
    Dim pty As Property

    On Error GoTo KeepEmOut_Err
```

```
   Set db = CurrentDb
   db.Properties("AllowBypassKey").Value = False

KeepEmOut_Exit:
   Exit Sub

KeepEmOut_Err:
   If Err.Number = 3270 Then        'Error code for "Property not found"...
      'so we'll create it ourselves
      Set pty = db.CreateProperty("AllowBypassKey", dbBoolean, False)
      db.Properties.Append pty
   Else
      MsgBox Err.Description
      Resume KeepEmOut_Exit
   End If

End Sub
```

# Summary

If you look back over this chapter, you'll see that we have covered a quite a few topics. We have looked at:

❑   Using functions to determine whether a variable holds an array

❑   Multi-dimensional arrays and advanced single-dimension arrays

❑   Transferring recordsets into arrays using the GetRows() method.

❑   Passing arguments by reference and by value, and the advantages of each method

❑   Enhancing the functionality of Access through use of DLLs

❑   User-defined and application-defined DAO properties

We are now getting to the stage where our code is getting a little complex. In one or two of the procedures in this chapter, we came into situations where the things we were trying to do might have caused errors to occur, so we had to put in some code to handle those situations. In fact, you will find out that even seemingly innocuous lines of code can sometimes cause errors to occur.

Now is probably the time to stop for a moment and spend some time looking at how we can make our VBA code more robust. That is why the next chapter will look at how we can ensure our code and applications work in the way they were intended to, by using sound debugging and error-handling techniques.

# Exercises

**1.** Modify the frmCriteria form by giving it a custom property of type Long and called TimesOpened. Then you should try to write some code that increments the value of this new property whenever the form is opened.

The Kernel32 dynamic link library contains a function called GetWindowsDirectory which returns the path to the **Windows** directory. You can declare the function like this in VBA:

```
Private Declare Function GetWindowsDirectoryA Lib "kernel32" _
    (ByVal strBuffer As String, ByVal lngSize As Long) As Long
```

The first argument should be passed as a fixed-length string and will be populated by the function with a string representing the path to the **Windows** directory. You should populate the second variable (lngSize) with the length of strBuffer before you call the GetWindowsDirectory function. The GetWindowsDirectoryA function returns a long integer denoting the length (max. 255) of the value it has placed in strBuffer.

**2.** Use this function to create a VBA procedure called GetWinDir that accepts no arguments and simply returns the path to the Windows directory.

**3.** What is the difference between, and effect of, passing an argument ByVal & ByRef?

**4.** What is the default method of passing an argument in VBA?

# CHAPTER 12

# Finding and Dealing with Errors

So far in this book, we've talked a lot about programming, code, recordsets, and so on – all the things that can make your applications great. However, one important concept is that of errors. You've probably encountered several already, and that's perfectly understandable. So what you need to know is how to stop those errors from occurring, and how to find the problems when they do occur.

One point to remember is that there is no such thing as bug-free software. We'd love to believe it's possible, but programs get more and more complex every year, and that means more people working on them and more lines of code. The law of averages dictates that there must be some errors somewhere. Humans are fallible, so their software probably is too, and that includes both beginners and seasoned professionals.

Therefore, in this chapter we are going to look at:

- ❑ How to prevent errors from occurring
- ❑ The different types of error that you might face
- ❑ How to handle those errors when they occur
- ❑ How to use the error events to control errors

## Planning for Errors

Despite the fact that we've said that errors will occur, it is possible to plan for errors. Someone once said that it's impossible to make anything foolproof because fools are so ingenious. We all make mistakes. We all do things that were unplanned. How many times have programmers thought "I don't need to add error code for this – the user will never do it"; or perhaps you think that nothing could go wrong with your code, only to be proved wrong at a later date.

So, errors don't just mean mistakes, or things you didn't think of, but also things the user does that you as a developer haven't accounted for. Perhaps they are using the application in a way that you just didn't think they would. Users don't really care about your code – they only see the visible portion of the application. So part of planning for errors is also planning for the way the application will be used, and planning for change, because applications do change over time.

# The Design

If you've just said 'Design, what design?' then you're starting out on the wrong foot, and you're probably not alone. Remember back in Chapter 2 how much we talked about design. The design is the most fundamental part of your application, and in some cases, can actually take longer to produce than the application itself. The importance of requirements gathering and design cannot be overstated, because it's during this that you should work out what the application is supposed to do, and how it can do it. That might seem an obvious point, but how many times have you created a small application only to realize once it was finished that you'd missed something out. Or you suddenly think of something extra to add that would really help.

One of the most common causes of errors is change. Every change you make has the potential for adding errors, not only in the new code, but also in the existing code. Therefore, if you can avoid change, you reduce the possibility of errors. One of the ways to reduce change is to plan ahead.

## User Analysis

Another obvious point, but working out what the users want is pretty important. One simple way to do this is to just sit and watch them work; see what they do and how they do it. There's no point creating a wonderful application if they have to change completely the way they work. This isn't the most time effective approach, but it can be instructive. Surveys and questionnaires also work well as user requirements analysis tools.

## Table Design

We've said this before, but plan ahead. Try to think of the fields that might be required, rather than the fields that are required. If you collect sales figures, for example, do you just collect the address of the purchaser? What if you want to analyze by region (East, Central, West, and so on) as well as by state? Make sure you add these future fields, even if you don't use them at the moment. It's a lot easier to combine fields together than it is to split them apart.

## Queries

In previous versions of Access it was a good idea to create a query for every table, and then base your forms upon the query. This allowed you to change the table without having to change the forms, because you could just change the query. Any field changes could easily be coped with by aliasing the fields. Access 2002 has a really cool feature that can automatically rename all occurrences of an object. You can turn this on from the General tab on the Options dialog, accessible from the Tools menu:

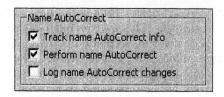

Selecting the first option allows Access to keep track of all of the objects and where they are used (except in code modules). The second option, if ticked, will automatically change all uses of an object name. If you don't want these changes automatically done, then leave this blank. If tracking is on, Access will track the changes to objects, and if AutoCorrect is on, then Access will be able to find all occurrences of the object and change them accordingly. The third option allows a table called **Name AutoCorrect Log** to be created with details of all changes that Access makes.

> **One thing to be aware of is that name tracking doesn't extend to modules. So any object names used within modules are not affected by the AutoCorrect tool.**

## Forms and Reports

The key to creating maintainable reports is to keep it simple. We strongly believe in the 80/20 rule, which states that 80% of the people use 20% of the functionality. Your aim is to deliver an application that gives 100/100. You might find that the whole application doesn't achieve this, but that's normal. Not everyone uses all of the application, so try to target your forms accordingly.

With forms it's easy to try to fit everything onto one screen, so that it's there for the user, but do they really need it? If they do, does the cluttered screen make it harder to navigate? You may also find that a complicated form can make it harder to understand how events are fired and in what order, and thus complicate your programming. Would a second screen, or a Tab control, make things easier?

## Modules

Using modules sensibly can ease maintenance. The idea is to put all of your functions that are related into a single module. So put all of your string handling functions into one place. This makes them easier to find later, and naturally keeps related items together.

If you have global variables, then consider a separate module just for their declaration. After all, if they are used everywhere it doesn't matter which module they are declared in, but it means that you can always go directly to the declaration if you need to. This works well for public constants and enumerated types too.

It's a fairly obvious solution, but one that works well.

## Data-Driven Design

This is another of those 'plan ahead' ideas. Think about information that is fairly static, but may one day change: sales tax, for example. This may be fixed at the moment, but it could change. One way to solve this is to use a constant, so that you only have to change it in one place. An even better way is to store information like this in a table. When the application starts you can read your configuration information and it's then available to the code. If any of the values do change, you've only got to edit a field. No messing about with code and recompiling, and so on, and you could even design a form to allow users to make changes to these settings, perhaps in an 'Admin' mode. One small change and the next time the users log into the application it's done.

Another great advantage of using data-driven design is that it's easier to accommodate historical data. Consider a sales system and the use of sales tax. If you have a table storing your sales, you might need to work out the total cost of an order, including the sales tax. If last year sales tax was 8% but it was changed to 9% this year, you will have to store the date that it changed, otherwise when you look at past orders you might use the wrong sales tax.

# Object-Oriented Techniques

We're not really going to talk much about these techniques since they are covered in the next chapter, but it's worth pointing out that object orientation isn't something to be scared of. You've already done some object oriented programming in this book, even though you might not have been aware of it.

All that needs to be said here is that object-oriented techniques can pay dividends to you as a developer. You will find that you can reuse your code more easily, and you'll find it easier to work with, thus reducing maintenance. The idea of an object that is completely self-contained means that all other programs see of the object is what you want them to see. You are free to change the inside in any way you feel fit, as long as the outside view stays the same.

If you think forward you might be able to create objects that will be usable in future projects. This not only saves the time taken to create future applications, but also reduces the maintenance because pre-built objects should be error free.

# Option Explicit

This has already been mentioned a couple of times so far, but it's worth mentioning again. You should ensure that this is the default for all modules in the VBE. It's available on the Options dialog from the Tools menu, and is shown as the second option below, Require Variable Declaration.

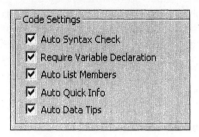

This option means that the OPTION EXPLICIT statement is placed in any new modules you create. With that statement safely installed, you cannot use a variable unless it has previously been declared, and thus allows VBA to pick up things such as typing mistakes, and incorrectly used variables. For example, consider the following:

```
Public Function Circumference(dblRadius As Double) As Double

   Circumfrence = 2 * 3.1414926 * dblRadius

End Function
```

I'm sure you've all made similar mistakes – did you spot this one? The function name has been typed incorrectly when returning the function value. Running this without OPTION EXPLICIT would not cause an error, but the function would always return 0 as the answer; however, with OPTION EXPLICIT at the top of our module, we would get a Variable Not Defined compile error, which would highlight the problem straight away. A simple example, but imagine a longer function, with many variables. You can see how it would be harder to track down. With Option Explicit set at the top of the module, VBA would warn you about undeclared variables.

Note that selecting the **Require Variable Declaration** option in the above dialog will not affect existing modules, only new ones, so if you have already created some modules, you'll need to go back and add the OPTION EXPLICIT statement. In general it is the first executable statement in a module, and resides in the General Declaration section of the module.

## Syntax Checking, Statement Completion, and Code Tips

VBA also supplies a handy set of options for syntax checking, statement completion, and tips. These are the ones shown in the code settings dialog above.

- ❑ **Auto Syntax Check** – turning this on (which is the default) causes VB to automatically verify correct syntax after you enter a line of code. This can be mighty frustrating sometimes, when you know that you haven't completed the line yet, but wanted to select text elsewhere, perhaps to copy and paste something. However, I generally keep it on, because in the main it's useful to know about a syntax error as soon as you have it.

❑ Auto List Member – this is also sometimes referred to as "IntelliSense autocompletion", which just rolls off the tongue! But it certainly is a useful feature. Turning it on causes VB to displays a list that contains information that would logically complete the statement you are writing. You can then use the arrow keys to select the one you want, and press *Tab* to complete the statement. This not only makes you a faster typist, but it means you avoid silly typos. You can also force this to happen by pressing *Ctrl + Spacebar* on the keyboard.

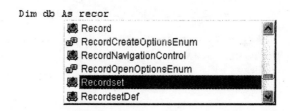

❑ Auto Quick Info – when enabled this displays information about functions and their parameters as you type them – it comes in quite handy as a quick reference.

```
iif(
   Iif(Expression, TruePart, FalsePart)
```

❑ Auto Data Tips – this displays the value of the variable over which your cursor is placed, and is used in Break mode (more on this later).

```
Circumference = 2 * 3.1414926 * dblRadius
                                dblRadius 23
```

## Comments

This always causes contention among programmers. We tend to put comments in as we go along, partly because we have bad memories. There are some people who put in no comments whatsoever ("If it was hard to write, it should be hard to read"), and there are others who go overboard, commenting every line.

Effective comments are those that are used judiciously. You have to find your own happy medium, but here are some tips:

❑ You could put a comment at the top of each procedure describing what it does, what arguments it takes, and so on. For example:

```
'
' Purpose:     To calculate the circumference of a circle
' Arguments:   dblRadius   The circle radius
' Returns:     The circumference
```

```
' Author:       David Sussman
' Date:         15 December 1998
' Modification History:
' Who      When        Why
' DMS      15 Dec 98   Corrected spelling of return value

Public Function Circumference(dblRadius As Double)

  Circumference = 2 * 3.1414926 * dblRadius

End Function
```

This gives a very clear picture of what the procedure is supposed to do, and what changes have been made to it. The procedure shown above only has one line of code, but for larger procedures you can see this would be useful.

❏ Comment variables, preferably on the same line, describing what they will be used for. For example:

```
Dim objRecSales As Recordset        ' recordset to hold sales figures
```

❏ Place comments on their own line, above the block of code to which they refer. For example: use comments for blocks of code, and describe functionality, rather than line by line.

❏ Do not comment the obvious. If the statement is self-describing and then you comment it why you are doing it? For example, the OpenRecordset command is obvious – it opens a recordset, but you may want to comment why you need the recordset in the first place.

❏ Keep your comments up to date. If you change the code, comment it. This is especially true in projects with multiple authors.

❏ Debug code, not the comments. Don't always rely on the comments, as they may not be accurate.

The most important thing is to be consistent. You may feel the code header shown earlier is a bit too unwieldy, but that's fine. Pick something that you feel happy with, and use it – everywhere.

# Compiling

Always remember to compile your project before delivering it. Not only does a compiled application run faster, but you'll also be able to get rid of any funny compilation errors you may have forgotten about.

# Testing

Many large organizations have departments devoted to testing. Others let their customers do it (that's what beta programs are for). In many cases, though, it's you, the developer, who often ends up testing products. This is a good thing. As a programmer you have to take responsibility for your code, and producing bug-free code is not only a matter of pride, but a time saver too. You'll be the one who has to fix the error, and you can guarantee that it will take longer to fix once you've forgotten what the procedure does. Putting the effort in at development time is nearly always quicker than waiting until the users find the errors.

Testing can take several forms, and if possible you should build time for these into your project plan.

## Functional Testing

Functional testing can involve checking that the whole application, or just a part of it, does what it is supposed to do. The aim is to test every possible condition in the program. There are three ways to achieve this and they should be used in the correct order:

❑ Test it yourself, as you understand how it is supposed to work.

❑ Give it to the users; after all, they are the ones who know what it should do.

❑ Give it to a third party, along with the specification. If they know nothing about it, apart from what is written, they will not make any assumptions. They also will not worry about upsetting you if it does not come up to scratch.

When testing the functionality of the application, you not only have to test individual items, such as procedures, forms, queries, and so on, but also how they fit together. Just because a query runs, it doesn't mean that the code that uses it works – in the code you may use a field that isn't in the query. You need to test the individual items, and then how they work together.

## Usability Testing

Usability testing really applies to the visible portions of the application. You need to know whether it is easy to use. Does it confuse the users? Does it follow the usual conventions? After all, if the users don't like the application, it doesn't matter how well it meets their requirements. You may have your own ideas about what is good but, at the end of the day, you must supply something that the user will be happy with. You may also wish to include the time it takes to accomplish a task as 'usability'. You may have to re-design your code if a particular function takes longer than acceptable to execute.

You should involve your users in the process of testing usability as soon as possible, preferably at the design stage – after all, what the application looks like and how it works are both part of the design. In some cases you can create dummy forms, just to show users what the application will look like.

## *Destructive Testing*

This is a fun stage. Give it to someone and ask them to break it. Tell them to try the unconventional. Search for that unplanned problem. If you are testing a form, then let someone who does not use forms, or even computers, play around. If you are testing some code, then give it to another programmer. They will love the chance to break your code. You can be sure that once they have found a few glaring bugs to gloat over, you'll soon start to tighten up your own checking. It may hurt your pride initially, but in the long run you'll become a better programmer.

## *Maintenance*

It is said that 60% of a programmer's time is spent maintaining old programs. When making changes to code, whether it is an old program or a new one, there are some important things to consider:

❑   Will the change you are making impact on anyone else? If it is a library routine then check with other people who are using your routine before making any changes. If there is an error in the code, other people might have coded around the error, so if you correct your code, theirs might stop working. You really want to avoid this situation if possible, and one way to achieve this is to create a new version of your library that is backwardly compatible without making a change to the interface. This way, current users of the system are not affected, and they have an option to update to the new version of the library.

❑   Keep focused on correcting the problem you are looking for. Don't get sidetracked if you find something else wrong.

❑   Only make one change at a time. Imagine correcting what you think are several problems, but when you run the code you get new errors. Which one of your changes caused this? If you track down problems one at a time, and test them one at a time, your overall maintenance time should be reduced.

❑   Comment your changes. Make sure that you add details of the change to the procedure header to show what you've done. You should also make sure that existing comments don't conflict with your changes – if they do, then change the comments to reflect the new functionality.

❑   Don't get distracted into 'tidying up' or improving code, unless that's the explicit reason you are modifying it. Remember that old axiom – if it isn't broke, don't fix it.

The above are really common sense, but you'd be surprised how often common sense flies out of the window when we have our heads stuck into code.

> One product you may want to consider if you want stronger control over code maintenance either within a team or even if you are just working by yourself is Microsoft Visual SourceSafe. This product integrates neatly with Access and provides a way of tracking and commenting (in an external database) all the changes that have been made to Access objects and modules, and by whom. It then allows you to rollback to previous versions if required. There are many other features too, which are beyond the scope of this book. Visual SourceSafe can be bought separately or as part of the Office XP Developer edition.

# Types of Errors

However well you have designed and tested your application, there are bound to be errors. It's a fact of life. The important thing is to learn from them, fix them quickly, and never make the same error again.

At this stage it's important to distinguish between errors and bugs, although the two terms are often used interchangeably. A bug is generally something unforeseen, unexpected, a coding mistake. An error can be the same, but it can also be something expected, something that we have realized might happen and we've catered for in our code.

We are going to look at three types of errors:

❑   Syntax Errors – These errors that are the result of you incorrectly structuring your code. For example you may have forgotten to put in a closing bracket on an expression.

❑   Compile Errors – These occur when the syntax is correct, but Access cannot compile the code for some other reason.

❑   Run-Time Errors – These are only found once the program is running. In these cases the language is syntactically correct, and can be compiled, but something happens to cause the program to halt.

## Syntax Errors

This is the simplest form of error, usually caused by typing mistakes. If you've graduated beyond the two-finger touch typing school, then you might find fewer typing errors, but the easiest way to handle these is to let VBA do it for you. Ensuring that variable declarations and syntax checking are on will save you the trouble of hunting these errors out.

You might also find times when you get a little confused between the various statements, but VBA will spot this too:

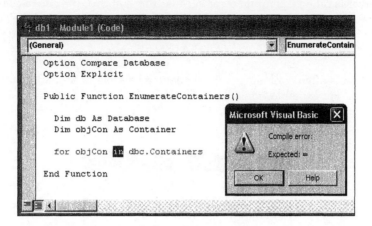

In this example, the Each has been missed out from the For...Each statement, so VBA assumes it's a standard For...Next loop, and is expecting the equals sign. If you give this a try, you'll find that the error message pops up when you press *Return* or *Enter* at the end of the line, and the line with the error turns red. You can click the **OK** button to cancel the error, and either fix the problem now or come back to it later.

## Compile Errors

Another type of problem often encountered cannot be found immediately. For example:

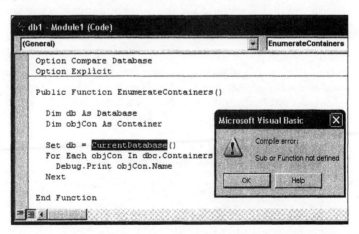

Notice that the CurrentDatabase function is highlighted, because VBA cannot find this function. This could either be because you meant to use the CurrentDb function, or because CurrentDatabase is a function of your own, but isn't visible. Perhaps it's not written yet, or maybe it's in another module and has been declared as Private instead of Public, or maybe you haven't referenced the library or application.

This type of error is called a compile error because the syntax of the above example is correct, but it cannot be compiled. Once the program is compiled, you know that the syntax is correct, and all functions that you've used have been found. However, there could be plenty of other errors lurking around.

Another error that is often confusing is the 'Expected variable or procedure, not module' compilation error. For example, consider the screenshot above. Let's assume we've fixed the compilation error shown and have saved the module. If we saved this module as EnumerateContainers and then tried to run the procedure, we'd get the following error:

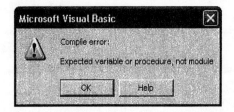

This is telling us that the name of the procedure we are trying to run is also the name of a module.

## Run-Time Errors

As the name suggests, run-time errors are only found once the program is running. In these cases the language is syntactically correct, and can be compiled, but something happens to cause the program to halt. The Auto Quick Info feature has eased a few of the run-time error problems, because it meant that you could see the order of parameters as you were typing. This has meant (hopefully) the end of passing in parameters in the wrong order.

Another run-time error, which probably is the most common, is the Type Mismatch error, which can be very confusing to beginners. If you remember way back to Chapter 4, we talked about variable types, and a type mismatch is where you assign a value of one type to a variable of another, and there is no implicit conversion rule, (such as there is between integers and doubles) You'll see this message if you do:

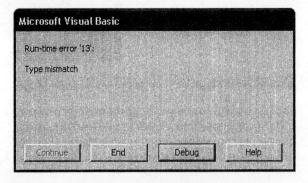

Clicking the *Debug* button will highlight the offending line:

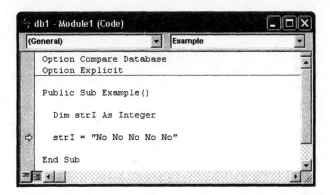

Here an integer variable is being assigned a string. Notice that although the variable is an `Integer`, its naming convention is wrong – it should be `intI`. This has probably contributed to the error in the first place, and shows the importance of a naming standard. It's possible that someone changed the variable type without changing its name.

## Semantic (or logic) Errors

Semantic errors are the hardest to find, because they represent errors in the logic of the program. This means that the code you've written is correct VBA code, but it's not doing what it's supposed to do. Sometimes these produce errors and other times there are no errors, but certain procedures in your application don't work as expected. If errors do occur then you may get an error dialog, and the opportunity to debug the program (note, however, that this is just the line where the error manifested itself, and may not actually be where the real problem lies) or worse still you may find that your code just produces incorrect results with no error at all.

Imagine a function using a variable that has been passed in as an argument. If the variable has the wrong value, then it's not the procedure that is using it that is wrong, but the calling routine. This sort of situation can leave you several layers deep, with functions calling other functions, so you often need to work backwards to find the root of it all. We'll show you how to track backwards later in the chapter.

Finding semantic errors is also a test on you. As a programmer, probably the person who wrote the code, you tend to test what you think the code should be doing, rather than what it actually is doing. This is not as odd as it seems, because we do tend to assume certain things. Don't get into the habit of skipping sections of code because you think you know what they do. When testing and debugging you should throw away your perceptions of the problem and start from scratch. Never think, "That can't be happening". It can, and does – not always, but if you take this approach, you'll be better for it.

Let's take a look at an example of some errors, and start to see how to track them down. We're going to create an example just to show you how lucky you really have to be to win the UK lottery. This uses 49 numbers from which you have to pick 6, in any order. The calculation for this is:

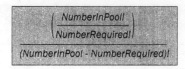

$$\left(\begin{array}{c} NumberInPool! \\ NumberRequired! \end{array}\right)$$
$$(NumberInPool - NumberRequired)!$$

Let's give this a go.

## Try It Out — Run-time and Semantic Errors

**1.** Create a new form, and set the Scroll Bars property to Neither, and the Record Selectors, Navigation Buttons, and Dividing Lines properties to No.

**2.** Put three textboxes and a command button on it, so it looks like this:

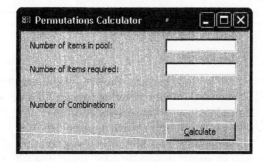

**3.** Name the textboxes txtPool, txtRequired, and txtCombinations. Call the command button cmdCalculate, and then save the form as frmCombinations.

**4.** Press the Code button on the toolbar to switch to the code editor and create a code module for this form.

Remember that pressing *Alt+F11* will also switch to the VBA IDE, but in this case the code module will not be created automatically.

**5.** Enter the following function:

```
Private Function Factorial (intNumber As Integer) As Double

  If intNumber < 0 Then
    Factorial = 0
  ElseIf intNumber = 0 Then
    Factorial = 1
  Else
    Factorial = intNumber * Factorial(intNumber - 1)
```

```
    End If

End Function
```

**6.** Now add the next function:

```
Private Function Combinations (intPool As Integer, _
  intRequired As Integer) As Double

  Combinations = Factorial(intPool) / _
    Factorial(intRequired) / _
    Factorial(intPool - intRequired)

End Function
```

**7.** Now in the `Click` event for the command button, add the following code:

```
txtCombinations = Combinations(txtPool, txtRequired)
```

**8.** Back in Access, switch the form back to form view and try the following numbers. Press **Calculate** to see what chance we in the UK have of winning our lottery.

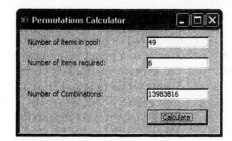

Yes, that's right. 14 million to 1! Not very favorable odds, but it shows the functions work OK. You might like to try the numbers from your local lottery.

**9.** Now change the number of items in the pool from 49 to 0 and try again.

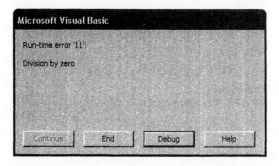

You're thrown back into the VBE with a division by zero error.

**10.** Press the Debug button to get taken to the line where the error was generated.

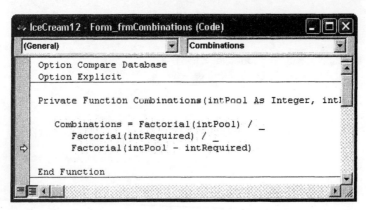

We know what the problem is, a division by 0, but where is it being generated and why? If you look at the above function and think about the arguments: `intPool` is 0, and `intRequired` is 6. This means that the final division here is the problem, as we're trying to get the factorial of a negative number, and our factorial program returns 0 if you try this.

Now for those of you with a math background, you might be starting to think about some problems we've got here. What do we correct? Should the `Factorial` function be corrected, because the factorial of a negative number isn't 0, it's infinity. So we've already introduced some error protection, but is it correct? Strictly speaking, no it's not, but what we've done is protect this function from raising errors that the user probably doesn't want to know about. The `Factorial` function could raise an error indicating a division by 0, but then we'd have to trap this error and act upon it (and we'll do this later in the chapter). For the moment a return value of -1 is fine. The division by 0 isn't acceptable though.

**11.** Press the Reset button on the toolbar (or select Reset from the Run menu) to stop the program running.

**12.** Change the code in the `Combinations` function to the following:

```
If intRequired = 0 Or (intPool - intRequired) < 0 Then
  Combinations = -1
Else
  Combinations = Factorial(intPool) / _
    Factorial(intRequired) / _
    Factorial(intPool - intRequired)
End If
```

**13.** Back in Access, try the same numbers again:

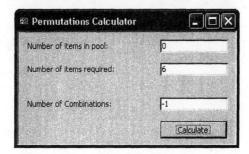

This is much better (although -1 isn't the correct answer) because for combinations to work, the number of items in the pool can't be 0 – it must be larger than the number of items required. All we've done is move the problem somewhere else. We could change the code for the command button so that it checks the number of combinations, and if it is -1 it displays a more informative error message, but for the moment we'll leave it as it is. We'll be coming back to this problem a little later.

## Locating Errors

One thing to remember when tracking down errors is that Access is event driven. That means code runs in response to events, so you might find that code corresponding to certain events is being run without you being aware of it. Consider opening a form. You've already seen that there's a Load event, generated when the form is loaded, but there are in fact four other events generated as well, in this order:

- ❑ Open
- ❑ Load
- ❑ Resize
- ❑ Activate
- ❑ Current

Closing a form generates:

- ❑ Unload
- ❑ Deactivate
- ❑ Close

So if opening the form appears to be a problem, don't forget to check the other events. You can see which events have code behind them because the events appear in bold in the event combo box in the code window:

Another good way not to miss code is to make sure you have the code window set to Full Module View – this can be set from the buttons at the bottom left of the code window:

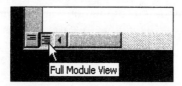

This shows all of the procedures for a single module together in the code window, with a line to separate them, and makes seeing all of the code much easier.

## Other Errors

There are occasions when other types of errors crop up, but with a bit of advance planning you can probably circumvent them. There are times, however, when you've no choice but to delve into the code line by line. Of course, the number of errors that occur is always in proportion to the importance of the application, and in inverse proportion to the time you have to fix them!

The cause of these other errors is almost limitless, but can include Dynamic Link Libraries (DLLs) and ActiveX controls. If the programmers who wrote these did a good job in testing them, you shouldn't see any problems, but as we've already said – writing bug-free software is very hard. Other problems, such as lack of memory, network problems, or registry problems, can cause some very odd things to happen.

Sometimes there is nothing you can do in these situations, but if you're stuck try the following steps:

❑    Check your code thoroughly, line by line, without any assumptions. Write down the state of variables as you go through to see what's changing.

❑    Try running the application on another machine. If it works, you could have a memory problem, or maybe an old version of a DLL or ActiveX control.

- ❑ Get someone else to check it for you. Even sitting down with someone else, with the code, trying to explain what it is doing can lead that light bulb above your head to flicker on, as you realize what the problem is.

- ❑ Buy a hat, fake glasses, and beard, and get those tickets to a technology-free sunny island!

The last of these shouldn't really be an option, however tempting it sounds. (Well, not the hat, glasses and beard part – but the sunny island sounds good!). If you are really stuck, then the Internet is wide and responsive, and the chances are that someone has either had a similar problem, or will be willing to help. One great place to look is the Microsoft Developer Network, which can be found at http://msdn.microsoft.com/. The newsgroups are also a great place, full of helpful people. The Access ones are named microsoft.public.access.*, and most ISPs support them.

# Debugging

So far in this chapter we've spent quite a lot of time discussing the different types of errors, and how to prevent them. Now you need to know how to track them down, and as you become more experienced, you'll find you get quite good at tracking down errors. In fact, you could say that making mistakes is a required part of the learning process, since it gives you first hand knowledge of the debugging process.

In this section we will learn how to use the VBA debugger to help track down errors in our code. The debugger enables us to pause the execution of code and then examine variables and logic line by line.

## *Program Execution*

VBA provides a number of ways to help you navigate through your code while it's running. When tracking down errors, this allows you to start the debugging process at a place where you know the code works. You can then gradually narrow down the areas that need checking, until you find the error.

All of the useful debugging facilities are located in two places within the Visual Basic Environment. The first is the Debug toolbar:

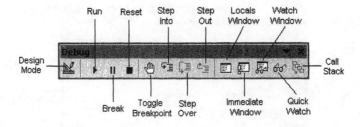

If this toolbar isn't visible, select the Toolbars option on the View menu.

The second set of facilities, which duplicates some of the debug toolbar, is available from the Debug menu:

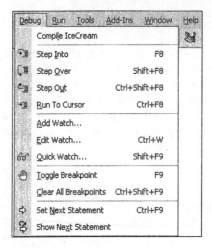

You can customize the toolbars and menus, but these are the default settings, and allow you a great deal of control over how you debug your program. Let's look at these facilities in more detail before we start using them.

## Breakpoints

Breakpoints are the heart of debugging, as they allow you to mark lines where you would like to suspend the program. This allows you to temporarily stop the program, perhaps to check some variables, or to start stepping through the code line by line. You can set breakpoints on a line in several ways:

❑   Clicking the Toggle Breakpoint button

❑   Selecting the Toggle Breakpoint option from the Debug menu

❑   Pressing *F9*

❑   Clicking in the border at the left of the module window

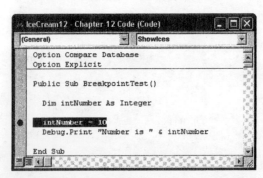

As shown, a breakpoint is identified by a red background, and a red dot in the border on the left of the module window (we know it's gray in the book).

All of these methods act as a toggle, so if there is already a breakpoint on the line it will remove the breakpoint. There is no limit to the number of breakpoints you can have. You cannot set breakpoints on variable declarations, but you can set them on the start and end lines of procedures. If you want to clear all the breakpoints you have set in one fell swoop, you can select Clear All Breakpoints from the Debug menu.

While the program is running and a line with a breakpoint is encountered, the program will halt and the breakpoint line will be highlighted. You can also halt the program by pressing *Ctrl+Break* while the program is running, which generates the following dialog:

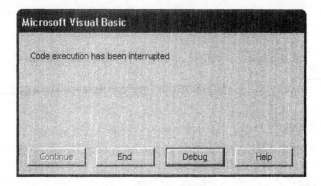

At this point you can continue with the program, end the program, or switch into debug mode, which stops the program after the line that is currently being executed.

## Assertions

An assertion is a statement used to test the value of an expression. When using the `Debug.Print` statement you probably saw `Assert` in the quick tips for `Debug`, allowing you to do `Debug.Assert`.

Assertions in VBA allow you to place expressions into your code that will be ignored if they are true, but will cause a breakpoint if they are false. For example, consider the following procedure:

```
Public Sub TestAssertion(intNumber As Integer)

    Debug.Assert intNumber = 10

End Sub
```

The expression we are testing for is if `intNumber` is 10. If it is, nothing happens, but if it isn't, a breakpoint is generated on the line. This allows us to have conditional breakpoints, and can be quite useful if you only want to halt execution under certain conditions.

## *The Stop Statement*

As well as breakpoints and assertions, you can use the Stop statement anywhere in your code to force VBA to suspend execution. This is exactly like putting a breakpoint on the line, and is quite useful as it allows you to clear all breakpoints from a program, but still make sure a program halts at a selected place. For example:

```
Private Sub Foo()

    Dim intI As Integer

    Stop
    For intI = 1 To 1000
        ...
    Next

End Sub
```

This would ensure that the code is halted on the Stop line, just before the loop.

Don't forget to remove any Stop statements before you release your product.

## *Continuing Execution* ▶

You can use the Continue button to continue execution of a halted program. Execution will continue from the current line until user input is required, or a breakpoint is reached.

## *Stopping Execution* ■

You can use the Reset button at any time to halt the execution of a running program. This doesn't place the program in debug mode, but stops all execution and resets all global and static variables.

## *Stepping through Code*

Stopping at a breakpoint is all very well, but you really need to look at lines of code as they are executed. Being able to move through the code one line at a time is a great way to examine variables, see what's happening, and generally understand how the program is working. This allows you to see exactly where problems lie. There are several ways of stepping through code:

| Symbol | Shortcut | Description |
|---|---|---|
| ⥅☰ | F8 | The Step Into button runs only the line that is currently highlighted, that is, the current line. If that line happens to be a procedure call, then it will step into the procedure, and allow you to continue single-stepping through the code within the procedure. |

| Symbol | Shortcut | Description |
| --- | --- | --- |
| | *Shift+F8* | The **Step Over** button runs only the line that is currently highlighted, that is, the current line. If that line is a procedure, then the procedure is executed, but single-stepping of the procedure does not occur. The next line to be single-stepped will be the line after the procedure call. |
| | *Ctrl+Shift +F8* | The **Step Out** button continues execution of a procedure until the line after the calling procedure. So if Procedure A calls Procedure B and you accidentally step into Procedure B, when you really meant to step over it, you can step out, which will place you back in Procedure A, and the line after the call to Procedure B. |
| | *Ctrl+F8* | **Run To Cursor** continues execution from the current line and halts on the line that contains the cursor. It's a bit like setting a temporary breakpoint. This button isn't shown on the Debug toolbar by default, but can easily be added, or accessed through the shortcut or from the **Debug** menu. |

The advantage of the **Step Into** method is that you can check every line in every procedure that is used. However, if you have a large number of procedures, then this is also a disadvantage as it's much slower to step through more lines of code, especially if the procedures contain loops. For example, with a loop counting from 1 to 5,000 you would have to step through the loop 5,000 times. **Step Over** allows you to run a procedure quickly, and is especially useful if you know the procedure works. This allows you to concentrate on debugging the procedures that you are unsure of. Using **Run To Cursor** is really useful for loops, since it allows you to continue execution until the line after the loop.

## Re-running Lines of Code

When you start debugging programs, and are single stepping through code, you might find lines of code that are wrong. If you are in debug mode, then you can change lines of code while the program is running, and re-run the line. This allows you to fix problems without having to stop the program and start again, which is a real boon if you've got a complex procedure. There are some changes that will force the program to stop, such as deleting variables, but for many cases you can edit as you go.

To re-run a line of code you can just grab the arrow in the code window border that indicates the current line and drag it to the new line:

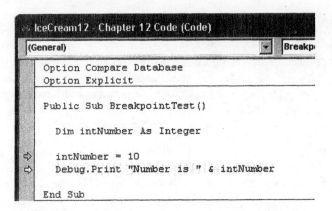

When the cursor is in the left margin, the cursor changes to an arrow and you can press the left mouse button, and without releasing the mouse button, drag it to the new line. Once on the new line release the mouse button, and the new line is highlighted as being the next line to be run.

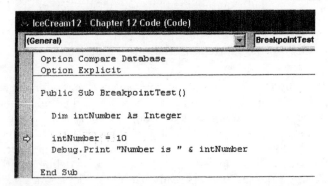

Now if you continue running the program it will run from the new line. This technique is also good for skipping lines of code.

### Skipping Lines of Code

As you've seen in the previous example, you can re-run lines of code, but a similar technique can be used to move the current line forward in a program, and skip the lines of code altogether. You can also place the cursor on the new line and press *Ctrl+F9* or choose Debug | Set Next Statement.

You should always be careful when skipping lines of code, especially if they contain procedures. Remember that this isn't like the Run To Cursor option where the code in between is run. Setting the next line forward in a program means that any lines you skip are not run, so if you are dependent upon what they do your code might not work in the way it is supposed to.

## Changing Code

VBA allows you to change code while the program is stopped, so you can correct any errors as they occur. What you can't do is change variable definitions while a procedure is running, since this would impact on the way that VBA stored the variables. If you need to change variable definitions, but don't want to reset your program and start from the beginning, then you can only do this in procedures that are not currently being executed. So, you could finish the current procedure, step out of it, change the variables, and then step back into it again.

Changing code is not just limited to a single line. You can create whole chunks of code, use code structures and loops, and move the current line around as you see fit.

If you try to change variables, or make another change that might cause the program structure to change (such as adding or deleting procedures), then you'll get a warning message:

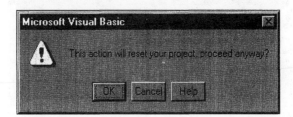

If you click the OK button your program will be stopped, just as if you'd pressed the Stop button. Pressing Cancel will undo the change you've just done that caused this warning.

### Commenting Out Lines

Another way to skip lines of code is just to comment them out by putting a comment character (') at the front of the line. If you comment out the currently active line, then VBA sets the next line as the active line. Uncomment the line again, and VBA moves the current line back – it's clever enough to realize that the line hasn't been run.

### Block Commenting

This is a trick that doesn't work while you're in debug mode, as it causes the program to halt, but it's pretty useful if you need to comment out a whole section of code. The normal way to do this would be to put a comment character at the beginning of each line, which is quite tedious. However, there's a much quicker way, using block commenting. This is a feature of the VBA editor that puts a comment at the beginning of a whole block of code. This doesn't appear on any menus by default so you will have to customize a menu to add this feature.

If you press the right mouse button when the cursor is over a toolbar or menu you can select the Customize… option. Select the Commands tab, and then select Edit from the Categories list box. If you now scroll the Commands list a little you'll see two items – Comment Block and Uncomment Block. Just drag these and drop them onto a menu or toolbar of your choice – the Edit menu is a good place.

Once these are on the menu you can highlight a whole section of code and then select **Comment Block** from the menu. All of the selected code will have a comment character placed at the beginning of the line.

## The Call Stack

The Call Stack is a list of procedures that are currently being executed. You might think it's obvious which procedure is being executed, but if you have highly-structured code, with several procedures, you might lose track of where you are. This is especially true if you have some generic procedures that are called from several places.

You can view the call stack by pressing the **Call Stack** button:

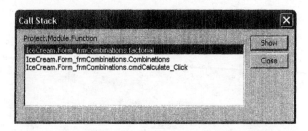

This shows what happens when we put a breakpoint in our `Factorial` routine. This is the current procedure so it is shown at the top. The first procedure called is shown at the bottom – in our case this is the `Click` event procedure for the `cmdCalculate` button. Any other procedures are shown in the order in which they were called, from the bottom upwards.

When this window is shown you can double-click (or select the procedure and click **Show**) on any procedure to be taken to the code for that procedure. For example, if we show the code for the command button:

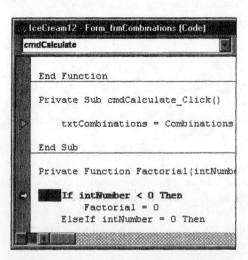

Here you can see that the first line in Factorial is highlighted, showing it is the current line, but that an arrow points to the line in the Click event that caused Factorial to be called. You can see this is a call to Combinations, which in turn calls Factorial.

## The Immediate Window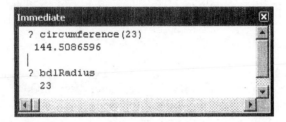

You've already seen and used the Immediate window, but since you'll be using it a lot more we ought to just examine the things that are possible in it. Quite simply it allows you to examine variables, change variables, and even run procedures.

If you want to output information to the Immediate window you use the Debug.Print statement, followed by the details you want printed. Within the window you can use Debug.Print, Print, or ? to see a value.

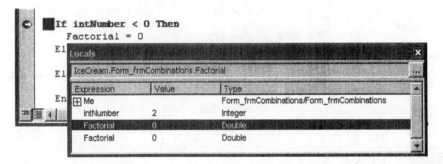

## The Locals Window

The Locals window contains all of the variables, and values, that are within the current scope. So that is all variables local to the current procedure, as well as global variables. For example, when our code was at a breakpoint in the Factorial function, the Locals window looks like this:

You can see there are three local variables, along with their values and data types. One, intNumber, is the function argument, and there are two local variables for the function name. Don't worry about this, as there are always two copies when using functions. At the top you can see Me, with a small plus sign next to it. As you know, Me corresponds to the current form, so clicking on the plus sign will expand Me to show you all of the properties for the form.

As you step through the program the values of the variables change, so you can see exactly what's happening. You can also double-click on the value and type in new values to see how that will affect things. Be careful though of using this window when examining a large and complex object (like a cell range in Excel) – it can take an eternity for VBA to iterate through all of the relevant child objects' properties when you click the button of the parent object to expand it.)

## The Watch Window

The Watch window is similar to the Locals window, but is used only for variables you choose. In fact, it's very similar to a window for assertions, since you can specify variables and conditions, and specify whether a break point is to occur when those conditions are met. You can also set breakpoints for when a variable changes, which can be extremely useful if a variable is being changed, but you're not sure where. You might not think this could be a problem, but with a large program and lots of variables, it's easy to lose track. This does slow down execution of the program though, but this is generally not a problem when you are debugging.

## Quick Watches

Quick watches are an easy way to add a watch to the Watch window. When the cursor is placed on a variable, or an expression is highlighted, you can press the Quick Watch button, or *Shift+F9* to see the value of the variable or the result of the expression, then click the Add button to add it to the normal Watch window.

## Hovering

This is the trick of holding the mouse pointer over a variable when the program is paused to see the contents:

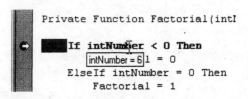

```
Private Function Factorial(intl
    If intNumber < 0 Then
        intNumber = 6 1 = 0
    ElseIf intNumber = 0 Then
        Factorial = 1
```

This is great for quickly finding out the value of variables.

---

**Try It Out**    **Debugging Code**

In this example, we're going to be looking at two procedures. The first, ShowIces, will print all of the ice cream names to the Immediate window. The second, ShowIngredients, prints the ingredients for each ice cream. If you don't want to type this code in you can find it in the IceCream.mdb database, in the Chapter 12 Code module.

**1.** Create a new module, and add a global variable.

```
Private m_db As Database
```

**2.** Now create the first procedure:

```
Public Sub ShowIces(blnQuantity As Boolean)

    Dim recIces As Recordset

    Set m_db = CurrentDb()
    Set recIces = m_db.OpenRecordset("tblIceCream")

    Do While Not recIces.EOF
      Debug.Print recIces("IceCream")
      ShowIngredients recIces("IceCreamID"), blnQuantity
      recIces.MoveNext
    Loop

    recIces.Close
    Set recIces = Nothing

End Sub
```

**3.** Now the second procedure:

```
Private Sub ShowIngredients(lngIceID As Long, blnShowQuantity As Boolean)

    Dim recIngredients As Recordset
    Dim strSQL As String

    strSQL = "SELECT tblIceCreamIngredient.Quantity, tblIngredient.Name " & _
      "FROM tblIngredient INNER JOIN tblIceCreamIngredient " & _
      "ON tblIngredient.IngredientID=tblIceCreamIngredient.fkIngredientID" & _
      " WHERE tblIceCreamIngredient.fkIceCreamID = " & lngIceID

    Set recIngredients = m_db.OpenRecordset(strSQL)

    Do While Not recIngredients.EOF
      Debug.Print vbTab; recIngredients("Name");
      If blnShowQuantity Then
        Debug.Print vbTab; recIngredients("Quantity");
      End If
      Debug.Print
      recIngredients.MoveNext
    Loop
```

```
    recIngredients.Close
    Set recIngredients = Nothing

End Sub
```

4. Now put a breakpoint on the first executable line in the first procedure. That's the one with `CurrentDb()` on it:

```
Set m_db = CurrentDb()
```

5. View the **Immediate** window (you can press *Ctrl+G* to open it if it is not already available, or select **View | Immediate Window**) and run our first function by typing in:

```
ShowIces True
```

6. When the code has stopped at the first line, view the **Locals** window:

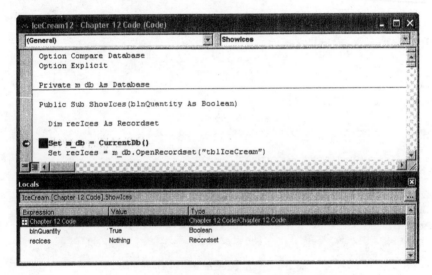

7. Press *F8* to step through the first line, and click on the plus sign next to **Chapter 12 Code** in the **Locals** window:

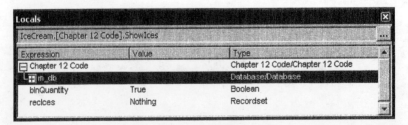

Notice that this has expanded to show all of the global variables in the module – in this case there's only one. You can see that recIces is a Recordset, and that because it hasn't been assigned yet, it has the value of Nothing.

**8.** Press *F8* again to step through the next line of code. This opens the recordset on the ice creams table. Keep an eye on the Locals window:

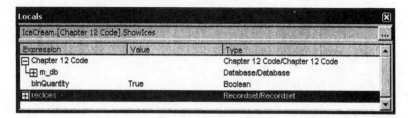

**9.** Notice that recIces is no longer set to Nothing. If you expand recIces, you'll see all of the recordset information. You can also verify this from the Immediate window. Try typing this:

```
?recIces("IceCream")
```

```
Immediate
ShowIces True
?recIces("IceCream")
Walnut Wonder
```

This prints out the value of the IceCream field for the current record.

**10.** Press *F8* again, and hold the cursor over recIces:

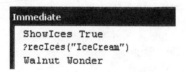

```
Do While Not recIces.EOF
    Debug.Print recIces("IceCream")
    Sho recIces("IceCream") = "Walnut Wonder" reamID"), blnQuantity
    recIces.MoveNext
Loop
```

This is a really quick way of getting to see what's in a variable.

**11.** Make sure the Debug toolbar is visible (just right-click over an existing toolbar and select Debug from the pop-up menu).

**12.** Press the Step Over button, or press *Shift+F8* to step over the Debug.Print line. For a line that is not a procedure call it doesn't actually matter whether you Step Over or Step Into. If you look at the Immediate window, you'll see that the ice cream name has been printed out.

**13.** Now you are on a procedure line. Let's first step over, so you can see what happens, so press *Shift+F8* again. Have a look at the Immediate window:

```
Immediate                                    ☒
ShowIces True
?recIces("IceCream")
Walnut Wonder
Walnut Wonder
    Sugar    0.16
    Cream, Double    1
    Walnuts    0.16
    Eggs    1.33
    Vanilla Extract    0.1
```

Notice that the `ShowIngredients` procedure has run, but that you didn't have to single step through it.

**14.** Press Step Into or Step Over four more times, so that you are back on the call to `ShowIngredients`. Now press Step Into to step into the procedure. See how you are now on the first line of the new procedure.

**15.** Press Step Into three times, until you are on the `While` statement. Keep an eye on the Locals window, just so you can see the values of the variables changing. Now click on the `Wend` statement and select Run To Cursor (either from the Debug menu, or by right-clicking for a pop-up menu). Notice how one set of ingredients has been printed to the Immediate window.

**16.** Select Step Out from the toolbar. This will run the rest of this procedure, and place us back in the calling procedure:

```
Set m_db = CurrentDb()
Set recIces = m_db.OpenRecordset("tblIceCream")

' loop through the ice creams printing out the ice cream name
' and calling a sub-procedure to print out the ingredients
Do While Not recIces.EOF
    Debug.Print recIces("IceCream")
    ShowIngredients recIces("IceCreamID"), blnQuantity
    recIces.MoveNext
Loop
```

**17.** Press *F8* three times, until you are back on the `Debug.Print` line. Highlight `recIces("IceCream")` and press the Quick Watch button, or *Shift+F9*:

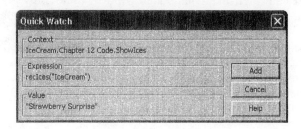

Notice how this shows another way of viewing the variable details. Press the **Cancel** button to close this dialog.

**18.** Switch into the **Immediate** window and type the following:

```
blnQuantity=False
```

This sets the value of the variable blnQuantity to False. Did you notice how the "auto list member" worked in the **Immediate** window, showing you the possible values for blnQuantity? That's because VBA knows this is a Boolean variable and that it can only have one of two values – True or False.

**19.** Press **Step Over** twice and look at the **Immediate** window again:

```
Admirable Apricot
    Milk, Full Fat
    Sugar
    Cream, Double
    Eggs
    Dried Apricots
```

Notice how the quantities are no longer shown. That's because we've changed the value of the Boolean variable that tells the ShowIngredients procedure whether the quantity should be printed.

**20.** Keep pressing **Step Into** until you are back in the ShowIngredients procedure. You want to be on the While statement.

OK, let's take a little breather here, and recap what we've done so far. Don't press any other keys or stop the program yet – we'll be continuing in a little while.

What we've done so far is use the stepping facilities to step over lines of code and step into procedures. Remember that **Step Over** doesn't mean the line isn't executed – it just means that if the line is a procedure call we don't step through the lines of that procedure.

You've also seen that the **Locals** window has a lot of information in it. Object variables, such as recIces, appear with a plus sign next to them, a bit like the Windows Explorer. You can use this plus sign to drill-down into the properties, examining the object in more detail.

You've also seen that you can use the Immediate window to not only view variables, but to change them as well. This allows you to perhaps correct variables that have the wrong values.

The process of stepping through each line and examining variables is time intensive, and often not a productive way to trap errors. For the next stage in the debugging process, we'll use watches, which allow us to run the program as normal, but watch individual variables, performing some action when these variables change. This allows us to target our debugging much more narrowly, and frees us from the drudgery of stepping through the code one line at a time.

---

**Try It Out**      **Debugging Code (continued)**

**1.** Highlight `recIngredients.EOF` and press the **Quick Watch** button. This shows the value of the `EOF` property is `False`, which is correct since we've only just opened the recordset, and we know there are some records in there.

**2.** Cancel the **Quick Watch** and highlight `Not recIngredients.EOF`, and press the **Quick Watch** button again.

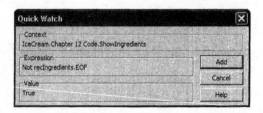

**3.** Now the value shows as `True`. Again, this is correct because we are watching a different expression, this time one that gives the opposite of the `EOF` flag. This shows that you can include more than a single variable in a watch expression.

**4.** Press the **Add** button to make this watch permanent.

**5.** Don't step any more yet, but highlight `recIngredients("Name")` on the following line and press the **Quick Watch** button. When the watch appears press **Add** to add this watch.

**6.** Now have a look at the **Watches** window. You can view this by pressing the **Watch** window on the toolbar, or selecting the same options from the **View** menu:

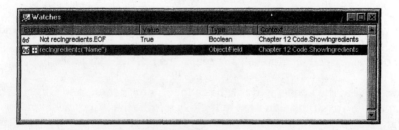

This is a little like the **Locals** window, but you can only see variables that you have added.

**7.** Press **Step Over**, going round the loop a few times, and notice how the value of the ingredient in the **Watches** window changes.

If you accidentally loop through too many times, you can position the yellow arrow to the `While Not recIngredients.EOF` line at the start of the loop. Before you can continue looping again, you will need to type `recIngredients.MoveFirst` in the **Immediate** window.

**8.** Highlight `recIngredients("Name")` watch in the **Watches** window, and from the **Debug** menu select **Edit Watch...**:

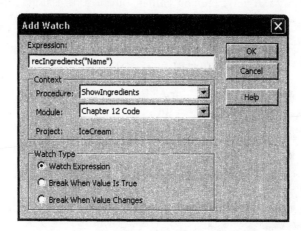

This allows you to edit the watch details. Notice that there are three Watch Types:

- ❏ **Watch Expression**, which is the type you've seen so far. This just shows the value in the watch window.

- ❏ **Break When Value Is True**, watches the expression, but if the value of the expression is `True`, the program halts and enters debug mode.

- ❏ **Break When Value Changes**, watches the expression, but if the value changes, the program halts and enters debug mode.

**9.** Click the last of these (**Break When Value Changes**).

**10.** Change the Expression so that it says `recIngredients("Name").Value`, and then click the **OK** button.

**11.** Press *F5* to continue running the program. Notice that the program halts on the `Wend` statement. This is the line after the `MoveNext`, which changes the record in the recordset, so the break is working.

But why did we have to add the .Value to the end of the expression? Well, Value is the default property, so in general use you can omit it, but when you need to break in a Watch expression, you have to add it in.

**12.** Select this watch in the **Watches** window, and from the Debug window **select Edit Watch...** (or use *Ctrl+W* for a quicker method).

**13.** Change the watch expression to `recIngredients("Quantity") > 1` and press **OK**.

**14.** Press *F5* to continue and see where it stops next. If you hover the cursor over `recIngredients("Quantity")` on the `Debug.Print` line you'll see the quantity is 1.33. So not only can you break on values, but on expressions too.

**15.** Press the **Stop** button. Notice how the **Locals** window is cleared, because there are now no active statements. The **Watch** window also changes to show <Out of Context> for the watches, because there is no active code.

**16.** From the **Debug** menu, select **Clear All Breakpoints**. This will clear all breakpoints, but not the breaks in the **Watches** window.

**17.** In the **Immediate** window run the procedure again, by typing:

```
ShowIces True
```

This will run the program until the Watch causes a break – remember that it is looking for a change in the Boolean value of `RecIngredients("Quantity") > 1`.

**18.** Press the **Call Stack** button on the **Debug** toolbar:

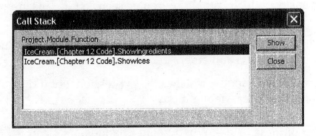

**19.** This shows that we are in the **ShowIngredients** procedure, but this was called from the **ShowIces** procedure. Select **ShowIces** and click the **Show** button:

```
While Not recIces.EOF
    Debug.Print recIces("IceCream")
    ShowIngredients recIces("IceCreamID"), blnQuantity
    recIces.MoveNext
Wend
```

Here you can see the arrow indicating the line in the ShowIces procedure that called ShowIngredients. The current executable line, however, hasn't changed, so pressing any of the **Step** buttons, or continuing, will not continue from the arrow in the diagram above, but from the current line.

**20.** Press *F8* to step and you're now switched back to ShowIngredients.

**21.** Place the cursor on the recIngredients.Close line and from the **Debug** menu select **Set Next Statement**. Notice how the highlight moves to that line. All of the code in the loop has been skipped.

**22.** Press the **Stop** button to halt the code.

Hopefully you can see that being able to step through the code in a variety of methods is extremely flexible. You can examine variables in several ways, monitor them closely, and even change them. As you use VBA, you'll become more familiar with using the various windows in the VBE.

# Error Handling

Now that you know how to prevent mistakes, and how to use debugging to find the ones you did not prevent, you really need to know how to handle errors gracefully. We've all seen those odd error messages with obscure numbers, but you should really try to present these in a more user-friendly manner. So the errors that we are going to look at now are the run-time errors that you can foresee.

For example, consider the situation of dealing with external data, perhaps linking an external text file. What happens if the text file is missing, or if it is stored on a network drive and the network has died? You need to be able to inform the user of the problem in a clear and concise way.

## The Err Object

When an error is generated in VBA, the details are stored in the Err object. This has several properties and methods that we can use to customize our error handling:

| Property | Description |
|---|---|
| Number | The unique error number |
| Description | Some descriptive text explaining what the error is |
| Source | The name of the object or application that generated the error |
| LastDLLError | A system error code returned from a Dynamic Link Library |

*Table continued on following page*

| Property | Description |
|----------|-------------|
| HelpContext | The context ID for the help topic in the help file |
| HelpFile | The name of the help file |

There are two methods:

| Method | Description |
|--------|-------------|
| Clear | Clears all of the property settings of the Err object |
| Raise | Generates a run-time error |

The most useful properties are Number and Description, although when generating your own error messages you might well set Source. Let's look at how we handle errors in code.

## Visual Basic Errors

You've already seen some examples of error handling code. Remember back in Chapter 6 when we first started looking at the objects in Access, and we were changing the font on forms. We used error handling there to ignore a certain error. If you use the Control Wizard to add controls to forms, some of the code they create also contains some default error handling.

Error handling is a way of catching run-time errors as they happen, and then dealing with them in a way appropriate to the application. The alternative is to let the user see the error message generated by Access, and most likely have them baffled and upset!

Before you can deal with errors in VBA, you need to announce your intention to handle them. For this you use the On Error statement and **labels**. A label is a marker in the code, a bit like a bookmark, that allows us to jump to certain places when an error occurs. You use On Error in one of three ways:

❑ On Error Goto 0 – disables any enabled error handler in the procedure.

❑ On Error Goto Label_Name – when an error is generated, causes execution to continue from the label named Label_Name. This is generally used for creating a central place to handle errors, as we will see shortly.

❑ On Error Resume Next – when an error is generated, cause execution to continue on the line after the one that generated the error. This can be useful for "in-line" error handling – that is, we can turn error handling on with this statement, try something that may cause an error, such as a database update, and then immediately check for the error and deal with it.

A label name follows the same naming rules as a variable, except that it ends with a colon, and it does not need to be unique within a module. The general rule is to either call the label after the name of the procedure and append _Err to the end of it, or use generalized labeling such as ErrHandler and ExitHere. For example:

```
Public Sub Foo()

   On Error Goto ErrHandler
   ' some code goes here

ErrHandler:
   ' Error handling code goes here

End Sub
```

However, this isn't a correct solution, because the label isn't a terminator of any sort, just a marker. So if no errors occurred, the code would just drop through the label and continue to run the error handling code, which could give some unusual results. There are two ways to get around this:

```
Public Sub Foo()

   On Error Goto ErrHandler
   ' some code goes here

   Exit Sub

ErrHandler:
   ' Error handling code goes here

End Sub
```

There is now an Exit Sub just before the error label, which forces the subroutine to exit immediately, without erroneously running the error code. Another solution, which is better, is:

```
Public Sub Foo()

   On Error Goto ErrHandler
   ' some code goes here

ExitHere:
   ' clean up code goes here
   Exit Sub

ErrHandler:
   ' Error handling code goes here
   Resume ExitHere

End Sub
```

This introduces a new label, `ExitHere`, which indicates the exit point of the procedure. Now we can use a new statement, `Resume ExitHere`, in the error handling code to say that, once the error has been handled, resume processing at the label indicated. This means that there is only one exit point in the procedure, which makes it easier if you need to do any tidying up, such as closing recordsets, clearing variables, and so on.

- ❑ If you have the Office XP Developer edition, you can install the "Visual Basic for Applications Add-Ins" These include a rather neat "Code Commenter and Error Handler Add-In" that will automatically add the above template to every procedure you create (after you have created them), together with comments on parameter info, author name and more. It is template based so that you can easily modify it to meet your exact requirements. We'll look at this in the next section.

There are three ways in which `Resume` can be used in error handling code:

- ❑ You can use `Resume` on its own, which tells VBA to try the statement that caused the error again. This allows you to handle an error, perhaps fixing the problem, and then try again. You should use this option with care, as you don't want to keep generating the error, as this would leave you stuck in a loop.

- ❑ You can use `Resume Next`, which is the same as when used in the `On Error` statement, telling VBA to continue at the line after the line that generated the error. This means that you can handle an error and then continue, as if nothing happened.

- ❑ You can use `Resume Label_Name` to jump to a label, where processing will continue.

OK, now that you've seen how the error handler will work, it's time to give it a go.

**Try It Out**     **Creating an Error Handler**

**1.** Create a new procedure, called `ErrorHandling`:

```
Public Sub ErrorHandling()

  Dim dblResult As Double

  dblResult = 10 / InputBox("Enter a number:")

  MsgBox "The result is " & dblResult

End Sub
```

**2.** Run this procedure from the Immediate window, or by pressing *F5* when the cursor is in the procedure, enter a number and press OK. This simply divides a number by 10. Not very exciting, but it will allow us to generate some errors.

**3.** Run the procedure again and enter 0:

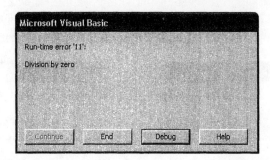

**4.** Press the **End** button, and run the code once more. This time don't enter anything, but just press **OK** straight away, and we receive a type mismatch error because the concatenation of `The result is` and `dblResult` fails when `dblResult` does not contain anything:

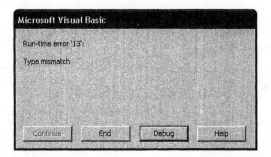

Press **End** once more. These are the two errors that we are going to trap.

**5.** Amend the code so that it looks like this:

```
Public Sub ErrorHandling()

   On Error GoTo ErrorHandling_Err

   Dim dblResult As Double

   dblResult = 10 / InputBox("Enter a number:")

   MsgBox "The result is " & dblResult

ErrorHandling_Exit:
   Exit Sub

ErrorHandling_Err:
   MsgBox "Oops: " & Err.Description & " - " & Err.Number
   Resume ErrorHandling_Exit

End Sub
```

**6.** Run the procedure again twice, re-creating the two errors – first entering 0 to get a division by zero, and then pressing OK without entering anything:

Notice that although the error details are the default ones, we've added a bit of our own code. There's also no option to debug – pressing OK just ends the procedure. Let's customize the error handling, checking for these errors.

**7.** Modify the code again, changing the error handling procedure to this:

```
ErrorHandling_Err:
  Select Case Err.Number
  Case 13          ' Type mismatch - empty entry
    Resume
  Case 11          ' Division by 0
    dblResult = 0
    Resume Next
  Case Else
    MsgBox "Oops: " & Err.Description & " - " & Err.Number
    Resume ErrorHandling_Exit
  End Select

Exit Sub
```

**8.** Now try to recreate the errors, and notice what happens. Entering 0 gives a result of 0, and a blank entry doesn't do anything – you're prompted again for a number.

### How It Works

Instead of VBA just displaying a default error message, we are checking the error Number:

```
Select Case Err.Number
```

From our previous examples we know the numbers of the two errors we need to trap. The first is for a Type Mismatch:

```
Case 13
  Resume
```

What we want to do here is just try again. A type mismatch indicates an incompatibility between variable types. In this case, we are trying to divide a number by an empty string, which is what is returned if nothing is entered in an InputBox. We just want the input box re-displayed; using Resume does this, because it continues on the line that caused the error. This sort of error is one reason why the results of an InputBox statement shouldn't be used directly in expressions.

For a division by 0, we also know the error number:

```
Case 11
   dblNumber = 0
   Resume Next
```

Here we just set the result of the division to 0 and the resume at the next line, which is the MsgBox statement.

For any other error we want to display the error details:

```
Case Else
   MsgBox "Oops: " & Err.Description & " - " & Err.Number
   Resume ErrorHandling_Exit
```

This uses a standard message box to display the error details, and then resumes execution at the procedure exit point. Since we don't know what the error is, it is safest just to end the procedure.

If you are handling errors you should always include an Else clause like this, to cater for unexpected situations, and so we are reporting unhandled errors back to the user.

## Using the Code Commenter and Error Handler Add-In

If you have bought Office XP Developer edition, then VBA comes with a rather neat Code Commenter and Error Handler Add-In that can add error handling code to all of your procedures automatically as well as put in a template for your comments.

It achieves this through templates that you create that contain a structure you want together with "tokens" that are replaced when you apply the template to your code.

To use this add-in you need to have run setup from the Office XP Developer CD and chosen to install the VBA Productivity Add-Ins. Once installed open the VBA window (Ctrl+F11) in Access and select Add-Ins | Add-In Manager. Now double-click on Code Commenter and Error Handler Add-In to load it:

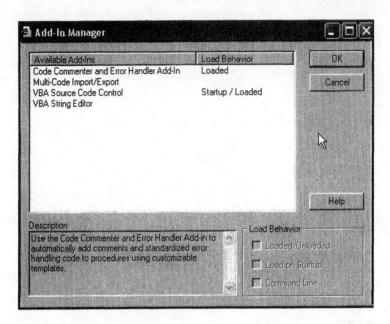

Click **OK** and then go back to the **Add-In** menu. You will see that the **Code Commenter and Error Handler Add-in** is now available.

The add-in can add an error handling template to all your procedures in the current project, procedures in the current module, or just the current procedure (the one that the cursor is in). It is quite simple to use but also very flexible because it is template based. Let's have a go at using it with a simple template of our own.

**Try It Out**     **Code Commenter and Error Handler Add-In**

**1.** Create the following function in a module:

```
Public Function MyFunction()
  'This function divides a number by a user entered number

  Dim dblResult      As Double    ' holds the result of the division

  dblResult = 10 / InputBox("Enter a number:")

  MsgBox "The result is " & dblResult
End Function
```

**2.** Click inside the function anywhere and Select Add-Ins | Code Commenter and Error Handler Add-in.

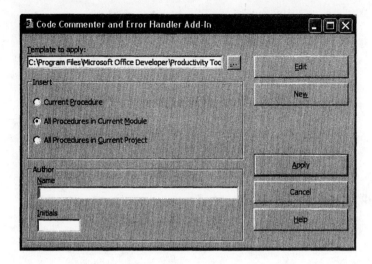

**3.** Click the New button to create a new template and open the template editor, then add the following. The text items prefixed with $$ are tokens that will be replaced later, and can be inserted by selecting them from the Insert menu

```
'$$ProcedureName Created by $$Author

$$HeaderComments
$$HeaderVariables

On Error Goto HandleErr

$$ProcedureBody

ExitHere:
  Exit $$ProcedureType

$$StartAuto
' Automatic error handler last updated at $$CurrentDate $$CurrentTime
HandleErr:
  Select Case Err.Number
    Case Else
      MsgBox "Error " & Err.Number & ": " & Err.Description, vbCritical,
"$$ProcedureAndModuleName"
  End Select
$$EndAuto
```

**4.** Close the Template Editor, and save the file as `Simple.eht`.

**5.** Now select your newly created `Simple.eht` template in the Template to Apply dialog.

**6.** Select Current Procedure from the Insert option buttons.

**7.** Enter your name in the Author textbox.

**8.** Click Apply.

You're done!

So what has it actually done. Well if look at your procedure now it will look like the following:

```
Public Function MyFunction()
'MyFunction Created by Ian Blackburn

   'This function divides a number by a user entered number

   Dim dblResult      As Double     ' holds the result of the division


On Error GoTo HandleErr

   dblResult = 10 / InputBox("Enter a number:")

   MsgBox "The result is " & dblResult

ExitHere:
   Exit Function

' Error handling block added by VBA Code Commenter and Error Handler Add-In.
DO NOT EDIT this block of code.
' Automatic error handler last updated at 03 December 2002 21:51:17
HandleErr:
   Select Case Err.Number
     Case Else
         MsgBox "Error " & Err.Number & ": " & Err.Description, vbCritical,
"Chapter 12 Code.MyFunction"
   End Select
' End Error handling block
End Function
```

We can see that it has taken our template and replaced the tokens (all those words prefixed with $$) with something more meaningful, and our procedure now has a nicely formatted error handler added to it, and the formatting has been improved somewhat. In fact there are many tokens that we can add to our templates as follows:

| Token | Meaning |
| --- | --- |
| $$Author | Author. Replaced with the current author name, that you enter in the dialog when you run the add-in. |
| $$Initials | Author initials from the add-in dialog. |

| Token | Meaning |
| --- | --- |
| $$CurrentDate | Current date, formatted as Windows short date. |
| $$CurrentTime | Current time, formatted as Windows short time. |
| $$HeaderComments | Header comments. This matches any number of comment lines or blank lines directly following the Sub, Function, or Property definition. |
| $$HeaderVariables | Header variables. This matches any number of Dim or Static lines directly following header comments. |
| $$ParameterList | Parameter list. Provides list of arguments to the current procedure. |
| $$ProcedureBody | The procedure body. |
| $$ProcedureName | The name of the procedure – it is replaced with the fully qualified procedure name, including the class name if it is a member of a class. |
| $$ProcedureAnd ModuleName | The name of the procedure and module in the form ModuleName.ProcedureName. Note that this token is not available from the Insert menu of the editor, but is a valid, useful token. |
| $$ProcedureType | Type of procedure. Replaced with Sub, Function, or Property as appropriate. |
| $$ProjectName | Project name. |
| $$StartAuto | Start auto. Used to flag the start of an inserted error handler. |
| $$EndAuto | End auto. Used to flag the end of an inserted error handler. |
| $$StartHeader | Start of header for Code Commenter and Error Handler. |
| $$EndHeader | End of header for Code Commenter and Error Handler. |

Note, however, that for the template to be valid, the file must contain at least the following tokens: $$ProcedureBody plus either $$StartHeader and $$EndHeader, or $$StartAuto and $$EndAuto, and these tokens must start on their own lines. If not then an error will occur when attempting to apply the file.

## Form Errors

The above examples have mentioned VBA errors, but in Access there are errors associated with forms. If an error occurs during processing in a form, such as an "Index or primary key cannot contain a Null value" error when adding a new record without a value for a primary key the Form_Error event is generated. This is just a normal event procedure, giving you the details of the error and allowing you to decide whether you want to handle the error, or whether you want Access to handle it:

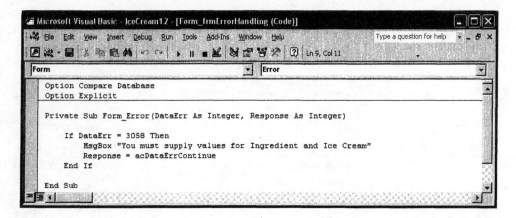

The first argument, DataErr, is the error number, and can be used in the same way as the Err.Number shown earlier.

The second argument, Response, is an output argument, so you set this in the procedure to tell Access what to do about the error. You can set it to acDataErrContinue and Access will ignore the error and continue with your code, allowing you to use your own error messages instead of the default ones. If you set it to acDataErrDisplay, which is the default, then Access displays its error message. Let's look at an example of this.

### Try It Out — The Form_Error Event

**1.** In the main database window, select Tables, and open tblIceCreamIngredient.

**2.** From the toolbar, select the AutoForm button:

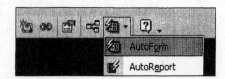

This creates a new form for you.

3. On the new form, add a new record (use the navigation buttons or New Record from the Insert menu).

4. Select Apples for the Ingredient ID and leave the Ice Cream ID blank.

5. Navigate to the previous record, and you'll see the following error:

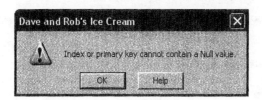

A pretty scary error message; and certainly not one we would like a user to see. The problem is that both of the ID fields are part of a unique primary key, which means that they both have to be filled in. We left one field blank, which is not allowed. We need to replace the default Access error message with one of our own.

6. Press OK to get back to the form and then press *Escape* to clear the record.

7. Switch the form into Design view and click the Code button on the toolbar to create a code module for this form.

8. In the form's Error event, add the following code:

```
If DataErr = 3058 Then
  MsgBox "You must supply values for Ice Cream and Ingredient IDs"
  Response = acDataErrContinue
End If
```

9. Back in Access, switch the form back into Form view and try the same procedure again – selecting only one of the ID values and then navigating away from the record. This time you get a more useful message:

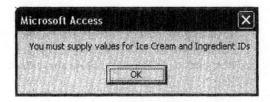

10. Close the form, saving it as frmErrorHandling.

Notice that when you save the form, the default name you are prompted to save it as is actually `tblIceCreamIngredient`. This is purely down to the fact that you created the form (using AutoForm) based upon this table.

**How It Works**

We know that the error number we need to trap is 3058. How to we know? Well there are two easy ways. The first is just to do what we did – create the same code as above, this time using an error number of 1, and put a breakpoint on the line. Then create the error, and when the breakpoint is triggered just see what the value of DataErr is, and then change the 1 to the correct number. The second method is to look up the error number, either in the help or in the error numbers table, as described in the next section.

Once we know what the error number is we can just output our own message, and set Response to tell Access that we are handling the error and it shouldn't display its own message. It's as simple as that.

You can use this technique for all sorts of errors that might violate the database, such as index errors or data integrity errors.

## Access and VBA Errors

If you want to know what the standard Access and VBA error numbers are, it's quite simple. There are two procedures in the MS Office XP Developer help files for this, under **Microsoft Access Visual Basic Reference: Error Codes**. Both of these procedures are in the **Chapter 12 Code** in IceCream.mdb. You should note that these procedures use ADO and ADO Extensions, so if you want to use them in your own databases you need to go to the **References** option in the **Tools** menu when in the VBE. Select both **Microsoft ActiveX Data Objects 2.1 Library** and **Microsoft ADO Ext. 2.5 for DDL and Security** (or a later version). Running these procedures create tables with the error numbers and descriptions in them.

> *To download extra documentation on Office XP including lists of error codes go to* http://msdn.microsoft.com/library/default.asp?url=/library/en-us/xpreskit/html/appa17.asp *and download the* OrkDocs.exe *file.*

## Data-Access Errors

So far we've talked about VBA errors, but there are plenty of occasions when errors are generated in response to data access, when using databases, recordsets, and so on, and in this case you need a way to access the error details. Remember how we said that the Err object relates to VBA errors? That means there must be another method for handling data-access errors.

### Data-Access Objects

When using DAO, there is an Errors collection, which contains Error objects. Each Error object contains a single piece of information about an error. When using DAO methods a single SQL statement can results in multiple errors being generated, and thus multiple Error objects in the Errors collection

This means that there are two places you must check for errors – the `Err` object and the `Errors` collection. If a DAO error occurs then `Err` is set to indicate this, as well as the `Errors` collection being filled. However, the reverse isn't true – a VBA run-time error only ever fills `Err`. You can examine the `Err.Source` property in VBA to determine if the error is a result of a DAO operation or something else.

**Try It Out — The Errors Collection**

**1.** Create a new procedure called `ShowErrors` and add the following code:

```
Public Sub ShowErrors()

  Dim db   As Database
  Dim recT As Recordset
  Dim errE As Error

  On Error GoTo ShowErrors_Err

  Set db = CurrentDb()
  Set recT = db.OpenRecordset("NonExistantTable")
  recT.Close

ShowErrors_Exit:
  Exit Sub

ShowErrors_Err:
  Debug.Print "Err = " & Err.Number & ": " & Err.Description
  Debug.Print

  For Each errE In DBEngine.Errors
    Debug.Print "Errors: " & errE.Number & ": " & errE.Description
  Next
  Resume ShowErrors_Exit

End Sub
```

**2.** Run the procedure from the **Immediate** window. You'll see two copies of the same error are printed:

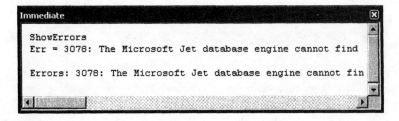

505

**3.** Now add the following line of code, directly before the `OpenRecordset` line:

```
Forms!frmCompany.Caption = "A new caption"
```

**4.** Run the procedure again:

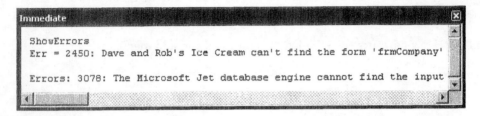

```
ShowErrors
Err = 2450: Dave and Rob's Ice Cream can't find the form 'frmCompany'

Errors: 3078: The Microsoft Jet database engine cannot find the input
```

### How It Works

The first time the procedure was run, we tried to open a recordset on a table that doesn't exist, so this generated an error. We jumped down to the error routine, which printed out the contents of both the `Err` object and the `Errors` collection. Since this was a DAO error, both of these are the same. This shows that when the DAO error is generated, the details are put into the `Err` object as well as the `Errors` collection.

The second time around though, the first error is that we try to set the property of a form that isn't open. This is a VBA run-time error – 2450. As soon as this is generated, the procedure jumps to the error routine, prints the error details, and exits. That means that the `OpenRecordset` hasn't been called. So why does the `Errors` collection still show an error? Remember how we said that a DAO method call clears the `Errors` collection – well we haven't yet done a DAO method call, so the `Errors` collection still holds the details of the previous errors.

This shows that the `Err` object and the `Errors` collection can hold different things, and that they both should be checked. The `Err` object always contains the details of the error, whether it is a VBA or a DAO error. You should compare the error number held in the `Err` object with that held in the `Errors` collection and if the numbers are different, then it is a VBA error. If the numbers are the same, you might want to loop through the `Errors` collection, in case there are any further DAO errors. In the example above, the DAO error only generated one error, but ODBC errors nearly always generate more. Have a look at this screenshot:

```
ODBCErr
Err = 3146: ODBC--call failed.

Errors: 547: [Microsoft][ODBC SQL Server Driver][SQL Server]INSERT statement c
Errors: 3621: [Microsoft][ODBC SQL Server Driver][SQL Server]Command has been
Errors: 3146: ODBC--call failed.
```

This shows the result of trying to add a record to a table linked with ODBC from a SQL Server database. The details we tried to add were incorrect and violated some SQL Server rules, so an ODBC error was generated. Notice that Err shows that this is an ODBC error, and this error matches the last error in the Errors collection. There are two other error messages that SQL Server has generated, and these have been added to the collection first. This means, that to have a proper error routine you should really check Err against the last Error object in the Errors collection, in a similar way to this:

```
Dim errE As Error

' ' '

If Err.Number = DBEngine.Errors(DBEngine.Errors.Count - 1).Number Then
   Debug.Print "Data Access Error"
   For Each errE In DBEngine.Errors
     Debug.Print "Errors: " & errE.Number & ": " & errE.Description
   Next
Else
   Debug.Print "VBA run-time Error"
   Debug.Print "Err = " & Err.Number & ": " & Err.Description
End If
```

This uses the Count property of the Errors collection to see how many errors there are. We subtract one from it because the Errors collection is zero based, and this gives us the last object in the collection. We can then compare this against the Err object to see whether it is a VBA error or a DAO error.

## ActiveX Data Objects

Although we are concentrating on DAO in this book, we need to briefly cover the same sort of things in ADO. Luckily there's not too much difference, as ADO has an Errors collection too, with similar properties, so you can use similar code.

With DAO, the Errors collection belongs to the DBEngine object, but in ADO it belongs to the Connection object. So our code might look something like this:

```
Dim db As New ADODB.Connection
Dim recT As New ADODB.Recordset
Dim errE As ADODB.Error

On Error GoTo ShowErrors_Err

db.Open "DSN=pubs", "sa", ""
recT.Open " NonExistantTable ", db, adOpenKeyset, _
   adLockOptimistic, adCmdTable
recT.Close

ShowErrors_Exit:
   Exit Sub
```

```
ShowErrors_Err:
  Debug.Print "Err = " & Err.Number & ": " & Err.Description
  Debug.Print

  For Each errE In db.Errors
    Debug.Print "Errors: " & errE.Number & ": " & errE.Description
  Next
  Resume ShowErrors_Exit
```

This example uses an ODBC DSN to connect to a SQL Server database, and the ODBC driver has good error reporting. The native OLEDB Providers seem to return less error information. For multiple errors, ADO also returns the error details in the opposite order to DAO, so you should compare the first member in the collection against Err, rather than the last.

## User Defined Errors

Much has been said about Access errors, but you can also define your own errors. This is very useful because it allows you to create a specific error in your procedure if something happens, then handle it in the same way as built-in errors. It also allows you to trigger the default error routines yourself without actually having an error occur.

Using the Raise method of the Err object generates user defined errors. All this does is cause the object to report an error in the normal way. The difference is that you must supply an error number. This can be a VBA standard error number, such as 13 for Type Mismatch, or one of your own that is outside the range VBA uses. The highest number is 65535, but VBA doesn't itself use anything above 31999 so you have plenty to choose from, however user-defined errors should always be outside the range of error numbers reserved by Access, DAO, and ADO.

**Try It Out          Raising Errors**

1. Open the ErrorHandling procedure that you were looking at earlier and modify the code to read as follows:

```
Public Sub ErrorHandling()

  Dim dblResult As Double
  Dim VarNumber As Variant

  On Error GoTo ErrorHandling_Err

  VarNumber = InputBox("Enter a number:")
  If Not IsNumeric(VarNumber) Then
    Err.Raise 32000
  End If
  dblResult = 10 / VarNumber
  MsgBox "The result is "& str$(dblResult)
```

```
ErrorHandling_Exit:
  Exit Sub

ErrorHandling_Err:
  Select Case Err.Number
  Case 13 ' Type mismatch - empty entry
    Resume
  Case 11 ' Divide by zero
    dblResult = 0
    Resume Next
  Case Else
    MsgBox Err.Description & " - " & Err.Number
    Resume ErrorHandling_Exit
  End Select

End Sub
```

Now, if the entry is not numeric, the error routine is called with an error number of 32000. However, to prevent conflicts with Access, make sure that you always use numbers 32000 and above for your code.

If you don't explicitly handle your user-defined errors, but simply use a message box to display the standard error text, you'll get the message **Application-defined or object-defined error**.

```
MsgBox Err.Description & " - " & Err.Number
```

For example, this would display the message **Application-defined or object-defined error –** 32000, if used in the previous procedure.

**2.** Now modify the error handling routine so that it has an extra selection:

```
Case 32000
  MsgBox "Must be a number"
  Resume ErrorHandling_Exit
```

**3.** Run the procedure and enter a letter. The new error handler processes the error number 32000 in exactly the same way as other errors. So now the function displays our own message.

## The Error Stack

Because Access is event-driven, it is constantly running small pieces of code that correspond to events. As each procedure is entered, the error handler is reset, and so any error is treated as the only error. Access does not keep a list of errors, but responds to them as they occur. This is fairly sensible, but you need to understand where Access looks for the error-handling code.

When an error occurs, Access backtracks through its currently active procedures looking for an error-handling routine and executes the first one it finds. If it does not find one, the default error handler routine is called.

For example, let's imagine that you have three procedures, A, B, and C. A calls B, and B in turn calls C. If C generates an error, Access will backtrack through B to A, looking for an error routine. If it does not find one in B or A, it calls the default routine.

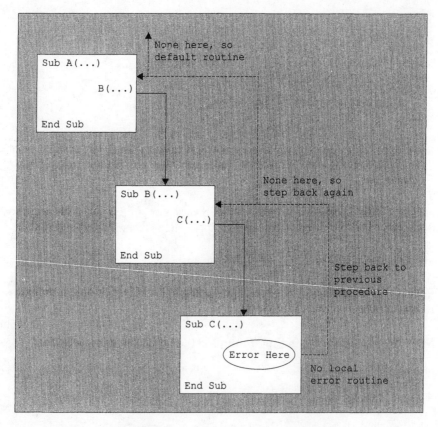

Note that this does not affect the flow of control in the program if no errors occur, as procedure C is still currently active. The backward arrows just show what Access does when searching for an error routine.

Now suppose that you need to add a little more meaning to this default error routine so you decide to create your own. Do you put a routine in each of A, B and C, or do you make use of the backtracking feature and just put it in A? Clearly, if you are dealing with similar errors, it makes sense to have one error routine and, because of the backtracking, it is also sensible to put it at the highest level.

Now imagine that you have the following error-handling code in procedure A, and none in the other procedures:

```
A_Err:
   Select Case Err.Number
   Case w ' Dangerous, so quit
     Resume A_Exit
   Case x ' Safe to carry on to next line
     Resume Next
   Case y ' Retry again
     Resume
   Case z ' A default error, let Access 2000 handle it
     Err.Raise q
   End Select
```

This seems straightforward, but there is one serious drawback. This can change the program flow. Neither `Resume` nor `Resume Next` continues execution in procedure C, as you would think, but at the current line in the procedure that handles the error. This is because the error handler is scoped to procedure A and sees the call to procedure B as a single line of code (which just happens to call another procedure; see diagram below).

So `Resume` will resume execution at the line that called procedure B – this is the current line in procedure A.

Likewise, `Resume Next` will continue on the line after the call to procedure B. Notice that neither method will return execution to procedure C. Have a look at this diagram to see what happens:

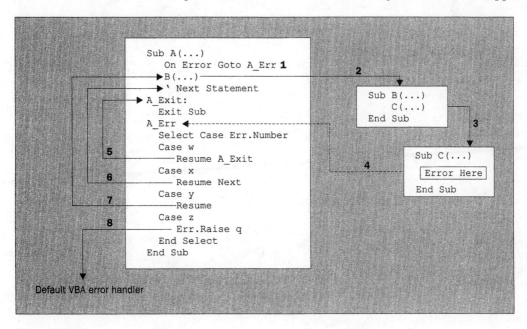

1. Error handling is initialized in `Sub A`

2. `Sub A` calls `Sub B`

3. `Sub B` calls `Sub C`

4. An error occurs in `Sub C` and the error handler in `Sub A` catches it

5. In this case execution is resumed at label `A_Err:`

6. `Resume Next` means execution will resume at the line after the call to `Sub B`

7. `Resume` means the call to `Sub B` is executed

8. `Err.Raise` takes us to the default VBA error handler

This clearly shows the danger of using a single routine for errors. However, it can also be useful – the thing to do is to be aware of this and plan accordingly. You can, for example, have a single error routine in A, and then another in C. The one in C would handle errors generated there, allowing continuation in non-fatal circumstances, whereas the one in A could be used to cope with errors from A and B. You could also use `Err.Raise` in C to force Access to move the error handler up to the next level. For example, look at the following code:

```
Sub C()

  On Error GoTo c_Err

  Dim intOne As Integer

  intOne = 123456789
  intOne = "wrong"

C_Exit:
  Exit Sub

C_Err:
  Select Case Err.Number
  Case 13
    MsgBox "C: Error " & Err.Number & ": " & Err.Description
  Case Else
    Err.Raise Err.Number, "C", Err.Description
  End Select
  Resume C_Exit

End Sub
```

This procedure has an error handler that checks the error number. If it is error 13 (Type Mismatch), then the error is displayed here, but any other error is handled by sending the error back up to the calling procedure. This is done by using the `Raise` method of the `Err` object, which in effect fires the error off again. The three arguments are the error number, the source (in this case the procedure C), and the description. The actual code of the procedure only consists of two lines, both of which generate errors. The first sets an integer variable to a very large value, which will cause an overflow – this is not error 13, and so will raise the error again. The second line generates error 13, and so would be handled here. In this example, you would have to comment out setting the variable to the large value before you could generate this error though, as they can't both happen. Let's look at a procedure that calls this one:

```
Sub B()

   Dim intI As Integer

   Debug.Print "In B"

   Call C

   Debug.Print "In B: setting intI to 123456789"

   intI = 123456789

End Sub
```

This procedure just calls procedure C and then generates its own error – an overflow. It has no error handling of its own, so Access will search back through the call tree to find an error handler, and in this example, it's in procedure A:

```
Sub A()

   On Error GoTo A_Err

   Debug.Print "In A"

   Call B

   Debug.Print "In A: 2 / 0 = " & 2 / 0
A_Exit:
   Exit Sub

A_Err:
   MsgBox "A (" & Err.Source & "): Error " & Err.Number & _
      ": " & Err.Description
   Resume A_Exit

End Sub
```

This does have an error handler, which displays the source of the error, the number, and the description. Let's review the procedures:

- ❑ A calls B, which calls C
- ❑ C has its own error handler, but this only handles error 13 – all others are sent back to B
- ❑ B does not have its own error handler, so it sends the error back to A
- ❑ The handler in A displays the error message

This shows you can handle some errors locally, but still have a general error handler to cope with the others. The Source property of the Err object allows you to identify where the error was generated.

# Debugging your Debugging Code

There may be times when you have added some error-handling routines but these themselves have errors in them. What you do in these circumstances is go to the **Tools** menu, pick **Options**, and then select the **Advanced** pane. Among the **Coding Options** group is **Break on All Errors**:

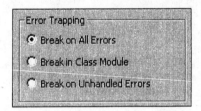

If you turn on this option, Access will ignore your error-handling routines and always use the default. This allows you to code error routines as you create your application, but have the option to turn your error routines off for debugging purposes.

# Summary

If you've been reading between the lines, you may have realized that the underlying message in this chapter is **planning**. A huge amount of effort goes into tracking down problems in software, and even a little forethought would reduce this wasted, and expensive, time. It always pays off in the end.

Part of this planning process is pre-empting the user. Try to think of the things that they do, so that your program is easy to use. Try not to get into the position where an error message leads them into thinking they've done something wrong – we call this rude software. It's just cruel popping up horrible error messages telling them they've done something wrong. If you can write your program in a way that doesn't allow them to do wrong things, then you've got less of a problem trying to handle those unforeseen errors.

So, in this chapter we've looked at:

❑ What errors are, and how you should design your program to minimize them

❑ The type of testing you should use

❑ How to debug your application if you do find errors

❑ How to write error-handling code

It would be great if you never had to reference this chapter again. Not because you've remembered what was in it, but because you don't need to. However you probably will have to do some debugging at one stage or another, so learning what to do and how to prevent it can only make your life easier. Another method of preventing errors is using object orientation, and that's the topic of the next chapter.

# Exercises

1. Examine the forms in the sample database. Do you think that any error routines could be removed and a global error routine used instead? What would be the disadvantage of this?

2. Having thought about a central error routine, create one. Give it two arguments: strProc, which should be the name of the procedure that calls the routine, and optionally, strDesc, for a general description. The routine should check to see if the error was a VBA error or a Data-Access error, and display any messages in a message box, along with the procedure that called the routine, and the additional text.

3. List three types of testing you can perform on an application. Now take any application you have created, and test it, using these three methods. Swallow you pride and ask a colleague to do the same – does you application pass?

# CHAPTER 13

# Using Classes

Back in Chapters 4 and 5, we introduced the concept of object-oriented programming. We looked at the Access object model and the Data Access Object hierarchy and how working with these different types of objects is really at the heart of programming in VBA. In this chapter, we are going to look at how we can create our own objects and how we can extend the functionality of Access and VBA.

For many people, the idea of object-orientation seems a bit scary. There are all those long words like **instantiation, encapsulation, inheritance,** and (my favorite) **polymorphism**. Not to worry – the implementation of class modules and user-defined objects in Access 2000 is actually fairly simple. It may not give you the flexibility of tools such as Visual C++, but what that means in turn is that it is very easy to pick up. Hopefully, this chapter will show you just how easy it is, and by the time you finish you should have added a very powerful tool to your programming armory.

We'll be looking at the following topics in this chapter:

- ❑ What objects are
- ❑ The benefits of object-based programming
- ❑ Building and instantiating custom objects
- ❑ Building object hierarchies through collections
- ❑ Custom properties and methods for forms
- ❑ Creating multiple instances of a form

# Class Modules and Custom Objects

Remember back in Chapters 4 and 5 we looked at the two primary groups of objects that we work with in Access. The Access objects themselves – including `Form`, `Report`, and `Module` objects – allow us to manipulate the composition of an Access application whereas the Data Access Object hierarchy – including `TableDef`, `QueryDef`, and `Recordset` objects – allows us to access and modify the data in tables programmatically. We are going to spend a little time now reviewing the basics in a little more detail, before we examine how Access provides developers with the capability to create their own custom objects through the use of class modules.

## What Are Objects?

Object-oriented development has been a hot topic for quite a few years now, but for many people the topic is one still shrouded in mystery. It often involves obscure jargon and seemingly acrobatic mental leaps and many of the tools that are provided to implement object-oriented development have a steep learning curve. The end result is that many regard it as a black art to be practiced only by the brave, which is a shame, because the principles behind object-orientation are really fairly straightforward, once you get beyond the jargon.

So let's start with the basics and find out what objects really are. There are many definitions of what an object is, but we'll use a simple one to start with and say this:

> An **object** is a self-contained entity that is characterized by a recognizable set of characteristics and behaviors.

For example, think of a dog as an object. Dogs are certainly recognizable by their characteristics and their behavior. If we were to put some of these down on paper we might come up with a list like this:

| Characteristics | Behaviors |
| --- | --- |
| They are hairy | They bark |
| They have four legs | They bite mailmen |
| They have a tail | They sniff things |
| Size | |
| Color | |
| Smell | |

Now, if you were to ask anyone what is hairy, has four legs and a tail, and barks, bites, and sniffs things, there aren't many people who wouldn't instantly know that you were talking about a dog – you would have described to them quite succinctly the characteristics and behavior of a dog.

In fact, what you would be describing was not any single dog. Rather, you were describing the characteristics and behavior of all dogs. In one sense, what makes a dog a dog is that it is like all other dogs. Sure, there are some minor differences, in size, color (and smell), but all dogs have a certain dogginess. Now, before you start to think that you are reading a book on canine philosophy, let's apply that to the world of software. An object-oriented programmer would have summarized those last couple of paragraphs like this:

❑ There exists a **class** called Dog

❑ **Instances** of this Dog **class** have the following **properties**: Hairiness, Four-Leggedness, Tailedness, Size, Color, Smelliness

❑ **Instances** of this Dog class expose the following **methods**: Bark, Bite, Sniff

OK, so let's look at some of that jargon. First of all – **classes**. A **class** is a type of blueprint or mold. In the case of animals that blueprint is genetic. If the objects we were talking about were candles, the blueprint would be the mold into which the wax is poured.

Individual dogs and candles are **instances** of their particular class, and as such they inherit the characteristics of the class to which they belong. Dogs bark because that is a characteristic of the Dog class. So we can now define a class.

*A **class** is a blueprint or template that defines the methods and properties of a particular type of object.*

Now, let's have a look at an object in the Data Access Object hierarchy with which we are already familiar – the Recordset object – and see how it fits into our model. First of all we can say that all Recordset objects have the same properties and methods. The properties include things like the RecordCount property, which is the number of records in the Recordset object, and the Updatable property, which indicates whether the Recordset object can be updated. The methods include the GetRows method, which takes a given number of records and places them into an array. All Recordset objects possess the same built-in methods and properties, because they are all derived from the same class. As Access developers we cannot see the class itself – all we see are the objects that are instantiated from that class. The class itself (CDaoRecordset) was defined by Microsoft developers using the language C. What we see in VBA are instances of that class.

# Why Use Objects?

In many respects, this question doesn't even make sense in modern programming. Everything that you manipulate in Access is an object, from forms and reports, to the controls that you place on those forms and reports, to the database and recordset objects that you use to manipulate data. You have already used many different objects in the lessons that you have completed so far, in fact if you use the properties and methods of forms and controls, you are using objects whether you realize it or not.

Given their ubiquitous nature, we need to understand and be comfortable with the lingo that surrounds them Hopefully, this section will blow away some of the mystique that surrounds the long words that plague object orientation. The major benefits of using classes to create custom objects in Access originate from the principles of abstraction, encapsulation, and polymorphism. We'll have a look at what those mean right now.

## Abstraction

One of the more important advantages of using classes is gained through something called **abstraction**. What that means is simply that users of the object shouldn't have to know the nitty-gritty of how the object does what it does. In other words, the developer doesn't need to worry about technicalities. It is a bit like turning an electric light on. People don't need to know anything about voltage, current, and resistance. All they need to know is how to flick a switch. They are removed from the physics that results in the bulb lighting and the room getting brighter.

We can see how this works with built-in DAO objects such as the `Recordset` object. All we need to do is to use the `Requery` method and somehow the `Recordset` object is repopulated with a more recent set of data. How does it do it? Who cares! All we need to know is that it works. And that is cool, because it means that we can spend more time developing our application rather than worrying about the low-level details of things like cursor functionality. The methods and properties of the object are called its **interface** because that is how it communicates with or interfaces to other objects.

> *The interface is that part of an object that is exposed on the outside to users of the object; it defines how we are allowed to interact with the object. The implementation is the code, internal to the class and invisible from the outside, which is responsible for defining how the object does what it does. If the lighting in your house was implemented as an object, the interface would consist of the light switches and lamps, and the implementation would consist of the electrical wiring.*

We can do the same with the custom objects that we build using class modules. In fact one of our goals when creating objects using class modules should be to keep the interface as simple as possible, irrespective of how complicated the implementation might be.

Abstraction means we can use objects without having to know the software details of how the object does what it does. This makes them easy to use and is one of the key advantages of using classes to define custom objects in Access. Such objects are often referred to as "Black Boxes" since you can't see past the interface to see how they really work inside.

## Encapsulation

Closely related to abstraction is the idea of **encapsulation**. Objects should encapsulate within them everything they need to allow them to do what they do. That means that they should contain their own methods, properties, and data – and it means that they don't need to rely on other objects to allow them to exist or to perform their own actions.

As we saw in Chapter 5, `Forms` and `Reports` are types of objects. They illustrate encapsulation quite well – if you use VBA for your event procedures you can import a form into another database and all the controls on the form and the code in its module go over with it. It's all encapsulated in the form.

Another good example of encapsulation is an ActiveX control such as the `Calendar` control. The `Calendar` control carries with it – or encapsulates – its own methods and properties, which are immediately accessible to you when you place it on a form. You could even think of this as a kind of software Plug-and-Play technology for developers: one programmer writes a component – and that component can simply be plugged into another program and function properly.

Encapsulation makes it easy to reuse classes because everything needed by the class to do it's job is available internally, there is no need to reference external code. This can not only speed up subsequent development projects that use these objects, but it also allows us to apply business rules consistently and makes group development much easier. This reusability is a key benefit of building our own custom objects in Access – if we do it right!

Of course there are cases where objects interact with or rely on other objects. As an example, the recordset object is not truly self contained since it requires the database object to open its dataset for it. You will find instances where you will need to develop systems of classes, each class doing its part in the larger task. The principal of encapsulation remains, however; as much as possible each class should contain all of the properties and methods required to do its part of the task, and should hide the complexity of the implementation details.

## Polymorphism

What a great word! The concept is pretty cool – it just means that you can have a whole load of disparate objects, but you can tell them all to do the same thing and they'll all know how to do it. Put another way, it means that objects can share the same methods and properties, but have different content behind the methods and properties to implement their behavior. For example, controls, forms, and pages in Access all have a SetFocus method. In all these cases, invoking the method shifts focus to the selected object, but the way they do it 'under the hood' is different in each case.

We can implement polymorphism in the custom objects we build in Access using class modules in two ways: through early binding and through late binding. We will look at both of these techniques later in this chapter.

> **The advantage of polymorphism is that we can present a familiar, consistent interface to the users of our custom objects, while hiding the differences in implementation.**

## Inheritance

Inheritance is mentioned here, as it is a fairly key concept of object-oriented design. What it means is that you can create a new class called a **subclass** that inherits all of the class's methods and properties. In the analogy we have been using, we could say that the Dog class is a subclass of the Mammal class. It therefore inherits the properties and methods of that class. The mammal class could have properties such as hairiness, four leggedness, and methods such as Runs and Eats. Such properties and methods can now be inherited from the Mammal class into a subclass Dog. The Dog class does not have to create such properties and methods since it can use the inherited ones.

> *Inheritance makes it easier to create new classes, as you are often able to simply sub-class an existing class and then add some specialization. However, there is no opportunity for this when using custom objects in Access, as VBA does not support it. Lack of inheritance is the largest single reason that VBA is not considered a true OO language.*

# The MyRectangle Class

That's enough of the theory. What we'll do now is build a fairly simple class so that we can analyze how Access implements the three features of OO that Access does provide us – abstraction, encapsulation, and polymorphism.

In fact, we will be creating a simple method of determining the area of a rectangle given its height and width. The formula that we use to calculate the area is quite straightforward:

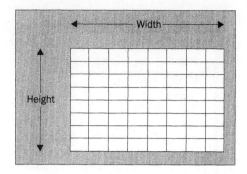

```
Area = Height x Width
```

However, we would like our programmers to be able to derive the area without having to remember even this bit of mathematics.

*This is, of course, a deliberately simple example. Later in the chapter, once we have got to grips with how class modules work, we will look at a more realistic example of using an object to hide the technicalities of some of the business rules used by the Ice Cream Shop.*

**Try It Out — Creating the MyRectangle Class**

**1.** Open up the `IceCream.mdb` database and switch to the VBA IDE by hitting *Alt+F11*.

**2.** Insert a new class module. You can do this either by selecting **Class Module** from the Insert menu or by hitting the **Insert Class Module** button on the toolbar.

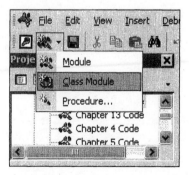

**3.** A new class called **Class1** should now appear in the **Project Explorer** window. If the **Properties** window is not visible, make it so by hitting *F4* and then change the name of the class to `MyRectangle`.

**4.** Now, in the code window, add the following declarations to the `Declarations` section of the class module.

```
Option Compare Database
Option Explicit

Private dblHeight As Double
Private dblWidth As Double
```

**5.** Next add the following two `Property Let` procedures making sure that you declare them with `Public` scope. Don't worry about the strange syntax; we will look at how they work in just a moment.

```
Public Property Let Height(dblParam As Double)
  If dblParam < 0 then
    dblHeight = -dblParam
  Else
    dblHeight = dblParam
  End if

End Property


Public Property Let Width(dblParam As Double)

  If dblParam < 0 then
    dblWidth = -dblParam
  Else
    dblWidth = dblParam
  End if

End Property
```

**6.** Now you should add the following three `Property Get` procedures as they appear below. Again, we will look at how they work later on.

```
Public Property Get Height() As Double

  Height = dblHeight

End Property

Public Property Get Width() As Double

  Width = dblWidth

End Property

Public Property Get Area() As Double

  Area = dblHeight * dblWidth

End Property
```

**7.** That is our class completed, so save the module as `MyRectangle` by hitting *Ctrl+S*.

**8.** Now create a new standard code module and call it `Chapter 13 Code`. Add the following procedure to the new module:

```
Sub ClassDemo()

Dim objRect As MyRectangle

Set objRect = New MyRectangle

objRect.Height = 5
objRect.Width = 8

Debug.Print "The area of a rectangle measuring " & objRect.Height & _
     " x " & objRect.Width & " is " & objRect.Area

Set objRect = Nothing

End Sub
```

**9.** Now run the `ClassDemo` procedure by typing its name in the Immediate window and hitting *Enter*. If you have typed everything in correctly, you should see the following result:

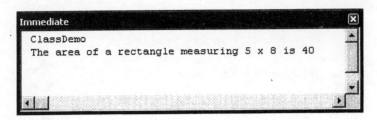

So there we have a fully functioning class that we can use to determine a rectangle's area whenever we want to!

## How It Works

In this exercise we created a MyRectangle class. This has three properties: Height, Width, and Area.

The first thing that we did was to create a new class by inserting a new class module into our project, a simple enough process. We then declared two private variables that would be used to store the dimensions of the height and width of the rectangle:

```
Private dblHeight As Double
Private dblWidth As Double
```

It is important to notice that these variables all have Private scope. That is to say that although available for use anywhere within the class module, they cannot be accessed from outside the class module. These are part of the implementation of the class; they are not part of its interface and their values can only be viewed or changed by code within the class module itself.

So how do developers specify the dimensions of the rectangle? The answer is that they set the object's Height and Width properties. We expose properties by using two special types of procedure. A Property Let procedure is used to expose a writeable property and a Property Get procedure is used to expose a readable property. In other words, we use a Property Let if we want developers to be able to let the object's property equal some value; and we use a Property Get if we want developers to be able to get (that is, read) the value of the property. If a property is to be readable and writeable then we use both a Property Get and a Property Let procedure.

We'll have a look first at one of the writeable properties:

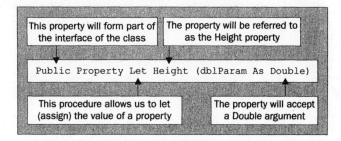

Before any methods or properties can be used, we must dimension the object and create an instance. We will look at that process in a few moments. Once the object has been created, a developer can set the value of the Height property like this:

```
objRect.Height = 5
```

When this happens, the value (5) is automatically passed into the Property Let procedure as the argument dblParam. One very important reason for using the property let/get instead of just making a class variable public is that we can do checking on the values passed in to prevent problems. In this example I checked whether the length passed in was negative, and if so, simply used the negative of the value passed in to correct the problem. We know that a length cannot be negative, and if we allowed it to be passed in we could end up with a negative area, so we correct that problem if it happens. We then place the original or corrected value into the module level Private variable dblHeight that we declared earlier.

```
If dblParam < 0 then
    dblHeight = -dblParam
Else
    dblHeight = dblParam
End if
```

The Area property is exposed as a read-only property. That means that we do not need a Property Let procedure, but use a Property Get procedure instead.

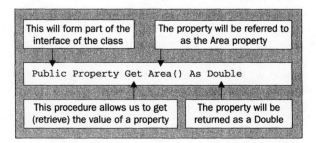

The value returned by the Area property is the result of multiplying the rectangle's height by its width.

```
Area = dblHeight * dblWidth
```

The Height and Width properties are readable and writeable because they each have a Property Get and a Property Let procedure. By contrast, the Area property is read-only because it has a Property Get procedure but no Property Let procedure.

Less commonly we may encounter write-only properties (that is properties whose values we can set but cannot inspect). The Password property of the User object in the DAO hierarchy is a write-only property. If we wanted to implement a write-only property in one of our class modules, we would do so by exposing the property via a Property Let procedure with no associated Property Get procedure.

> The point of this example is to show how you can hide a piece of logic behind a simple interface. In this case, the logic (working out the area of the rectangle) is very straightforward, but in many situations the logic stored within the implementation of object can be quite complex. In fact the more complex the logic, the more benefit can be realized by wrapping it up in an object with a simple interface.

That is really all there is to defining our class. What we end up with is a class that can be used to create MyRectangle objects. It has two read/write properties (Height and Width) and a read-only Area property.

When we want to use one of these MyRectangle objects, we create it using this syntax:

```
Dim objRect As MyRectangle

Set objRect = New MyRectangle
```

The first line creates a variable objRect designed to hold a **pointer** to the MyRectangle object. A pointer is a generic term for the thing that "points to" the actual memory used to store a variable. Note that at this stage the object has not been created, there is just a variable ready to reference the object once it is created. The second line is the one that actually instantiates (creates an instance of) a MyRectangle object and returns a reference to it as objRect.

You might have noticed as we were typing in the first line of code that the MyRectangle class actually appeared within the list of available object types.

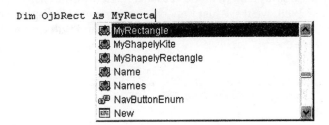

```
Dim OjbRect As MyRecta
```

The next step is to instantiate a `MyRectangle` and we do this by using the `New` keyword.

```
Set objRect = New MyRectangle
```

This is a key moment in the whole process. It is the programming equivalent of Dr. Frankenstein throwing the big switch on the wall and looking on in amazement as his creation comes to life. Whereas before we just had a lifeless class, we now have a living, breathing object. A `MyRectangle` object has been created and a reference to it is returned in the `objRect` variable. Oh, the rapture...

A little more prosaically, once the new `MyRectangle` object has been created, we can then set its `Height` and `Width` properties:

```
objRect.Height = 5
objRect.Width = 8
```

and then, we can inspect the object's `Height`, `Width`, and `Area` properties:

```
Debug.Print "The area of a rectangle measuring " & objRect.Height & _
       " x " & objRect.Width & " is " & objRect.Area
```

Again, notice that as we type in the lines above, we are prompted by IntelliSense with the names of the properties that we created because they form part of the object's public interface.

```
Debug.Print "The area of a rectangle measuring " & objRect.
                                                     Area
                                                     DoubleSides
                                                     Height
                                                     Width
```

Finally, once we have finished with our monster (sorry, object) we destroy it by setting it to `Nothing`, so releasing any resources that it was using up.

```
Set clsRect = Nothing
```

So, that's how easy it is to implement an object with readable and writeable properties. But what about methods? Well, we'll see just how easy that is now by implementing a new method for our `MyRectangle` object. The new `DoubleSides` method will double the height and width of the rectangle that we create.

**Extending the MyRectangle Class**

**1.** Open up the `MyRectangle` class module that we created in the previous exercise and add the following procedure definition:

```
Public Sub DoubleSides()

   dblHeight = dblHeight * 2
   dblWidth = dblWidth * 2

End Sub
```

**2.** Now open the `Chapter 13 Code` module, locate the `ClassDemo` procedure and add the following lines of code to it:

```
Debug.Print "The area of a rectangle measuring " & objRect.Height & _
     " x " & objRect.Width & " is " & objRect.Area

objRect.DoubleSides

Debug.Print "The area of a rectangle measuring " & objRect.Height & _
     " x " & objRect.Width & " is " & objRect.Area

Set objRect = Nothing
```

**3.** Now save the changes you have made and run the `ClassDemo` procedure in the **Immediate** window. This time the result you see should look like this:

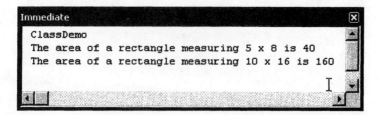

```
Immediate                                      ☒
ClassDemo
The area of a rectangle measuring 5 x 8 is 40
The area of a rectangle measuring 10 x 16 is 160

                                    I
◄                                            ►
```

As you can see, the `DoubleSides` method has doubled the rectangle's height and width (and the area has therefore increased four-fold).

To implement a method in our custom object, we simply need to add a public procedure to the class module. The procedure needs to be `Public`, because it forms part of the `MyRectangle` object's interface. This procedure can then be invoked as a method of the `MyRectangle` object.

It really is as simple as that!

Before we look in more detail at creating methods and properties, let's revisit those four concepts that we discussed earlier in relation to classes (abstraction, encapsulation, polymorphism, and inheritance) and see how they apply in this situation.

## Abstraction

The principle behind abstraction is producing a simple interface and hiding the complexity of the implementation. It's a bit like watching a swan gliding across the water. It looks so graceful you would think that there was nothing to it, but if you look underwater you will see that its legs are pumping away like there is no tomorrow! That's what we should aim for with our classes, a simple interface irrespective of the complexity of the implementation.

To be fair, the `MyRectangle` class does not contain any excessively complex logic. The calculation of the area is fairly straightforward. But that's because this is a deliberately simple example to show you how to build classes. In practice the logic implemented by a class's methods and properties might be exceedingly obscure and complicated. But users of the class won't need to worry about what is going on under the hood. They simply set or inspect the properties or invoke the methods and all the hard work is done by the object. Easy! Furthermore, by encapsulating all the functionality in one place, you can comment the code heavily and have a single place to go to discover how it works if you or your replacement ever has to revisit the implementation.

## Encapsulation

This is a strong point of the `MyRectangle` class. It is completely self-contained and doesn't rely on the existence of any other objects in order to allow it to operate properly. We could export this class into another database and it would function just as well there.

The other thing to notice is that the two key variables that hold the sizes of the height and width of the rectangle (`dblHeight`, `dblWidth`) are owned by the object itself (they are `Private`) and cannot be manipulated directly by external code. The only way that developers can interact with our `MyRectangle` object is through the interface we have defined, while the rest of the implementation is hidden away.

So our `MyRectangle` class scores highly for encapsulation.

## *Polymorphism*

This is a slightly tougher one. If you remember, polymorphism means that different objects can share the same methods and properties, but can have different content behind the methods and properties to implement their behavior. On its own the MyRectangle doesn't exhibit polymorphism, but we can see how we can introduce it if we define a new MyKite class.

A kite is a two-dimensional object whose area can be calculated by multiplying its height by its width and dividing by two:

```
Area = (Height x Width) / 2
```

So we can create a MyKite class to return an Area property like this:

```
Option Compare Database
Option Explicit

Private dblHeight As Double
Private dblWidth As Double


Public Property Let Height(dblParam As Double)

   dblHeight = dblParam

End Property


Public Property Let Width(dblParam As Double)

   dblWidth = dblParam

End Property


Public Property Get Height() As Double

   Height = dblHeight

End Property


Public Property Get Width() As Double

   Width = dblWidth

End Property


Public Property Get Area() As Double

   Area = (dblHeight * dblWidth) / 2
```

```
End Property

Public Sub DoubleSides()

   dblHeight = dblHeight * 2
   dblWidth = dblWidth * 2

End Sub
```

❑ You might find this section easier to follow if you build the MyKite class by using the code laid out in this section. Alternatively, you can find all of this code in the IceCream.mdb database.

Now if we wanted to determine the area of a kite, we could use our MyKite class to do this by writing a procedure such as this in a standard code module:

```
Sub ClassDemo2()

Dim objKite As MyKite

Set objKite = New MyKite

objKite.Height = 5
objKite.Width = 8

Debug.Print "The area of a kite measuring " & objKite.Height & _
      " x " & objKite.Width & " is " & objKite.Area

objKite.DoubleSides

Debug.Print "The area of a kite measuring " & objKite.Height & _
      " x " & objKite.Width & " is " & objKite.Area

Set objKite = Nothing

End Sub
```

If you run this code, you should see this in the **Immediate** window:

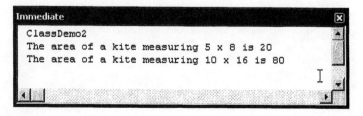

**533**

This should look fairly familiar! The MyRectangle class and the MyKite class share two read-write properties (Height and Width), a read-only Area property, and a DoubleSides method. We have implemented a form of polymorphism across our objects. So what good is that? Well, for one thing it makes it easier for the developer to learn how to use the objects, as there is just one interface to learn. We define the dimensions of the MyRectangle and MyKite objects with just the same syntax, and we can find their areas by inspecting the same property.

It also means that we can write a procedure that treats both MyRectangle and MyKite objects the same like this:

```
Function GetObjectArea(obj As Object, _
          dblHeight As Double, _
          dblWidth As Double) As Double


obj.Height = dblHeight
obj.Width = dblWidth
GetObjectArea = obj.Area

End Function
```

If we wanted to, we could pass a MyRectangle object to the GetObjectArea function:

```
Sub ClassDemo3()

Dim objRectangle As MyRectangle
Set objRectangle = New MyRectangle

Debug.Print "The rectangle's area is " & GetObjectArea(objRectangle, 5, 8)

Set objRectangle = Nothing

End Sub
```

Or we could pass a MyKite object in, just as easily:

```
Sub ClassDemo3a()

Dim objKite As MyKite
Set objKite = New MyKite

Debug.Print "The kite's area is " & GetObjectArea(objKite, 5, 8)

Set objKite = Nothing

End Sub
```

In both situations, the `GetObjectArea` function is able to use the object's `Height`, `Width`, and `Area` properties, irrespective of whether the object passed in is a `MyRectangle` object or a `MyKite` object.

```
obj.Height = dblHeight
obj.Width = dblWidth
GetObjectArea = obj.Area
```

The problem with this technique is that we have to use a generic object variable (the variable `obj` uses the `Object` data type). Because of this, VBA does not know what type of object will be stored in the variable and, as a result, we are not prompted with the names of the properties when we use the dot operator after the variable `obj`.

More importantly, if we mis-spell the name of one of the properties, VBA will not pick up this error when we compile our code. Instead, the first time we will know that we have got the property name wrong is when we try to run our code. So a line like this will not cause a compile-time error:

```
obj.Height = dblHeight
```

But when we try to run the `ClassDemo3` procedure, VBA will generate a run-time error.

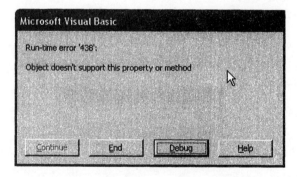

This is because VBA is using a technique known as **late binding**. Not only does late binding make it harder to ensure our code is error-free at design time; it also makes our code run slower. Fortunately, there is a better way to implement polymorphism.

*We will look at the performance implications of late binding later on in Chapter 19.*

## Polymorphism through Early Binding

Thus far the `MyRectangle` and `MyKite` objects share the same interface because we happened to give them both the same properties and methods. However, in VBA it is now possible to implement polymorphism through the use of the `Implements` keyword. We'll try this out for ourselves, and then investigate how it works and what its implications are.

**Using the Implements keyword**

1.  In the `IceCream.mdb` database insert a new class module and call it `Shape`.

2.  Add the following code in the code window of the `Shape` class:

```
Option Compare Database
Option Explicit

Public Property Let Height(dblParam As Double)
End Property

Public Property Get Height() As Double
End Property

Public Property Let Width(dblParam As Double)
End Property
Public Property Get Width() As Double
End Property

Public Property Get Area() As Double
End Property

Public Sub DoubleSides()
End Sub
```

3.  Now insert a new class module and call it `MyShapelyRectangle`.

4.  At the top of this new class module, add the following statement:

```
Option Compare Database
Option Explicit

Implements Shape
```

```
Private dblHeight As Double
Private dblWidth As Double
```

**5.** If you look in the object box at the top of the module window, you should see that there is now a reference to the Shape object.

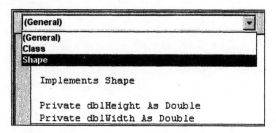

**6.** Select the Shape object and you should then be able to see the names of the available properties and methods in the procedure combo. Start by selecting the Height property:

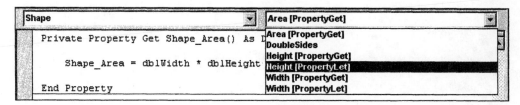

**7.** Add the following code to the Shape_Height property Let procedure and the Shape_Height property Get procedure:

```
Private Property Let Shape_Height(RHS As Double)

    dblHeight = RHS

End Property


Private Property Get Shape_Height() As Double

    Shape_Height = dblHeight

End Property
```

**8.** Now add the code for the remaining two properties and for the DoubleSides method. The completed module should now look like this:

```
Option Compare Database
Option Explicit
```

```
Implements Shape

Private dblHeight As Double
Private dblWidth As Double

Private Property Get Shape_Area() As Double

  Shape_Area = dblWidth * dblHeight

End Property

Private Sub Shape_DoubleSides()

  dblWidth = dblWidth * 2
  dblHeight = dblHeight * 2

End Sub

Private Property Let Shape_Height(RHS As Double)

  dblHeight = RHS

End Property

Private Property Get Shape_Height() As Double

  Shape_Height = dblHeight

End Property

Private Property Let Shape_Width(RHS As Double)

  dblWidth = RHS

End Property

Private Property Get Shape_Width() As Double

  Shape_Width = dblWidth

End Property
```

9. Next, create a new `MyShapelyKite` class and repeat Steps 4 to 8. However, this time, make sure to define the `Shape_Area` property so that it returns half of the width multiplied by the height. The resultant `MyShapelyKite` module should look like this:

```
Option Compare Database
Option Explicit

Implements Shape
```

```
Private dblHeight As Double
Private dblWidth As Double

Private Property Get Shape_Area() As Double

  Shape_Area = (dblWidth * dblHeight) / 2

End Property

Private Sub Shape_DoubleSides()

  dblWidth = dblWidth * 2
  dblHeight = dblHeight * 2

End Sub

Private Property Let Shape_Height(RHS As Double)

  dblHeight = RHS

End Property

Private Property Get Shape_Height() As Double

  Shape_Height = dblHeight

End Property

Private Property Let Shape_Width(RHS As Double)

  dblWidth = RHS

End Property

Private Property Get Shape_Width() As Double

  Shape_Width = dblWidth

End Property
```

**10.** Now open the code module Chapter 13 Code, which you created earlier in this chapter, and add the following three procedures:

```
Function GetShapeArea(shp As Shape, _
          dblHeight As Double, _
          dblWidth As Double) As Double

shp.Height = dblHeight
shp.Width = dblWidth
GetShapeArea = shp.Area
```

```
End Function

Sub ClassDemo4()

Dim shpRectangle As Shape
Set shpRectangle = New MyShapelyRectangle

Debug.Print "The rectangle's area is " & GetShapeArea(shpRectangle, 5, 8)

Set shpRectangle = Nothing

End Sub

Sub ClassDemo4a()

Dim shpKite As Shape
Set shpKite = New MyShapelyKite

Debug.Print "The kite's area is " & GetShapeArea(shpKite, 5, 8)

Set shpKite = Nothing

End Sub
```

**11.** Finally, run the `ClassDemo4` and `ClassDemo4a` subprocedures in the Immediate window. You should see the correct results:

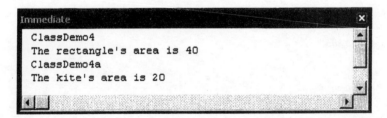

So now we have two separate objects, the `MyShapelyKite` and the `MyShapelyRectangle` objects, sharing a single common interface define by the `Shape` class module. "So what?" you might say! Well, just as in the previous example, we can treat these two objects the same (that is they can both be passed in to the `GetShapeArea` procedure). The key difference, however is that this time we are using **early binding**. That means that not only will our code execute more quickly at run time, but also we are much less likely to make mistakes when we write our code in the first place. Let's look at how it works.

The first thing that we do in this exercise is to create a dummy interface class called Shape. The purpose of this class is purely to provide a common interface that other classes can then use to provide their own interface services.

As you can see, the only thing that this class contains is the definitions for the methods and properties that will appear in the interface.

```
Option Compare Database
Option Explicit

Public Property Let Height(dblParam As Double)
End Property

Public Property Get Height() As Double
End Property

Public Property Let Width(dblParam As Double)
End Property

Public Property Get Width() As Double
End Property

Public Property Get Area() As Double
End Property

Public Sub DoubleSides()
End Sub
```

As in the previous examples, the interface for this class will contain read-write Height and Width properties, both of which accept a Double value, and one read-only Area property, which returns a Double. There is also a DoubleSides method.

Note how the Shape class contains only the definitions for the methods and properties. There is no code to explain how these methods and properties will be implemented. So the interface is now totally separate from the implementation (Object Nirvana!).

The next step is to instruct VBA that the MyShapelyRectangle and MyShapelyKite classes will use the Shape class to provide their interface. We do that by using the Implements keyword in the Declarations section of the MyShapelyRectangle and MyShapelyKite class modules.

```
Implements Shape
```

When you insert an `Implements` statement into a class module, VBA then causes the interface elements (that is, the method and property declarations) to be inherited by the class in which the `Implements` keyword is placed. This means that both the `MyShapelyRectangle` and `MyShapelyKite` classes inherit the `Height`, `Width`, and `Area` properties and the `DoubleSides` method defined in the `Shape` class. That is why this method of sharing interfaces is sometimes referred to as **interface inheritance**.

We need to be careful when using interface inheritance to make sure that the class inheriting the interface provides handlers for every element of the interface defined in the dummy interface class. In our example, that means that the `MyShapelyRectangle` and `MyShapelyKite` methods must provide handlers for the `Height`, `Width`, and `Area` properties and the `DoubleSides` method defined in the `Shape` class. Failure to implement any property or method defined in the dummy interface class will cause a compile error.

In order to implement a handler for the inherited interface element, we simply provide a `Private` procedure with the name of the procedure modified to indicate that it represents an inherited element. So whereas our `MyRectangle` class originally implemented its own native `Height` property like this:

```
Public Property Let Height(dblParam As Double)
```

the new `MyShapelyRectangle` now implements the `Height` property that it has inherited from the `Shape` dummy interface class like this:

```
Private Property Let Shape_Height(RHS As Double)
```

As you can see, the first difference is that the name of the procedure is prefixed with the name of the class from which the interface element has been inherited. More interestingly, the property is now declared with the `Private` keyword. So, why is it private? The answer is that the `MyShapelyRectangle` object is now all implementation and no interface. We only want developers to manipulate the object via the `Shape` interface, so that is why the `Shape` class is the only module that will contain public procedures. In case you're wondering, you can define a public function in `MyShapelyRectangle`. Its existence does not cause a compile error but it cannot be seen outside of the class, and trying to reference it as a method will give a compile error.

*If you are wondering why VBA gives the parameter the somewhat obscure variable name RHS, it is because the parameter represents the value on the Right Hand Side of the equals sign in the property assignment, for example shpKite.Height = 8.*

One of the key advantages of interface inheritance is that it allows **early binding**. Because both the `MyShapelyRectangle` and `MyShapelyKite` objects share the same `Shape` interface, we can define a variable as a `Shape` and then use it store references to both `MyShapelyRectangle` and `MyShapelyKite` objects.

So, whereas before we had to pass the generic object like this:

```
GetObjectArea (obj As Object, ...
```

We can now pass it like this:

```
GetShapeArea (shp As Shape, ...
```

The advantage of this technique is that, because VBA knows that we will be dealing with objects that use the Shape interface, it can prompt us with the names of the objects' methods and properties as we are typing code in the GetShapeArea procedure.

```
Function GetShapeArea(shp As Shape, dblHeight As Double, dblWidth As Double)

shp.Height = dblHeight
shp.
```

In fact, we can use the very same variable within the same subroutine to contain a reference first to MyShapelyKite object, and then to a MyShapelyRectangle object, as shown in the code sample below:

```
Sub ClassDemo4b()

Dim shp As Shape

'First we use shp to refer to a MyShapelyKite object
Set shp = New MyShapelyKite

shp.Height = 8
shp.Width = 5
Debug.Print "The kite's area is " & shp.Area

Set shp = Nothing

'And then we use it to refer to a MyShapelyRectangle object
Set shp = New MyShapelyRectangle

shp.Height = 8
shp.Width = 5
Debug.Print "The rectangle's area is " & shp.Area

Set shp = Nothing

End Sub
```

In this example, we would again be prompted with the names of the methods and properties because we are using a Shape object variable:

That shows that VBA is now using early binding, which means that not only will it prove easier for us to write error-free code at design time but also that our code will execute more quickly at run time.

## Inheritance

The fourth and final feature that we noted earlier was characteristic of object-oriented development was inheritance. Unfortunately the current version of VBA does not support inheritance in the traditional sense. True inheritance allows us to take an existing class and derive a subclass from it, which inherits both interface and implementation details from the original class. Although VBA allows us to implement interface inheritance through the use of the Implements keyword, there is no easy way to inherit functionality from another class.

# The PaymentStats Class

So far we have covered what might seem like a lot of new ground to many of you. If this is your first experience with object-oriented programming, then you might find the wealth of new terminology somewhat overwhelming. So what we'll do now is to look at how we can implement a class in the Ice Cream database. Hopefully, this will help to reinforce some of the concepts that we have covered earlier, while allowing us to look at some more of the features of class-based development in VBA.

## The Business Need

As you know, the database that we are using throughout this book is IceCream.mdb, a database that contains stock and sales information for an ice-cream making company. Anyone who has been involved in running a company will know that one of the most important functions within a company is collecting payments. Invoicing clients on a timely basis is fine, but, as the saying goes, "Cash is King!" If clients don't pay their bills in a timely fashion, then a company can very soon find itself facing cash-flow problems.

For this reason, the Dave and Rob's Ice Cream Company employs a credit collection agency, "Harry, Grabbit, and Scarper", to collect payment on their outstanding invoices. The Finance Director at Dave and Rob's know that the company will be OK if it can ensure that 90% of its invoices are paid within 40 days of the order being received. So Dave and Rob's has a service-level agreement in place, which states that every month, if Harry, Grabbit, and Scarper fails to collect 90% of invoices within 40 days, then it will be fined $1,000 for every percentage point of invoices not collected within that period.

For example, if Harry, Grabbit, and Scarper only collects 84% of invoices issued in September within 40 days, then it will have to pay a fine of (90 − 84) * $1,000.00 = $6,000.00.

The Finance Director would therefore like to be provided with the following information on a monthly basis for presenting to board meetings:

❑ What percentage of invoices, for orders placed within that month, were collected within 40 days?

❑ Did Harry, Grabbit and Scarper hit the targets in the service-level agreement and, if not, what fine does it owe us?

The Finance Director would also like to know:

❑ What is the shortest delay between a client placing an order in that month and paying for it?

❑ What is the longest delay?

❑ What is the average delay?

## The Object Model

To help us to answer these questions, we will build a custom object. This object, which we will call `PaymentStats`, will contain a month's payment information and will expose a number of simple properties, which allow us to determine the information requested by the Finance Director.

The following table details the properties that our `PaymentStats` object will need to expose:

| Property | Data Type | Read/Write | Comments |
| --- | --- | --- | --- |
| MeanDelay | Double | Read Only | Stores the average delay (in days) between invoicing (`DateOrdered`) and payment (`DatePaid`) |
| MinimumDelay | Integer | Read Only | Stores the minimum delay (in days) between invoicing and payment |
| MaximumDelay | Integer | Read Only | Stores the maximum delay (in days) between invoicing and payment |

The `PaymentStats` object will also need to return the percentage of invoices paid within 40 days and the fine payable by Harry, Grabbit, and Scarper, but these will be implemented as methods.

| Method | Arguments | Return Data Type | Comments |
| --- | --- | --- | --- |
| Percentile | Days (Integer) | Single | Returns the percentage of invoices paid within the number of days specified by the Days argument |
| FinePayable | Days (Integer) Percent (Single) UnitFine (Currency) | Currency | Returns the size of the fine payable calculated according to the following formula: [UnitFine] times ([Percent] minus percent of invoices paid within [Days] days) |

The reason that these two methods are exposed as methods, rather than properties, is that because they are implemented as methods, we can pass parameters to them. We could have implemented a Percentile property to return the percentage of invoices paid within 40 days. However, that is fairly inflexible. If we changed the service-level agreement to say that 90% of invoices had to be paid within 35 days, we would need to re-write the way that the Percentile property was implemented. By implementing Percentile as a method, we can still return a value, but we can parameterize the method to allow us to specify the delay for which we want the percentile returned.

The same argument applies for the FinePayable method. By implementing it as a method rather than a property we can vary the number of days, the percentage cut-off, and the unit fine per percentage point by which the credit collection company missed its target.

If we are concerned about the fact that developers will have to remember extra arguments when calling these methods, we can implement them as optional arguments with default values. In other words, for the Percentile method, we can make the Delay optional (that is, the programmer can choose to feed it a value or not) but set the default to 40. That way, if there is no argument provided, 40 will be used. This reduces the chances for error but still allows the programmer to change the delay if needed.

Finally, we will need a method for loading the payment data into the PaymentStats object before we perform the various calculations.

| Method | Arguments | Return Data Type | Comments |
|--------|-----------|------------------|----------|
| LoadData | Month (Integer)<br><br>Year (Integer) | N/A | Loads payment data for the specified Month of the specified Year. |

## Building the Interface

The first step is to create the interface for the new PaymentStats object. Once we have done that we can add the implementation.

**Creating the PaymentStats Class Interface**

**1.** Open up the IceCream.mdb database and switch to the VBA IDE by hitting *Alt+F11*.

**2.** Insert a new class module. You can do this either by selecting Class Module from the Insert menu or by hitting the Insert Class Module button on the toolbar.

**3.** In the Properties window, rename the class PaymentStats.

**4.** Add the following code to create the declarations for the three properties:

```
Option Compare Database
Option Explicit

Public Property Get MeanDelay() As Double
End Property

Public Property Get MinimumDelay() As Integer
End Property
```

**547**

```
Public Property Get MaximumDelay() As Integer
End Property
```

**5.** Now add the declarations for the three methods:

```
Public Sub LoadData(Month As Integer, Year As Integer)
End Sub

Public Function Percentile(Optional Days As Integer = 40) As Single
End Function

Public Function FinePayable(Optional Days As Integer = 40, _
          Optional Percent As Single = 90, _
          Optional UnitFine As Currency = 1000) As Currency
End Function
```

**6.** Save the changes you have made to this class module and then open up the standard code module Chapter 13 Code.

**7.** Add the following procedure that we will use to create an instance of the PaymentStats class, load it with data, and then retrieve the information we want.

```
Sub ShowPaymentStats(intMonth As Integer, intYear As Integer)

Dim objPayStats As PaymentStats
Set objPayStats = New PaymentStats

objPayStats.LoadData intMonth, intYear

Debug.Print "  Min Delay: "; objPayStats.MinimumDelay
Debug.Print "  Max Delay: "; objPayStats.MaximumDelay
Debug.Print " Mean Delay: "; objPayStats.MeanDelay
Debug.Print " 40 day %ile: "; objPayStats.Percentile
Debug.Print "Fine Payable: "; objPayStats.FinePayable

End Sub
```

**8.** Next compile the project by selecting **Compile Ice Cream** from the **Debug** window.

**9.** Finally, run the **ShowPaymentStats** procedure by typing the following in the **Immediate** window and hitting **Enter**.

```
ShowPaymentStats 12, 2002
```

You should see the results shown next.

```
Immediate                                              [x]
ShowPaymentStats 12, 2002
   Min Delay:   30
   Max Delay:   43
  Mean Delay:   35.571
 40 day %ile:   85.714              I
Fine Payable:   4286.0031
```

## How It Works

OK, so there is not a lot of functionality here at the moment, but at least we have got the interface sorted out. The ShowPaymentStats procedure accepts two arguments, intMonth and intYear, which between them denote the month whose data is to be analyzed.

The first two lines of the ShowPaymentStats procedure instantiate the PaymentStats class.

```
Dim objPayStats As PaymentStats
Set objPayStats = New PaymentStats
```

We then invoke the LoadData method, which will load the appropriate month's data into the object.

```
objPayStats.LoadData intMonth, intYear
```

Next, we inspect the three properties of the PaymentStats object.

```
Debug.Print "  Min Delay: "; objPayStats.MinimumDelay
Debug.Print "  Max Delay: "; objPayStats.MaximumDelay
Debug.Print " Mean Delay: "; objPayStats.MeanDelay
```

Finally we invoke the two methods that return values.

```
Debug.Print " 40 day %ile: "; objPayStats.Percentile
Debug.Print "Fine Payable: "; objPayStats.FinePayable
```

Notice that we are not supplying arguments to these two methods. That is because the arguments have been declared as Optional and have default values. This means that the two lines above are equivalent to these:

```
Debug.Print " 40 day %ile: "; objPayStats.Percentile 40
Debug.Print "Fine Payable: "; objPayStats.FinePayable 40, 90, 1000
```

**549**

## Implementing the Logic

Now that we have implemented the interface for the PaymentStats class, we can set about implementing its functionality. That's what we will do in this next exercise.

**Implementing the PaymentStats logic**

1.  Open up the code window for the PaymentStats class module and add the following private variable declarations at the top of the class module:

```
Option Compare Database
Option Explicit

Private varSalesArray As Variant
Private lngTotalRecords As Long
Private lngTotalDelay As Long
Private dblMeanDelay As Double
Private intMinDelay As Integer
Private intMaxDelay As Integer
Private sngPercentile As Single
```

2.  Now add the following code to the procedure that defines the LoadData method:

```
Dim rec As Recordset
Dim strSQL As String

strSQL = "SELECT DatePaid - DateOrdered AS PaymentDelay " & _
    "FROM tblSales " & _
    "WHERE Month(DateOrdered) = " & Month & " " & _
    "AND Year(DateOrdered) = " & Year & " " & _
    "AND Not IsNull(DatePaid) " & _
    "ORDER BY DatePaid - DateOrdered"

Set rec = CurrentDb.OpenRecordset(strSQL, dbOpenSnapshot)
If rec.RecordCount Then
  rec.MoveLast
  rec.MoveFirst
  varSalesArray = rec.GetRows(rec.RecordCount)
End If
rec.Close

If VarType(varSalesArray) And vbArray Then
  CalcStats
End If
```

3.  Next add the CalcStats procedure to the class module, making sure to define it as a Private subprocedure:

```
Private Sub CalcStats()

Dim i As Integer

'Determine total records
lngTotalRecords = UBound(varSalesArray, 2) + 1

'Determine total dispatch delay
lngTotalDelay = 0
For i = 0 To lngTotalRecords - 1
   lngTotalDelay = lngTotalDelay + varSalesArray(0, i)
Next

'Determine mean payment delay
dblMeanDelay = lngTotalDelay / lngTotalRecords

'Determine minimum and maximum delays
intMinDelay = varSalesArray(0, 0)
intMaxDelay = varSalesArray(0, lngTotalRecords - 1)

End Sub
```

**4.** Now we need to put in the code that will return values from the three properties:

```
Public Property Get MeanDelay() As Double

MeanDelay = dblMeanDelay

End Property

Public Property Get MinimumDelay() As Integer

MinimumDelay = intMinDelay

End Property

Public Property Get MaximumDelay() As Integer

MaximumDelay = intMaxDelay

End Property
```

**5.** Finally, we need to implement the logic to return values from the `Percentile` and `FinePayable` methods. To do this, modify these two procedures so that they look like this:

```
Public Function Percentile(Optional Days As Integer = 40) As Single

Dim i As Integer
```

```
If VarType(varSalesArray) And vbArray Then
  Percentile = 100
  For i = 0 To lngTotalRecords - 1
    If (varSalesArray(0, i)) > Days Then
      Percentile = 100 * i / lngTotalRecords
      Exit Function
    End If
  Next
End If

End Function
```

```
Public Function FinePayable(Optional Days As Integer = 40, _
            Optional Percent As Single = 90, _
            Optional UnitFine As Currency = 1000) As Currency

Dim i As Integer
Dim sngPercentActual As Single

If VarType(varSalesArray) And vbArray Then
  sngPercentActual = Percentile(Days)
  If sngPercentActual < Percent Then
    FinePayable = (Percent - sngPercentActual) * UnitFine
  End If
End If

End Function
```

That is the class completed! All that remains is to test it out by re-running the
ShowPaymentStats procedure and inspecting the results for December 2002. You can do this
by typing *ShowPaymentStats 12, 2002* in the **Immediate** window. You should see the
following results:

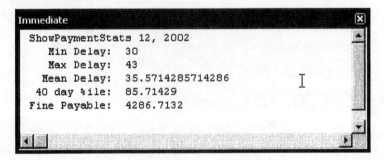

Now there is quite a lot of material to cover here, but most of it uses techniques that we have already encountered.

```
Private varSalesArray As Variant
Private lngTotalRecords As Long
Private lngTotalDelay As Long
Private dblMeanDelay As Double
Private intMinDelay As Integer
Private intMaxDelay As Integer
Private sngPercentile As Single
```

First up, we declare the variables that we will be using within this class. Note that these are all declared as private. That means that the variables can only be viewed within the class module and are not viewable from outside it, in other words we've encapsulated the data storage. Remember, we don't want to expose any of the details of the implementation; all we want to expose is the interface we defined earlier.

The next step is to build the `LoadData` method for loading the sales data into our object. We do this by creating a `Recordset` object, which extracts the payment delay for all orders that were placed in the month specified by the programmer. (For purposes of simplicity we have chosen to exclude orders that have not been paid for yet).

```
strSQL = "SELECT DatePaid - DateOrdered AS PaymentDelay " & _
    "FROM tblSales " & _
    "WHERE Month(DateOrdered) = " & Month & " " & _
    "AND Year(DateOrdered) = " & Year & " " & _
    "AND Not IsNull(DatePaid) " & _
    "ORDER BY DatePaid - DateOrdered"
```

Note that we are retrieving the records ordered in such a way that the orders with the smallest payment delay are retrieved first and the orders with the greatest payment delay last.

We retrieve the records using a read-only cursor. However, we have to be alive to the possibility that there might be no records for the particular month that we have selected. That is why we test the `Recordset` object's `RecordCount` property before we attempt to extract the records into a variable.

```
Set rec = CurrentDb.OpenRecordset(strSQL, dbOpenSnapshot)
If rec.RecordCount Then
  rec.MoveLast
  rec.MoveFirst
  varSalesAray = rec.GetRows(rec.RecordCount)
End If
```

If you can remember that far back, we saw in Chapter 5 that – even though not all of the records might have been returned immediately – the RecordCount will always give you an indication of whether at least one record has been returned. That is because, when the OpenRecordset method is invoked, VBA will always wait until at least the first record in a non-empty recordset is returned before it passes control to the next line of code. So, the RecordCount property of the query will only be 0 if there will definitely be no records in the recordset.

If the query does return records, we need to retrieve them into a variable. However for this operation, we need to make sure that all of the records have finished being retrieved and the easiest way to ensure this is to use the MoveLast method of the Recordset object. Now that is all well and good, but the GetRows method – which is what we will use to copy the records from the Recordset object into the variable – copies rows from the current record onwards. That is why we then need to invoke the MoveFirst method to move back to the beginning of the Recordset object before we invoke the GetRows method.

So, by this stage we have retrieved details of the payment delays for orders placed in the specified month and we have copied them into the variant varSalesArray. Now that we have done that we can perform some the calculations in the CalcStats procedure.

```
If VarType(varSalesArray) And vbArray Then
   CalcStats
End If
```

Of course, we only want to perform these calculations if we were successful in retrieving any records. That is why we use the VarType function to determine what type of variable varSalesArray is. The varSalesArray variable was originally declared as a variant and would have had a VarType of 0 – the default empty data type for uninitialized variables. However, once a value is assigned to varSalesArray, the VarType changes to match the data type of the value held by the variable. Now we saw in Chapter 9 that when an array is placed in a variant variable, the number representing the variable's VarType is incremented by 8192, which is represented by the intrinsic constant vbArray. So, the expression VarType(varSalesArray) And vbArray will return 0 (False) if varSalesArray does not contain an array and it will contain a non-zero value if it does contain an array.

> For more information on using logical operators with the VarType function, have a look back at Chapter 9. If you are still not sure how this works, don't worry. You can achieve a similar effect by replacing the expression VarType(varSalesArray) And vbArray with VarType(varSalesArray) >= vbArray.

So, if varSalesArray contains an array, we run the CalcStats procedure. This is a fairly straightforward procedure.

```
lngTotalRecords = UBound(varSalesArray, 2) + 1
```

The first step is to determine the total number of records that we have copied into our varSalesArray array. The GetRows method creates a two dimensional array, the first dimension of which represents the number of fields in the original Recordset object and the second represents the number of rows. The array created by GetRows is zero-based, so although the expression UBound(varSalesArray, 2) will return the index of the last element of the array in the dimension representing the rows, we need to add 1 to this to determine the number of elements and therefore the number of rows returned.

Having determined the total number of records, we then loop through the array to determine the total of all of the payment delays added together.

```
lngTotalDelay = 0
For i = 0 To lngTotalRecords - 1
  lngTotalDelay = lngTotalDelay + varSalesArray(0, i)
Next
```

This value is stored in the variable lngTotalDelay. It is then very easy to determine the average payment delay:

```
dblMeanDelay = lngTotalDelay / lngTotalRecords
```

The next step is to determine the minimum and maximum payment delays.

```
intMinDelay = varSalesArray(0, 0)
intMaxDelay = varSalesArray (0, lngTotalRecords - 1)
```

These values will be located in the first and last elements of the array because our query returned the records ordered by the magnitude of the payment delay.

So, let's take stock of where we are at the moment. If the LoadData method is invoked, the payment delays for the specified period are returned and the values loaded into an array. From this we determine the mean delay, the minimum delay, and the average delay. These are calculated in the CalcStats function (called by the LoadData method after the data has been loaded into the object) and are stored in three private variables (dblMeanDelay, intMinDelay, and intMaxDelay). If we want to expose these to the outside world, we need to return them as the values of the relevant properties of the PaymentStats object.

```
Public Property Get MeanDelay() As Double
  MeanDelay = dblMeanDelay
End Property

Public Property Get MinimumDelay() As Integer
  MinimumDelay = intMinDelay
End Property
```

```
Public Property Get MaximumDelay() As Integer
   MaximumDelay = intMaxDelay
End Property
```

Now that is most of the functionality of the class implemented. All we need to do now is to return the percentage of payments made within a certain number of days and any fine that is due. The `Percentile` method returns the percentage of payments made and relies on the fact that our array is ordered by the magnitude of payment delay.

Because this calculation is carried out every time this method is invoked, we need to check again that the `varSalesArray` variable contains an array.

```
If VarType(varSalesArray) And vbArray Then
   .
   .
   .
End If
```

If it does, then we loop through the array until we find the first element with a payment delay greater than the payment delay specified as an argument to this method:

```
For i = 0 To lngTotalRecords - 1
   If (varSalesArray(0, i)) > Days Then
   .
   .
   .
   End If
Next
```

As soon as we find one, we know that this and all future elements will have a payment delay greater than the one specified. So we can say that the percentage of elements with a payment delay of less than or equal to the specified payment delay is 100 times the current index of the array ($i$) divided by the total number of elements in the array (`lngTotalRecords`).

```
Percentile = 100 * i / lngTotalRecords
```

Of course, if a payment delay is specified that is greater than all of those in the array, this line of code will never be reached. That is why we started by initializing the value of `Percentile` to 100 (meaning 100%).

```
Percentile = 100
```

The final stage is to calculate the fine payable. To do this, we must again check that there are elements in the array. After all, there is nothing to stop someone invoking the `FinePayable` method prior to invoking the `LoadData` method.

Then we find the percentage of payments made within the specified period represented by the argument Days (which defaults to 40 days):

```
sngPercentActual = Percentile(Days)
```

Finally we take the difference between the percentage specified by the user (which defaults to 90) and the percentage of payments actually made. If fewer payments than the specified percentage have been made then we multiply the difference by the UnitFine (which defaults to $1000).

```
If sngPercentActual < Percent Then
  FinePayable = (Percent - sngPercentActual) * UnitFine
End If
```

That is the class finished. So we test it out by loading it with data and inspecting its properties. If you have typed all of our code in correctly, you should see the right results!

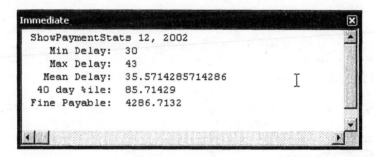

You should be able to see that we could use the same class to give us a listing of all of the fines payable by our credit collection agency in 2002, simply by running the following procedure:

```
Sub ShowFines(intYear As Integer)

Dim i As Integer
Dim objStats As New PaymentStats

For i = 1 To 12
  objStats.LoadData i, intYear
  Debug.Print MonthName(i, True) & _
  " Fine Payable: "; FormatCurrency(objStats.FinePayable, 2, , , vbTrue), _
  objStats.Percentile(40)
Next

End Sub
```

If you run this in the **Immediate** window, you should see these results:

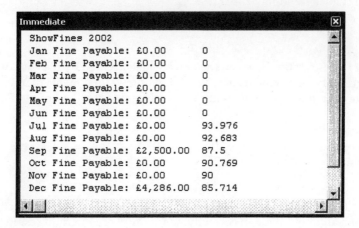

```
Immediate                                                              ☒
ShowFines 2002
Jan Fine Payable: £0.00        0
Feb Fine Payable: £0.00        0
Mar Fine Payable: £0.00        0
Apr Fine Payable: £0.00        0
May Fine Payable: £0.00        0
Jun Fine Payable: £0.00        0
Jul Fine Payable: £0.00        93.976
Aug Fine Payable: £0.00        92,683
Sep Fine Payable: £2,500.00    87.5
Oct Fine Payable: £0.00        90.769
Nov Fine Payable: £0.00        90
Dec Fine Payable: £4,286.00    85.714
```

## Finishing Touches

So far, we have seen how to create objects with custom methods by using either public functions or public subprocedures. Public subprocedures are used for methods that simply perform an action (for example PaymentStats.LoadData), whereas public functions are used for methods that return a value, such as PaymentStats.FinePayable.

We have also looked at how to expose properties by using Property Get and Property Let procedures. We will use that knowledge to implement an Accuracy property that will allow us to specify the number of decimal places that will be used when returning values from the PaymentStats object.

### Try It Out — Adding a Writeable Property

**1.** Add the following variable declaration to the Declarations section of the PaymentStats object we just created.

```
Private intMaxDelay As Integer
Private sngPercentile As Single
Private intAccuracy As Integer
```

**2.** Now add the following procedure, which will allow us to inspect the value of the Accuracy property

```
Public Property Get Accuracy() As Integer

Accuracy = intAccuracy

End Property
```

**3.** Next we will add a procedure to allow us to assign a value to the Accuracy property of the PaymentStats object.

```
Public Property Let Accuracy(DecimalPlaces As Integer)

If DecimalPlaces < 0 Or DecimalPlaces > 9 Then DecimalPlaces = 3
intAccuracy = DecimalPlaces

End Property
```

**4.** The next step is to use the Accuracy property to modify the way that properties are returned. So we will modify the line in the Percentile property that returns the value so that it now looks like this:

```
If (varSalesArray(0, i)) > Days Then
   Percentile = Round(100 * i / lngTotalRecords, intAccuracy)
   Exit Function
```

**5.** Then modify the MeanDelay property so that it looks like this:

```
Public Property Get MeanDelay() As Integer

MeanDelay = Round(dblMeanDelay, intAccuracy)

End Property
```

**6.** Save the changes to the PaymentStats object and switch to the Chapter 13 Code module.

**7.** Finally, modify the ShowPaymentStats subprocedure to include a line to specify the number of decimal places that will be used in returning values from the PaymentStats object.

```
Sub ShowPaymentStats(intMonth As Integer, _
          intYear As Integer, _
          Optional intDecimalPlaces As Integer)

Dim objPayStats As PaymentStats
Set objPayStats = New PaymentStats

objPayStats.Accuracy = intDecimalPlaces
objPayStats.LoadData intMonth, intYear

Debug.Print " Min Delay: "; objPayStats.MinimumDelay
Debug.Print " Max Delay: "; objPayStats.MaximumDelay
Debug.Print " Mean Delay: "; objPayStats.MeanDelay
```

```
Debug.Print " 40 day %ile: "; objPayStats.Percentile
Debug.Print "Fine Payable: "; objPayStats.FinePayable

End Sub
```

**8.** Now, when you run the ShowPaymentStats procedure in the **Immediate** window, it should return the **MeanDelay** property and Percentile method to the specified number of decimal places.

```
Immediate                                              ☒
ShowFines 2002
Jan Fine Payable: £0.00        0
Feb Fine Payable: £0.00        0
Mar Fine Payable: £0.00        0
Apr Fine Payable: £0.00        0
May Fine Payable: £0.00        0
Jun Fine Payable: £0.00        0
Jul Fine Payable: £0.00        93.976
Aug Fine Payable: £0.00        92.683
Sep Fine Payable: £2,500.00    87.5
Oct Fine Payable: £0.00        90.769
Nov Fine Payable: £0.00        90
Dec Fine Payable: £4,286.00    85.714
```

You may find it odd that the accuracy of the fine payable is to 4 decimal places rather than 2 – after all it is a currency value we wish to display. We've left that for you to change as an exercise at the end of this chapter.

## How It Works

A value is passed in via the DecimalPlaces argument and is stored in the intAccuracy variable.

```
intAccuracy = DecimalPlaces
```

It is later used as an argument to the Round function when modifying the result of the MeanDelay property procedure and the Percentile method.

*Because the FinePayable method uses the Percentile method in its calculations, the value it returns is also affected by the use of the Accuracy property.*

The only thing we need to check is that an appropriate value is passed in as the Accuracy argument. If the value is too high or too low, we simply choose to use 3 decimal places instead.

```
If DecimalPlaces < 0 Or DecimalPlaces > 9 Then DecimalPlaces = 3
```

Once the `Accuracy` argument has been added to the interface of the `PaymentStats` object, we can use it in the `ShowPaymentStats` procedure.

```
objPayStats.Accuracy = intAccuracy
```

If we then want to inspect the value of `intAccuracy`, we can do so through the `Public Property Get Accuracy()` procedure, which makes the `Accuracy` property readable.

Of course, now that we are using the private `intAccuracy` variable – exposed as the `Accuracy` property – to regulate the number of decimal places in answers returned by the `MeanDelay` property and `Percentile` method, we need to consider what will happen if we do not assign a value to this property. For example, if we ran the `ShowPaymentStats` procedure without assigning a value to the `Accuracy` property, we would get these results:

```
  Min Delay: 30
  Max Delay: 43
 Mean Delay: 36
 40 day %ile: 86
Fine Payable: 4000
```

That is because the `intAccuracy` variable, like all integer variables, is initialized to 0 if no one explicitly assigns a value to it. So, by exposing the `Accuracy` property, we have made the default accuracy for the `PaymentStats` to be zero decimal places. We will look in a few moments at how we can keep the `Accuracy` property readable and writeable, but allow it to default to a different value.

## Benefits of an Object-Oriented Approach

At this stage it is worth looking at the benefits that this approach offers the developer when compared to alternative techniques. If we had not decided to use an object-oriented approach to solving this problem, how could we have done it?

The most likely approach is that we would have used a series of functions, so that our code would have looked something like this:

```
Debug.Print "  Min Delay: "; GetMinimumDelay(intYear, intMonth)
Debug.Print "  Max Delay: "; GetMaximumDelay(intYear, intMonth)
Debug.Print " Mean Delay: "; GetMeanDelay(intYear, intMonth)
Debug.Print " 40 day %ile: "; GetPercentile(intYear, intMonth)
Debug.Print "Fine Payable: "; GetFinePayable(intYear, intMonth)
```

In this case, each of the five functions would accept a year and month as an argument and return the requested statistic relating to the sales data for that period. Each of these five functions would need to fetch the required subset of data from the sales table and analyze it to determine the correct value of the required statistic. That's five potentially expensive queries to be executed compared to the single one required by our object-based approach.

If we had wanted to minimize the number of times we fetched data from the database, we could incur the one database hit up front like this:

```
Dim varMonthlyDataArray As Variant

varMonthlyDataArray = GetMonthlyData(intYear, intMonth)

Debug.Print "  Min Delay: "; GetMinimumDelay(varMonthlyDataArray)
Debug.Print "  Max Delay: "; GetMaximumDelay(varMonthlyDataArray)
Debug.Print " Mean Delay: "; GetMeanDelay(varMonthlyDataArray)
Debug.Print " 40 day %ile: "; GetPercentile(varMonthlyDataArray)
Debug.Print "Fine Payable: "; GetFinePayable(varMonthlyDataArray)
```

In this situation, the initial `GetMonthlyData` function would return an array containing the month's sales data and the five subsequent functions would each return the required statistic from that data. Although more efficient from a data access point of view, there is still a major drawback compared to the object-oriented approach.

The drawback is this: if we want to use this functionality in another database, with the procedural approach shown above, we have to copy all six procedures into our new database; with the object-based approach we only have to copy one class module. Because the class encapsulates within itself everything it needs in order to function properly, it provides a significantly more manageable way of building applications than the procedural approach. Now, the `PaymentStats` class is only a very simple business object and the benefits that this encapsulation offers over the procedural approach, although noticeable, are not necessarily compelling. But the more complex the object becomes (and, therefore, the more discrete procedures that can be replaced by a single object) the more convincing the argument for an object-oriented approach becomes.

Another key benefit of the object-oriented approach is the way that it makes programming more intuitive in the VBA programming environment. The ability of VBA to expose an object's properties and methods to a developer via the Auto List Members feature of IntelliSense (those funny pop-up thingies) means that the object-oriented approach is likely to yield fewer design-time errors and so lead to faster development than the procedural approach. Also, the more complex the object becomes, the more noticeable will be the benefits that this approach offers over the traditional procedural approach.

Using class modules will inevitably involve a slight development overhead compared to the traditional procedural approach, especially if you are new to the concepts of object orientation. For very simple processes, this overhead may not be worth entertaining, but for more complex processes the use of an object-oriented approach will make subsequent programming more intuitive, will increase the possibilities for code reuse and will make code maintenance significantly easier. How can you say no to that?

# *Differences between Classes and Modules*

We have seen so far that class modules resemble standard modules, in that they contain a Declarations section and can contain `Public` and `Private` procedures. In class modules, `Private` procedures are used to construct the implementation of the class and `Public` procedures are used to expose methods in the interface of the class.

Unlike standard code modules, however, class modules can contain `Public Property` procedures, which are used to expose properties in the interface of the class. `Public Property Get` procedures are used to make properties readable and `Public Property Let` procedures are used to make properties writeable.

> *In fact, there is also a third type of `Public Property` procedure, the `Public Property Set` procedure, which is used to make properties writeable in situations where the property returns a reference to an object.*

However, there is another, more fundamental way in which standard modules and class modules differ. Standard modules are in scope for the duration of the VBA project to which they belong. That means that if a variable, constant, or procedure is declared with `Public` visibility in a standard code module, then that variable, constant, or procedure will remain publicly visible for the whole of the time that the Access database in which that code module is located remains open. Standard code modules do not need to be explicitly loaded or instantiated; they are always there and always accessible.

By way of contrast, class modules provide templates for objects, rather than being objects in their own right. That means that we need to explicitly create an instance of an object based on a class before we can access any of the public procedures (methods) or properties in the object's interface.

The process of creating a new instance of an object from a class is called instantiation, and we have already seen this in action several times already. For example, we created an instance of the `PaymentStats` class. First, we declared a variable to hold a reference to the new `PaymentStats` object once it was created:

```
Dim objPayStats As PaymentStats
```

Then we actually created an instance of the object and place a reference to it in the `objPayStats` variable:

```
Set objPayStats = New PaymentStats
```

It is worth remembering that it is the second of these lines that actually causes the object to come into existence. You might sometimes see this alternative method of instantiating objects being used:

```
Dim objPayStats As New PaymentStats
```

However, it is recommended that you avoid using this technique for a number of reasons. When you use the Dim...As New... syntax, VBA creates a variable to hold a reference to the new object, but it does not actually create an instance of the object until the object is next referenced in code. In fact, when you use this syntax, every time that you subsequently refer to the objPayStats variable, VBA checks to see whether the object has been instantiated. If it has, VBA uses the existing object; if not, VBA creates a new instance. The overhead of checking for the existence of this object every time it is referenced means that this method is noticeably slower than specifically instantiating the object straight away using the Set...= New... syntax.

The other disadvantage of the Dim... As New... syntax is that it is sometimes difficult to keep track of when the object is actually instantiated as this only happens the next time that the object is referenced after the Dim... As New... statement.

### The Class Initialize and Terminate Events

The more perceptive of you will have noticed that class modules contain a couple of events that do not appear in standard code modules. These are the Initialize and the Terminate events of the Class object. You can see these if you look in the object and procedure combo boxes for the code window of a class module.

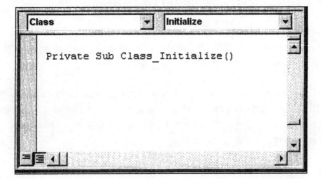

The Class_Initialize event fires whenever a class object is instantiated and the Class_Terminate event is fired whenever the object is destroyed.

> **Objects can be destroyed either explicitly (by setting the object variable to Nothing) or implicitly when the variable containing the object goes out of scope. Bear in mind that if an object has several variables all containing a reference to it, the object will only be destroyed when all of the variables containing a reference to it go out of scope. We will examine this in more detail later when we look at how to create multiple instances of a form.**

A frequent use of the `Class_Initialize` event is to initialize the value of variables within the new object. For example, we could use the `Class_Initialize` event of the `PaymentStats` object to ensure that the initial value of the `Accuracy` property is something other than 0. To do this, we would add the following code to the `Class_Initialize` event of the `PaymentStats` object.

```
Private Sub Class_Initialize()

intAccuracy = 3

End Sub
```

Now, whenever a new instance of the `PaymentStats` object is created, a value of 3 is instantly assigned to the `Private` variable `intAccuracy`. This is exposed as the `Accuracy` property, and is used to limit the number of decimal places that will be used when returning values via the `MeanDelay` property and the `Percentile` method.

Access's trash collector is notoriously unreliable and there are developers who always close any objects that have a close method and set their pointers to nothing. If your class has such variables and you want to do your own cleanup, the `Class_Terminate` event is a good place to do so since it will fire if the class is destroyed, allowing you to ensure that objects that you have pointers to will be cleaned up.

# Forms as Class Modules

We mentioned earlier in the book that all forms and reports are able to have class modules associated with them. In fact, forms and reports do not have associated class modules by default. The class module is only created when you first attempt to view or enter code in the form's class module. You can actually tell whether a form or report has an associated module by inspecting its `HasModule` property. This returns `True` or `False` to indicate whether the object has an associated class module. This property is read-only at run-time but can be written to at design time.

You can also tell whether a form or report has an associated class module by looking in the **Project Explorer** window in VBA. To open the explorer window from the code editor, tap *Ctrl-R* or click **View | Project Explorer** from the menu. If the form or report has a class module it will be listed as a **Microsoft Access Class Object**.

## Creating Custom Properties for Forms

We create custom properties for forms and reports in just the same manner as we do for other classes. The easiest way to see this is to try it out for yourself – so let's do it! In the following example, we will create a `Maximized` property for the form `frmSales` and define what happens when the property is set.

**Try It Out** — **Creating a Custom Form Property**

**1.** Open the `Chapter 13 Code` module that we have been using in this chapter and type the following declaration in the Declarations section of the form's module:

```
Public Declare Function IsZoomed Lib "User32" (ByVal hWnd As Long) As Integer
```

**2.** Now open the code module for the form `frmSales` and type in the two new procedures listed below:

```
Public Property Get Maximized() As Boolean

    If IsZoomed(Me.hWnd) Then
        Maximized = True
    Else
        Maximized = False
    End If

End Property
```

```
Public Property Let Maximized(blnMax As Boolean)

   If blnMax Then
      Me.SetFocus
      DoCmd.Maximize
   Else
      Me.SetFocus
      DoCmd.Restore
   End If

End Property
```

**3.** Close `frmSales`, saving the changes that you have made. Then open it up in **Form** view. Make sure it isn't maximized and it should look something like this:

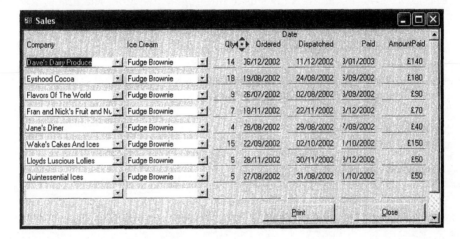

**4.** The important thing to notice on this form is that the control buttons in the top right corner indicate that the form is not maximized.

**5.** Now switch to the **Immediate** window by hitting *Ctrl+G*.

**6.** Inspect the form's `Maximized` property by typing the following in the **Immediate** window and hitting the *Enter* key.

```
?forms("frmSales").Maximized
```

**7.** It should return `False`, indicating that the form is not maximized.

**8.** Now switch back to Access and maximize `frmSales`. Then inspect its `Maximized` property again in the **Immediate** window. This time it should return `True`, indicating that the form is maximized.

**9.** Finally set the form's `Maximized` property to `False` in the **Immediate** window with the following statement.

```
forms("frmSales").Maximized=False
```

**10.** If you switch back to Access, you should see the form has returned to its normal non-maximized state.

In order to create a custom form property, we use the now-familiar `Property Let` and `Property Get` procedures. The `Property Let` procedure allows us to set the property's value and the `Property Get` procedure allows us to interrogate its value. The first procedure we wrote was the `Property Get` procedure.

```
Public Property Get Maximized() As Boolean
```

The procedure creates a property called `Maximized`, which can be either `True` or `False`, and which is `Public`, that is, visible to all procedures.

```
If IsZoomed(Me.hWnd) Then
   Maximized = True
Else
   Maximized = False
End If
```

These next lines are responsible for determining the value returned to anyone interrogating the value of the `Maximized` property. If `IsZoomed(Me.hWnd)` returns a non-zero value, then the `Maximized` property is returned as `True`, otherwise it is returned as `False`.

`IsZoomed()` is simply an API function, a procedure in an external DLL. The DLL, `User32`, contains procedures that handle interaction of Windows programs with user interfaces, and so is responsible for tasks such as window management.

The `IsZoomed()` procedure takes the handle of a window as an argument. It returns `False` if the window is not maximized and a non-zero value if it is maximized. A handle is simply a unique long integer identifier generated by Windows and used to allow it to keep track of individual windows and controls. We get the handle of the form's window by using the form's `hWnd` property. You probably won't come across this property very much, and when you do it will almost invariably be when you want to pass the handle to an API function.

To set the property we use the `Property Let` statement.

```
Public Property Let Maximized(blnMax As Boolean)
```

Again, we can see from the opening line of this procedure that the property's name is `Maximized` and that it has a `Boolean` datatype.

As for the rest of the procedure, it is fairly straightforward.

```
If blnMax Then
   Me.SetFocus
   DoCmd.Maximize
Else
   Me.SetFocus
   DoCmd.Restore
End If
```

If the value to which `Maximized` is being set is non-zero, we need to maximize the form. If the value is being set to `False`, we need to restore the form.

As you can see, creating custom form properties is just the same as creating properties for other class modules and is a fairly simple task once you have got your mind around the syntax of the `Property Let` and `Property Get` statements.

## Custom Form Methods

As well as custom form and report properties, you can also create custom form and report methods. To create a custom method, you simply write a procedure within the form (or report) module and expose it outside the form by making it `Public`.

So, to create a `Maximize` method that increases the size of the form in the manner described above, simply type this code into the form module of `frmSales`:

```
Public Sub Maximize()

   Me.Maximized = True

End Sub
```

Because this procedure has been made `Public`, it can be invoked from outside the form in the following manner:

```
forms("frmSales").Maximize
```

and there you have a custom form method! Now that wasn't too hard, was it?

# Creating Multiple Instances of Forms

Now we'll move on to another feature that is exposed to us through the object-oriented nature of Access and VBA – the ability to create multiple instances of a single form. When you open a form, you are creating an **instance** of that form. The first instance is called the **default instance**. Most of the time, that is the only instance you will need, but there may be occasions when you want to have multiple instances of the same form open at the same time.

Typically, you will create multiple instances of forms when you want to view two records alongside each other. We will try that out now by creating a pop-up form to give details of the ingredients of ice creams that appear in the `frmSales` form.

**Try It Out**     **Creating Multiple Instances of a Form**

1.  In the `IceCream.mdb` database, make a copy of the `frmsubIceCreamIngredients` form, call it `frmIceCreamPopup`, and open it up in design view.

2.  Open the Properties window and change the form's Pop Up and Has Module properties to Yes.

3.  Next change the form's RecordSource property to the following SQL string.

```
SELECT *
FROM tblIceCreamIngredient
WHERE fkIceCreamID=[forms]![frmSales]![fkIceCreamID]
```

4.  Now close the form, saving changes when prompted to do so.

5.  Next, switch to VBA by hitting *Alt+F11* and open `Form_frmSales`, the class module for the `frmSales` form.

6.  Add the following code to the Declarations section of the class module.

```
Private colForms As New Collection
```

7.  Now add the following code to the DblClick event handler for the fkIceCreamID control.

```
Private Sub fkIceCreamID_DblClick(Cancel As Integer)

Dim frmPopup As Form_frmIceCreamPopup

Set frmPopup = New Form_frmIceCreamPopup
```

```
frmPopup.Caption = fkIceCreamID.Column(1)
frmPopup.Visible = True

colForms.Add frmPopup

End Sub
```

**8.** Now switch to Access and close the `frmSales` form, saving changes when prompted to do so.

**9.** Next, open the `frmSales` form and double-click on the combo box containing the name of an ice cream for one of the sales records. This should cause a form to appear detailing the ingredients of that ice cream.

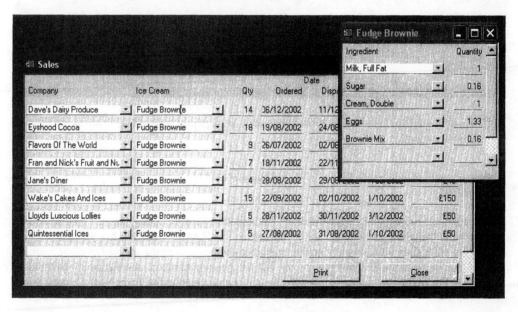

**10.** Move the pop-up form to one side and double-click on the name of a different ice cream on the `frmSales` form. This should cause a second pop-up form to appear.

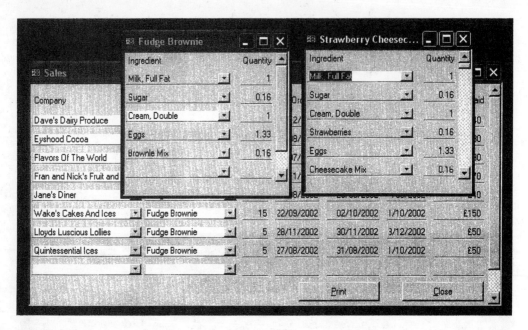

**11.** Now close the `frmSales` form. This should automatically close both of the pop-up forms as well.

This is not as confusing as it might look at first glance. After creating the `frmIcecreamPopup` form, the first thing we have to do is to make sure that the new form has a class module. The reason for that is that we can only create instances of (as opposed to simply open) forms with a class module behind them. That is why we set the form's `HasModule` property to `True`. We also change the form's `Popup` property to `True` to ensure that the form will always remain topmost on the screen.

We then modify the pop-up form's `RecordSource` property to ensure that it will only display details of the selected ice cream.

Next, we add the code to the `frmSales` form to create a new instance of the pop-up form every time the ice cream combo box is double-clicked. Most of this code should seem straightforward. The only unusual line is the one in which we add the variable referring to the pop-up form to a collection declared at the form level.

```
Private Sub fkIceCreamID_DblClick(Cancel As Integer)

Dim frmPopup As Form_frmIceCreamPopup
```

```
    Set frmPopup = New Form_frmIceCreamPopup

    frmPopup.Caption = fkIceCreamID.Column(1)
    frmPopup.Visible = True

    colForms.Add frmPopup

    End Sub
```

Form instances perish when the variables referencing them go out of scope. The variable frmPopup was declared at the procedure level, and so will go out of scope when the procedure exits. In other words, the fkIceCreamID_DblClick procedure creates a form instance that dies immediately as the procedure ends.

In order to prolong the lifetime of the form instance, we add it to a collection that was declared at the form level (that is, in the Declarations section of the form module for frmSales).

```
    Option Compare Database
    Option Explicit

    Dim colForms As New Collection
```

We can then add the form instance to the collection.

```
    colForms.Add frmPopup
```

This variable will only go out of scope when the form frmSales is closed. Any form instances that are added to the collection survive beyond the end of the procedure that created them, but perish when frmSales is closed because, at that point, the collection variable colForms goes out of scope.

One thing to be careful of is that when you create multiple instances of a form, the syntax for referring to the form by name – forms("frmIceCreamPopup").SomeProperty is no longer valid since there are two instances of the form in memory. Trying to refer to a form opened multiple times using this syntax will result in a run-time error.

In fact you can "see" the form by using the syntax forms(Y) (if you know what Y is) but since the index Y changes as forms open and close you cannot reliably refer to forms using this syntax. In the example above we stored a pointer to the forms in our own collection. If you need to reference one of these instances, you will need to do so by going through that collection. In fact you could use the Key property of the collection to "name" the pointer to the form as you add it to the collection, for easy reference later:

```
    colForms.Add frmPopup, frmPopup.Name & 1
```

# Collections – Creating a Hierarchy

In fact, collections have another use in object-oriented programming in VBA. You can use collections to create an object hierarchy, just like the Data Access Object hierarchy. For example, if you cast your mind back to the MyRectangle class that we created earlier in this chapter, we could have created a Sides collection to contain a Side object for each of the four sides of the rectangle.

To do this, we would first need to create a public collection in the Declarations section of the MyRectangle class to contain the child objects.

```
Public Sides As New Collection
```

Next we would need to create a new Side class, with the appropriate methods and properties. For example, we could create a Side class with a Length property – corresponding to the length of the side in centimeters – and an ImperialLength property corresponding to the length of the side in inches.

Finally, we would need to add a new instance of the Side class to the Sides collection of the MyRectangle object for each of the four sides of the rectangle when the object was instantiated.

> It is left to you as an exercise to implement this Sides collection, but if you want to see how it works you can see it implemented in the final version of the MyRectangle object in the Solutions database.

One thing that may not be immediately obvious is that a collection used in this way simply stores a pointer to the instance of the object in memory. We are accustomed to dimensioning a variable and referencing the object's properties via this variable:

```
Dim Side as MySide
Set Side = Sides(1)
  Side.Length = 1.5
```

However since the collection holds a pointer to the object, you can reference object properties directly in the collection without first dimensioning a variable and using the variable.

```
Sides(1).Length = 1.5
```

The advantage of dimensioning the variable is that you get early binding and IntelliSense operation with the variable, whereas if you reference the object properties or methods directly in the collection, you are using late binding and you cannot see the IntelliSense help. The advantage of directly referencing the object in the collection is that you don't need to dimension the variable and perform the set statement, which will be faster for single property references.

Which method to use will be personal preference, however if you will be using a `With ...End With` construct to manipulate many different object properties, dimension the variable will make the code faster and more intuitive.

# Getting the Most from Class Modules

To finish with, here are five closing thoughts to help you on your way when using objects and collections. It really is worthwhile getting to grips with class modules as they are a key part of Microsoft's programming strategy across all its development products.

## Hide Your Data

Make sure that you declare everything privately unless you really want to expose it as a method or property of the class. Public variables act like properties, in that they can be inspected or set from outside the module. However, unlike properties – which have clearly defined `Property Let` and `Property Get` statements – there is no way of detecting when a public property is being set or inspected. As an aside, for troubleshooting purposes, a breakpoint can be set in the `Property Let`, which allows you to find out exactly when and from where the value is being set. So, if you want to expose something, use a property or a method to do so.

If you accidentally expose something you shouldn't, then several things could happen:

- ❏ Code outside your object might accidentally alter data within your object.

- ❏ This could cause your object to behave in a way other than how it should and can be a beast of a bug to track down.

- ❏ Procedures that use your objects may rely on those wrongly-exposed properties for their functionality.

- ❏ This makes maintenance a nightmare. You expect to have to check procedures that access your object when you modify your class's interface, but you don't want to have to check that they will still work whenever you modify the implementation as well.

- ❏ Bad values could be introduced, with no way for you to check or fix the values, or even discover who was setting the bad value.

## Don't Overdo It

Although objects are useful in some situations, that's no reason for using them everywhere. Creating an instance of an object and invoking a method of that object not only consumes more memory than calling the function in a standard module, but is also more time-consuming. So use class modules judiciously.

## *Avoid Get and Set Methods*

It is not good practice to create objects with lots of methods whose names begin with `Get` and `Set`. For example, we could have implemented a `GetAccuracy` and `SetAccuracy` method to allow developers to inspect and set the value of the accuracy to be used in the `PaymentStats` object. But if you want users of your objects to 'get' some form of information about of your object, then you should formally expose that information as a property, and if you want users to alter properties of your object, you should make those properties writeable.

## *Get the Object Model Right*

It is easy to just wade in and create models without thinking through exactly what your object model should look like. But the same warning applies to designing objects that applies to designing databases: design time is the best time to design! If you have to redesign your object model halfway through the build process, the chances are that you will then have to change all the code that uses those objects. That's seldom cheap and it's never, ever fun.

## *Make it Look Easy*

We mentioned earlier that one great advantage of using objects is that they offer the possibility of abstraction. In other words, the code inside the object might be quite complex, but the interface the object presents to users is very straightforward. Although it required knowledge of geometry to design the implementation of the `Area` property of the `MyRectangle` class, no such knowledge is required to use the property. The implementation might be complex, but the interface is easy. What's more, implementing polymorphism, through the use of the `Shape` interface class, meant that the `MyShapelyRectangle` and `MyShapelyKite` objects exposed identical properties and methods and so were easier to use. If you knew how to use one, you knew how to use the other.

# Summary

That's pretty good going! In sixty pages you've got to grips with object-oriented programming! Obviously this chapter doesn't cover everything to do with OOP in Access, but we have covered a good deal of material and certainly enough to get you started.

If you are coming to this from a traditional programming background, you might find it takes a little time to feel totally comfortable with the way it works. But don't worry, just read the chapter again, try out the code and don't be afraid to experiment. After all it's often only when you get down to cutting code for yourself that you really understand how it all fits together.

# Exercises

**1.** In the PaymentStats class you added a write-only property, Accuracy. Make sure that the accuracy is applied to the FinePayable method.

**2.** Try to modify the MyRectangle class so that it contains a Sides collection. This collection should contain a Side object for each of the four sides of the rectangle. The MyRectangle should create these when it is created.

Each of these Side objects should have a Length property (the length of the side in centimeters, which is specified when the Height and Width properties of the MyRectangle are set) and a read-only ImperialLength property which specifies the length of the side in inches (1 inch = 2.54 cm). When you have made these modifications, you should be able to use this procedure to print the area of the rectangle and the lengths of the three sides.

**3.** In the Property Let of the Rectangle and Kite classes, add checking to ensure that no negative numbers are passed in, or if they are, that you fix them before they can be used.

# CHAPTER 14

# WithEvents and RaiseEvent

Events are the life-blood of Windows and of Access forms and controls. Responding to events is an integral part of Access development. You have already seen dozens of examples where we ran our own code on a button click event or a combo after update. In a sense, writing our own event handlers to make our forms or controls do useful things is one of the key differences between a developer and a power user. Access has many wizards that can build up command buttons and similar controls for us, but to be able to do that ourselves, to really *understand* event handlers, is the key to really controlling our applications.

WithEvents is one of the best-kept secrets in Access. Do a keyword search of WithEvents in any of the Access or VBA help files and you get nothing! If you find anything at all, it will be simply that it is a keyword – no explanation of what it does, where or why you would use it. Start looking in all of the books in the bookstores. Most of them don't even mention the term anywhere. So what are they and why would we use them? Once you learn the how and why, you soon realize that handling events in classes is a tremendously powerful encapsulation tool, making it difficult to understand why they have been kept so quiet.

In Chapter 12 we learned how to build our own classes to encapsulate behaviors that would be useful to implement in multiple places in our databases. What if we could somehow marry classes and object events into a tightly integrated, completely encapsulated system that performed some useful behavior for us? Imagine being able to build a class that could cause a control to do exactly the same thing on any form we wanted. For example, we could build a class that allows us to handle the Enter and Exit events for textboxes. As the textbox gets the focus we could do something like change the font or font color or background color. That is the exact purpose of WithEvents – handling an object's events inside of classes other than the form classes.

WithEvents requires us to think about events a little differently than we have before. Events have more power than we commonly believe and can be used in ways not understood by the average Access developer. In order to learn these things we need to do a little reviewing of what we currently understand, learn some new terms, and stretch our imaginations just a bit. The next couple of pages will require a little more concentration, but once you learn the terms and concepts, the actual implementation is simple. When we say simple, we mean that we only need to use about eight lines of code in a class module and five lines in the form's module, as shown below, to start using WithEvents.

### Class code:

```
Private WithEvents mcbo As ComboBox

Public Function init(lcbo As ComboBox)
  Set mcbo = lcbo
  mcbo.AfterUpdate = "[Event Procedure]"
End Function

Private Sub mcbo_AfterUpdate()
  MsgBox "this is the combo After Update event"
End Sub
```

### Form code:

```
Dim fclsCboSimple As clsCboSimple

Private Sub Form_Open(Cancel As Integer)
  Set fclsCboSimple = New clsCboSimple
  fclsCboSimple.init Combo0
End Sub
```

As you can see from the above code, the implementation is really simple, so bear with me. WithEvents provides the developer with considerable capabilities, and learning how to use this simple concept will literally move you to a new level of development ability.

In this chapter we will be looking at the following:

❑ Reviewing events

❑ What WithEvents is

❑ Why we use WithEvents

❑ How to build a simple class that uses WithEvents

❑ How to build a Record Selector class that demonstrates reusability

❑ How to have our class raise an event of its own!

# Event Review, Some Terms and Facts

There are some terms that we will need to learn in order to get a handle on WithEvents, and be able to discuss event handling among ourselves. As you know, objects can cause events to happen. This process is called *sourcing* an event. One thing that may not be obvious is that an event acts very similar to a radio broadcast of a message. The following is a simplified version of what really happens.

An event occurs, which could be the click of a mouse. Windows takes that click and determines what program of all those currently running "owned" the piece of screen that the click occurred on, and notifies that program (Access in this case) that the click occurred, passing in a "handle to window" of the object clicked on. That program (for our purposes Access, but also Word or Excel, or almost any other Windows program) discovers which of its controls corresponds to that "handle to window" and notifies that control that the mouse clicked on it. Everything that happens from the click to the instant the event is broadcast is irrelevant to us. What we care about is that the control "broadcasts" its click event! And by broadcast we do mean broadcast. Any class inside of Access can (potentially) hear the event. It is important to understand the concept of an event being broadcast because it is possible (and even common) to handle an event in more than one class.

The process of "listening" or receiving program control from an object event is called *sinking* the event. Only classes can sink events. This is the really weird part of this whole "secret" thing – only classes can sink events, and only the WithEvents keyword allows a non-form class to sink events. (And the WithEvents keyword isn't explained anywhere in all of Access documentation!) Form classes don't need the WithEvents keyword to sink events for objects physically placed on the form, but they will need to use the WithEvents keyword to sink events generated by any objects that cannot be physically placed on the form, such as DLLs, OCXs, and classes that can be directly referenced.

Up to this point, the only place you have handled events has been in the module of a form. It turns out that form modules are classes, and the event handlers that we create in these classes are also called **event sinks**. So an object *sources* events, and a class *sinks* events. An event handler and an event sink are just different terms for the same thing. As an interesting aside, the terms source and sink come from electronics where transistors source and sink current.

By the way, a class is an object, and as such it too can source an event! Yes, your own classes can raise (source) events that other classes in your application can sink. That is powerful stuff as we will see towards the end of this chapter.

But first let's review a little of what we already know. A combo on a form has many possible events that it can source; `Click`, `GotFocus`, `AfterUpdate`, and so on. Back in Chapter 3 we learned how to use the property box of a control to select an event property, then click the builder button (the ellipsis to the right of the property) and select code builder. This caused Access to do two things. First of all it built an event handler shell sub for us in the form's module. The empty event handler shell is also known as an *event stub*. It is called a stub because it contains only the `Sub` and `End Sub` lines with no real code inside of it. It also placed the text [Event Procedure] in the event property of the property sheet.

Having created the event stub, we can now place code into the sub that the code builder built for us. When that event fires for that object, program control is transferred to the event handler sub and our code begins to run.

An interesting and little known fact is that it is the very existence of the text [Event Procedure] in the object's event property that causes (or allows) Visual Basic to allow the event to fire. We can literally turn off the broadcasting of an individual event simply by deleting that [Event Procedure] text in the event property, and turn it back on by setting [Event Procedure] back in the property. Even if you have an event stub for a combo's click event (for example) in the form's module, simply delete the [Event Procedure] in the combo's `Click` event property and the event will never fire (source the event). As the event never even fires, the click event code will never run. Put [Event Procedure] back in the property and the event starts firing again. We will be using this little known fact to turn on an object's event broadcasting from right inside our classes from code in our class's `Init` event.

# What is WithEvents?

`WithEvents` is a Visual Basic keyword, and is declared as below:

```
Private WithEvents mcbo As combo
```

`WithEvents` tells the class that an object will be sourcing events, and that we want to sink those events in this class. By adding the `WithEvents` keyword to a statement that would normally just declare `mcbo As combo`, the keyword is literally telling the class to dimension the object "with events". In other words, this object is capable of sourcing events and we will be sinking at least some of those events inside of this class. Once an object is declared using the `WithEvents` keyword, *any or all* of its events can be sunk (handled) in the class. Which you sink will depend entirely on which events you need to handle to perform the task.

Since only classes can sink events, the `WithEvents` keyword can only be used in classes. You cannot declare a control `WithEvents` in a normal module, or you will get a compile error when you attempt to compile the project.

Of course you are probably wondering how the class knows *which* combo to sink events for. The answer to that comes in the `Init` event we define for the class.

```
Public Function init(lcbo As ComboBox)
   Set mcbo = lcbo
   mcbo.AfterUpdate = "[Event Procedure]"
End Function
```

Notice that we are passing in a combo box to the function, and inside the init event we set our own mcbo to the lcbo passed in. Thus we have told the class to sink events for whatever combo is passed in. By the way, there is nothing magic about the name Init for the function; it can be whatever you wish. Simply understand that real classes are going to be more complex than the simple examples you have seen so far in this book and it is common practice to initialize all of the variables for the class in an Init statement immediately after setting the class variable.

Having dimensioned the combo WithEvents in the class and told the class which combo to sink events for, you can now create event handlers in the class, and control will be transferred to your event handler when the control fires that event.

```
Private sub mcbo_AfterUpdate()
   msgbox "this is the after update event"
End Sub
```

Of course you can sink as many of the object's events in the class as you wish. To keep things simple we are just showing you one for now.

An event handler that you write in your class is identical in every way to an event handler that the code builder writes. It must be private, it must be a sub, and it must use the name of the object sourcing the event (mcbo in this case) with an _ (underscore) and then the event property name (AfterUpdate). If the event passes in any parameters you must also recreate these parameters as well. The easiest way to get an event handler built is to simply place a control of the type you desire in a form, name the control exactly what you will call it in your class, open the properties box for that control, then use the code builder to build the event stub. Now cut the event stub out of the form's module and paste it into your own class. The code builder will also build any parameters that Access requires for that event. After a while you will get used to seeing the event stub and will be able to build your own. If you ever have problems though, just remember you can always fall back on Access to build one for you.

Once you learn and start using WithEvents you are going to discover all kinds of classes written by other developers that raise events that you can sink in your own classes. Want to zip and unzip files? Yep, there's a class out there and guess what, it raises events when it is done doing various things. You will learn all about raising events at the end of this chapter.

# Why Use WithEvents?

Simply put, `WithEvents` allows us to sink events for objects in classes of our choosing instead of just in form modules. All of a sudden we can create a class that provides our project with all of those advantages that classes give us – encapsulation of properties, methods, and behaviors (including object event sinks) – but apply them to forms, controls, and other objects as well!

For example, in a project for an insurance company, the client wanted a set of 5 checkboxes to record properties of a claim. It could be a worker's compensation claim, car-related (an accident), an illness, an accident / injury, or a maternity claim. That's what they wanted! Thinking about it and discussing it with the client it became obvious that certain rules had to be applied, that is, that these couldn't just be clicked willy-nilly without affecting other check boxes. Some of the rules were that if it was an illness it wasn't an accident (and vice versa), if it was maternity, it was listed as an illness and (therefore) wasn't an accident (don't go there!), if it was workers comp it wasn't an illness but was an accident, and so on. So when the auto-related checkbox was checked the accident had to be checked and the illness had to be unchecked. If maternity was checked, then the accident and auto had to be unchecked and illness checked, and so on. Using `WithEvents` (the click event) for all of the checkboxes, we were able to encapsulate the entire set of rules into a single class that was then used on several different forms (see `frmChkBoxes` in `WithEvents.mdb`).

A form has its own class module, but even in this case you really don't want to place common functionality in each form's module. We can build a class to sink the form's events and have all form functionality that is common across all (or a set of) our forms encapsulated in that class. This makes it much easier to maintain, and one place to go to update the behaviors.

Controls on the other hand don't have a class of their own, which is one of the big drawbacks to Access controls! Suppose you wanted to have a common behavior for a combo's `NotInList` event. Perhaps you simply want the combo to inform the user that they can't edit the list, or perhaps you want to open a form that allows the user to edit the data behind the combo. Sure you can create functions that sit in a library to handle these things, but by wrapping them up in a class, you know exactly where to go to edit combo functionality, and of course you can move the class from project to project (or store it in a library!).

A couple of things to know about event sinks:

❑ For physical objects (controls) on forms, you don't need the `WithEvents` keyword. To sink an object's events in any other class or even a non-control's events in a form's class module, you must use the `WithEvents` keyword.

❑ If you have an event stub in a form class for a control event, that event stub will get control first, before your class.

❑ It is possible to sink object events in multiple classes! You can literally sink an event for a control on form A over on form B! Or you can define a class that handles events for an object, and then create multiple instances of that class passing in a reference to the same object. Thus you can have one, five, ten, or a hundred instances of a class all sinking the click event for the same button, or the after update event of the same combo. This can actually be quite useful since your own classes can raise events and in fact we will show you an example of that later.

❑ If you sink events in multiple instances, control passes to the classes in the order instantiated for Access 97, but in *reverse order of instantiation* for Access 2000 and Access 2002. What this means is that each class will eventually get control but the order that the classes gets control depends on the order that the classes are instantiated.

❑ Visual Basic is a single-threaded language. Each event sink must finish processing before the next event sink can get control. If the code in the class sinking the event takes 30 seconds to do something, *your program will appear to hang* for thirty seconds before control passes on to the next event sink for that control's event. No other processing will occur anywhere in your program until the event handler finished its processing! This isn't a reason not to use events (or `WithEvents`), but it is a warning to make sure event handlers – *all* event handlers *everywhere* – finish what they are doing as rapidly as possible. If they are going to take very long, *let the user know* or you will have users rebooting their machine because it's "hanging".

## The Simple Combo Class

Enough theory, let's have some fun. In order to demonstrate just how simple `WithEvents` really is, we are going to build a very simple class that handles the `AfterUpdate` event of a combo box. Don't get too excited though; all this class will do for us is put up a message box when the after update fires, but that is enough to demonstrate the process. It also allows you to see exactly how simple this stuff really is. Once we understand what we are doing and how and why it works, we will then move on to a slightly more complex combo class that is truly useful – a combo record selector. Ok, let's get to work.

**Try It Out**     **Creating the Simple Combo WithEvents Class**

**1.** Open up the `IceCream.mdb` database and switch to the VBA IDE by hitting *Alt+F11*.

**2.** Insert a new class module. You can do this either by selecting **Class Module** from the **Insert** menu or by hitting the Insert Class Module button on the toolbar.

**3.** A new class called `Class1` should now appear in the Project Explorer window. If the Properties window is not visible, make it so by hitting *F4* and then change the name of the class to `MySimpleCbo`.

**4.** Now, in the code window, add the following code to the class module. Then save the class module.

```
Option Compare Database
Option Explicit

Dim WithEvents mcbo As ComboBox

Public Function init(lcbo As ComboBox)
  Set mcbo = lcbo
  mcbo.AfterUpdate = "[Event Procedure]"
End Function

Private Sub mcbo_AfterUpdate()
  MsgBox "This is the combo After Update event"
End Sub
```

**5.** Next, switch to the database window and create a new blank form in design view. Add a combo control to the form. The default combo name will be **Combo0**.

**6.** Now open the properties box for the combo, set the row source type to `Value List`, and set the row source to `1;2;3`. This will provide us some simple data for the combo, so that the `AfterUpdate` event can be generated.

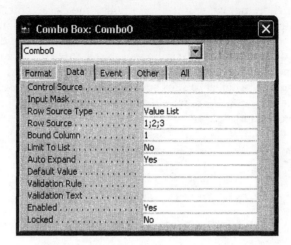

**7.** Save the form as `frmSimpleCombo`. Open the module for the form and insert the following code:

```
Option Compare Database
Option Explicit

Dim fMySimpleCombo As MySimpleCbo

Private Sub Form_Open(Cancel As Integer)
  Set fMySimpleCombo = New MySimpleCbo
  fMySimpleCombo.init Combo0
End Sub
```

**8.** Close the form, and then reopen it. Drop down the combo and select one of the numbers. A message box will pop up saying "This is the combo After Update Event".

## How It Works

That's all there is to `WithEvents`! We built a simple class that dimensions a combo control `WithEvents`.

```
Dim WithEvents mcbo As ComboBox
```

We built an `Init` function that we will use to initialize the class, which tells the class exactly which combo we want to respond to. This `Init` function stores the pointer (a pointer is a variable that holds a memory address that allows you direct access to the data held in that address) of the combo passed in to the combo variable that we declared using `WithEvents` in the class header. Remember we also said that simply setting the object's event property to [Event Procedure] causes the object to start sourcing the event, so in order to make sure that the combo is sourcing the `AfterUpdate`, we simply use code to set the control's `AfterUpdate` property to [Event Procedure].

```
Public Function init(lcbo As ComboBox)
    Set mcbo = lcbo
    mcbo.AfterUpdate = "[Event Procedure]"
End Function
```

Finally we build an event stub for the event we want to sink – the `AfterUpdate` in this case.

```
Private Sub mcbo_AfterUpdate()
    MsgBox "this is the combo After Update event"
End Sub
```

In the form's class module we dimension a `fMySimpleCombo` class variable.

```
Dim fMySimpleCombo As MySimpleCbo
```

Then in the form's `Open` event we set our class variable to be equal to a *new* instance and initialize the class instance.

```
Private Sub Form_Open(Cancel As Integer)
    Set fMySimpleCombo = New MySimpleCbo
    fMySimpleCombo.init Combo0
End Sub
```

We then saved the form, closed it and reopened it, so that when we select something from the combo the combo's `AfterUpdate` event fires. The biggest difference between what you already knew and what we have learned in this chapter is that the event is sunk in our own class – `fMySimpleCombo` instead of in the form's module as we would normally expect to happen. Notice that nowhere in the form's module is there any event sink for the combo, but we still get the event to perform work for us.

Think about this... if we had another form (or simply another class), and we dimensioned the same class in that form, but we passed in the combo form's (`frmSimpleCombo`) `Combo0`... event what do you think would happen? That is correct, the class on that other form would sink the event for the combo on `frmSimpleCombo`. In effect you can spy on a control on a completely different form using this technique. We have no idea why you would want to do that but if you ever did, now you know how!

# The Record Selector Class

Now that you have seen how simple it is to use `WithEvents`, it's time to build a class that is actually quite useful, amazingly simple, and yet clearly demonstrates the whole reusability thing.

The record selector class will take control of a combo's `AfterUpdate` event and use the event to find the primary key (PK) of a record, and use the PK to find and display that record in the form. In other words use a combo to select a record for display. Once we have this class working you will discover that we can then use the class on virtually any form that displays data from a table, such as `frmIceCream`, `frmIngredients`, `frmCompany`, and so on, as long as it uses a single field PK. From that we can clearly see the reusability and maintenance advantage of doing this in a class rather than with functions scattered in a library, or, even worse, in code scattered throughout your forms.

**Try It Out** — **Creating the Simple Combo WithEvents Class**

**1.** Open up the `IceCream.mdb` database and switch to the VBA IDE by hitting *Alt+F11*. Insert a new class module.

**2.** Change the name of the class to `MyRecordSelector` using the properties window.

**3.** Now, in the code window, add the following code to the class module. Then save the class module

```
Option Compare Database
Option Explicit

Dim WithEvents mcboRecSel As ComboBox
Dim mtxtRecID As TextBox
Dim mfrm As Form

Public Function init(lfrm As Form, lcboRecSel As ComboBox, ltxtRecID As
TextBox)
   Set mfrm = lfrm
   Set mtxtRecID = ltxtRecID
   Set mcboRecSel = lcboRecSel
   mcboRecSel.AfterUpdate = "[Event Procedure]"
End Function

Private Sub Class_Terminate()
   'clean up pointers to form and control objects
   Set mcboRecSel = Nothing
   Set mtxtRecID = Nothing
   Set mfrm = Nothing
End Sub

Sub mcboRecSel_AfterUpdate()
Dim strSQL As String
```

```
    'BUILD AN SQL STATEMENT
    strSQL = mtxtRecID.ControlSource & " = " & mcboRecSel
  With mfrm
      ' Find the record that matches the control.
      .RecordsetClone.FindFirst strSQL
      'SET THE FORMS BOOKMARK TO THE RECORDSET CLONES BOOKMARK
      '("FIND" THE RECORD)
      .Bookmark = .RecordsetClone.Bookmark
  End With
End Sub
```

4. Switch to the database window and open frmCompany in design view. Add a combo and a textbox to the form in the form header section.

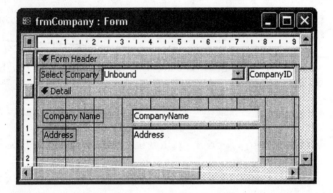

5. Open the properties sheet for the textbox and set the **Name** property to txtRecID. Then set the **Control Source** to CompanyID.

6. Select the label for the combo and change it to display Select Company. Then view the properties sheet for the combo box and change the **Name** property to cboRecSel. Set the **Row Source** property to:

```
SELECT tblCompany.CompanyID, tblCompany.CompanyName FROM tblCompany ORDER BY
tblCompany.CompanyName;
```

7. On the **Format** tab of the property sheet, set the **Column Count** property to 2 and the column widths to "0cm;1cm".

8. Open the form's code module and place the following code in the header:

```
Dim fMyRecordSelector As MyRecordSelector
```

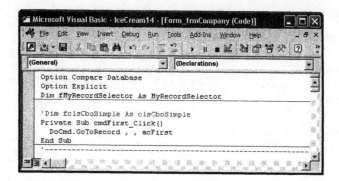

**9.** Next, go to the bottom of the form's code module and insert the following code into the form:

```
Private Sub Form_Close()
  Set fMyRecordSelector = Nothing
End Sub

Private Sub Form_Open(Cancel As Integer)
  Set fMyRecordSelector = New MyRecordSelector
  fMyRecordSelector.init Me, cboRecSel, txtRecID
End Sub
```

**10.** Save the form, close it, and reopen the form.

**11.** Select a company name in the record selector. The class module we just created will sink the combo box's `AfterUpdate` event. Using that event the class module will run code that causes the form to find and display the record for the company selected in the combo box.

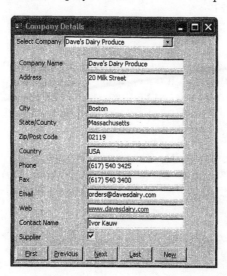

This time we pass into the class `Init` function a reference to the form, the combo, and the textbox. Notice that only the combo is dimensioned `WithEvents`. We will not be sinking any events for the form or the textbox; in fact the only event we will sink is the combo's `AfterUpdate` event.

```
Dim WithEvents mcboRecSel As ComboBox
Dim mtxtRecID As TextBox
Dim mfrm As Form

Public Function init(lfrm As Form, lcboRecSel As ComboBox, ltxtRecID As
TextBox)
   Set mfrm = lfrm
   Set mtxtRecID = ltxtRecID
   Set mcboRecSel = lcboRecSel
   mcboRecSel.AfterUpdate = "[Event Procedure]"
End Function
```

Once again we save the object pointers passed into the class global variables for the corresponding objects. And of course, we set the `mcboRecSel.AfterUpdate = [Event Procedure]` so that we know that event sourcing is enabled by the record selector `AfterUpdate` event.

The terminate event cleans up the pointers to the objects.

```
Private Sub Class_Terminate()
   'clean up pointers to form and control objects
   Set mcboRecSel = Nothing
   Set mtxtRecID = Nothing
   Set mfrm = Nothing
End Sub
```

The combo box's `AfterUpdate` event sink is where all the action is. As you can see, however, it isn't complicated. Basically we build a SQL statement that we will use to find the record in the form. The control source of the `txtRecSel` control on the form tells us what the field name is for the PK of the table. The `cboRecSel` value will be the PK of the record selected. We use these two values to construct our SQL string.

Then with the `mfrm` object, we use the `RecordsetClone.FindFirst` method to find the record using the SQL statement we created in the step above. Having found the record, we now set the form's bookmark equal to the `RecordsetClone`'s bookmark. That step causes the form to display the record found.

```
Sub mcboRecSel_AfterUpdate()
Dim strSQL As String
```

```
'BUILD A SQL STATEMENT
strSQL = mtxtRecID.ControlSource & " = " & mcboRecSel
With mfrm
  ' Find the record that matches the control.
  .RecordsetClone.FindFirst strSQL
  'SET THE FORMS BOOKMARK TO THE RECORDSET CLONES BOOKMARK ("FIND" THE
  'RECORD)
  .Bookmark = .RecordsetClone.Bookmark
End With
End Sub
```

All in all the process is remarkably simple. The nice part though is that you can now add this record selector functionality to any form simply by copying the two controls into any form that displays records from a table or query and which has an AutoNumber PK. Set the SQL statement of the combo to use data from the new form's RecordSource (table / query) and bind txtRecID to the PK field of the RecordSource. Dim the class in the form's header, initialize the class in the form's Open event, and destroy the class in the form's Close event. It is very quick and easy to add this functionality to the next form that you want to have a record selector.

# RaiseEvent

So we have now seen how objects such as controls on a form (or a form itself) can source events, and we have discovered how to sink those events inside our own classes using the WithEvents keywords. But how can we create our own events and why might we want to?

The RaiseEvent keyword is the answer to how. The why is just a matter of imagination. Let us give you an example of how we used RaiseEvent one time to get your imagination cranking.

We needed to interface a bar code reader to an Access database and we needed ironclad control over the process so we decided to use a serial port bar code reader.

The bar code reader we selected connected to a COM (serial) port and transmitted a string of characters with a Carriage Return terminator at the end of the bar code. In order to use this however we needed to somehow "talk to" the serial port. We discovered that Visual Basic (that is, Visual Basic such as Visual Basic 6, not VBA) comes with a ComCtl OCX, a control that can be dropped on a form, and which can monitor a single serial port. The ComCtl OCX raises events that basically tell us that a character or set number of characters have been received on the COM port.

In order to provide black box encapsulation and a simple interface to the database system, we created a class that could initialize the baud rate, start and stop bits, and other parameters of the ComCtl OCX, turn on and off receiving data on the COM port, as well as sink the events that the ComCtl OCX generated (using WithEvents of course!).

The problem though is that we wanted the ComCtl and its class to deal only with the data coming from (and going to) the serial port, not deal with the bar coding stuff itself. In other words, we wanted to be able to use that same class for any application that needed to talk to the COM port, not build a class that could only interface the COM port to a bar code reader. Done correctly we would have a ComCtl class that could be used for interfacing a bar code reader to one system, while the exact same class could interface a serial modem to another system, or a gauge multiplexer to a different system.

We could then build a second class that understood bar code stuff and could "listen" for messages from my ComCtl class saying that data had arrived. The ComCtl class handled the port, by setting it up, getting the data from the ComCtl OCX and broadcasting a message that data had arrived, while my bar code class listened for messages saying that data had arrived and processed the data however it wanted to.

In order to do that we needed our ComCtl class to be able to raise its own events when it was finished getting data from the ComCtl OCX. It turns out this is absolutely trivial by using the RaiseEvent keyword!

# A Simple Example

In order to keep things simple we're not going to use the ComCtl class. What we will do instead is create a class that can broadcast messages for other classes. Once we have that working we will set up two forms that can talk to each other using this message class. So, when we type in a textbox on FormA, it will appear on FormB. Type in a textbox in FormB and it will be displayed on FormA. This will all be done by using RaiseEvents in our Message class (the event source) and WithEvents in our forms (the event sinks). All this in two lines of code and it will roll into one everything we have learned in this chapter. By the way, we actually use this class in our own systems to solve some tricky inter-form communications problems.

**Try It Out**       **RaiseEvent example**

In order to save space and time, we have created a database called WithEvents.mdb to demonstrate the concepts. Let's get started.

**1.** Create a new class module and enter the following code, then save it, calling it clsMsg:

```
Option Compare Database
Option Explicit

Public Event Message(varFrom As Variant, varTo As Variant, _
                     varSubj As Variant, varMsg As Variant)
Public Event MessageSimple(varMsg As Variant)

Function Send(varFrom As Variant, varTo As Variant, _
          varSubj As Variant, varMsg As Variant)
```

```
    RaiseEvent Message(varFrom, varTo, varSubj, varMsg)
End Function

Function SendSimple(varMsg As Variant)
  RaiseEvent MessageSimple(varMsg)
End Function
```

**2.** Now insert another module and enter the following code:

```
Option Compare Database
Option Explicit

Public gclsMsg As clsmsg

Function InitClsMsg()
Static blnInitialized As Boolean
  If blnInitialized = False Then
    Set gclsMsg = New clsmsg
    blnInitialized = True
  End If
End Function
```

Save the module as basInitMsg.

**3.** Now create two forms frm1 and frm2, each with just two textboxes in each form. Call one of the textboxes txtSend and the other txtReceive. Change the caption property of each box to Send Message and Receive Message respectively:

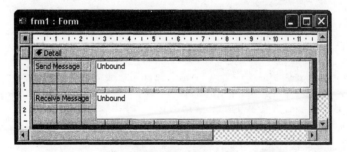

**4.** Open the code view for frm1 and add the following code:

```
Option Compare Database
Option Explicit
Private WithEvents fclsMsg As clsMsg

Private Sub Form_Close()
  Set fclsMsg = Nothing
End Sub
```

```
Private Sub Form_Open(Cancel As Integer)
  InitClsMsg
  Set fclsMsg = gclsMsg
End Sub

Private Sub txtSend_AfterUpdate()
  fclsMsg.Send "frm1", "frm2", "Just a test", txtSend.Value
End Sub

Private Sub fclsMsg_Message(varFrom As Variant, varTo As Variant, _
                            varSubj As Variant, varMsg As Variant)
  If varTo = "frm1" Then
    txtReceive = varMsg
  End If
End Sub
```

**5.** The code for `frm2` is almost identical with just the following lines altered:

...

```
Private Sub txtSend_AfterUpdate()
  fclsMsg.Send "frm2", "frm1", "Just a test", txtSend.Value
End Sub

Private Sub fclsMsg_Message(varFrom As Variant, varTo As Variant, _
                            varSubj As Variant, varMsg As Variant)
  If varTo = "frm2" Then
    txtReceive = varMsg
  End If
End Sub
```

Save both the forms and close them.

**6.** Now, reopen `frm1` and `frm2` in Form view. In the **Send Message** box on `frm2` type in anything you want. Notice that as soon as you press *Enter* the message is immediately displayed on `frm1`. Likewise click into the **Send Message** textbox on `frm1` and type in anything you want. Notice that it is immediately displayed on `frm2`.

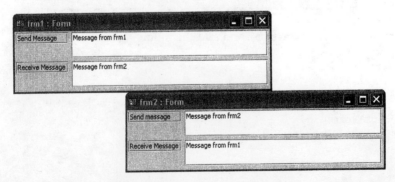

```
Public Event Message(varFrom As Variant, varTo As Variant, _
                        varSubj As Variant, varMsg As Variant)
Public Event MessageSimple(varMsg As Variant)
```

We declare two different public events, `Message` and `MessageSimple`. The `Message` event has full to / from / subject / message parameters whereas the `MessageSimple` has only a single simple message parameter.

```
Function Send(varFrom As Variant, varTo As Variant, _
                varSubj As Variant, varMsg As Variant)
  RaiseEvent Message(varFrom, varTo, varSubj, varMsg)
End Function

Function SendSimple(varMsg As Variant)
  RaiseEvent MessageSimple(varMsg)
End Function
```

Then there are two methods of the class, the `Send` and the `SendSimple`. Notice that each method accepts the same parameters as the event declared in the header and just passes them on to the `RaiseEvent` inside of the method.

We need to have a global variable for the message class as well as an `init` function, all this is stored in the `basInitMsg` module. This will allow us to have a single class instance that gets and sends messages, and everybody that uses the class will just get a pointer to this global variable.

```
Option Compare Database
Option Explicit

Public gclsMsg As clsmsg

Function InitClsMsg()
  Static blnInitialized As Boolean
  If blnInitialized = False Then
    Set gclsMsg = New clsmsg
    blnInitialized = True
  End If
End Function
```

Notice that `InitClsMsg` has a static boolean flag that stores whether or not we have already initialized the class so that we only do it once. This allows many different forms or classes to call the `Init` so that they can be set up in any order and only the first one that calls the function actually performs the initialization.

Finally the two demo forms, frm1 and frm2, both have pretty much identical code. Notice that we dimension a fclsMsg variable inside the form using the WithEvents keyword. This tells the form's class that the fclsMsg object will be sourcing events and we want to sink those events inside of this (the form's) class.

```
Option Compare Database
Option Explicit
Dim WithEvents fclsMsg As clsmsg
```

In the Open event we call the InitClsMsg function, which will initialize the message class if that has not been done yet, and then we get a pointer to that global message class.

```
Private Sub Form_Open(Cancel As Integer)
  InitClsMsg
  Set fclsMsg = gclsMsg
End Sub
```

Close simply cleans up behind us.

```
Private Sub Form_Close()
  Set fclsMsg = Nothing
End Sub
```

The txtSend textbox is used to transmit messages so in the AfterUpdate we call fclsMsg's Send method, passing a string saying who we are (frm1), who we are sending the message to (frm2), what the message is about (Just a test), and the message itself which is the value of the txtSend (whatever was typed in).

```
Private Sub txtSend_AfterUpdate()
  fclsMsg.Send "frm1", "frm2", "Just a test", txtSend.Value
End Sub
```

And finally... we sink the Message event that fclsMsg raises. Notice that *every* message sent on this message channel will cause this event to fire, even the messages that we send. Since that is the case, we need to only listen to or look for the messages sent to frm1 (if we are looking at the code in frm1). Obviously frm2 would only look for messages sent to frm2. When a message comes in with our name in the varTo parameter we place it into the txtReceive and the message will be displayed.

```
Private Sub fclsMsg_Message(varFrom As Variant, varTo As Variant, _
        varSubj As Variant, varMsg As Variant)
  If varTo = "frm1" Then
    txtReceive = varMsg
  End If
End Sub
```

And that's it!

One other thing to think about is that the messages don't have to be text. Because we are passing into variant parameters, the message could be a number, string, even a pointer to a word document or a recordset. As long as the receiving class knows what is coming and how to use it, it can be passed over this message channel. And of course, your class can simply raise its own event directly, it doesn't need to use a message channel like this.

And finally, notice that using `WithEvents` we don't have the problem of having to have the recipient there to take the message. We could have done this inter-form communication simply by writing code that poked the values directly into the textbox on the other form. But what happens if the other form is closed? Well, we would get a run-time error. Using `WithEvents` / `RaiseEvent`, if the other form is closed nothing happens. Again, we can build a system that sends a message without even having the receiver loaded. Clean, encapsulated, and doesn't depend on the existence of the matching interface to work. "I've done my part, if anyone is interested here's the data."

You might be scratching your head asking when you would ever really use this message class... maybe never. This was really just intended as a simple demo without any clutter to demonstrate how `WithEvents` and `RaiseEvents` work together to form a complete system. Furthermore it demonstrates that *more than one class can sink an event*! You could have one or a hundred forms watching the message channel and all of them will receive the message. Which one, if any, actually uses the message is up to you. In fact you could have a class that isn't even on a form watching the message channel and doing something when it gets a message. My bar code processor is a classic example of that.

On the other hand, imagine a form that is hidden when open. Its purpose is to watch the free disk space (using its timer event, once an hour) and transmit a message to the database application when the space gets too low. The form's class simply sends a "Low Disk" message using the message class above. An error logger class that logs the disk usage in a table is sinking events from the message class and when it sees a message addressed to itself, logs the problem and generates an e-mail to the network administrator warning them that they need to free up some disk space before the database fails.

The point is that we are looking at classes as black box systems with complex internal workings but a simple interface. `WithEvents` and `RaiseEvent` allow us to communicate directly from one object to another, or from one object to many other objects if that is what we need. Each class (object) doesn't need to know about who will use the event, nor how the event will be used (or even if it will be used). The object simply does its job and raises an event saying "I have finished my task", possibly passing parameters as well. Whether anyone is listening at the moment or using the event to trigger other actions is entirely irrelevant to the object that raises the event. This is no different from a combo box that has a dozen or more events. The combo is capable of raising its events regardless of whether anyone uses them. If no one is sinking those events, no problem, but if someone needs them they are there. Thus the combo doesn't know, nor care, who may be listening to its events. Furthermore the combo doesn't know, nor care *how* any of its events will be used.

# Summary

Events are vitally important to Windows and Access. As developers we quickly learn how to build event handlers in forms for the various form and control events we use to customize our forms and, by now, events are probably old hat.

What we have done in this chapter is taken event handling to the next level and shown you how to sink events directly in a class of your own making. This ability combined with your evolving knowledge of classes will undoubtedly make you a better programmer. Class objects allow you to encapsulate behaviors and properties for objects so that you can use these behaviors throughout your system with just a few simple lines of code to instantiate the class.

We have learned how to:

❏ Use the keyword `WithEvents` to allow our class to sink events for an object.

❏ Build an `init` procedure to accept references to objects and save them in a class's local variable.

❏ Build the event sink itself and apply logic to cause the event sink to perform some action.

❏ Hook the class into a form, initialize in `Open`, and clean up in `Close`.

❏ Raise an event of our own in order to signal to a listener that something has happened, passing parameters to the listeners if we need to.

As you've seen, this is mostly just an extension of information you learned in earlier chapters. You already know how to handle events generated by objects, and how to build classes. This chapter simply put the two concepts together and showed how to handle events in any class you want rather than only in form classes. However it truly is a revolutionary step for most developers, giving them the power to do things that simply weren't possible before.

# Exercises

**1.** Add the record selector controls and class to `frmIceCream` and `frmIngredients`. This will demonstrate to you the value of reusability and how easy it is to get a coherent look and feel across your forms using your new class.

**2.** Think about other ways you could use `WithEvents` to encapsulate functionality into a class for use in your projects. Add an event handler for the record selector's combo box to sink the `NotInList` and display an error message to the user that the data they tried to find in the combo isn't a valid record. This will replace the annoying "the text you entered isn't an item in the list" with a more user-friendly message.

**3.** Implement a `NotInList` handler class for combos to open a form to edit the data in the table behind the combo.

**4.** Notice that although the combo control does select a record, it doesn't stay "synched" with the form if you page down through records in the form. Add a public method to the combo's class to set the combo equal to the PK in the textbox and call that method from the form's `Current` event so that the combo stays synched to the form.

# CHAPTER 15

# Libraries and Add-Ins

This chapter is all about code libraries. We're all familiar with libraries of books, and the concept of code libraries is similar. A book library is a public place, and after a quick registration process, you can borrow books. You can join many different libraries, giving you a wider range of books to select from. The books are generally arranged according to subject (Fiction, Reference, and so on) and there is usually a full index allowing you to quickly find what you are looking for.

A code library is much the same. It will contain code, forms, tables, and so on, and after registering it, you can use the items in the library as though they were in your current database. This means you can use other people's code as well as your own. You've already seen the advantages to code reuse, so this just takes it one step further.

In this chapter we'll be looking at the following:

- ❑ Creating a library database
- ❑ Referencing library databases
- ❑ Creating class libraries
- ❑ Using Add-Ins
- ❑ Creating your own Add-Ins

## Library Databases

All of the code (as well as the forms) we have written so far only works in the database in which it was written. There is nothing wrong with this, since in most cases it's exactly what is required, but given the advantages of code reuse, wouldn't it be good to share your hard work among other Access applications of yours, or even allow others to use it?

A library database is just a repository of these fragments of code, forms, and so on, which you would like to use elsewhere. It allows you to write normal VBA code, in a normal Access database, and then allow it to be used in any other Access database. The advantages of doing this are enormous. By inserting functions and classes that are generic (can be used in more than one project) directly into a project ends up causing maintenance nightmares. Imagine that you create a class that does some wonderful thing, perhaps calculating state taxes. You drop that directly into several database projects. When it is time to update the formulas, you are now faced with remembering which projects used that class, then opening each one of those projects and fixing the formula in each project. Had you placed the class in a library and distributed the library with your projects, all you have to do is update the formulas in your library and you are done. Since all of the projects use the library, you have fixed all of the projects with a single edit.

## Creating a Library Database

One of the first things I do when starting a new Access project is to create some error logging routines. Instead of just flashing up a message telling the user what the problem is, they also log the error to a table. There are two really good reasons for this:

❑ It's a great development tool. If errors occur during your development and testing they will be logged into a table, so you don't have to keep writing them down (and invariably losing the bit of paper).

❑ It's a great feature during run time. Very often users fall into the habit of just clicking on an error message and trying again, or phoning you to tell you something is wrong, but not writing down the error message. With this sort of logging you don't have to worry because the details will all be stored for you.

Since this feature is pretty useful, let's create a library database to do this. If your fingers are feeling a little tired there's a ready-made database called `ErrorLogging.mdb` for you.

### Try It Out — Creating a Library Database

**1.** Start Access and create a new database. This should be a standard, blank database. Call the database `ErrorLoggingXP`.

**2.** Create a new code module and save it, calling it `ErrorLoggingRoutines`. Starting with Access 2000, the default method of dealing with records is ADO. This book teaches DAO, and so we have to unselect the ADO library and set the DAO library. From the Tools menu, select **References**. Unselect the **Microsoft ActiveX Data Objects 2.1 Library**, scroll down a little, and select **Microsoft DAO 3.6 Object Library**. Click the OK button to close the dialog.

**3.** Add the following globals to the module:

```
Private Const m_ERROR_TABLE As String = "tblErrorLog"

Private m_UserDb As Database
Private m_recErrLog As Recordset
```

**4.** Write this procedure which creates a table to hold the error details:

```
Private Sub CreateErrorTable()

   On Error GoTo CreateErrorTable_Err

   Dim tblE As TableDef
   Dim strSQL As String

   Set m_UserDb = CurrentDb

   Set tblE = m_UserDb.TableDefs(m_ERROR_TABLE)
   Set tblE = Nothing

CreateErrorTable_Exit:
   Exit Sub

CreateErrorTable_Err:
   If Err.Number = 3265 Then
      strSQL = "CREATE TABLE " & m_ERROR_TABLE & " (" & _
         "ErrorID       AUTOINCREMENT, " & _
         "UserName      TEXT(50), " & _
         "ErrDate       DATETIME, " & _
         "ErrNumber     INTEGER, " & _
         "Description   TEXT(255), " & _
         "Source        TEXT(50))"
      m_UserDb.Execute strSQL
   Else
      Err.Raise Err.Number, "ErrorLogging:CreateErrorTable", _
         Err.Description
   End If


   Resume CreateErrorTable_Exit

End Sub
```

**5.** Now create a new procedure, to log the errors, with the following code:

```
Public Sub ErrorLog()

   Dim lngNum As Long
   Dim strDesc As String
   Dim strSource As String
```

```
        Dim errE As Error

        lngNum = Err.Number
        strDesc = Err.Description
        strSource = Err.Source

        CreateErrorTable

        Set m_recErrLog = m_UserDb.OpenRecordset(m_ERROR_TABLE)

        If lngNum = DBEngine.Errors(DBEngine.Errors.Count - 1).Number Then
            For Each errE In DBEngine.Errors
                WriteError errE.Number, errE.Description, errE.Source
            Next
        Else
            WriteError lngNum, strDesc, strSource
        End If

        m_recErrLog.Close

    End Sub
```

**6.** Next, create another procedure, to actually write the errors to the Error table:

```
Private Sub WriteError(lngNum As Long, strDesc As String, strSource As String)

    With m_recErrLog
        .AddNew
        !UserName = Trim$(CurrentUser())
        !ErrDate = Now()
        !ErrNumber = lngNum
        !Description = Trim$(strDesc)
        !Source = Trim$(strSource)
        .Update
    End With

End Sub
```

**7.** Save the module, and from the **Debug** menu select **Compile ErrorLogging**.

**8.** Close the database and open `IceCream.mdb`. Create a new module and add the following code. You should recognize this from our debugging code earlier in the book:

```
Sub TestErrorLogging()

    Dim db    As Database
    Dim recT As Recordset
    Dim errE As Error
```

```
On Error GoTo TestErrorLogging_Err

    'open current database
    Set db = CurrentDb()

    'set a property on a form that isn't open - this will generate a VBA error
    Forms!frmCompany.Caption = "A new caption"

    'open a table that doesn't exist - this will generate a DAO error
    Set recT = db.OpenRecordset("NonExistentTable")
    recT.Close

TestErrorLogging_Exit:
    Exit Sub

TestErrorLogging_Err:
    ErrorLog

End Sub
```

**9.** From the **Tools** menu select **References**. Select the **Browse** button and change the **Files of type** drop down to Microsoft Access Databases (*.mdb).

**10.** Pick `ErrorLogging` from this dialog:

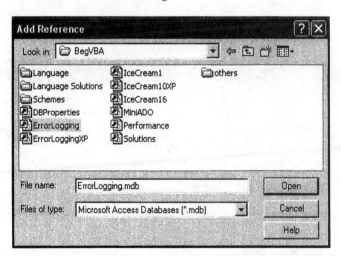

**11.** Click the **Open** button, and you'll be returned to the **References** dialog showing the `ErrorLogging` database selected:

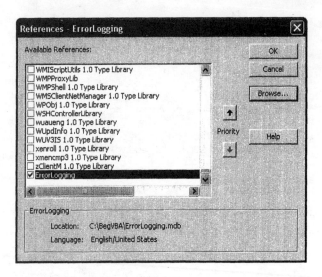

**12.** Press the OK button to close this dialog. From the **Immediate** window, run the procedure. Nothing visible will happen.

**13.** Now comment out the line (by placing a single apostrophe at the start of the line) that sets the `Caption` (see line in bold in step 8), and run the procedure again.

**14.** Switch back to Access and you should notice a new table – `tblErrorLog`. If it's not there, press F5 to refresh the window.

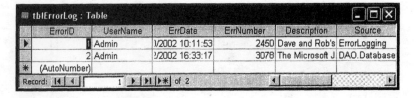

**15.** Notice that although the code is actually in another database, it has created a table in the local database and added rows for each error.

## How It Works

Let's look at the global variables first, and then the `CreateErrorTable` routine, since this is what actually creates the table in the database:

For the globals, we define a constant, which defines the name of the error logging table. Using a constant means we can easily change the name if required. Then there are two global variables. The first will point to the database that the user currently has open, and the second will be a recordset, pointing to the error logging table, that we will use to add records to the error logging table.

```
Private Const m_ERROR_TABLE As String = "tblErrorLog"

Private m_UserDb As Database
Private m_recErrLog As Recordset
```

In the `CreateErrorTable` procedure, the first thing to do is to set some error handling. This is because we need to see if the error log table already exists, and the simplest way to do that is to just set a variable to point to it. If it doesn't exist, and an error is generated, we can trap that error:

```
On Error GoTo CreateErrorTable_Err
```

Once the error handling is active, we define a couple of variables. The first will point to the error table, and the second will hold the SQL string that creates the table.

```
Dim tblE As TableDef
Dim strSQL As String
```

Now we need to open the database. Notice that we use the `CurrentDb` function here; as `CurrentDb` points to the database currently open in the database window in Access. We want to build the error table in the client's database, not in the library database. So, even though this code is in a different (library) database, we still use the active database. If we wanted to access tables and so on in the database where the code is, we could use the `CodeDB` function.

```
Set m_UserDb = CurrentDb
```

Now we need to see if the table exists. The `TableDefs` collection holds all of the existing tables, so we simply set our variable to point to the error logging table. If it exists then we can clear the reference, and exit:

```
Set tblE = m_UserDb.TableDefs(m_ERROR_TABLE)
Set tblE = Nothing

CreateErrorTable_Exit:
    Exit Sub
```

If the table doesn't exist, then the error handling comes into place. We check for error number 3265, which means that the object we were looking for (`tblErrorLog`) wasn't found in the collection (the `TableDefs` collection).

```
CreateErrorTable_Err:
    If Err.Number = 3265 Then
```

If the table wasn't found we need to create it, so we construct a SQL statement to do this, and then `Execute` the SQL statement. We used the `CREATE TABLE` method here because it's quite simple – some other methods for creating tables were discussed in Chapter 8.

```
        strSQL = "CREATE TABLE " & m_ERROR_TABLE & " (" & _
            "ErrorID      AUTOINCREMENT, " & _
            "UserName     TEXT(50), " & _
            "ErrDate      DATETIME, " & _
            "ErrNumber    INTEGER, " & _
            "Description  TEXT(255), " & _
            "Source       TEXT(50))"
        m_UserDb.Execute strSQL
    Else
```

Since it is possible to get an error and not yet have a table to log errors into, if any other type of error is found then we use the default VBA error handler.

```
        Err.Raise Err.Number, "ErrorLogging:CreateErrorTable", _
            Err.Description
    End If

    Resume CreateErrorTable_Exit
```

Now that you've seen how the table is created, let's look at the error logging routine itself, `ErrorLog`:

The first three variables will hold the error details, from the `Err` object. We need to save them because as you've just seen, the table creation routine uses error handling and using `On Error` clears `Err`. The last variable will hold the error details if the error is a data access error.

```
    Dim lngNum As Long
    Dim strDesc As String
    Dim strSource As String
    Dim errE As Error
```

The first thing to do is to store the error details, and then call the routine that creates the error table.

```
    lngNum = Err.Number
    strDesc = Err.Description
    strSource = Err.Source

    CreateErrorTable
```

Now we know that the error table exists, we can open it.

```
    Set m_recErrLog = m_UserDb.OpenRecordset(m_ERROR_TABLE)
```

Now we can use the same routine you saw in the debugging chapter, where we check to see if the error number matches the last error in the `Errors` collection. If it does, then this is a data access error, so we loop through the collection, calling the `WriteError` routine for each error. If it isn't a data access error, we just call the `WriteError` routine with the details from `Err`.

```
If lngNum = DBEngine.Errors(DBEngine.Errors.Count - 1).Number Then
    For Each errE In DBEngine.Errors
        WriteError errE.Number, errE.Description, errE.Source
    Next
Else
    WriteError lngNum, strDesc, strSource
End If

m_recErrLog.Close
```

The routine that actually writes the error details to the table is quite simple:

```
Private Sub WriteError(lngNum As Long, strDesc As String, strSource As
String)

    With m_recErrLog
```

Since we are adding a new record we use the `AddNew` method – this creates a blank record for us to add the details to.

```
        .AddNew
```

We then set the user details. The `CurrentUser` function returns the name of the current user. If you're not using security then this will always be `Admin`, but if security is set up this will be the name of the user that logged into Access. For more details on this, see Chapter 17.

```
        !UserName = Trim$(CurrentUser())
```

Next we set the date and time using the `Now` function:

```
        !ErrDate = Now()
```

And now the actual details of the error:

```
        !ErrNumber = lngNum
        !Description = Trim$(strDesc)
        !Source = Trim$(strSource)
```

Finally, we can update the record with the new details.

```
        .Update
    End With

  End Sub
```

So that's it. Let's just summarize the concept:

❑   A library database is a normal Access database.

❑   Any procedures in the library database that you want other databases to use should be `Public` procedures. All other procedures should be `Private`.

❑   To use a library database you create a Reference to it, from the Tools menu in the VBE.

## Considerations

One thing to beware of when using library databases is name clashes. It's quite possible that you might have a public function in your library database that has the same name as a function in a database that is using the library database. If this happens then Access uses the local procedure, and not the procedure in the library database.

There are two ways to get around this problem. The first is to qualify the procedure name with the module name when you use it. So, assume that `ErrorLog` existed in both the local database and the library database. Calling `ErrorLog` like this:

```
ErrorLog
```

would use the local procedure. But calling it like this:

```
[ErrorLoggingRoutines].ErrorLog
```

would call the one in the library database, because we have put the module name in front of the procedure call.

The second method is to make sure your procedures won't clash, by uniquely naming them. For example:

```
Public Sub logErrorLogging()
```

This puts a unique identifier in front of each public procedure. If you make sure that each library database you create has a unique identifier then you should never get clashes, unless someone else is using the same naming convention in their database libraries, and you use it!

> *On the book's CD, in the Error Handling folder, you can find a wizard that automatically inserts error handlers into existing VBA code. To install the wizard, follow the instructions in the ReadMe.txt file.*

# Class Libraries

Previously, we extolled the virtues of object orientation, and how classes can promote not only good programming, but also good code reuse as well. Since we've shown that using library databases is just another way of promoting code reuse, it seems sensible that that we should use classes within a library database. The unfortunate fact is, though, that although classes can be used outside of the database within which they reside, they cannot actually be instantiated. However, there is a way around this, because we know that normal procedures can be used outside of their own database, so we can provide a wrapper function in the library database that just instantiates the object, and passes it back to the calling object.

So, what we can't do is this:

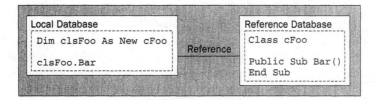

But what we can do is this:

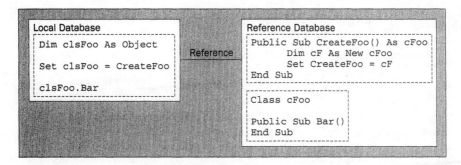

The class is exactly the same, but there is now a public function, in a normal module, that instantiates the class object. The disadvantage of this method is that you can't use early binding, since Access has no knowledge of what the class is. Despite this, though, it's a very good way of using classes in multiple databases.

## An ADO Class Library

Although we're concentrating on DAO in this book, there are some things that ADO can do easily that DAO can't, and one of these is the User Roster. This allows us to see which users are logged into a database – extremely useful if you need to make changes or shut down a server. A set of support libraries was shipped with older versions of Access, but the ADO way is much simpler.

If you want to use ADO, you know that you need to have the ActiveX Data Objects reference set in the VBE, and the same applies with DAO, where you need the Data Access Objects reference set. Having the two set together isn't a problem, but can lead to some confusion. For example, consider the following line of code:

```
Dim recIces As Recordset
```

Does this refer to a DAO `Recordset` or an ADO `Recordset`? In fact, if you don't specify the data access method, then DAO is the default. To clarify which method you want to use, you can prefix the object with its type:

```
Dim recIces As DAO.Recordset
Dim recIces As ADODB.Recordset
```

This makes it very clear, but it looks a little ugly. If all we are using ADO for the user roster, then it seems sensible to put this into a class library. That way the class library can have the reference to ADO, so we don't need this reference in our database, which makes things simpler. In real life, however, it is preferable to simply explicitly define which data access method you are using, so that if the code gets copied into another library, there is no confusion (or compile error). For our purposes though, we are going to create a new library.

## Try It Out — Creating a Class Library

1. Create a new database called MiniADO.

2. Create a new class module (from the Insert menu), and add the following code:

```
Private Const JET_SCHEMA_USERROSTER = "{947bb102-5d43-11d1-bdbf-
00c04fb92675}"

Public Sub GetUserRoster(vUserList As Variant, lReturnType As ReturnType)

    Dim conADO As ADODB.Connection
    Dim recADO As ADODB.Recordset

    Set conADO = CurrentProject.Connection

    Set recADO = conADO.OpenSchema(adSchemaProviderSpecific, , _
        JET_SCHEMA_USERROSTER)

    If lReturnType = RETURN_ARRAY Then
        vUserList = recADO.GetRows
    Else
        vUserList = recADO.GetString(adClipString, , ",", vbCrLf)
    End If
```

```
    recADO.Close
    conADO.Close

End Sub
```

**3.** In the **Properties** window, set the class **Name** to `clsADO` and the **Instancing** to `2 - PublicNotCreatable`.

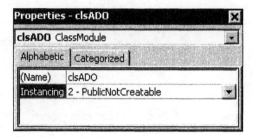

**4.** Save this module as `clsADO`.

**5.** Create a normal module, and add the following code:

```
Public Enum ReturnType
    RETURN_ARRAY
    RETURN_STRING
End Enum

Public Function CreateMiniADO() As clsADO

    Dim cADO As New clsADO

    Set CreateMiniADO = cADO

End Function
```

**6.** Save this module as `MiniADOEntryPoints`.

**7.** Close this database and open `IceCream.mdb`.

**8.** Add a reference to `MiniADO.mdb` as before.

**9.** In the code module for this chapter, add a new procedure:

```
Public Sub WhosIn()

    Dim objMiniADO As Object
    Dim varUsers As Variant
```

```
Set objMiniADO = CreateMiniADO

    objMiniADO.GetUserRoster varUsers, RETURN_STRING

    Debug.Print varUsers

End Sub
```

**10.** From the Immediate window, run this procedure:

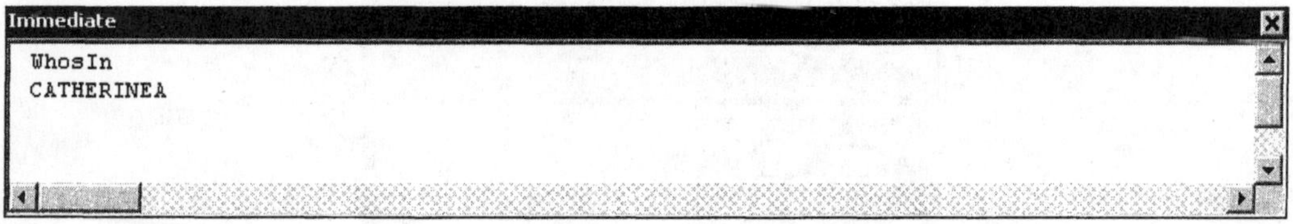

```
Immediate                                                    [X]
WhosIn
CATHERINEA


◄                                                             ►
```

This shows only one user logged in. The columns (separated by commas) are: Computer Name, Login Name, Connected, and Suspect State, although you can only see the first one here.

**11.** Now open another copy of the same database and run the procedure again:

```
Immediate                                                    [X]
WhosIn
CATHERINEA
EWANB

◄                                                             ►
```

The above diagram shows two machines accessing the database: the first machine is called **CATHERINEA** and the second machine is called **EWANB**. At this stage, you might not think this is too useful, since both users are Admin. However, that's only because we haven't set up security. Once you look at Chapter 17 on multi-user issues, you'll see how to set up security to allow users to log into an Access database under user names. When no security is involved, all users are Admin, although the machine name shows up correctly. So, even if you aren't using security, you can still get a good user list if you name your machines correctly.

### How It Works

Let's look at the class first. At the top of the class we define a constant, which is the special key, called a GUID. A GUID (**G**lobally **U**nique **ID**entifier) is a special number that is unique across the whole world, and this is used by the operating system to identify objects, components, libraries, and so on. Generally you don't need to know about them, as most objects have a proper name, but this user roster doesn't have a name – just a GUID.

```
Private Const JET_SCHEMA_USERROSTER = "{947bb102-5d43-11d1-bdbf-
00c04fb92675}"
```

Next comes the definition of the method, taking two arguments. The first is a variant, which will hold the user details, and will either be returned containing a string or an array. The second argument identifies whether a string or an array of the user details is to be returned.

```
Public Sub GetUserRoster(vUserList As Variant, lReturnType As ReturnType)
```

Now we have two ADO objects – one for the `Connection` to the database, and one for the `Recordset` of connected users.

```
Dim conADO As ADODB.Connection
Dim recADO As ADODB.Recordset
```

Next, we connect to the current database. The `CurrentProject` object is an Access object that points to the currently open database – not the library database. The `Connection` property of this object contains the ADO connection details.

```
Set conADO = CurrentProject.Connection
```

Now that we are connected to the database, we need to get the users, and for that we use the `OpenSchema` method. Schemas are really just collections of like objects, and most databases have schemas for tables, queries, users, and so on – they describe what the data is and how it is stored. ADO has provided this method to access these details, and it also allows the data provider (in this case the JET database engine) to specify its own schemas as well as the default ones. This is done using `adSchemaProviderSpecific` as the first argument of the `OpenSchema` method. The second argument allows us to filter the results – we've left this empty because we want all of the users returned. The third argument is the special key that tells the data provider (JET) what to return.

```
Set recADO = conADO.OpenSchema(adSchemaProviderSpecific, , _
    JET_SCHEMA_USERROSTER)
```

At this stage `recADO` contains a recordset of the user details. We can't just return this recordset, because the whole purpose of this class is to encapsulate ADO, allowing it to be used from another database without setting ADO references. So we want to return the recordset as a comma-separated string, or as an array. That's where the second argument to the `GetUserRoster` procedure comes in – you'll see where the values are defined in a minute.

If the return type is to be an array, then we call the `GetRows` method of the recordset. This is exactly the same as the `GetRows` method of the DAO recordset, and converts a recordset into an array. We assign the result of the `GetRows` method to the variant parameter passed into the `GetUserRoster` procedure – remember that this is a `Variant`, and variants can hold different variable types.

```
If lReturnType = RETURN_ARRAY Then
    vUserList = recADO.GetRows
```

If the return type isn't to be an array, then it must be a string. In this case we use the `GetString` method of the recordset, which converts a recordset into a string. The two important arguments to this method are the last two. The first of these identifies the separator (or delimiter) between the fields, in this case a comma, and the latter identifies the separator between the rows, in this case a carriage return and new line.

```
Else
    vUserList = recADO.GetString(adClipString, , ",", vbCrLf)
End If
```

The last thing to do is close both the recordset and the connection.

```
recADO.Close
conADO.Close

End Sub
```

That's it for the class – it has just one method. One thing to notice is the setting for the `Instancing` property of the class – we set this to `2 - PublicNotCreatable`. This defines the class as `Public`, meaning it can be used outside of the database in which it is defined, but that it cannot be created in another database. Unfortunately Access doesn't allow Public Creatable classes, where they can be instantiated and used outside of their own database. It's for this reason that we have to have a normal module with a public procedure to create the object.

Let's now look at the normal module associated with the class. Firstly there's an `Enum` statement, to define the two possible return types for the list of users.

```
Public Enum ReturnType
    RETURN_ARRAY
    RETURN_STRING
End Enum
```

Now we have a `Public` function, which returns a type of the `MiniADO` class. In this function we simply instantiate a new object of that class type, and then return this object.

```
Public Function CreateMiniADO() As clsADO
```

```
      Dim cADO  As New clsADO

      Set CreateMiniADO = cADO

  End Function
```

So, at this stage we have finished the class library. We have a class with one method, and a function that creates an instance of the class for us. Let's look at how it's used now, in the WhosIn procedure.

Firstly there are two variables. The first is a generic object, which will hold the MiniADO class. Remember that we can't define this as clsADO because the class can't be seen outside of its own database, and it's in the library database. The second variable is a variant that will hold the user details.

```
      Dim objMiniADO As Object
      Dim varUsers As Variant
```

To instantiate the class, we have to call the public function in the library database. This creates the class object and returns it to us.

```
      Set objMiniADO = CreateMiniADO
```

Then we call the GetUserRoster method of the class.

```
      objMiniADO.GetUserRoster varUsers, RETURN_STRING
```

Finally, we can print out the user details.

```
      Debug.Print varUsers
```

If you want to return an array of the user details all you have to do is change RETURN_STRING for RETURN_ARRAY, and after the GetUserRoster method is called, varUsers will hold an array of the details. In this case, you would use the normal array indexing methods to access the details:

```
      Debug.Print varUsers(0,0)
```

This would print out the machine name of the first user. Remember that this array is like a recordset, so the first array index is the rows, and the second index the columns.

As you can see, creating class libraries is fairly simple. The only downside is the instancing problem, but using a function to create the class object can circumvent this. We used this method here to encapsulate some ADO functionality, and another good area is API functions, or general programming libraries.

### *An Undocumented Secret*

Having shown you the official method of using classes located in libraries (the wrapper function to return a pointer to the class), we will now discuss another method that is officially unsupported, and is undocumented, but widely used.

Class modules have some properties that can't be seen or manipulated from inside the VBA editor. However, any module can be exported to a text file, and from a text editor, we can open that exported module and see and manipulate the properties that can't be manipulated from inside Access. Two of these properties will allow us to modify our class modules such that they can be directly used from our front end while residing in a class library, including directly instantiating them, using early binding, and so on.

The first thing we need to do is export the class to a text file. To do this, click on the class that you want to export and choose **Export** from the file menu. The **Export Module As** dialog will open.

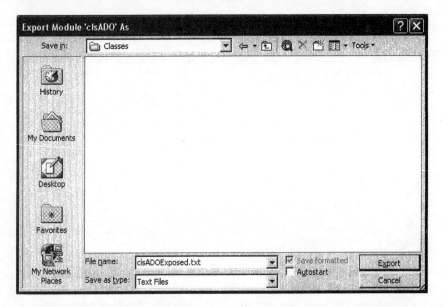

Notice that I started by exporting **clsADO**, but added **Exposed** to the end of the name. In the next step, we will pull this text file back into our library and it can't have the same name as the original class module. Make sure that you change the **Save as type** to **Text Files**, and then add a .txt to the end of the file name. Click **Export** and you will have saved the class module to the text file in the directory you selected. I have added a **Classes** directory under **My Documents** to hold all the class files that I export.

Once you have exported the class module to a text file, you can open the file with Notepad. When you do so, you will notice a bunch of lines above the normal Option statements that are usually at the top of the class when viewed from inside Access.

```
 clsADOExposed - Notepad
File  Edit  Format  View  Help
VERSION 1.0 CLASS
BEGIN
  MultiUse = -1  'True
END
Attribute VB_Name = "clsADO"
Attribute VB_GlobalNameSpace = False
Attribute VB_Creatable = False
Attribute VB_PredeclaredId = False
Attribute VB_Exposed = True
Option Compare Database
Option Explicit

Private Const JET_SCHEMA_USERROSTER = "{947bb102-5d43-11d1-bdbf-00c04fb92675}"

Public Sub GetUserRoster(vUserList As Variant, lReturnType As ReturnType)
```

The ones we are specifically interested in are:

**Attribute VB_Name = "clsADO"**
**Attribute VB_Creatable = False**
**Attribute VB_Exposed = True**

Using Notepad, we set the **VB_Name** to whatever we want the class to be called inside Access. The other two we will set to **True**. Notice that in this case **VB_Exposed** is already **True**, but this won't necessarily be the case with other classes that you might want to use this method on, and both properties must be set to **True** for this trick to work.

```
 clsADOExposed - Notepad
File  Edit  Format  View  Help
VERSION 1.0 CLASS
BEGIN
  MultiUse = -1  'True
END
Attribute VB_Name = "clsADOExposed"
Attribute VB_GlobalNameSpace = False
Attribute VB_Creatable = True
Attribute VB_PredeclaredId = False
Attribute VB_Exposed = True
Option Compare Database
Option Explicit

Private Const JET_SCHEMA_USERROSTER = "{947bb102-5d43-11d1-bdbf-00c04fb92675}"

Public Sub GetUserRoster(vUserList As Variant, lReturnType As ReturnType)
```

Save the text file and close Notepad.

In order to get the class text file back into the Access library, we need to insert a new class module (from the Insert menu), then choose File... from the Insert menu. We use the Insert File dialog to navigate to and select the text file we just created, and then click Open.

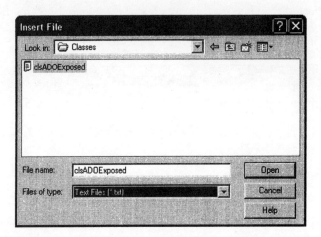

Doing so will import the text module into the new class module.

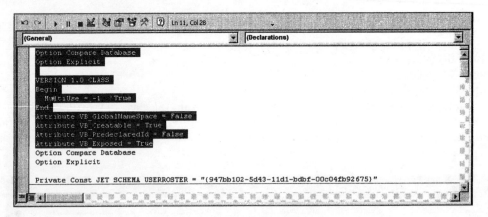

We have a little cleanup to do. Select and delete everything from the top Option Compare statement down to above the second Option Compare, then save the class module.

You're done!

To recap, for reasons known only to them, Microsoft does not allow us to see these class "properties" from inside the VBA editor (though they can be seen from inside VB's (the language) editor). Therefore, in order to work with them in Access, you exported the class to a text directory on the hard disk, which allows you to edit the class in an external editor. You edited these two class properties to set them to True. You then imported them back into Access, cleaning up some stuff that the import leaves exposed, and which, if left exposed, would cause compile errors. Because you have edited those hidden properties to True, you can now reference the class directly outside of the library.

Let's look at how it's used now, in the WhosInExposed procedure.

As before, there are two variables. The first is a typed class variable, which will hold the `MiniADO` class. Remember that we can now define this as `clsADOExposed` because the class can be seen outside of its own database (the library database). The second variable is a variant that will hold the user details.

```
Dim clsMiniADO      As clsADOExposed
Dim varUsers        As Variant
```

To instantiate the class we no longer have to use (or have) the `Public` function in the library database. We simply use the normal `Set MyVar = new ...` syntax

```
Set clsMiniADO = new clsADOExposed
```

Then we call the `GetUserRoster` method of the class.

```
clsMiniADO.GetUserRoster varUsers, RETURN_STRING
```

Finally, we can print out the user details.

```
Debug.Print varUsers
```

So there you have it, an undocumented way to expose classes so that they can be seen outside of the library that they reside in. Doing this gives us all the advantages of direct instantiation: early binding and IntelliSense. Using the "object and wrapper" method, we can not get any help from Access in seeing the names of methods or properties of the classes in our libraries, whereas with the new method we have code completion as well as the parameter prompting that occurs with early binding. In addition, we no longer have to build wrappers for the classes that we place into libraries. All in all, a very useful trick to have up our sleeve.

# Add-Ins

Add-Ins are another form of library, and although they contain objects such as code, tables, and forms, they are generally complete tools, rather than collections of code. Library databases are generally for the developer to use, but Add-Ins are usually for the end-user. They generally provide features, which while being useful to some users, are not really required as a central part of Access. By building these features into an Add-In you get the benefit of extra functionality combined with the ability to load it at will.

There are different types of Add-Ins, and which you use depends upon the task you need to accomplish. If you are creating objects, the Add-In will probably be a wizard or a builder, such as the controls wizards, form creation wizard, or the color builder. If you need to do more than this, or something that is completely separate from other objects, then creating an Add-In from scratch is probably the way to go. From here on, we're going to take an in-depth look at an example Add-In. We'll see how we can put it together and then use it in any database we want.

# The Language Converter Add-In

Let's imagine that you've just spent six months building your new application, and it's finally finished. The users have done their own testing and are really happy with it, and so is your manager. In fact, with a surprising amount of common sense, your manager has agreed that this application will be used in all of the company's offices around the world. "Great," you think, "at last, recognition for all of that hard work." So you start writing up installation instructions, only to be told that the application has to work in the native language of the company office. Oh boy. How do you manage that? All of the forms and reports will have to be translated, and your foreign language ability is well, shall we say, slightly lacking. Also, how do you manage the various copies of the application? Will you have to keep a copy for each language? But then what happens if you need to make a change? It's not looking good, is it?

Fear not, because this can all be done automatically (apart from the translation, of course). We can write an Add-In that allows the users to add new languages, edit the language details, and change all of the application's details. But how?

Remember how we looped through the controls on a form and changed the Font property? Well, the Caption is just another property, so this can be changed too. Here's how it's going to work:

❑ We create a language table in the database, with the following columns: FormName, ControlName, ControlType, DateUpdated. These are the basic columns that hold the details of each control on each form.

❑ Then, for each language, we add another column.

❑ We loop through all of the forms and controls, and add a row into our table or each control that has a Caption property, setting the language field to the actual caption.

At this stage we have a table that looks something like this:

| FormName | ControlName | ControlType | DateUpdated | English | French |
|---|---|---|---|---|---|
| frmClipCursor | cmdClip | Command button | 1/10/2002 02:40:26 | &Clip | |
| frmClipCursor | cmdUnclip | Command button | 1/10/2002 02:40:26 | &Unclip | |
| frmClipCursor | frmClipCursor | Form | 1/10/2002 02:40:26 | Cursor Clip Example | |
| frmCombination | cmdCalculate | Command button | 1/10/2002 02:40:26 | &Calculate | |
| frmCombination | frmCombinatior | Form | 1/10/2002 02:40:26 | Permutations Calculator | |
| frmCombination | Label1 | Label | 1/10/2002 02:40:26 | Number of items in pool: | |
| frmCombination | Label3 | Label | 1/10/2002 02:40:26 | Number of items required: | |
| frmCombination | Label5 | Label | 1/10/2002 02:40:26 | Number of Combinations: | |
| frmCompany | cmdFirst | Command button | 1/10/2002 02:40:26 | &First | |
| frmCompany | cmdLast | Command button | 1/10/2002 02:40:26 | &Last | |
| frmCompany | cmdNew | Command button | 1/10/2002 02:40:26 | Ne&w | |
| frmCompany | cmdNext | Command button | 1/10/2002 02:40:26 | &Next | |
| frmCompany | cmdPrevious | Command button | 1/10/2002 02:40:26 | &Previous | |
| frmCompany | frmCompany | Form | 1/10/2002 02:40:26 | Company Details | |
| frmCompany | Label11 | Label | 1/10/2002 02:40:26 | Country | |
| frmCompany | Label13 | Label | 1/10/2002 02:40:26 | Phone | |
| frmCompany | Label15 | Label | 1/10/2002 02:40:26 | Fax | |
| frmCompany | Label17 | Label | 1/10/2002 02:40:26 | Email | |
| frmCompany | Label19 | Label | 1/10/2002 02:40:26 | Web | |

Record: 1 of 102

We can now add text for the other language columns. To change the language, we can open the form in design mode, loop through the controls, and set the `Caption` property of the control to the value in the table.

This may sound rather complex, but it's quite easy. Let's give it a go.

*If you don't feel like typing all of these procedures in, then have a look in the `Lang.mda` database on the CD – they are all in there.*

**Try It Out** — **The Language Converter Add-In**

**1.** Create a new database called `LangXP.mda`. Notice that this is an `mda` file and not an `mdb`. There is no physical difference between an `mdb` and an `mda` file, but Add-Ins are generally given the `mda` suffix to differentiate them from standard Access databases.

*While we are on the subject of extensions, it is worth knowing that Access uses the extensions MDA and MDE to apply a filter to its Find dialog when setting references to files in the Addin manager and other places within Access. Generally speaking, addins and libraries both use MDA for the uncompiled version, and MDE for the compiled version. However, you can rename any file from MDB to MDA or MDE, MDE to MDB, and so on. Be careful, however. Just because you rename a file to MDE, it doesn't make it one. This is a case where the extension is supposed to mean something specific, that is, that it is compiled. It is also useful to know that developers have been known to rename their MDB databases (particularly a data "back end") to some custom extension like ROC or BIZ. This has the effect of "hiding" the fact that it is an Access database from prying eyes. However, it can be opened by Access just like any other database using Open with from the right-click menu of Explorer.*

Back to the subject at hand, you can make sure you create the correct type by selecting **All Files (\*.\*)** in the **Save as type** field on the new database dialog. If you don't do this, you'll get a database called `LangXP.mda.mdb`.

| File name: | Lang.mda |
| --- | --- |
| Save as type: | All Files |

**2.** Create a new table with the following fields:

| Field Name | Type | Length |
| --- | --- | --- |
| FormName | Text | 30 |
| ControlName | Text | 30 |

*Table continued on following page*

| Field Name  | Type      | Length |
|-------------|-----------|--------|
| ControlType | Text      | 20     |
| DateUpdated | Date/Time |        |
| English     | Text      | 255    |
| French      | Text      | 255    |

**3.** Set the primary key to be both `FormName` and `ControlName`. You can do this by highlighting these two fields and pressing the **Primary Key** button:

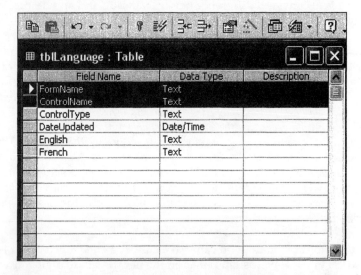

**4.** Once set, the fields show the key symbol against them:

| Field Name  | Data Type | Description |
|-------------|-----------|-------------|
| FormName    | Text      |             |
| ControlName | Text      |             |
| ControlType | Text      |             |

**5.** Set the `Allow Zero Length` property for the `English` and `French` columns to `Yes`:

| | |
|---|---|
| Validation Text |  |
| Required | No |
| Allow Zero Length | Yes |
| Indexed | No |
| Unicode Compression | Yes |

**6.** Save this table as `tblLanguage`, and close it.

**7.** Create a new module, and from the **Tools** menu pick **References**. Clear the box against **Microsoft ActiveX Data Objects 2.1 Library**, scroll down, and tick the box against **Microsoft DAO 3.6 Object Library**. Click **OK** to close the **References** dialog.

**8.** In the empty module, add the following constant:

```
Private Const wcs_LANGUAGE_TABLE As String = "tblLanguage"
```

**9.** Add the following procedure, which will loop through all of the forms:

```
Public Sub LangEnumerateForms(bolExtract As Boolean, strLang As String)

    Dim db As Database
    Dim recLang As Recordset
    Dim objAO As AccessObject
    Dim objCP As Object

    ' open the database and language recordset
    Set db = CurrentDb()
    Set recLang = db.OpenRecordset (wcs_LANGUAGE_TABLE)
    recLang.Index = "PrimaryKey"

    ' enumerate the forms
    Set objCP = Application.CurrentProject
    If bolExtract Then
       For Each objAO In objCP.AllForms
          LangExtractControls recLang, strLang, objAO.Name
       Next objAO
    Else
       For Each objAO In objCP.AllForms
          LangSetControls recLang, strLang, objAO.Name
       Next objAO
    End If

    ' close up
    recLang.Close

End Sub
```

**10.** Now another procedure, this time to loop through the controls on a form, extracting the caption into our language table:

```
Private Sub LangExtractControls(recLang As Recordset, strLang As String,
strFormName As String)
    Dim frmF As Form
    Dim ctlC As Control
```

```
Dim strControlName As String
Dim datNow As Date
Dim intControlType As Integer
   ' open the form, hidden, in design view
DoCmd.OpenForm strFormName, acDesign, , , , acHidden
datNow = Now()

' add the form caption
Set frmF = Forms(strFormName)
With recLang
   .Seek "=", strFormName, strFormName

   ' Add or update the form in the language table
   If .NoMatch Then
      .AddNew
   Else
      .Edit
   End If

   ' set the details
   !FormName = strFormName
   !ControlName = strFormName
   !ControlType = "Form"
   !DateUpdated = datNow
   .Fields(strLang) = frmF.Caption
   .Update

   ' now loop through the controls
   For Each ctlC In frmF.Controls

      ' we are only interested in the controls
      ' with a Caption property
      intControlType = ctlC.ControlType
      If ControlHasCaption(intControlType) Then

         ' find the control in the language table
         strControlName = ctlC.Name
         .Seek "=", strFormName, strControlName

         ' Add or update the control in the language table
         If .NoMatch Then
            .AddNew
         Else
            .Edit
         End If

         ' set the details
         !FormName = strFormName
         ! ControlType = ControlTypeName(intControlType)
         !DateUpdated ControlName = strControlName
         ! = datNow
         .Fields(strLang) = ctlC.Caption
         .Update
```

```
        End If
     Next
  End With

  ' close the form and save it
  DoCmd.Close acForm, strFormName, acSaveYes

End Sub
```

**11.** Now the opposite function, to loop through the controls setting the `Caption` property with the text in our languages table:

```
Private Sub LangSetControls(recLang As Recordset, _
          strLang As String, strFormName As String)

  Dim frmF As Form
  Dim ctlC As Control
  Dim strControlName As String
  Dim intControlType As Integer

  ' open the form, hidden, in design view
  DoCmd.OpenForm strFormName, acDesign, , , , acHidden

  ' add the form caption
  Set frmF = Forms(strFormName)
  With recLang
     .Seek "=", strFormName, strFormName

     ' Add or update the form in the language table
     If .NoMatch Or IsNull(.Fields(strLang)) Then
        frmF.Caption = ""
     Else
        frmF.Caption = .Fields(strLang)
     End If

     ' now loop through the controls
     For Each ctlC In frmF.Controls

        ' we are only interested in the controls
        ' with a Caption property
        intControlType = ctlC.ControlType
        If ControlHasCaption(intControlType) = True Then
           ' find the control in the language table
           strControlName = ctlC.Name
           .Seek "=", strFormName, strControlName

           ' Add or update the control in the language table
           If .NoMatch Or IsNull(.Fields(strLang)) Then
           ctlC.Caption = ""
           Else
              ctlC.Caption = .Fields(strLang)
```

```
            End If
        End If
    Next
End With

    ' close the form and save it
    DoCmd.Close acForm, strFormName, acSaveYes

End Sub
```

**12.** Now a function to determine if the control has a `Caption` property or not:

```
Private Function ControlHasCaption(intCtlType As Integer) As Boolean

    Select Case intCtlType
        Case acCommandButton, acLabel, acToggleButton
            ControlHasCaption = True
        Case Else
            ControlHasCaption = False
    End Select

End Function
```

**13.** Finally, a function to return the type name of controls with a `Caption` property.

```
Private Function ControlTypeName(intCtlType As Integer) As String

    Select Case intCtlType
        Case acLabel
            ControlTypeName = "Label"
        Case acCommandButton
            ControlTypeName = "Command button"
        Case acToggleButton
            ControlTypeName = "Toggle button"
    End Select

End Function
```

At this stage, the Add-In is functionally complete, so compile the code and make sure you save it – call it **Language Handling**. There are some things we need to do, though, before we can use it as an Add-In, so let's give it a test before turning it loose on another database.

**14.** Create a new form in this database, adding the following controls:

❑ A textbox

❑ A listbox

❑ A combo box

❑    A label

❑    A command button

❑    A toggle button

It doesn't matter what's in these controls. I made mine look like this:

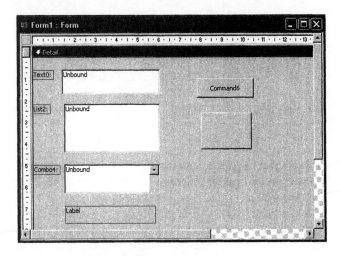

**15.** Save the form as `Form1`. Then switch back to the VBA IDE, and from the Immediate window run your new code, by typing:

LangEnumerateForms True, "English"

**16.** The code will run quite quickly, and when it's done, switch back to Access and open the languages table:

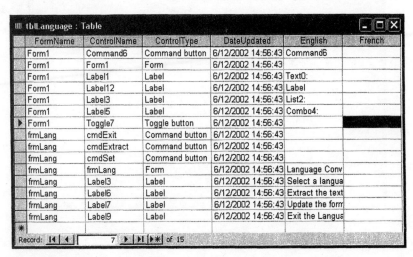

| FormName | ControlName | ControlType | DateUpdated | English | French |
|----------|-------------|-------------|-------------|---------|--------|
| Form1 | Command6 | Command button | 6/12/2002 14:56:43 | Command6 | |
| Form1 | Form1 | Form | 6/12/2002 14:56:43 | | |
| Form1 | Label1 | Label | 6/12/2002 14:56:43 | Text0: | |
| Form1 | Label12 | Label | 6/12/2002 14:56:43 | Label | |
| Form1 | Label3 | Label | 6/12/2002 14:56:43 | List2: | |
| Form1 | Label5 | Label | 6/12/2002 14:56:43 | Combo4: | |
| Form1 | Toggle7 | Toggle button | 6/12/2002 14:56:43 | | ▮ |
| frmLang | cmdExit | Command button | 6/12/2002 14:56:43 | | |
| frmLang | cmdExtract | Command button | 6/12/2002 14:56:43 | | |
| frmLang | cmdSet | Command button | 6/12/2002 14:56:43 | | |
| frmLang | frmLang | Form | 6/12/2002 14:56:43 | Language Conv | |
| frmLang | Label3 | Label | 6/12/2002 14:56:43 | Select a langua | |
| frmLang | Label6 | Label | 6/12/2002 14:56:43 | Extract the text | |
| frmLang | Label7 | Label | 6/12/2002 14:56:43 | Update the form | |
| frmLang | Label9 | Label | 6/12/2002 14:56:43 | Exit the Langua | |

Record: 14 ◀  7  ▶ ▶I ▶*  of 15

**17.** Add some values into the French column. If your language ability is like mine (I once got 7% in a French exam!) then you can do something like this:

| English | French |
| --- | --- |
| Command6 | le command |
| | le form |
| Text0: | le text |
| Label | le label |
| List2: | le list |
| Combo4: | le combo |
| | le toggle |
| | le command |
| | |

And please. No feedback from linguistic experts (or French people, come to think of it). This is just for testing. If you can speak French (and as you can see, I can't!) you might like to add some proper translations.

**18.** Close the language table and switch back to the Immediate window. Now run the language converter in its other mode – setting the language for the forms:

LangEnumerateForms False, "French"

**19.** When this has run, switch back to Access and view the form:

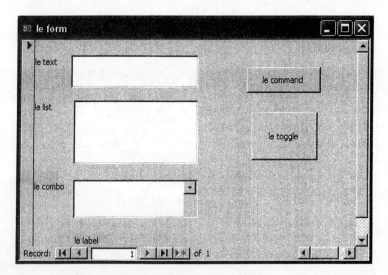

There you have it – easy conversion. You can add languages to the language table, and all you have to do is add a new language column, then add the new details in the new language column. The great beauty of this method is that you can create multi-lingual applications even if you can't speak the language the application needs translating into. All you need is someone who can speak the language to add the correct translations.

Let's have a quick look at how this works before we convert it into an Add-In.

## How It Works

Although it looks a little complex, it's actually quite simple. All it does is this:

❑ **Extract Language Mode – extracting the existing captions for the form and controls**

Pull out the caption for the form, and store it in the appropriate column in the languages table. Set the other details for the form (control name, type, and modification date). If no previous record exists for the form, a new one is created.

Similarly, loop through all the controls on the form, checking for any that have captions (by calling another function). A record is created (or edited) for each control that has a caption. Set the details as above (calling a function to determine the control type).

❑ **Set Language Mode – changing the language of the captions on the form and controls**

Change the caption of the form to that specified in the form's record, in the relevant language column.

Loop through the controls, checking for any that have captions (as above). For each of these, find the right control in the language table, and change its caption as specified in the correct language column.

Some of the techniques we've used have been explained before, so they shouldn't need too much detail.

Let's start with the LangEnumerateForms procedure. Depending on the argument passed to this procedure, we're either in extract language mode (mode 1) or set language mode (mode 2). The first thing we do here is to open both the database and the language table. Then we set the current index to be the primary index – that's because we will be using the Seek method later on.

```
Set db = CurrentDb()
Set recLang = db.OpenRecordset("tblLanguage")
recLang.Index = "PrimaryKey"
```

**633**

Now we need to loop through all of the forms using the `AllForms` collection, calling the correct procedure for each one, depending on our mode. If the `bolExtract` argument is `True`, we're in mode 1, so we call `LangExtractControls`; but if `bolExtract` is `False`, then we're in mode 2, so we call `LangSetControls`.

```
Set objCP = Application.CurrentProject
If bolExtract Then
    For Each objAO In objCP.AllForms
        LangExtractControls recLang, strLang, objAO.Name
    Next objAO
Else
    For Each objAO In objCP.AllForms
        LangSetControls recLang, strLang, objAO.Name
    Next objAO
End If

' close up
recLang.Close
```

## Mode 1

Let's now look at `LangExtractControls`. Opening the form in Design view, and being exposed to the user's view, is very distracting, if not downright disconcerting, so we open the form, hidden, in Design view. We also set a variable to hold the current date and time – this will allow us to see when the form details were last extracted.

```
DoCmd.OpenForm strFormName, acDesign, , , , acHidden
datNow = Now()
```

Next we set a form variable to point to the newly opened form. We then use the `With` statement on the language recordset. Both of these are for speed and clarity, as they are not only quicker, but they also make the code easier to read. Remember that the `With` statement allows us to just use the property or method name, in this case of the recordset, without repeating the recordset name.

```
Set frmF = Forms(strFormName)
With recLang
```

Now we look for the form name in the languages table. Forms have a `Caption` property, so we want to extract this:

```
.Seek "=", strFormName, strFormName
```

The `Seek` method sets the `NoMatch` property to `True` if the item sought wasn't found. So, if we don't find an existing record, we'll want to add a new one. Otherwise, we just want to edit the existing record.

```
If .NoMatch Then
    .AddNew
Else
    .Edit
End If
```

We are now on the correct record (either a new one or an existing one), so we want to set the details. We set the `FormName` and `ControlName` to the name of the form (remember this is the form's `Caption` property), the `ControlType`, and the `DateUpdated`.

```
!FormName = strFormName
!ControlName = strFormName
!ControlType = "Form"
!DateUpdated = datNow
```

We then need to set the value for the correct language, so we use the `Fields` collection of the recordset, using `strLang` as the index to this collection – `strLang` contains the name of the language, and was passed into this procedure as an argument.

```
.Fields(strLang) = frmF.Caption
```

Finally, for the form, we update the record.

```
.Update
```

At this stage all we have done is added (or updated) a single record in the languages table (the one for the form), so we now need to loop through the controls:

```
For Each ctlC In frmF.Controls
```

We are only interested in controls that have a caption, so we call the `ControlHasCaption` function – this returns `True` if the control has a `Caption` property. We'll look at this function in a little while.

```
intControlType = ctlC.ControlType
If ControlHasCaption(intControlType) = True Then
```

Now, in a similar way to the form, we use `Seek` to find the record in the languages table for this control, and we either add a new record, or update an existing record, depending upon whether it was found or not:

```
strControlName = ctlC.Name
.Seek "=", strFormName, strControlName
```

```
          If .NoMatch Then
              .AddNew
          Else
              .Edit
          End If
```

Once on the correct record, the details need updating. The `FormName` and `ControlName` are pretty obvious, as is the date. For the `ControlType` we call a separate function, `ControlTypeName`, to identify the type of control – again, we'll look at that function in a while.

```
          !FormName = strFormName
          !ControlName = strControlName
          !ControlType = ControlTypeName(intControlType)
          !DateUpdated = datNow
```

Then, as with the form, we set the field for the correct language:

```
          .Fields(strLang) = ctlC.Caption
```

Then we update this record, and move on to the next control.

```
              .Update
          End If
      Next
  End With
```

Finally, we close the form, saving the changes.

```
  DoCmd.Close acForm, strFormName, acSaveYes
```

It's really only a few steps. Let's see how the opposite function, `LangSetControls`, works.

### Mode 2

As with the previous function, we open the form in Design mode.

```
  DoCmd.OpenForm strFormName, acDesign, , , , acHidden
```

The next thing to do is get the text from the language table and set the `Caption` property of the form. As before, we use `Seek` to find the correct record.

```
  Set frmF = Forms(strFormName)
  With recLang
      .Seek "=", strFormName, strFormName
```

If no record was found (`NoMatch` is `True`), or if the entry for this language is empty, then we set the `Caption` to an empty string, otherwise we set the `Caption` to the value of the language field.

```
If .NoMatch Or IsNull(.Fields(strLang)) Then
    frmF.Caption = ""
Else
    frmF.Caption = .Fields(strLang)
End If
```

Now we need to loop through the controls, again only checking the ones that have a caption.

```
For Each ctlC In frmF.Controls
    intControlType = ctlC.ControlType
    If ControlHasCaption(intControlType) = True Then
```

Like the form, we use `Seek` to find the record, and set the caption to the value of the field in the language table, or to a blank string if the control wasn't found in the language table:

```
        strControlName = ctlC.Name
        .Seek "=", strFormName, strControlName

        If .NoMatch Or IsNull(.Fields(strLang)) Then
            ctlC.Caption = ""
        Else
            ctlC.Caption = .Fields(strLang)
        End If
    End If
    Next
End With
```

Finally, we close and save the form.

```
    DoCmd.Close acForm, strFormName, acSaveYes

End Sub
```

### The Supporting Functions

The only things left now are the two supporting functions. The first just identifies those controls that have a `Caption` property. Note that we define these ourselves.

```
Private Function ControlHasCaption(intCtlType As Integer) As Boolean

    Select Case intCtlType
    Case acCommandButton, acLabel, acToggleButton
        ControlHasCaption = True
    Case Else
```

```
      ControlHasCaption = False
   End Select

End Function
```

The second returns a string for the control type. This isn't really required, but it makes it easier to see in the language table what type a control is.

```
Private Function ControlTypeName(intCtlType As Integer)

   Select Case intCtlType
   Case acLabel
      ControlTypeName = "Label"
   Case acCommandButton
      ControlTypeName = "Command button"
   Case acToggleButton
      ControlTypeName = "Toggle button"
   End Select

End Function
```

That's all there is to this basic Add-In. There are still two things to do, however. The first is to give our Add-In a form of its own, so that other people can use it without resorting to the code windows. The second is to add some Access bits and pieces that will allow this database to be used as an Add-In.

## Creating the Add-In

1. Delete the test form and any records in the languages table.

2. Create a new form, making it look like this:

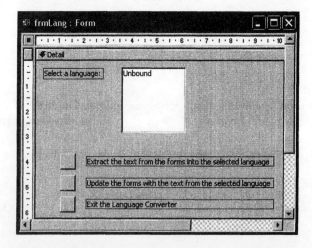

**3.** Name the listbox `lstLang`, set its Row Source Type to Value List and its Row Source to English;French:

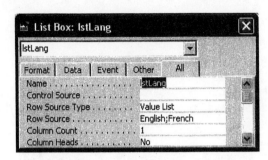

**4.** Name the three command buttons `cmdExtract`, `cmdSet`, and `cmdExit`, in order of top to bottom.

**5.** In the form Design view, press the `Code` button to create a code module for this form, and switch to the VBE.

**6.** In the `Click` event for `cmdExit`, add the following line of code:

```
DoCmd.Close
```

**7.** In the `Click` event for `cmdExtract`, add the following code:

```
If lstLang.ListIndex = -1 Then
    MsgBox "Please select a language"
Else
    LangEnumerateForms True, lstLang
End If
```

**8.** In the `Click` event for `cmdSet`, add the following code:

```
If lstLang.ListIndex = -1 Then
    MsgBox "Please select a language"
Else
    LangEnumerateForms False, lstLang
End If
```

**9.** Save the form as `frmLang`.

**10.** That's all we need for the user form. It allows the user to pick a language and then either extract or set the caption details. Now we need a public function to open this form, so create a new module, and add the following code:

```
Public Function wrox_Lang()

    DoCmd.OpenForm "frmLang"

End Function
```

**11.** Save this module as `Language Entry Point`.

**12.** Finally, let's set the database properties, so that the Add-In shows up nicely in the Add-In Manager. So, back in Access, select **Database Properties** from the **File** menu, and set them like this:

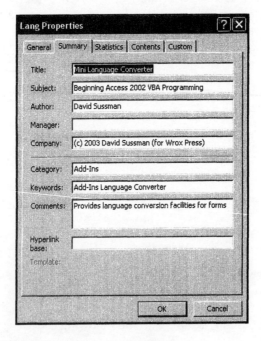

You can change the author and company if you like.

Now on to the final piece of the Add-In.

**Try It Out**   **Creating the USysRegInfo Table**

To use a database as an Add-In you need to create a special table, called `USysRegInfo`. This is a system table, so is not normally seen, and it needs to contain four columns and three rows. Rather than create this table yourself, it's a lot easier to just import it from the supplied language converter, `Lang.mda`, from the CD. You don't really need to know much about this table, except it's this table that Access uses to store some of the details for the Add-In.

*If you are interested in knowing more, do a web search on* **USysRegInfo** *and you should find an article on the Microsoft site called* Creating the USysRegInfo Table for a Microsoft Access 2000 Add-In *with lots of interesting details.*

**1.** In Access, from the **Tools** menu, select **Options**.

**2.** From the **View** tab, make sure the **System Objects** checkbox is selected. This allows us to see system objects, which are normally invisible.

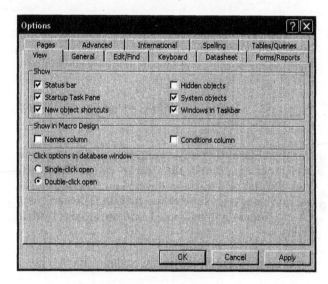

**3.** From the **File** menu, select **Get External Data**, and then **Import**.

**4.** From the **File** dialog, find and select `Lang.mda` on the CD, and press the **Import** button.

**5.** From the **Import Objects** dialog, on the **Tables** tab, select **USysRegInfo**, and press the **OK** button.

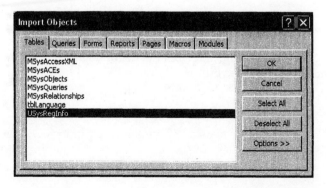

**6.** Open up the newly imported table:

| Subkey | Type | ValName | Value |
|---|---|---|---|
| HKEY_CURRENT_ACCESS_PROFILE\Menu Add-Ins\Mini Language &Converter | 0 | | |
| HKEY_CURRENT_ACCESS_PROFILE\Menu Add-Ins\Mini Language &Converter | 1 | Expression | =wrox_Lang() |
| HKEY_CURRENT_ACCESS_PROFILE\Menu Add-Ins\Mini Language &Converter | 1 | Library | |ACCDIR\Lang.mda |

USysRegInfo : Table — Record: 1 of 3

This table must contain these details for an Add-In to work, as the Add-In Manager uses these values to update the registry. The Subkey column shows the name of the Add-In – in this case we've called it **Language Converter** – the ampersand identifies the hot key, so the **C** will be underlined.

You can ignore the Type and ValNames columns, as long as the values you enter are the same as shown.

The Value column, for the bottom two rows, contains the important details. The first, for the Expression, identifies the entry point of the Add-In. This is the function that Access will call when the Add-In is run. It must be a Public Function. The second Value, for the Library, identifies the directory and database name of the Add-In. The name is Lang.mda, and |ACCDIR\ means that the Add-In will be copied into the Access Add-Ins directory. We'll see this happening a little later.

The Language Converter Add-In is now complete, so let's give it a go.

**Try It Out — Using the Language Converter**

**1.** Close the Add-In, and open up a database. Any one with forms will do. You might like to copy a database you've already got; that way your changes won't be permanent.

**2.** From the **Tools** menu, select **Add-Ins**, and then **Add-In Manager**. The list of installed Add-Ins will probably be blank, unless you've already used some.

**3.** Press the **Add New...** button, and from the file dialog select the Lang.mda you've just created, and press the **Open** button.

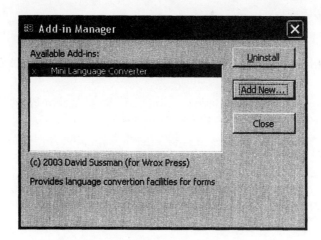

**4.** The Add-In is now installed. Notice the details at the bottom of this dialog – these come from the database properties that we set in the Add-In.

**5.** Press the Close button.

**6.** Before the Add-In can be used, you'll need a language table in this database, so from the File menu, select Get External Data, and then Import.

**7.** From the File dialog, find Lang.mda, and press the Open button.

**8.** From the Import Objects dialog, select tblLanguage from the Tables tab, and press the OK button. This imports the language table into the local database.

**9.** From the Tools menu, select Add-Ins, and then Mini Language Converter. The main screen pops up just as it did when testing.

**10.** Select English and press the Extract button. This will extract all of the captions from the forms.

**11.** Open the language table to have a look at what it's done.

**12.** Add some text to the French column, and then try setting the captions to French.

So, there you have it. Some code which is fairly simple, in a standalone database, which can be shipped to any office, in any country, and works with any database. Your boss will be very impressed, so go for that pay rise!

### *The Complete Language Converter Add-In*

There are a number of small faults with the language converter as it stands:

❑ You have to manually create, or import, the language table into any database in which you wish to use the converter. The table should really be created automatically for you.

❑ To add new languages you have to edit the table. This should also be automatic, removing what could be a complex task for a user.

❑ To edit the details you have to open the table manually. A nice form to allow editing would be better.

Although not major faults, these could be considered bad programming, since they give the user tasks to perform which could either be eliminated or smoothed. There are two ways around this problem:

❑ As an exercise, add these facilities to the converter you've just created.

❑ Use the `Language.mda` converter supplied on the CD. This is a fully completed version, which looks like this:

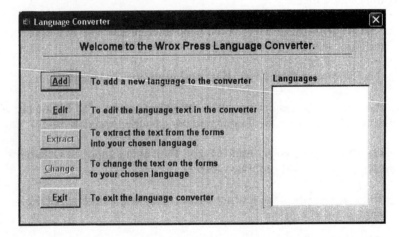

The code is only slightly different from the converter you've just created, and it has a few extra facilities. But you're well on the way to creating this yourself, so why not give it a try?

## *The Color Schemes Add-In*

Another Add-In that's quite useful is the Color Schemes one. Do you like the way Windows allows you to select the appearance of various screen items? So do I, so I thought a similar facility for Access forms might be a good idea.

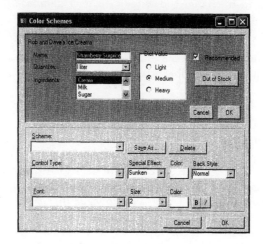

This uses a very similar technique to the language converter, looping through the controls on a form and setting the various properties. In fact, the above form is more complex than the code that applies the scheme.

We're not going to look at the code here, but you might like to browse through it. You can find it on the CD, called Schemes.mda.

## Creating Add-Ins Summary

Although creating Add-Ins is quite simple, it's worth reiterating a few points.

- ❑ You must have a USysRegInfo file in the Add-In. The Add-In Manager requires this to be able to load your Add-In. You can copy this table from any other Add-In and just modify the values.

- ❑ The entry function pointed to in USysRegInfo should be a Public Function.

- ❑ Make all of your procedures Private, unless you want them exposed to calling databases.

- ❑ If your Add-In takes several steps, then display your forms as dialog boxes (set the WindowMode argument to acDialog). This prevents the user from continuing until your form has finished.

- ❑ Bound objects are bound to the data in the Add-In. So a form based on a table shows the records in the table in the Add-In. If you need to use bound forms you can link user tables into the Add-In database for the duration of processing. The Color Schemes Add-In does this.

- ❑ If you are creating recordsets, then remember that CurrentDB() points to the user database, and CodeDB() points to the Add-In database. You can also use the new Access objects CurrentData and CurrentProject to point to the user database, and CodeData and CodeProject to point to the Add-In database.

**645**

- ❏ Don't let your Add-In change the state of the user database. This doesn't apply to Add-Ins that change forms, but to Access options. If you need to change any global options, keep a copy of what they are so they can be reset when your Add-In finishes.

- ❏ Create error-handling code. Your Add-In is meant to make the user's life easier, so don't dump them out to horrible error messages.

If you stick to these few basic rules, you should be OK.

## Updating your Add-In

There's one think to watch during the development of Add-Ins, and that's the location of the Add-In that's running. Office XP is a very user-based application, so when you install an Add-In, it copies it into its own directory. Under Windows 98 this is:

`\Windows\Application Data\Microsoft\Addins`

Under Windows NT, this is:

`\WinNT\Profiles\username\Application Data\Microsoft\AddIns\`

Under Windows 2000/XP, this is:

`\Documents and Settings\username\Application Data\Microsoft\AddIns\`

This means that once installed, there are two copies of the Add-In. One in the original directory, and one in the AddIns directory, so any changes you do must be done in the right place.

There's no problem with leaving the Add-In installed and editing the mda file directly in the AddIns directory, but you must close down any instances of Access that have been using the Add-In. That's right – close Access. Just closing the database doesn't free the lock. However, when you have finished making your changes, don't forget to update the "master" copy of the Add-In in your original development environment. Most of us forget that the copy being used is in our username path and ship out the copy in the development directory, so that one had better have all your changes.

These aren't major problems, but can be a bit of a pain. Just bear them in mind while you are developing your Add-Ins.

## Summary

In this chapter we've looked at ways to extend the functionality of Access, both from a programmer's point of view, by using library databases, and from a user's point of view, by using Add-Ins. Both of these use standard Access databases, so there's no major difference between what you do in these databases and what you do in normal databases.

What we've concentrated on is:

❑ Using library databases to provide common functionality to many databases. This allows you to provide routines to other Access programmers, and is especially useful for supplying routines to power users, who are good at using Access, but haven't mastered VBA yet.

❑ Using object-oriented features, by providing class libraries. These extend the benefits of classes, putting them in a more distributable format.

❑ Using Add-Ins to extend the functionality of Access, providing users with a richer working environment.

As you've seen, there's not a great deal of complexity involved in using libraries and Add-Ins, just a few points to follow and a few points to watch out for.

Now it's time to look at extending the functionality of Access by using other applications, such as Word and Excel.

# Exercises

**1.** Think about how you could use the language converter so that the language is changed as the form is opened, rather than a permanent change. If used with security, you could store a table of user names, along with their preferred language, and as each form is opened, run a procedure that changes the controls. You've already seen how quick this is, so there'll be virtually no slow down from the user's point of view.

**2.** Add a facility to allow message boxes to have language facilities. This is fairly easy to do, as you could just add records into the language table, using a unique name for each message box. Then instead of calling MsgBox with a direct string, you could replace the string with a call to a function that looked up the language string in the table.

**3.** Currently the language converter only works with forms. Try extending it so that it works for reports as well.

**4.** Try our secret tip (exposing classes in libraries) to export the Shape class out to the MiniADO.mdb library, and then modify the other classes that use Shape. Hint... don't forget to delete (or rename) the Shape class from the Ice Cream database before using the one in the library. Remember that our scope rules say to search the current database before going out to a library, so if you don't delete the one in the current database, you will never use the one in the library.

# C H A P T E R 16

# Automation

Life, it seems, is getting more and more hectic for everyone. Every business needs a competitive advantage and that generally revolves around its business processes. The more efficient you can make them, the quicker, and therefore cheaper, they are to perform. One way to achieve this is to automate and reuse existing processes. That's really what a lot of programming is anyway: the automation of complex or monotonous processes.

In this chapter we are going to see how object orientation can be used at a much higher level than you've seen so far. We've talked about code and object reuse, but here we are going to look at application reuse. All of the Microsoft Office applications have the ability to be used as objects from within VBA, so that means we can use things that Microsoft has written for us.

What we're going to look at here is:

- ❑  What exactly automation is
- ❑  Understanding how to use other applications
- ❑  How to use Outlook for mail and appointments
- ❑  How to use charts
- ❑  How to use Word for reporting

## What Is Automation?

Even though you may not realize it, you've already seen automation in action, as using any standalone object is a form of automation. Remember when you went into the References and selected the DAO Library and then defined a variable as type Recordset? Well, that's just using an existing object.

So, in VBA and programming terms, automation is just the use of other objects. At the application level that means using such things as Outlook to send mail messages, or perhaps embedding an Excel chart on an Access form. What these do is just use some existing functionality, but instead of this functionality coming from a class, or a small object, it comes from an application. So you must get into the habit of thinking of everything as an object, even applications.

There are two descriptions that you might hear about when dealing with automation, and they are **Automation Server** and **Automation Client**.

> *Automation used to be called OLE Automation, so you might hear of OLE Servers and OLE Clients, but these days it's generally just referred to as Automation.*

An Automation Server is the object you are using (it has nothing to do with physical machines), and an Automation Client is the one using the object. So, if you have some VBA code in an Access module, and that code uses Microsoft Excel, then Access is the Client, and Excel is the Server.

## Interfaces and Object Models

Objects have **interfaces**, and these define what parts of the object the programmer can see – this usually means the methods, properties, and events. Remember when we looked at classes the Public procedures became methods and the Property procedures became properties? That's the interface – the view the user of the object has. All of the Private procedures and Private variables are part of the object, but they are not part of the interface, because they cannot be seen outside of the object.

An object model is just another way of saying interface, and is usually a diagram showing the objects and collections. For example, a portion of the DAO object model is shown below:

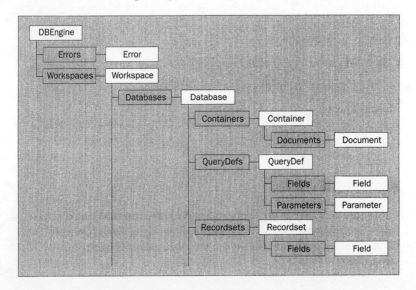

The `Objects` are shown shaded and the `Collections` are in white. This sort of diagram allows us to clearly see the hierarchy of objects, and makes it easier to find our way around the objects. For example if we have a `Recordset` object we know it has a `Fields` collection. This means we can instantly know that code like this will work:

```
For Each objField in objRec.Fields
Next
```

Understanding the object model is paramount to using automation. All of the Office applications have an object model, but we won't be including them in the book, as they are far too large. They are well covered in the Office documentation (make sure you install the VBA Help for all of the applications), and we've also included the most relevant sections of them on the CD.

> Of course, Wrox have a range of Office VBA books available – check out www.wrox.com for more details.

# Object References

Before you can use an Automation Object you need to create a reference to the appropriate object library. An **object library** is usually a DLL or OCX file that contains the code for the object. You can see which objects are installed on your machine by switching to the VBA IDE and selecting References... from the Tools menu:

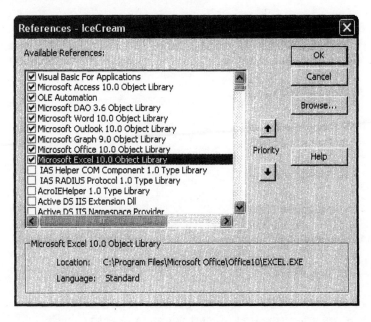

In the example above, the database has nine references set – these are the ones with check marks against them. You can easily set a reference by just checking an item, and unchecking an item removes the reference – it doesn't remove the object library, just the reference. You saw in the previous chapter that you can use the **Browse...** button to browse for other objects that are not already registered – such as an Access Add-In.

> **To complete the exercises in this chapter you should ensure that you at least have the references for Outlook, Word, Graph, and Office set, just like the picture above. You can scroll down through the list to find the libraries that you need.**

# Creating Automation Objects

Because automation objects are just objects, you can create them in the same way as you've created other objects. For example, to create a recordset object variable you use a `Dim` statement:

```
Dim objRec As Recordset
```

Similarly, to create an instance of an application object, you generally use this format:

```
Dim objApp As application_name.Application
```

Here, *application_name* would be `Word`, `Outlook`, or `Excel`. Using this just creates a variable to hold an object of the appropriate type, and doesn't actually create the object. This method is generally used when the object already exists, and you are just using your own variable. For example, consider a `Field` in a recordset – you would declare the variable like this:

```
Dim objFld As Field
```

This doesn't create a new `Field` object, but just creates a variable to hold an existing `Field`. This means that you cannot do this:

```
objFld.Name = "NewField"
```

If you try this you will get an error (Error 91 – Object variable or With block variable not set). That's because `objFld` is not an object, just an object variable – it hasn't been instantiated. If you want to create a new object then you use the `New` keyword. For example:

```
Dim objFld As New Field
```

You can then set the field name because the object has been instantiated. In reality the object is instantiated when you access the first property or method of the object.

So, the rules are:

❑ If you are going to point to an object that already exists, just use the normal syntax.

❑ If you are creating a new instance of an object, then you must use the New keyword. We usually do this in the Set statement rather than in the Dim statement, though either works.

# Microsoft Outlook

You saw in Chapter 10 how easily mail can be sent from within Access, using DoCmd.SendObject, but this is rather restrictive. It doesn't allow you to set options on the message, or do anything complex – it's really just designed for sending objects. To achieve a greater degree of control over the mail procedure you can use the Outlook object model to send messages.

To use Outlook there are only a few objects you need to know about:

| Object | Description |
|---|---|
| Outlook.*Application* | The main Outlook application. |
| MailItem | A mail message. |
| AppointmentItem | A diary appointment. |
| NoteItem | A note. |

In fact, most of the folders in Outlook have an associated Item object.

Using Outlook programmatically means that we can build sending mail into existing processes. Consider the ingredients table, which has the UnitsInStock and ReOrderPoint fields. Every time an order is placed the UnitsInStock field should be decreased, and if it drops below the ReOrderPoint, then an order could be mailed automatically. This would prevent the ingredients from ever running out. Or you could run this as a weekly procedure, so that you don't send lots of small orders to the same supplier. That's what we'll do here. We'll create a query that shows us which items are below the reorder point, and then we'll create a mail message to our supplier requesting these items.

*If you are an AOL user, then you won't be able to use Microsoft Outlook to send mail messages. AOL uses a proprietary mail system. You can still run through the exercise, but you won't actually be able to send mail.*

**1.** Create a new query, adding `tblIngredient` and `tblSupplierList`. Add `fkCompanyID` from `tblSupplierList`, and `Name` and `ReOrderPoint` from `tblIngredient`.

**2.** In the **Criteria** field for `ReOrderPoint` add the following:

```
> [UnitsInStock]
```

The query should now look like this:

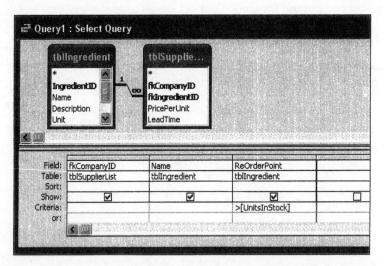

**3.** Close the query, saving it as `qryReOrder`. Now create a new query, adding `tblCompany`, `tblSupplierList`, and `tblIngredient`.

**4.** Add `CompanyID`, `CompanyName`, `ContactName`, and `Email` from `tblCompany`, and `ReOrderPoint` from `tblIngredient`.

**5.** For the **Criteria** for `ReOrderPoint` add the following:

```
> [UnitsInStock]
```

The query should now look like this:

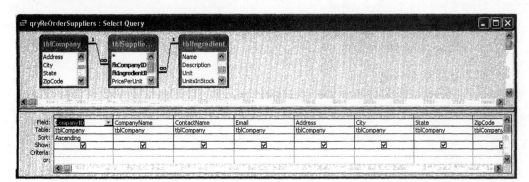

6. View the properties of the query. You can do this by the **Properties** button on the toolbar, or by selecting **Properties** from the **View** menu, or **Properties** from the context menu (right mouse button).

7. Change the **Unique Records** property to **Yes**. Now close the query, saving it as `qryReOrderSuppliers`.

8. Create a new module. From the **Tools** menu select **References**, check **Microsoft Outlook 10.0 Object Library**, and press **OK** to close the dialog.

9. Create a new procedure called `ReOrder` in the empty module. Add the following code:

```
Public Sub ReOrder()

Dim db As Database

Dim recReOrder As Recordset

Dim recSupps As Recordset
Dim objOutlook As New Outlook.Application
Dim objMessage As MailItem
Dim strSQL As String
Dim strOrder As String
Dim strItems As String

Set db = CurrentDb()

Set recSupps = db.OpenRecordset("qryReOrderSuppliers")

While Not recSupps.EOF
    strSQL = "SELECT * FROM qryReOrder " & _
        "WHERE fkCompanyID = " & recSupps("CompanyID")
    Set recReOrder = db.OpenRecordset(strSQL)
```

```
        strItems = "Item" & vbTab & "   Quantity"
    While Not recReOrder.EOF
        strItems = strItems & vbCrLf & recReOrder("Name") & _
            vbTab & recReOrder("ReOrderPoint")
        recReOrder.MoveNext
    Wend
    recReOrder.Close

    strOrder = "Dear " & recSupps("ContactName") & _
        vbCrLf & vbCrLf & _
        "Once again we are running short of the following items:" & _
        vbCrLf & vbCrLf & _
        strItems & _
        vbCrLf & vbCrLf & _
        "I'd be grateful if you could deliver " & _
        "these as soon as possible." & _
        vbCrLf & vbCrLf & _
        "Many Thanks" & _
        vbCrLf & vbCrLf & _
        "Dave"

    If Not IsNull(recSupps("Email")) Then
        Set objMessage = objOutlook.CreateItem(olMailItem)
        With objMessage
            .To = recSupps("Email")
            .Subject = "New Order"
            .Body = strOrder
            .Send
        End With
    End If

    recSupps.MoveNext
Wend

recSupps.Close
Set recSupps = Nothing
Set recReOrder = Nothing
Set objOutlook = Nothing
Set objMessage = Nothing

End Sub
```

**10.** Save the module as `Email`. Now switch to the `Immediate` window and try the procedure out, by typing `ReOrder`, or by pressing the Play button on the menu bar.

**11.** When the procedure has finished, open Outlook and have a look in either your **Outbox** or your **Sent Items** folder. You should have a mail message there somewhere The procedure sends one mail message to each supplier with an e-mail address (here, there's only one supplier). Where the message appears depends on whether you've got a connection set up:

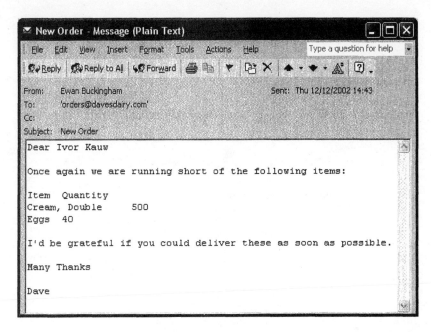

Admittedly the order details could be formatted a little nicer, but that's not a great deal of trouble. We're really concentrating on sending the message here.

## How It Works

Let's first look at the queries we created. The first, qryReOrder, shows the ingredients that need reordering. We've included the ReOrderPoint in this query because we are going to order the same number of items that the ReOrderPoint contains. The second query, qryReOrderSuppliers, shows the supplier details – contact name and e-mail address. Setting the Unique Records property to Yes ensures that we only see one record for each supplier. If this value was No then we would see a row for each supplier, for each product that needed reordering. We want one entry for each supplier because we are going to send a single mail message to each supplier with all of the order details on it.

Now on to the procedure. The first thing it does is declare all of the variables. The first three you've seen before – a database object and two recordsets. We need a recordset for the suppliers and one for the order items. Next comes the two Outlook objects – the main Outlook application, and a mail message item. Finally there are three strings – to hold a SQL query, the full order text and the order details:

```
Dim db As Database
Dim recReOrder As Recordset
Dim recSupps As Recordset
Dim objOutlook As New Outlook.Application
```

```
Dim objMessage As MailItem

Dim strSQL As String
Dim strOrder As String
Dim strItems As String
```

Once the variables are declared, we can open the database and create the recordset of suppliers:

```
Set db = CurrentDb()
Set recSupps = db.OpenRecordset("qryReOrderSuppliers")
```

We now need to loop through each supplier:

```
While Not recSupps.EOF
```

We need to create a list of order items for this supplier, so we create a SQL string, based on qryReOrder. Once the SQL string is set we create a recordset from it:

```
strSQL = "SELECT * FROM qryReOrder " & _
    "WHERE fkCompanyID = " & recSupps("CompanyID")
Set recReOrder = db.OpenRecordset(strSQL)
```

Now we have a recordset containing ingredients for a particular supplier, and we want a list of these in our mail message, so we create a string containing the item to be ordered and the quantity to order. We simply loop through the recordset adding these details to a string. We use the intrinsic constants vbCrLf and vbTab to provide new lines and tabs in the string. Once the loop is finished we can close the recordset, because all of the details we need are now in the string:

```
strItems = "Item" & vbTab & "   Quantity"
While Not recReOrder.EOF
    strItems = strItems & vbCrLf & recReOrder("Name") & _
        vbTab & recReOrder("ReOrderPoint")
    recReOrder.MoveNext
Wend
recReOrder.Close
```

We can't just send a message with a list of the ingredients, so we add the contact name as some more text, again using intrinsic constants to format this text. We use a separate string for the items and for the full order details, because we'll be using the items later in the chapter:

```
strOrder = "Dear " & recSupps("ContactName") & _
    vbCrLf & vbCrLf & _
    "Once again we are running short of the following items:" & _
    vbCrLf & vbCrLf & _
    strItems & _
    vbCrLf & vbCrLf & _
```

```
"I'd be grateful if you could deliver " & _
"these as soon as possible." & _
vbCrLf & vbCrLf & _
"Many Thanks" & _
vbCrLf & vbCrLf & _
"Dave"
```

The string is now complete, so the mail message can be created. If the e-mail address field in the database is empty, then obviously we can't send an e-mail order. We didn't omit records that have no e-mail address in the query because we are going to modify this procedure later on, and we want to make sure it copes with all suppliers, and not just those that have e-mail addresses.

```
If Not IsNull(recSupps("Email")) Then
```

The variable `objOutlook` is an instance of the Outlook application. One of the methods this has is `CreateItem`, which creates an item of a specific type – in this case we use an intrinsic constant to specify a mail item:

```
Set objMessage = objOutlook.CreateItem(olMailItem)
```

We now have a mail message item, so we can set some properties. The `To` property is the e-mail address of the recipient, and the `Subject` property is the subject line. The `Body` property is the actual body of the message, so we set this to the string we have created. We then use the `Send` method to send the message:

```
With objMessage
    .To = recSupps("Email")
    .Subject = "New Order"
    .Body = strOrder
    .Send
End With
End If
```

That's the end of one supplier, so we move on to the next:

```
    recSupps.MoveNext
Wend
```

And that's the end of the suppliers, so we close the recordset and clean up any object references, to free the memory they use:

```
recSupps.Close
Set recSupps = Nothing
Set recReOrder = Nothing
Set objOutlook = Nothing
Set objMessage = Nothing
```

Pretty easy, huh? In fact the section of code that actually sends the message is far simpler than the code that creates the message body.

Another way of achieving the aim of ordering by e-mail would be to create a file, perhaps a saved report or a Word document, containing the order details, and then attach that to the mail message. We'll look at that method in a little while, when we look at Word.

Next we'll look at how to create appointments in Outlook, which will hopefully cure you of some of those horrible yellow notes you've got stuck all around your monitor! What we'll do is add a reminder to our Outlook diary, reminding us when the orders we've just placed are due – they are usually expected within three days.

### Try It Out — Using Automation for Appointments

**1.** Open the Email module you've just created.

**2.** Create a new Private procedure, as follows:

```
Private Sub MakeAppointment(objOApp As Outlook.Application, _
    strCompany As String, strBody As String)

    Dim objAppt As AppointmentItem

    Set objAppt = objOApp.CreateItem(olAppointmentItem)
    With objAppt
        .Subject = "Order due from " & strCompany
        .Body = strBody
        .Start = Date + 3 & " 8:00"
        .End = Date + 3 & " 8:00"
        .ReminderSet = True
        .Save
    End With

End Sub
```

**3.** Add a new line to the ReOrder procedure, after the mail message has been sent, just before moving to the next supplier which calls the new MakeAppointment sub:

```
    End With
End If

MakeAppointment objOutlook, recSupps("CompanyName"), strItems

recSupps.MoveNext
Wend
```

**4.** Save the module, and run it again.

**5.** Open Outlook and have a look at the calendar, for three days from now:

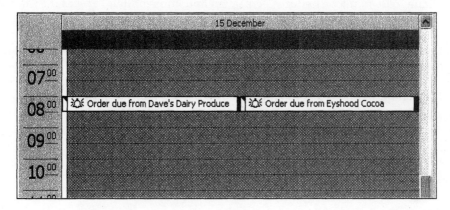

**6.** Open one of the appointments to look at it in detail:

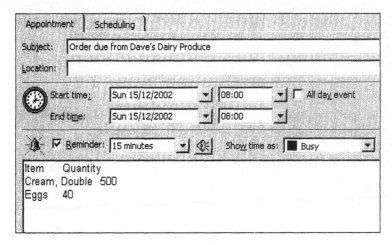

Notice how the start and end times are the same, and that the body of the appointment mirrors the details from the order?

Let's first look at the MakeAppointment procedure, which takes three arguments. The first is the Outlook application object. This could have been declared as a global variable, but since it's only going to be used in two procedures, it seems sensible to pass it as an argument. The second argument is the company name, and the third the body of the appointment.

```
Private Sub MakeAppointment(objOApp As Outlook.Application, _
    strCompany As String, strBody As String)
```

The first thing to do in the procedure is create an appointment item. This is the same method as we used to create a mail item – all we do is use a different constant:

```
Dim objAppt As AppointmentItem
Set objAppt = objOApp.CreateItem(olAppointmentItem)
```

Now we can set the appointment details. The Subject of the appointment is a note that the order is due from the company, and the Body contains the details passed in as the third argument. We'll see what these are in a minute:

```
With objAppt
    .Subject = "Order due from " & strCompany
    .Body = strBody
```

We set the Start and End times of the appointment to be today's date, as returned by the Date function, with three days added to it (remember from our early chapters on data types that adding a number to a date adds that number of days). We also append the time to this string, since without an explicit time, the appointment defaults to midnight:

```
    .Start = Date + 3 & " 8:00"
    .End = Date + 3 & " 8:00"
```

We then ensure that a reminder flag is set so that the appointment will pop up a reminder at the appropriate time and date, and then we save the appointment:

```
    .ReminderSet = True
    .Save
End With

End Sub
```

To create the appointment, we simply call this function:

```
MakeAppointment objOutlook, recSupps("CompanyName"), strItems
```

We pass in the Outlook application object, the company name, and the list of ingredients.

Once again you can see that using automation to use the facilities of Outlook is extremely simple. With only a few extra lines of code we now have an automatic reminder system. You could also use this sort of thing for adding payment reminders when you send out orders to customers.

# Microsoft Word

Using automation to drive Microsoft Word is more complex than Outlook, because it has such a large object model. There are literally hundreds of options that you can use, and it's often very confusing for the beginner. This is not really surprising considering the large number of things that you can do in Word – format text, insert tables, etc. In some respects, because Word is such a visual tool, you wonder whether it's really worth delving into the object model?

The answer to that conundrum is obviously going to be yes, otherwise there wouldn't be anything about it in this chapter, but there are two ways to combine the use of Word and Access. The first, using Mail Merge, has Word as the client requesting data from Access. You get the option to put Access fields in document templates, and then merge these into a document. However, this has always been rather restrictive. You can produce form letters, where the data from each row in the data source is inserted somewhere among the letter text. This is pretty much the way all that junk mail you receive works. You can also create a Catalog, where each row of data is shown after the previous one – exactly like a catalog. What's more difficult, however, is the combination of these two methods. Think about what we've just done with Outlook. We had a parent record (the supplier) and some child records (the order items). This isn't so easy to set up using a mail merge.

So a good way to achieve this is using the second way of combining Access and Word – using automation from Access to push the data into Word documents. This involves starting Word, in much the same way as we started Outlook, creating documents, and adding text to them. This is perfect to fill the gap in our re-ordering setup. At the moment orders are only placed for those suppliers who have e-mail addresses, so for those that don't have e-mail we need some form of paper order. What we'll do is create a Word document containing the order details, and print this out. This can then be faxed or sent to the supplier.

Let's give it a go. The following example uses the Word template `Order.dot`, which is on the accompanying CD. We use a template just to give us the basic layout of the report. This should be copied into the directory where you have placed the other samples. The example also saves documents in this directory *as well as printing them out*.

> *If you have installed your samples in another location then you should change* `C:\BegAccessVBA2002` *to the appropriate directory.*

## Try It Out     Creating a Word Document

1. Modify the query `qryReOrderSuppliers`, and add the `Address`, `State`, `City`, `PostCode`, and `Country` fields.

2. Now create a new module.

3. Add the following global variables:

```
Private Const m_strTEMPLATE As String = " Order.dot"

Private m_objWord As Word.Application
Private m_objDoc As Word.Document
```

**4.** Now the main procedure, to create the order letter:

```
Public Sub CreateOrderLetter(recSupp As Recordset, recItems As Recordset)
Dim m_strDIR As String

    m_strDIR = CurrentProject.Path & "\"
    Set m_objWord = New Word.Application
    Set m_objDoc = m_objWord.Documents.Add(m_strDIR & g_strTEMPLATE)

    InsertTextAtBookMark "ContactName", recSupp("ContactName")
    InsertTextAtBookMark "CompanyName", recSupp("CompanyName")
    InsertTextAtBookMark "Address", recSupp("Address")
    InsertTextAtBookMark "City", recSupp("City")
    InsertTextAtBookMark "State", recSupp("State")
    InsertTextAtBookMark "PostCode", recSupp("PostCode")
    InsertTextAtBookMark "Country", recSupp("Country")

    InsertItemsTable recItems

    m_objWord.PrintOut Background:=False

    m_objDoc.SaveAs FileName:= m_strDIR & recSupp("CompanyName") & _
        " - " & FormatDateTime(Date, vbLongDate) & ".DOC"
    m_objDoc.Close
    m_objWord.Quit

    Set m_objDoc = Nothing
    Set m_objWord = Nothing

End Sub
```

**5.** Next comes a function to insert some text at a specific point:

```
Private Sub InsertTextAtBookMark(strBkmk As String, varText As Variant)

    m_objDoc.Bookmarks(strBkmk).Select
    m_objWord.Selection.Text = varText & ""

End Sub
```

**6.** And now a procedure to insert a table:

```
Private Sub InsertItemsTable(recR As Recordset)

    Dim strTable As String
    Dim objTable As Word.Table

    strTable = "Item" & vbTab & "Quantity" & vbCr
    recR.MoveFirst
    While Not recR.EOF
        strTable = strTable & recR("Name") & vbTab & _
            recR("ReOrderPoint") & vbCr
        recR.MoveNext
    Wend

    InsertTextAtBookMark "Items", strTable
    Set objTable = m_objWord.Selection.ConvertToTable(Separator:=vbTab)
    objTable.AutoFormat Format:=wdTableFormatClassic3, AutoFit:=True, _
        ApplyShading:=False

    Set objTable = Nothing

End Sub
```

**7.** The code for Word is now finished, so we just need to call the main function when we run our ReOrder procedure. Don't forget to save this module – call it **Word Functions**.

**8.** Open the **Email** module you created earlier.

**9.** In the ReOrder procedure, add the following highlighted line. It should go after the string of items has been created, but before the recordset of items is closed:

```
While Not recReOrder.EOF
    strItems = strItems & vbCrLf & recReOrder("Name") & _
        vbTab & recReOrder("ReOrderPoint")
    recReOrder.MoveNext
Wend

CreateOrderLetter recSupps, recReOrder

recReOrder.Close
```

**10.** Save this module and run it. It should take a little longer this time, and you might see a printing window, indicating that the order letter is being printed out.

**11.** When the procedure is finished have a look in C:\BegAccessVBA2002 (or wherever you installed your samples) for two new documents, which you can view in Word:

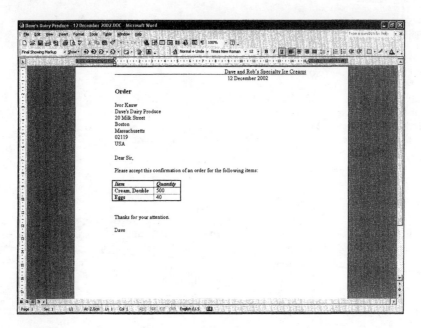

You can see that we now have a pretty good Word document, with a table of the orders.

## How It Works

The first thing to do is look at the Word template:

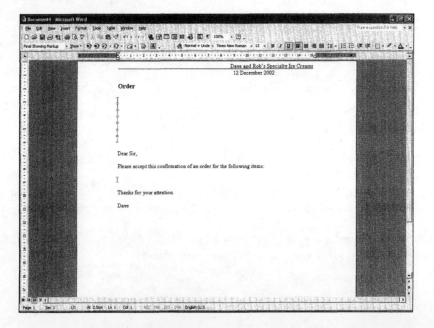

What you'll notice here is the large I symbols – these represent bookmarks.

*If you don't see the bookmarks, then from the **Tools** menu select **Options**, and on the **View** tab select **Bookmarks** in the **Show** section:*

If you select **Bookmarks** from the **Insert** menu you'll see a list of them:

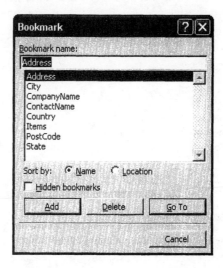

Bookmarks in Word documents are just the same as bookmarks you place in books – that shopping receipt or envelope you tuck into a book to remind you where you are. This is the same – they allow you to jump to specified places in the document. Using automation we can jump to these bookmarks and insert text. Notice there's only one for the list of items. Although there are many items, what we'll be doing is inserting a table, so we only need one bookmark.

OK, let's take a look at the code, starting with the global variables. Firstly there are constants, defining the directory and the Word template to be used. Using a constant means that if we change the directory we don't have to crawl through the code looking for where we've used it:

```
Private Const g_strTEMPLATE As String = "Order.dot"
```

Next come two Word object variables. The first is the main Word application, and the second will be the Word document. These correspond to the main Word window, and to an individual document within Word. We've used global variables here because they will be used in several procedures:

```
Private m_objWord As Word.Application
Private m_objDoc As Word.Document
```

Now let's look at the main procedure, which takes two arguments, both recordsets. The first is the recordset of the suppliers, and the second the items to be ordered for the supplier:

```
Public Sub CreateOrderLetter(recSupp As Recordset, recItems As Recordset)
```

Once in the procedure, the first thing we do is get the path to the project, then create an instance of Word – this actually starts Word, but hides it from view so you can't see it. After starting Word we use the Documents collection, and Add a new document. The argument we pass into the Add method is the name of the template that we want our new document to be based on.

```
Dim m_strDIR As String

    m_strDIR = CurrentProject.Path & "\"
  Set m_objWord = New Word.Application
  Set m_objDoc = m_objWord.Documents.Add(m_strDIR & g_strTEMPLATE)
```

*The Documents collection just contains a list of all documents currently open, just like the Access Forms collection, which contains a list of all open forms.*

At this stage we now have a new document based upon our template. That means that it has the default text from the template, but has empty spaces where the bookmarks are, so that's what we do next. Insert some text into the bookmarks. We call another function to do this, and we'll look at that in a moment, but you can see we are inserting the details from the supplier recordset into specific bookmarks.

```
    InsertTextAtBookMark "ContactName", recSupp("ContactName")
    InsertTextAtBookMark "CompanyName", recSupp("CompanyName")
    InsertTextAtBookMark "Address", recSupp("Address")
    InsertTextAtBookMark "State", recSupp("State")
    InsertTextAtBookMark "PostCode", recSupp("PostCode")
    InsertTextAtBookMark "Country", recSupp("Country")
```

Next is another function call, this time to insert the order items as a table. We'll look at that in a moment too:

```
    InsertItemsTable recItems
```

At this stage all of the text has been inserted, so we print out a copy of the order, setting the Background argument to False. This ensures that we wait for Word to finish printing before we continue. This is important, as the next thing we do is save the document and quit Word, and you can't quit if the document is still being printed. We've used Background as a named argument as it makes it much clearer what we are doing:

```
    m_objWord.PrintOut Background:=False
```

Once the document is printed it needs to be saved. The file name we use is the company name plus the current date. In real life you'd probably have an order number in there somewhere:

```
m_objDoc.SaveAs FileName:= m_strDIR & recSupp("CompanyName") & _
    " - " & FormatDateTime(Date, vbLongDate) & ".DOC"
```

Once saved, we can close the document, quit Word, and clear any object references:

```
m_objDoc.Close
m_objWord.Quit

Set m_objDoc = Nothing
Set m_objWord = Nothing

End Sub
```

So that's it. We open a new document based upon a template, add some text at specified positions, print the document, and then save it. Let's see how the text is actually inserted.

To use the bookmarks in the document we use the `Bookmarks` collection. This is just like the `Controls` collection on a form, and for a document, contains one entry for each bookmark in the document. We use the name of the bookmark to index into the collection, and use the `Select` method to make the bookmark the current selection. This would be the equivalent of just clicking on the bookmark in the Word document:

```
Private Sub InsertTextAtBookMark(strBkmk As String, varText As Variant)

    m_objDoc.Bookmarks(strBkmk).Select
```

Once this is done the `Selection` object is activated, containing the currently selected items. When typing documents the selection is visible as a highlight, for example when you select a word or sentence. The `Selection` object has a property called `Text`, which contains the text in the selection. We then set the text of the selection to the text we want to insert. We've appended an empty string onto the text because the text comes from the database, and might contain a null value. Adding this empty string just prevents any errors about null values:

```
    m_objWord.Selection.Text = varText & ""

End Sub
```

So that's how to add text at a bookmark. Let's see how to insert a table. This procedure takes a recordset of the order items, which we will use to create a table. The method we are going to use to create the table is similar to the way you might do it in Word, by just typing in the items, separated by tab characters, and then selecting the **Convert Text to Table** option from the **Table** menu. We use this method because it's actually simpler than creating a table, and then moving around the cells inserting the data:

```
Private Sub InsertItemsTable(recR As Recordset)
```

We have two variables. The first is a string, into which we will build up the table, separating the table columns by tab characters, and the table rows by carriage return characters. We've actually already done this procedure once, when we added these details to the mail message, but we're doing it again here to emphasize the method used to create tables:

```
Dim strTable As String
```

The second variable is another word object – a `Table`, which represents, unsurprisingly, a Word table:

```
Dim objTable As Word.Table
```

Now we create the string containing the table details, by looping through the recordset adding the ingredient name and the number of items to reorder:

```
strTable = "Item" & vbTab & "Quantity" & vbCr
recR.MoveFirst
While Not recR.EOF
    strTable = strTable & recR("Name") & vbTab & _
        recR("ReOrderPoint") & vbCr
    recR.MoveNext
Wend
```

Then we insert this string into the position marked by the `Items` bookmark:

```
InsertTextAtBookMark "Items", strTable
```

At this stage the document looks like this:

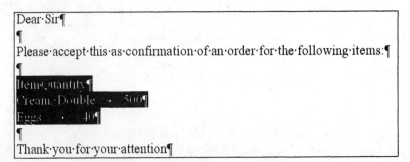

The inserted text is highlighted, so we now need to convert it into a table. To do this we use another method of the `Selection` object, `ConvertToTable`, using the `Separator` argument to tell the method what character is to be used as the column separator:

```
Set objTable = m_objWord.Selection.ConvertToTable(Separator:=vbTab)
```

Now the document looks like this:

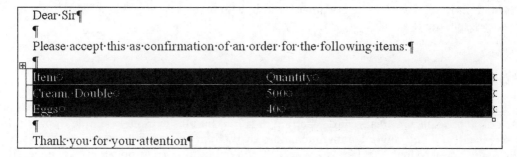

The text has been converted into a table, but it's not a particularly nice table, so it needs a little formatting. We use the `AutoFormat` method of the table, supplying three arguments. The first, `Format`, identifies the auto format style to use, in this case the Classic 3 style. The second argument, `AutoFit`, is a Boolean, and indicates whether the columns of the table should be automatically sized to fit their contents. The third argument, `ApplyShading`, is another Boolean, identifying whether or not shading is to be used on the table:

```
objTable.AutoFormat Format:=wdTableFormatClassic3, AutoFit:=True, _
    ApplyShading:=False
```

The table is nicely formatted, so we've really finished our work. All that's left to do is tidy up the object reference:

```
Set objTable = Nothing

End Sub
```

That's all there is to it. The final piece is to call all of this code from within our e-mail procedure:

```
CreateOrderLetter recSupps, recReOrder
```

Here we simply call the procedure passing in the recordsets of the suppliers and order items.

## Word Summary

As mentioned at the beginning of the section, using automation with Word can be complex, but we've only used a few features here, and managed to get quite a degree of flexibility. Using bookmarks as place markers for text insertion allows the Word document to change without affecting your code. As long as the bookmarks are in the document, then your code will still work.

This is actually quite a powerful concept, because you could use it to create a very flexible report writer. Often, one of the complaints of users is that the reports you've written don't quite do what they want. You could easily create a set of queries and some code that allows users to create their reports using Word. Just give them a list of queries and fields in each query, and they can add bookmarks to Word that match those fields. Your report writer code could search through the bookmarks in the document, and if it finds one that matches a field, could insert the text from the field.

# Microsoft Excel

Microsoft Excel, again because of its complexity, has a large object model, so we're only going to look at one specific area – charts. Getting data into Excel is extremely simple from within Excel itself, and you can link data much more easily than you can with Word, so that's why we're not going to look at it here. However, if you're building an application, you generally have to provide some form of reporting, for all those managers and accountants. They like that sort of thing.

One of the great things about Access is that you can use objects from other applications on your forms. This is particularly useful for adding charts to your applications. So in this example, we're going to do our automation a little differently. Instead of creating an instance of an application, we're going to put the instance on a form, as a visible object.

### Try It Out — A Chart on a Form

1. In Access, create a new query without any tables or queries on it. From the Query menu, select **SQL Specific**, and then **Union**.

2. Type the following SQL statement into the blank window:

```
SELECT -1 As CompanyID, "<All>" As CompanyName
FROM tblCompany
UNION
SELECT CompanyID, CompanyName
FROM tblCompany
ORDER BY CompanyName
```

3. Close the query, saving it as `qryCompanyLookup`. Create another new query, adding `tblCompany` and `tblSales`.

4. Add the `CompanyName` and `Quantity` fields, then into the next empty field add the following:

```
MonthName: Format([DateOrdered], "mmmm")
```

**5.** From the Query toolbar select **Crosstab Query**.

**6.** In the `CompanyName` column, set the **Total** entry to **Group By** and the **Crosstab** entry to **Row Heading**. Then, in the `MonthName` column set the **Total** entry to **Group By** and the **Crosstab** entry to **Column Heading**. Finally, in the `Quantity` column set the **Total** entry to **Sum** and the **Crosstab** entry to **Value**.

**7.** Your query should now look like this:

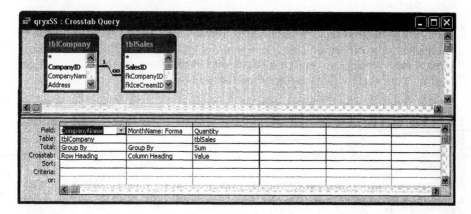

**8.** From the **View** menu select **Properties**, and add the following into the **Column Headings** field:

```
January;February;March;April;May;June;July;August;September;October;November;
December
```

*Note: This should all be on the same line when you type it in.*

**9.** Close the query, saving it as **qryxSS**.

**10.** Create another query, based upon **qryxSS**. Add all of the fields to the query, and change each of the month fields so that the name is the abbreviated month name, and they use the `Nz` function to return `0` if the field is null. This might be easier to do in SQL view, where the query will look like this:

```
SELECT qryxSS.CompanyName,
Nz(January,0) AS Jan, Nz(February,0) AS Feb, Nz(March,0) AS Mar,
Nz(April,0) AS Apr, Nz(May,0) AS May, Nz(June,0) AS Jun,
Nz(July,0) AS Jul, Nz(August,0) AS Aug, Nz(September,0) AS Sep,
Nz(October,0) AS Oct, Nz(November,0) AS Nov, Nz(December,0) AS [Dec]
FROM qryxSS;
```

**11.** Close the query, saving it as `qryxSalesSummary`. Now create a new form and add a combo box at the top. Name the combo box `cboCompany`, and change the label accordingly.

**12.** Set the Row Source Type to Table/Query and the Row Source to `qryuCompanyLookup`. Then set the Column Count to 2 and Columns Widths to 0.

**13.** Put a checkbox next to the combo box. Call it `chkLegend` and change the label to `Show Legend`.

**14.** From the toolbox select Unbound Object Frame and draw a large frame on the form, underneath the other two controls. From the Insert Object dialog, make sure that Create New is selected, and pick Microsoft Graph 2000 Object, before pressing the OK button. Your form will now look something like this:

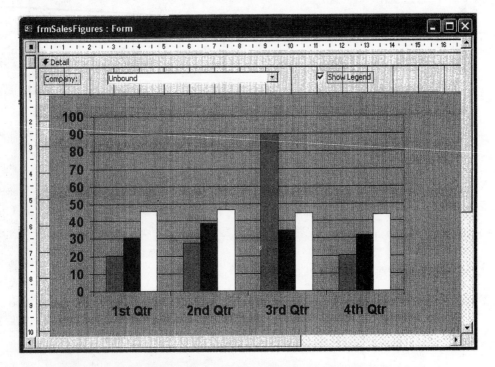

*Don't worry about what the data is or what the graph looks like. We'll be changing that later.*

**15.** Click on the form background, to the side of the new object, and the graph deactivates. Now view the properties for the graph object. Set the Name to `ctlChart`, the Row Source Type to Value List, and the Column Heads to Yes. Then save the form as frmSalesFigures.

**16.** Press the **Code** button to create a code module, and from the **Tools** menu select **References**. Make sure the **Microsoft Graph 10.0 Object Library** is checked, before pressing the **OK** button. Now add the following module level variable to the new module:

```
Private m_objChart As Graph.Chart
```

**17.** In the Click event for chkLegend add this code:

```
m_objChart.HasLegend = chkLegend
```

**18.** In the Load event for the Form add the following:

```
Set m_objChart = ctlChart.Object
```

**19.** In the Unload event for the Form add the following – this will clear the memory used by the object variable:

```
Set m_objChart = Nothing
```

**20.** In the Change event for cboCompany add the following:

```
Private Sub cboCompany_Change()

    On Error Goto cboCompany_Change_Err

    Dim strSQL As String

    If cboCompany = -1 Then
        strSQL = "qryxSalesSummary"
    Else
        strSQL = "SELECT * FROM qryxSalesSummary WHERE CompanyName=""'" & _
            cboCompany.Column(1) & """'"
    End If

    ctlChart.RowSource = strSQL
    ctlChart.RowSourceType = "Table/Query"

    With m_objChart
        .ChartArea.Font.Size = 8
        .HasLegend = chkLegend

        If cboCompany = -1 Then
            .ChartType = xl3DColumn
            .Refresh
            .Axes(xlSeriesAxis).HasTitle = False
        Else
            .ChartType = xl3DColumnStacked
```

```
            .Refresh
        End If

        With .Axes(xlCategory)
            .HasTitle = True
            .AxisTitle.Caption = "Month"
        End With

        With .Axes(xlValue)
            .HasTitle = True
            .AxisTitle.Caption = "Total Sales"
        End With

    End With

cboCompany_Change_Exit:
    Exit Sub

cboCompany_Change_Err:
    If Err.Number = 1004 Then
        m_objChart.Refresh
    Else
        Err.Raise Err.Number, Err.Source, Err.Description, _
            Err.HelpFile, Err.HelpContext
    End If

End Sub
```

**21.** Save the code and switch back to Access. Now switch the form into form view. The Company combo box will be empty, so select **Amethyst Group**:

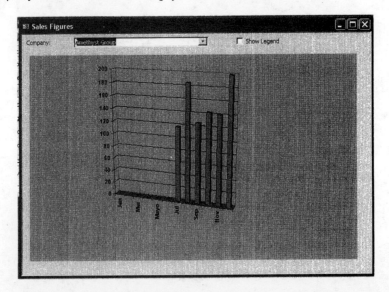

Pretty cool, huh? A chart of all sales for this company. Now select <All> from the combo box:

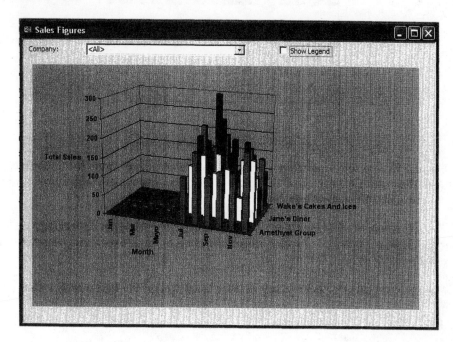

Even cooler. Clicking the **Show Legend** check box shows the legend for the various companies – they aren't all shown because there isn't room to show them all – this also happens with the month names.

## How It Works

Let's first start with the queries, starting with qryuCompanyLookup. This is a UNION query, which joins two sets of data together. Why do we want to do this? Well, what we want on the form is a way for the user to choose either a single company or all companies. You could have a combo box of companies and a checkbox for all companies, but this just seems a bit confusing. What's better is a single combo that shows <All> as the first record, and then the companies underneath that. So that's what this query does.

The first SELECT statement is used to produce the <All>, and shows a feature of SQL that you might not have seen before – you don't actually have to select data from a table. Here we are selecting two values of our choosing. Notice that we've used column aliases, giving our two values proper column names. That's because the columns in the two select statements must match:

```
SELECT -1 As CompanyID, "<All>" As CompanyName
FROM tblCompany
```

On its own this gives:

| CompanyID | CompanyName |
|---|---|
| 1 | <All> |
| -1 | <All> |
| -1 | <All> |
| -1 | <All> |
| -1 | <All> |
| -1 | <All> |
| -1 | <All> |
| -1 | <All> |
| -1 | <All> |
| -1 | <All> |

This is because we are selecting from a table but not selecting columns from that table, so we get a row in the output for each row in the table. But, because we are supplying our own values for the columns, all of the rows are the same:

> *This in fact points to a bug in JET SQL, because you should be able to do* `SELECT -1 As CompanyID, "<All>" As CompanyName` *without the* `FROM` *clause. However, JET reports this as an error.*

Next we use the `UNION` statement to say that we want to join the first query with the second:

```
UNION
```

The second query is a normal `SELECT` statement.

```
SELECT CompanyID, CompanyName
FROM tblCompany
ORDER BY CompanyName
```

Having looked at the diagram above you might think that our combo box would show several rows of <All>, but by default a `UNION` query only shows unique records, so all of the duplicate values are stripped out.

This `UNION` technique is a great way to allow users to select one or all values from a table. One thing to note about `UNION` queries is that both of the queries must contain the same number of columns, otherwise errors will be generated.

OK, let's look at the crosstab query now. Crosstab queries allow us to make a row value become a column. So if we look at a non-crosstab version of this query:

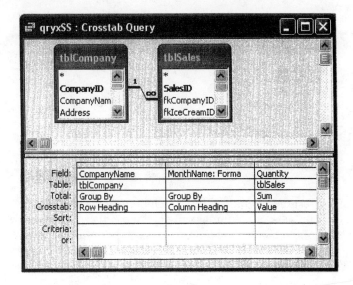

This gives a result of:

What we want is one row for each company, with the month names as columns. So a crosstab query allows us to specify three things:

- ❑ Row Heading, which will be CompanyName.

- ❑ Column Heading, which will be MonthName.

- ❑ Value, which will be SumOfQuantity.

However, on its own this just gives us:

| Company Name | July | August | September |
|---|---|---|---|
| Amethyst Group | 118 | 185 | 126 |
| Eyshood Cocoa | | 11 | |
| Flavors Of The World | 131 | 163 | 119 |
| Jane's Diner | 148 | 100 | 160 |
| Lloyds Luscious Lollie | 193 | 153 | 242 |
| Quintessential Ices | 215 | 159 | 195 |
| Wake's Cakes And Ic | 165 | 295 | 136 |

*qryxSS : Crosstab Query*

What about all of the rest of the months, for which there is no data? They don't appear for that very reason – there is no data. A column is only created if there is a `MonthName` for it. To get column names for all of the months we have to specify the columns, and we do this by setting the `Column Headings` property of the query. This makes sure that we get a column for each month, even if there is no data.

This, however, still isn't complete, as cells with no data show up as empty, rather than 0. This isn't a problem here, but will be a problem when we try to create the graph. So, what we do is create another query based on our crosstab query, using the `Nz` function to return 0 if the column is null. Only now do we have the correct query.

Let's move onto the form now. The combo box just takes its values from the union query, and the checkbox is straightforward too. The Object Frame might be a new control to you though. You already know what objects are, so this is just a way to embed one of these objects on a form. In this case our object frame is used to contain a graph. If you've ever used graphs in Excel, then this isn't really any different, because the graph is a separate object. When you create a graph in Excel you are embedding a graph object in your spreadsheet.

Like many other controls the graph control on the form can be bound to a data source. To stop the graph trying to display data when it first loads we set the `Row Source Type` property to `Value List`. We also set the `Column Heads` property to `Yes` – for some reason this is required for the data to display correctly, but the reason is not documented.

Now let's move onto the code, starting with the global variables. To save lots of unnecessary referencing, we have a variable that will point to the chart:

```
Private m_objChart    As Graph.Chart
```

So when the form loads we can do this:

```
Set m_objChart = ctlChart.Object
```

This points to the chart object. This is an important point because you have to differentiate from the chart control and the chart object. The chart control is the visible control on the form, which is what Access controls. This includes things such as the height, width, border, etc., and is really how we, as the user, see the control. The chart object is the underlying chart, and is what controls the chart itself.

For the checkbox we only have one line of code – to change whether the chart has a legend or not, using the `HasLegend` property:

```
m_objChart.HasLegend = chkLegend
```

Now comes the real guts, as this is the code for the `Change` event of the combo box. Firstly we set some error handling – I'll explain why later:

```
Private Sub cboCompany_Change()

On Error Goto cboCompany_Change_Err
```

Next we declare a string, which will hold the SQL statement – this is what we are going to use as the source of the chart data:

```
Dim strSQL    As String
```

Now we need to set this SQL statement. Remember how our union query has `-1` as the `CompanyID` for the `<All>` value – this allows us to identify in code whether `<All>` has been selected. If it has, we want to use all of the data from the crosstab query – remember that this contains data for every company:

```
If cboCompany = -1 Then
    strSQL = "qryxSalesSummary"
```

If a company has been selected we only want to show values for that company, so we build a SQL string just picking out the correct values:

```
Else
    strSQL = "SELECT * FROM qryxSalesSummary WHERE CompanyName=""'" & _
        cboCompany.Column(1) & """'"
End If
```

We now set the source of the data for the chart, also setting the type of data to be a table or a query. We couldn't do this at design time because the source of the data wasn't known and an error would have occurred. Now we know the source of the data, it's safe to set it here:

```
ctlChart.RowSource = strSQL
ctlChart.RowSourceType = "Table/Query"
```

Now we need to set some properties of the chart:

```
With m_objChart
```

We start with the font size. The `ChartArea` property applies to the whole chart, so allows us to set the font size for all aspects of the chart:

```
.ChartArea.Font.Size = 8
```

Then we set the legend property.

```
.HasLegend = chkLegend
```

If the user selects all companies, then we need to show a multi-dimensional graph. So we set the `ChartType` property to be a `3D Column`.

```
If cboCompany = -1 Then
    .ChartType = xl3DColumn
```

Next we `Refresh` the chart, because we want to set some properties that are dependent upon the chart type. One of those is setting a title for one of the axis. When you have a 2D graph you only have the X and Y axes, but a 3D graph has a Z axis as well. This axis doesn't exist if the chart is 2D, but does if 3D, so we use `Refresh` to ensure that all axes are visible. We then turn off the `Title` for this axis.

```
.Refresh
.Axes(xlSeriesAxis).HasTitle = False
```

For a single company, we want a two-dimensional graph, so we use a different `ChartType`.

```
Else
    .ChartType = xl3DColumnStacked
    .Refresh
End If
```

Now we can deal with the X and Y axes, making sure that the title is visible, and the caption for the axis is set appropriately.

```
With .Axes(xlCategory)
    .HasTitle = True
    .AxisTitle.Caption = "Month"
End With

With .Axes(xlValue)
    .HasTitle = True
    .AxisTitle.Caption = "Total Sales"
```

```
        End With
    End With
```

That's it, so we can simply exit.

```
cboCompany_Change_Exit:
    Exit Sub
```

The error handling here is a bit of a kludge, and is purely included to get around a timing problem. We've already mention that we use `Refresh` to ensure that properties are updated. There are occasionally times when trying to set a property occurs before that property is available, and an error is generated. So, we check the error number to see if it means that the property isn't available, and just `Refresh` to ensure it is. Any other error is sent back to the default error handler.

```
cboCompany_Change_Err:
    If Err.Number = 1004 Then
        m_objChart.Refresh
    Else
        Err.Raise Err.Number, Err.Source, Err.Description, _
            Err.HelpFile, Err.HelpContext
    End If

End Sub
```

The final thing to do is to clean up the object reference when the form is closed.

```
Set m_objChart = Nothing
```

That's all there is to it. Although it may look complex, we are really only dealing with a few properties. If you create a chart in Excel and use the dialog boxes and toolbars to modify the properties, you'll see a similar kind of result.

## Graph Summary

The main properties we've looked at have been:

- ❑ `ChartType` identifies what type of chart you want to see.
- ❑ `HasLegend` identifies whether or not a legend is shown on the chart.
- ❑ `Axes(xlCategory)` identifies the X axis.
- ❑ `Axes(xlValue)` identifies the Y axis.
- ❑ `Axes(xlSeriesAxis)` identifies the Z axis, if it exists.

`Axes` is a collection containing objects of type `Axis`, so these have their own properties too.

## *Office Assistant*

Since we're near the end of the book, and the rest of this chapter has been pretty sensible, let's just have a quick look at the Office Assistant to lighten the load a little. You need to make sure that the Office Assistant is installed for this example.

To save you a lot of unnecessary typing, import the form `frmAssistant` from `IceCream.mdb`. Switch to the code module, and from the **Tools** menu pick **References**, making sure you check the **Microsoft Office 10.0 Object Library** before pressing the **OK** button. Now switch back to Access and open the form in form mode. Use the combo box to select the action for your assistant. Pretty fun, eh? You can look at the code here in more detail if you like, to see how you can use the Office Assistant yourself.

# Summary

There is quite a lot of important code in this chapter, building on some of the techniques you've learned earlier in the book. In previous chapters we've looked at classes and building your own objects, but this chapter focuses on using objects that have been built by other people – in this case Microsoft. We know that using classes is a great way to promote code reuse and provide ready made functionality to other programmers, and using Automation just takes this one step further.

In this chapter we've looked at the following topics:

❑　What Automation is and how it works.

❑　How you can use the functionality of existing applications.

❑　Using Outlook to send e-mail messages and make appointments.

❑　Using Word as a basic report writer.

❑　Combining Excel Charts with Access to provide graphs on forms.

The important thing about using automation is the Object Model. Once you have a basic understanding of the object model of the application you are using, then almost anything is possible.

Now it's time to turn our sights back towards Access, and see how it handles multiple users, and the security of those users.

# CHAPTER 17

# Multi-User

In this chapter we will be looking at a number of different issues that face developers as they develop applications for a multi-user environment. The most obvious of these is the issue of record locking; what happens when two users want to update the same record at the same time? We will look at how we can programmatically control shared access to data and how we can gracefully handle errors that arise when two users attempt to access the same data at the same time.

Then we will go on to look at the whole issue of security. Broadly speaking, security is implemented within database applications for two reasons. It allows us, as developers, to restrict unauthorised access to areas of the database that we wish to remain off-bounds and it allows the application to identify users so that it can both personalise their interaction with the database and audit their use of application and database resources.

Finally, we will look at another development-related issue – compilation. This is the process of wrapping up or packaging an application before it is developed so that it runs more efficiently and is less susceptible to accidental design changes than it would be if it were in an uncompiled state.

## Multi-Developer Issues

In this chapter, we are going to tackle the question of how Access functions in a multi-user environment. But we'll just take a moment to look at another multi-user aspect – how does Access work as a **multi-developer** product? So far, we have concentrated on the functionality that Access, DAO, and VBA provide for the user and developer but we have been considering these from quite an isolated viewpoint. To a large degree that is inevitable. After all, developing applications does tend to be a fairly personal experience. Sure, we may work in project teams and, yes, we may have weekly design meetings where we collaborate on various aspects of the design and development of the product we are working on, but when it comes down to the nitty-gritty of cutting code – most of us tend to work on our own.

Over the years there have been various formal attempts to get us all to program together (for example "peer review programming" where code is first written solo and then discussed and modified in groups or "extreme programming" where programmers take it in turns to write code with the others watching every move). None of these have yet been proven particularly successful.

I am not suggesting that the cubicle culture – familiar to anyone who reads Dilbert cartoons – is the ideal way to work, but a lot of the design and development process is a fairly cerebral process and lends itself to isolated, concentrated effort rather than a more communal approach.

To a large degree this has been exacerbated by the limited support that Access has traditionally offered for team development – Access was just not accepted or supported by Microsoft as a serious development language. Earlier versions of Access allowed multiple developers to make design changes to Access objects and code in the same open database but implemented it through a complex procedure behind the scenes that fooled Access into thinking that only one developer at a time was making those changes. Now that Access has matured and is being used for even major projects, industrial-strength source code tools such as Visual SourceSafe and Code Librarian, and full integration with Visual Studio have finally been made available by Microsoft. These do not ship with any of the standard versions of Access 2002 though – you will need the Microsoft Office XP Developer Edition. That is because Access 2002, in line with the other Office XP applications, does not allow multiple developers to make native design changes to Access objects and code in the same open database. So, if you want to develop in teams, you are going to need the Developer Edition.

The historical upshot of this approach is that many developers tend only to consider the multi-user aspects of their applications towards the end of the development and testing cycle. Even if they design their applications in teams, using the latest team development tools, many developers build their code alone. They also do their system testing alone and it is really only when user acceptance testing starts and two or three people use the database for real at the same time that multi-user problems start to show. Then, the application is rolled out in production to thirty users and it comes to a grinding halt. The developer says out loud "That's odd!", while they are really thinking "Oh <expletive deleted>!" and it is back to the drawing board, do not pass "Go" and do not collect $200...

# Record Locking in Access 2002

## What is Locking Anyway?

Locking is a mechanism that controls the editing of records. It allows multiple users to share and modify data safely. It does this by blocking one user's changes to records while they are being modified by another.

Without the use of locking two users could both make different changes to the same record. What happens when they finish editing and save the changes? The data that gets saved last will overwrite the first without any warning. This is a dangerous thing to allow. You can imagine a table of customers where perhaps one user changes an account's telephone number and another other the name of the sales rep assigned to it at the same time – both changes equally valid – one of them arbitrarily overwritten by the other! Locking helps to mitigate these problems.

In fact locking can also apply to a single user who happens to be using the same data from multiple applications or perhaps even from within the same application on multiple forms, say. It is useful anywhere that multiple editing of the same data can occur.

One other thing to bear in mind is that locking never prevents reading of data, only editing and/or writing. This allows other users to view records and perform reports etc. however many records are currently being edited by others. It also doesn't affect adding new records as these do not truly exist in the table until they have been saved by the application that created them.

There are a number of different forms of locking, which we will go through in detail below.

## Page Locking vs. Record Locking

If you have used Microsoft Access before, you might have noticed that the **Advanced** page of the **Tools/Options...** dialog box now contains a checkbox that was not present in previous versions:

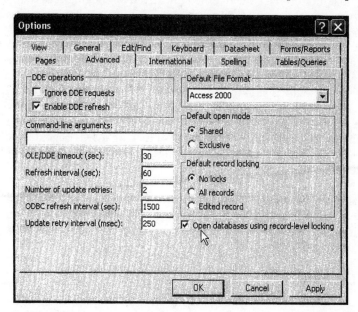

We can now decide whether we want use record-level locking or page-level locking when we open databases.

In previous versions of Access, Microsoft employed a **page-level locking** strategy. That is to say that instead of placing locks on individual records, Access placed locks on the underlying data page on which the record resided. Data pages were 2Kb in length and could contain multiple records. What that means is that the act of placing a lock on a data page could lock a great many records apart from those that were actually being edited.

Well, page-level locking does have some advantages. The process of obtaining and releasing locks is an expensive process in terms of both the CPU activity and the memory overhead required to maintain the lock structure. Because page-level locking locked multiple records it meant that fewer locks were typically required than if record-level locking had been implemented. Fewer locks means less work for the processor and less memory overhead. However, it also means less concurrency (the ability for multiple users to access the same data at the same time). Microsoft believed that page-locking offered the best tradeoff to this problem.

By contrast, **record-level locking** places locks on individual records. So, if one record is locked, other users can still access all other records in the base table including the records on the same page as the locked record. To many people this will seem like an overwhelmingly obvious approach. Why did previous versions of Access not employ record-level locking in the first place?

Several things have changed since the days of page-level locking in early versions of Access. Dramatic improvements in processor performance, coupled with reductions in memory prices mean that for most modern PCs the overhead incurred by locking is less onerous than it once was. Record-level locking is a relatively less expensive option than it was originally.

Coupled to the improvement in PC performance is the fact that Access now offers full Unicode support. That means that Access can now support the characters that appear in a variety of international languages rather than simply supporting the 256 commonly used characters of the ANSI character set. The downside to this, however, is that Access now uses 2 bytes rather than 1 for each character. In order to support this, the size of data pages has grown from 2 Kb to 4 Kb. Now if locking a 2 Kb page full of records when only one record is being updated is a controversial move, then just think of the effect of locking a 4Kb page. In a table with relatively short records – say, an average of 20 bytes in length – then a 4 Kb page would contain approaching 200 records.

Another important factor behind choosing record-level locking is to maintain compatibility with Microsoft SQL Server, which also supports it. The use of this feature therefore allows developers to migrate applications from Access to SQL Server without having to worry about changes in locking strategies.

## Record-Level Locking

As we mentioned before you can choose record-level locking by checking the Open databases using record-level locking checkbox on the Advanced page of the Tools/Options... dialog box in Access. Leaving it unchecked selects page-level locking.

> Note that the option selected only applies to the future opening of databases and does not affect the one currently open, which continues to use whichever option was selected when it was first opened.

Which should you select? For most people, the default – record-level locking – will be the preferred choice because of the benefits it offers in terms of concurrency. Actually, if a database has been opened in record-level locking mode, JET will still use page locks in those situations where it is more appropriate to do so.

Specifically, if you perform set-based operations such as UPDATE, INSERT, or DELETE queries, then JET will temporarily switch to a page-locking mechanism as this will help to perform the query more effectively, regardless of the option selected. If, however, you are performing a cursor-based operation (such as looping through all of the records in a recordset and updating records individually) then JET will use record-level locking.

However, there are a couple of caveats. Firstly, due to the limitations of Access, you will only be able to realize the concurrency benefits of record-level locking in code if you place your data modification statements inside transactions.

> *A **transaction** is a method of programmatically grouping together a number of data modification statements into a single unit. They are normally used to promote database consistency, by ensuring that either all of the statements in the transaction are executed successfully, or none of them are. A discussion of transaction usage is a little beyond the scope of this chapter, but if you want to know more about transactions, you should take a look at the topic "BeginTrans, CommitTrans, Rollback Methods" in the Visual Basic help file.*

Secondly, and potentially more confusingly, in a multi-user environment, the decision as to whether a database will be opened with page or row locking is determined by the first person that opens the database. So if the first person to open a database has record-level locking specified as an option, then the database will be opened with record-level locking and this option will apply to all other users who then access the database while it is open, irrespective of the locking level that they might have specified as an option. After the last person closes this database, the level of locking selected the next time the database is opened will be decided again by the person who opens the database first.

> **What this means is that in a multi-user environment there is no easy way of determining whether a database that you have opened in is in record-level or page-level mode!**

To change the granularity of locking to record-level or page-level programmatically simply use the SetOption method of the Application object like this:

```
Application.SetOption "Use Row Level Locking", True
```

> *This has exactly the same effect as checking the **Open databases using record-level locking** checkbox on the **Advanced** page of the **Options...** dialog box in Access. Don't forget that changing this setting, either manually or programmatically, has no effect on any database that is currently open. Therefore, you must set this option before you open the database that you wish it to apply to.*

So, now that we have looked at the way that Access provides a method of altering the granularity of locking, let's have a look at when JET places and releases locks.

## Optimistic and Pessimistic Locking

Access 2002, just like previous versions of Access, employs two methods of locking records – optimistic and pessimistic locking:

- ❑   With **pessimistic** locking, Access locks a record (or the page the record is on) whenever someone starts to change the contents of that record. This could be as a result of changes made to a form, table view, programmatically, or via any other method.

- ❑   With **optimistic** locking, Access only tries to place the lock when someone tries to save the changes that they have made. Again this occurs no matter what method was used to save the changes.

Let's look at an example to clarify the difference between the two. Suppose John and Mary are both using the same database and are editing records in the same table. If John decides just to view record #30 then, irrespective of the type of locking strategy involved, Mary will still also be able to look at the contents of that record (locking doesn't affect read operations remember).

However, suppose John now decides to edit the contents of that record by typing a new value in one of the fields on his form. If pessimistic locking is being employed, Access will now lock that record so that only John can change it.

> **Pessimistic locking implies that when a user edits a record, Access pessimistically assumes that someone else will also want to edit that same record and so needs to lock it.**

Mary will now see the 'record locked' indicator on her form, a circle crossed through, which tells her that she can't edit the record. The screenshot fragment below shows that the record with the CompanyID of 1 has been locked for editing by another user or process:

| | | CompanyID | Company Name | |
|---|---|---|---|---|
| ⊘ | + | | Fran and Nick's Fruit and Nuts | 37 V |
| | + | 2 | Candy's Cones | 26 V |
| | + | 3 | Dave's Dairy Produce | 20 N |

Access simply will not allow Mary to type anything into any of the fields for the record that is locked. In fact, she will not be able to edit that record until John has finished with record #30 and has saved his changes.

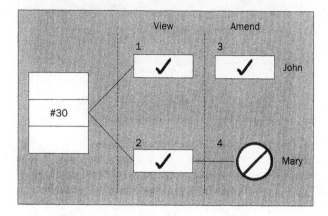

However, if an optimistic locking strategy were being used, Mary would have been able to make changes to record #30, even while John was editing it.

> **Optimistic locking implies that, when a user edits a record, Access optimistically assumes that no-one else will want to edit the same record, and so it doesn't lock it.**

This can be a very dangerous scenario. Assume that both John and Mary are now editing the same record – what happens when John tries to save the record? Nothing out of the ordinary... he is able to save the record as if nothing had happened. But what happens when Mary tries to save the record?

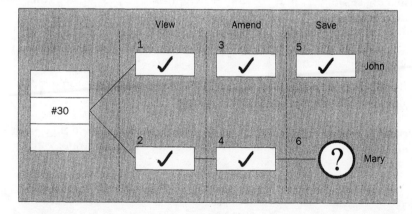

The answer is that when she tries to save a record that has changed since she opened it, she is presented with this dialog box:

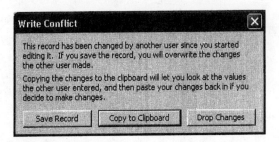

Sometimes, when a dialog box pops up you instantly know what is wrong and what you need to do. But this one carries a rather complicated message. You really need to think twice about how to respond to it and for those seeing it for the first time, it can be quite confusing. Essentially, the dialog box is telling Mary that she has three choices:

❑ She can save her record. This will overwrite the changes that John has just made without John being aware of the fact.

❑ She can copy her changes to the clipboard. These can then be pasted into another application like Word or Excel so that they can be saved for reviewing and/or reapplying. To reapply all the changes the record can be pasted back into the table without having to retype anything. Normally, however, you will want to save only some or merge the changes in some way – this has to be done manually.

❑ Or she can just call it a day and drop the changes she has just made. In this case, John's amended record will remain in the table but the changes that she has made will be lost.

## Choosing a Locking Strategy

So which locking strategy should you choose? Optimistic or pessimistic? There is no simple answer, but in general:

❑ If it is unlikely that any two users will want to amend the same record simultaneously, use optimistic locking.

❑ If it is likely that two or more users may want to amend the same record simultaneously, choose pessimistic locking.

You are probably getting fed up with us saying this again, but developing Access applications involves a large degree of compromise. When choosing a locking strategy, the compromise is one of concurrency versus complexity.

|  | Optimistic Locking | Pessimistic Locking |
|---|---|---|
| **For** | Locks are only in place for a short time, increasing concurrency. | If you are have started to modify a record, you know that you will be able to save those changes. |

|  | Optimistic Locking | Pessimistic Locking |
|---|---|---|
| Against | You cannot guarantee that you will be able to save a record once you have started to modify it. This leads to complex decision-making to decide which changes will receive priority and be committed. | Locks are in place for a long time (from when a user **starts** to edit a record until the changes are saved or cancelled). This means concurrency is reduced and users may have to wait longer before they can access data. |

> Using record-level locking makes pessimistic locking a significantly less expensive strategy in terms of concurrency than it was in some previous versions of Access where only page-level locking was available.

## Setting the Default Record Locking Mechanism

To choose a particular locking strategy for your Access environment, you should select the appropriate option from the Advanced page of the Options... dialog box:

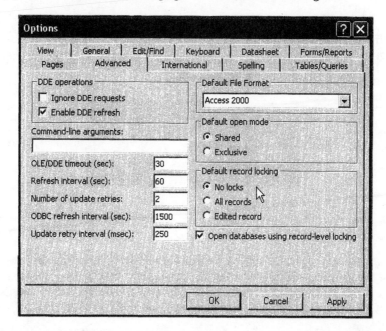

No Locks invokes **optimistic locking**. A record is locked only when it is actually being saved.

All Records (exclusive locking) causes the entire table or tables, which form the recordsource of the object, to be locked when any record is edited. This is fairly extreme and generally should only be used by the administrator, when performing maintenance.

Edited Record invokes **pessimistic locking**. A record will be locked as soon as someone starts to edit it. This is normally the best compromise option.

### Changing the Default Locking Mechanism

**1.** Open up `IceCream.mdb` and make sure the Default Record Locking option on the Advanced page of the Tools | Options... dialog box is set to No Locks. Click the OK button.

**2.** Create a new module called `Chapter 17 Code` and type the following procedure into it:

```
Sub SetLocking ()

    Application.SetOption "Default Record Locking", 2

End Sub
```

**3.** Run this procedure by typing `SetLocking` in the Immediate window.

**4.** Now open the Advanced page of the Options... dialog box again. The Default Record Locking option should now be Edited Record:

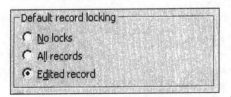

### How It Works

There are three different settings for the Default Record Locking option in Access. The table below shows the different options and the VBA statement that is used to set each of those options. As with all multi-select options, the value used in the SetOption method corresponds to the zero-based order in which the option appears on the Tools/Options... dialog box.

| This option... | ...is also known as... | ...and is set like this |
|---|---|---|
| No Locks | Optimistic Locking | `Application.SetOption "Default Record Locking", 0` |

| This option... | ...is also known as... | ...and is set like this |
|---|---|---|
| All Records | Exclusive Locking | `Application.SetOption "Default Record Locking", 1` |
| Edited Records | Pessimistic Locking | `Application.SetOption "Default Record Locking", 2` |

In order to determine what the current locking option is, you can use the `GetOption` method of the `application` object. Here's a procedure you can write to allow you to set and then read the **Default Record Locking** option:

```
Sub SetAndGetLocking(strLockType As String)

    Dim intLockIndex As Integer
    Dim strLockDesc As String

    'Convert the string argument into a option index
    Select Case strLockType
        Case "Optimistic"
            intLockIndex = 0
        Case "Exclusive"
            intLockIndex = 1
        Case "Pessimistic"
            intLockIndex = 2
        Case Else
            intLockIndex = -1
    End Select

    'Set default record locking option
    If intLockIndex <> -1 Then
        Application.SetOption "Default Record Locking", intLockIndex
    End If

    'Now determine and display default record locking option
    Select Case Application.GetOption("Default Record Locking")
        Case 0
            MsgBox "The default locking method is optimistic."
        Case 1
            MsgBox "The default locking method is exclusive."
        Case 2
            MsgBox "The default locking method is pessimistic."
    End Select

End Sub
```

If you run this procedure by typing the following in the **Immediate** window,

```
SetAndGetLocking "Exclusive"
```

**697**

the default locking option will be set to Exclusive (All Records) and you will see this dialog box:

# Implementing Record Locking on Forms

So far, we have only really considered the record-locking mechanism that applies to the tables and queries in your database. But you can also specify the locking method used by individual forms and reports. You do this by setting the `RecordLocks` property of the object concerned. For example, look at this code:

```
Dim frm As Form

DoCmd.OpenForm "frmCompany"
Set frm = Forms!frmCompany
frm.RecordLocks = 2
```

This will set pessimistic locking (Edited Records) for the `frmCompany` form. In other words, as soon as someone edits a record using `frmCompany`, Access will attempt to lock that record (or the data page that the record is on if page-level locking is implemented). This will prevent anyone else from editing that record (or page), whether from `frmCompany` or any other forms, or with a query or directly within the table where that record exists.

The `RecordLocks` property uses the same three arguments as the `Application.SetOption` method. They are described below:

| This option... | ...is set like this... | ...and has this effect |
| --- | --- | --- |
| No Locks | `.RecordLocks = 0` | The default setting. Tries to obtain a lock on the underlying data only when a user attempts to save an amended record. |
| All Records | `.RecordLocks = 1` | Tries to lock all records in the underlying table(s) whenever someone has the form open. This option is only really useful when the form is designed to modify all of the records in the table itself (such as for some kind of maintenance, perhaps resetting sales bonus points once a year for the whole sales team). It should certainly only be used when absolutely necessary. |

| This option... | ...is set like this... | ...and has this effect |
|---|---|---|
| Edited Records | .RecordLocks = 2 | Tries to obtain a lock whenever someone starts to amend a record on the form. The lock stays in place until the user finishes editing the record. |

If you don't explicitly set the RecordLocks property for a form, report or query, the object inherits the default record locking option that was in place when the object was created.

# Recordsets and Record Locking

Earlier in the book we looked at how we could create Recordset objects. The basic syntax for creating a Recordset object is as follows:

```
Set rs = db.OpenRecordset(source, type, option, lockedits)
```

The *source* argument simply defines where the records will come from that will populate the recordset. This can be the name of a table or query, or a SQL string. You should be familiar with this by now, but what of the other arguments? Well, let's take a more detailed look now at the other arguments that we can supply to the OpenRecordset method and, in particular, how these arguments affect the way that locking is handled.

## The Type Argument

In Chapter 8 we said that there were four different types of recordset that JET provides. To specify the type of recordset we wish to open, we use the appropriate *type* argument with the OpenRecordset method. The following four intrinsic constants can be used for that type argument to create JET Recordset objects:

- ❑ dbOpenTable
- ❑ dbOpenDynaset
- ❑ dbOpenSnapshot
- ❑ dbOpenForwardOnly

You should be familiar with these arguments by now. If you feel a little unsure of the differences between these types of Recordset objects, you should run through that chapter again. As far as we are concerned right now, however, the major difference is that you cannot edit the records in a snapshot or forward-only Recordset object.

## *The Option Argument*

The third argument affects the updateability of the recordset is as a whole. Valid choices for this argument, together with their meanings, are shown below:

| This option... | ...has this effect |
|---|---|
| dbDenyWrite | No one else can modify or add records while we have the recordset open. |
| dbDenyRead | No one else can read data in the table while we have the recordset open. |
| dbSeeChanges | If one person tries to save changes to a record that another user has modified since the first user started editing it, Access generates a run-time error. |
| dbAppendOnly | We can only add records to the recordset and cannot view or amend existing ones. We can only use this option with dynaset-type recordsets. |
| dbInconsistent | We can modify all columns on both sides of the join in a dynaset built from multiple tables. This can leave the recordset in an "inconsistent" state as these changes may violate the join rules. It is recommended that you avoid using this option if at all possible for this reason. |
| dbConsistent | We can only modify columns that leave the dynaset consistent. So we can't alter the joined field on the 'many' side of a one-to-many join to a value that doesn't appear on the 'one' side. |

If you need to, you can combine two or more of these options in a single statement like this:

```
Set rs = db.OpenRecordset(strSQL, dbOpenDynaset, dbConsistent + dbDenyRead)
```

There are a few other valid constants you can supply as the *option* argument, but they are either for use with non-Access databases or are present only for backwards compatibility.

## The LockEdits Argument

The final argument is used to specify the type of record locking that will be used when we – or other users – try to edit records that appear in the recordset.

| This argument... | ...has this effect |
|---|---|
| dbReadOnly | No one else can amend records that appear in our recordset so long as we have the recordset open. |
| dbPessimistic | A pessimistic locking strategy is applied (see earlier). No one else can amend records that appear in our recordset if we are in the process of editing them. Similarly, we can't edit a record in our recordset if someone else is already editing it. |
| dbOptimistic | An optimistic locking strategy is applied (see earlier). Two or more users can try concurrently to amend a record that appears in our recordset. However, only the first person to save their changes will be successful. When other users try to save a record that the first user has changed, Access generates a run-time error. |

*Again, there are another couple of arguments as well, but they are only for use with ODBCDirect, so we don't need to worry about them.*

So, if we wanted to create a dynaset-type recordset based on the table tblSales that would allow us to add and edit records to the table, but didn't allow anyone else to view the records in tblSales while the recordset was open, we would use the following code:

```
Dim db As Database
Dim rec As Recordset

Set db = CurrentDB()

Set rec = db.OpenRecordset("tblSales", dbOpenDynaset, dbDenyRead)
.
.
.
rec.Close

db.Close
```

## The LockEdits Property

Once a recordset is open, we can also change its locking behavior by setting its `LockEdits` property. To change the locking behavior for a recordset to optimistic locking, we set the `LockEdits` property of the recordset to `False`. To apply a pessimistic locking strategy, we set the `LockEdits` property of the recordset to `True`.

For example, the following piece of code opens a recordset and changes the locking behavior of the recordset to optimistic:

```
'This opens a recordset with pessimistic locking (default)
Set rec = db.OpenRecordset("Country", dbOpenDynaset)

'This line sets the locking behavior to optimistic locking
rec.LockEdits = False

...'Do something with the records

rec.Close       'Close the recordset
```

Although the `LockEdits` argument of the `OpenRecordset` method and the `LockEdits` property of a `Recordset` object do the same thing, the difference is when they are used. The `LockEdits` argument of the `OpenRecordset` method can only be used when you open a recordset, whereas you can set the `LockEdits` property of a recordset any time after the recordset has been opened, until the recordset is closed.

> Some recordsets, such as those based on tables in ODBC data sources, do not support pessimistic locking. Attempting to set the **LockEdits** property of such a recordset to **True** will cause Access to generate a run-time error.

# Handling Record-Locking Errors

It is all very well to say that, when a recordset is opened with the `dbDenyWrite` option, no one else can add or edit records in the underlying table(s), but what actually happens when a procedure attempts to open an exclusively locked table? The answer is that a run-time error occurs and, if we don't have any error handling, our application will stop. It is important, therefore, to know the types of record-locking errors that can occur at run time, and how our error-handling code should deal with them.

## Optimistic Locking Errors

With optimistic locking we should not encounter any errors when attempting to edit a record – only when we try to update or add one.

### Likely Errors

If we are using optimistic locking, the three most common error codes we will encounter are 3186, 3197, and 3260.

Error 3186 – Could not save; currently locked by user <xxx> on machine <xxx>

This error only occurs when optimistic locking is being used. It indicates that we are trying to save a record that is locked.

Error 3197 – The Microsoft Jet database engine stopped the process because you and another user are attempting to change the same data at the same time.

This error occurs when we try to use the Update method but another user has changed the data that we are trying to update. The other user will have changed the data between the time we used the Edit method and the Update method. This is the same situation that led to the **Write Conflict** dialog box that we saw at the start of this chapter.

Error 3260 – Couldn't update; currently locked by user <xxx> on machine <xxx>

This error will occur if we use the Update method to try to update a record we have added or changed, but where another user has since locked that record.

If page-level locking is in place, this error may also occur when we use the AddNew method to add a record to a recordset where the page on which the new record resides is locked.

> *You might have noticed that errors **3186** and **3260** have similar causes. In fact, although they can occur at subtly different times, as far as we are concerned we should handle them in exactly the same way.*

### How to Deal with Optimistic Locking Errors

For error codes 3186 and 3260, we should wait a short period of time and then attempt to save the record again. If we still can't save the record after several attempts, we should cancel the operation, inform the user of what has happened and let them do something else.

For error code 3197, we should requery the database to see what the new value of the record is, display it to the user and ask them if they want to overwrite the record with their own changes. Depending on your particular application it might be possible to automatically resolve the problem by checking which fields conflict and performing some kind of a merge. In practice however, unless the two edits are in fairly self contained parts of the record (for example, one has changed sales info and the other accounts info) this is unlikely to work well and you will have to resort to human intervention to sort the problem out. If the users are not likely to be well trained, or if it is very likely that they will be editing the same records at the same times, then you may have no other option but to resort to pessimistic locking.

The following sample of code illustrates how we can gracefully handle the type of errors that occur when we are using optimistic locking:

```
Function OptErrors() As Boolean

    Dim db As Database
    Dim rec As Recordset
    Dim intLockRetry As Integer
    Dim i As Integer
    Dim intRetVal As Integer
    Dim recClone As Recordset

    Const LOCK_RETRY_MAX = 5
    Const LOCK_ERROR$ = "Could not save this record. " & _
                        "Do you want to try again?"
    Const SAVE_QUESTION$ = "Do you want to save YOUR changes?"

    On Error GoTo OptErrors_Err

    Set db = CurrentDb()
    Set rec = db.OpenRecordset("tblCountry", dbOpenDynaset, ,dbOptmistic)

    '
    ' This is the main body of your code
    '

OptErrors = True

OptErrors_Exit:
    Exit Function

OptErrors_Failed:
    OptErrors = False

    'This is where you put code to handle what
    'should happen if you cannot obtain a lock

    GoTo OptErrors_Exit

OptErrors_Err:
    Select Case Err.Number
        Case 3197                       'Data has changed

            'Make a copy of the recordset
            Set recClone = rec.OpenRecordset()

            'Move to amended record
            '...

            'Display amended record
            '...
```

```
                'Ask user what to do
                intRetVal = MsgBox(SAVE_QUESTION$, vbExclamation + vbYesNo)

                'If the user wants to save their changes
                If intRetVal = vbYes Then
                    'Try to update again
                    Resume
                Else
                    'Else just call it a day
                    Resume OptErrors_Failed
                End If
        Case 3186, 3260

                'Record is locked so add 1 to counter
                'indicating how many times this happened
                intLockRetry = intLockRetry + 1

                'Have you already retried too many times?
                If intLockRetry < LOCK_RETRY_MAX Then

                    'If you haven't, then wait for a short period
                    For i = 0 To intLockRetry * 1000
                    Next

                    'Now try again
                    Resume

                Else

                    'But if you have already tried 5 times
                    'ask if user wants to retry.
                    'If they say yes then...
                    If MsgBox(LOCK_ERROR$, vbExclamation + vbYesNo) = vbYes Then

                        intLockRetry = 0   '...set counter to 0
                        Resume                'and do it over

                    Else        'But if they have had enough
                                'just call it a day

                        Resume OptErrors_Failed

                    End If

                End If
            Case Else           'Catch all other errors
                MsgBox ("Error " & Err.Message & ": " & str(Err.Number))
                Resume OptErrors_Failed
        End Select

End Function
```

## Pessimistic Locking Errors

If we are using pessimistic locking, we can normally guarantee that we will be able to save any record that we have opened with the Edit method. For this reason, we shouldn't encounter error 3186. However, we may come across the other two errors.

### Likely Errors

Error 3197  The Microsoft Jet database engine stopped the process because you and another user are attempting to change the same data at the same time.

When using pessimistic locking, this error occurs if we try to use the Edit method on a record but the data in the record has changed since it was last accessed. This may happen, for example, if someone has changed or deleted the record since we opened the recordset.

Error 3260  Couldn't update; currently locked by user <xxx> on machine <xxx>

Don't be misled by the word 'update' in the message. If we are using pessimistic locking, this error will occur if we try to use the Edit or AddNew methods on a record where the record (or page) is already locked by someone else.

### How to Deal with Pessimistic Locking Errors

For error code 3260, we should wait a short period of time and then attempt to edit the record again. If we still can't edit the record after several attempts, we should give the user the choice of continuing to attempt to edit the record or canceling the operation.

For error code 3197, we should requery the database to see what the new value of the record is and try the Edit method again. If the record had only been changed, we should be able to edit it now. If it was deleted though, we will encounter error code 3167 (Record is deleted).

The function below contains an error handling routine that should take care of these errors:

```
Function PessErrors() As Integer

    Dim db As Database
    Dim rec As Recordset
    Dim intLockRetry As Integer
    Dim i As Integer

    Const LOCK_RETRY_MAX = 5
    Const LOCK_ERROR$ = "Could not save this record. " & _
                        "Do you want to try again?"

    On Error GoTo PessErrors_Err

    Set db = CurrentDb()
    Set rec = db.OpenRecordset("tblCountry", dbOpenDynaset)
```

```
'
' This is the main body of your code
'

PessErrors = True

PessErrors_Exit:
    Exit Function

PessErrors_Failed:
    PessErrors = False
    'This is where you put code to handle what should
    'happen if you cannot obtain a lock after many attempts

    GoTo PessErrors_Exit

PessErrors_Err:
    Select Case Err
        Case 3197           'If data has changed, then
            rec.Requery     'simply refresh the recordset
            Resume          'and try again.
        Case 3167
            'You have not got much choice
            'if someone else has deleted this record
            MsgBox "Someone else has deleted this record"
            Resume PessErrors_Failed
        Case 3260
            'But if the record is locked, add 1 to counter
            'indicating how many times you have retried
            intLockRetry = intLockRetry + 1

            'Have you already retried 5 times?
            If intLockRetry < LOCK_RETRY_MAX Then

                'If not then wait for a short period
                For i = 0 To intLockRetry * 1000
                Next

                'Now try again
                Resume

            Else
                'If you have already tried 5 times
                'ask the user if they want to retry
                'If they hit the yes button then...
                If MsgBox(LOCK_ERROR$, 'vbExclamation + vbYesNo) = vbYes Then

                    'Set counter to 0 and do it over again
                    intLockRetry = 0
                    Resume
```

```
            Else
                'But if they have had enough
                'just call it a day
                Resume PessErrors_Failed

            End If

        End If
    Case Else
        MsgBox ("Error " & Err & ": " & Error)
        Resume PessErrors_Failed
    End Select

End Function
```

## Deadlocks

Deadlock is the name for the potentially disastrous situation where two users get stuck, each waiting for the other to unlock a required table. Maybe an example might help to make things a little clearer:

John's program needs to lock records A and B to perform an update operation. Mary's program needs to lock records B and A to perform a different update operation.

John's program locks record A. Mary's program locks record B. John then attempts to lock record B. Mary attempts to lock record A.
The result is a *deadlock*. Both users get stuck waiting for the other to complete, which they can't do because they're waiting for the other to complete, who can't complete...

Unfortunately Access currently has no built-in methods for detecting and dealing with a deadlock gracefully. There are, however, a number of techniques to help prevent this situation arising in the first place:

**1.** Only use locks where absolutely necessary and only apply them for as short a time as necessary. Obvious advice but all too often ignored!

**2.** Try to write all code so that it always locks tables and records in the same order. In the example above deadlock would be avoided if this technique had been employed as Mary would not have locked record B before attempting to lock record A (which was already locked by John). This is sensible but will not get you out of every hole and may mean that you have to hold more tables or records locked for longer if you need to use them in a different order.

3.  Add error trapping code so that if the attempt to lock the second table fails the whole operation is abandoned and the locks on all other tables and records are released. This is fine if there are only a couple of tables involved but can get messy if the operation is very complex and uses several tables. In addition, in order for this to work well you must lock *all* tables or records required *before* beginning any editing or undoing changes may become extremely complex or even impossible. This will also increase the likelihood of locking out other users of course.

4.  Write all updates using transactions. Transactions are beyond the scope of this book but essentially they allow the *rollback* (or cancellation) or the entire operation much more easily than coding by hand.

## Other Solutions

Possibly the best solution to the problems of concurrent editing is to try to avoid it completely if at all possible! Normalization, or the splitting of data down to its atomic (or indivisible) parts, can really help here. While a full discussion of normalization is completely beyond the scope of this book (it would fill several large tomes and be very, very boring to read!) a simple example may help to demonstrate the principle:

Consider a customer table, perhaps similar to tblCompany in the Ice Cream database. You may require several contact names and numbers stored in each record rather than the one we have at the moment. To do this you could simply add more fields to the table **but**, if instead of this you create a new table tblCompanyContacts, use this to store individual contact names and numbers, and then link them to the main tblCompany then you have just *normalized* that part of the data.

Obviously this has just added an extra layer of complication to your application. You will need a sub-form to display the list of contacts alongside the main company info for example. The payoff comes when a user needs to edit a contact number though. They will only need a lock on that particular contact record and not the entire company record, which is much less likely to affect anyone else. Two users can also edit two different contacts completely without problems. There are other advantages too; there are also now no limits to the number of contacts you can store for each company, 1, 2, 100, 1000, and storage will only be used as required (if you had to allow 100 extra contact fields "just in case" you will soon be buying more hard disk space!).

> *You can apply these normalization techniques on many occasions in order to help solve locking problems but as always there is a tradeoff; although normalization can remove duplicated data it always makes the database more complicated and this can adversely affect performance, particularly for complex reports that may now need to collate information together from several tables instead of one or two. As always, there is no simple answer; you must make the decision based on the needs of your users.*

Well, that's about all we are going to say about record locking. I hope you have managed to keep track! In practice, managing locking is not too tricky provided that you take the time to think, before you start building the database, about how users are going to be interacting with it. Predicting usage patterns is as vital a part of the analysis process as any. If you take the time to do it properly, then you will be able to produce a more appropriate database (and code) design and you will end up – all things being equal – with happier customers.

# Security

So far in this chapter, then, we have looked at the way in which Access handles record locking, when multiple users are attempting to use the database at the same time. We will now take a look at another key issue that raises its head in a multi-user scenario – how Access enforces security.

## Why Security?

The first question that needs to be answered is "Do I need to secure my database?" This is a question that you should ask when designing any database. Implementing security adds a maintenance overhead – so does your application merit it? Quite often the answer will be that it doesn't. The ease with which database applications can be created with Access means that they are now frequently used for fairly trivial functions, which don't always require security. However, if you are concerned about any of the following issues, you should consider implementing some method of securing your application:

❑ **Your database contains confidential information that you don't want unauthorized personnel to view.**

Frequently, databases are used to store confidential information about personal or financial details. Such data needs to be protected from accidental or deliberate access by people who aren't authorized to view it. Your organization may even be legally required to do so.

❑ **You want to protect your database objects from accidental change.**

It may have taken you a lot of time to create your database application. The last thing you want is for one of the users of the application to modify the design of a form or query so that the application no longer works.

❑ **You want some of your users to be able to use certain functionality within your application but don't want this to be generally available.**

Often, your application will contain functionality that is only appropriate to a subset of users. For example, you may wish only Grade 3 managers to be able to use the application to approve expense checks.

❑ **You want to implement an audit trail to monitor who has been doing what in your application.**

As well as building an audit trail specifically for security purposes, you may find it useful to build one for use during the application's testing cycle or initial rollout, so you can log how people have been using the application.

Security can be defined as a method of restricting the access that users have to a database and the objects within that database. You are probably already familiar with the methods of securing an Access database using the menu commands and standard Access dialogs. The main two ways of securing a database in this way involve:

❑ Creating a password for the database

❑ Establishing user-level security

Over 90% of the time you will perform these tasks through the user interface. These two options can be reached from the Security option on the Tools menu:

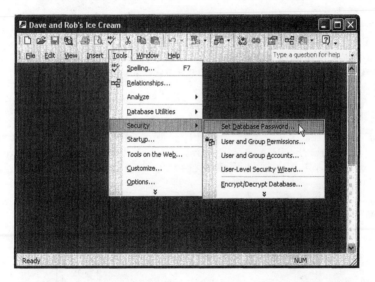

However, there may be occasions when it is preferable to administer these tasks from within VBA code. For example, you might wish to provide the users of your application with the ability to change the database password for themselves. Instead of expecting users to set the database password via the toolbar, you might wish to provide a simple password form that would allow users to enter the new database password. You could then add a procedure that programmatically changed the database password when the user hit the OK button on the form.

We will start by looking at the code that we would use to set a database password programmatically, and after that we'll examine the security model that Access employs and how it can be manipulated in VBA code.

# Setting a Database Password from VBA

To set a database password from VBA, we simply apply the `NewPassword` method to a `Database` object representing the database. This method takes the existing password and the new password as its arguments.

```
Set db = CurrentDB()
db.NewPassword "", "Valerie"
```

The code above would add a password (`Valerie`) to a database that previously didn't have one. To change this password, we would use this syntax.

```
Set db = CurrentDB()
db.NewPassword "Valerie", "Smith"
```

To clear the password, we would specify an empty string for the new password:

```
Set db = CurrentDB()
db.NewPassword "Smith", ""
```

It should be noted that setting a password in this way is not recommended in a live application as it is possible for a hacker to extract the password from it relatively easily.

# Protecting Your Code

Access 2002 also provides us with the capability to protect the code in the VBA project associated with our database. To set the VBA project password, select the Protection tab from the dialog that appears when you choose <ProjectName> Properties from the Tools... menu **in the VBE**:

If you select the Lock project for viewing checkbox and enter a password, subsequent users of the database will not be allowed to view the VBA code for the database unless they enter the specified password.

If, instead, you enter a password but leave the Lock project for viewing checkbox unchecked, users will be able to view and amend the VBA code for the database, but will not be able to display the <ProjectName> Properties dialog.

> *In Access 2002 it is not possible to assign permissions to individual modules – you will need the Office XP Developer edition to achieve this.*

## The Access Security Model

So let's have a look now at how we can use user-level security to assign permissions to users and groups on individual database objects.

The Access security model consists of two elements:

**1.** The workgroup information file

**2.** User and group permissions

The workgroup information file (WIF) contains:

- ❑ The names of all users in the workgroup
- ❑ The names of all groups in the workgroup
- ❑ Information about which users belong to which groups
- ❑ Each user's password (in encrypted form)
- ❑ A unique SID (Security ID) for each user and group (in a binary format)

## Using the User-Level Security Wizard

This wizard, new to Access 2002 (previously you had to find and use a less helpful separate utility WRKGADM.EXE), allows you to simply and easily set up a security regime for your database. To initiate it select Tool, Security, and then User-Level Security Wizard:

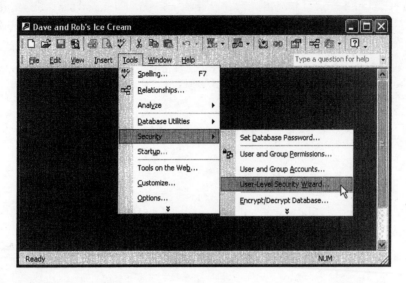

Once started simply follow through each of the stages. They are pretty straightforward and self explanatory so we won't go through them here. Help is available via the Help button on the dialogue itself if you get stuck.

Once you have created your security regime you can inspect and modify it by selecting Tools, Security, and then User and Group Permissions or Accounts.

These wizards are useful and quick tools but we want to see how to do all this from VBA so we can manipulate users and groups from within our own programs. So, rather than taking you through each and every screen of the wizards we'll just dive into the VBA code detail. All the comments regarding Users, Groups, etc. apply equally to the WIF created by the wizard in any case.

## Manually Making a Workgroup Information File (WIF)

OK, I know I just said we were going to look at how to do this stuff in VBA – but there is one operation that you are unlikely to need it for and that's setting up the WIF as this only needs doing once (except for very specialist applications). There are two options for doing this:

**1.** Use the User-Level Security Wizard and set basic user and groups up, then use VBA to modify them as required.

**2.** Use the Workgroup Administrator method explained below.

*If you really do have a need to use VBA code to change the WIF or create a new one please refer to the Visual Basic Help file and search for CreateNewWorkgroupFile, SetDefaultWorkgroupFile, and SystemDB.*

To manually create and/or set the location of the workgroup information file without going through the User-Level Security Wizard select Tools, Security, and then Workgroup Administrator:

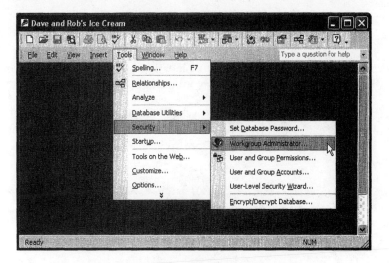

You will then be asked whether you wish to create a new WIF or utilize an existing one:

If you select Create then you will be presented with the following dialogue:

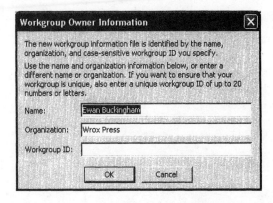

Enter a name for your **Workgroup** under **Workgroup ID** and press **OK**. You will then be asked for a path and filename for the WIF. The default is:

```
C:\Documents and Settings\[user name]\Application
Data\Microsoft\Access\System.mdw
```

It would make a lot of sense to change this to a location where all potential users had access to it. The same directory as the database itself would seem the obvious place.

Permissions for using individual data objects within a database are stored in the database that contains the objects. We'll look at how you modify these permissions a little later. First, we are going to look at how to modify the user and group information in the workgroup information file through VBA.

> *It is recommended that you make sure that the WIF is stored safely and periodically backed up as if it is lost or corrupted then you will have to re-create the User and Group Accounts with exactly the same Personal IDs that were originally assigned. If the new workgroup information file is not created exactly as the original file, you will not be able to open the database with the workgroup file.*

## Manipulating Users and Groups

The Data Access Object hierarchy, which we have already noted to be central to VBA coding, contains the following security objects:

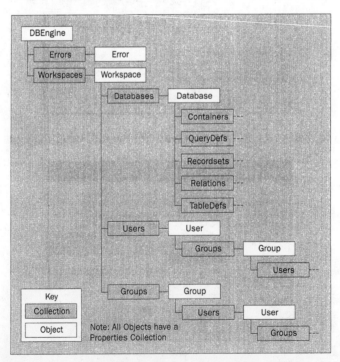

The most striking feature of this hierarchy is its seemingly recursive structure. A User object contains a Groups collection and a Group object contains a Users collection. The hierarchy is implemented in this way to allow for the many-to-many relationship between Users and Groups. A user can belong to one or more groups, each of which can contain many users.

Notice also that the Users and Groups collections belong to the Workspace object, rather than the Database object. Although the properties for individual objects are contained within each database, users and groups are defined within the workgroup information file and are available to all databases that are opened in the security context (Workspace) defined by that workgroup information file. So we can think of the Workspace as being the object that is primarily responsible for access to user and group maintenance in VBA.

So, let's have a look at how we can use these data-access objects to perform the following tasks:

- ❏ Create new users and groups
- ❏ Add users to groups
- ❏ Change a user's password

> **Note that for the following examples to work, you must be logged in with permissions to allow the creation and modification of users. The same rules apply for creating and modifying users and groups in VBA as they do when you use the Security menu options. Normally it is only members of the Admins group who should modify security options.**

## Enumerating Users and Groups

To enumerate all of the users and groups in the current Workspace, we simply need to loop through the Users and Groups collections.

```
Sub EnumGroupsAndUsers()

Dim grp As Group
Dim usr As User

For Each usr In DBEngine(0).Users
    Debug.Print usr.Name
    For Each grp In usr.Groups
        Debug.Print vbTab; grp.Name
    Next
Next

End Sub
```

Note how we can use DBEngine(0) to refer to the default workspace. We can do that because Workspaces is the default collection of the DBEngine object, so that line of code is equivalent to:

```
For Each usr In DBEngine.Workspaces(0).Users
```

If we were to run this procedure in a database while using the default `system.mdw` workgroup information file that is installed with Access, we would see the following in the **Immediate** window:

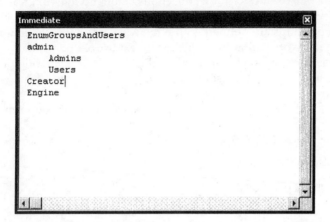

As expected, we see the `admin` user. By default, Access will attempt to log on all users with a user name of `admin` with a blank password. If you want Access to display the logon dialog in order to allow users to log on with a different user name, you should first change the password of the `admin` user. This will cause the default login mechanism to fail and the login dialog box will be displayed.

As you can see, the `admin` user is a member of the two built-in groups, `Admins` and `Users`. We can verify this much if we switch to Access and display the **User and Group Accounts...** dialog from the **Tools | Security...** menu.

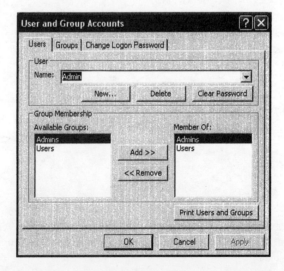

But what of the two other users whose names we saw in the Immediate window? Creator and Engine are actually a couple of internal system accounts. They are used by JET and are not accessible to users and so do not appear when viewing and setting users and groups through the graphical interface. They are mentioned here not because we will use them at all, but simply to alert you of their presence. So, leaving aside the Creator and Engine user accounts we have one built-in user (admin) and two built-in groups (Admins and Users). Let's see how we programmatically add new users and groups.

## Creating a New User

Creating a new user is very straightforward – you simply use the CreateUser method against the Workspace object. For example, the following piece of code can be used to create a user called Mark Fenton:

```
Sub UserAdd()

    Dim wks As Workspace
    Dim usrMark As User
    Dim strUsersPID As String

    Set wks = DBEngine(0)
    strUsersPID = "1234abcd"

    'Start by creating a new User account
    Set usrMark = wks.CreateUser("Mark Fenton")

    'Now set the User's properties
    usrMark.Password = "Doctor"
    usrMark.PID = strUsersPID

    'Append User to the Users collection of this workspace
    wks.Users.Append usrMark

End Sub
```

As before with the database password, I would not recommend using this technique in a live application. Placing passwords in source code means that they can be extracted by a hacker fairly easily.

As you can see, the first step is to create a new user object. We do this by applying the CreateUser method to the workspace object and supplying the name of the new user:

```
Set usrMark = wks.CreateUser("Mark Fenton")
```

The next step is to set the properties of the new User object. The properties you can set are the Password property, the PID property, and the Name property. Note that we set the Name property of the user object when we created it with the CreateUser method.

The PID property is a string of between four and twenty characters, which is used to uniquely identify a user:

```
usrMark.PID = strUsersPID
```

The Password property, a string of up to fourteen characters, corresponds to the password that the new user will need to enter. This is simply an additional way of verifying the user's identity and is *not* the same as the database password.

```
usrMark.Password = "Doctor"
```

After you have set these three properties, you are ready to append the User object to the collection of Users already defined in the current workspace. This will save the User, and its properties, in the workgroup information file.

```
wks.Users.Append usrMark
```

If you type the procedure into a new module and then run it, you can check the existence of the new user by going to the **User and Group Accounts...** section of the **Security** submenu on the menu:

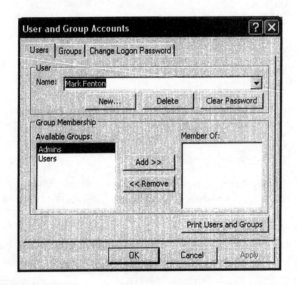

Notice, however, that the new user has not been added to any groups. That's not really surprising, as we never added the user to any groups in our code! We'll see next how we can create a new group and then add a user to that group.

## Creating a New Group

A group is used to collect together users to whom you wish to assign the same permissions. For example, you may have thirty different registrars who will use your database, each of whom you want to define as a user in an Access workgroup. It would be very tiresome if you then had to assign permissions on every single database object to each of the thirty users. So, instead, you can create a group called `Registrars`, add the thirty users to it, and then assign database object permissions just to that group.

> **Wherever possible, you should assign permissions to groups rather than to individual users. Indeed, it is often better to create a group even if it currently only has one user in it – it makes it much easier to change the user or add a user at a later date without having to re-enter or copy permissions individually. It is also recommended that you create an Administration group rather than separately assigning administration permissions to individual users. Having a group to do this makes it easy to add or remove users from the group and also makes it a cinch to keep track of who currently has these important privileges.**

Creating a group is a very similar process to the one we employed above for creating new users:

```
Sub GroupAdd()

    Dim wks As Workspace
    Dim grpRegistrars As Group
    Dim strGroupPID As String

    Set wks = DBEngine(0)
    strGroupPID = "5678"

    'Start by creating a new Group account
    Set grpRegistrars = wks.CreateGroup("Registrars")

    'Now set the Group's properties
    grpRegistrars.PID = strGroupPID

    'Append Group to the Groups collection of this workspace
    wks.Groups.Append grpRegistrars

End Sub
```

First we create a group object within the current workspace:

```
Set grpRegistrars = wks.CreateGroup("Registrars")
```

**721**

Next we set the properties for the group. The only two properties of a group are the Name property and the PID property. We set the Name property when we create the group, just as we did when we created the new user.

```
grpRegistrars.PID = strGroupPID
```

Finally we save the group by appending it to the Groups collection in the current workspace:

```
wks.Groups.Append grpRegistrars
```

## Adding a User to a Group

Once we have created the Registrars group, we want to add our new user to it. The following piece of code will achieve this:

```
Sub AddUserToGroup()

    Dim wks As WorkSpace
    Dim usrMark As User

    Set wks = DBEngine(0)
    Set usrMark = wks.CreateUser("Mark Fenton")

    wks.Groups("Registrars").Users.Append usrMark

End Sub
```

First, we declare an object variable of type User and use it to reference the user object that we want to add to the Registrars group:

```
Set usrMark = wks.CreateUser("Mark Fenton")
```

All of the details concerning the user object Mark Fenton were set in the procedure `UserAdd`, so now it's just a case of appending the user object to the `Users` collection, which belongs to the `Registrars` group.

```
wks.Groups("Registrars").Users.Append usrMark
```

If you run the procedure and then look at the **User and Group Accounts** section again, you will see that Mark Fenton is now a member of the `Registrars` group.

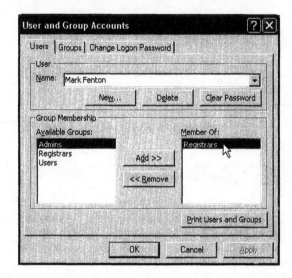

Also, if you refer back to the DAO hierarchy, you will realize that we could have achieved this the other way round:

```
Sub AddUserToGroup()

    Dim wks As WorkSpace
    Dim grpRegistrars As Group

    Set wks = DBEngine(0)
    Set grpRegistrars = wks.CreateGroup("Registrars")

    wks.Users("Mark Fenton").Groups.Append grpRegistrars

End Sub
```

In this example, we append the `Registrars` group object to the `Groups` collection that belongs to the user called **Mark Fenton**.

## Changing a Password

To change our user's password we simply use the `NewPassword` method of the user object:

```
Dim wks As WorkSpace
Set wks = DBEngine(0)

wks.Users("Mark Fenton").NewPassword "Doctor", "Nurse"
```

To clear Mark Fenton's password, we supply an empty string as the new password:

```
Dim wks As WorkSpace
Set wks = DBEngine(0)

wks.Users("Mark Fenton").NewPassword "Doctor", ""
```

> **To change a user's password you must be logged on to that database either as that user or as a member of the Admins Group.**

Now that we have got this far, we should be able to create a form that allows the users of our database to change their password.

**Try It Out** — **Creating a 'Change Password' Form**

> **I strongly recommend you read through this exercise thoroughly before entering any code, as you will be changing the Admin User's password – you wouldn't want to be locked out of your own database by mistake now would you? Indeed, I would urge you to backup your database before you proceed or to use a test database instead.**

**1.** In the `IceCream.mdb` database, create a new blank form in Design view and set the following properties for it:

**2.** Add three **TextBox** controls. Call them `txtOldPwd`, `txtNewPwd`, and `txtVerify` and change the text of their labels to read **Old Password**, **New Password**, and **Verify New Password**.

**3.** Now select the three textboxes (hold down shift as you click on each item) and change them to password input boxes by changing their **Input Mask** property to **Password**.

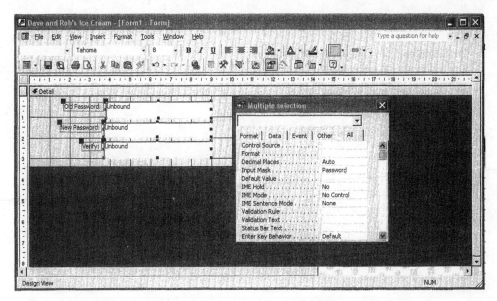

**4.** Add the following code to the form's `Load` event handler:

```
Private Sub Form_Load()

    Me.Caption = Me.Caption & " (" & CurrentUser & ")"

End Sub
```

**5.** Now add two command buttons. Call them `cmdCancel` and `cmdChange` and change their captions to **Cancel** and **Change**. Make sure that the Command Button Wizard isn't enabled when you create these buttons.

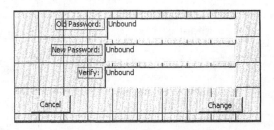

**6.** Next, add the following routines to the Click event handlers of each button. This code for the Cancel button:

```
Private Sub cmdCancel_Click()

    DoCmd.Close

End Sub
```

**7.** and this code for the **Change** button:

```
Private Sub cmdChange_Click()

Dim strOld As String
Dim strNew As String
Dim strVerify As String
Dim strMsg As String

strOld = Nz(txtOldPwd, "")
strNew = Nz(txtNewPwd, "")
strVerify = Nz(txtVerify, "")

If ChangePassword(strOld, strNew, strVerify) = True Then

    If strNew = "" Then
        strMsg = "Your password has been cleared"
    Else
        strMsg = "Your password has been changed"
    End If

    MsgBox strMsg, vbOKOnly

    txtOldPwd = Null
    txtNewPwd = Null
    txtVerify = Null


End If

End Sub
```

**8.** Next, write the code for the function that we referred to in the cmd_Change_Click procedure:

```
Function ChangePassword(strOld As String, _
                        strNew As String, _
                        strVerify As String) As Boolean
```

```
Dim wks As Workspace

On Error GoTo ChangePassword_Err

Set wks = DBEngine(0)

If strNew <> strVerify Then
    MsgBox "Your new password and the verification of your " & _
        "new password do not match." & _
        vbCrLf & vbCrLf & _
        "Please try again.", vbExclamation
End If

wks.Users(CurrentUser).NewPassword strOld, strNew

ChangePassword = True

ChangePassword_Exit:
    Exit Function

ChangePassword_Err:
    MsgBox "Cannot change this password.  Please ensure that " & _
        "you have typed the old password correctly.", _
        vbExclamation
    Resume ChangePassword_Exit

End Function
```

**9.** Close the form and save it as `frmPassword`.

**10.** Finally, open the form and try it out!

> **Beware! If Access does not ask you for a password when you start it up, then Access will log you on as Admin with an empty password. Once you change the Admin password to something other than an empty password, Access will always ask for a login and password when it starts. So when you use the password form, if you are changing the password for the Admin user, make sure you write it down (remember that it's case-sensitive), because if you forget it you won't be able to get back in. To stop Access asking you for a login and password when it starts, set the password for Admin back to an empty string.**

If you followed the description of how to change passwords in the section above this example, you should have no problem understanding how the code works. The form simply allows a user to either enter a new password, change an existing one, or clear the current password.

The code behind the cmdCancel button shouldn't need any explanation.

The cmdChange button is used to change the password of the user who is currently logged on. The user must enter their current password in txtOldPwd and new password in txtNewPwd. The user must also enter it again in the txtVerify box to ensure that no mistake has been made. When the cmdChange button is clicked, the procedure in the Click event of the button starts by converting any null strings into empty strings:

```
strOld = Nz(txtOldPwd, "")
strNew = Nz(txtNewPwd, "")
strVerify = Nz(txtVerify, "")
```

We do this because Access treats textboxes that contain no text as if they contained the value Null. Now that might be appropriate for forms that are used to enter values into a database, but it is not appropriate in this situation. The NewPassword method of the User object, which we will use to change the user's password can only accept string values and Null is not a valid string value. If we want the user to have a blank password, we need to use an empty string ("") instead.

The simplest way to convert Null values into any other value is to use the Nz (Null-to-zero) function. This function accepts two arguments and checks whether the first is Null. If it is not Null, the function returns that first argument as its return value; but if the first argument is Null, the function returns the value of the second argument.

For example, if the value of txtNewPwd is Null, then Nz(txtOldPwd, "") returns an empty string. But, if the value of txtNewPwd is not Null, then Nz(txtOldPwd, "") returns txtNewPwd.

Once we have converted any Null values into empty strings, we call the ChangePassword function and determine whether it returns True or False.

```
If ChangePassword(strOld, strNew, strVerify) = True Then
```

If it returns True then we know that the password has been successfully changed, so we can display a message to the user stating that the password has either been changed or cleared (changed to a blank password). If it returns False then the attempt has failed for some reason. We should really do something about this (like maybe ask the user to try again) but for brevity we have not bothered here:

```
If strNew = "" Then
    strMsg = "Your password has been cleared"
Else
    strMsg = "Your password has been changed"
End If

MsgBox strMsg, vbOKOnly
```

Lastly we clear the values from the three textboxes on the form.

```
txtOldPwd = Null
txtNewPwd = Null
txtVerify = Null
```

Now that is simple enough, but how does the ChangePassword function work? Well, again it is fairly straightforward. The first task is to get hold of a reference to the current Workspace object.

```
Set wks = DBEngine(0)
```

Remember that the Workspace object is the object that gives us access to the Users collection and we need to use a User object if we are to change the current user's password.

We then perform a check to ensure that the new password and the confirmation of the new password have been entered correctly. If they are different, we display a warning message and exit the ChangePassword function.

```
If strNew <> strVerify Then
    MsgBox "Your new password and the verification of your " & _
        "new password do not match." & _
        vbCrLf & vbCrLf & _
        "Please try again.", vbExclamation
End If
```

Once we have performed that check, we can try to change the password:

```
wks.Users(CurrentUser).NewPassword txtOldPwd, txtNewPwd
```

If the attempt is successful the function returns True:

```
ChangePassword = True

ChangePassword_Exit:
    Exit Function
```

However, if an error occurs, it is trapped in the error handler. An error here will almost certainly be caused by the user supplying an incorrect current password, so we display an appropriate message:

```
ChangePassword_Err:
    MsgBox "Cannot change this password.  Please ensure that " & _
           "you have typed the old password correctly.", _
           vbExclamation
    Resume ChangePassword_Exit
```

> Notice that the **ChangePassword** function only returns **True** if the password has been successfully changed. That is because the value of the **ChangePassword** function is only set to **True** once the password has been changed. If the function exits before this point (either because the new password and confirmation are different or because of some other error) the function will return **False**. That is because the function returns a **Boolean** value and the initial value of all **Boolean** variables is **False**.

This form is still only very rudimentary in many ways, but it does illustrate how you can very quickly provide a simple interface to allow users to maintain their own passwords.

## Setting Object Permissions with Visual Basic

Now that we have created users and groups and have learned how to assign them passwords, we shall take a look at how to give those users and groups permissions on objects. We said earlier that permissions for using specific objects within a database are held within each individual database. But how do we find out what those permissions are and how do we set them?

The keys to retrieving and setting permissions are Documents and Containers. As you may know, a Document is an object that contains information about a specific object in the database. A Container is an object that contains information about a collection of objects in the database. You will not be surprised to know that some of the information held by Document objects and Container objects is information about permissions.

### Try It Out — Retrieving Permissions

**1.** In the IceCream.mdb database, add the following procedure to the Chapter 17 Code module:

```
Sub ShowPerms()

    Dim objContainer As Container
    Dim objDoc As Document
```

```
    For Each objContainer In CurrentDb.Containers
        Debug.Print "--> Container: " & objContainer.Name
        For Each objDoc In objContainer.Documents
            Debug.Print "Document: " & objDoc.Name & "   ";
            objDoc.UserName = "Admin"
            Debug.Print "Perms: " & objDoc.AllPermissions
        Next
    Next

    Debug.Print "Done"

End Sub
```

**2.** Run the procedure from the Immediate window. You will get a large output similar to the following:

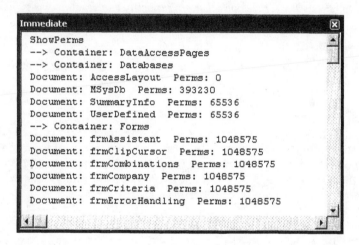

## How It Works

The procedure loops through all the Container objects within the database and assigns a reference to each of them in turn to the variable objContainer. It then prints the Name of the Container object.

```
For Each objContainer In CurrentDb.Containers
    Debug.Print "--> Container: " & objContainer.Name
```

It then loops through all of the Document objects within the Container object referenced by objContainer and assigns them in turn to the variable objDoc.

```
For Each objDoc In objContainer.Documents
```

It then displays the name of the Document object and the permissions in that Document object for the Admin user:

```
Debug.Print "Document: " & objDoc.Name & "   ";
objDoc.UserName = "Admin"
Debug.Print "Perms: " & objDoc.AllPermissions
```

To display the permissions for a specific user you must first set the UserName property of the Document object you are inspecting to the user's name. The semicolon at the end of the first Debug.Print statement tells Access not to move onto a new line for the next Debug.Print statement.

> *Note that we inspect the AllPermissions property of the document. The AllPermissions property reflects those permissions explicitly assigned to the user and those the user inherits from the group to which they belongs. The Permissions property only reflects the permissions that are explicitly and separately assigned to a user.*

## Analyzing the Output

Don't panic if you're a bit confused by the output you get in the Immediate window. We'll go through this now.

### Containers and Documents

Containers are not the same as collections. For example, the Forms **collection** contains references to those forms that are currently open, and it contains information about the design and properties of those forms. The Forms **container**, by contrast, has a Document for every saved form in the database – whether it is loaded or not – and this Document contains information about the form's owner and permissions.

Each database will have within it the following nine containers: DataAccessPages, Databases, Forms, Modules, Relationships, Reports, Scripts, SysRel, and Tables.

Of these, three (Databases, Tables, and Relations) are defined by JET, whereas the other six (DataAccessPages, Forms, Modules, Reports, Scripts, and SysRel) are defined by the Access application.

Now the contents of most of these containers are fairly obvious but you might be confused by the Relationships and SysRel containers. Well, the Relationships container holds information about all the relationships that have been defined between the tables in the current database, while the other container object, SysRel, is used internally by Access to store information about the layout of the System Relationships window. We need not concern ourselves with that here. You should also note that there is no separate container for queries. Instead, these appear within the Tables container.

So much for containers, but what about the documents? If you look at the names of these Document objects, you will recognize most of them as saved objects within the database. There are a few oddities, however, such as AccessLayout, SummaryInfo, and UserDefined. These are all in the Databases container that refers to the current database.

The SummaryInfo Document has a Properties collection, which contains the properties on the **Summary** page of the **Database Properties...** dialog box, found on the **File** menu. Similarly, the UserDefined Document has a Properties collection containing the user-defined properties, found on the **Custom** page of the same dialog box. Finally, the AccessLayout Document is a system document used internally by Access.

So that explains the unfamiliar documents and containers. The rest of them apply to familiar objects and collections within the database.

### Permissions

The next thing we must explain is the permission values. What does a Permissions property of 1048575 for frmCompany mean? To find out, we must use some intrinsic constants. Have a look at the following intrinsic constants which represent user permissions:

| This constant... | ...equals... | ...and means that |
| --- | --- | --- |
| dbSecNoAccess | 0 | The user can't access the object at all. |
| dbSecDelete | 65536 | The user is able to delete the object. |
| dbSecReadSec | 131072 | The user can read the security information about the object. |
| dbSecWriteSec | 262144 | The user is able to alter access permissions for the object. |
| dbSecWriteOwner | 524288 | The user can change the Owner property setting of the object. |
| dbSecFullAccess | 1048575 | The user has full access to the object. |

You will no doubt have spotted that 1048575 is represented by the constant dbSecFullAccess, indicating that, in our previous example, Admin has full permissions for the form we created earlier, frmCriteria.

So, if we wanted, we could now alter our function so that it only shows whether or not a user has permission to, say, delete documents. In this case, it would read like this:

```
Sub ShowNoDelPerms()

    Dim objContainer As Container
    Dim objDoc As Document

    For Each objContainer In CurrentDb.Containers
        Debug.Print "--> Container: " & objContainer.Name
        For Each objDoc In objContainer.Documents
            If (objDoc.AllPermissions And dbSecDelete) = dbSecDelete Then
                Debug.Print "Can Delete Document: " & _
                        objDoc.Name & "   ";
                objDoc.UserName = "Admin"
                Debug.Print "Perms: " & objDoc.AllPermissions
            Else
                Debug.Print "Cannot Delete Document: " & _
                        objDoc.Name & "   ";
                objDoc.UserName = "Admin"
                Debug.Print "Perms: " & objDoc.AllPermissions
            End If
        Next
    Next

    Debug.Print "Done"

End Sub
```

To check whether the user has permission to delete the object associated with a document, we compare the document's AllPermissions property with the constant dbSecDelete using the And operator:

```
If (objDoc.AllPermissions And dbSecDelete) = dbSecDelete Then
```

If the result of this expression is True, the user has permission to delete the document.

The main thing to remember here is not that you have to understand how these logical operators work at a low level but that you need to know how to use these operators to determine permission values.

To determine if a user has permissions represented by one of the security constants on a certain object we use the And operator. So the following expression will return True if the user **does** have the permission represented by the security constant and will return False if the user **does not** have that permission:

```
(objDoc.AllPermissions And <security constant>) = <security constant>
```

## Setting Permissions

We can also set permissions as well as retrieve them. Suppose we want to make sure that one of our users, Mark Fenton, doesn't accidentally delete the frmPassword that we so carefully created earlier on. To do this, we can modify the Permissions property of the document for frmPassword. This is what the following procedure does:

```
Sub ProtectItFromMark()

    Dim db As Database
    Dim Doc As Document

    Set db = CurrentDb()
    Set Doc = db.Containers("Forms").Documents("frmPassword")

    Doc.UserName = "Mark Fenton"
    Doc.Permissions = dbSecFullAccess And Not dbSecDelete

End Sub
```

The first thing to notice about this piece of code is the way in which we select the document whose permissions we wish to alter. In the previous example, we simply looped through the container and document collections in turn. But if you want to, you can select a specific document or container by name. In this example, we are selecting the document for the object called frmPassword. Because this is a form, its document will be located in the container called Forms, hence the line:

```
Set Doc = db.Containers("Forms").Documents("frmPassword")
```

We then need to specify the user to whom these permissions should apply:

```
Doc.Username = "Mark Fenton"
```

Finally, we specify the permissions we want to give Mark. Here we are saying that we want Mark to be able to do everything but delete the form:

```
Doc.Permissions = dbSecFullAccess And Not dbSecDelete
```

Again, you don't need to understand exactly why And Not removes permissions. What you need to remember is that it works. The following code fragments show how to add and remove permissions for objects.

To replace all permissions on an object with a new single permission, use this:

```
Set Doc.Permission = <security constant>
```

To replace all permissions on an object with a new set of permissions, use this:

```
Set Doc.Permission = <security constant> Or <security constant>
```

To add a new single permission while retaining the existing permissions, use this:

```
Set Doc.Permission = Doc.Permission Or <security constant>
```

To add a new set of permissions while retaining the existing permissions, use this:

```
Set Doc.Permission = Doc.Permission Or <security constant> Or _
                     <security constant>
```

To remove a single permission from the existing permissions, use this:

```
Set Doc.Permission = Doc.Permission And Not <security constant>
```

To remove a set of permissions from the existing permissions, use this:

```
Set Doc.Permission = Doc.Permission And Not (<security constant> Or _
                     <security constant>)
```

There are many ways you can manipulate object permissions through VBA. After all, there are 25 security constants! But the principle is the same whichever you use. The full range of security constants is shown below:

| | | |
|---|---|---|
| acSecMacExecute | dbSecDBAdmin | dbSecReadSec |
| acSecMacReadDef | dbSecDBCreate | dbSecReadDef |
| acSecMacWriteDef | dbSecDBExclusive | dbSecReplaceData |
| acSecFrmRptExecute | dbSecDBOpen | dbSecRetrieveData |
| acSecFrmRptReadDef | dbSecDelete | dbSecWriteSec |
| acSecFrmRptWriteDef | dbSecDeleteData | dbSecWriteDef |
| acSecModReadDef | dbSecFullAccess | dbSecWriteOwner |
| acSecModWriteDef | dbSecInsertData | |
| dbSecCreate | dbSecNoAccess | |

We don't have space here to go through every constant in detail (and in any case it would be deeply dull!) but you can get a full description of all of them by going to the Microsoft Developer's Network (MSDN) web site at http://msdn.microsoft.com and doing a search for the keywords "DAO Security Constants".

## Workspaces

Finally, a quick note about workspaces. Many of the code snippets in this last section have started with the following line:

```
Set wks = DBEngine(0)
```

This means that any code that follows that uses the wks workspace object will execute in the current workspace. In other words, it will run in the security context of the currently logged on user. There are times, however, when we might want to run some code in the security context of a different user. For example, our database may contain a function that lists the groups to which the user belongs. The problem is that we need to be logged on with administrative privileges to do this.

The way to impersonate another user in code is to create a new workspace, which we do like this:

```
Set wks = DBEngine.CreateWorkspace("MyWorkspace", "Admin", "Glenfarclas")
```

This has the effect of programmatically logging us on as the user called Admin with a password of Glenfarclas and creates a workspace called MyWorkspace. Any operations performed on users or groups within that workspace will be executed as if they were being performed by the user called Admin, irrespective of how the current user is currently logged on to Access.

In fact, if you want to try this out, you can have a go in one of the exercises at the end of this chapter!

# Compiling

One of the final issues that we will discuss in this chapter is the ability to protect your source code by saving a database as an MDE file. An MDE file is, in essence, a pre-compiled version of the database. But before we look at MDE files in more detail, let's just take a moment or two to see how Access projects are compiled.

We saw earlier in Chapter 12 how compiling our code can alert us to any errors we may have made in our code. Some errors can be detected by Access as we are writing our code. For example, let's suppose we type the following line of code in a module:

```
DoCmd openform "frmSwitchboard"
```

As soon as we try to move off this line of code onto a new line, Access will alert us with a message box informing us that the line of code contains a syntax error.

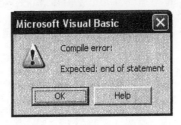

In this case, the error was generated because we omitted the period between the words DoCmd and OpenForm. Despite the misleading message box that Access displays, this isn't really a compile error; it is a **syntax** error. By default, Access will check the syntax of every line of code you enter and flag any errors it notices like the one above. If you want to, you can disable this automatic syntax checking by unchecking the Auto Syntax Check box under the Tools | Options… dialog.

Be wary of disabling automatic syntax checking. There are occasions when it can be useful to disable it. For example, you might be pasting a large chunk of code from, let's say, Access Basic into the module window and you know it will need a fair bit of rework before it will work in VBA. In that case you won't want message boxes appearing every time you move from one line to another.

But in most other situations, you will want automatic syntax checking enabled. Most of the errors it determines are genuine mistakes and are much more easily corrected on the spot.

Whereas syntax errors are easily recognizable as soon as they occur, there are other types of errors that can creep into our code that cannot be detected until later on. For example, what if we create a Do...Loop structure and forget to put the Loop statement at the end? We certainly wouldn't want Access to flag the error when we move off the line containing the Do statement. So when should these errors be detected? The answer is that these are compile errors and are detected when VBA attempts to compile the project. We'll look now at what compilation actually involves and the implications of the different types of compilation afforded to us by VBA. Then we'll look at ways of compiling our code programmatically.

## What is Compilation?

So what happens when a VBA project is compiled? Normally when programmers talk about compiling an application, they mean that the human-readable code is converted into native machine-readable code that can be executed directly. Access works slightly differently, in that the VBA code that we write is not converted directly into machine-readable code but is instead converted into an intermediate format called p-code (or pseudo-code). When the application is run, the p-code is interpreted (translated into machine-readable code also called native code or machine code – the code that the particular processor inside your PC actually uses) line-by-line by a run-time DLL.

Many developers regard p-code as an unnecessary evil and bemoan the performance degradation that results from VBA not being compiled into native machine code. In point of fact, although native code can be substantially faster than interpreted p-code for computationally-intensive operations, which rearrange lots of bits and bytes all over the place, most of the VBA code we write is no slower in p-code than native code. After all, the VBA functions we use already reside in a run-time library which is highly optimized machine code, so there won't be too much overhead there. In any case, once you start calling subprocedures, DLLs, or other objects, the overhead of setting up things like stack frames makes the difference between p-code and native code performance negligible. Add to that the fact that the average application spends less than 5% of the time running code and you will see that the p-code versus natively compiled argument doesn't hold that much water when it comes to VBA projects in Access.

All the same, the process of compilation still causes the code we have written to be checked for syntax and integrity; and it's that stage of the process that is most noticeable to us. If structures without an End If, variables that haven't been declared, calls to procedures that don't exist – these are all the types of error that are detected and flagged to us when we compile our code. In fact, the whole process of checking the syntax and integrity of the code and then compiling it into p-code can be quite lengthy, especially where large amounts of code are involved.

> *If compiling code takes time and highlights errors in our code, the corollary is that trying to run uncompiled code will be just as slow (because the code will have to be compiled when it is run) and may contain bugs. So, get into the habit of regularly compiling your code and always compile it before you distribute a finished application.*

## How do we Compile Code?

Compiling a project is a simple enough process. The easiest way is to simply choose the Compile <ProjectName> item from the Debug menu in the VBE.

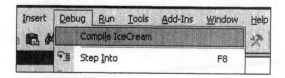

This menu item is only available whenever the project is in an uncompiled state. If the project is fully compiled, the Compile <ProjectName> item is disabled on the menu bar.

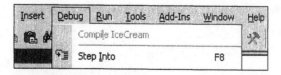

Personally, I prefer to put a button on the toolbar that allows me to see whether my code is compiled and to compile it with just a single click. To do this, select Customize... from the Add or Remove Buttons on the VBE toolbar:

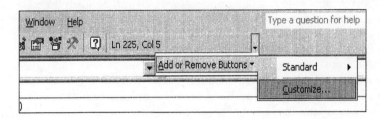

Then, simply locate the Compile Project button from the Debug category and drag it onto the toolbar.

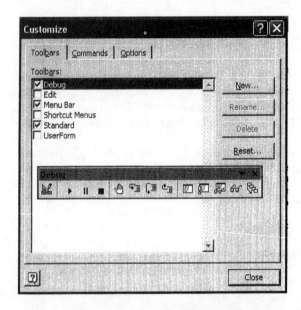

Lo and behold, you now have a toolbar button that allows you to compile your code at a simple click and – much more usefully – whose status indicates whether a project is compiled or not.

*In previous versions of Access this button was on the toolbar by default. Its removal in the current version of Access is a consistency issue; because none of the other implementations of VBA (in Word, Excel etc.) have historically had this button on the toolbar it has been removed from VBA in Access. Frankly, I would prefer to have seen it added to the toolbar by default. After all, the first thing that all the developers I know do when they install Access is to add the button anyway!*

### Compile On Demand

You may have noticed two options – Compile On Demand and Background Compile – on the General tab of the Tools | Options... dialog in the VBE.

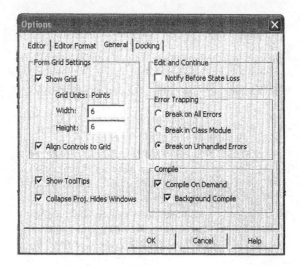

If VBA needs to execute a procedure and the procedure is in a module that is not compiled, it will automatically compile the module before it runs the procedure. It has to because VBA code is not machine-readable, so the VBA has to be converted into p-code that can then be interpreted into a machine-readable format.

If the Compile On Demand option is checked, then VBA will load and compile only those modules that contain procedures that are potentially called by the about-to-be-executed procedure.

However, if the Compile On Demand option is not checked, then VBA will load and compile all modules in the project. This can cause a notable performance hit, if your database contains a lot of uncompiled code, so you are advised to leave the Compile On Demand option checked at all times.

If on-demand compiling is enabled, you can also use the Background Compile checkbox to instruct VBA to use idle time to compile a project in the background, so reducing the number of times that you will need to compile your project explicitly.

## When does Code Decompile?

By this stage, you might be wondering whether the Compile On Demand option really makes much difference. Surely if you compile your code before you ship your application you won't have any decompiled code, so you won't have to worry about how long it takes to compile. Most of the time that's fine. However, there are one or two things that your users can do that may cause code in your application to decompile. These include:

- ❑ Adding a form, report, control, or module

- ❑ Modifying the code in a form, report, control, or module

- ❑ Deleting a form, report, control, or module

❑ Renaming a form, report, control, or module

❑ Adding or removing a reference to an object library, or database

If any of these occurs and the project needs to be recompiled, your users could experience a significant delay if they then have to wait for the entire project to be recompiled. In such a case, selecting the Compile On Demand option could make a big difference to perceived performance.

# Using MDE files

A feature introduced in Access 97 was the ability to save a database as an MDE file. When you save a database as an MDE file, Access creates a new database, into which it places a copy of all the database objects from the source database except for the modules. It then compiles all of the modules in the source database and saves them in their compiled form in the target database, which it then compacts. The target database does not contain a copy of the source VBA code, only compiled p-code. Obviously it takes time and effort to create the MDE file and so you would normally only do this when you are ready to deploy the application to the users.

There are three main benefits to be gained from using an MDE file instead of the database file:

❑ The p-code is smaller than the source VBA code, so the MDE file will take up less space and therefore have a smaller memory footprint when running and be easier to distribute to the target machine(s).

❑ The modules are already compiled, so performance of the database will be optimal.

❑ Users are unable to perform certain modifications to MDE files (see Restrictions on MDE Files) and they have no access to the source (uncompiled) code. This presents excellent opportunities for tightening the security of your application.

*Note, however, that an MDE is not an executable file. In other words, it cannot be run as a standalone application in the way that an .exe file can be – you still need Access to be installed on every machine that will use the file.*

## Saving a Database as an MDE file

Saving a database as an MDE file couldn't be easier. But you must meet certain prerequisites before Access will allow you to do so. The prerequisites are as follows:

❑ You must use a workgroup information file that contains users defined to have permission to access the database.

❑ You must be logged on as a user with Open and Open Exclusive permissions for the database.

❑ You must be logged on as a user with Modify Design or Administer privileges for tables in the database (or you must own the tables in the database).

❑ You must be logged on as a user with Read Design permissions for all objects in the database.

*If you use the replication features of Access, you should also note that you cannot convert a replicated database to an MDE file until you have removed all of the replication system tables from the database.*

If all these criteria are met, then you can save the database as an MDE file. The process of creating an MDE file requires that Access should be able to exclusively lock the database, so you should make sure that no one else is using the database as well.

Then you simply select the Make MDE File... option from the Database Utilities item on the Tools menu:

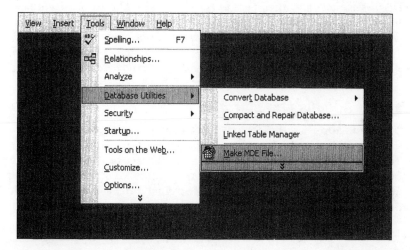

In the Save MDE As dialog that then appears, you should type the name and location that you want for the new MDE file, and that's it!

## Restrictions on MDE Files

We noted earlier on that there are various actions that will cause code in a database to decompile. Because MDE files can only contain compiled code, those actions that cause code to decompile are not allowed in a database that has been saved as an MDE file. In other words, users cannot perform any of the following actions in databases saved as MDE files:

- ❑ Add a form, report, control or module
- ❑ Modify the code in a form, report, control or module
- ❑ Delete a form, report, control or module
- ❑ Rename a form, report, control or module
- ❑ Add or remove a reference to an object library or database
- ❑ Change the Project Name for the database in the Tools | Options... dialog

However, users are free to import or export tables, queries, and macros to or from MDE or non-MDE databases.

When using MDE files, you should also note that future versions of Access may not be backward compatible with Access 2002 MDE files. In other words, if you create an MDE file with Access 2002, you may not be able to open it or run it in future versions of Access, nor may there be a way to convert it to newer versions of Access. In practice this should not be too great a problem as you can always recreate the MDE file using the new version and redeploy it; providing that everyone is using compatible versions that is.

> *These two limitations – the fact that you cannot modify forms, reports, or modules, and that MDE files are not guaranteed to be upgradeable – should make you realize the importance of hanging on to your source code. When you save a database as an MDE file, you should **always** make sure that you keep a copy of the original source database, because you will need it if you want to make any changes to the design of forms, reports, or modules or if you want to use the database with future versions of Access.*

## Using MDEs with Add-Ins and Libraries

A final consideration applies if the database that you are saving as an MDE file contains references to other databases as either add-ins or libraries. In short, before you save a database as an MDE file, you should save as MDE files any databases to which the source database contains references, and then redirect the references to the MDE files rather than to the original add-ins or libraries. Only then can you save the original database as an MDE file. The example below should clarify the situation.

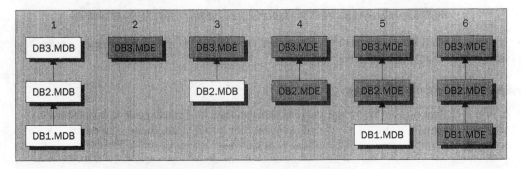

Let us suppose that we have a database DB1.MDB, which contains a reference to DB2.MDB, and that DB2.MDB in turn contains a reference to DB3.MDB (stage 1). The first step is to save DB3.MDB as an MDE file (stage 2) and then set a reference from DB2.MDB to the new compiled DB3.MDE (stage 3). Once you have set the reference, you can then save DB2.MDB as an MDE file (stage 4) and set a reference to it from DB1.MDB (stage 5). Only once you have done that, can you save DB1.MDB as an MDE file (stage 6).

## Encrypting

There remains one final method of preventing unwanted access to the data in a database and that is to encrypt the database. Although methods such as protecting databases or projects with passwords and setting security on DAO objects are useful methods of limiting access to a database, there is nothing to prevent someone from simply opening up an Access database in an editor such as Notepad. In fact, you can get a lot of data out of an Access database just by looking at the raw data in a basic text editor like Wordpad as we have below:

```
___€?_€O_€___€o_,   __ _    ÿþWake's Cakes And Icesÿþ72 High Street
Birminghamÿþ827 2AAU K ÿþ+44 121 789 4562ÿþKaren Waked X X X X F B 9 9 _ _
w__
   ÿþJane's Dineryÿþ1827 East 1st Avenue
DenverC O ÿþ80206ÿþUSAÿþ303 322-1070ÿþJane Donnelly_ P P P P B = 6 2 _ _
   □__     ÿþQuintessential Icesÿþ14 Hambledon Road
GodalmingÿþSurreyÿþGU8 1AAU K ÿþ+44 1428 121212ÿþChris Quink _ _ _ _ N J A 9
 __
   □__ _  ÿþLloyds Luscious Lolliesÿþ18-20 Alverston RoadÿþLondonÿþE5 9JWU K
ÿþ+44 181 745 1322ÿþ+44 181 745 1765ÿþJanine Lloyd{ m m m [ I E = 5
```

In order to prevent this low-level access, you can encrypt a database. This is simple enough to do. Just close down the database that you want to encrypt and select Encrypt/Decrypt Database... from the Tools | Security menu in Access.

You will be prompted for the name of the database you want to encrypt and the name of the file you want to save the encrypted database as.

Encrypted databases can be used from within Access just like unencrypted databases but their contents are indecipherable when viewed as plain text. There is a slight overhead in terms of performance (Microsoft claims no more than 15% slower) incurred when using a database in an encrypted state and you will need to bear this in mind if you decide to encrypt database applications for which execution speed is a priority.

# Summary

Well then, in this chapter we have looked at the many problems that can arise when more than one person wants to use a database at the same time. In fact they aren't so much problems, as issues. They only become problems when you ignore or forget about them.

The key to producing an Access database that will function as happily with ten people using it as with one, is to plan ahead. If you bear in mind the issues we have looked at in this chapter, and apply them to your databases from the moment you start building them, you should have very few problems. On the other hand, if you wait until the last moment to add a veneer of multi-usability on top of your database, you will spend some very long days and nights trying to iron out problems which wouldn't have arisen if you had been a little more far-sighted in the beginning!

This chapter has covered:

- ❏ The difference between page-level and row-level locking
- ❏ The difference between optimistic and pessimistic locking
- ❏ How to apply locking
- ❏ The locking errors you are likely to encounter and how to deal with them
- ❏ How to use the user and group objects to secure a database
- ❏ How to set and change passwords
- ❏ Compiling projects
- ❏ Creating and using MDE files
- ❏ Encrypting databases

That was quite a lot of ground we covered there! Obviously some of these subjects could fill whole chapters in their own right so we could only really scratch the surface here but you should have enough to make a good start.

# Exercises

1. Earlier in this chapter we looked at how it was possible to use the `CreateWorkspace` method to allow us to act in the security context of another user. One potential use of this is to allow us to create a procedure that lists all of the groups to which the current user belongs. The potential problem is that only members of the `Admins` group have permission to view this information. See if you can write a procedure that lists all of the groups to which the current user belongs even if the user is not a member of the `Admins` group.

2. The password form we created in this chapter is still fairly rudimentary. You can probably think of many ways to improve it. For example, some security systems force you to change your password at monthly intervals and will not allow you to reuse any of your, say, five previous passwords. See if you can modify the password form so that it enforces these two rules.

**Hint**: If you decide to store users' passwords in a table you need to make sure that you will be able to read the table from code, but that normal users won't be able to read the data in the table.

# C H A P T E R 18

# The Internet

There is no one who can deny the pervasive nature of the Internet, and whether you love it or loathe it, there's no doubt it will be with us for a long time to come. It has already proven to be an important tool for many businesses and there are a great many ways in which it can aid your work practices. In many organizations one of the requirements when working with databases is to make that data available via a web browser, and given the growth of the Internet this development of database interfacing with the browser will continue to expand.

In Chapter 14, we saw how e-mail can easily be integrated into Access applications, easing communications and improving the ordering system via automation. Now we need to look at the other features of Access that can integrate with the Internet.

In particular we are going to look at:

- ❑ How to publish data to an Intranet using Data Access Pages
- ❑ Using XML to export both Data and Schema
- ❑ How to publish your data using Active Server Pages
- ❑ Using Hyperlinks within Microsoft Access

## The Internet

We're sure you know what the Internet is by now, but let's start with a few definitions so that we're all on common ground:

- ❑ **HyperText Markup Language (HTML)** is the format in which most Internet documents are written. It is a fairly simple language and is really just designed for the layout of documents (the Markup part), and the linking of documents to each other (the HyperText part).

- ❑ A **hyperlink** is what identifies the connection between one HTML document and another.

- ❑ The **Dynamic HyperText Markup Language (DHTML)** was created to overcome the rather static nature of HTML, where there is no ability for HTML pages to interact with the user. The Dynamic ability is provided by programming code embedded into the HTML page. DHTML also includes topics like Cascading Styles, downloadable fonts, and other dynamic technologies which can be used to bring life to otherwise static HTML pages.

- ❑ A **browser**, or **web browser**, is a program that displays HTML pages. The two most popular are Microsoft Internet Explorer and Netscape Navigator.

- ❑ A **web server** is a computer system that is used to store HTML pages, graphics, ASP pages, and so on, and sends them to a browser when the browser requests them.

- ❑ **Active Server Pages (ASP)** is Microsoft's technology for web servers, which allow programming code to run on the web server before the web page is sent to the browser. Note that classic ASP 3.0 has been superceded in most of the Microsoft documentation and focus by ASP.NET. However, Access 2002 still uses classic ASP. We hope to see significant changes in Office 11.

- ❑ A **web site** is a collection of related web pages. The Wrox Press web site, for example, can be found at http://www.wrox.com/. Most web addresses are preceded by www.

- ❑ A **Uniform Resource Locator (URL)**, or **web address**, is the address given to a web site, or a page within it. For example, the URL for the books catalog page at the Wrox Press website is http://www.wrox.com/Store.

There are also a number of protocols that are used around the Internet. A protocol is simply the name given to the way computers can communicate with each other. For example:

- ❑ **HyperText Transfer Protocol (HTTP)** is the main protocol for transferring web pages between the web server and the web browser. That's why many URLs start with http:

- ❑ **File Transfer Protocol (FTP)** allows you to download, and upload, programs and files to web servers. FTP addresses start with ftp:

- ❑ **Mail**, which allows mail to be sent over the Internet. A URL that represents a mail address starts with mailto:

There are many other protocols, but they don't play as important a role for us when we're working with VBA.

# Data Access Pages and Access XP

Although not specifically a VBA topic, publishing data to the web is one of the most common database/Internet-related activities, and so deserves a mention. If you want to publish data to the Internet then you need to consider one important point – how dynamic is your data, that is, does it change frequently or is it static? For example, a staff contact listing which may not change a great deal over time as opposed to daily sales figures which will obviously change frequently. The publishing approach taken will depend on how dynamic your data is.

If your data is static, that is, does not change, then you could use plain HTML files and then update these on a regular basis, say once a month. If you need the very latest data, then there are several options available to you from within Microsoft Access: you can use ASP files to show the latest data every time the web page is viewed, or you can use Data Access Pages (DAPs), which show a live view of the data. Both HTML and ASP files give the advantage that any browser can view the page, whereas Data Pages only work in Internet Explorer 5 or above. Data Pages are restrictive to say the least – they are best used in an intranet, and only then if you can guarantee the browser being used will be Internet Explorer. However, when working in an intranet environment where you know that your users will be using Internet Explorer 5 and above, DAPs provide you with a useful tool to distribute data to the users. As you will see later, DAPs also provide you with a virtual codeless solution, that is, they are created using the Access interface. However, in order to create greater functionality you will need to learn VBScript at some point.

> An intranet can be viewed as an internal Internet with access provided to those within a company or other organization. Increasingly we are seeing inter-company intranets between a large organizations and, for example, their suppliers where common information can be shared privately.

In our view, unless you are tied into a completely Microsoft solution, DAPs are of little benefit. Sometimes you will know in advance which browser the user will view your site with. It is also possible to use browser detection software such as BrowserHawk (available from http://www.cyscape.com/products/) to detect the browser the user is entering a site with, so you can then redirect them to another set of pages more appropriate for that browser. This, of course, is an option, but you need to be prepared to maintain and manage two or three different sets of web pages.

> Do not confuse Data Access Pages (DAPs) with Access Data Pages (ADPs). Access Data Pages are a specific file type (.adp) used to interface with SQL Server databases as opposed to Data Access Pages which are used to interface with a web browser.

# DAP Connection Files

A Data Access page is peculiar to Microsoft Access and is not available for use with any other database. As we have said, it is also a total Microsoft Solution requiring the full range of Microsoft software from the server to the client. DAPs can also be used when working with SQL Server and SQL Server Desktop via Microsoft Access Data Project files. At a high level, DAPs contain HTML and ActiveX controls. The ActiveX controls allow you to bind to Microsoft Jet, SQL Server, and SQL Server Desktop data stores. One of the more important of the controls is the Data Access Control, which interacts with Internet Explorer, permitting you to actually display the data. This is why it is impossible to get a DAP to work with, for example, Netscape Navigator. The interaction with the browser is just not there.

The following diagram provides an overview of how a DAP works:

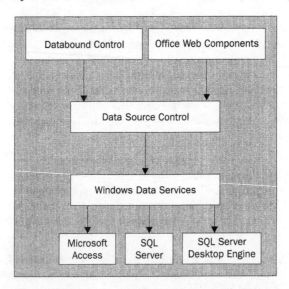

Before creating our Data Access Pages it is useful to know how the actual connection information is stored. This is the ADO connection string that will be used on the web to get at the actual data. (ADO Connection strings are discussed in Chapter 21). Microsoft Access provides you with a database option which makes it very simple to edit or create the string. This option will create a particular file type known as an Office Data Connection or .odc file. The ODC file can be opened and edited in a text editor, which makes it very easy to change the connection string if required. You can also view the contents of the ODC file by opening it using Microsoft Internet Explorer. To create a database connection file which points to an Access Database, open a database file and using the main menu select Tools | Options. In the Options dialog, click on the Pages tab. From here it is simply a matter of following the wizard:

1. Check the Use Default Connection File box.

2. Click on the Browse button.

**3.** Click on the New Source button.

**4.** Select Other/Advanced, and click Next >>.

**5.** Select Microsoft Jet 4 OLEDB Provider.

**6.** Click Next >>.

**7.** Use the button beside the Select or enter a database name to navigate to the required database.

**8.** The User name will be defaulted to Admin with a blank password. If you are using Access security you may change this by removing the check marks in the appropriate box.

**9.** Click the Test Connection to ensure all is well.

**10.** Click OK.

**11.** In the Choose Data dialog simply click Next>. This option is available when working with SQL Server, and you have the opportunity of selecting from a number of databases on the server. It is disabled when working with Jet.

**12.** The final dialog allows you to enter a File Name for the odc file and a textual Description about the connection. Click Finish to close the dialog and save the connection file.

If at some point you need to change the connection information, it is simply a matter of opening the ODC file in Notepad and manually changing the database location section. A section of which is highlighted in the following figure. Note that much of the connection information is not visible in this example.

# What's New in Access 2002 DAPs

In Access 2000, DAPs were viewed as a version one technology, and, in some cases, by Access Developers as marketing fluff. With Access 2002, Microsoft brings several new features to DAPs in an effort to increase their uptake, including:

❑ An Office 2000 or 2002 license is now no longer required. Users, however, still require the Office web controls to view and interact with a DAP. This, though, does not present great problems. When installing Office XP, the web controls are installed as part of the setup. A user without the controls will be prompted to download the files from the Microsoft web site. See
http://office.microsoft.com/downloads/2002/owc10.aspx.

❑ Multiple levels of undo.

❑ Ability to save existing forms and reports as Data Access Pages.

❑ Improved DAP designer.

❑ Ability to select multiple fields from the table selector.

❑ New Autosum feature when working with aggregate values.

### What are the Office Web Components?

The web components are assets of COM objects used to place spreadsheets and pivot tables on the Internet. Using the controls, a user can use this functionality without having Microsoft Office XP installed. Make sure you have at least version 2.5 of the Microsoft Data Access Components on your machine before the install.

## New DAP Events

In additional to the above there are also several new events available to you in Access 2002.

❑ `AfterDelete`
Fires after a record is deleted or the deletion is cancelled. This event is commonly used to show a message to the user that the deletion was successful.

❑ `AfterInsert`
Fires after a new record is added. In this case, you may want to "grab" the username of the individual who entered the record or simply update an audit table with the date and time the insert took place.

❑ `BeforeDelete`
Fires before a record is deleted or the deletion is cancelled. You may want the user to confirm they actually want to delete a record before continuing. This event would permit you to send a message to the user requesting that they confirm the deletion before actually deleting the record.

❑ `BeforeInsert`
Fires when you type the first character into a control, but before the record is actually inserted into the database. Commonly used as a validation trigger.

❏ Dirty

Fires when the record changes, but before the `BeforeUpdate` event. It can be used to trigger code when data or text items in a combo box change. For example, enabling or disabling controls on a page based on data entered by the user.

❏ Focus

Fires when a DAP section receives the focus. For example, when moving from one record to another the focus event could be used to change the background color.

❏ RecordExit

Fires when all `AfterUpdate` events fire, but before the record becomes non-current. Can be used to ensure that any necessary validation has been carried out before you close a form. Commonly used when working with Master Detail pages, when you need to work with an embedded sub form in the DAP. For example, a customer record can be displayed on the top half of the form, and the multiple orders can be displayed on the bottom half of the form. A sub form is normally used to display the many records.

*A Master Detail page is commonly used to display one record and its associated many records.*

The best way to understand Data Access Pages is to actually create one.

---

**Try It Out**      **Creating a Simple Data Access Page**

Remember, to view Data Access Pages you require at least Internet Explorer 5.

**1.** In an open database, select the **Pages** in the **Objects** bar.

**2.** Select **Create data access page by using wizard** – you can double-click to start it.

**3.** Select **tblIceCream** as the table, selecting all fields. You don't need to add any grouping or sorting, so just keep clicking **Next** and finally **Finish**. After the wizard has finished you'll see your Data Access Page in design view:

Notice how much this looks like the standard form and report designer, but in fact it's an HTML page, with embedded ActiveX objects. The DAP designer contains some features that would be very useful in standard Access forms design. For example, selecting View | Field List from the main menu opens a drag and drop interface to your database object, tables, queries, and views. One additional trick it has is that it can "read" existing relationships between tables and allow you to create relationships on the fly. Adding a field is a simple matter of dragging and dropping the field from the list to the DAP.

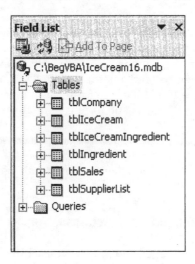

**4.** Finally save this page as tblIceCream and view it by right-clicking on the page and selecting Web Page Preview:

> When you save the DAP it is not saved within your MDB file. The first time you create a DAP you will be prompted for a folder in which to save this and any further pages you create. DAPs are not actually part of your MDB file and are therefore stored outside the MDB file in their own folder. Remember a DAP is actually a HTML page containing ActiveX objects, not an Access object. There are no particular conventions when saving DAPs but it is handy to save all the files in a sub folder of your main project folder. That way you know where they are when you need to find them.

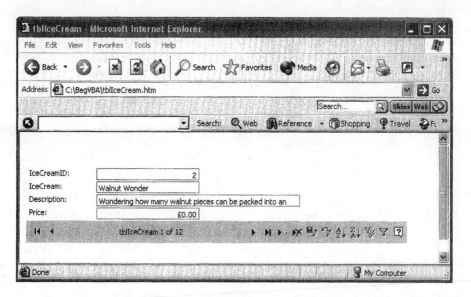

This looks very much like a normal Access form. It shows a single record at a time, and the navigation bar works just like the Access form equivalent. As you can see, creating a basic DAP is a fairly simple process. It is also possible to export a report as a Data Access Page.

## Try It Out     Saving a Report as a Data Access Page

This time we will take an existing report which shows the ice creams and the ingredients required for production. The report is available in the Chapter 16 example database. In the **Database** window, select **Reports**.

1. Select the rptIceCreamIng report

2. Either right-click and select **Save As** or chose the same from the **File** menu

3. Enter a name for the new object

4. Select **Data Access Page** from the dialog drop-down list

5. Click **OK** to proceed

6. Using the **New Data Access Page** dialog accept the default folder or navigate to the required folder and click **OK**

Microsoft Access will generate the DAP based on the selected report.

Notice within the DAP the format of the report has been changed. Rather than a static Access Master Detail report when all the data is presented to you at once, the new DAP file is actually interactive. In order to see the ingredients for each ice cream, click on the plus (+) symbol to expand the data tree. This process gives you a dynamic version of a standard Access Master Detail form which is viewable via the Web. The DAP will always contain the latest version of your data, and all your users need do is refresh the page within the browser to view the latest information.

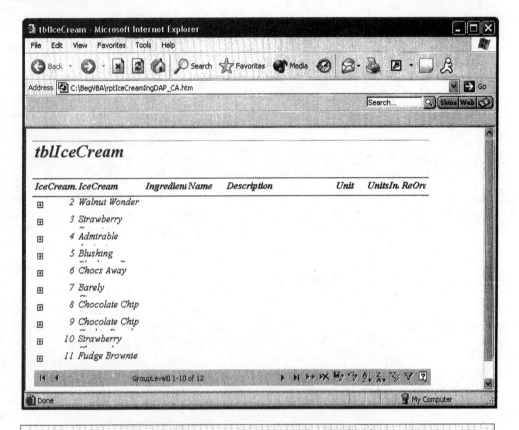

In order to complete the DAP, you will have to go into design view and amend some items, for example, you can change the default title from tblIceCream to something more meaningful. Textboxes also need to be resized, in particular, you may need to expand some of them in order to display the full ingredients and remove the default line wrap put in by the wizards.

When your data is not dynamic, but there is a requirement to display it via the Web, then one simple approach is to save it as a static HTML page. For multiple page sets, Microsoft Access will add the required page navigation links for you.

## Try It Out — Creating HTML Files

**1.** In the database window, select tblIceCream.

**2.** From the File menu, select Export.

**3.** From the Export dialog, change the Save as type to HTML Documents (*.html; *.htm).

**4.** Press the Export button to create the HTML file.

**5.** The new HTML file isn't automatically displayed, so switch to Windows Explorer and find the file, then double-click it to launch Internet Explorer.

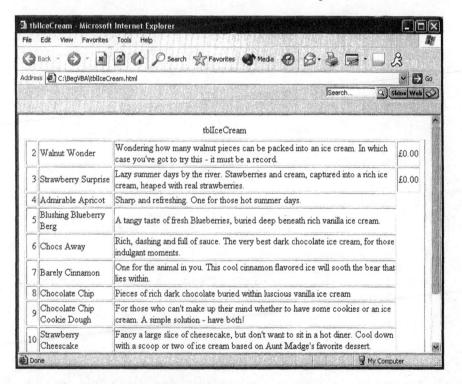

You now have a static HTML file, which will not change if the data changes. In addition the file, unlike a Data Access Page is viewable by any browser. However, once the data changes, you must then republish the HTML page in order to let users see the latest data. However, for data that does not change often, saving as HTML offers you an easy route to the Internet. Unlike ASP, standard HTML requires no execution on the web server as it is simply text and no translation process is required. Another important feature of static HTML is that there are no database connections to maintain. For completeness, we will show a fragment of the HTML produced from the above example.

```
<HTML DIR=LTR>
<HEAD>
<META HTTP-EQUIV="Content-Type" CONTENT="text/html; charset=Windows-1252">
<TITLE>tblIceCream</TITLE>
</HEAD>
<BODY>
<TABLE DIR=LTR BORDER>
<CAPTION>tblIceCream</CAPTION>
<TR>
<TD DIR=LTR ALIGN=RIGHT>2</TD>
<TD DIR=LTR ALIGN=LEFT>Walnut Wonder</TD>
<TD DIR=LTR ALIGN=LEFT>Wondering how many walnut pieces can be packed into an
ice cream.  In which case you've got to try this - it must be a record.</TD>
<TD DIR=LTR ALIGN=RIGHT>£0.00</TD>
<TD></TD>
</TR>
<TR>
<TD DIR=LTR ALIGN=RIGHT>3</TD>
<TD DIR=LTR ALIGN=LEFT>Strawberry Surprise</TD>
<TD DIR=LTR ALIGN=LEFT>Lazy summer days by the river.  Stawberries and cream,
captured into a rich ice cream, heaped with real strawberries.</TD>
<TD DIR=LTR ALIGN=RIGHT>£0.00</TD>
<TD></TD>
</TR>
<TR>
<TD DIR=LTR ALIGN=RIGHT>4</TD>
<TD DIR=LTR ALIGN=LEFT>Admirable Apricot</TD>
<TD DIR=LTR ALIGN=LEFT>Sharp and refreshing.  One for those hot summer
days.</TD>
<TD></TD>
<TD></TD>
</TR>
<TR>
<TD DIR=LTR ALIGN=RIGHT>5</TD>
<TD DIR=LTR ALIGN=LEFT>Blushing Blueberry Berg</TD>
<TD DIR=LTR ALIGN=LEFT>A tangy taste of fresh Blueberries, buried deep
beneath rich vanilla ice cream.</TD>
<TD></TD>
<TD></TD>
</TR>
<TR>
```

The HTML tags used here are standard tags used to create a HTML table. The only additional tag which may appear odd is the DIR=LIT. This tag simply states that the language direction is Left to Right. The following HTML tags are used to create a table:

❑   TABLE – the beginning of a HTML table structure

❑   <TR> – the beginning of a Row

❑   <TD> – the beginning of a HTML table cell

- ❑   `</TR>` – the end of a table row
- ❑   `</TD>` – the end of an individual cell
- ❑   `</TABLE>` – the closing tag ending the table construct

# XML

Everywhere you look now you will find references to XML as the savior of the Internet. In this section, we will look at how we can use Microsoft Access 2002 to both import and export XML files. First we will have a quick overview of what XML is and why it is so useful. For a detailed look at XML, see *Beginning XML 2nd Edition*, from Wrox Press (ISBN 1-861005-59-8).

## *What is Extensible Markup Language (XML)*

XML is a markup language very similar to HTML in that it uses a set of tags that permit you to work with structured data. With HTML you are restricted to using the tags that comprise the language. This restriction does not apply when using XML as you can create any tags you like. First let's take a look at a simple XML file exported from within the Ice Cream database. Note that this file is incomplete:

```
<?xml version="1.0" encoding="UTF-8"?>
<dataroot xmlns:od="urn:schemas-microsoft-com:officedata"
xmlns:xsi="http://www.w3.org/2000/10/XMLSchema-instance"
xsi:noNamespaceSchemaLocation="companyxml.xsd">
<tblCompany>
  <CompanyID>1</CompanyID>
  <CompanyName><![CDATA[Fran and Nick's Fruit and Nuts]]></CompanyName>
  <Address>37 Walnut Grove</Address>
  <City>Nutbush</City>
  <State>Tennessee</State>
  <ZipCode>38053</ZipCode>
  <Country>USA</Country>
  <Phone>(423) 935 9032</Phone>
  <Fax>(423) 935 9001</Fax>
  <Supplier>1</Supplier>
</tblCompany>
<tblCompany>
<CompanyID>2</CompanyID>
...
```

The above XML file is simply a copy of the Customers table. When viewed within Internet Explorer it takes on a different appearance.

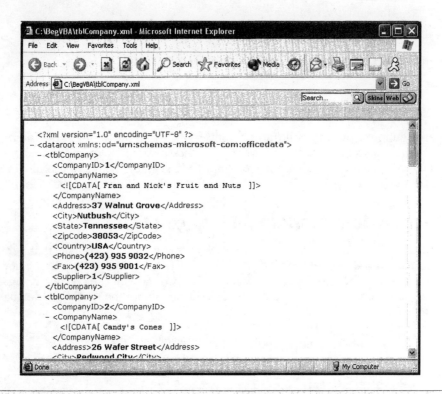

> It is important to note that this is a raw XML file which has not been
> formatted manually. The XML file is using the default format template
> supplied by Internet Explorer which permits you to expand and contract the
> XML element by clicking on a plus or minus sign.

As you can see this is similar to HTML and tags are used to layout the page. Note the minus
signs to the left of the page. Clicking the symbol will contract the tree, changing the symbol to a
plus sign. Clicking the plus sign has the opposite effect and expands the data tree.

Properly formatted XML is said to be well-formed and meets the following requirements:

- ❑ An XML declaration must be the first line in the file.
- ❑ All XML tags must have an opening and a closing tag.
- ❑ Tags cannot contain comments.
- ❑ Tags are case-sensitive.
- ❑ All elements must be properly nested.
- ❑ All documents must have a root tag. This is the first tag in the document.

## *Advantages to XML*

So why bother – what are the advantages to using XML in the first place? Before looking at some XML examples, let's have a quick overview of the advantages of XML.

❑ You can define your own XML tags to suit your purpose. For example, the following is a valid XML fragment :

```
<Person>
  <Type>Male</Type>
  <height>Big</height>
  <Hair>Black</Hair>
  <eyes>blue</eyes>
</Person>
```

❑ Many databases can actually store XML documents (Oracle, DB2, SQL Server).

❑ XML is an Open Standard – http://www.w3c.org/XML/.

❑ It is widely used in business to transfer data. For example, a form of XML has been used by the press industry to exchange news information for many years. Have a look at this page which is used by the British Broadcasting Corporation to deliver news content www.bbc.co.uk/syndication/feeds/news/ukfs_news/technology/rss091.xml.

❑ Permits different systems to interoperate.

❑ Designed for the Internet.

❑ Has a very small footprint in the browser.

❑ Separates content and appearance.

## *How to Export a Table as XML*

Exporting a table to XML is a simple process, and at this level very little about XML needs to be known. Let's see how to export the Customer table as XML. Firstly, in the **Database** window select tblCompany. With the table highlighted:

**1.** Click on File on the main Access menu

**2.** Select File | Export

**3.** In the Export Table dialog use the Save As Type drop-down list and select XML Documents

> Note that Access will add the table name to the dialog as the default file name. You may change this if required.

**4.** Click the Export button

Now this is where things get interesting. We are given a few different ways that we can export the data as XML:

❑ Data (XML)

❑ Schema of the data

❑ Presentation of your data (XSL)

### Data

This option will create a simple XML file containing only the table data, as shown in the screenshot below:

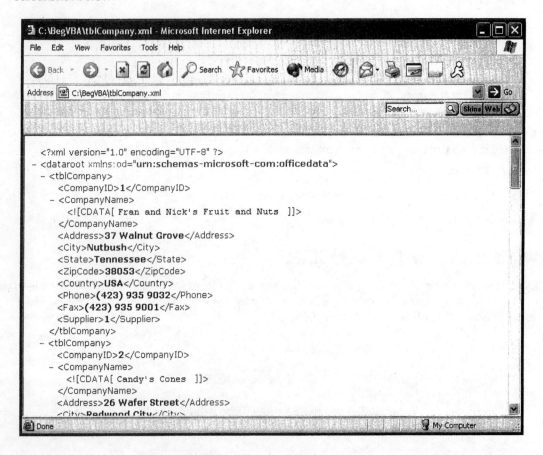

This form of XML export uses the default presentation template in Internet Explorer to display the data in a tree structure. If you also select the **Presentation of your data** checkbox:

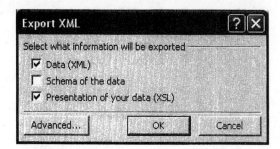

Then you also generate an XSL and HTML file. This option is available only if the **Data** checkbox is selected. The XSL file is much like a HTML template and controls the presentation of your XML data. Rather than use the default template in IE the browser will use the defined XSL file to present your data.

> **XSL can be compared to a Cascading Style Sheet used with HTML and deals only with the layout and presentation of the data contained in your XML file in a process called transformation. Without your own XSL file, the XML file will be displayed using the browser default.**

### Schema of the Data

This option permits you to export the structure or Schema of the table instead of the data. You may export both the schema and the data in a single operation by checking the **Data** and **Schema of the data** boxes in the **Export XML** dialog. If you want to select **Schema of data** only, you can then import the resulting file back to Access or SQL Server 2000 Desktop (which is provided free of charge on the Office XP CD-ROM) and have an unpopulated copy of the company table. The XML schema file contains the structure of your Access table including data types, indexes, field names, and any constraints you may have placed on a field. For example, limiting the number of characters allowed in a text field. We will look at this shortly as it provides you with a very easy technique to move schema between different and at times diverse databases.

Clicking on the **Advanced** button will close the initial XML dialog and open a new dialog. This gives you several additional options when exporting. For example, when exporting a schema you can choose to **Include primary key and index information** from the file. Note that once you open the advanced dialog you will be unable to return to the initial export screen. The advanced dialog also permits you to include the schema information within the XML file rather than as a distinct document.

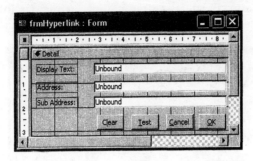

It is also possible to use VBA to import and export data as XML. There are two new methods available, `ExportXML` and `ImportXML`. For these examples we have set a reference to Microsoft ADO 2.7.

## Try It Out — Exporting the Company Table to XML

**1.** Open a new module and enter the following code into the module window:

```
Sub ExportcustXML()

    Application.ExportXML ObjectType:=acExportTable, _
    DataSource:="tblCompany", _
    DataTarget:="c:\Companyxml.xml", _
    SchemaTarget:="CompanySchema.xml", _
    OtherFlags:=1

End Sub
```

This procedure will export the Customers table as XML. The resulting file `CompanyXML.xml` will be saved to C:\ or any folder specified within the argument. In addition, we are also creating a schema file, `CompanySchema.xsl`. The `OtherFlags` option, currently set to one offers you additional control over the way the file is exported.

### Other Flags

| Option | Comment |
|--------|---------|
| 1 | Will include any related tables on the many side of a relationship with the named table |
| 2 | Creates relational properties |
| 3 | Creates an ASP wrapper as opposed to a HTML wrapper |
| 4 | Creates extended schema properties |

**2.** Creating a generic procedure:

We can also create a nice simple generic procedure for exporting objects as follows. In this case, all that is required is that you pass the table name and the save path to the procedure, and off you go. Enter the following procedure into the module window:

```
Sub ExportXML (tabl As String, path As String)
   Application.ExportXML ObjectType:=acExportTable, _
   DataSource:=tabl, DataTarget:=path
End Sub
```

This procedure automates the manual example just seen, and provides you with more flexibility when it is called. The resulting file will look no different to that produced manually. Importing an XML file is just as easy.

**Try It Out**      **Importing an XML File**

Before we import an XML file using ADO, we need to export a new copy. We will discuss the reasons for this shortly.

**1.** In the Database Window, select tblCompany

**2.** From the main menu select File | Export

**3.** Select XML Documents from the Save As Type dialog, accepting the default name for the file

**4.** Save the file to C:\

**5.** In the dialog, accept the default option of Data and Schema of the data, and click OK to finish the export

**6.** Open a new module and enter the procedure shown below:

```
Sub ImportXML()
   Application.ImportXML "C:\tblCompany.xml"
End Sub
```

This procedure will create a perfect copy of the customer table which already exists within the database. In this case, the table name will be suffixed with the number 1. Each time you run the procedure the table will be recreated as tblcustomer2, tblcustomers3, and so on. In addition, there are three arguments available when using ImportXML:

- ❏ `acStructureAndData`, which creates the table and populates it with data

- ❏ `acStructureOnly`, creates the table structure only

- ❏ `acAppendData`, will simply append the XML data to an existing table

OK, so why did we not use the XML file we created earlier via ADO? Well try it and see what happens, you can't import it. ADO creates a type of XML file that is not recognized by Microsoft Access. Access 2002 uses a specific type of XML called element-centric XML, as opposed to the attribute-centric XML used by ADO. Therefore it is not possible to import ADO produced XML without first transforming it using XSLT. XSLT is discussed in *Beginning XSLT* by Wrox Press (ISBN: 1-861005-94-6).

### Creating a Generic Import XML Routine

As with `ExportXML` we can also create a simple generic procedure which can be used to import XML files.

```
Sub ImportXML(path As String)
   Application.ImportXML DataSource:=path, _
   ImportOptions:=acStructureAndData
End Sub
```

In this case all that is required is the full path to the XML file being imported.

In order to execute the above procedure, open the **Immediate** window while in the VBE. Press *Ctrl+G* or select **View | Intermediate Window** using the main menu option. We will import the XML file created in the example above. Simply enter the following into the **Immediate** window:

ImportXML("C:\ tblCompany.xml")

Return to the database window and notice that a new `tblCompany` has been created based on the XML file. If you have been testing, you should notice that the table name is followed by a number.

As you can see Access 2002 offers several ways to use XML within a database. In these brief examples we have exported data to XML and then imported an XML file back into Microsoft Access. But what's the point in it all? Well as we seen above, when we looked at the advantages of XML, you are not restricted to exporting and importing to simply Microsoft Access. Suppose a client is using IBM DB2, Oracle, or even SQL Server. XML provides you with a way to export data and table structures in a way that is now universally understood by most major database systems in use with business. You can be almost certain that your client can then read into their system your Access data, or even recreate the table structures in their systems. The use of XML files both to view and share data via the browser is expected to increase, and we can expect to see the XML features of Access improve with the next version.

## *Reports and XML*

When you need to have reports available via the Internet, XML offers you another tool in the arsenal. Similar to how we can save reports as DAPs, it is also possible to save reports as XML files via the Access interface. In this way we can, again, make data available via the Internet. For static data, we provide a link to the XML file as opposed to a connection to the database. However, remember that the data is static and the user will be viewing information at a specific point in time, but then again, that's generally the purpose of a report anyway.

The process used to export a report to XML is identical to that used with a table: select the report, right-click, and choose Export. However, in this case, you will return a variety of documents including a HTML file, the XML File and an XSL stylesheet. Generally to view the data you select the HTML file which acts as the template for the other file groups.

### Try It Out    Exporting a Report as XML

1.  Select the Ingredients report from the Database window

2.  Select File | Export from the main menu

3.  Select XML Documents from the Save as type list

4.  Click the Export button

5.  Accept the default Data in the Export XML dialog

6.  Click OK

7.  Navigate to the folder you saved the files to, and open Ingredients.html using a web browser

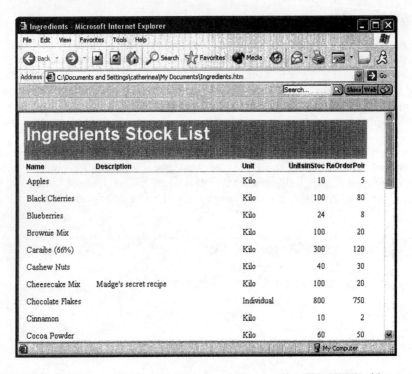

Notice that we are opening a HTML file, not the XML directly. The HTML file contains a script which calls the required XML and XSL files for viewing. The relevant lines are show as bold in the script below.

```
SCRIPT event=onload for=window>
    objData = new ActiveXObject("MSXML.DOMDocument");
    objData.async = false;
    objData.load("Ingredients.xml");
    if (objData.parseError.errorCode != 0)
    alert(objData.parseError.reason);
    objStyle = new ActiveXObject("MSXML.DOMDocument");
    objStyle.async = false;
    objStyle.load("Ingredients.xsl");
    if (objStyle.parseError.errorCode != 0)
    alert(objStyle.parseError.reason);
    document.open("text/html","replace");
    document.write(objData.transformNode(objStyle));
```

## *Active Server Pages*

Publishing live data to the Internet means that every time the web page is viewed, the data is fetched from the database. This has the advantage of the data always being up-to-date, but the downside is that it takes longer to set up and has a slightly longer loading time. We should also say that we are just touching the surface of ASP in this section. This is a massive subject, which is mostly outside the scope of this book. For an excellent study of Microsoft Access and ASP try *Beginning ASP Databases* from Wrox Press (ISBN 1-861002-72-6).

To use Active Server Pages (ASP) you will need either Microsoft Internet Information Server (IIS) or Microsoft Personal Web Server. IIS5 is available with Windows 2000 Server and Windows XP Professional. Microsoft Personal Web Server may be used for testing and development purposes only, if required. Many developers who have moved onto Windows 2000 and XP Professional operating systems have the advantage in that a full version of IIS is available for use when working with the web. That being the case, Personal Web Server may not be available on your machine and you will use IIS.

Just for information ASP is also available for Unix using a third party product. Details are available at http://www.sun.com/software/chilisoft/. It has also been reported that Microsoft ASP.NET is being developed to also run on Unix-based web servers.

> **The following example requires the use of an *ODBC System DSN* and an *IIS Virtual Directory*. To keep this chapter focused, we've included this information as an Appendix on the CD, for those of you that are not familiar with this.**
>
> **Please also ensure that you have both IIS and MDAC 2.7 installed on your machine before you attempt this example.**

### Try It Out — Creating ASP Files

1. In the Tables window of the example database, select tblIceCream

2. Select File | Export from the main menu

3. From the Export dialog change the Save as type to Microsoft Active Server Pages

4. Save the file in a folder below your C:\Inetpub\wwwRoot directory (if this directory doesn't appear, you probably don't have IIS installed correctly – see the appendices)

5. Press the Export button to open the ASP Options dialog:

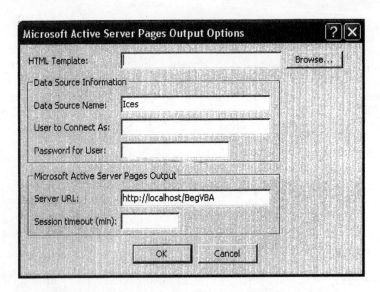

Since the data is updated every time the ASP page is loaded, you need to fill in some details:

| Field | Description |
|---|---|
| HTML Template | If you've got an HTML template you can enter its name here. This can help give your ASP pages a consistent look. |
| Data Source Name | This can be an ODBC DSN (as shown) or ADO connection string. ADO is discussed in Chapter 21. This is how the ASP page connects to the Access database to get the data. |
| User and Password | If you have security set on your Access database you should enter a user name and password here, otherwise you can leave them blank. |
| Server URL | This allows you to enter the default URL of the web server that will host this page. Unlike HTML pages, which can be viewed directly by a browser, an ASP file must be processed by the web server before the browser can use it. |

After entering a DSN and the server URL shown in the above figure, you can view the web page by opening it in a web browser. In the case of this example, we have created a folder on the web server called BegVBA. The example file is placed in there. The URL localhost is the common URL used to specify the server running on the development machine. If you save the file in a folder other than BegVBA remember to use that folder name.

**6.** Enter the URL: http://localhost/BegVBA/tblIceCream.asp

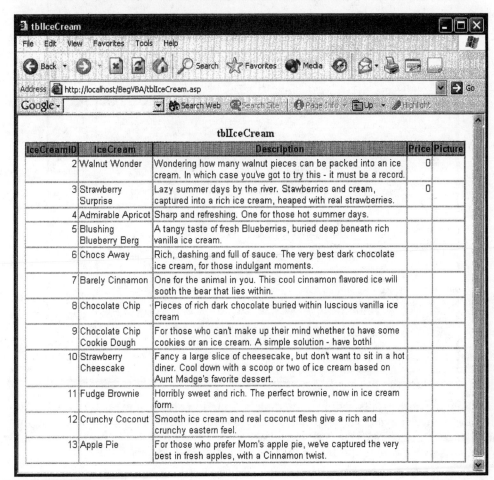

This looks pretty similar to the previous static example, but this time the data will be fetched from the database every time the web page is viewed. In order to actually see the changes you will need to amend one of the records in the table. In this case, we have added some text to the Walnut Wonder record, but you can alter any record that you choose.

**7.** When you're done, hit the Refresh button in your browser. See how the changes you've just made are carried across.

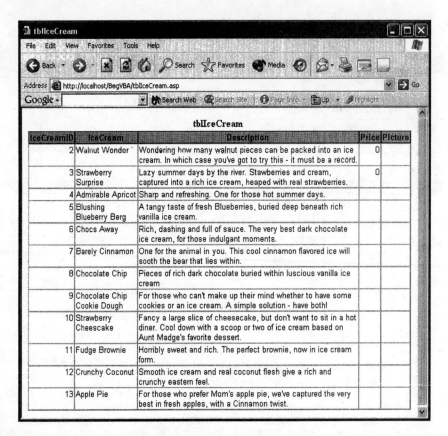

Notice how the new data is visible immediately. You don't have to export this again, because each time this web page is viewed, the data is fetched directly from the database. Again for completeness a fragment of the ASP script taken from the above file is shown below. Note the use of the <% to indicate to the server that what follows is executable ASP code:

```
<%
If IsObject(Session("ice_conn")) Then
    Set conn = Session("ice_conn")
Else
    Set conn = Server.CreateObject("ADODB.Connection")
    conn.open "ice","",""
    Set Session("??ice_conn") = conn
End If
%>
<%
If IsObject(Session("tblCompany_rs")) Then
    Set rs = Session("tblCompany_rs")
Else
    sql = "SELECT * FROM [tblCompany]"
```

```
        Set rs = Server.CreateObject("ADODB.Recordset")
        rs.Open sql, conn, 3, 3
        If rs.eof Then
            rs.AddNew
        End If
        Set Session("tblCompany_rs") = rs
    End If
    %>
```

# Uploading Data

Being able to create HTML and ASP files is only the first step; step two involves getting your files onto a web server. Many people use third-party FTP clients to upload the files to the server. In addition to the third-party software it is also possible to actually FTP files from within Microsoft Access. There are several ways to do this.

> *Those of you with the Office 2002 Developers edition can use an ActiveX Control called the Internet Transfer Control. This control allows you to perform simple file transfer using FTP or HTTP protocols.*

However, a pure Microsoft Access approach is also available. Dev Anish and Terry Craft have made a free addin available which will permit you to transfer files to the Internet without the use of ActiveX controls. This feature has the advantage that, when distributing your database, you do not need to worry about ActiveX controls on the user PC. You simply include the FTP library with your database and set a reference to it. This is discussed in Chapter 13. We have included both the database and the library files on the book CD (FTP2002 is the MDB file, and InetTransferLib the library file containing the required modules. Further information is available from *The Access Web* site at http://www.mvps.org/access/. A ReadMe file has also been included which provides some examples of usage. The library exposes two objects: HTTP which is used to download from the server, and FTP which is used to both upload and download files. Note that some default FTP and HTTP clients have been added to the code in the example database. You will need to change these in order to get the tool to function.

Using the library is a straightforward process, but make sure you view the ReadMe file for more information and instructions on providing this functionality in your own database. Make sure you set a reference to the MDA library file before actually trying it out.

Before anything else let's install the files.

**1.** Create a new folder on your PC.

**2.** Copy the files FTP2002 and InetTransferLib.mda from the chapter section of the CD-ROM to the new folder.

**3.** Open the FTP2002 database file.

**4.** Within the FTP2002.mdb file, open a new module.

**5.** Click Tools | References.

**6.** Click the Browse button and navigate to InetTransferLib.mda.

**7.** Select InetTransferLib.mda and click OK.

That's the first few steps done. We have now installed the database and library files and set a reference to the library. The next step is to actually move some files.

**8.** Open frmTestCases

This form offers you three choices:

❑ FTP Upload – calls `TestFTPUpload()`.This opens a file dialog and you can then select a file to transfer to the web server. Note that a dummy ftp location has been entered into the procedure. You will need to replace this with a valid server address. Until you do this the function will return an error.

❑ FTP Download – calls `TestFTP()`. This button will navigate to a specific FTP site and download a named file. For this example, I have set the path and file names within the procedure to ftp://ftp.microsoft.com/softlib/index.txt which is the Index file from the Microsoft FTP service.

❑ HTTP Download – calls `TestHTTP()`.

**9.** Click the FTP Download button to open the standard windows Save dialog.

**10.** Enter a name for the downloaded file.

**11.** Click OK to save the file locally.

## *How to Use Hyperlinks*

If you've looked at the Company table, then you've already seen a hyperlink field:

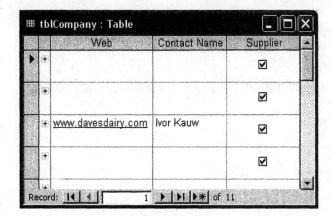

As you can see this field is designed to hold the web address of the companies and, because the field is a hyperlink, clicking on the field will launch your web browser to point at this web site.

**Try It Out**     **Using Hyperlink Fields**

**1.** Open the `tblCompany` table in design mode.

**2.** Change the **Data Type** property for the Email column from **Text** to **Hyperlink**. Make sure the **Allow Zero Length** property is set to **Yes**.

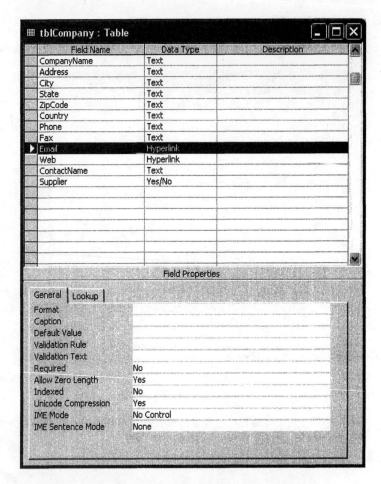

**3.** Save the changes and switch the table into datasheet view.

**4.** Find **Dave's Dairy Produce** and notice the **Email** and **Web** fields.

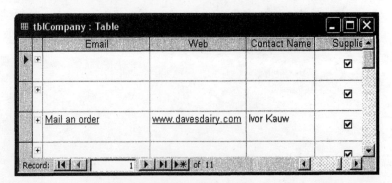

Although they look similar, we want one to behave like an e-mail address, launching our e-mail program when clicked, and one to behave like a web address, launching the web browser when it's clicked. Since there is nothing in the properties of the hyperlink field to identify this, we have to use the hyperlink itself, and that's where the protocols come in. The default protocol is `http`, so at the moment Access thinks the e-mail address is a web address. That means you can't just click in the column to edit the field, as this tries to jump to the hyperlink.

**5.** To get around this, click in the Email column for either of the empty records either side of the Dave's Dairy record, and use the cursor keys to move to the Email column for Dave's Dairy.

**6.** Enter the following into the Email column:

```
mailto:sales@davesdairy.com
```

**7.** Click on the new mail hyperlink, and you'll see your mail program load with the e-mail address already in the To: field.

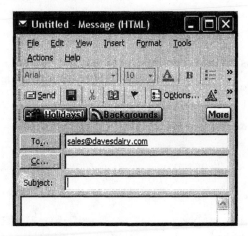

You can see that the Hyperlink column type is extremely useful, as it gives you, and your users, quick access to web pages and mail addresses. If you want to hide even more complexity from your users you can use the display part of the hyperlink to show different text. Rather than delete and retype the hyperlink, let's edit it in a different way.

With your mouse over the e-mail address column, click the right mouse button and select Hyperlink, and then Edit Hyperlink from the next menu. This brings up the Edit Hyperlink window:

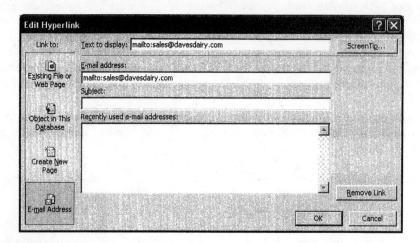

If you now change the Text to display field and press the OK button, you'll see that what's displayed in the column is now the text you typed in, rather than the e-mail address.

## Hyperlinks in VBA

You've seen how easy it is to use hyperlinks in tables, but you might be wondering how you can use them in your code. The Hyperlink data type is more like an object, with several properties and methods:

| Item | Type | Description |
|------|------|-------------|
| Address | Property | The main hyperlink address. |
| EmailSubject | Property | The Subject line if the hyperlink is an e-mail. |
| ScreenTip | Property | The Screen Tip or Tool Tip text to display for the hyperlink. This requires IE4 or later to work. |
| SubAddress | Property | The sub-address of the hyperlink. |
| TextToDisplay | Property | The visible text to show on the screen. |
| AddToFavorites | Method | Add the hyperlink to the favorites folder. |
| CreateNewDocument | Method | Creates a new document associated with the hyperlink. |
| Follow | Method | Follows the hyperlink, opening the program (browser, mail, and so on) associated with the hyperlink. |

## Custom Hyperlink Form

You've seen the Edit Hyperlink dialog, which allows all of the values for a hyperlink to be edited, but you may not want your users using this form. After all, it looks fairly confusing and has more information than the user will require. This process, creating a new form, simplifies the process for the end user. Let's make a more user-friendly form for editing hyperlinks.

**Try It Out** — **Editing Hyperlinks**

1.  Open frmCompany in design view, and add two small buttons to the right of the Email and Web fields. You might need to widen the form a bit to get the buttons on:

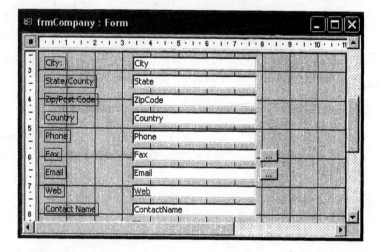

2.  Name these buttons cmdEmail and cmdWeb. If you make these as small as the diagram, then you might need to reduce the font size to make the dots show up – 7-point seems to work well.

3.  In the Click event for cmdEmail add the following code (make sure you get the number of commas correct – there are five of them).

```
Private Sub cmdEmail_Click()
  DoCmd.OpenForm "frmHyperlink", , , , , acDialog, "Email"
End Sub
```

4.  In the Click event for cmdWeb, add the following code:

```
Private Sub cmdWeb_Click()
  DoCmd.OpenForm "frmHyperlink", , , , , acDialog, "Web"
End Sub
```

**5.** Save and close this form. Now create a new form and add three textboxes and four text buttons:

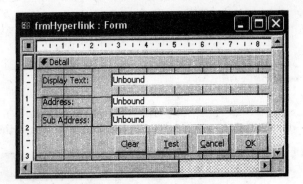

**6.** The textboxes should be named `txtDisplay`, `txtAddress`, and `txtSubAddress`, and the command buttons `cmdClear`, `cmdTest`, `cmdCancel`, and `cmdOK`.

**7.** Set the **Record Selectors** and **Navigation Buttons** properties for the form to `No`. Now save the form as `frmHyperlink`.

**8.** Create a code module for the form by pressing the code button, and add the following global variable:

```
Option Compare Database
Option Explicit

Dim m_ctlHyperlink As Control
```

**9.** Now we'll place code for each of our command buttons in their respective event procedures. First, in the `Click` event for `cmdCancel`, add the following:

```
Private Sub cmdCancel_Click()
    DoCmd.Close
End Sub
```

**10.** Next, in the `Click` event for `cmdOK`, add the following:

```
Private Sub cmdOK_Click()
    m_ctlHyperlink = txtDisplay & "#" & txtAddress & "#" & txtSubAddress
    DoCmd.Close
End Sub
```

**11.** Now add the following line to the `Click` event of the `cmdTest` button:

```
Private Sub cmdTest_Click()
  m_ctlHyperlink.Hyperlink.Follow
End Sub
```

**12.** Next, add this code to the `Click` event of the `cmdClear` button:

```
Private Sub cmdClear_Click()
  txtDisplay = ""
  txtAddress = ""
  txtSubAddress = ""
End Sub
```

**13.** To wrap up the procedure, add this code to the `Load` event for the `Form`:

```
Private Sub Form_Load()
  Set m_ctlHyperlink = Forms!frmCompany.Controls(OpenArgs)
  With m_ctlHyperlink.Hyperlink
    txtDisplay = .TextToDisplay
    txtAddress = .Address
    txtSubAddress = .SubAddress
  End With
End Sub
```

**14.** Save the module, switch back to Access, and save and close the form.

**15.** Now open `frmCompany` in form view, and view the record for **Dave's Dairy**.

**16.** Press the button alongside the **Mail** field, which will bring up the **Edit Hyperlink** form below

**17.** Enter the information into the textboxes as shown below:

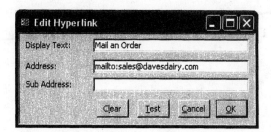

**18.** Just press the **Test** button to launch the mail program.

So with just a few lines of code, you've made a simpler form for editing hyperlinks and made the link a lot more readable.

**How It Works**

We've done two things here. The first has been to modify the company form, because that's where the hyperlinks are shown. The second has been to create a new form to allow editing of those hyperlinks. Let's first look at the new code in the company form, behind the two buttons that open the hyperlink form:

```
DoCmd.OpenForm "frmHyperlink", , , , , acDialog, "Email"

DoCmd.OpenForm "frmHyperlink", , , , , acDialog, "Web"
```

You've seen forms being opened before, but this format does require a little explanation. The last two arguments are the ones we're interested in. The arguments specified by the commas tell Access to simply use the default argument. DoCmd.OpenForm takes the following arguments: FormName, View, FilterName, WhereCondition, DataMode, WindowMode, OpenArgs. acDialog tells Access that the form is to be opened modally, as though it were a dialog form – that means that you have to close the form before you can continue. The last argument is a string that gets passed into the hyperlink form, and is used to identify which control we are editing the hyperlink for.

Let's now look at the code for the hyperlink form. Firstly there's a global variable, m_ctlHyperlink, which is a Control. This will point to the actual control on the calling form – this will be either the Email or Web address control.

Now for the Form_Load procedure. Firstly we set this global variable to point to the control on the previous form. We're using a special variable called OpenArgs here – this contains the value that was passed in as the last argument of the OpenForm command shown earlier. In this case it's the name of a control, so we can use this to index into the forms Controls collection:

```
Set m_ctlHyperlink = Forms!frmCompany.Controls(OpenArgs)
```

Now we want to display the various parts of the hyperlink on our form. For this we refer to the Hyperlink property of the control, which allows us to access the various hyperlink elements.

```
With m_ctlHyperlink.Hyperlink
  txtDisplay = .TextToDisplay
  txtAddress = .Address
  txtSubAddress = .SubAddress
End With
```

When the user presses the OK button we want to be able to update the hyperlink control. We can't use the Hyperlink property and its elements as we did when the form was opened because the individual elements are read-only, but we can combine the elements together, using the hash symbol to separate them.

```
m_ctlHyperlink = txtDisplay & "#" & txtAddress & "#" & txtSubAddress
DoCmd.Close
```

The **Clear** button simply clears the values from the form fields. This saves the user having to clear them individually.

The last piece of code is for the **Test** button, when we want to launch the application associated with the hyperlink. For this we use the `Follow` method of the `Hyperlink` property.

```
m_ctlHyperlink.Hyperlink.Follow
```

That's all there is to it! An easier form, with only a few lines of code. Although we've only shown this code working for the e-mail address, it works the same way for Web addresses. Why not try adding some real Web URLs to see it in action?

# Summary

In this chapter we've looked at how Access can be used to interface to the Internet. The rise of the Internet has meant that more and more people are creating web sites and learning new technologies, such as HTML, ASP, and so on. To make a web site dynamic it must be driven by data, and the ease of using Access has fueled the desire for people to know Access.

What we've covered are the major areas where Access can be used in this respect, notably:

- ❑ The use of XML to both import and export data and schema

- ❑ The various types of Internet document that you can create when exporting data from Access

- ❑ The use of Data Access Pages primarily for Intranet as opposed to Internet use

This really is only the tip of the iceberg as far as Internet and data go, but to delve further you'll need to study an Internet book. The next topic we're going to look at is how to optimize your code, and put those finishing touches to your database to make sure everything is as polished as possible.

# Exercises

**1.** We want to publish a list of our ice creams to our internet site, and we want to use plain HTML files. Add some code to the ice creams form, so that any time an ice cream entry is changed, a new HTML file is generated.

**2.** Export the customer table as HTML and, using the FTP database, move the resulting HTML files to your web sever.

# CHAPTER 19

# Optimizing Your Application

*Chambers 20th Century English Dictionary* defines optimization as:

*"Preparing or revising a computer system or program so as to achieve the greatest possible efficiency."*

That is the focus of this chapter. We shall be looking at the different methods available to you as a developer to ensure that your database application operates as efficiently as possible.

In particular, we will cover:

- ❑  What makes a piece of code efficient
- ❑  How to measure the speed of a program
- ❑  Some coding tips for creating faster programs
- ❑  What to bear in mind when writing networked applications

## Efficiency

The Performance Analyzer (which you can access from the menu bar by clicking **Tools | Analyze** and then selecting **Performance**) is a useful enough tool. It can help you to a large degree in identifying potential problems with database performance, and it is always useful to run it against a poorly performing database application. However, the Performance Analyzer doesn't help you with several other factors that you should consider, one of these being optimization of your VBA code.

If our aim is to achieve maximum efficiency, the key question is, of course, "What constitutes efficiency?" This is a more complex question than it may at first appear. Listed below are four of the most frequently cited benchmarks for evaluating the efficiency of a database application:

❑   Memory footprint (that is, size)

❑   Real execution speed

❑   Apparent speed

❑   Network traffic

It is nearly always possible to optimize your application with respect to one of these benchmarks, but how do you optimize with respect to them all? The simple answer is that you can't – and you shouldn't try to, because it is not achievable.

One of the key tasks at the start of a development project is to devise a list of coding priorities. Which of the factors listed above are most important for the successful implementation of the application? Which would it be nice to have? And which are irrelevant?

To the four factors listed above, you can add another five:

❑   Portability

❑   Robustness

❑   Scaleability

❑   Maintainability

❑   Reusability

And perhaps most important are scheduling factors. Although not optimal, poor performance might be an acceptable price to pay if only the application can be delivered within schedule.

Of course, none of these factors will necessarily help to increase the efficiency of the application – optimizing a piece of code for portability or robustness may well cause the code to run slower or consume more memory than before.

In fact, these various factors can all pull in separate directions. Consider these two bits of code:

```
If (bln1 = True And bln2 = True) Or (bln1 = False And bln2 = False) Then
    blnResult = False
Else
    blnResult = True
End If
```

And:

```
blnResult = (bln1 Xor bln2)
```

Both of these examples produce the same result. However, the first can take approximately four times as long to execute as the second. If you were optimizing for speed, you would go for the latter. This example shows a clear-cut difference in performance, many others will not be so obvious, but it serves as a good illustration of what can be achieved.

On the other hand, many developers, especially inexperienced ones with no knowledge of bitwise comparisons, would find the first example easier to follow. If you were optimizing for maintainability (and thus easier to read code), you would probably choose the first one (especially given that, on a typical machine, both examples execute in little more than a thousandth of a second). If you chose the second one, you would almost certainly want to add a comment to explain the code.

This chapter, then, is not going to tell you the optimal way to write your code. That will depend on the coding priorities that you determine for your application. What this chapter will do is to highlight the impact, in terms of the four most frequently cited coding priorities, of various coding practices.

> All of the code that is used in this chapter can be found in the `Performance.mdb` database that accompanies this book.

# Reducing Memory Overhead

A modern desktop computer running Access will typically have anywhere between 32 and 512 MB of memory (RAM). This is where all of your application's code is executed. The more memory your computer has, the more likely it will be that the data needed by an application will be available in memory, and therefore the less frequently the application will need to read from and write to the disk. Reading and writing to disk is a relatively slow process and the less disk access is required, the faster the program will typically run.

As a general rule, more memory equals better performance. In the dim and distant past, computers were limited to around 32 or 64 kilobytes of memory. To put this in perspective, that is about 2000 times less than the amount in the machine that I am using to produce this chapter. Even if you had an operating system or program able to use 96 MB of RAM in those days – and that is much more than was utilized in many mainframes – the sheer cost of the memory would have torn your scheme to shreds.

It's not surprising, therefore, that with such limited memory available, programmers spent a great deal of time shoe-horning their quart of code into the pint pot that was their computer. The key phrase was 'disciplined programming'; the language was typically assembler or machine code (almost impenetrable to the layman) and the results produced were a testimony to the ingenuity and patience of the programmers involved.

But these days we live on easy street... if a program is running slowly, just spend $20 on another 64 MB of RAM for your machine! This isn't a completely heinous attitude – after all, it might cost $40,000 in man-days to recode the program so that it runs as quickly on the old machine as if you just bought the memory.

However, that is not to say that we should let this newfound freedom allow us to churn out sloppy code. Memory, although relatively cheap, is still precious. The less memory your program takes up, the faster it, and all the other programs running simultaneously, should perform.

Additionally, if you are writing an application that will be used by a thousand users, then every extra megabyte of memory required by your application equates to 1000 MB of memory across all those machines.

In other words, for most projects, producing an application with a small memory footprint is still a very real coding priority.

You should, therefore, bear the following guidelines in mind when developing any application:

- ❑ Use the right data type
- ❑ Group procedures into modules
- ❑ Reclaim memory where possible
- ❑ Don't load unnecessary modules/libraries
- ❑ Save the database as an MDE file

## Use the Right Data Type

Different types of variable take up different amounts of memory. The size of the memory taken up by each of the data types is shown in the table below:

| Data type | Storage size | Range |
| --- | --- | --- |
| Byte | 1 byte | 0 to 255 |
| Boolean | 2 bytes | True or False |
| Integer | 2 bytes | -32,768 to 32,767 |
| Long | 4 bytes | -2,147,483,648 to 2,147,483,647 |
| Single | 4 bytes | -3.403E38 to -1.401E-45; 0; 1.401E-45 to 3.403E38 |
| Double | 8 bytes | -1.798E308 to -4.941E-324; 0; 4.941E-324 to 1.798E308 |
| Currency | 8 bytes | -922,337,203,685,477.5808 to 922,337,203,685,477.5807 |
| Decimal | 12 bytes | -7.923E28 to 7.923E28 (varies with number of decimal places in number stored) |
| Date | 8 bytes | January 1, 100 to December 31, 9999 |

| Data type | Storage size | Range |
|-----------|--------------|-------|
| Object | 4 bytes + the size of the object | A reference to any object |
| Fixed String | 1 byte per character | Up to approx. 65,400 characters |
| Variable Length String | 10 bytes + 1 byte per character | Up to approx. 2 billion characters |
| Variant (numeric) | 16 bytes | As double |
| Variant (string) | 22 bytes + 1 byte per character | As variable length string |

As you can see, variables of type Long take up twice as much memory as variables of type Integer. But then again, optimization is a question of compromise – Long variables can hold a much wider range of values than Integer variables can.

The problem of memory usage becomes even more marked when dealing with arrays. This line:

```
ReDim adbl(9, 9) As Double
```

declares an array containing 100 elements and takes up around 800 bytes of memory, compared to the 200 or so bytes taken up by this one:

```
ReDim aint(9, 9) As Integer
```

*For more detailed information on calculating the memory requirements of arrays, refer back to the Memory Considerations section in Chapter 11.*

As a rule, if memory footprint size is a coding priority – as it nearly always is – you should choose the smallest variable that can hold the values that you will be dealing with. To remind you to explicitly assign types to variables, you should tick the **Require Variable Declaration** option on the **Editor** tab in the VBA **Tools/Options...** dialog. This is also a good coding practice, because it avoids variable name mismatch, and minimize the bugs caused by this problem.

It has been said before – but I make no apology for saying it again – always, always be wary of the Variant data type. Although there are situations in which it is useful – and sometimes necessary – to use a Variant data type, you should bear in mind that not only does it take up significantly more memory than the other data types, but it can also lead to errors in your code going undetected. For example, I'll wager that no one reading this will be able to accurately predict what 10 values the following procedure will print in the **Immediate** window... Try it out and see how many you guessed correctly!

```
Sub AreYouSure()

Dim v1 As Variant
Dim v2 As Variant
Dim v3 As Variant

v1 = 1
v2 = "1"
v3 = "(1)"

Debug.Print v1 + v2
Debug.Print v1 + v3
Debug.Print v2 + v3
Debug.Print
Debug.Print v1 & v2
Debug.Print v1 & v3
Debug.Print v2 & v3
Debug.Print
Debug.Print v2 + v1 + v3
Debug.Print v2 & v1 + v3
Debug.Print (v1 & v2) + v3
Debug.Print v1 + (v1 & v2) + v3

End Sub
```

The answers are as follows:

| | |
|---|---|
| v1 + v2 | = 2 |
| v1 + v3 | = 0 |
| v2 + v3 | = 1(1) |
| | |
| v1 & v2 | = 11 |
| v1 & v3 | = 1(1) |
| v2 & v3 | = 1(1) |
| | |
| v2 + v1 + v3 | = 1 |
| v2 & v1 + v3 | = 10 |
| (v1 & v2) + v3 | = 11(1) |
| v1 + (v1 & v2) + v3 | = 11 |

# Group Procedures into Modules

VBA only loads modules or classes when a procedure in that module or class is called. This is called loading on demand. Therefore, if you have a routine that calls three procedures and they are all in separate modules, all three modules will be loaded into memory. By judiciously grouping related procedures into the same module, you can minimize the number of modules loaded into memory at any one time.

## Reclaim Memory Where Possible

You can use the Erase statement to reclaim the memory used by a dynamic array. When you have finished with the array, using the Erase statement will discard the data in the array and free up the memory that it had been using.

The Erase statement doesn't reclaim space from static (fixed-size) arrays. However, it does reinitialize them. For more information on reinitializing arrays, refer back to Chapter 11.

You can also reclaim the memory used by object variables when you have finished with them. You do this by setting them to a special value called Nothing.

```
Set objExcel = Nothing
```

*Remember, however, that the memory used by an object cannot be reclaimed if there is another reference to the object elsewhere in code. We used this to our advantage when we examined classes where we prevented an instance of a popup form from being destroyed by placing a reference to it in a collection declared at the module level of another form. This ensured that the popup form was not destroyed until the second form was closed and the collection went out of scope.*

## Don't Load Unnecessary Libraries

We saw earlier how library databases can be a useful way to store and re-use frequently needed procedures. They can also be used to house wizards and add-ins, such as the control and form-design wizards that ship with Access. However, each of these library databases needs to be loaded into memory when used and that can have a significant hit on the amount of memory that is being used. So, to reduce the memory footprint of your installation, you should use the Add-In Manager (available from the **Tools/Add-Ins** menu in Access) to unload any library databases or add-ins that are not essential.

## Save as an MDE

Previously, we looked at the final touches that you should apply to your application before you give it to the end users of the databases. One of those things is converting your database into an MDE file. This conversion compiles any modules within the database and then strips out the original source code. This in turn has the twin advantages of making your database more secure and reducing the memory footprint of your application, because the source is not kept.

*Bear in mind that you cannot modify the design of MDE files and that you should always keep an original source version of your database in MDB format.*

## *A Final Recommendation – Buy More Memory!*

No, it's not cheating! It is recommended that you have 32MB (Win98), 40MB (WinME, NT4 or later), 72MB (Windows 2000), or more of memory if you are running Access

If you are running on a network, or intend to use other Windows applications at the same time, you will find that the extra few dollars it will cost to buy another 32 or 64MB will be well worth it.

# Increasing Execution Speed

Reducing the amount of memory that your Access database and its code occupy may result in both it and other Windows applications running faster. But, if fast execution is a real coding priority, there are other methods you can consider:

- ❑ Use constants
- ❑ Use specific object types (early binding)
- ❑ Use variables, not properties
- ❑ Avoid slow structures
- ❑ Beware of `IIf`
- ❑ Use integer arithmetic where possible
- ❑ Use inline code
- ❑ Use `DoEvents` judiciously
- ❑ Use the `Requery` method, not the `Requery` action
- ❑ Use `Me`
- ❑ Speed up database operations

We'll look at these in more detail and provide some code samples that prove the point. The code samples have been included so that you can gauge the impact of these techniques for yourself. After all, computers differ greatly in terms of the amount of RAM, processor speed, cache size, disk speed, and so on. These differences are reflected in the performance of VBA on those machines. Don't take my word for it; try out these examples for yourself!

Looking at the results below, you might be forgiven for wondering whether it is worth bothering with some of the improvements. After all, if it only takes three milliseconds to perform an operation, why bother going to the effort of optimizing your code so that it only takes one millisecond? After all, who's going to notice? Well, although it's fair to say that the difference may not be noticeable in a single line of code, it might be if that code is executed many times. For example, you may be looping through all the controls on a form to check for a certain condition. Or you might be looping through all the records in a recordset. Get into the habit of coding efficiently all the time – then it won't be a struggle to do it when it really matters.

## *Timing the Code Samples*

The simplest method for timing how long a piece of code takes to execute is to use the `Timer` function. For example, we could use the following sample of code to time how long it takes for a `For...Next` structure to loop through 100,000 values.

```
Sub TimeLoop()

Dim sngStart As Single
Dim sngEnd As Single
Dim lngLoop As Long

sngStart = Timer

For lngLoop = 0 To 100000
Next lngLoop

sngEnd = Timer

Debug.Print "It took " & Format$(sngEnd - sngStart, "0.000") & " secs."

End Sub
```

The `Timer` function returns a `Single` indicating the number of seconds elapsed since midnight. In the example above, we save the value of `Timer` in the variable `sngStart` before the loop commences:

```
sngStart = Timer
```

And then save the value of `Timer` in the variable `sngEnd` when the loop has finished:

```
sngEnd = Timer
```

By subtracting one from the other, we can determine how long it took for the loop to execute:

```
Debug.Print "It took " & Format$(sngEnd - sngStart, "0.000") & " secs."
```

Now you could include this code in all of the procedures that you want to time. However, if you will be doing a lot of code timings, you might want to set up a test harness like this…

## Try It Out — Creating A Test Harness

**1.** Open a standard code module and type in the procedure `TestPerformance` listed below:

```
Sub TestPerformance(lngIterations As Long, intRuns As Integer)

Dim intLoop As Integer
Dim lngLoop As Long
Dim sngStart As Single
Dim sngCorrection As Single
Dim sngTime As Single
Dim sngTimeTotal As Single

sngStart = Timer
For lngLoop = 1 To lngIterations
    EmptyRoutine                 '<--- This is an empty procedure
Next
sngCorrection = Timer - sngStart

For intLoop = 1 To intRuns
    sngStart = Timer
    For lngLoop = 1 To lngIterations
        TestProc                 '<--- This is the procedure we are testing
    Next
    sngTime = Timer - sngStart - sngCorrection
    Debug.Print "Run " & intLoop & ":  " & sngTime & " seconds"
    sngTimeTotal = sngTimeTotal + sngTime
Next

Debug.Print
Debug.Print "Correction : " & Round(sngCorrection, 3) & " seconds"
Debug.Print
Debug.Print "AverageTime: " & Round(sngTimeTotal / intRuns, 3) & " seconds"

End Sub
```

**2.** Also, create two procedures called `EmptyRoutine` and `TestProc`, looking like this:

```
Sub EmptyRoutine()

End Sub


Sub TestProc()

Dim sngTime As Single

sngTime = Timer
```

```
Do While sngTime + 5 > Timer
    DoEvents
Loop

End Sub
```

**3.** Now, open the **Immediate** window, type in the following code to run the `TestPerformance` procedure and hit *Enter*.

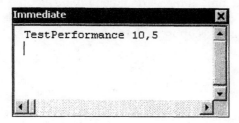

**4.** The results of running the `TestProc` procedure 10 times in 5 different test runs will (eventually) be shown in the **Immediate** window.

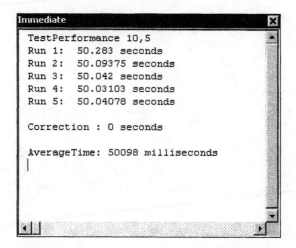

The `TestPerformance` procedure accepts two arguments. The first of these is the number of times that the procedure we want to test (`TestProc`) will be executed in each run; the second argument indicates the number of runs that we want to time.

The important part of this procedure is a loop that runs the code to be tested a certain number of times:

```
For lngLoop = 1 To lngIterations
    TestProc
Next
```

In this case, `TestProc` is the name of the procedure that we wish to test. When you want to time a different procedure, simply substitute its name at this point of the `TestPerformance` procedure.

The difference between the time at the start and end of this loop is then displayed. However, the loop itself has its own overhead. For this reason, we also use another loop to monitor the overhead that is incurred by executing the loop.

```
sngStart = Timer
For lngLoop = 1 To lngIterations
    EmptyRoutine
Next
sngCorrection = Timer - sngStart
```

The `EmptyRoutine` function is simply a procedure that contains no code.

The overhead that is recorded is then stored in a variable called `sngCorrection` and is used to correct the eventual timings that the function displays after each of the test runs:

```
sngTime = Timer - sngStart - sngCorrection
Debug.Print "Run " & intLoop & ":   " & sngTime & " seconds"
```

> *Don't forget, if you do not want to build this `TestProcedure` function, you can find the code for this – and everything else in this chapter – in the `Performance.mdb` database.*

You will notice that the code we test is in a `For...Next` loop which iterates many times. We need to do this because, although the `Timer` function is very accurate, each function executes extremely quickly and so executing many iterations of the function increases the accuracy of our measurement.

The sample timings shown in this chapter were produced on a 2GHz Pentium machine 1 70GB IDE disk (7.2ms access) and 512MB RAM. These timings can also be found in the `Performance.xls` spreadsheet accompanying this book.

> If you want to test these code samples for yourself, just substitute the name of the procedure that you want to time in place of **TestProc** in the **TestPerformance** procedure.

When testing the execution speed of your code, you should make the test conditions as realistic as possible. In other words, test the application on the same specification of computer that will be used in production, load up any other applications which the users will be running, use realistic volumes of data, and (if possible) have realistic numbers of users accessing the shared data in the database. Also, run your tests three or four times to see if performance varies from run to run. You might find that the first run of the following examples will give varying results as the code and any data has to be loaded into memory before it can be run. On subsequent runs, the code and data should already be in memory so the speed will improve and the results will be more consistent. Bear in mind that you are looking for relative improvements in timings when testing a block of code; there is not a single target figure that you are usually aiming for, just an improvement over pervious recordings.

Anyway, that's enough about timing our code. Let's get on with looking at methods for improving our code's performance…

## Use Constants

If you use values in your code that do not change, then you should consider assigning them to constants rather than to variables. As well as the overhead incurred by dimensioning the variable, whenever a variable is encountered in a line of VBA code, Access needs to access the memory location that contains the variable in order to determine the value of the variable. In contrast, the value of a constant is resolved and written into the code at compile time. As a result, reading values from constants generally works out slightly quicker than reading values from variables. The following code illustrates this; the first one uses constants only, and should be quickest, and the second uses string variables.

> *Like variables, constants can be declared at the procedure or at the module level and can have either* Public *or* Private *scope.*

```
Sub ConstantsNotVariables()

Const sDummy = "This is a string which is saved as a constant " & _
               "rather than as a variable. This means that it is " & _
               "resolved and written into the code at compile time."

Const sDummy2 = "This is a string which is saved as a constant " & _
                "rather than as a variable. This means that it is " & _
                "resolved and written into the code at compile time."

If sDummy = sDummy2 Then
End If

End Sub


Sub VariablesNotConstants()

Dim sDummy As String
Dim sDummy2 As String
```

```
    sDummy =  "This is a string which is saved as a variable " & _
              "rather than as a constant. This means that it has to be " & _
              "retrieved every time it needs to be used."

    sDummy2 = "This is a string which is saved as a variable " & _
              "rather than as a constant. This means that it has to be " & _
              "retrieved every time it needs to be used."

    If sDummy = sDummy2 Then
    End If

    End Sub
```

To test this out, add the previous procedures to a module and then modify the
TestPerformance procedure we created earlier to call the VariablesNotConstants
procedure. Execute it from the Immediate window (View | Immediate Window) by typing
TestPerformance 30000,5. Make a note of the timings, and the average. Now modify the
TestPerformance to run the ConstantsNotVariables procedure and run it again.

The results below confirm our beliefs. When run through 30,000 iterations of each procedure,
using constants was 1.6 times faster, than using variables.

| Procedure | Iterations | Elapsed Time | Improvement |
|-----------|-----------|--------------|-------------|
| VariablesNotConstants | 30,000 | 93 ms | |
| ConstantsNotVariables | 30,000 | 58 ms | 1.6 times |

# Don't be Vague!

Although the use of 'loose' data types such as Variant and Object can make it easier to write
generic code, they are usually slower to use than more specific data types.

## Use Specific Object Types (Early Binding)

Previously, we looked at the difference between using early and late binding. The two
procedures that we looked at were GetObjectArea (which used late binding), and
GetShapeArea (which used early binding).

```
Function GetObjectArea(obj As Object, _
                       Side1 As Double, _
                       Side2 As Double, _
                       Side3 As Double) As Double
```

```
        obj.Construct Side1, Side2, Side3
        GetObjectArea = obj.Area

    End Function
```

Although this code will run, it is not very efficient. Because the object variable obj has been declared As Object, Access does not know what type of object it is. This in turn means that whenever we try to inspect or set a property value, or invoke a method against that object at runtime, Access must first check whether or not that property or method is appropriate for the object.

```
Function GetShapeArea(shp As Shape, _
                    Side1 As Double, _
                    Side2 As Double, _
                    Side3 As Double) As Double

    shp.Construct Side1, Side2, Side3
    GetShapeArea = shp.Area

    End Function
```

The second procedure uses what is known as **early binding**. This time around, Access knows what type of object shp is. This means that it can determine at compile time which properties and methods are appropriate to it. Because Access only has to perform this check once, and it does it prior to runtime, the difference in execution speed at run time between code using the two methods can be very significant.

*A secondary advantage of early binding is that because Access can determine which properties and methods are appropriate at compile time, any errors in your code which result from misspelling property or method names are caught at compile time rather than appearing as run-time errors. In addition, without early binding, you won't see the auto-complete features of VBA, such as Auto List Members and Auto Quick Info.*

The procedures we use to test these two techniques are shown below:

```
Sub UseLateBinding()

Dim tri As Triangle
Set tri = New Triangle

GetObjectArea tri, 5, 6, 7

End Sub


Sub UseEarlyBinding()

Dim shp As shpTriangle
Set shp = New shpTriangle
```

```
GetShapeArea shp, 5, 6, 7

End Sub
```

| Procedure | Iterations | Elapsed Time | Improvement |
|-----------|-----------|--------------|-------------|
| UseLateBinding | 30,000 | 2053 ms | |
| UseEarlyBinding | 30,000 | 406 ms | 5.1 times |

## Use Variables, Not Properties

You can realize similar performance benefits if you use variables to refer to forms, controls, and properties. If you are going to refer to a form, report, or control more than once in a procedure, you should create an object variable for the object and then refer to that instead of the object itself.

The following procedure opens the Switchboard form and determines whether the name of various command buttons on that form is `"Blobby"`. If any of the buttons does have that name, then code execution will stop on the line that performs the comparison for that button.

> The `Assert` method of the `Debug` object is useful for debugging and causes code execution to stop when a given expression (like `frm.cmdExit.Name <> "Blobby"`) evaluates to False.

```
Sub UseFormVariables()

Dim frm As Form_frmSwitchboard
Set frm = Forms("frmSwitchboard")

Debug.Assert frm.cmdExit.Name <> "Blobby"
Debug.Assert frm.cmdIceCreams.Name <> "Blobby"
Debug.Assert frm.cmdIngredients.Name <> "Blobby"
Debug.Assert frm.cmdMaintenance.Name <> "Blobby"
Debug.Assert frm.cmdReports.Name <> "Blobby"
Debug.Assert frm.cmdSuppliers.Name <> "Blobby"

Set frm = Nothing

End Sub
```

Alternatively, we could have rewritten this code to take advantage of the With structure.

```
Sub UseFormVariablesAndWith()

Dim frm As Form_frmSwitchboard
Set frm = Forms("frmSwitchboard")

With frm
    Debug.Assert .cmdExit.Name <> "Blobby"
    Debug.Assert .cmdIceCreams.Name <> "Blobby"
    Debug.Assert .cmdIngredients.Name <> "Blobby"
    Debug.Assert .cmdMaintenance.Name <> "Blobby"
    Debug.Assert .cmdReports.Name <> "Blobby"
    Debug.Assert .cmdSuppliers.Name <> "Blobby"
End With

Set frm = Nothing

End Sub
```

Code written using either of these two syntaxes will execute considerably faster than code that uses the long-hand syntax.

```
Sub UseLongHandSyntax()

Debug.Assert Forms!frmSwitchboard!cmdExit.Name <> "Blobby"
Debug.Assert Forms!frmSwitchboard!cmdIceCreams.Name <> "Blobby"
Debug.Assert Forms!frmSwitchboard!cmdIngredients.Name <> "Blobby"
Debug.Assert Forms!frmSwitchboard!cmdMaintenance.Name <> "Blobby"
Debug.Assert Forms!frmSwitchboard!cmdReports.Name <> "Blobby"
Debug.Assert Forms!frmSwitchboard!cmdSuppliers.Name <> "Blobby"

End Sub
```

In this situation the With...End With syntax is only fractionally faster than the first method which simply uses object variables. This is because of the overhead involved in setting up the With structure. However, you would find that if you were to add more and more references to the specified object between the With and End With statements, then this structure would become even more efficient.

| Procedure | Iterations | Elapsed Time | Improvement |
|---|---|---|---|
| UseLongHandSyntax | 30,000 | 5582 ms | |
| UseFormVariables | 30,000 | 3687 ms | 1.5 times |
| UseFormVariablesAndWith | 30,000 | 3634 ms | 1.015 times |

# Avoid Slow Structures

Another way to make your VBA code run faster is to avoid using slow structures. What does this mean? Well, most languages offer the programmer several different methods of performing a single task. If real execution speed is a coding priority, you should test each of these different methods for speed and decide which to use accordingly. For example, in Chapter 13, we discovered that there are two methods of determining the area of a triangle, given the lengths of all three sides.

## Method A: (Trigonometrical Method)

```
Function Area1(dblSide1 As Double, _
               dblSide2 As Double, _
               dblSide3 As Double) As Double

Dim dblAngle1 As Double

dblAngle1 = ((dblSide2 ^ 2) + (dblSide3 ^ 2) - (dblSide1 ^ 2)) _
            / (2 * dblSide2 * dblSide3)
dblAngle1 = Atn(-dblAngle1 / Sqr(-dblAngle1 * dblAngle1 + 1)) + 2 * Atn(1)

Area1 = dblSide2 * dblSide3 * Sin(dblAngle1) * 0.5

End Function
```

## Method B: (Heron's Formula)

```
Function Area2(dblSide1 As Double, _
               dblSide2 As Double, _
               dblSide3 As Double) As Double

Dim dblSemiPerim As Double

dblSemiPerim = (dblSide1 + dblSide2 + dblSide3) / 2

Area2 = Sqr((dblSemiPerim) * _
        (dblSemiPerim - dblSide1) * _
        (dblSemiPerim - dblSide2) * _
        (dblSemiPerim - dblSide3))

End Function
```

Both functions return identical results, but the first of these executes noticeably faster. In this situation, there would seem to be little reason not to choose the first method. However, in other situations you might find that the faster method conflicts with another of the project's coding priorities, so you may have to compromise. Even if this is the case, though, the time spent timing the code will not have been wasted, as you will be able to use this knowledge in future projects.

| Procedure | Iterations | Elapsed Time | Improvement |
|---|---|---|---|
| Area2 (Heron's Formula): | 30,000 | 61 ms | |
| Area1 (Trigonometrical Method): | 30,000 | 7 ms | 8.7 times |

Other examples of potentially slow structures are now described.

## Immediate If (IIf)

The Immediate If (IIf) function is often viewed as a quick and easy way to return one of two values depending on whether an expression evaluates to True. We looked at this function in Chapter 4. Its syntax is:

```
value = IIf(Expression, TruePart, FalsePart)
```

TruePart is returned if Expression is True, and FalsePart is returned if Expression is False. This is the same as writing:

```
If Expression Then
   value = TruePart
Else
   value = FalsePart
EndIf
```

However, the key difference between the two formats is that the IIf function will always evaluate both TruePart and FalsePart, whereas the normal If structure will only evaluate the part which is returned. To see the implications of this, consider these two portions of code:

```
Function IIfTest(lngNumber As Long)

Dim lngRetVal As Long

lngRetVal = IIf(lngNumber = 5, 10, _
                DMin("Quantity", "tblSales", "AmountPaid > 180"))

End Function


Function IfTest(lngNumber As Long)

Dim lngRetVal As Long

If lngNumber = 5 Then
   lngRetVal = 10
Else
   lngRetVal = DMin("Quantity", "tblSales", "AmountPaid > 180")
```

```
    End If

    End Function
```

Both of these procedures do the same thing. They evaluate the variable lngNumber and if it is equal to 5, the procedure sets the value of lngRetVal to 10. If it isn't, the procedure sets the value of lngRetVal to a value that it looks up in the tblSales table.

The difference between the procedures is that the first one will always look up the record from tblSales whether it's required or not. So whenever these procedures are called with lngNumber equal to 5, the first one will be considerably slower.

| Procedure | Iterations | Elapsed Time | Improvement |
| --- | --- | --- | --- |
| IIfTest (10) | 3,000 | 38366 ms | |
| IfTest (10) | 3,000 | 38320 ms | 1.001 times |
| IIfTest (5) | 3,000 | 37668 ms | |
| IfTest (5) | 3,000 | 2 ms | 18834 times |

## Use Integer Arithmetic Where Possible

The speed with which arithmetic calculations are performed depends on the data type of the variables concerned and the type of operation being performed.

In general, however, Integer and Long variables are faster than Single and Double variables. These, in turn, are faster than Currency variables. Variant variables are considerably slower, with most operations taking typically twice as long as with other data types.

Although the difference in execution times for a single operation is very small, it will become more noticeable for repeated operations (such as within large loops).

Another useful tip is to use Integer division wherever possible. Integer division uses the (\) symbol rather than the (/) one and always returns an integer, which will be faster than the Double that normal division always returns.

## Use In-Line Code

Earlier on, we noted that variables could be passed as arguments to procedures by reference or by value. When a variable is passed by reference (the default), the procedure that is called is passed a pointer to the memory location of the variable being passed. In contrast, when a variable is passed by value, a copy of the variable is made and is passed to the procedure. Although passing variables by value has its uses, it is fractionally slower than passing by reference.

Both of these methods are slower, however, than placing the code inline (within the body of the original procedure). The downside of inline code is that it is more difficult to maintain if you have the same code appearing inline in multiple procedures. In addition, having the same code appearing inline in multiple procedures will increase the memory footprint of your code. But if your chief coding priority is execution speed, you should seriously consider using in-line code, particularly if this code is frequently called or within a loop structure.

The following procedures can be used to illustrate the difference between the three methods described above:

```
Sub TestPassingByValue()

Dim dbl1 As Double
Dim dbl2 As Double

dbl1 = 1234

'Placing the argument in parentheses passes it by value
dbl2 = FourthPower((dbl1))

End Sub

Sub TestPassingByReference()

Dim dbl1 As Double
Dim dbl2 As Double

dbl1 = 1234

'Passing by reference
dbl2 = FourthPower(dbl1)

End Sub

Sub TestPassingInLine()

Dim dbl1 As Double
Dim dbl2 As Double

dbl1 = 1234

'Inline coding
dbl2 = dbl1 ^ 4

End Sub

Function FourthPower(dblVal As Double)

FourthPower = dblVal ^ 4

End Function
```

| Procedure | Iterations | Elapsed Time | Improvement |
|---|---|---|---|
| TestPassingByValue | 30,000 | 57 ms | |
| TestPassingByReference | 30,000 | 45 ms | 1.27 times |
| TestPassingInLine | 30,000 | 15 ms | 3.8 times |

## Use DoEvents Judiciously

When a VBA procedure is running, it will act very selfishly and hog the Access limelight unless you tell it otherwise. For example, if you were to run the following portion of code, you would find that Access was locked up until the code finished running.

```
Sub NoDoEvents

Dim lngCounter As Long
Dim i As Integer

For lngCounter = 1 to 1000000
    i = Rnd*12
Next lngCounter

End Sub
```

This routine takes approximately 1.7 seconds to execute on my computer. But it is considered good etiquette (and common sense) to yield control to Windows every so often. For example, while your routine is running you may wish to cancel it, pause it for a moment, or do something else. If your routine ignored all your requests then you wouldn't be very happy. What you need is a way to allow other events to be processed while your routine runs.

This can be achieved with the DoEvents statement. This instructs Windows to process any messages or keystrokes that are currently queued. In the following portion of code, whenever the loop reaches the DoEvents statement, control passes to Windows which checks to see whether any other application has any messages or keystrokes waiting to be processed. It then passes control back to the procedure.

```
Sub AllDoEvents

Dim lngCounter As Long
Dim i As Integer

For lngCounter = 1 to 1000000
    i = Rnd*12
    DoEvents
```

```
    Next lngCounter

    End Sub
```

Although this is good practice, it does take up time. In fact, the routine, which checks for events every time the loop is passed through, takes *over 50 minutes* to run! If you want to use the `DoEvents` statement, do so sparingly. The portion of code shown above can be rewritten like this:

```
    Sub SomeDoEvents

    Dim lngCounter As Long
    Dim i As Integer

    For lngCounter = 1 to 1000000
        i = Rnd*12
        If lngCounter Mod 50000 = 0 Then DoEvents
    Next lngCounter

    End Sub
```

Now, control passes to Windows every 50,000 loops. This means 20 times in the 2.4 seconds or so that the loop now takes to finish, which leaves you with a well-behaved and yet fast bit of code. The `DoEvents` adds only 0.7 seconds to the execution time of this code.

| Procedure | Iterations | Elapsed Time | Difference |
| --- | --- | --- | --- |
| NoDoEvents | 1 x 1,000,000 | 169 ms | |
| AllDoEvents | 1 x 1,000,000 | 801554 ms | +13.36 min |
| SomeDoEvents | 1 x 1,000,000 | 328 ms | +0.159 sec |

Obviously, the number of `DoEvents` statements that you actually use will vary depending on the degree of interactivity that the procedure demands. For example, a procedure that runs for 10 minutes at the dead of night when everyone is in their beds and while no other applications are running will typically require less interactivity (and thus fewer `DoEvents` statements) than a procedure which updates the screen to display real-time stock prices to a user.

> *Whenever you yield control to the processor from within a procedure, you should always write your code in such a way that the procedure will not be executed again from a different part of your code before the first call returns. If it does (this is called **reentrancy**) your code will probably not work the way you intended it to and the application may either hang or crash.*

## *Use the Requery Method, not the Requery Action*

Another method of speeding up your procedures is to avoid using the Requery action to display up-to-date values in a form or control. Use the Requery method instead. This is quicker as it simply reruns the query behind the form or control instead of closing it, reopening it and then rerunning it, as the Requery action does. The actual measured difference will depend on the size and complexity of the form, and the underlying query.

```
DoCmd Requery ctlText.Name        'This is slow

ctlText.Requery                   'This is much quicker
```

## *Use Me*

When you use the Me keyword to refer to a form within an event procedure, Access only searches in the local namespace (that is the objects that are currently available in the open form) for the form. This means that the form is found more quickly than if the full reference to the form is specified.

```
Forms!frmFoo.BackColor = QBColor(9)     'This is slow

Me.BackColor = QBColor(9)               'This is quicker
```

## *Speed Up Database Operations*

Whereas the optimizations you can realize through changing the syntax of your VBA are sometimes marginal, optimizing your database calls almost always leads to substantial performance benefits. The reason for that is simple. Database calls generally take longer to execute than normal VBA statements because they involve accessing the hard disk as opposed to changing the contents of the computer's memory, so a 10% improvement in performance in both will be more noticeable in the case of the database call. We'll look below at some of the ways you can improve the way that VBA code interacts with your database.

### *Creating Test Data*

When you run your performance testing, you should replicate both the expected data volumes and the conditions of the production environment as closely as you can. It may not always be possible to obtain a copy of live data to perform your testing against, so you may need to generate test data.

There are two stages to producing a set of test data: creating the test table(s) and populating the test table(s). To see how easy it can be to build large volumes of test data, let's try it out for ourselves.

**Try It Out — Creating Test Data**

**1.** Create a new database in which to store the test data that we will create. Call the new database `PerformanceXP.mdb`.

**2.** In the `PerformanceXP.mdb` database, switch to VBA by hitting *ALT+F11*.

**3.** Display the **References** dialog by selecting **References...** from the **Tools** menu. When the dialog appears, uncheck the reference to **Microsoft ActiveX Data Objects 2.5 Library** and check the reference to the **Microsoft DAO 3.6 Object Library**. Then hit the **OK** button.

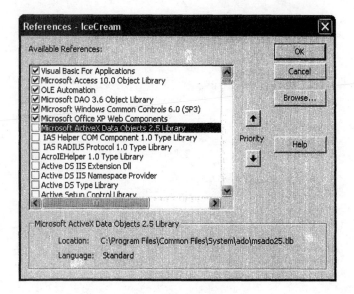

**4.** Next, create a new module by selecting **Insert/Module** from the toolbar.

**5.** Add the following procedure to the new module. This will be used to create the test table.

```
Sub BuildPerformanceTable()

On Error GoTo BuildPerformanceTable_Error
```

```
Dim db As Database
Dim tdf As TableDef
Dim fld As Field
Dim idx As Index

Set db = CurrentDb()

'Try to delete the tblPerformance table
db.TableDefs.Delete ("tblPerformance")

'Create a new tabledef object
Set tdf = db.CreateTableDef("tblPerformance")

'Create and save an ID counter field
Set fld = tdf.CreateField("ID", dbLong)
fld.Attributes = fld.Attributes Or dbAutoIncrField
tdf.Fields.Append fld

'Create and save an unindexed 255-character text field
Set fld = tdf.CreateField("UnindexedText", dbText, 255)
tdf.Fields.Append fld

'Create and save an indexed 255-character text field
Set fld = tdf.CreateField("IndexedText", dbText, 255)
tdf.Fields.Append fld

Set idx = tdf.CreateIndex("TextIndex")
Set fld = idx.CreateField("IndexedText")
idx.Fields.Append fld
tdf.Indexes.Append idx

'Create and save an integer field
Set fld = tdf.CreateField("Num1in100", dbInteger)
tdf.Fields.Append fld

'Create and save another integer field
Set fld = tdf.CreateField("Num1in1000", dbInteger)
tdf.Fields.Append fld

'Create and save (yet) another integer field
Set fld = tdf.CreateField("Num1in10000", dbInteger)
tdf.Fields.Append fld

'Create and save a Yes/No field
Set fld = tdf.CreateField("YesNo", dbBoolean)
tdf.Fields.Append fld

'Save the tabledef into the database
db.TableDefs.Append tdf
```

```
BuildPerformanceTable_Exit:
    Exit Sub

BuildPerformanceTable_Error:
    Select Case Err
        Case 3265        'Item not found in this collection
            Resume Next
        Case Else
            MsgBox "The following unexpected error occurred:" & vbCrLf & _
                Err.Description & " (Error " & Err.Number & ")", vbCritical
            Resume BuildPerformanceTable_Exit
    End Select

End Sub
```

**6.** Next, add the following procedure to the new module. This will be used to insert the data into the newly created table:

```
Sub PopulatePerformanceTable(lngRecords As Long)

Dim lngRecordLoop As Long
Dim intLoop As Long
Dim recPerformance As Recordset
Dim strText As String

Set recPerformance = CurrentDb.OpenRecordset("tblPerformance", _
                                             dbOpenDynaset, _
                                             dbAppendOnly)


For lngRecordLoop = 1 To lngRecords

    'Prepare to add new record
    recPerformance.AddNew

    'Add string up to 5 chars long into [UnindexedText] field
    strText = ""
    For intLoop = 1 To (1 + Int(5 * Rnd))
        strText = strText & Chr$(65 + Int(26 * Rnd))
    Next intLoop
    recPerformance("UnindexedText") = strText

    'Add string up to 255 chars long into [IndexedText] field
    strText = ""
    For intLoop = 1 To (1 + Int(255 * Rnd))
        strText = strText & Chr$(65 + Int(24 * Rnd))
    Next intLoop
    recPerformance("IndexedText") = strText

    'Add integer between 1 and 100 into [Num1in100] field
    recPerformance("Num1in100") = 1 + Int(100 * Rnd)
```

```
    'Add integer between 1 and 1000 into [Num1in1000] field
    recPerformance("Num1in1000") = 1 + Int(1000 * Rnd)

    'Add integer between 1 and 10000 into [Num1in10000] field
    recPerformance("Num1in10000") = 1 + Int(10000 * Rnd)

    'Add True or False into [YesNo] field
    recPerformance("YesNo") = (Rnd < 0.5)

    'Save new record
    recPerformance.Update

Next

recPerformance.Close

MsgBox lngRecords & " rows were added to the tblPerformance table." & _
    vbCrLf & _
    "It now has " & CurrentDb.TableDefs("tblPerformance").RecordCount & _
    " records."

End Sub
```

**7.** Check that there are no compilation errors in the code that you have just typed in by selecting **Compile PerformanceData** from the **Debug** menu.

**8.** Now make sure that the **Immediate** window is visible by hitting *Ctrl + G*. Run the procedure to create the test table by typing the following into the **Immediate** window and hitting *Enter*.

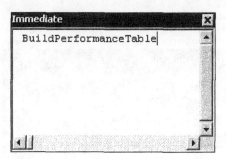

9. Check that the table has been created by switching back to Access. You can do this by hitting *Alt + F11*. The new table should appear in the **Database** window. If it does not appear, you might have to refresh the **Database** window by hitting *F5*:

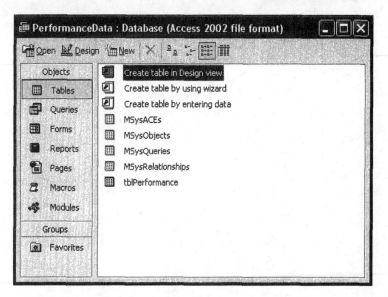

10. Now, switch back to VBA and populate the table with test data. To do this, type the following into the **Immediate** window and hit *Enter*.

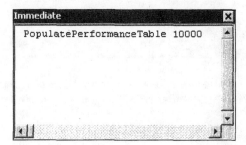

**11.** When the procedure has finished executing, a message box will inform you of the fact.

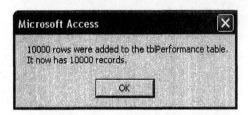

Microsoft Access

10000 rows were added to the tblPerformance table.
It now has 10000 records.

OK

**12.** Switch back to Access and open the table. It should contain 10,000 records of random-looking data.

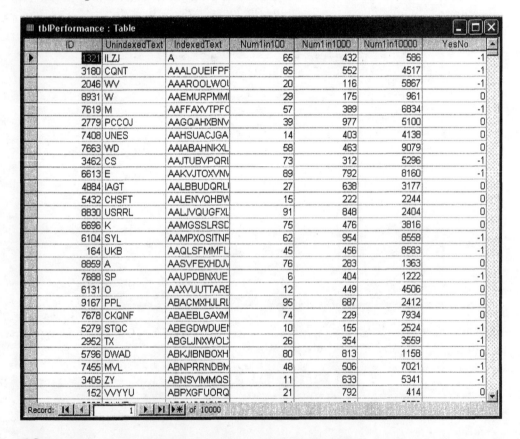

| ID | UnindexedText | IndexedText | Num1in100 | Num1in1000 | Num1in10000 | YesNo |
|---|---|---|---|---|---|---|
| 1321 | ILZJ | A | 65 | 432 | 586 | -1 |
| 3180 | CQNT | AAALOUEIFPF | 85 | 552 | 4517 | -1 |
| 2046 | WV | AAAROOLWOI | 20 | 116 | 5867 | -1 |
| 8931 | W | AAEMURPMMI | 29 | 175 | 961 | 0 |
| 7619 | M | AAFFAXVTPFC | 57 | 389 | 6834 | -1 |
| 2779 | PCCOJ | AAGQAHXBNV | 39 | 977 | 5100 | 0 |
| 7408 | UNES | AAHSUACJGA | 14 | 403 | 4138 | 0 |
| 7663 | WD | AAIABAHNKXL | 58 | 463 | 9079 | 0 |
| 3462 | CS | AAJTUBVPQRI | 73 | 312 | 5296 | -1 |
| 6613 | E | AAKVJTOXVNV | 89 | 792 | 8160 | -1 |
| 4884 | IAGT | AALBBUDQRLI | 27 | 638 | 3177 | 0 |
| 5432 | CHSFT | AALENVQHBW | 15 | 222 | 2244 | 0 |
| 8830 | USRRL | AALJVQUGFXL | 91 | 848 | 2404 | 0 |
| 6696 | K | AAMGSSLRSC | 75 | 476 | 3816 | 0 |
| 6104 | SYL | AAMPXOSITNF | 62 | 954 | 8558 | -1 |
| 164 | UKB | AAQLSFMMFL | 45 | 456 | 8583 | -1 |
| 8859 | A | AASVFEXHDJ\ | 76 | 283 | 1363 | 0 |
| 7688 | SP | AAUPDBNXUE | 6 | 404 | 1222 | -1 |
| 6131 | O | AAXVUUTTARE | 12 | 449 | 4506 | 0 |
| 9167 | PPL | ABACMXHJLRL | 95 | 687 | 2412 | 0 |
| 7678 | CKQNF | ABAEBLGAXM | 74 | 229 | 7934 | 0 |
| 5279 | STQC | ABEGDWDUEI | 10 | 155 | 2524 | -1 |
| 2952 | TX | ABGLJNXWOL\ | 26 | 354 | 3559 | -1 |
| 5796 | DWAD | ABKJIBNBOXH | 80 | 813 | 1158 | 0 |
| 7455 | MVL | ABNPRRNDBN | 48 | 506 | 7021 | -1 |
| 3405 | ZY | ABNSVIMMQS | 11 | 633 | 5341 | -1 |
| 152 | VVYYU | ABPXGFUORQ | 21 | 792 | 414 | 0 |

Record: 1 of 10000

**13.** Finally, save the module and take a look at the size of the database in Explorer. You should see that it is a little under 700KB. Not a bad amount of test data for five minutes' work!

## How It Works

Don't be daunted by the length of the two procedures we use in this example. They are actually fairly straightforward. The first of these, the `BuildPerformanceTable` procedure, builds an empty table with the following structure:

| Field | Datatype |
|-------|----------|
| ID | AutoNumber |
| UnindexedText | Text(5) |
| IndexedText | Text(255) |
| Num1in100 | Integer |
| Num1in1000 | Integer |
| Num1in10000 | Integer |
| YesNo | Yes/No |

It creates this table by using DAO, which is the reason that we replace the default reference to ADO with a reference to DAO in step 3.

The first task in the `BuildPerformanceTable` procedure is to delete any existing tables with the name `tblPerformance`. Although not necessary in the exercise above, this step is useful if you are going to execute this procedure more than once.

```
db.TableDefs.Delete ("tblPerformance")
```

However, it could be that there was no existing table with that name (such as when this procedure is run for the first time), in which case this line of code would normally cause run-time error 3265 to occur.

That is why our error handler contains a test for that specific error code.

```
BuildPerformanceTable_Error:
    Select Case Err
        Case 3265          'Item not found in this collection
            Resume Next
        Case Else
            MsgBox "The following unexpected error occurred:" & vbCrLf & _
                Err.Description & " (Error " & Err.Number & ")", vbCritical
            Resume BuildPerformanceTable_Exit
    End Select
```

If the error does occur, we simply ignore the error and resume execution on the next line of code in the main body of the procedure. Any other errors that occur cause a generic message box to display the error code and description.

The next step is to create the table and append the seven fields to it. This is all fairly straightforward and should hold few surprises for you.

> *If you aren't quite sure how this table creation process works, it is described in much more detail in Chapter 8.*

Once we have created the table, we need to populate it with random data. That is what the `PopulatePerformanceTable` procedure does.

If you have read the previous chapters in this book, then there should be little to surprise you in this procedure. The first step is to open the `Recordset` that will be used to insert new records into:

```
Set recPerformance = CurrentDb.OpenRecordset("tblPerformance", dbOpenDynaset, _
dbAppendOnly)
```

The important feature to notice here is the fact that the `Recordset` has been opened with the `dbAppendOnly` flag. This indicates that an empty `Recordset` should be opened for the sole purpose of adding new records. This speeds up the opening of the `Recordset`, especially in situations where the underlying table contains a large number of records.

The next step is to prepare to insert the specified number of records. The basic structure for adding new records looks like this:

```
For lngRecordLoop = 1 To lngRecords

    'Prepare to add new record
    recPerformance.AddNew
    .
    .
    .
    'Save new record
    recPerformance.Update

Next
```

If you remember back as far as Chapter 6, you will recall that there are three steps to adding records to a `Recordset`. First, a new record is placed into the copy buffer:

```
recPerformance.AddNew
```

Next, the fields in the copy buffer are amended. Finally, the contents of the copy buffer are appended to the table.

```
recPerformance.Update
```

That's straightforward enough, but how do we generate the random data that we will insert into the table? The key to it is the Rnd statement.

## Generating Random Numbers

The Rnd statement generates a pseudo-random number which is greater than or equal to 0 and less than 1. We can take advantage of the Rnd function to define both a random length and a random value for data to be inserted. Inserting a random integer between 1 and, say, 100 is simple enough:

```
recPerformance("Num1in100") = 1 + Int(100 * Rnd)
```

The Int function truncates numbers rather than rounding them. So, if a number generated by the Rnd function satisfies this condition:

$0 \leq r < 1$

then (100*Rnd) yields this:

$0 \leq r < 100$

and Int(100*Rnd) yields an integer such that:

$0 \leq r \leq 99$

To yield an integer between 1 and 100, rather than between 0 and 99, we simply add 1.

```
1 + Int(100 * Rnd)
```

So adding random numbers poses no problems. But how do we add random text strings? The answer is to use to the Chr$ function. This returns a character based on its ANSI code. The American National Standards Institute (ANSI) character set used by Microsoft Windows contains 256 characters. The first 32 characters (from 0 to 31) represent special characters such as tab and backspace characters. The next 96 characters (from 32 to 127) correspond to the letters and symbols on a standard U.S. keyboard. The final 128 characters represent special characters, such as letters in international alphabets, accents, currency symbols, and fractions.

If you look at the ANSI character set, you will notice that the letters A-Z have ANSI codes ranging from 65-90. So, if we want to generate a random letter between A and Z we need to generate an integer between 65 and 90 and pass that number to the Chr$ function. That is just what this line does:

```
strText = strText & Chr$(65 + Int(26 * Rnd))
```

If we want our string values to be of random length between 1 and 5 characters, we simply need to execute this line of code a random number of times between 1 and 5.

```
For intLoop = 1 To (1 + Int(5 * Rnd))
    strText = strText & Chr$(65 + Int(24 * Rnd))
Next intLoop
```

*You can also determine a character's ANSI code by using the Asc function, for example, Asc("A") returns 65.*

In some situations you might want to be able to generate a reproducible series of random numbers. You can easily do this by resetting the Rnd function. We can do this by passing a negative number to the Rnd function. For example, the following procedure will always generate the same random numbers.

```
Sub PseudoRandom()

Dim i As Integer

Rnd (-2)
For i = 1 To 5
    Debug.Print Rnd
Next

End Sub
```

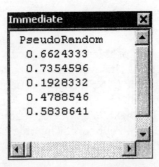

To generate a different series of reproducible random numbers, simply pass a different negative number to the Rnd function.

*Of course, the numbers returned by* Rnd *– just like the numbers returned by any mathematical algorithm – are not truly random. They are pseudo-random. However, they are random enough for the purpose of generating test data!*

## Populating the Test Table

To fill the table with random data, we simply need to run the PopulatePerformanceTable procedure, passing to it as an argument the number of records that we wish to insert. When the procedure has finished executing, it displays a message box explaining the number of records it has added and the total number of records now in the table.

Be careful not to get carried away when running this procedure. On a PC with a 300 MHz Pentium processor and 64MB of memory this procedure will add records at a rate of nearly 250 per second. Put another way, that means that the database will grow at a rate of around 10MB per minute!

Something else to be wary of is the fact that deleting and recreating tables can quickly lead to database bloat. That is a condition that arises when unused space is not reclaimed as objects are deleted, and it manifests itself in ever increasing database sizes. To reduce database bloat, you should compact the database regularly, a task described in more detail later on in this chapter. Fortunately, the auto-compact feature in Access 2002 means that bloated databases will automatically be compacted when they are closed.

So now we have a relatively straightforward method for generating large volumes of test data at great speed. Now let's look at some ways that we can improve access to that data.

## Use Indexes

Adding an index to a field can be an excellent way of improving the performance of searches on that field. Although adding indexes slows updates and increases locking contention, very often this overhead is more than offset by the performance benefits gained if the fields are frequently used for query searches.

The following procedure counts the number of records in which the IndexedText field begins with the letter X, using the set of 10,000 records that we created in the previous exercise:

```
Sub IndexedSQL()

Dim strSQL As String
Dim rec As Recordset

strSQL = "SELECT Count(*) FROM tblPerformance WHERE IndexedText LIKE 'X*'"
Set rec = CurrentDb.OpenRecordset(strSQL, dbOpenDynaset)
rec.Close

End Sub
```

Whereas this procedure runs the same query against the UnindexedText field:

```
Sub UnindexedSQL()

Dim strSQL As String
Dim rec As Recordset

strSQL = "SELECT Count(*) FROM tblPerformance WHERE UnindexedText LIKE 'X*'"
Set rec = CurrentDb.OpenRecordset(strSQL, dbOpenDynaset)
rec.Close

End Sub
```

On my computer the indexed search took 188ms the first time it was run and only 38ms for subsequent executions. By way of contrast, the unindexed search took over 5 seconds the first time and only 38ms subsequently.

| Operation | Elapsed Time | Improvement |
|---|---|---|
| UnindexedSQL (1st run) | 5375ms | |
| IndexedSQL (1st run) | 188 ms | 28.66 times |
| UnindexedSQL (subsequent runs) | 38 ms | |
| IndexedSQL (subsequent runs) | 38 ms | 1.3 times |

> The vast difference between the first and subsequent executions of these searches shows the impact of caching. The first time that these searches are performed, the data has to be physically read in from disk, whereas for subsequent searches the data only needs to be read in from memory – a substantially faster operation.

## Use Appropriate Recordset Types

Another way of increasing the performance of data access in code is to use a more efficient type of Recordset object, a subject we have already looked at in Chapter 6.

```
Sub TestSnapshot()

Dim strSQL As String
Dim rec As Recordset

strSQL = "SELECT * FROM tblPerformance WHERE IndexedText > 'N*'"
Set rec = CurrentDb.OpenRecordset(strSQL, dbOpenSnapshot)
rec.MoveLast
rec.Close

End Sub
```

The procedure above returns all of the records from the `tblPerformance` table that have a value in the `IndexedText` field which begins with an N or any letter alphabetically after N.

Because dynaset-type `Recordset` objects only cache a copy of the key values of the result set, they will typically open more quickly than snapshot-type `Recordset` objects in situations where the result set is larger than, say, 500 records.

```
Sub TestDynaset()

Dim strSQL As String
Dim rec As Recordset

strSQL = "SELECT * FROM tblPerformance WHERE IndexedText > 'N*'"
Set rec = CurrentDb.OpenRecordset(strSQL, dbOpenDynaset)
rec.MoveLast
rec.Close

End Sub
```

Where the result set is extremely large, or where the base tables are located on the other side of a slow network, the difference can be quite significant.

The following table indicates the results of running these two procedures against a `tblPerformance` table with 30,000 rows (of which approximately half are returned by the query).

| Procedure | Elapsed Time | Improvement |
| --- | --- | --- |
| TestSnapshot (1$^{st}$ run) | 8266 ms | |
| TestDynaset (1$^{st}$ run) | 734 ms | 11.3 times |
| TestSnapshot (subsequent runs) | 72 ms | |
| TestDynaset (subsequent runs) | 16 ms | 4.5 times |

If you cannot use a dynaset-type `Recordset` object, you might find that you achieve slightly better performance if you use a forward-only `Recordset` object.

These only allow you to scroll downwards through a recordset and you cannot use certain methods (for example, `MoveLast`) against recordsets created like this. Although this means that you cannot use forward-only recordsets in all situations, the fact that they do not need a complicated cursoring mechanism means that they will often outperform conventional recordsets.

In a multi-user environment, you might also see some small advantage from using read-only recordsets.

Still better performance gains, however, can be achieved by opening an append-only recordset. These recordsets are empty and can only be used to add new records, rather than for inspecting existing records. Because append-only recordsets do not require any records to be retrieved, they will typically open significantly faster than fully-populated recordsets, especially when the base table contains many records.

The performance of any of the `Recordset` types described in this section is highly dependent on the size of the base table, the restrictiveness of the criteria, and which fields are indexed. In short, there is no substitute for performance testing on your own database.

## Use Bookmarks

Each record in a recordset is automatically assigned a `Bookmark` when the recordset is opened. If you are in a recordset and know that you will want to move back to the record that you are currently on, you should save the record's `Bookmark` to a variable. By setting the `Bookmark` property of the `Recordset` object to the value you saved in the variable, you will be able to return to the record far more quickly than you would be able to if you used any of the `Find` or `Seek` methods.

*Bookmarks are stored as arrays of byte data and so should be saved as byte arrays rather than strings. Although you can save a Bookmark to a string variable, comparing a record's Bookmark to a Bookmark stored in a string variable will not yield correct results, unless the comparison is performed as a binary comparison. You can also use variants for bookmarks, but the extra work VBA has to do with the variant type will mean performance is not as good as using a byte array. For more information on using Bookmarks and performing binary comparison, refer to Chapter 6.*

## DAO or ADO?

In Chapter 6 we examined DAO in detail, and in Chapter 21 we will be examining ADO in detail, including a discussion on when to use ADO in preference to DAO. One of the factors you will consider when making that choice will be performance. So let's have a look at how ADO performs compared to DAO when using the Jet database engine. Firstly let's compare updating data in a loop using DAO against using ADO. Before the following code will work, you need to make sure that you have a reference to **Microsoft ActiveX Data Objects 2.7** by selecting **Tools | References** in the VBA editor:

```
Sub ADOUpdates()
Dim strSQL As String
Dim con As ADODB.Connection
Set con = CurrentProject.Connection
Dim rec As New ADODB.Recordset
strSQL = "SELECT * FROM tblPerformance where indexedtext > 'N%' "
rec.Open strSQL, con, adOpenKeyset, adLockOptimistic
Do Until rec.EOF
    rec("num1in10000") = rec("num1in10000") * 0.9
    rec("num1in1000") = rec("num1in1000") * 0.9
    rec("num1in100") = rec("num1in100") * 0.9
```

```
    rec.Update
    rec.MoveNext
Loop
rec.Close
End Sub


Sub DAOUpdates()
Dim strSQL As String
Dim rec As DAO.Recordset
strSQL = "SELECT * FROM tblPerformance where IndexedText > 'N*'"
Set rec = CurrentDb.OpenRecordset(strSQL, adOpenDynamic, dbOptimistic)
Do Until rec.EOF
    rec.Edit
    rec("num1in10000") = rec("num1in10000") * 0.9
    rec("num1in1000") = rec("num1in1000") * 0.9
    rec("num1in100") = rec("num1in100") * 0.9
    rec.Update
    rec.MoveNext
Loop
rec.Close
End Sub
```

Note that the `adOpenKeyset` cursor is equivalent to the `dbOpenDynaset` recordset type, and that `adLockOptimistic` equates to `dbOptimistic`. Note also that ADO does not need to begin editing with the `rec.Edit` method.

| Operation | Elapsed Time | Improvement |
|-----------|--------------|-------------|
| ADOUpdates | 569 ms | |
| DAOUpdates | 425 ms | 1.34 times |

For this test we can see that DAO performs better than ADO. In fact DAO makes much more efficient use of the Microsoft Jet database engine than ADO can. One of the reasons for this is that the internal ADO calls made to retrieve schema information about the table you are querying are relatively inefficient when applied against Jet, and that adds overhead. Also in ADO, every `Connection` object uses a separate Jet session, whereas, by default, DAO objects use the same Jet session. Each session has an overhead and a separate read cache, so we can see that ADO requires more work to get started, and that the read cache, which makes subsequent runs so much faster, cannot be shared between each connection.

Microsoft quotes that for many operations using Jet databases DAO is 5 to 10 times faster than ADO, and for queries and updates against tables with a large number of columns ADO is 30 percent to 80 percent slower than the equivalent query using DAO (see Q225048 – http://support.microsoft.com/default.aspx?scid=kb;en-us;Q225048).

# Increasing Apparent Speed

Although you may be able to do much to increase the real execution speed of your VBA code and your database calls, there is only so far you can go. So what happens if you have optimized your application for real execution speed and it still appears sluggish? One option is to increase the application's **apparent** speed. This is how fast the user *thinks* the application is, rather than how fast it really is.

> *Users of an application do not get upset when the application is slow. They get upset when they* ***notice*** *that it is slow! There is a big difference.*

Consider the following ways of making an application appear more quickly:

- Using a startup form
- Using gauges
- Removing code from form modules
- Pre-loading and hiding forms
- Caching data locally

## Startup Forms and Splash Screens

One trusted method of distracting users from the fact that an application is taking a long time to perform some task is to distract them with some fancy graphics. After all, Microsoft, and most all other software suppliers, do it all the time. What happens when you start up Access, Word or Excel? You see a startup form or splash screen.

"Gosh! That's pretty. I wish my application looked so professional!" you think to yourself. And by the time you have snapped out of your reverie, the application has loaded.

If there had been no splash screen you would have probably thought to yourself, "What on earth is happening? Why does it take so long for this application to start?"

Once the database has opened, you can also configure a database form to be the **start-up form**. A start-up form is simply an Access form that is displayed as soon as a database is opened.

## Using a Start-Up Form

To make a form the start-up form, simply specify its name in the Display Form/Page box on the Tools/Startup... dialog in Access.

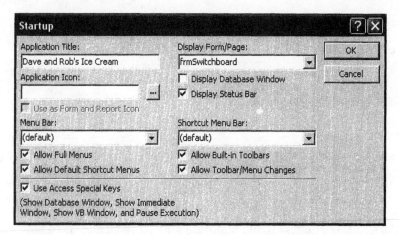

The example above will cause `frmSwitchboard` to be displayed as soon as Dave and Rob's Ice Cream database has been opened (but after the Access splash screen and logon dialog box).

A word of warning – don't overload your startup form with too many controls or complex `Load` event code or else it will take too long for the form to appear, and you will have defeated the object of the exercise!

# Use Gauges

Another way that you can distract users – and reassure them that *something* is happening – is to show a meter displaying the progress of operations that are being performed. The `SysCmd` function provides a simple way of doing this. There are three steps involved in displaying a progress meter in the status bar of your application:

❑ Initialize the meter and specify its maximum value and text to be displayed

❑ Repeatedly update the meter to show progress

❑ Remove the meter

The following code illustrates one way of displaying a progress meter:

```
Sub ShowProgress()

Dim i As Integer
Dim j As Integer
Dim intRnd As Integer
```

```
'Initialise Progress Meter and set Maximum to 300
SysCmd acSysCmdInitMeter, "Testing...", 300

For i = 0 To 300
    'Perform some processing or other...
    For j = 0 To 10000              'Your real code
        intRnd = Rnd * 10 + 1       'would replace
    Next j                          'this test loop

    'Update Meter to Show Progress
    SysCmd acSysCmdUpdateMeter, i
    DoEvents
Next i

'Remove Meter from Status Bar
SysCmd acSysCmdRemoveMeter

End Sub
```

This procedure causes a gradually filling progress meter to be displayed with the text Testing...

*The progress meter is displayed in the status bar of the main Access window, so you will have to switch from the VBA IDE to Access if you want to see it. Note that another alternative to this progress meter is the Common Control that gives progress bars everywhere.*

Of course, you do not need to set up a loop to update your progress meter. Instead you could structure your procedure like this:

```
Sub ShowProgress()

'Initialize Progress Meter and set Maximum to 30
SysCmd acSysCmdInitMeter, "Testing...", 30

'Perform some processing or other...
....
'Update Meter to Show Progress
SysCmd acSysCmdUpdateMeter, 5

'Perform more processing...
....
'Update Meter to Show Progress
SysCmd acSysCmdUpdateMeter, 10

'And yet more...
....
'Update Meter to Show Progress
SysCmd acSysCmdUpdateMeter, 15
```

```
    .
    .
    .

    'Remove Meter from Status Bar
    SysCmd acSysCmdRemoveMeter

    End Sub
```

The three constants `acSysCmdInitMeter`, `acSysCmdUpdateMeter`, and `acSysCmdRemoveMeter`, which are used to initialize, update, and remove the status bar, are intrinsic to Access. In other words, they are built into the Microsoft Access 10 Object Library. Since our project has a reference to that library, we do not need to declare these constants anywhere in our code.

> *Note also that the progress meter will only be shown if the status bar is visible in your database. To make it visible, select **Startup** from the **Tools** menu option (available when the database window is active) and tick the **Display Status Bar** option. You will have to reopen the database for this to take effect.*

## Remove Code from Form Modules

Users are likely to get irritated if they click a button to open a form and it then seems to take ages for the form to appear. This usually happens when a form has substantial amounts of code in its module, which delays the form's loading. In this situation, you might consider removing the code from the form module and placing it in a standard code module. This will cause the form to load more quickly, as code will only be loaded on demand after the form has opened.

## Pre-Load and Hide Forms

Alternatively, if you find that you use a form frequently and it takes a long time to load and unload, you might choose to load the form during the application's startup and then make it visible and invisible instead of loading and unloading it.

This technique will slow down the startup of your application, but will appear to increase its subsequent performance. You can even delay the loading of the form until after the main form has already appeared. While the user is looking at the main form, the other form can be loading in the background.

This method works well if apparent speed is a coding priority, but it does increase the complexity of the application. You should also bear in mind that having several forms loaded concurrently will increase the application's memory usage.

## Setting the HasModule Property to False

If you have forms and/or reports that have no code in their modules at all, then you can improve performance by settings their HasModule property to False. This will also reduce the size of your database a little. For forms that only contain links to other forms, consider using macros or hyperlinks rather than VBA, then set the HasModule property to False. One word of warning, if you do set this property to False, using either VBA or the design, Access deletes the code module and any code it contains.

## Cache Data Locally

A **cache** is just an area of memory (or hard disk space) that is used to hold values that have been retrieved from somewhere else, ready to be used again. For example, Windows places the data that comes from your hard disk into a cache made up of an area of memory. Often a program uses the same data over and over again. This way it can just read it from the cache the next time, instead of having to fetch it from the hard disk again. Of course, reading from memory is much quicker and more efficient that reading from a hard disk.

So you can increase an application's performance by caching data in one form or another. In decreasing order of speed (in other words, fastest first), the three methods of data retrieval are:

❑ Reading data from memory (for example variables, arrays)

❑ Reading data from local tables, or external files

❑ Reading data from tables across the network

If you want to increase the perceived speed of your application, think about how you can cache data to 'move it up' a level.

If you keep frequently accessed, non-volatile data (in other words, data that doesn't change much) in a table on a network server, you might consider copying that data to the local client machine to make the application run faster. However, you will need to make sure that whenever data is updated on the server, it is also updated on all client machines as well (and vice versa).

Similarly, if you have data in a lookup table which you frequently access in VBA code, you could create an array to hold that data with the GetRows method. This could make retrieving the data substantially faster. However, it will also increase the memory usage of your application.

*Both these methods increase the **apparent** speed of your application. They may not increase the actual speed, because there will be a performance overhead involved in the process of caching the data in the first place. Remember that caching only works well if you need to read the data several times. If you only read it once, caching will slow your application down.*

# Network Considerations

So far, we have concentrated on writing code that fits into as small an amount of memory as possible, and can be executed as quickly as possible – or at least appears to do so. But that is only part of the story. One of the major reasons why Access database applications run slowly has nothing to do with memory footprints or code execution speed. Instead, the albatross around the neck of many applications is the vast amount of data that needs to be read from disk and passed across a network.

A network has two major drawbacks. Firstly, performance across a network – particularly a slow one – can be worse than performance against local tables. Secondly, you might find that your application generates a lot of network traffic. This will not make you popular with other users of the network, who find that their applications have slowed down considerably because of the log-jam. If either of these causes you a problem, consider:

❑  Searching on indexed fields in attached tables

❑  Putting non-table objects on the local machine

❑  Disabling AutoExpand

## *Search on Indexed Fields in Attached Tables*

One method of minimizing the amount of data that an application has to read from disk is to ensure that fields used in the queries are indexed. If you run a query with a criterion against a field that is indexed, Access will be able to determine the exact data pages which contain the records it needs to retrieve in order to run the query. It will retrieve only the data pages that contain those records.

However, if you are running a query that uses a criterion against a field which is not indexed, Access will need to read into memory every single record in the underlying table to see whether it meets the criterion. If the table is large and is on a network server, this will result in large amounts of network traffic, and a very slow and frustrating query.

To look at an example of this in a little more detail, consider the following query:

```
SELECT *
FROM tblPerformance
WHERE ID=4000
```

If the ID field in tblPerformance is indexed, then the Jet engine knows that it will only need to retrieve the pages containing records with an ID of 4000 from the tblPerformance table.

However, if the ID field is not indexed, then Jet will have to read the whole of the tblPerformance table from disk and transfer it into the memory of the PC running the query. If the tblPerformance table is on a network server, this means that the whole table will need to be transferred across the network. Once it is in local memory, Jet can determine which records match the criterion by going through each record in turn and checking whether the ID field is equal to 4000. This is known as a full table scan and is slow.

Imagine if the tblPerformance table contained half a million records, each approximately 260 bytes long. A table scan on an attached table would mean reading (500,000 x 260 bytes =) 130MB across the network and trying to fit them into local memory...

As a rule, therefore, always use indexes on fields which are involved in joins or which have criteria applied to them in queries.

## Put Non-Table Objects on the Local Machine

Another way to minimize the amount of network traffic that a networked application generates is to place tables on the network server, but to place other objects into a local copy of the database. Then all users can share the data in the tables, but all other objects (queries, forms, reports, macros, and modules) will reside on the local computer. Consequently, when that object is activated – say, when a form is opened – the computer only needs to read it into memory from its local disk. This will generally be quicker than loading it over the network and will also mean a noticeable reduction in network traffic.

The downside of this strategy is that you will have to distribute a new copy of the database to each user whenever you revise the code or any of the objects in it. Despite this, most applications benefit from this sort of segmentation.

## Disable AutoExpand

The AutoExpand property of a combo box forces Access to fill it automatically with a value that matches the text you have typed. Although this is a neat feature and can make the process of filling in forms less of a chore, it comes at a price – the table that supplies the values has to be queried as the user types in text. If the table on which the combo box is based resides across the network, the result may be a substantial increase in network traffic, especially if the combo box contains many values.

# Finishing Touches

All of the tips so far have been aimed at specific coding priorities. Some increased real execution speed, or reduced network traffic, and others reduced the memory footprint of the database application.

In some cases, a single optimization may bring many benefits. For example, changing a variable's data type from variant to integer will reduce memory demands *and* may increase execution speed.

However, in other cases, an optimization may have an antagonistic effect. It may bring a benefit *and* incur a cost. For example, loading forms and hiding them will increase the apparent execution speed of your application, but it will also increase your application's memory footprint. In that situation you must decide what your priorities are and act accordingly.

The final section of this chapter concentrates on the things that you can do which will always benefit your application – irrespective of your coding priorities. These include:

- ❑ Compacting the database
- ❑ Compiling all modules
- ❑ Opening databases exclusively

## Compact the Database

Over a period of time you may find that the performance of your database slowly degenerates. This may be because the database has become fragmented.

Fragmentation occurs when objects are deleted from a database, but the space used by those objects isn't reclaimed. The database becomes like a Swiss cheese – full of little holes. As pretty a simile as that may be, it also means that your database slows down. It's not damaged in any way, but performance suffers. This is because it is physically slower to read non-contiguous (fragmented) data from a disk than it is to read contiguous data.

Compacting a database removes any unused space (the holes in the cheese!) and makes all the data pages in the database contiguous. This has two benefits:

- ❑ Database performance improves
- ❑ The size of the database file is reduced

As well as allowing you to compact a database from the menu bar – just select **Compact and Repair Database…** from the **Database Utilities** submenu on the **Tools** menu – Access 2002 now provides you with the ability to compact databases automatically when they are closed. In order to turn on this feature, simply check the **Compact on Close** checkbox on the **General** tab of the Access **Tools/Options…** dialog box.

You can also compact a database from VBA, using the `CompactDatabase` method of the `DBEngine` object:

```
DBEngine.CompactDatabase "c:\myold.mdb","c:\mynew.mdb"
```

*For optimal performance, you should occasionally use a disk defragmentation program (such as the Disk Defragmenter supplied with Windows 98 or later) before compacting your database.*

## Compile All Modules

You have been working feverishly all weekend to get that database application finished for Monday's demonstration to the board. You tested the application last night – making sure you tested it in a production environment – and it was really zippy. There's an hour to go and you think you might as well run that little library routine of yours to add fancy headers to the procedures. It only takes a couple of minutes to run and you've done it so often you know that it's bug free.

The time comes, the board members sit down and you hit the icon to start your application... and wait... and wait... and wait...

"Whaaaaat!" you scream, inwardly, of course. "What's happened to my speedy app???" It's suddenly performing like a three-legged dog... in a coma. Looks like you forgot to recompile your application!

When you make any changes to code in a standard code module or a class module (including form and report modules), the module has to be recompiled before it can be run. To compile the code in all the modules in your database, choose Compile <ProjectName> from the Debug menu in the VBA IDE.

If you don't explicitly compile your code in this manner, VBA compiles your code at run time. This can cause a significant delay, especially if there is a lot of code in the module being compiled. This delay is reduced, however, if you have checked the Compile On Demand box, and the Background compile checkbox on the General page of the Tools/Options... dialog in the VBA IDE (we discussed these options in Chapter 12). In this case, VBA only compiles the parts of the code that are called by the procedure that is executing – the call tree – rather than all of it, but uses idle time during run time to finish compiling the project in the background. So there is less delay. However, to be safe, you should always compile all your code before delivery. After all, compilation will also detect compile-time errors such as a For... statement without a corresponding Next statement.

*You can increase performance further still by saving your database as an MDE file. We looked at MDE files – and the whole area of compilation – in more detail in Chapter 18.*

## Open Databases Exclusively

If you are the only person who will be using the database at any one time, you should open the database **exclusively**. This means that your application will perform better because Access will not have to spend time monitoring whether other users want to lock records. You can ensure that databases are opened exclusively by default by selecting Exclusive as the Default Open Mode on the Advanced page of the Access Tools/Options... dialog.

If you use a command line to start your application, you can use the /Excl switch to achieve the same result.

```
c:\access\msaccess.exe c:\abwrox\code\wrox.mdb /Excl
```

If you are opening the database in VBA, set the Exclusive argument to True when using the OpenDatabase method:

```
Set db = DBEngine(0).OpenDatabase("c:\abwrox\code\wrox.mdb", True)
```

# Summary

Producing an application is one thing. Producing an application that runs (or at the very least, appears to run) quickly and doesn't hog the whole of your computer's memory is quite another – but this is what will make or break your application. Users are impatient beings, and to them there is nothing worse than an inefficient program.

This chapter has covered several tips and tricks for improving the general speed of your code. Before you start to put your application together, you should decide what your coding priorities are, and then follow the guidelines drawn up here to achieve them. Remember that optimizing for one priority, such as maintainability, may adversely affect a secondary aim, such as the speed of your code – it is up to you to decide which is more important.

> *Remember, also, that you can spend forever tweaking your application to go a fraction faster, but will it be worth the amount of time you're putting in? Do you have a deadline to meet? Is it worth it?*

So, in this chapter we have covered:

- ❑ How to reduce memory overhead by choosing the right data types, reclaiming memory and grouping procedures strategically
- ❑ Which coding techniques to employ to increase execution speed
- ❑ Tricks such as using a startup screen and progress gauges to distract the user and make it appear that an application is running quicker
- ❑ How to make a networked application more efficient

# Exercises

1. We can write a procedure in a number of ways according to our coding priorities. Try to write a procedure that tells you the delivery day for corn syrup (the second Wednesday of every month) for a given year and month. Now rewrite the procedure so that it is optimized for:

   ❑ Real execution speed
   ❑ Maintainability
   ❑ Reusability

2. Create a form and place a button on it. Now write a procedure that prints to the debug window the number of fields and records in each table in the database when the button is clicked. Now add a gauge to the status bar to display the progress of this operation.

3. List the following:

   ❑ Six ways of reducing memory overhead
   ❑ Five ways of increasing execution speed
   ❑ Three finishing touches that can improve performance

   Now take a database that you have previously created and see if you can apply any of these techniques to it. Measure the before and after performance to see how well you have done!

# C H A P T E R 20

# Moving to Client-Server

Many Microsoft Access developers are finding that they are required to work with databases other than Microsoft Access. The push to have corporate data made available via the Internet, Access databases growing beyond the limitations of Access, and greater numbers of users have all lead to a need to move to other Relational Databases. For many Access developers, this means SQL Server. We will look at SQL Server 2000 or Microsoft SQL Server Desktop Engine, formerly MSDE, which is provided free with Microsoft Office XP.

In this chapter we will introduce you to the Client-Server Model and using Microsoft Access to develop solutions that are based on SQL Server data storage either using the full version of SQL Server or the free version, SQL Server Desktop Engine. In this set up, Microsoft Access is used as the front-end to the database housed on SQL Server. It's worth bearing in mind that they are both the same database engine with some slight, but significant, differences. We will be looking at Access Data Projects, the Microsoft Access file type used to develop against SQL Server backends. We will also provide an overview of Stored Procedures, User Defined Functions, Views, and Transact SQL. In addition, we will also step through the Microsoft Access 2002 Upsizing Wizard in order to move the Ice Cream example database to SQL Server 2000.

As this is but a single chapter, we cannot cover all the information you will need, but we hope sufficient information is provided to get you started on the road to client-server development using Microsoft Access 2002 as your development platform.

> **All the examples and code shown in this chapter apply equally to both SQL Server 2000 and SQL Server Desktop.**

# What is Client-Server?

Let's start off by saying that Microsoft Access is a file based database as opposed to a client-server database. All requests for data are processed on the client by Jet (Jet being the database engine behind the Access interface) compared to a database like SQL Server, where all requests for data are processed on the server by the database engine, then passed to the client. For example, if you place a copy of an Access database on a network server and then provide say twenty users with front-end applications, all processing of data will take place on each user's PC independently of the database backend on the server. Just think of the network traffic this causes as each user downloads data to the local PC! Using the Client-Server architecture, processing is carried out on the database server, in this case SQL Server, leading to improvements in speed and the reduction of data being passed along the wire to the client PC. However, as we shall see, moving up to bigger and better software does not always lead to performance improvements, and, at times, can even see a performance drop as developers continue to build applications as if they where using Access, for example, not restricting the records retrieved from the server. Using SQL Server, you could be pulling thousands of records across the network as opposed to hundreds. In addition, when you use the common front-end backend setup with Access and have multiple users, you also have the problem of many different processes writing to a single database file; a failure in any process can collapse the entire application.

# Jet vs. SQL Server: Why Move?

First off let's be clear on what both SQL Server and SQL Server Desktop are. **SQL Server 2000** is the flagship database product from Microsoft. It is suitable for use in installations holding massive amounts of data and with up to thousands of users. **SQL Server Desktop**, supplied free of charge on the Office XP CDs, is also SQL Server 2000, but with two very serious limitations:

❑ There is no front-end user management interface. SQL Server is the Database Management System, just like JET. The full version of SQL Server is supplied with Enterprise Manager, SQL Query Analyzer, and other tools used to both manipulate data and manage the installation. In order to manage an instance of SQL Server Desktop, you must either use command-line tools or work via code. You could, of course, purchase some of the third-party management tools available via the Internet. The following table lists some tools you may find useful, but, of course, we endorse none of them.

| Tool | URL | Comment |
| --- | --- | --- |
| MSDE Query | http://www.msde.biz/download.htm | Free Download |
| dbManager | http://utenti.lycos.it/asql/DownLoad2k.html | VB 6 Free Download |

| Tool | URL | Comment |
| --- | --- | --- |
| MSDE Manager | http://www.whitebearconsulting.com/Downloads.htm | 30 day evaluation |
| MSDE TinyAdmin | http://www.sbh.de/eng/tools_msdetinyaframe.asp | Shareware |

Another option available to you is to build your own management interface to the Database server using Microsoft Access. However, this requires a fairly high level of knowledge of how SQL Server operates and of its objects. Using the Access interface you can manage tables, relationships, and associated properties, but you cannot manage areas such as security.

❑ SQL Server Desktop is rigged so that performance falls after a number of concurrent threads are running on the server. Once the limit is reached (more than 5 processes) performance slows until a thread is freed to bring you back within the limits. This process is called Target Benchmark Users or TBU. There is no indication given to the user that processing has slowed down. Therefore, there is no limit to the number of users who can work with SQL Server Desktop. A common mistake made when talking about TBU and SQL Server Desktop is that the limit refers to users. It does not – it refers to concurrent threads of execution.

> It has been strongly suggested that the sole reason for SQL Server Desktop is to get Access developers to move up to the full version of SQL Server 2000. One thing it does provide, however, is a free training tool for developers to use before laying out their cash on a full server license. Rumor also has it that there will be no further development of the Jet database engine used by Access.

## Advantages of SQL Server

There are many reasons to move your Jet database up to SQL Server, including:

❑ Movement of all or most of your data processing to the database server itself as opposed to processing on each client machine.

❑ Improved security with SQL Sever through the use of roles and groups, which are far in excess of the security features used by Microsoft Access.

❑ The Access 2002 interface makes working with SQL Server 2000 objects very easy. Graphical tools are provided which allow you to create Stored Procedures, Views, User Defined Functions, and Database Diagrams.

❑ Management of multiple databases via Enterprise Manager.

❑ Improved backup – can cope with massive databases as opposed to the 2GB limits of MS Access. There are SQL Server databases being used with terrabytes of data.

❑ Scalable for use on the Internet. Microsoft SQL Server 2000 will handle hundreds of users with no problems, has built in support for XML, and is a true client-server database engine, unlike Access which is a file-based system.

❑ Improved data manipulation language, Transact SQL (T-SQL is SQL Server's version of the Microsoft SQL language, and is discussed briefly later in this chapter).

❑ Use of stored procedures and views to secure access to tables by users. Using views we can restrict the user to just the data they require and "hide" sensitive data.

❑ Users have no access to the database file, unlike an MDB file. In this way it is impossible for the user to mess with the table or the table structure as they are safely tucked away and protected by the database server.

> **On one occasion a client tried to open the MDB file in Microsoft Word. Why? I have no idea. I do know it cost close to $2,000 to have the database fixed.**

## Disadvantages of SQL Server

Of course, things are not all rosy, and there are several disadvantages to moving your database, including:

❑ New skills must be learned, including T-SQL, Stored Procedures, SQL Server Management and ADO, particularly if you're working with Access Data Projects

❑ SQL Server license costs are not cheap, and you may also be required to purchase additional hardware, such as dedicated servers, to run the database.

❑ Management of the database server is not as easy as with Microsoft Access. You could have hundreds of users and multiple databases to manage when using SQL Server.

❑ Your existing applications may need to be rewritten, or, at least, changed in some ways in order to be fully compatible with SQL Server and the client server model in general.

❑ Not all Access features are supported by SQL Server, for example, functions such as `format` need to be changed before they will run on SQL Server.

> **We will be looking at the issue of Access functions shortly when we upsize the Ice Cream database to SQL Server 2000.**

# Access Data Projects

It has been the belief of many Microsoft Access developers for some time that Access was being repositioned by Microsoft as a development tool for SQL Server. This belief has been strongly reinforced by Access 20002 and the ability to work directly with SQL Server via Access Data Projects. Access now provides you with a super tool for working with the server.

## Database Files

Unlike an Access database, a SQL Server database contains two files. If you check out `C:\Program Files\Microsoft SQL Server\MSSQL\Data` once you have upsized the Ice Cream database, you will notice that there are two files, `FileName.mdf` and `FileName.ldf`.

> **Do not simply move these files to a new folder. Unlike Access it doesn't work like that and there are procedures to follow before you can move a SQL Server database file.**

The `mdf` file is the actual database file used by SQL Server. The `ldf` file contains details of your actions on the database. The `ldf` file is the log file containing a record of all the transactions that have taken place on your database. As a result, its importance cannot be overstated. When backing up SQL Server, you backup both of these files. Again a detailed discussion of this process would fill a book, never mind a chapter, so it is outside the scope of this book. For a good solid grounding in SQL Server, see *Beginning SQL Server 2000 Programming*, published by Wrox Press (ISBN 1-86100-523-7).

> **Your best friend when moving to SQL Server will be the help files provided; known as Books Online, they provide a great deal of information and example files that will assist you in the move to this environment. Books Online is available on the SQL Server 2000 installation CD and is also available on the Internet at http://www.microsoft.com/sql/techinfo/productdoc/2000/default.asp. If you are installing the SQL Server Desktop Engine, then download Books Online as it is not available on the Office XP CD.**

## What is an Access Data Project (ADP)?

An **ADP** is a specific file type available with Access to enable you to develop front-end applications to data held on SQL Server. The ADP file itself stores user objects such as:

❑ Forms

❑ Reports

❑ VBA Code

Data is held within SQL Server, together with any stored procedures, functions, and views, and all the management of the database, including security, is carried out on the server. It is worth noting that an ADP is only available when working with SQL Server. For those working with other Relational Database Management Systems, ADPs are not available. Just like Data Access Projects, we are dealing with a total Microsoft Solution.

> **SQL Server provides you with features, such as linked servers, to deal with data held in other RDBMS. A linked server allows you to connect to another database, for example Oracle, and use its tables as if they where part of SQL Server 2000. For more information see SQL Server Books Online available for download from www.microsoft.com/sql.**

The interface to SQL Server 2000 has been greatly improved in this version of Access with graphical tools now available to enable you to work in a more 'Access-like' environment. For example, building a stored procedure is just as easy as building an Access Query. A stored procedure is precompiled SQL that is stored on the database server – we will discuss these shortly. However, the ability to work with SQL Server security has been removed from the Access Interface, and must now be handled either via code, T- SQL, or using the SQL Server Enterprise Manager.

> **Transact or T-SQL is SQL Server's version of the SQL language. You will notice many differences, including the ability to use conditional logic within your SQL statements.**

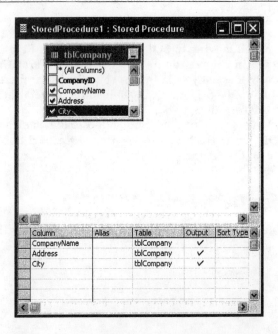

As can be seen from the figure, the interface to create a stored procedure is identical to that used to create a standard Access Query. The same interface is also used to create views and user defined functions. Stored Procedures, Views, and user defined functions are discussed later in this chapter. The single most important point to remember when working with Access Data Projects is that the Jet database engine is now no longer in the picture, and that you are now working with SQL Server.

# Creating an Access Data Project

There are a few approaches you can take when working with SQL Server and Access. You can simply link to the SQL Server tables in the same way as you would link to an Access backend, or you can move completely into the world of ADPs. For this section, we are going to upsize the IceCream database directly to SQL Server 2000 using the Microsoft Access Upsizing Wizard.

> Remember if you're using Microsoft Access Security, your Access Data Project file will be unable to use it. You will need to recreate your security system using SQL Server Security. However, if security is in place in the mdb file, ensure you log in as the Admin user in order to have the required permissions to upsize.

## What's New in Access 2002 for ADPs?

It is really more a case of what's new in SQL Server 2000. Microsoft has made the process involved in upsizing your Access Database easier with this release. The following Access features are now supported in SQL Server:

### Extended Properties

The following Access properties will now be upsized to SQL Server:

❑ Decimal Places

❑ Format

❑ Caption

❑ Row Source Type

❑ Row Source

❑ Column Headings

❑ List Rows

❑ Input Mask

❑ Limit to list

- ❑ Column Width

- ❑ List Widths

SQL Server 2000 now supports the Cascading Update and Delete features for relationships long used with Microsoft Access. Cascading Update permits you to change a Primary Key and have that change reflected in the related tables. Cascading Delete permits you to delete a record and have the database delete all related records.

Within Access itself there are some changes:

- ❑ The ability to build stored procedures, functions, and views graphically.

- ❑ You can no longer work with SQL Server security from within Microsoft Access, as was the case with Access 2000.

- ❑ Database Diagrammer is now available from within Access. This is a bit like the Access relationship window, but with a lot more functionality. The Database Diagrammer can be viewed as an application development tool. From within the Diagrammer we can build and amend tables, set relationships, build constraints, and even delete tables.

# Installing SQL Server Desktop Engine

Before you can move to SQL Server, you must, of course, have the database server installed. In this section, we will briefly look at installing SQL Server Desktop Engine, which is available on the Office XP CD. The full version of SQL Server 2000 is available for evaluation download at www.microsoft.com//sql.

Installing the Engine from the Office is very easy, simply locate the setup.exe file located in X:/MSDE/setup.exe (X representing your CD Rom Drive) and execute. It really is as simple as that. Once you restart you PC, you will find the SQL Service Manager running in the task bar.

The service manager is used to start and stop the database service. Note in the figure opposite, we have checked the Auto-start to ensure the service starts when the PC boots up. The full install of SQL Server is slightly more complicated, but for an enterprise-level product, surprisingly straightforward. Full details are available from www.microsoft.com. Once the engine is installed you can check all is well by installing the demonstration databases available with Microsoft Access XP. To install the demonstration ADPs:

- ❑ Open Microsoft Access

- ❑ Click Help on the main menu

- ❑ Select Northwind Sample Access Data Project

The sample database will be installed to the database server and the ADP will open.

# Running the Upsizing Wizard

One of the great benefits of Access 2002 is its ability to interact with SQL Server. This process has been improved with each release of Microsoft Access, and Access 2002 continues the process. The Upsizing Wizard was introduced to Access in Version 2, but not actually included as part of the Access Menu until Access 2000. Over this period the wizard has been improved but is still limited in how it will move your database to SQL Server. In this section we look at how to move your Access file to SQL Server 2000.

## Before you Start

Of course, before you begin the move to SQL Server, that is running the upsizing wizard on your MDB file, there are a few things to do:

- ❑ Make sure you backup the mdb file.

- ❑ Ensure you have administrator privileges in both Access and SQL Server in order to upsize your access database. Administrator privilege is required in SQL Server, as you will be creating many new server objects.

- ❑ Check the data in your Access tables. It is with dates that most upsizing problems occur.

- ❑ Access and SQL Server use different data ranges. For example, 01/April/100 is a valid date in Microsoft Access, but not in SQL Server. The date range in SQL Server covers the period 1 Jan 1753 to 31 Dec 9999 while Access permits date values in the range 1 Jan 100 to 31 Dec 9999. We know; you validate all the dates entered into your application. Just as well because if the Wizard hits one of these dates in a table then the table will not be upsized.

- ❑ Ensure each table has a unique index, otherwise it will be read-only when upsized. Each table should have the index set. If you have established Primary Keys, then you should be OK. This one tends to catch out many Access users moving to SQL Server for the first time.

❑    Make sure you have no spaces in table names. Spaces in table names result in you having to enclose the table name in square brackets when referencing them in SQL Server. Just another added hassle you can do without.

A really useful tool is Upsizing Pro which is available from: http://www.ssw.com.au/ssw/UpsizingPRO/Default.aspx. Upsizing Pro is used before you upsize and highlights any problems you may have with your mdb file before you actually upsize. This tool can save you hours of work looking through tables and code, and is well worth investing in.

The upsizing wizard is designed to move your tables to SQL Server by hook or by crook, everything else, forms, reports and queries are secondary to that main task, and the result can be a bit hit and miss as we shall see. Let's get right to it, and as we go, you will see some of the problems that can arise when moving databases.

**Try It Out      Using the Upsizing Wizard**

**1.**    To run the upsizing wizard from the Access main menu select Tools | Database Utilities | Upsizing Wizard to begin the process.

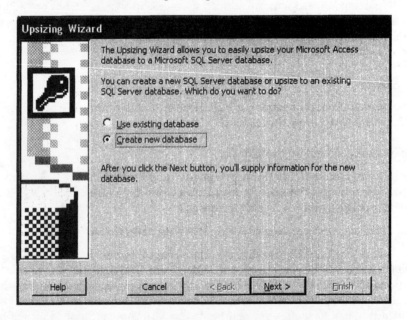

**2.**    The first step in the process requires you to either create a new SQL Server database or work with an existing database. On this occasion we will create a new database. Accept the default Create new database and click Next.

**3.** You will then be prompted to select the name of the SQL Server instance to use to store the database. In the majority of cases, you will have a single instance, so you can simply accept the default database. If not, always check that your connection is to the correct instance of SQL Server on your machine. At this point, you will also be asked to select the security model for the server data, either Windows Authentication or SQL Server security. Unless you have a good reason for using SQL Server security, you should select **Use Trusted Connection**. A trusted connection connects to the database as a Windows Administrator. For this example, I am logged into my machine as the Windows Administrator. You may accept the suggestion or enter a new name for the database. Click **Next** to proceed.

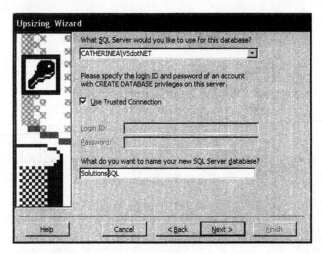

**4.** You are now required to select the tables to be upsized to SQL Server. In this case, we will select all the tables with the exception of **tblPasswords**. Remember in the new ADP you will be using SQL Server security, so this table is no longer required, as it is an Access security table created in this example database. Use the arrow buttons to move the required tables from the **Available Tables** list to the **Export to SQL Server** list. Once done click **Next** to proceed.

In addition to the data the upsizing wizard can also export several table attributes:

❑ **Indexes**
Microsoft Access table indexes will be upsized to SQL Server Indexes. You may then be required to manually adjust the index once the process is complete, as in the case of Primary Keys, you should ensure that the index type used is an SQL Server Clustered Index. With a Clustered Index your data is stored in a predefined order, for example, by Town, assuming the index is set on the Town field. As a result, each table can have a single clustered index. This ordering of the table data leads to very fast retrieval as SQL Server has to read fewer rows when searching. A Non Clustered index simply maintains a key that points to the actual data. When retrieving data from SQL Server, must first look up the keyed indexes on your tables.

❑ **Defaults**

If you have used default values within the table design, for example, Date(), to insert the current date, the wizard will attempt to upsize them to their SQL Server equivalent. Note that a failure to do this results in the entire table being skipped and not exported to SQL Server.

❑ **Validation Rules**

Again the upsizing wizard will attempt to upsize any table validation rules you have set on the database tables. Validation rules are often used at the table level in Access to restrict the data that can be added. For example, with a field Order_Date, the validation rule could say that the Order_Date <=Date(). That means that you cannot enter orders for dates earlier than today. Validation rules such as this will be upsized to SQL Server constraints. If you want your validation rules upsized then accept the default choice and let the wizard take care of things.

❑ **Table Relationships**

SQL Server 2000 can now use both Cascade update and delete options, long available with Microsoft Access. DRI, Declarative Referential Integrity, is almost the same method used by Access to enforce relationships. Again accept the default choice.

❑ **Timestamps**

A SQL Server Timestamp field is added to your table and updated by SQL Server whenever a change to data takes place. If you accept the default, a timestamp field will be added to any table containing a single, double, or OLE data type.

**5.** The last option in this screen permits you to instruct the wizard to simply export the table structure and leave the actual data behind in Access. The data would then have to be manually imported into SQL Server later. On this occasion, we want the tables and the data, so accept the default and click Next to continue.

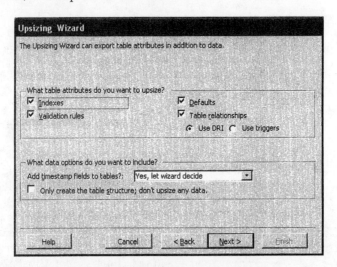

**6.** This next screen in the upsizing process also provides you with several options:

### Create a new Access client/server application

This moves everything into the world of SQL Server. Tables will be moved to the server and a new SQL Server database will be created. All user objects, forms, reports and any VBA code will be migrated into a new ADP on the client side. You may also use the **Browse** button to select a location for the ADP file or accept the default. On this occasion, I have created a folder for the database and simply navigated to that location. If you have created a folder for the ADP, then navigate to it now.

### Link SQL Server tables to existing application

In this case, you simply create a link to the SQL Server database tables and your file type remains the standard Access `mdb` file. All local tables will be retained with the prefix `_local` added to the table name and stored in the `mdb` file.

### No application changes

Export the tables, but make no changes to the Access application. This option creates the table structure on SQL Server, but little else. No changes will be made to the `mdb` file, that is, links will not be made and no connection will be provided to SQL Server.

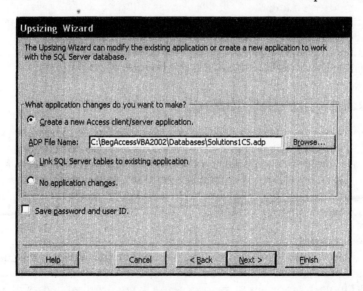

7. Click **Next** to proceed. The final screen in the process asks if you want to **Open the new ADP file** or **Keep the MDB file open**. Select your option, and click Finish to generate the ADP. The choice of which option to use depends on what you want to do. If you want to begin working with the new ADP file right away, then select **Open the new ADP file**, otherwise select **Keep the MDB file open**.

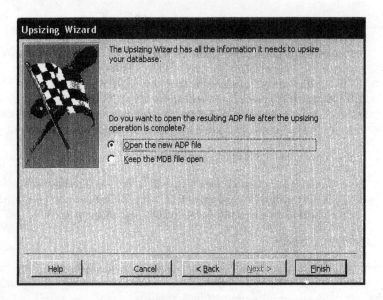

**8.** In addition to generating the ADP files Access will produce an Upsizing report. Make sure you print this file as it contains a record of all changes made during the process, including information on any objects that did not upsize. Print this out *NOW*. The report will be saved as an Access Snapshot file in the same folder as the ADP file. You cannot save the report using the Access Menus, so it really is a case of print it, export it, or lose it.

## What's New in your Database?

From here on in, when we refer to a database we are referring to the database as a SQL Server 2000 database and an ADP file, as opposed to Microsoft Access. When you reopen the database, you will find that you have left the world of Jet behind and that there are several new things you will need to learn or relearn. The database window, while looking the same, will contain many different objects, and this is apparent when you come to create queries. Queries are now replaced by SQL Server objects, including:

❑ Stored Procedures
A stored procedure is precompiled SQL stored on the server, not within your ADP front-end application. Access 2002 permits you to create stored procedures using graphical tools. In addition to the procedure being precompiled, SQL Server will create an execution plan, which gives the fastest way to get at the data. Each time the stored procedure is executed, this plan is used. Thus the speed of data retrieval increases.

❑ Views
A view is a window into data. Usually used to shield users from complex SQL statements and also to hide specific data; for example, you could create a view of a salary table which hides the manager's salary from other employees. A view can be treated just like a normal database table.

- ❑ User-Defined Function
  A user-defined function is simply a function created by you. SQL Server comes with hundreds of system functions such as GETDATE (). New to SQL Server 2000 is the ability to create your own functions.

- ❑ Database Diagrams
  The best way to explain this is to equate it to the Access Relationship window on steroids. From within this tool, you can actually create the structure of entire applications. Existing relationships in your upsized database will not be visible until you create a new diagram.

- ❑ ActiveX Data Objects (ADO)
  DAO will no longer get you by. You will have to move all your code to ADO when working within an ADP. ADO is discussed in Chapter 21.

The following table also highlights some areas that also tend to catch out the Access developer moving to ADPs.

| Access | SQL Server | Comment |
|--------|------------|---------|
| & | + | Concatenation |
| * | % | Wildcard |
| # | ' | Date separator |

# Results of Upsizing the IceCream Database

This database upsizes fairly well. All the database tables and table fields upsize with no problems. However, there are one or two areas where you will have to manually recreate some objects. The following queries must be recreated manually. Note that the upsizing report will also show you the T-SQL that was attempted, which serves as a great start when repairing the damage.

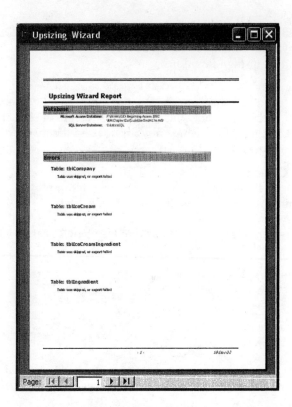

The upsizing report provides you with much needed information about the entire process. All of the options you have chosen are displayed in the report. In addition, the following information is provided:

❑ Tables
A listing of all tables, including the Access data type and the SQL Server data type they are converted to.

❑ Indexes
Access Indexes upsized to SQL Server Indexes.

❑ Queries
For each query successfully upsized, you are shown the SQL Server object the query is converted to, including the SQL statement. For each query that fails to upsize, the report shows the SQL Server-generated SQL that was used in the attempt.

The upsizing report is a valuable tool which can assist you in tracking down problems with objects that fail to upsize.

The following table lists the Query Objects in the original Microsoft Access database and the resulting SQL Server objects. We also show those objects that were not upsized.

| Access Query Name | SQL Server Object | Comment |
| --- | --- | --- |
| qryAllSalesFigures | FUNCTION qryAllSalesFigures() | User-Defined Function |
| qryChapter4Sales | FUNCTION qryChapter4Sales() | User-Defined Function |
| qryCompanyLookup | FUNCTION qryCompanyLookup() | User-Defined Function |
| qryExample | FUNCTION qryExample() | User-Defined Function |
| qryIngredientLookup | FUNCTION qryIngredientLookup() | User-Defined Function |
| qryReOrder | qryReOrder | SQL Server View |
| qryReOrderSuppliers | Not Upsized | Uses DISTINCTROW – Not Supported |
| qryResults | qryResults | SQL Server View |
| QrySalesSummary | Failed to Upsize | Access-Specific Function calls particularly the Format function |
| qryuCompanyLookup | qryuCompanyLookup | Stored Procedure |
| qryxSS | Failed to Upsize | Crosstab Query |

As you can see we have a wide mixture of SQL Server objects to deal with, many of which may be new to you. The next section looks at each of the above objects and provides you with the opportunity to actually create them using the Access interface.

# SQL Server Objects

Now that we have upsized the database, we will look at the major objects your queries will be changed to.

## Views

Think of a view as a window into your data. Views allow you to create 'tables' on the fly, usually to permit users to have access to a subset of data. Views can have many advantages:

- ❑ Hide complex SQL from users
- ❑ Used to limit direct access to tables
- ❑ Reduce data returned from the server
- ❑ Group date from different table together

For example, consider the following T-SQL statement:

```
SELECT
dbo.tblCompany.CompanyName, dbo.tblCompany.Address, dbo.tblCompany.City,
dbo.tblCompany.State, dbo.tblCompany.ZipCode,
dbo.tblSales.fkIceCreamID, dbo.tblSales.Quantity, dbo.tblSales.DateOrdered,
dbo.tblSales.DateDispatched, dbo.tblSales.DatePaid
FROM
dbo.tblCompany INNER JOIN
dbo.tblSales ON dbo.tblCompany.CompanyID = dbo.tblSales.fkCompanyID
```

Look at the next bit of SQL:

```
SELECT
dbo.vw_sales.*
FROM
dbo.vw_sales
```

This returns the same records as the above SQL, but this time we are using the view that will be created in the next example. Note that we don't have to worry about the complex SQL this time. A simple SELECT statement is all that is required.

> Note the use of the prefix dbo before each table name. dbo is the table owner. It is possible for different users to create objects with the same name. For example, user Martin could create a table called Customer; user Patricia could also create a table of the same name. When referencing the tables, you would prefix the table name with the table owner name, for example, Martin.Customer. When creating Stored Procedures in an Access 2002 ADP, your table will have the prefix of dbo; in this case, this is the system administrator. It is good practice to have all tables owned by dbo rather than have multiple table owners.

## Try It Out — Creating a View

Microsoft Access 2002 uses the "Query Builder" to create views in ADPs. This is a very handy tool when working with SQL Server and a big advance over Access 2000. To create a view in the ADP:

**1.** Select Queries | New.

**2.** In the dialog, select Design View.

**3.** Click OK to open the Query Window.

**4.** Creating the view is a simple matter of selecting the tables and indicating the fields required. Select tblcompany and tblSales and close the dialog.

**5.** Select the fields you would like from both tables (click the checkbox beside the field names).

Your window should look as follows. In order to view the SQL statement being generated select View | Show Panes | SQL Pane from the main menu, or click the SQL button on the toolbar.

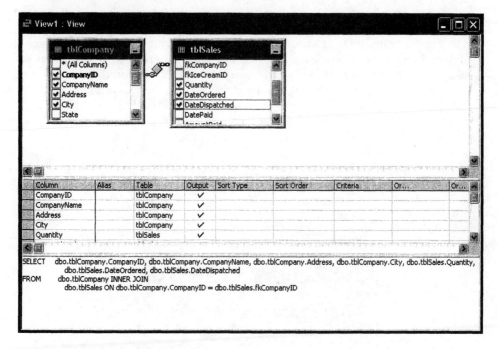

You must now save the view.

**6.** Execute the code by clicking Run in the main menu.

**7.** Save the view as vw_SalesExample in response to the prompt. You must save the view before you can execute it.

When you come to use the view, you simply treat it as a table in the normal way. However, there is one important difference; usually this view cannot be updated as it uses multiple tables, so you need to be careful when using a view as the record source for a form. However, a view that is based on a single table is updateable once you change some of its properties.

**Try It Out**     **Updating Data via a View**

1. For this example, create a view using Microsoft Access which selects all the fields from `tblCompany`. To select all fields from a table, right-click the mouse button and select **All Columns** from the context menu. Simply follow the instructions from the earlier example, only this time select a single table. Save the view as `vw_Customer`. Once you have created the view, run the form wizard to create a simple form based on `vw_Customer`. On this occasion, the data can be updated via the view as the view is based on a single table.

   In order to permit a normal user to edit data via a view-based form, it is important that you change one of the view properties. When working with views, the usual setup is to grant permission to the users on the view only, without giving permission to the underlying table. That being the case, the user has no permissions to work directly with the table data. SQL Server will therefore not permit any updates to the table. When you try to update the data via the form, SQL Server will attempt to update the table directly. If your user has no permissions on the table, the update fails. However, by changing one of the view properties, we can force Access to update the table via the view instead.

2. To see the property sheet for the view click **Queries**, then select the **View** in the Database window.

3. Open the view in **Design View**.

4. Select **View | Properties** using the main menu.

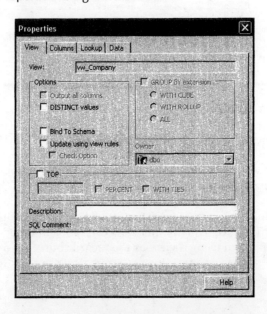

**5.** Check the box beside **Update using View Rules** to enable this option.

**6.** Close the dialog and save the changes.

The view can now be used as the record source of a form to display company data. Any user with access to the view, but not the base table, will now be able to use the customer form based on vw_company, even though they do not have permission on the actual customer table on SQL Server.

Again, views provide you with access to data without giving users permissions to actually access tables directly. We know several developers who base all ADP applications on views rather than tables. One additional benefit to this is that the user does not even see the table in the database window. As far as they are concerned the table doesn't exist. So are there any problems with views? Of course there are:

❑ Views do not allow ORDER BY because a view is a virtual table, and tables, like views, cannot be ordered.

However, the use of the SQL TOP command can circumvent this restriction. For example, the following is the syntax to add an ORDER BY to one of the views created earlier:

```
SELECT
TOP 100 PERCENT dbo.tblCompany.CompanyID, dbo.tblCompany.CompanyName,
dbo.tblCompany.Address, dbo.tblCompany.City,
dbo.tblSales.Quantity, dbo.tblSales.DateOrdered,
dbo.tblSales.DateDispatched
FROM
dbo.tblCompany INNER JOIN
dbo.tblSales ON dbo.tblCompany.CompanyID
= dbo.tblSales.fkCompanyID
ORDER BY dbo.tblCompany.CompanyID
```

❑ Views do not permit parameters.

❑ If you try to add a parameter to a view within the graphical designer, then SQL Server responds with an error. Try it out in the Access Interface. As we shall see, User-Defined Functions offer you similar functionality, which replaces the need for parameter views.

## User-Defined Functions (UDFs)

SQL Server supports two types of UDFs – Scalar Functions and Inline Table Valued Functions. As usual with Access, there are a number of ways to design the function, but for Inline Functions, you can use the graphical Query Builder. SQL Server also provides you with hundreds of built-in functions. Below is a brief sample of the more useful functions:

| Access | SQL Server |
|--------|-----------|
| Day() | DatePart(dd,date) |
| Month() | DatePart(m,date) |
| Date() | Convert(varchar, getdate(),101) |
| Now() | GetDate() |
| Month | DatePart(mm,date) |
| UCase | Upper() |
| LCase | LCase() |
| Ltrim | (Ltrim) |

In addition to standard functions, SQL Server also provides the following System Functions:

| Function | Comment |
|----------|---------|
| @@IDENTITY | Returns the Primary Key of the last record inserted |
| @@ERROR | Returns the error number of the last statement called |
| @@ROWCOUNT | Returns the number of records affected by an SQL statement |
| @@ServerName | Returns the name of the server |

> While @@IDENTITY returns the value from the last insert, it really means THE LAST insert. If two users insert a record, the result of running @@IDENTITY will be the latest insert, which may not be the one you require. SQL Server 2000 provides a new function to return the identity value of the last insert: Scope Identity. This returns the identity value from the context in which it is called.

SQL Server Books online provides copious information on the hundreds of functions available in SQL Server 2000.

Functions are classified as either deterministic or non deterministic. A deterministic function will always return the same value when called. A non-deterministic function on the other hand returns a different value when called. For example, GetDate() will always return a different value when you call it, as it will always include the date and time portion of a date which is always different. This distinction is important when creating your own functions as there are restrictions placed on function use. For example:

❑ Scalar Functions
Scalar functions return a single data value (not a table) with a RETURNS clause. Scalar functions can use all scalar data types, with exception of timestamp and user-defined data types

❑ Inline Functions
Inline functions are much like a SQL Server view, only on this occasion you can pass parameters to the function. Again, Access permits you to create the function using the graphical interface. An Inline Function returns a data type in the form of a table and you can then reference the function in the SELECT statement of a SQL statement.

**Try It Out** — Creating an Inline Function

From the Database window:

**1.** Select Queries | New.

**2.** Select Design In-Line Function from the dialog.

**3.** Add the Company and Sales tables, using the Add Table dialog. At this point (once you select the fields), your function should look like the following:

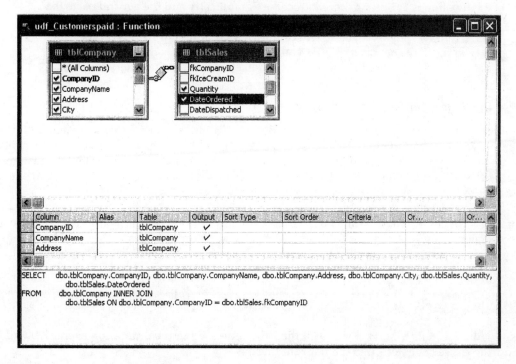

**4.** Close and save the function as `udf_Customerspaid`. The u prefix indicates that this is a user created function.

The function is executed just as you would a standard Access query. Simply double-click on it in the Database window, or select the function and click Run on the Access tool bar.

The function can be used in place of a table. For example, the following stored procedure uses the function output as if it were a standard table:

```
CREATE PROCEDURE dbo.usp_CustPaid
(@ID int)
AS
SELECT
CompanyID, CompanyName, Address, City, Quantity, DateOrdered
FROM
dbo.udf_Customerspaid() udf_Customerspaid
WHERE
(CompanyID = @ID)
```

In addition, the function can also be used in the JOIN clause of an SQL Statement.

> If you're still learning SQL, the easy way to create the SQL statement used by the function is to build a Stored Procedure graphically and the cut and paste the SQL from the procedure into the function. This way you know the syntax is correct. In fact any time you're working with VBA and SQL strings this is a good way to check the syntax of SQL if you receive an error message. In fact why bother typing it in the first place? Cut and paste it in from the Query Builder.

## Multi-Line User-Defined Functions

In this case you get no help from the Query Builder, and must enter the code by hand. Multi-Line UDFs allow you to build up very sophisticated functions, which, in this case, return a table data type that you can define yourself. Our next example returns the sales from two customers whose IDs are passed to the function. Shortly we shall see this function type applied to one of the queries that failed to upsize in our IceCream database.

Another form you will have to amend is `frmSalesFigures` – those data sources are set to the old Access query. Simply change the form and the combo box record sources to `usp_qrysalessummary` to fix the form and all will be well. What? It didn't work! Let's see why...

**Try It Out**     **Fixing the Combo using a UDF**

The combo box fails to work because of the VBA code used in the OnChange event. We will not show the entire code here, just the relevant lines:

```
If cboCompany = -1 Then
  strSQL = "qryxSalesSummary"
Else
  strSQL = "SELECT * FROM qryxSalesSummary WHERE CompanyName=""" & _
    cboCompany.Column(1) & """"
End If
```

Note that again we are using the old Access query as the source for `strSQL` in the initial `If` statement, otherwise we are running a `SELECT` statement filtered by column 1 of the combo box. Later we will use a stored procedure to replace the sales summary query. On this occasion we are going to write a UDF that returns a table to carry out the same function. The following is the text of the UDF:

```
CREATE Function dbo.SalesSummary
()
Returns @salessummary TABLE
(

CompanyName NvarChar(50),
MonthName nvarchar (20),
Quantity Int,
MonthNumber Int
) as
Begin
INSERT @salessummary
SELECT
  dbo.tblCompany.CompanyName, DATENAME(MONTH, dbo.tblSales.DateOrdered) AS
MonthName,
SUM(dbo.tblSales.Quantity) AS Quantity,
MONTH(dbo.tblSales.DateOrdered) AS MonthNumber
FROM
dbo.tblCompany INNER JOIN
dbo.tblSales ON dbo.tblCompany.CompanyID = dbo.tblSales.fkCompanyID
GROUP BY dbo.tblCompany.CompanyName, DATENAME(MONTH,
dbo.tblSales.DateOrdered), MONTH(dbo.tblSales.DateOrdered)
ORDER BY dbo.tblCompany.CompanyName, DATEPART(m, dbo.tblSales.DateOrdered)
RETURN
END
```

To create the function in the Access interface:

1. From the database window, click Queries | New

2. Select Create Text Table Valued Function in the dialog

3. The function template opens with some boilerplate structure already in place:

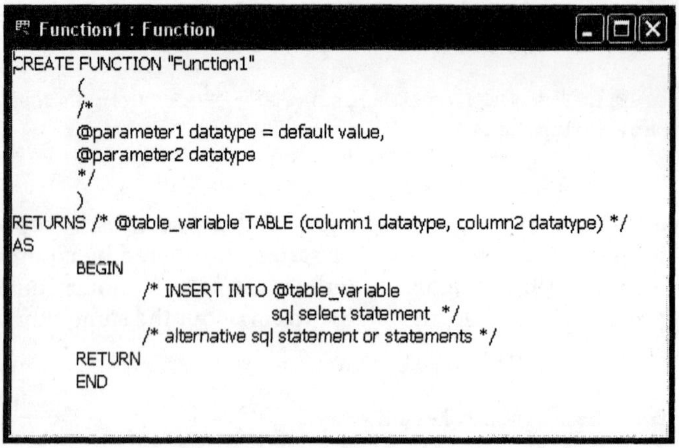

```
Function1 : Function                                    [_][□][X]
CREATE FUNCTION "Function1"
        (
        /*
        @parameter1 datatype = default value,
        @parameter2 datatype
        */
        )
RETURNS /* @table_variable TABLE (column1 datatype, column2 datatype) */
AS
        BEGIN
                /* INSERT INTO @table_variable
                              sql select statement  */
                /* alternative sql statement or statements */
        RETURN
        END
```

**4.** The easiest way to proceed is to delete the template text and enter the function shown above.

**5.** Save and close the function accepting the default name which you have already defined in the CREATE statement.

**6.** Double-click the function name in the Database window to execute it.

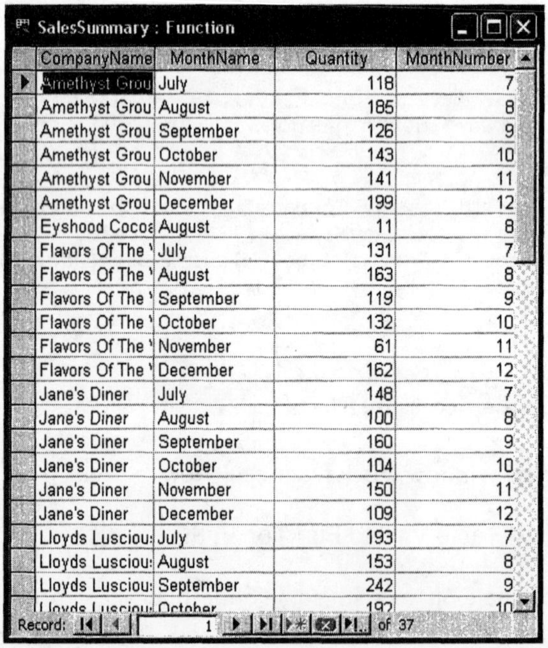

| CompanyName | MonthName | Quantity | MonthNumber |
|---|---|---|---|
| Amethyst Grou | July | 118 | 7 |
| Amethyst Grou | August | 185 | 8 |
| Amethyst Grou | September | 126 | 9 |
| Amethyst Grou | October | 143 | 10 |
| Amethyst Grou | November | 141 | 11 |
| Amethyst Grou | December | 199 | 12 |
| Eyshood Cocoa | August | 11 | 8 |
| Flavors Of The ' | July | 131 | 7 |
| Flavors Of The ' | August | 163 | 8 |
| Flavors Of The ' | September | 119 | 9 |
| Flavors Of The ' | October | 132 | 10 |
| Flavors Of The ' | November | 61 | 11 |
| Flavors Of The ' | December | 162 | 12 |
| Jane's Diner | July | 148 | 7 |
| Jane's Diner | August | 100 | 8 |
| Jane's Diner | September | 160 | 9 |
| Jane's Diner | October | 104 | 10 |
| Jane's Diner | November | 150 | 11 |
| Jane's Diner | December | 109 | 12 |
| Lloyds Lusciou: | July | 193 | 7 |
| Lloyds Lusciou: | August | 153 | 8 |
| Lloyds Lusciou: | September | 242 | 9 |
| Lloyds Lusciou: | October | 192 | 10 |

SalesSummary : Function

Record: 1 of 37

The date functions used are discussed following the next example *Stored Procedures*.

# Stored Procedures

Stored Procedures form the backbone of many SQL Server applications and are widely used to provide data access to the tables. Using stored procedures, we can grant access to the procedure while protecting our table structure. All interaction between the user and the data is via the stored procedures the user is given permission to use. Another advance in Access is the ability to build simple stored procedures via the user interface. However, for more complex procedures, those that contain additional logic, you are still required to write them by hand.

## What Is a Stored Procedure?

A stored procedure is a SQL query that is stored on the database server, a bit like an Access Query or `QueryDef` object. However, SQL Server stored procedures differ in many ways, not least the fact that using T-SQL we can build conditional logic into the SQL, using `CASE`, `IF...THEN...ELSE` and other programming structures. The first time a stored procedure is executed, SQL Server creates an execution plan, which is the optimal way to actually retrieve your data or perform the function of the procedure. This plan remains in memory and is reused by the procedure on each execution.

### The Query Builder

The actual window will have changed slightly, but the basic operation remains the same. The window is still divided into two panes, the top pane is used to display the tables, while the bottom pane is used to display the fields of output and any criteria or sorting you wish to apply. You may also add a SQL pane by selecting **View | Show Panes | SQL** using the main menu or by clicking the **SQL** button on the toolbar.

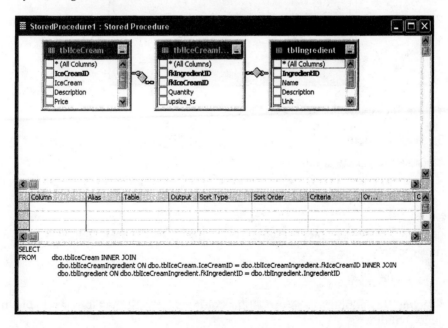

You may also notice that beside each field/column name there is a checkbox. To select a field, simply check the box. If you wish to select all the fields, check the first box **\*(All Columns)**.

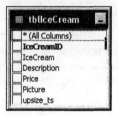

There are also several properties you can set for a stored procedure. From the main menu, select View | Properties to open the **Properties** dialog for this stored procedure.

There are three tabs available to you on the dialog:

❑ Stored Procedure

❑ Stored Procedure Parameters

❑ Data

### Stored Procedure Tab

Using this page, we can set some properties that affect the stored procedure and the way in which it returns data:

❑ Output all Columns

Selecting this option will return all the columns from all the tables available in the query windows.

- ❏ **DISTINCT Values**

  Removes duplicate values form the output.

- ❏ **Set NOCOUNT on** (Remember to set it back to **OFF** when you are done with the query).

  Indicates whether SQL Server returns a count of the records returned by the stored procedure to the client. Setting NOCOUNT to ON, the count is not returned. For stored procedures which do not return data, this can lead to large performance improvements when NOCOUNT is set to ON.

- ❏ TOP is used to select a group of records, for example, the top 10 customers. If we also click the **PERCENT** box, we would then return the top 10% of customers.

- ❏ **Description and Comment**

  This is a free text field to allow you to add notes to the procedure.

### Stored Procedure Parameters Tab

This tab is only available once you have added a parameter to the procedure. However, once you have added a parameter, it is added to this tab.

You can also provide a **Default** parameter, which will be used if there is no input to the procedure by the application or the user.

### Data Tab

There are several properties available under the **Data** tab:

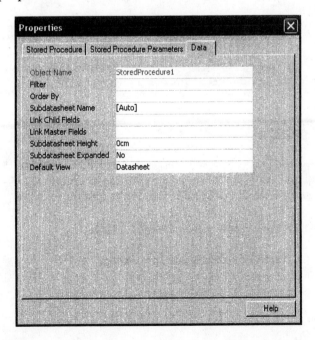

❑ Filter

When data is returned to the client, the filter will be applied. This is a WHERE clause without the WHERE keyword.

❑ Order By

A field or fields used to order the result set on the client.

❑ Subdatasheet Name

The help file recommends setting this file to Auto; however, many users have seen performance fall as a result when using this setting in Access 2000 and have agreed within the Microsoft Newsgroups that this setting should be place at None.

❑ Link Child Fields

Shows the fields used to link the subdatasheet selected in the property above.

❑ Link Master Fields

Related field in the subdatasheet.

❑ Subdatasheet Height

Height of the subdatasheet.

❑ Subdatasheet Expanded

Expands the subdatasheet when viewed in data view.

❑ Default View

The default view for the subdatasheet.

As you can see there are several stored procedure properties that you can set within Query Builder itself. Let's move on and create a procedure in our ADP

**Try It Out     Creating a Stored Procedure**

Access 2002 provides the Query Builder, which can be used to graphically build stored procedures. We also see examples of stored procedures in Chapter 21 on ADO. In this section, we will look at working with the Graphical Builder in a bit more detail.

**1.** From the Database window, select Queries | New.

**2.** Select Design Stored Procedure from the dialog.

This opens the graphical stored procedure tools. This is one of the major advances Access 2002 has made. The ability to create stored procedures is similar to that we used to create Access Queries. The window you use is very similar to the Query Builder in Access. You still have the **Add Table** Dialog, only on this occasion you will find two new items, **Views** and **Functions**. You can also use these server objects when building a stored procedure.

**3.** Select tblIceCream and tblCreamIngredient and tblIngredient.

**4.** Select any fields in addition to tblIngredient.IngredientID as the additional fields are not important to this example.

**5.** In the Sort Type, select tblIceCream.IceCream as the sorting field.

**6.** In the criteria cell for the Price value enter = @IngID.

**7.** Close and save the procedure as usp_ingredients.

Once the stored procedure has been saved, it can then be used as the record source for forms and reports. However, unlike an Access Query, it cannot be used as the basis for another stored procedure. However, it is possible to call one stored procedure from within another. If you do need this functionality, then create a view or a UDF instead.

> Remember before your users can execute any object on SQL Server they need to have the required permissions granted. The easy way to do this is by using Enterprise Manager, the graphical administration tool that comes with the server. However, those using SQL Desktop Engine will find that they have no user interface with which to manage the instance of the server unless they have downloaded the evaluation edition of SQL Server 2000, which does include a non-time-expired copy of the Enterprise Manager. However, its continued use does break Microsoft SQL Server license requirements. We will be looking at programming security at the end of this chapter.

> A word on parameters: Parameters in stored procedures are indicated using the at symbol (@). They can be of several types – input parameters as above, or output parameters, which can be passed from the procedure.
>
> When you are using a parameter to pass a value into a stored procedure, do not use the default property in the procedure property sheet. The default is supposed to be used if the user or application does not pass a parameter to the procedure; however, it does not work when used in the Access interface. Using the default value results in the procedure no longer requesting a parameter as it goes directly to the default.

**8.** Finally we have got here. Execute the query using a value of 31 for the parameter. One record should be returned.

# Fixing the Queries

As we have said, some of the queries in the Access database no longer work, mainly due to the use of the Format function, which is not supported by SQL Server. In this section, we will look at the T-SQL required to repair the queries. This is where the upsizing report comes in handy. Instead of having to check each and every form/report, we simply check the upsizing report for failed queries.

## qryxSS

This query failed to upsize because T-SQL does not support the Access TRANSFORM, PIVOT, or FORMAT syntax. SQL Server does not support Access Crosstab queries. The highlighted keywords cause the problem here as they are not supported by SQL Server.

```
TRANSFORM Sum(tblSales.Quantity) AS SumOfQuantity
SELECT tblCompany.CompanyName
FROM tblCompany INNER JOIN tblSales ON tblCompany.CompanyID =
tblSales.fkCompanyID
GROUP BY tblCompany.CompanyName
PIVOT Format([DateOrdered],"mmmm") In
("January","February","March","April","May","June","July","August","September
","October","November","December");
```

Before we look at the solutions to the above problems, let's look quickly at some other problems you may face when upsizing. In general, the following will always fail to upsize:

❑ Queries containing DISTINCTROW

❑ Crosstab queries

❑ Pass-through queries

❑ DDL queries

Queries that reference forms controls will also cause problems. It is common practice to pass parameters to queries from forms, for example, many developers use forms to collect dates for reports. When such a query is upsized, your Access SQL is replaced by T-SQL.

For example, consider the following query, which collects a company's name using a form and filters the results:

```
SELECT tblCompany.CompanyName, tblCompany.Address, tblCompany.City
FROM tblCompany
WHERE (((tblCompany.CompanyName)=[forms]![frmcompany]![txtname]));
```

When upsized the form reference parameter will be changed to:

```
@forms_frmcompany
```

As you can see, this will not work, as you have lost the reference to the form value.

## Fixing qrySalesSummary

We will use the same technique to fix both `qrySalesSummary` and `qryxSS`. This involves the use of the T-SQL `CASE` structure.

## qryxSS

This is a standard Crosstab query, which is unsupported by SQL Server. We will use the T-SQL `CASE` statement to replace this query, but return the same answer. This query is used as the basis for `qrySalesSummary`, which in turn is used to provide the recordset for the report `Sales Summary`.

**Try It Out**   **Replacing qryxSS with a Stored Procedure**

Because this stored procedure is fairly complex, we are unable to use the graphical tools to create it. The graphical tools allow you to create basic SQL procedures via the interface. In this case, we will be using conditional logic including the `CASE` statement. As the graphical tools are just not smart enough to do this for us, we will have to enter the SQL manually into the procedure window. Using SQL, this is as close as you will get to re-creating a "crosstab query" in SQL Server. Third-party products are available that use complex stored procedures to produce output very similar to that of Access.

**1.** To create the procedure, click **Queries | New**.

**2.** Select **Create Text Stored Procedure**.

**3.** Enter the following SQL into the Stored Procedure:

```
Create Procedure usp_qryss
AS

SELECT tblCompany.CompanyName,
CASE Month(DateOrdered) WHEN 1 THEN SUM(tblSales.Quantity)
  ELSE 0 END AS 'January',
CASE Month(DateOrdered) WHEN 2 THEN SUM(tblSales.Quantity)
  ELSE 0 END AS 'February',
CASE Month(DateOrdered) WHEN 3 THEN SUM(tblSales.Quantity)
  ELSE 0 END AS 'March',
CASE Month(DateOrdered) WHEN 4 THEN SUM(tblSales.Quantity)
  ELSE 0 END AS 'April',
```

```
CASE Month(DateOrdered) WHEN 5 THEN SUM(tblSales.Quantity)
   ELSE 0 END AS 'May',
CASE Month(DateOrdered) WHEN 6 THEN SUM(tblSales.Quantity)
   ELSE 0 END AS 'June',
CASE Month(DateOrdered) WHEN 7 THEN SUM(tblSales.Quantity)
   ELSE 0 END AS 'July',
CASE Month(DateOrdered) WHEN 8 THEN SUM(tblSales.Quantity)
   ELSE 0 END AS 'August',
CASE Month(DateOrdered) WHEN 9 THEN SUM(tblSales.Quantity)
   ELSE 0 END AS 'September',
CASE Month(DateOrdered) WHEN 10 THEN SUM(tblSales.Quantity)
   ELSE 0 END AS 'October',
CASE Month(DateOrdered) WHEN 11 THEN SUM(tblSales.Quantity)
   ELSE 0 END AS 'November',
CASE Month(DateOrdered) WHEN 12 THEN SUM(tblSales.Quantity)
   ELSE 0 END AS 'December'
FROM tblCompany INNER JOIN
tblSales ON tblCompany.CompanyID =tblSales.fkCompanyID
GROUP BY tblCompany.CompanyName,month(DateOrdered)
```

## How It Works

There is a lot of SQL here, and it demonstrates one or two areas of T-SQL. Note the use of the CASE structure within the SQL statement. The CASE statement checks the value of the DateOrdered field. If the field contains a quantity the value is summed using the SUM(Quantity) statement, otherwise it is set to 0 or NULL. Finally, we use an alias for the result based on the month concerned. The output from the procedure can be seen below:

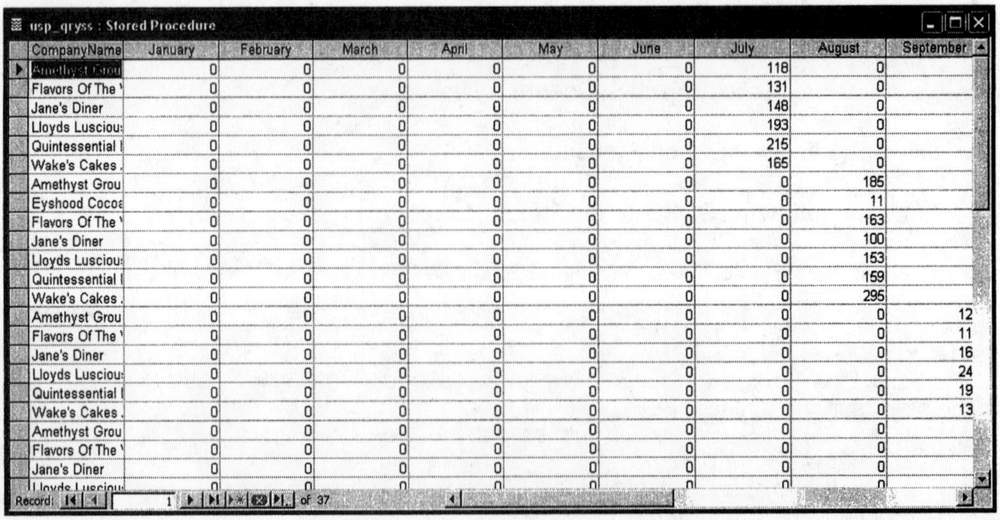

| CompanyName | January | February | March | April | May | June | July | August | September |
|---|---|---|---|---|---|---|---|---|---|
| Amethyst Grou | 0 | 0 | 0 | 0 | 0 | 0 | 118 | 0 | |
| Flavors Of The | 0 | 0 | 0 | 0 | 0 | 0 | 131 | 0 | |
| Jane's Diner | 0 | 0 | 0 | 0 | 0 | 0 | 148 | 0 | |
| Lloyds Lusciou | 0 | 0 | 0 | 0 | 0 | 0 | 193 | 0 | |
| Quintessential | 0 | 0 | 0 | 0 | 0 | 0 | 215 | 0 | |
| Wake's Cakes | 0 | 0 | 0 | 0 | 0 | 0 | 165 | 0 | |
| Amethyst Grou | 0 | 0 | 0 | 0 | 0 | 0 | 0 | 185 | |
| Eyshood Cocoa | 0 | 0 | 0 | 0 | 0 | 0 | 0 | 11 | |
| Flavors Of The | 0 | 0 | 0 | 0 | 0 | 0 | 0 | 163 | |
| Jane's Diner | 0 | 0 | 0 | 0 | 0 | 0 | 0 | 100 | |
| Lloyds Lusciou | 0 | 0 | 0 | 0 | 0 | 0 | 0 | 153 | |
| Quintessential | 0 | 0 | 0 | 0 | 0 | 0 | 0 | 159 | |
| Wake's Cakes | 0 | 0 | 0 | 0 | 0 | 0 | 0 | 295 | |
| Amethyst Grou | 0 | 0 | 0 | 0 | 0 | 0 | 0 | 0 | 12 |
| Flavors Of The | 0 | 0 | 0 | 0 | 0 | 0 | 0 | 0 | 11 |
| Jane's Diner | 0 | 0 | 0 | 0 | 0 | 0 | 0 | 0 | 16 |
| Lloyds Lusciou | 0 | 0 | 0 | 0 | 0 | 0 | 0 | 0 | 24 |
| Quintessential | 0 | 0 | 0 | 0 | 0 | 0 | 0 | 0 | 19 |
| Wake's Cakes | 0 | 0 | 0 | 0 | 0 | 0 | 0 | 0 | 13 |
| Amethyst Grou | 0 | 0 | 0 | 0 | 0 | 0 | 0 | 0 | |
| Flavors Of The | 0 | 0 | 0 | 0 | 0 | 0 | 0 | 0 | |
| Jane's Diner | 0 | 0 | 0 | 0 | 0 | 0 | 0 | 0 | |
| Lloyds Lusciou | 0 | 0 | 0 | 0 | 0 | 0 | 0 | 0 | |

Record: 1  of 37

As we can see, it's not as compact as the Access Crosstab, but not too shabby at all. The failure of SQL Server to support native Crosstabs has been a major complaint from Access developers. For some reason the SQL Server development team have so far refused to add PIVOT and TRANSFORM to T-SQL.

# qrySalesSummary

This query uses the Access FORMAT function and thus fails to upsize to SQL Server.

```
SELECT tblCompany.CompanyName, Format([DateOrdered],"mmmm") AS MonthName,
Sum(tblSales.Quantity) AS SumOfQuantity, DatePart("m",[DateOrdered]) AS
MonthNumber
FROM tblCompany INNER JOIN tblSales ON tblCompany.CompanyID =
tblSales.fkCompanyID
GROUP BY tblCompany.CompanyName, Format([DateOrdered],"mmmm"),
DatePart("m",[DateOrdered])
ORDER BY tblCompany.CompanyName, DatePart("m",[DateOrdered]);
```

In order to reproduce this query as a SQL Server stored procedure, we must replace the Access-specific functions and add one or two SQL Server functions. We are going to use the Datepart, DateName, and Month functions to recreate this query. Once we have recreated the query as a stored procedure, we will repair the Sales Summary Report. In order to repair the query, we need to look as some SQL Server functions.

### DATENAME

In the original query, MonthName: Format([DateOrdered],"mmmm") is the Access function used to return the month. We change this when using SQL Server and instead use the DATENAME(MONTH, dbo.tblSales.DateOrdered) function. The DATENAME function returns the part of the date specified as the first parameter to the function call. The following options are available using DateName:

| Function | Result |
| --- | --- |
| DATENAME(MONTH, DateOrdered) | Returns the Month |
| DATENAME(Quarter, DateOrdered) | Returns the quarter |
| DATENAME(week, DateOrdered) | Returns the week number |
| DATENAME(day, DateOrdered) | Returns the day |
| DATENAME(year, DateOrdered) | Returns the year |

*MONTH*

We then use the MONTH function to return the month number of the DateOrdered field. The MONTH function simply returns an integer representing the month passed to the function. For example, January will be 1, February 2, and so on. This is equivalent to DatePart(mm,dateordered), but we are using it to illustrate the functions available to you in SQL Server. The rest of the procedure is standard, as in Microsoft Access SQL, and should pose no problem to you.

**Try It Out** — **Recreating QrySalesSummary as a Stored Procedure**

**1.** From the database window, click **Queries | New**.

**2.** Click Design Stored Procedure.

**3.** Select tblCompany and tblSales from the **Add Table** dialog.

As we shall be using SQL Server functions, we will enter the field information manually.

**4.** Click in the column pane (bottom half of the Query window).

**5.** Use the drop-down list to select the **CompanyName** field.

**6.** In the next row, enter the following: DATENAME(MONTH, dbo.tblSales.DateOrdered). The alias is entered as **MonthName**.

**7.** In row three, select **Quantity** using the dropdown.

**8.** In the row for **Quantity**, select **SUM** in the **Group By** column.

**9.** In the next free row, enter MONTH(dbo.tblSales.DateOrdered) with an alias of **MonthName**.

**10.** In the final row enter DATEPART(m, dbo.tblSales.DateOrdered).

**11.** At this point your stored procedure should look like that shown next:

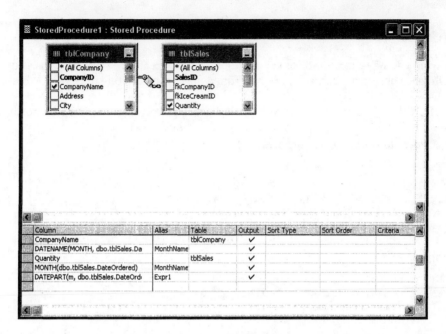

**12.** Close and save the procedure as usp_qrySalesSummary.

Execute the query. The results are shown below:

## How It Works

Most of what you have just completed is no different from creating a standard Access query. The main difference here is the use of SQL Server functions to replace non-supported Access functions.

The SQL for the usp_qrySalesSummary stored procedure is also shown below for information:

```
PROCEDURE dbo.usp_qrySalesSummary
AS
SELECT
dbo.tblCompany.CompanyName, DATENAME(MONTH,
dbo.tblSales.DateOrdered) AS MonthName,
SUM(dbo.tblSales.Quantity) AS Quantity,
MONTH(dbo.tblSales.DateOrdered) AS MonthNumber
FROM
dbo.tblCompany INNER JOIN
dbo.tblSales ON dbo.tblCompany.CompanyID = dbo.tblSales.fkCompanyID
GROUP BY dbo.tblCompany.CompanyName,
DATENAME(MONTH, dbo.tblSales.DateOrdered),
MONTH(dbo.tblSales.DateOrdered)
ORDER BY dbo.tblCompany.CompanyName,
DATEPART(m, dbo.tblSales.DateOrdered)
```

The next step in the process, once we have written the stored procedure and tested its output using our original database for comparison, is to repair the **Sales Summary** Report by changing the record source of the report to the stored procedure created. Once we do this, there will be one or two other items that require tweaking.

## Try It Out       Changing Report Sales Summary Record Source

Because the query QrySalesSummary was not upsized, this report will have lost its record source. We are now going to replace it with the Stored Procedure just created:

1. Open the **Sales Summary** report in **Design** View.

2. Open the reports **Property Sheet**.

3. Click on the **Data** tab.

4. Click in the **Record Source** property.

5. Select usp_qrySalesSummary from the drop-down list. This is the Stored Procedure created in the earlier example.

Switch to standard report view. Now we get some errors. The first error message we receive informs us that a field does not exist. This is because the report is looking for a field named `SumOfQuantity`. This happens because when the original query was written no alias was used for the field. We have to create an alias called `Quantity` using the line `SUM(dbo.tblSales.Quantity) AS Quantity`:

1. Open the textbox `SumOfQuantity`.

2. Open the **Controls** properties sheet.

3. Click the **Data** tab.

4. Click in the **Control Source** and using the drop-down list select **Quantity**.

5. Close and Save the Report.

That's it, you're done! View the report and you should find that it is identical to its Access counterpart.

So, we're dealt with the queries. Is there anything else causing problems? Let's look at each object in turn.

# Forms

Forms based on single tables have upsized with no problems. However, it is better to replace the table with a stored procedure. In this way, using SQL Server security, we can grant our users access to the stored procedure rather than the table itself, thus adding an additional level of security.

> When working with the record source of a form it is better, if you intend to upsize, to use a fixed query rather than SQL. When your database is upsized stored procedures or functions will be created. This is very useful if you are using the same SQL in several objects. Instead of multiple stored procedures (one for each SQL string) only one is created. This makes managing these objects much simpler.

## frmIceCreamPopup

This pop-up form is called from `frmSales` and provides additional detail on the price. The form is populated using the following SQL statement in the original database:

```
SELECT *
FROM tblIceCreamIngredient
WHERE
(((tblIceCreamIngredient.fkIceCreamID)=[forms]![frmSales]![fkIceCreamID]));
```

*Note the use of the form value as the criteria in the SQL statement. When the database is upsized this SQL statement changes and must be corrected to get the form to perform as intended. The changed SQL statement is as follows:*

```
SELECT tblIceCreamIngredient.*
FROM tblIceCreamIngredient
```

You can see that the WHERE clause has been removed. We are going to replace the WHERE clause and use the forms Input Parameters property to pass the ID value from our sales form, fkIcecrream.

---

**Try It Out**     **Creating a Stored Procedure**

In order to do this we are going to create a new stored procedure to act as the form's record source. Close the form, saving any changes. Then in the Database window:

1. Click Queries.

2. Click New.

3. Select Design Stored Procedure from the dialog.

4. Create the stored procedure shown below.

5. Save the procedure as usp_popup.

Changing the form's record source:

6. Open frmIceCreamPopup in Design view.

7. Click the Data tab.

8. Select the stored procedure usp_popup in the recordsource drop-down list.

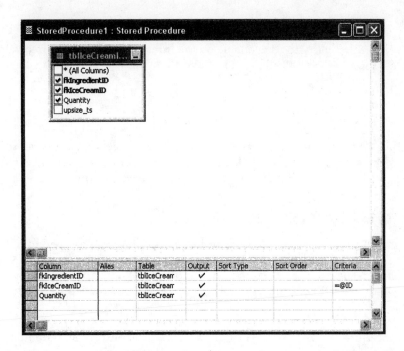

*Note the use of @ID as the T-SQL parameter. We are going to use the input parameter of the form to pass the ID value from frmsales to this procedure.*

9. Close the query builder and save the changes. Remember this form is called from frmsales and is passed a reference to the fkIceCreamID to filter the records returned. With frmIceCreamPopup in Design view:

10. Open the Property Sheet.

11. Click the **Data** tab to view the **Input Parameter** property.

12. Enter the following into the **Input Parameter** property:

```
@ID Int,=[Forms]![ frmSales].fkIceCreamID
```

13. Open frmSales.

14. Double-click the **Ingredients** combo box.

*Note that the value in the combo box is passed to the form using the above syntax and the results are now filtered.*

# When you have No GUI

There are several third-party tools available on the Internet ranging from freeware to expensive proprietary solutions. However, all is not lost and there are ways in which you can work with both SQL Server and MSDE via code.

## SQLDMO

**SQL Distributed Management Objects (SQLDMO)** is an object model we can reference from an ADP to work with SQL Server and MSDE. In order to work with this object model, you must set a reference to it in your project. We'll show you how to do this now.

## System Stored Procedures

In addition to SQLDMO there are many **system stored procedures** designed to return information about your server and its databases. System stored procedures are supplied with SQL Server and can be executed from the client interface. Where appropriate, we will demonstrate both the SQLDMO method and the system stored procedure when working with database objects.

All system procedures are prefixed as sp_procedurename and are stored in the master database on SQL Server.

### Security Procedures

| Procedure Name | Description |
| --- | --- |
| sp_addlogin | Adds a new user to the database |
| sp_grantlogin | Adds a Windows NT user or group |
| sp_password | Changes a user's password |
| sp_defaultdb | Changes a user's default database |
| sp_addroleAdds | Adds a new role to the current database |
| sp_addrolemember | Adds a new member to the role |
| sp_droprolemember | Removes a user from a role |

## System Management

| Procedure | Description |
|-----------|-------------|
| sp_columns | Lists the columns for the specified table |
| sp_tables | Lists the tables in the current database |
| sp_defaultdb | Changs the default database for a user |

To view a full range of system stored procedures, please see Books online.

## To Set the Reference to SQLDMO

**1.** Open a code Module.

**2.** In the VBE, select Tools | References.

**3.** Select Microsoft SQLDMO Object Library and check the checkbox.

**4.** Click OK to set the reference.

That's it – the reference is set and you're ready to go.

> For the rest of this section, we will be using the Microsoft Access database, which will contain the examples and the example code, IceAdmin.

In the remainder of this chapter, we will show you how you can:

❑ Connect to SQL Server

❑ View databases and database objects

❑ Amend database objects

**Try It Out**     **Connecting to SQL Server and Displaying the Available Databases**

In this example, we will create some code to connect to SQL Server and list all the available databases.

**1.** Enter the following into the code window:

```
Dim IceServer As New SQLDMO.SQLServer
Dim dbs As New SQLDMO.Database
IceServer.LoginSecure = True
```

```
IceServer.Connect "HOME"
For Each dbs In IceServer.Databases
Debug.Print dbs.Name
Next
```

> **Remember to set a reference to Microsoft SQLDMO library.**

*Note that the name of the server may differ.*

**2.** Running the above code will list the available databases on the HOME SQL Server to the Immediate window.

### How It Works

The Dim statements should be familiar by now, so we will look at the other new items:

```
IceServer.LoginSecure = True
```

Because we're using Windows Integrated security we tell the procedure this by setting the LoginSecure property to True. If we were using SQL Server Security, then we would have to change the syntax and pass a username and password to the procedure. For example:

```
IceServer.connect ,servername,username,password
```

*Many book examples show a blank password value for examples like this. Do not leave passwords blank on any installation of SQL Server. Many hackers use this blank password as a means to get into the server. In addition users have been known to play around with logins. You do not want an unauthorized user to login into your server as an sa or system administrator. Unless of course you like working weekends!*

Using the **Connect** property of the Server object, we pass the name of our SQL Server to the procedure:

```
IceServer.Connect "HOME"
```

The next statement uses a For Each loop to iterate the available databases on the named server, printing them out to the Immediate window:

```
For Each dbs In IceServer.Databases
Debug.Print dbs.Name
```

We then use the `Next` statement to move through the available databases in the collection and print the name of each out:

```
Debug.Print dbs.Name
```

Within an ADP we can also execute a system stored procedure, which will return similar information.

## Try it Out — Executing a System Stored Procedure

The `sp_databases` system stored procedure returns information on the databases on a SQL Server. The procedure will return the database name, database size, and remarks. This data is held within the SQL Server system tables. For this example, we are simply going to execute the stored procedure from within another stored procedure. From the Database window:

**1.** Click **Queries**.

**2.** Click **New**.

**3.** Select **Create Text Stored Procedure**.

**4.** Replace the template with the following:

```
ALTER PROCEDURE usp_listtables

AS

Exec sp_databases
```

**5.** Execute the procedure responding to the **Save As...** prompt.

In addition to listing the databases, we can also view the tables in a specific database. Again we will use both methods to view tables and their columns.

## Try it Out — Listing Columns and Tables

Again we will first use SQLDMO to list the tables in the `Icecream` SQL Server database. The code to do this is very similar to that used to list the databases. The only changes we need to make are to loop through the table collection for a specific database rather than loop through the database collection:

```
Sub listtables()
```

```
Dim IceServer As New SQLDMO.SQLServer
Dim IceTable As New SQLDMO.Table
dbName = "Icecream2002SQL"

IceServer.LoginSecure = True
IceServer.Connect "HOME"

For Each IceTable In IceServer.Databases(dbName).Tables

If IceTable.TypeOf = SQLDMOObj_UserTable Then

Debug.Print IceTable.Name

End If

Next

End Sub
```

### How It Works

As before we are using a trusted connection to SQL Server:

```
IceServer.LoginSecure = True
```

Then connecting to the server known as HOME:

```
IceServer.Connect "HOME"
```

We then use a For Each loop to iterate through the tables. In doing so, we use the SQLDMOObj_UserTable property to check that the table is a user table and not a system table. If it is a user table, we print it out to the debug window.

When executed, the above code will list all the user tables within the Ice Cream SQL Server database to the Immediate window.

## SQLDMO and Security

Not only can we work with tables and columns, we can also use SQLDMO to work with security.

## A Note on Security

When you leave the world of Jet behind, you also leave behind Microsoft Access's security model and move into the world of SQL Server security. SQL Server security is much more sophisticated than that of Access, but also has much in common with it. Security on the server is multi-layered and comprises:

### Logins

Users must have a valid login to the server. This can be either a Windows login or a SQL Server login. Windows Authentication is supported by default. When working in a total Windows Operating System environment this is the recommended way to proceed; however, some concerns have been expressed about how connection pooling is handled by SQL Server, which can lead to performance problems.

### Users

Once given permission to access the server, you must then create a user with specific database permissions.

### Roles

Roles are defined job functions within SQL Server. For example, all clerical staff could be assigned to a clerical role. If you are using Windows security with SQL Server, than it is possible to assign a Windows group to a role.

SQL Server 2000 can use two types of security model:

❑ Windows Authentication, which maps all users and groups to Windows accounts

❑ A mixed model, where you can use both Windows and SQL Server security to manage security

For all examples in this chapter, we will be using Windows Authentication.

> **A full discussion of security is outside the scope of this chapter, but it is an area you must get familiar with before you make any application live. SQL Server Books Online provides information on the various security issues and the latest security information can be found at http://microsoft.com/sql/default.asp.**

### Try It Out — Adding a Login to SQL Server

Creating the login and user with SQLDMO is a three step process:

❑ Connect to the server

❑ Create a new login

❑ Add the new login to the server

**1.** Enter the following procedure into a new module in the module window. Remember you need a reference set to SQLDMO for this to work.

```
Sub IceLoginAdd()

    Dim IceServer As New SQLDMO.SQLServer
    Dim newlog As SQLDMO.Login
    Dim login_name As String
    Dim password As String
    Dim default_databse As String

    default_database = "Icecream2002SQL"
    password = "mypassword"

    login_name = "Ice1"
    IceServer.LoginSecure = True
    IceServer.Connect "HOME"
    Set newlog = New SQLDMO.Login

    newlog.Name = login_name
    newlog.Database = default_database
    newlog.SetPassword "", password
    IceServer.Logins.Add newlog

    Set newlog = Nothing
    IceServer.Disconnect
    Set IceServer = Nothing

End Sub
```

## How It Works

The first step is to dimension all our variables before use. This process should be very familiar to you by now:

```
Dim IceServer As New SQLDMO.SQLServer
Dim newlog As SQLDMO.Login
Dim login_name As String
Dim password As String
Dim default_databse As String
```

The next line may, however, be new to you:

```
default_database = "Icecream2002SQL"
```

When they login into SQL Server, users are given access to a default database. In this case, the default database for this login is our upsized `IceCream` database. Failure to set a default database could lead to the user accessing the master database used to manage SQL Server. You need to be careful that this does not happen.

Next we assign the password and login for this user to the variables `password` and `login_name`:

```
password = "mypassword"
login_name = "Ice1"
```

Note that plain text has been used for the password for illustration only. When creating passwords in SQL Server use strong passwords, that is, a mixture of text and numbers.

Finally we create the new login with password:

```
Set newlog = New SQLDMO.Login
newlog.Name = login_name
newlog.Database = default_database
newlog.SetPassword "", password
```

Once done, we clean up after ourselves by resetting the server and closing the connection. That's the login created. Now we need to create a user for the database. In this case, we are going to add our new login ICE1 to the database as a user.

The above example uses **Mixed Security** to establish the login. However, it's also useful to know how to carry out the same procedure for Windows Authentication. In this next example, we will use most of the same code, only this time we will create a login for an existing Windows User. Before we look at adding users, let's have a very quick overview of database roles.

### Database Roles

Roles within SQL Server allow you to group individuals who require the same permissions into specific named roles. For example, you may have a group of users who can only read data from the database, or others who have both read and write permissions. You could simply group your users together and assign them to a role with read-only permissions. However, this gives you very little flexibility, unless, of course, this is a requirement for that group of users. In addition, if you have a low number of users you may find that creating a role for, for example, two of the users to be too much bother, and it is much simpler to give permissions to individual user. Database Roles are particularly useful when you have a large number of users and they make the management of permissions on database objects very straightforward.

SQL Server 2000 comes with some database roles already in existence. We will be using these for our examples. The default roles are:

| Role | Comment |
| --- | --- |
| db_owner | Has the highest level of control on all databases |
| db_accessadmin | Can manage user and group security |

*Table continued on following page*

| Role | Comment |
|------|---------|
| db_datareader | Can read data from all tables within a database |
| db_datawriter | Can change and add data to the database |
| db_ddladmin | Can change or remove objects |
| db_securityadmin | Can manage database roles and permissions on objects |
| db_backupoperator | Can backup the database |
| db_denydatareader | Cannot select data |
| db_denydatawriter | Cannot change data |

Once we create a login to the server, we can then create a user account for the specific database and assign our user to one of the existing database roles. In order to create the new user, we need to create a new user object and add the user to its collection. Once this is done, we then add our user to one of the fixed database roles. This fits into the three-tier model of security: create the login to the server, then create the user, and assign the user to a specific database. Once we grant the user permission to access the database, we must then provide access to the objects within that database. In this case we are doing that via a database role.

> All database users are by default members of the *public role* and you cannot delete this role. What you can do, however, is to set permissions for this role. In that way a basic set of permissions on database tables and objects is available by default for every user added to the database.

## Try It Out          Create the Whole Works

For this example we are going to:

- ❑ Create a server login
- ❑ Create a user
- ❑ Assign the user to a database
- ❑ Assign the user to a default database role

**1.** Right let's go! Enter the following code into a module:

```
Public Sub Createsecurity()

    Dim databasename As String
    Dim loginname As String
    Dim username As String
    Dim DbRole As String
    Dim default_databse As String
    Dim iceserver As SQLDMO.SQLServer
    Dim logIn As SQLDMO.logIn
    Dim IceUser As SQLDMO.User

    'Connect to the Icecream Databse on SQL Server
    'We are using Windows security so we set login to true

    Set iceserver = New SQLDMO.SQLServer
    iceserver.LoginSecure = True
    iceserver.Connect "HOME"

    'Make sure the new login is to the correct default database
    default_database = "Icecream2002SQL"

    'Add the login
    Set logIn = New SQLDMO.logIn
    logIn.Name = "Martin"
    logIn.SetPassword "", (reid01)
    iceserver.Logins.Add logIn

    'That's the login to the database server created.
    'The default database is set to the IceCream example

    'Now we must create the user account

    Set IceUser = New SQLDMO.User
    IceUser.Name = "MReid"
    IceUser.logIn = logIn.Name
    iceserver.Databases(default_database).Users.Add IceUser

    'Now assign the user to a fixed database role
    'Set up our user to be a data reader only
    DbRole = "db_datareader"
    iceserver.Databases(default_database).DatabaseRoles(DbRole).AddMember
    IceUser.Name

End Sub
```

**How It Works**

We have already seen the login code, and the details on connecting to the database. We shall therefore only look at creating the user, and assigning them to a database role. This is done with the following code:

```
Set IceUser = New SQLDMO.User
IceUser.Name = "MReid"
```

The first line of this code adds the user to the `Users` Collection of the database. We then assign the username `MReid` to the new user. The following two lines then assign the user to one of the fixed database roles, in this case `db_datareader`, which permits the user to read data from any table within the Ice Cream SQL database.

```
IceUser.logIn = logIn.Name
iceserver.Databases(default_database).Users.Add IceUser
```

# Summary

This chapter took you a long way and like any single chapter can only cover some of the material you require. This is particularly true of the move to SQL Server, a topic which has filled many other Wrox books from cover to cover. We have looked at upsizing the Ice Cream database, looking at what can go wrong and how to fix some of the problems, then covered Stored Procedures and User-Defined Functions, and had a brief look at using SQLDMO to create users and logins to your ADP. We have also seen that SQL Server Desktop 2000 comes without a user interface; this is perhaps one of its major weaknesses, but we saw how we can overcome this using SQLDMO.

This will get you started on the road to SQL Server and Access Data Projects. Access 2002 provides you with an excellent interface when working with the larger server and lots of graphical tools are available to assist you in the move.

The best advice we can give you about making the move to SQL Server is to plan ahead. Look at your database, look at the tables and data types and the data and plan the move before actually doing anything.

# CHAPTER 21

# ActiveX Data Objects – ADO

Back in Chapter 6 when we discussed DAO, ActiveX Data Objects (ADO) was briefly touched upon. However, it is important for future programming with Microsoft Access and your own development as a programmer that you have a basic understanding of ADO. In this chapter we will examine ADO and how it relates to Microsoft Access 2002. We will look at what ADO is, the basic Object Model, how we can use ADO with Access 2002 and some of the basic code structures used in VBA. We will also touch on some of the main differences with DAO.

All code is included in the ADO `IceCream.mdb` database Note that this database is in Access 2002 format so cannot be used in earlier versions of Access. We are also using ADO 2.7 and have all the latest Microsoft Access Data Components installed. For information on the latest MADC updates please visit http://www.microsoft.com/data/.

## Universal Data Access

One of the main ideas behind ADO is the ability to permit you to access data wherever it is held. This is not strictly limited to databases but applies to data held in text files, spreadsheets, and in other structured forms. In many organizations data is held in many different forms and on many different applications. Universal Data Access (UDA) is designed as a means to make accessing this data easier. Universal Data Access is a strategy rather than a technology, and ADO and OLE DB are the means used to make that strategy work.

# Object Linking and Embedding Database (OLE DB)

OLE DB is the technology on which ADO operates. It is designed to work with almost any data store for which an OLE DB provider exists. OLD DB simply works as a translation service, taking your ADO instructions and translating them into the language of the target databases or non-database data stores. ODBC, which is commonly used to communicate with databases, was limited to only that type of data storage. OLE DB on the other hand permits you to "speak" to the *system* storing the required data. Furthermore, ODBC is an older technology designed from the ground up to interact with SQL relational databases, while OLE DB is the latest technology from Microsoft. In addition to interacting with databases it is designed to provide access to data wherever the data is being held.

## So, What is OLE DB?

OLE DB can be thought of as a component or set of components, which can provide you with access either to a database or non-database data store. OLE DB providers are available for many current applications, for example, Oracle, SQL Server, DB2, and other non-database data stores such as Excel or text files. Its functionality can be broken down into four components:

- ❑ **Data provider** – Provides access to data held on different systems and file formats.

- ❑ **Data consumer** – The application that uses OLE DB methods to interact with the data. For example Microsoft Access would be the consumer when working with SQL Server, where SQL Server holds the data you require.

- ❑ **Data service provider** – Generally any third-party component that provides query or cursor facilities.

- ❑ **Business component** – A COM-based object that performs some business function and which in itself can be a data consumer.

ODBC is still there, but OLE DB is the preferred method for working with data held in relational databases. In fact specific optimized providers are available when you are working with ADO.NET, SQL Server, Oracle, and Jet. ADO is a mature technology and we are currently at version 2.7. Its worth noting that the default ADO library installed with Access 2002 is ADO 2.1 and you will have to change this reference to Microsoft ADO 2.7 to take advantage of the updated library. In general OLE DB will give you greater performance when working with both SQL and non-SQL data. The diagram opposite shows how using OLE DB native providers bypasses ODBC thus speeding up access to your data store. In this case an OLE DB Data Store refers to both relational databases and non-database data, such as data held in Microsoft Excel.

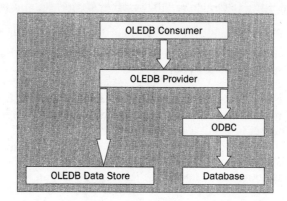

As shown in the figure above, we have the OLE DB Consumer at the top level, which for our purposes is a Microsoft Access database. Using a specific OLE DB provider from within Access we can then access data held in any system, including relational databases, for which we have an OLE DB provider. When you are using an OLE DB provider directly you are said to be using a Native Provider (for example connecting to Oracle using the Oracle OLE DB Provider). However there is an OLE DB provider for ODBC that can be used with a DSN (Data Source Name) that points to your database. For example, given a DSN of Ice we could create the connection as:

```
Conn.ConString ="DSN=Ice"
Conn.Open
```

The major advantage and performance gain is due to the fact that the native OLE DB provider communicates with the database in its own "native language" and bypasses the translation required when using ODBC.

## ADO vs. DAO

Before looking at ADO let's take a moment to compare DAO and ADO, and provide some information for those moving over. ADO may prove more valuable when you're working with data held in systems and file formats other than Microsoft Access, and in particular, when working with SQL Server and Access Data Projects; when DAO is not available ADO is your only choice. If you are working with Internet-based applications you will again use ADO in your Active Server Pages. However one thing to watch out for when you are referencing both DAO and ADO object libraries, for example when moving a database from DAO to ADO, is that you may need to retain some DAO code while the conversion process is ongoing. However, because both libraries have object names in common you must prefix your DAO objects as such. For example, Dim rs as DAO.recordset, in this way no confusion with libraries can arise. The following short list shows you when you need to use ADO:

❑ When you're dealing with non-relational data stores

❑ Working with Access Data Projects and SQL Server 2000

❑ If you are connecting to Oracle or DB2 or other "large" Relational Databases

❑ If you access your data via the Web

❑ If you intend, at some point, to move up to SQL Server you will already be half way there if you're using ADO for your coding

Many DAO objects, such as recordsets, are still available using ADO, but you may find that how they are referred to and how you use their methods and properties has changed. For example to open a recordset in DAO we could use:

```
Dim rs As DAO.Recordset
Set rs = CurrentDb.OpenRecordset("tblcompany", dbOpenDynaset)
```

Using ADO we would still be using a recordset but the syntax to open a recordset is slightly different:

```
Dim rs As New ADODB.Recordset
rs.Open "tblcompany", CurrentProject.Connection, adOpenStatic
```

As you can see we are still using a recordset but the way in which it is referenced and opened has changed.

If you're working purely in the world of Jet at the moment DAO still remains the language of choice as it is optimized for use with the Jet engine and will improve performance. However, you can expect that DAO will no longer be enhanced by Microsoft. So the features you have now are likely to be the last and ADO will be the main focus of Microsoft for programming data access. The following table lists some of the major DAO methods with their ADO counterparts. This table is not exhaustive but intended as a guide only to the major objects.

| DAO Object | Property | ADO Object | Property |
|---|---|---|---|
| DBEngine | IniPath | ADO Connection | Jet OLEDB:Registry Path2 |
| DBEngine | LoginTimeout | ADO Connection | ConnectionTimeout |
| DBEngine | SystemDB | ADO Connection | Jet OLEDB:System Database2 |
| DBEngine | Version | ADO Connection | Version |
| DBEngine | BeginTrans | ADO Connection | BeginTrans |
| DBEngine | CommitTrans | ADO Connection | CommitTrans |
| DBEngine | Rollback | ADO Connection | RollbackTrans |

| DAO Object | Property | ADO Object | Property |
|---|---|---|---|
| DBEngine | CreateDatabase | ADO Catalog | Create |
| DBEngine | CreateWorkspace | ADO Connection | Open |
| DBEngine | OpenDatabase | ADO Connection | Open |
| Recordset | AddNew | ADO Recordset | AddNew |
| Recordset | CancelUpdate | ADO Recordset | CancelUpdate |
| Recordset | Clone | ADO Recordset | Clone |
| Recordset | Close | ADO Recordset | Close |
| Recordset | CopyQueryDef | ADO Recordset | Source |
| Recordset | Delete | ADO Recordset | Delete |
| Recordset | Edit | N/A | N/A |
| Recordset | FindFirst | ADO Recordset | Find |
| Recordset | FindLast | ADO Recordset | Find |
| Recordset | FindNext | ADO Recordset | Find |
| Recordset | FindPrevious | ADO Recordset | Find |
| Recordset | Move | ADO Recordset | Move |
| Recordset | MoveFirst | ADO Recordset | MoveFirst |
| Recordset | MoveLast | ADO Recordset | MoveLast |
| Recordset | MoveNext | ADO Recordset | MoveNext |
| Recordset | MovePrevious | ADO Recordset | MovePrevious |
| Recordset | OpenRecordset | ADO Recordset | Open |
| Recordset | Requery | ADO Recordset | Requery |
| Recordset | Seek | ADO Recordset | Seek |
| Recordset | Update | ADO Recordset | Update |

As can be seen many of the properties used in ADO are much the same to their DAO equivalents. How you actually interact with them, though, may change as we shall see when we discuss many of the objects.

# What is ADO?

ADO is a Microsoft technology designed to permit you to access data wherever it is stored, for example, SQL Server, Oracle, Excel, and Word. ADO may also be used when working with Microsoft technologies on the Internet, for example with .NET languages. Many ADO examples to be found on the Web are often used in the context of Active Server pages, or even ASP.NET and ADO.NET. The future of programming, with Microsoft technologies, not only in database access but also in web-based applications, lies in the realm of ADO and we will see an increased focus with the .NET languages. One of the nice things about ADO is that, unlike many other Microsoft technologies, the object model is fairly small. In the case of ADO you only have five objects to worry about. However while it has fewer objects than the DAO object model it does have more methods and properties that you can use.

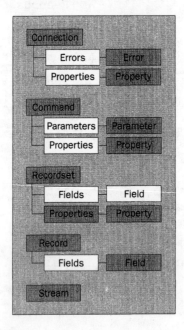

In this section we will look at the main objects, that is, those you will use every day, in some detail. Record and Stream while important are really topics for a more detailed discussion than we can give here.

## Connection

This is the top of the ADO food chain. Without the Connection object you have nothing. Creating a connection is fairly simple. Access, as usual, provides you with a nice shortcut when creating a connection. For example, the following snippet of code creates a connection used by the current database:

```
Set Conn = CurrentProject.Connection
```

This statement simply sets a reference to the current database connection being used. We then create a recordset based on a SELECT statement to retrieve the required data. The code is a shorthand way to provide all the required connection information and it saves us having to provide the required connection information to Access. The actual connection information required by ADO to create the connection is shown below for information. If you do not use the current project connection you then have to create the connection string manually.

```
Provider=Microsoft.Jet.OLEDB.4.0;User ID=Admin;Data
Source=C:\BegAccessVBA2002\Databases\IceCream21.mdb;
Mode=Share Deny None;
Extended Properties="";
Jet OLEDB:System database=""
Jet OLEDB:Registry Path=SOFTWARE\Microsoft\Office\10.0\Access\Jet\4.0;
Jet OLEDB:Database Password="";
Jet OLEDB:Engine Type=5;
Jet OLEDB:Database Locking Mode=0;
Jet OLEDB:Global Partial Bulk Ops=2;
Jet OLEDB:Global Bulk Transactions=1;
Jet OLEDB:New Database Password="";
Jet OLEDB:Create System Database=False;
Jet OLEDB:Encrypt Database=False;
Jet OLEDB:Don't Copy Locale on Compact=False;
Jet OLEDB:Compact Without Replica Repair=False;
Jet OLEDB:SFP=False
```

As you will see in the following examples, however, not all of the options in the demonstrated connection are required.

If you need to work with data held outside the current database, you must create your own connection string. For example to work with a database stored in C:\Beg Access2002VBA you could create a connection string as follows

```
Provider-Microsoft.Jet.OLEDB.4.0;
User ID = Admin
Data Source = C\Beg Access2002VBA\ADOExample.mdb
```

> **A great list of all the connections strings you could possibility require is available at** http://www.able-consulting.com/ADO_Conn.htm.

This code can be used to create a connection to our data either in a relational database or other file format, such as a Microsoft Excel Spreadsheet. The connection is used to provide the relevant information required by the data provider. To connect to Microsoft Access, the following connection string can be used:

```
"Provider=Microsoft.Jet.OLEDB.4.0;" & _
    "Data Source=C:\Beg Access2002VBA\ADOExample.mdb;" & _
```

```
            "User Id=admin;" & _
            "Password="
```

When working with Microsoft Access you have a couple of choices when working with connections. You can create your own connection as above or you can use the same connection as that used by Microsoft Access. To use the same connection as the current database you would use the following:

```
CurrentProject.Connection
```

This statement permits you to use the connection used by the database you're currently working in. All the properties of the connection are filled in "on the fly" by Access.

In order to connect to a secured Access database you must specify the location of the System.mdw file. For example:

```
.Open "Provider=Microsoft.Jet.OLEDB.4.0;" & _
"Data Source=C:\BegAccess2002VBA\ADOExample.mdb;" & _
"Jet OLEDB:System Database=YourSystem.mdw", & _
"Username", "Password"
```

To connect to an SQL Server 2000 database you would use the following:

```
With conn
   .Provider = "SQLOLEDB"
   .ConnectionString = "User ID=sa; Password='MyPassword" & _
   "Data Source=Martin; Initial Catalog = Martinhome"
End With
```

> **DO NOT leave the password blank as it is a major security hole in your code. Always set a strong password for this username when working with SQL Server. The SA user is the system administrator user and has full permissions on all objects within SQL Server. In fact better advice is to not use this account at all. It is used here to illustrate this point in the hope that more developers will heed the advice.**

Access 2002 provides you with a new connection; the AccessConnection. When working with Microsoft Access both the AccessConnection and the CurrentProject.Connection return different OLE DB strings. The AccessConnection will use the Microsoft Jet OLE DB data provider (Microsoft.Jet.OLEDB.4.0) and the Microsoft Access 10 OLE DB service provider (Microsoft.Access.OLEDB.10.0). The CurrentProject.Connection, on the other hand, uses just the Microsoft.Jet.OLEDB.4.0 provider.

> Note that the `AccessConnection` property does not support Jet and Replication Objects code, it does not support ADO extensions for security (ADOX), and finally it does not support the ADO `Seek` method.

## Connection Properties

Each ADO object has a set of provider-specific properties, which are added to this collection. These include, for example, the `Name` property, which will return the name of the provider. Using the property for a specific provider means we can meet that individual provider's requirements. The `Properties` collection applies to a number of ADO objects as shown in the object model previously. The most often seen property will be the connection string, which provides three types of information; the name of the provider to use, security information such as the username and password, and any information specific to the provider being used. The following table shows the more common connection properties you will use when working with Microsoft Access 2002.

| Property | Comment |
|---|---|
| `Data Source` | The path and file name of the database to be used. |
| `Mode` | Instructions on how to open the database. See the table below for what is available here. |
| `Prompt` | Can be used to prompt the user for specific information, such as, for example, if a password is required. |

The following table outlines the mode options available to you when you use the mode property. The default is shared use of the database.

| Mode | Description |
|---|---|
| `adModeUnknown` | Permissions not set or cannot be determined. |
| `adModeRead` | Read-only permissions on the data. |
| `adModeWrite` | Write-only permissions on the data. |
| `adModeReadWrite` | Read/Write permissions on the data. |
| `adModeShareExclusive` | Stops others opening a connection. |
| `adModeShareDenyWrite` | Stops others opening a connection with Write permission. |
| `adModeShareDenyRead` | Stops other opening a connection with Read permission. |

## *Errors*

The collection contains errors returned by the OLE DB Provider. The `Error` object has the following properties, which can provide you with information about the error returned.

| Property | Description |
|---|---|
| Description | A description of the current error. |
| HelpContext | The location of the help file for the associated with an error. |
| NativeError | The specific provider error number. |
| Number | The error code. |
| Source | The name of the object that actually created the error. |
| SQLState | The SQL state for any given error. For example syntax errors. |

There are several errors that can occur when connecting to your data. The most common of these that you will need to trap and deal with are incorrect usernames and passwords, and system and server failure. The following generic code example shows how to trap errors by looping through the ADO `Errors` collection. This is just like trapping errors using the DAO `Errors` collection where we can loop through the errors collection dealing with each error as it arises.

**Try It Out**     **Catching a Connection Error**

In this example we are going to force a connection error by running a `SELECT` statement against a non-existent table, to demonstrate the `Errors` collection within ADO. In this case we will simply print out the error messages to the immediate window. For this example we are going to add some error code to the procedure created to populate the customer form above. We have yet to cover some of the objects you are using but don't worry as we will come to all of them in the following pages.

In the database window:

**1.** Open the `IceCream.mdb` example database and select Forms from the list of objects.

**2.** Open the form `frmCompanyADOerr` in design view (this form is supplied in the `IceCream.mdb` database file). Opening this form in normal view will trigger the error.

**3.** Ensure that the form as a whole is the focus and then select View | **Properties** using the main menu and click on the Event tab on the form property sheet.

**4.** Click on the ellipsis button (...) beside the On Open property.

**5.** Look at the On Open event procedure shown below. The error code has been highlighted in the example.

This code populates the form using an ADO recordset as opposed to binding the form directly to tblCustomer.

```
Private Sub Form_Open(Cancel As Integer)
    Dim conn As ADODB.Connection
    Dim rs As ADODB.Recordset
    Dim adoerr As ADODB.Error

    On Error GoTo ADOError

    'Reuse the same connection used by Access
    Set conn = CurrentProject.Connection

    'Create the new recordset
    Set rs = New ADODB.Recordset

    'Create the recordset basing it on an SQL statement
    With rs
        Set .ActiveConnection = conn
        .Source = "SELECT * FROM tblCompany12"
        .LockType = adLockOptimistic
        .CursorType = adOpenKeyset
        .CursorLocation = adUseServer
        .Open
    End With
    Set Me.Recordset = rs
Exit Sub
'Trap the error by checking if the error collection contains any errors
'Print each error to the debug window

ADOError:
    With conn
        If .Errors.Count > 0 Then
            For Each adoerr In conn.Errors
            Debug.Print "The Error is", adoerr.Number, adoerr.Description
            Next
        End If
    End With
    Set Me.Recordset = rs
    Set rs = Nothing
    Set conn = Nothing
End Sub
```

**6.** Open the Immediate Window.

**7.** Keep the module open and return to your form.

**8.** Change from design view to normal form view. Because we have changed the table name to a non-existent table we generate an error.

**9.** Return to the module and examine the Immediate window. The error message below should be displayed.

The Error number is -2147217865. The Microsoft Jet database engine cannot find the input table or query 'tblCompany12'. Make sure it exists and that its name is spelt correctly.

**How It Works**

For this example we have created a SQL statement that attempts to retrieve records from a non-existent table in the database SELECT * FROM tblCompany12, which is certain to cause an error. Once an error occurs the procedure passes control to ADOError where the contents of the Errors collection are checked.

```
If .Errors.Count > 0 Then
```

If the count of the errors in the collection is greater than 0 then we have an error and we then use the For loop to iterate through the collection while there are errors to process. We check the errors collection of the connection object:

```
For Each adoerr In conn.Errors
```

With each error found, we print the error number and error description:

```
Debug.Print "The Error is", adoerr.Number, adoerr.Description
```

We then move on to the next error using the Next statement. Once all errors have been processed we exit the For loop

# Command

The Command object is used to ask questions of or update your data. Using the Command object we can define the command to execute, indicate if we are using parameters for queries (or stored procedures if working with SQL Server 2000), and inform the command object about the connection we are using. The command object has a parameters collection used to pass parameters to the query. Just like the other objects, the Command object has properties and methods.

## Command Properties

| Property | Comment |
| --- | --- |
| ActiveConnection | The connection string or object used by the connection. |
| CommandText | An Access query or SQL Server Stored procedure to be executed. |
| CommandType | The type of command to be executed. |
| CommandTimeout | Time in seconds to wait before the query execution is stopped. |
| Name | The name of a command object. This can be referenced as if it were a method on the Command object's ActiveConnection property. |
| Prepared | Set to True to run the command as a prepared statement. In this case a precompiled copy of your query will be saved by the provider. This can slow down the initial execution of the command but later executions should be faster. |
| State | Returns details on whether the command object is open or closed. |

Let's look at some of these properties in a bit more detail.

### ActiveConnection

The ActiveConnection indicates to ADO which connection it is to use for the execution of a query or to return a recordset.

### CommandText

The CommandText contains the command to be issued to a specific provider. This can be an SQL string, an Access Query, or a SQL Server 2000 Stored Procedure.

**Try It Out — Working with a Command**

The following procedure in the **Chapter 21 Code** module illustrates working with the Command object.

```
Sub runcmdobj()
    Dim cmd as ADODB.Command
    Dim strSQL as String
    Set cmd = New ADODB.Command
    strSQL =  "SELECT * FROM tblcompany"
    'Reuse the current Access connection
    Set cmd.ActiveConnection = CurrentProject.Connection
    Cmd.CommandText=strSQL
```

```
    cmd.Execute
    Set cmd = Nothing
End Sub
```

In the above example we are simply assigning our SQL string `"SELECT * FROM tblcompany"` to the variable `strSQL`. The line `Set cmd.ActiveConnection = CurrentProject.Connection` defines the connection as the current connection used by the database. We set `CommandText` to the SQL string and with the final command `cmd.Execute`, we call the `Execute` method of the command object to actually run the SQL Statement. Note that the command text can be a SQL string as in the above example, but it could, for example, also be a call to a stored procedure on SQL Server. The `Execute` method will return a recordset but in the case of this example the recordset is not stored and will be lost when we execute the code. Later when we discuss recordsets we will look in more detail at working with them, as these are probably one of the most common ADO objects you will use. In this example we have also omitted the `CommandType` property and simply accepted the default of `adCmdUnknown`. We will be looking at `CommandType` in the next section. Of course, as usual, things are not always as straightforward and there are many different types of command that can be executed.

## CommandType Property

This property simply returns the type of command being executed. The following table shows the common types available to you. It is better from a performance point of view to always tell the server which type of command you are going to run, because specifying the command type leads to a performance gain as the server knows exactly what it is receiving.

| Type | Comment |
| --- | --- |
| adCmdTable | A table name. In this case an SQL statement, based on the table name, is created by the ADO Command object. When working with the Jet OLE DB provider you can use acCmdTableDirect to bypass this stage. |
| adCmdStoredProc | A stored procedure name. |
| adCmdTableDirect | A table name. Must be used if you're using the ADO Seek method. Using the Seek method on any other type of recordset will result in an error. |

| Type | Comment |
|------|---------|
| adCmdUnknown | Unspecified. Performance can suffer as the provider must evaluate the command. If you fail to specify an option adCmdUnknown will be used as the default. This can slow your application down as the OLE DB provider is required to provide information on the type of command to be executed. |
| adCmdtext | A SQL statement to be executed. |
| adCmdFile | Used when working with a persisted recordset. |
| adCmdUnspecified | This is the default value and no information is passed about how to evaluate the command. |

When you don't state the CommandType property ADO has a best guess as to the actual type of command you are running. This can impact on performance and slow down execution. However when working with SQL strings many developers believe the performance gain is so small as to be irrelevant. For example we could amend our former example and place a CommandType statement in the procedure:

```
Sub runcmdobj()
   Dim Cmd as ADODB.Command
   Dim strSQL as String
   Set Cmd = New ADODB.Command
   strSQL =  "SELECT * FROM tblcompany"
   Set Cmd.ActiveConnection = CurrentProject.Connection
   Cmd.CommandText=strSQL
   Cmd.CommandType = adCmdText
   Cmd.Execute
   Set Cmd = Nothing
End Sub
```

### CommandTimeout

If anything goes wrong, you don't want to be sitting about all day waiting for a SQL statement to execute. This property allows you to specify a time in seconds to wait before stopping execution. The default is currently 30 seconds. In the example above we could instruct ADO to wait 40 seconds before terminating execution of the command with the following code:

```
Cmd.CommandTimeout = 40
```

### Name

We can give our command a name and then refer to it. This name uniquely identifies a command object. For example, for our example above:

```
    Cmd.Name ="MartinsCommand"
```

### Prepared

This property returns a Boolean property of `True` or `False` which indicates if a complied version of the command should be saved. The default is `False`. If complied prior to execution the command should executer faster each time it is executed.

```
    Cmd.Prepared=True
```

### State

The `State` property returns a value that indicates the current state of the connection object.

```
    Cmd.State
```

## Command Methods

| Method | Comment |
|---|---|
| Cancel | Stops the execution of a statement. |
| CreateParameter | Creates a parameter for a query or stored procedure. |
| Execute | Runs the command query or stored procedure. |

As the `Cancel` method is fairly obvious (it simply cancels the execution of a command (using `Cmd.Cancel`), we will concentrate on the other methods.

We will take the next two methods slightly out of order and look at the `Execute` method first as it will place many of our later examples into context including those used with `CreateParameter`.

## Execute

The `Execute` method can be used to create recordsets and run SQL commands, for example `INSERT` and `DELETE`. We have already used the `Execute` syntax in the previous example:

```
    Set Cmd.ActiveConnection = CurrentProject.Connection
    Cmd.CommandText=strSQL
    Cmd.CommandType = adCmdText
    Cmd.Execute
    Set Cmd = Nothing
```

The options for the `Execute` method are as follows.

### RecordsAffected

This does not apply when you are returning records as a recordset. It is designed to inform you of how many records have been affected by an Action Query, such as how many records your statement deleted. If you need to know how many records are returned in a recordset you can use `RecordCount`.

### Parameters

This is optional and uses an array of input parameters.

### Options

This provides the type of command in the `CommandText` property, such as `adCmdtext`. When executing a command that does not return records, you can use `adExecuteNoRecords` to let ADO know that you are not concerned with any records returned. `adExecuteNoRecords` is not supported by the `CommandType` property, which is why it is used here.

---

**Try It Out**     **Executing an Update Statement**

**1.** Enter the following code as a new procedure in the **Chapter 21 Code** module.

```
Public Sub usingexe()
    Dim Cmd As ADODB.Command
    Dim strSQL As String
    Dim recs As Long

    Set Cmd = New ADODB.Command
    strSQL = "UPDATE tblCompany SET CompanyName = 'The Amethyst Group'" _
        & "WHERE CompanyName = 'Amethyst Group'"

    Set Cmd.ActiveConnection = CurrentProject.Connection
    Cmd.CommandText = strSQL
    Cmd.CommandType = adCmdText
    'Get the records affected by the statement and tell ADO that
    'a recordset is not required.
    Cmd.Execute RecordsAffected:=recs, Options:=adExecuteNoRecords
    'Print out the result to the debug window
    Debug.Print recs & " Updated"
    Set Cmd = Nothing
End Sub
```

**2.** Using the immediate window execute the code. From within the module window press *Ctrl + G* to open the Immediate window. Enter the procedure name "`usingexe`" into the Immediate Window, and press return to execute the code.

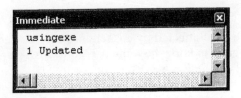

**3.** Just to prove it works, open `tblcompany` and check out the amended name:

| | CompanyID | Company Name | Address | City | State/County |
|---|---|---|---|---|---|
| + | 1 | Fran and Nick's Fruit and Nuts | 37 Walnut Grove | Nutbush | Tennessee |
| + | 2 | Candy's Cones | 26 Wafer Street | Redwood City | California |
| + | 3 | Dave's Dairy Produce | 20 Milk Street | Boston | Massachusetts |
| + | 4 | Eyshood Cocoa | 14 Bournville Street | Birmingham | Alabama |
| + | 6 | The Amethyst Group | 42 Melville Street | Edinburgh | Midlothian |
| + | 7 | Flavors Of The World | 23 Eastcote Lane | London | |
| + | 8 | Lloyds Luscious Lollies | 18-20 Alverston Road | London | |
| + | 9 | Quintessential Ices | 14 Hambledon Road | | Surrey |
| + | 10 | Jane's Diner | 1827 East 1st Avenue | Denver | CO |
| + | 11 | Wake's Cakes And Ices | 72 High Street | Birmingham | |
| * | (AutoNumber) | | | | |

`tblCompany : Table`

Record: 5 of 10

`Execute` is commonly used with SQL strings and the connection objects, particularly with SQL statements that do not return records, such as `INSERT`, `DELETE`, and `UPDATE`. We have already discussed many of the features of `Execute`, but it's worth noting that when you use `Execute`, ADO will create a recordset even if one is not required. You now have the ability to improve performance slightly using `adExecuteNoRecords`.

### CreateParameter

In addition to executing simple SQL statements we can also pass parameters using the `Command` object. In order to work with parameters we can use the `CreateParameter` method of the `Command` object. This provides you with a very flexible method when using ADO and SQL, including Microsoft Access Queries and SQL Server 2000 stored procedures. The formal syntax for `CreateParameter` is:

```
Set parameter = command.CreateParameter (Name, Type, Direction, Size, Value)
```

| Option | Description |
|---|---|
| Name | An optional value containing the name of the parameter. |
| Type | An optional `DataTypeEnum` that provides the data type of the parameter. |

| Option | Description |
|---|---|
| Direction | Specifies an Input, Output, or Input/Output parameter. |
| Size | An options value that specifies the size of the parameter. |
| Value | The value for the parameter object. |

So, to pass a `CompanyID` to a parameter we could use the following:

```
Set param =Cmd.CreateParameter("CompanyID", adInteger, adParamInput,,ID)
```

Note that we have accepted the default values of `Size` and `Direction` neither of which apply to Microsoft Jet. It is also very important to know that your parameter is not automatically added to the `Parameters` collection. In order to add the parameter to the collection you must append it.

```
Cmd.Parameters.Append param
```

Your parameters must be appended to the parameters collection in the same order that they are defined in your query or SQL Server stored procedure.

In our example, the procedure simply deletes one record from the IceCream Customer table based on the Primary Key value, `CompanyID` passed in to the procedure. Before getting to the next code example we will need to create an Access query that accepts a single parameter and then deletes the required company from `tblcompany`.

---

**Try It Out**     **Deleting a Company Record from tblcompany**

Create a Delete Query that accepts a single parameter, `CompanyID`, and save it as `qryDeleteCompany`:

1. In Queries click the New button, and then in the New Query dialog select **Design View** and then OK.

2. In the Show Table dialog add `tblcompany` and then **Close**.

3. In the main menu select Query | Delete Query; this will change the query into a Delete Query.

4. Double-click the * symbol in `tblcompany` to select all records.

5. Double-click `CompanyID` to add it to the query.

**911**

**6.** In the `Criteria` cell for `CompanyID` enter `[Enter ID]` as the user prompt.

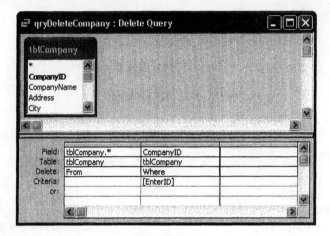

**7.** Close and save the query as `qryDeleteCompany`.

**8.** Click Modules.

**9.** Click New.

**10.** Enter the following code into the ADO module:

```
Public Sub DeleteCust(lngID As Long)
   Dim cmd As ADODB.Command
   Set cmd = New ADODB.Command
   With cmd
   .ActiveConnection = CurrentProject.Connection
   .CommandText = "qryDeleteCompany"
   .CommandType = adCmdStoredProc
   .Execute , Parameters:=lngID
   End With
End Sub
```

In this case we set the `CommandType` argument to `adCmdStoredProc`. That way the server knows what to expect.

**11.** In the Immediate window enter `DeleteCust(14)` and press *Enter*.

The customer record with a Primary Key value of 14 is then deleted. (Note that if you use a value that does not exist or a company with current related sales records then you will receive an error message.)

**12.** Open `tblcompany` and you will find that the entry with the `CompanyID` of 14 has been deleted.

This is a simple way to pass a value to the procedure if you have a single value. If you need to pass multiple values you can use the VBA Array function to pass multiple values, for example:

```
cmd.Execute Parameters:=Array("Joes Dinner", "24 New Road", London")
```

The order of the parameters must be identical to those stated in the stored procedure. We can also use the more common approach for the `Parameters` collection of the command object to pass multiple parameters to a procedure.

For this example we will again reuse qryDeleteCompany, and pass the parameter to the procedure as part of the command object using CreateParameter.

**1.** Open the **Chapter 21 Code** module and enter the code below:

```
Public Sub DeleteCustParam()
    'Using CreateParameter to delete a company record
    Dim cmd As ADODB.Command
    Dim prm As ADODB.Parameter
    Set cmd = New ADODB.Command
    With cmd
        .ActiveConnection = CurrentProject.Connection
        .CommandText = "qryDeleteCompany"
        .CommandType = adCmdStoredProc
        'Create the parameter
        Set prm = cmd.CreateParameter(Name:="MyParam", Type:=adInteger, _
                                Direction:=adParamInput)
        'Append the parameter to the parameters collection
        .Parameters.Append prm
        prm.Value = 16
        .Execute
    End With
End Sub
```

This is a modified version of the previous example and is used to illustrate how you can use the CreateParameter methods.

**2.** To execute the procedure enter DeleteCustParam in the Immediate Window and press *Return*.

### How It Works

The main body of the code is similar to the other examples we have seen. The changes are contained within the With construct. The following line creates our parameter object;

```
Set prm = cmd.CreateParameter(Name:="MyParam",
Type:=adInteger,Direction =AdParamInput)
```

We provide a name to the parameter, specifying its type as an `Integer` and direction as `adParamInput`. The parameter is not automatically added to the parameters collection and we therefore have to add it ourselves using `Append`. The line `cmd.Parameters.Append prm` appends our parameter to the collection. We then provide the value for the parameter, `prm.value=16`, which is the Primary Key value for the record we wish to delete, and then execute the code using `.Execute`. The more information we can provide about the parameter the better the code will perform as ADO will not have to query the provider to find out such details. The following parameter direction property settings are available to you when specifying the direction of a parameter.

| Direction | Comment |
|---|---|
| AdParamInput | Default. Input parameter. |
| AdParamOutput | Output parameter. |
| AdParamInputOutput | Indicates a two-way parameter. |
| AdParamReturnValue | A return value. |
| AdParamUnknown | Direction is not known. |

### Execute

We can use the `Execute` method of the `Command` object to open a query. Let's try a quick example and execute a simple Query in our Access Database.

> When running queries that do not return records you can use `adExecuteNoRecords`. Doing so informs ADO that the command being run doesn't require a recordset to be built, thus improving performance.

### Try It Out — Executing a Query

The Query will update those companies in `tblcompany` whose `Country = "England"` to `Country = "UK"`. Of course you will first have to create the Update query.

1. Create a new query in Design view.

2. In the Show Table dialog add `tblcompany` and then close.

**3.** In the main menu select **Query | Update Query**, this will change the query into a Update Query.

**4.** Create the query shown below:

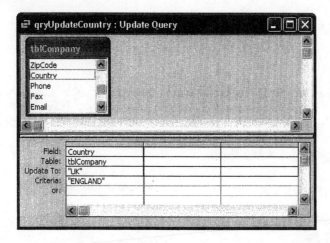

**5.** Close and save the query as `qryUpdateCountry`.

**6.** Open the ADO module and enter the procedure below:

```
Sub UsingQuery()

    'Running an Update Query using adExecuteNoRecords
    'This query changes the country field in tblcustomers to UK
    'Where it is currently set to England

    Dim conn As ADODB.Connection
    Dim recs As Long

    'Use the current connection for this database
    Set conn = CurrentProject.Connection

    'Execute our update query using the execute method of the
    'connection object
    With conn
        .Execute "qryUdateCountry", recs, adExecuteNoRecords
        .Close
    End With

    Set conn = Nothing
    'Return a message to the screen telling us how many records got updated.
    'Should be 4
    MsgBox recs & " record(s) affected."

End Sub
```

**7.** Run the procedure in the Immediate window by typing:

UsingQuery

**8.** You will get a dialog box appearing telling you the numbers of records updated.

# Recordset

Once you execute a query ADO will construct a `Recordset` object, which by default is read-only and is used to hold the records returned by your query. It is within the `Recordset` object that we can add, delete, amend, and search for records returned in response to our query. This is the object you will probably see most often when working with ADO and Access 2002. The syntax to open a recordset is as follows:

```
Rst.Open Source,Connection,CursorType,LockType,Options
```

| Parameter | Description |
| --- | --- |
| Source | Where the data is to come from. |
| Cursor Type | The type of cursor to use to move through the recordset when opened. |
| LockType | The type of record-locking to use. |
| Option | Similar values to the `CommandText` options seen earlier. |

## Cursor Type

There are several ways in which you can open a recordset, set the cursor location, and allocate a locking strategy. Each of the options is shown in the tables below.

*A cursor is a structure within memory that contains your recordset. How you interact with the recordset depends on the type of cursor you open.*

| Cursor Type | Comment |
| --- | --- |
| adOpenForwardOnly | This is the fastest (and the default) of the cursor types but only supports forward movement through the recordset via `MoveNext`. Changes made to the recordset once it is opened are not available. |
| adOpenStatic | All fields are returned to the client. Works very like a DAO snapshot recordset type. |

| Cursor Type | Comment |
|---|---|
| adOpenKeyset | Returns the Index key of the recordset only and then the full data set as required. Supports full movement but additions to the recordset are not visible once it is opened. A data buffer of records surrounding the current record pointer is also returned. |
| adOpenDynamic | Creates fully scrollable recordsets with full navigation. All changes are visible. However, this is not supported by the Jet engine. If you try to open a dynamic recordset using Jet, it will work, but if you check the Cursor Type property of the resulting recordset object, you'll find that it is adOpenKeyset. This is sometimes referred to as "graceful degradation". |

It's worth noting that even if the provider you are using does not support the cursor, it will still open one.

So which cursor type do you use? Well it depends on what you want to do but more that that it depends on the performance. The less complex the cursor the less work ADO has to do in the background. For example, in a forward-only cursor because you do not need to move backwards you simply forget the records you have passed as you have no need to have ADO remember them. However, in a cursor that supports full movement, the cursor and the resulting records must be managed for you, in case you need to nip back to another record. In addition to the cursor type, we can also specify the location of the cursor. This will be new to DAO users as you don't have to worry about cursor locations using DAO. When working with Microsoft Access remember server-side cursors will also be created on your machine as Jet always runs on the local machine (that is, the one sitting in front of you now).

| Cursor Location | Comment |
|---|---|
| adUseClient | ADO creates and manages the cursor for you. If you are using disconnected recordsets then this is the option to use. |
| adUseNone | Provided for backward compatibility and now no longer used. |

## Locking

The following table shows the locking strategy available to you when editing records via the recordset.

| Locking | Comment |
| --- | --- |
| adLockReadOnly | You cannot update, add, or delete records. If you leave the parameter out this is the default recordset returned by ADO. It is also the best option if you do not need to change or work with the recordset. |
| adLockPessimistic | Data can be updated. As soon as you begin to edit a record it is locked and remains so until you either finish the edit or cancel the update |
| adLockOptimistic | Data is updateable but no locks are used until you actually begin to save the record. As soon as the changes are saved the lock is released. |
| adLockBatchOptimistic | All updates are cached locally until the UpdateBatch method is used. All updates are then committed to the database at once. |

Now we will have a look at creating some recordsets.

**Try It Out**     **Using ADO to Populate a Form in the IceCream.mdb file**

**1.** In the Ice Cream Database (IceCream21.mdb) copy the frmCompany and paste it back into the database window as frmCompanyADO. To copy the form, select the form name and right-click, and in the context menu that appears select Copy from the context menu. To paste the form right-click again and select Paste from the menu. Remember for this example you need to have a reference set to the ADO 2.7 object library.

**2.** Enter frmCompanyADO as the new name for the form, and then click OK to save the new form.

**3.** Open frmCompanyADO in Design View.

**4.** From the main menu select View | Properties to open the form's property sheet (or press F4). Click the Data tab.

**5.** Delete the table name from the Record Source property.

**6.** Click on the Event tab and delete the procedure from the On Current property.

**7.** Go to the On Open event for the form and click the ellipsis button (...) to open the **Choose Builder** dialog.

**8.** Select Code Builder and click **OK**.

**9.** In the module window enter the ADO code shown below into the code stub in the module:

```
Private Sub Form_Open(Cancel As Integer)

   Dim conn As ADODB.Connection
   Dim rs As ADODB.Recordset

   Set conn = CurrentProject.AccessConnection
   Set rs = New ADODB.Recordset
   With rs
      Set .ActiveConnection = conn
      .Source = "SELECT * FROM tblCompany"
      .LockType = adLockOptimistic
      .CursorType = adOpenKeyset
      .CursorLocation = adUseServer
      .Open
   End With
   'Set the form's Recordset property to the ADO recordset
   Set Me.Recordset = rs
   Set rs = Nothing
   Set conn = Nothing
End Sub
```

**10.** Close the form accepting all changes.

We have created a form bound directly to the company table. We then removed the record source of the form and replaced it with ADO code, which will provide the record source. Copying the form using Cut and Paste is just a quick way to create the form without having to manually create the objects to hold the field data.

The data is still available on the form but is now provided using an ADO recordset as opposed to being bound directly to the table.

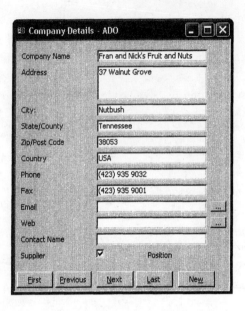

## How It Works

The first thing we do is declare our variables; `conn` and `rs`. `conn` will be used to refer to the connection being used and `rs` is used to refer to the recordset being manipulated.

```
Set conn = CurrentProject.AccessConnection
```

Here we are setting the connection to the database. In DAO we would have used the following code:

```
Dim db as Database and Set db = Currentdb()
```

Once we have set up the connection and defined the recordset, we then get to the bones of our code and using the `With` syntax we set the properties of the recordset collection.

`With` provides you with a short way to manipulate and set the properties of a collection. To refer to a property you simply prefix it with a dot separator as follows:

```
With rs
   Set .ActiveConnection = conn
   .Source = "SELECT * FROM tblCompany"
   .LockType = adLockOptimistic
   .CursorType = adOpenKeyset
   .CursorLocation = adUseServer
   .Open
End With
```

`With rs` informs ADO which object collection we are going to work with. In this case, it is the recordset collection.

We then set the connection. We are going to use the same connection as Access:

```
Set ActiveConnection = conn
```

After this we inform ADO about the SQL statement we are going to use – in this case, we used a SQL string to provide the recordset. We could also have used a table name, a query, or a SQL Server stored procedure.

We next set the locking type of the recordset being returned – the functionality is the same as DAO but the syntax has changed slightly.

| DAO Locking | ADO Locking |
| --- | --- |
| dbReadOnly | adLockReadOnly |
| dbPessimistic | adLockPessimistic |
| dbOptimistic | adLockOptimistic |

Then we set the cursor type and cursor location, and then opened the recordset. Just as with DAO we must open the recordset in order to manipulate it. We then stopped the manipulation of the recordset collection using the `With` statement.

Finally we set the forms record source to the recordset that had been opened:

```
Set Me.Recordset = rs
```

Finally we closed and cleaned up all objects by setting them to `Nothing`.

Using Access 2002 and ADO we now have a fully updateable recordset bound to our customers form as opposed to a table. Just like most things in the programming world, there are several ways to open and work with recordsets and the following examples show you various ways to proceed.

As well as working with SQL strings as in the above example we can also work with Access Queries. So, in the above example we could replace `tblcompany` with a query that selects all records. Using an existing Access query, `qryExample`, we can create a recordset as:

```
Dim rs as ADODB.Recordset
Set rs = New ADODB. Recordset
rst.Open "qryExample", CurrentProject.Connection
```

Notice that on this occasion we are also passing the `CurrentProject` connection to the recordset. The `Open` method of the `Recordset` object will open a connection when passed a valid connection property. However, it's worth noting that a command object is created by ADO in the background to handle this process.

We can also use parameters in our SQL string, for example:

```
strSQL = "Select * FROM tblcompany WHERE CompanName = " & txtCompanyName
rs.Open strSQL, conn, Options:=acCmdText
```

## Moving Around in Recordsets

As you have already seen we can use the `rs.MoveNext` statement to move to the next record in the recordset. In addition to `MoveNext` we can also `MoveFirst`, `MoveLast`, and `MovePrevious`.

| Property | Description |
|---|---|
| MoveFirst | Moves to the first record in the recordset. Works with all the cursor types. |
| MoveLast | Moves to the last record in a record. The cursor being used must support both forward and backwards movement. |
| MoveNext | Moves to the next record in a recordset. If the EOF (End-of-File) property is `True` and you use this method then you will get an error. |
| MovePrevious | Moves back one record. If you are at the first record then BOF (Beginning-of-File) will be `True` and an error will be created. |

## Inserting Records

We have seen a basic example of retrieving a recordset using ADO, but we can also insert records into our tables. The next example inserts a single record in the company table, `tblCompany`, using the `AddNew` method of the recordset.

*Unlike DAO when you move to a new row or close the recordset your changes are committed to the database. However it is good practice to always deliberately update the row using the `Update` method. To discard the changes you must call the `CancelUpdate` method before moving off the current record.*

The syntax is very simple:

```
With rs
   .AddNew
   .Fields("FieldName") = "Value"
```

```
      .Fields(FieldName") = "Value"
      .Update
   End With
```

## Try It Out       Adding a New Customer Record

**1.** Open the Chapter 21 Code module and add the following code:

```
Public Sub addCustomer()
   Dim conn As ADODB.Connection
   Dim rs As ADODB.Recordset

   Set conn = CurrentProject.Connection
   Set rs = New ADODB.Recordset

   rs.Open "tblCompany", conn, adOpenDynamic, adLockOptimistic, adCmdTable

   With rs
     .AddNew
     .Fields("CompanyName") = "Liams Diner"
     .Fields("Address") = "44 Long Road"
     .Fields("City") = "New York"
     .Update
   End With
End Sub
```

**2.** Open the Immediate window and type in addCustomer.

**3.** Open tblCompany and you will see that the new record has been entered in the table.

*An important point to remember is that if you are using AutoNumber Primary Keys then you do not need to add this field to the AddNew statement. The Primary Key will be added by the database itself.*

## How It Works

In this case we are using the AddNew method of the recordset to insert one record. We are using the With syntax to avoid full references to the recordset each time. The AddNew method will add a row to the table. An important difference between DAO and ADO to remember here is that ADO will save the record when you move off it. However, we are using the Update method to save the record "just in case". Leaving a save record pending and closing a recordset will result in an error.

Another approach is to this is to use a `Variant` array. In this case ADO actually handles the `Insert` for you. For example, if you were to use the following code using an array as opposed to using the ADO fields collection to actually pass the values for insertion. The changes to the code are highlighted below.

```
Public Sub addCustomerArray()

    Dim conn As ADODB.Connection
    Dim rs As ADODB.Recordset

    Set conn = CurrentProject.Connection
    Set rs = New ADODB.Recordset

    rs.Open "tblCompany", conn, adOpenDynamic, adLockOptimistic, adCmdTable

    varfields = Array("CompanyName", "Address", "City")
    varValues = Array("Aines Diner", "26 Long Road", "Belfast")

    rs.AddNew varfields, varValues
    rs.Update

End Sub
```

## Updating Records

The next example uses a SQL string to update the `CompanyName` field in `tblCompany` table.

**Try It Out      Updating Records using ADO**

**1.** Add the following code into the **Chapter 21 Code** module:

```
Public Sub ADOUpdate()
    Dim rs As ADODB.Recordset
    Dim strSQL As String
    Set rs = New ADODB.Recordset
    strSQL = "SELECT CompanyName, Address, City FROM tblCompany
            WHERE (CompanyName = 'Liams Diner')"
    rs.Open strSQL, CurrentProject.Connection, adOpenKeyset, adLockOptimistic
    With rs
      !CompanyName = "Williams Diner"
      .Update
    End With
    rs.Close
End Sub
```

**2.** Open the Immediate window and type in `ADOUpdate` to run the code.

**3.** Open `tblCompany` and you will see that the record for Liams Diner's name has been changed from `Liams Diner` to `Williams Diner`.

Note that in this case we have added the `CurrentProject.Connection` to the `Open` method rather than as a separate code line. ADO will create the connection for us using the recordset's `Open` method.

Many developers recommend not using recordsets to update records. They prefer to work with queries or stored procedures (if using Access as a front-end to an MSDE database for example). At times you may also want to update more than one record. If that is the case simply enclose the `Update` statements in a `Do` statement testing for the EOF or End-of-File. The `If` statement is also used to actually test the fields' value:

```
Do Until rs.EOF
   If rs!fieldname = "Field Required" Then
      rs!fieldname ='New Value'
      rs.Update
   End if
   rs.MoveNext
Loop
```

## Deleting Records

Deleting a record using ADO is very similar. In this case we need to move to the row targeted for deletion and then use the `Delete` method of the recordset object to actually remove the record using `rs.Delete`.

---

**Try It Out     Deleting a Record**

**1.** Open the **Chapter 21 Code** module by double-clicking it or open a new module. Enter the following ADO into the module window:

```
Public Sub RemoveCompany()
   Dim rs As ADODB.Recordset
   Dim strSQL As String
   Set rs = New ADODB.Recordset

   rs.Open "SELECT * FROM tblCompany WHERE CompanyID=13", _
      CurrentProject.Connection, adOpenStatic, adLockOptimistic
   With rs
      'Make sure we have a record by checking the RecordCount property
      If .RecordCount > 0 Then
         'Delete the record
         .Delete
      End If
   End With

   'Close and clean up
   rs.Close
   Set rs = Nothing
End Sub
```

2. Change the `CompanyID` to that of the company you want to delete.

3. Run the code from the Immediate window and then open `tblCompany` to see that the record has been deleted.

## Finding Records

ADO supports a couple of ways to search for records, `Find` and `Seek`, and of course using SQL. There is much discussion about which is the best way to find records. Personally when working with Access or SQL Server we tend to opt for the Stored Procedure or Query approach as opposed to using `Find` or `Seek`. In this section we will provide a quick overview of the three methods.

### SQL

Perhaps the best way to actually find records is to use the tried and tested method of the SQL `WHERE` clause. It has been stated on many developer's lists that working experience has proven this method to be the best in terms of speed and flexibility. You can use a SQL string, or pass criteria to a query or stored procedure to filter the recordset. One other advantage in using queries to filter records is when you come to upsize the database to an Access Data Project your queries will be converted to stored procedures, saving you from having to amend code.

### Find

Let's take a look at the `Find` method. In this example, `Find` is used to limit the recordset to a single record, that for the customer Candy's Cones. The `Find` method permits you to use a single field value as the criterion for your recordset.

---

**Try It Out**     **Using Find**

1. Open the Chapter 21 Code module or open a new module. Enter the following code into the module:

```
Public Sub GetCompany()

    Dim rs As ADODB.Recordset
    Dim strSQL As String
    Set rs = New ADODB.Recordset

    strSQL = "SELECT tblCompany.CompanyName, tblCompany.Address," _
        & "tblSales.Quantity, tblSales.DateOrdered" _
        & " FROM tblCompany INNER JOIN tblSales ON tblCompany.CompanyID" _
        & " = tblSales.fkCompanyID"

    rs.Open strSQL, CurrentProject.Connection, adOpenKeyset, adOpenDynamic

    With rs
        Find "CompanyName='Eyshood Cocoa'"
    End With
```

```
        Debug.Print rs!CompanyName & " " & rs!Quantity & " " & rs!DateOrdered

        rs.Close
        Set rs = Nothing

    End Sub
```

**2.** Run the code from the Immediate window by typing **GetCompany** and pressing *Enter*.

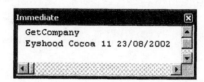

The `Find` method has one obvious drawback; you can only use one field value as the criterion. However you can also add a `WHERE` clause with the `Find` method, for example:

```
    rs.Find("CompanyName LIKE 'A*'")
```

Note that only one record is returned by the above examples even if there are multiple matches. In order to return all the records, you need to enclose the `Find` statement in a `Do` loop. This is unlike a SQL `WHERE` clause when we can pass multiple values to the `WHERE` string.

### Seek

The `Seek` method can also be used to find records. `Seek` is mainly used with records that return tables. It is supported by the Jet engine but not by SQL Server. In order to work with the `Seek` method you must also use the `Index` property as your search fields must also have an index set. For example if we wanted to search by `CompanyName` and `City`, then we would create an index on `tblCompany` and include the fields `CompanyName` and `City`. We would then base our search on both fields.

### Try It Out — Using Seek

For this example we have copied the table `Customers` from the Northwind example database. This table is included in the chapter database.

**1.** Enter the following code into the **Chapter 21 Code** module or create a new module for this purpose.

```
Sub UsingSeek()
    'Using seek to find a record
    Dim rs As ADODB.Recordset
    Dim conn As ADODB.Connection
```

```
Dim strSQL As String
Set rs = New ADODB.Recordset
Set conn = CurrentProject.Connection

With rs
   .Open Source:="Customers", ActiveConnection:=conn,
   CursorType:=adOpenKeyset, LockType:=adLockOptimistic,
   Options:=adCmdTableDirect
   .Index = "CompanyName"
   .Seek ("Antonio Moreno Taquería")
End With

Debug.Print rs!CompanyName & " " & rs!ContactTitle & " " & rs!ContactName

End Sub
```

**2.** Run the code from the Immediate window by typing UsingSeek and pressing *Enter*.

The only new lines at this stage are:

❑    .Index – where we pass the name of the index to ADO

❑    .Seek – passing the value we wish to search for

We then print out the value to the Immediate window. The problem with Seek is that it is only supported by Jet 4 and then support is ropey at best. The advice is to use either the Find method or our own preference, SQL with stored procedures and queries.

## Fields

Each recordset comprises a Fields collection, made up of individual field objects. Each field of data in your table will have a corresponding field object. The field object contains a Value property, which is where your data actually resides. The Value property is also used to place any new or amended data before it is passed back to the database.

## Record

Can be used to represent one row of data or a file or directory structure.

## Stream

A `Stream` object can be used to manipulate the binary data stream, for example an e-mail or image file, which makes up a file or object.

# Disconnected Recordsets

So far we have concentrated on pulling data directly out of a database and at times changing it and reinserting it into the database. The basic idea behind a disconnected recordset is to grab the data, save or persist it locally, manipulate it, and save it back to the database thus reducing the number of connections required to the database. Once we disconnect the recordset from its source we can save it to disk. The basic steps involved are shown below but like everything connected with Microsoft Access there are other ways to do this.

1.  Get a recordset in the usual way.

2.  Close the connection.

3.  Save the recordset locally to file.

4.  Change the recordset in some way.

5.  Reconnect and update the database.

The next example does just that. In this case we have created a simple form based on the company table using the Access form wizard. Once the form is created we simply remove the recordsource (`tblCompany`) using the form's property sheet and enter the following code into the form `On_Open` event.

**Try It Out     Adding a Record via a Disconnected Recordset**

1.  Use the form wizard to create a new form based on `tblcompany`. Select all the fields and click **Finish**. Save the form as `frmCompanyAutoform`.

2.  Open the form in design view and then open the Properties window.

3.  On the **Data** tab delete `tblcompany` as the form's Record Source.

4.  Click **Event** and go to the **On Open** event.

5.  Click the build (...) button and then select Code Builder.

6.  Enter the following code into the code sheet:

```
Private Sub Form_Open(Cancel As Integer)
   Dim conn As ADODB.Connection
   Dim rs As ADODB.Recordset
   Set conn = CurrentProject.AccessConnection
   Set rs = New ADODB.Recordset
   rs.CursorLocation = adUseClient
   rs.Open "Select * from tblcompany", conn, _
     adOpenForwardOnly, adLockOptimistic
   Set rs.ActiveConnection = Nothing
   Set Me.Recordset = rs
End Sub
```

**7.** Use the form to change a few records then examine the table.

None of your changes will appear in the table because you are working with a copy of the recordset held in memory. The recordset contains the changes but cannot as yet write the changes back to our database. We now need to add some code to actually perform the update back to the table. Before going into the code we need to have a quick word on working with batches.

When working with the database we do not have to write all changes back to the source as and when they occur. With a disconnected recordset this is possible to achieve but the better way would be to send all the changes to the database in one go. In order to do this we perform a batch update. Without a batch update the recordset can be changed but immediately "forgets" the update has taken place. It simply treats the new value as if it has always been part of the recordset. However when we use batch updates the recordset remembers the changes and as a result can write them back to our database. To turn batch updating on we set the `locktype` to `adLockBatchOptimistic`.

We are going to make some changes to the above code to allow us to update the recordset. The changes required to the procedure above are shown highlighted below.

```
Private Sub Form_Open(Cancel As Integer)
   Dim conn As ADODB.Connection
   Dim rs As ADODB.Recordset
   Set conn = CurrentProject.AccessConnection
   Set rs = New ADODB.Recordset
   rs.CursorLocation = adUseClient
   rs.Open "Select * from tblcompany", conn, & _
     adOpenForwardOnly, adLockBatchOptimistic
   'Kill the connection
   Set rs.ActiveConnection = Nothing

   'Set the form record source to our disconnected recordset
   Set Me.Recordset = rs

   'Reopen the connection to the database
   Set conn = CurrentProject.AccessConnection
   rs.ActiveConnection = conn
```

```
    'Update the database with any changes from the recordset
    rst.UpdateBatch

    rs.Close
    conn.Close
    Set rs = Nothing
    Set conn = Nothing
End Sub
```

An optional value can also be used with `UpdateBatch` that determines how many records will be affected by the statement.

| Option | Comment |
|---|---|
| AdAffectCurrent | Write pending changes only for the current record. |
| AdAffectGroup | Write pending changes for the records that satisfy the current Filter property setting. |
| adAffectAll | (Default) Write pending changes for all the records in the Recordset object, including any hidden by the current Filter property setting. |

This section only introduced the topic of disconnected recordsets. Disconnected recordsets provide you with a way to download records to locally manipulate those records and write the changes to the server at a later time. There are also three options which can be used with `UpdateBatch`.

# Summary

In this chapter we have introduced you to the world of ADO. We have looked at connections, commands, and recordsets. Whole books have been written on ADO and it's difficult in a single chapter to cover all the ground. We briefly introduced one of the more interesting features of ADO, that of the use of disconnected recordsets. We also looked at searching recordsets for records using `Find` and `Seek` and the perhaps better way restricting records using either the `WHERE` clause of a SQL string or passing parameters using stored procedures or queries.

# Exercises

1. Using ADO add a complete record to the company table (`tblCompany`).

2. Using a command object execute a Query that populates a form with customers living in London.

# INDEX

# Index

## A Guide to the Index

More important entries have **bold** page numbers.